HEAT & COLD

MASTERING THE GREAT INDOORS

ABOUT THE AUTHORS

Barry Donaldson is executive vice-president of Tishman Research Corporation in New York City. He received a bachelor of arts degree from Colgate University and a master's degree from the Yale University School of Architecture. Mr. Donaldson, an ASHRAE member since 1982, belongs to a number of professional societies including the National Institute of Building Sciences and the Illuminating Engineering Society.

Bernard Nagengast is a consulting engineer in Sidney, Ohio. He has a bachelor of science degree in environmental engineering and a master's degree in business administration from California Polytechnic State University. Mr. Nagengast is a well-known author and lecturer on the history of heating, ventilating, air-conditioning, and refrigerating technology. He has been a member of ASHRAE since 1968. He is a member of The Society for the History of Technology, The Society for Industrial Archaeology, and The Newcomen Society.

The late **Gershon Meckler**, elected to ASHRAE membership in 1950, was president of Gershon Meckler Associates, an engineering design consulting firm in the Washington, D.C., area. He held more than 50 patents and was the author of 80 technical papers and the co-author of five books. A 1949 engineering physics graduate of Pennsylvania State University, Mr. Meckler died in 1994.

Heat and Cold: Mastering the Great Indoors is the result of more than 20 years of research by the authors. Its publication by ASHRAE was sponsored by the ASHRAE Historical Committee as a special project to commemorate the 100th anniversary of the Society's founding.

HEAT & COLD

MASTERING THE GREAT INDOORS

A Selective History of Heating,
Ventilation, Air-Conditioning and Refrigeration
from the Ancients to the 1930s

Barry Donaldson & Bernard Nagengast
with an Introductory Essay by Gershon Meckler

American Society of Heating, Refrigerating
and Air-Conditioning Engineers, Inc.

ISBN 1-883413-17-6

©1994 American Society of Heating, Refrigerating
and Air-Conditioning Engineers, Inc.
1791 Tullie Circle NE
Atlanta, GA 30329

PRINTED IN THE UNITED STATES OF AMERICA

_____ *ASHRAE Publications* _____

Frank M. Coda, *Publisher*   **W. Stephen Comstock,** *Director*

_____ *Special Publications Staff* _____

Mildred Geshwiler, *Editor*
Lynn Montgomery, *Associate Editor*
Michelle Moran, *Associate Editor*
Stefanie Frick, *Secretary*

Ron Baker, *Production Manager*

TABLE OF CONTENTS

ACKNOWLEDGMENTS

The authors would like to express their thanks to the many people who have contributed to this effort and to the American Society of Heating, Refrigerating and Air-Conditioning Engineers and the Historical Committee of the Society, which sponsored this publication.

We would like to thank Everett Barber for his inspiration in starting on this long journey. Many thanks also to Wesley Haynes for his excellent work on the history of heating and ventilating the New York State Capitol.

We would also like to thank the many manufacturers and industry representatives who provided histories of their companies and ancestor companies.

A special thanks to Rebecca Stanton, who assisted with background research and did all of the production and initial editorial work on the manuscript for this book.

The reference collections of the following institutions were useful, and the authors wish to thank their staff for their kind assistance in locating material.

Boston Public Library
Carrier Collection, Department of Manuscripts and
    Archives Cornell University Library
Cleveland, Ohio, Public Library
Historical Archive and Library, American Society of
    Heating, Refrigerating and Air-Conditioning
    Engineers
Library of the Refrigeration Service Engineers Society
Montgomery County, Ohio, Historical Society
New Haven Colony Historical Society, Connecticut
Ohio State University Library
Refrigeration Research Corporation Museum
The Air Conditioning and Refrigeration Industry
    Museum, Los Angeles
The Baker Library, Harvard University
The Cincinnati, Ohio, Public Library
The Dibner Library, Smithsonian Institution
The Engineering Societies Library
The Florida State Archives
The General Electric Hall of History
The General Motors Institute, Collection of Industrial
    History
The International Institute of Refrigeration
The John Crerar Collection at the Library of the
    University of Chicago
The Library of Congress
The Library of the Franklin Institute
The New York Public Library
The Philadelphia Public Library
The Smithsonian Institution Library
The St. Louis Public Library
Yale University Department of History
    of Science and Medicine
Amos Memorial Library, Sidney, Ohio

Although many individuals provided suggestions and information, the following were particularly helpful with their assistance: Cooky and Carol, for their patient support during the preparation of the manuscript; our processing assistants, Melinda McCullough and Patricia Tinsler; the ASHRAE staff: W. Stephen Comstock, Lawrence Darrow, Micki Geshwiler, Anthony Giometti, Emily Walker, Lynn Montgomery, and Michelle Moran; the past chairmen and members of the ASHRAE Historical Committee; and the following individuals:

Janet Alford
Susan Appel
John Bernaden (Johnson Controls)
Neville Billington (Heritage Group of the Chartered
    Institution of Building Services Engineers)
Ed Bottum, Sr.
Anne Boutwell
Gail Cooper
Ruth Schwartz Cowan
Hans Luigder Dienel
Cecil Elliott
Frank Faust
G. Ralph Fehr (deceased)
Lynette Haessely (Landis & Gyr Powers)
Valentine Kartorie
Clovis Linkous
Geoff Luscombe (Australian Institute of Refrigeration,
    Air Conditioning and Heating)
Gershon Meckler (deceased)
Anne Millbrooke (United Technologies Archive)
Jane Morley
Brian Roberts (Heritage Group of the Chartered
    Institution of Building Services Engineers)
Vivian Sherlock
Jay Smilac
Mike Stapp (Honeywell)
Ray Thornton
The Twining Family
Robert Vogel
Marsha Watson (Dometic Corporation)
George Wise (General Electric Co. Research and
    Development)
William Worthington (Smithsonian Institution)
Paul Yunnie (Heritage Group of the Chartered
    Institution of Building Services Engineers)
Kenneth Hickman (York International Corp.)
Steven Shafer
Edwin Scott, Jr.

SCIENTIFIC ROOTS OF HVAC&R

GERSHON MECKLER, P.E.

At least 750,000 years ago, our ancestor *Homo erectus* knelt in a cave and applied his wits to building and sustaining a hearth fire. Thus began the long, slow, pre-science evolution of technology to provide indoor comfort: first heating, later cooling and ventilating.

Before modern science emerged in the late sixteenth and the seventeenth and eighteenth centuries, the evolution of heating and cooling technology—the accumulation of practical, useful knowledge or "know-how"—was a ponderous, iterative, trial-and-error process marked from time to time by leaps of inventive insight. Despite the methodological limitations, given human ingenuity the pre-science results were impressive, as the early chapters of this book attest.

Central heating in the large, public Roman baths of the first and second centuries A.D. is a fascinating example. The Romans knew a lot. But, as D. Lindberg points out, the word "know" is tricky; knowing *how* to do something is quite a different matter from knowing *why* the thing acts as it does.[1]

The two kinds of knowing—knowing how and knowing why—imply very different capabilities. Science provides the "why," the fundamental principles or laws of nature that enable us to understand the forces producing the result we see and to invent new applications that were not apparent from previous experience.

Without scientific understanding, technological progress is tied to practical experience and is limited to the "next steps" that are within mental reach based on past practice. *With* fundamental scientific understanding, those boundaries fall away and the realm of the possible expands dramatically.

This introduction outlines the major scientific advances that enabled the craft-based technology of the past to evolve into the science-based one of today. Without science-based technology, modern heating, ventilating, air-conditioning, and refrigerating (HVAC&R) systems would not be possible.

SCIENTIFIC UNDERPINNINGS OF HVAC&R

The scientific underpinnings of modern HVAC&R systems emerged from a brilliant stream of experimentation and discovery in the three hundred years between 1600 and 1900. Among the scientific building blocks were fundamental discoveries about gas laws governing the interactions of pressure, volume, and temperature; the nature of heat; and the laws of thermodynamics, that is, the dynamic relations among heat, work, and energy.

A remarkable characteristic of this period was the close ties and mutual stimulus between scientists and engineer-inventors. Historically this was a period of unprecedented symbiosis between science and technology.

Not only were there many personal, collegial, and student-teacher relationships between significant figures in science and technology—something else quite powerful was also at work. As D.S.L. Cardwell writes in *From Watt to Clausius: The Rise of Thermodynamics in the Early Industrial Age*:

> The development of machines like the steam-engine in the eighteenth century almost forced man to recognise the enormous power, the *puissance*, of heat, the grand moving-agent of the universe. The sight of a primitive steam-engine tirelessly pumping ton after ton of water out of a mine . . . did more for science than all the speculations of the philosophers about the nature of heat since the world began. . . . Thus a great scientific revolution was effected as a result of man's experiences of an enormously important technological development: the invention of the heat-engine.[2]

Steam engine technology has a special place in the HVAC&R lineage. It both spurred and demonstrated major advances in understanding heat and the relation of heat and work, ranging from Thomas Newcomen's use of atmospheric pressure (1712) and James Watt's introduction of a separate condenser (1777) to Sadi Carnot's seminal work in thermodynamics (1824), including the concept of the reversible engine.

Only after the new science of thermodynamics was fully formulated in the mid to late 1800s did a mature engineering science and modern HVAC&R systems become possible. Based, for the first time, on a fundamental understanding of the principles governing the interaction of heat, work, and energy, mathematical relationships were formulated and new analytic tools developed to make practical use of this knowledge. It became possible, increasingly, for inventors to develop smaller, much more efficient and practical equipment tailored to specific needs and for engineers to predict design performance with a high probability of success.

Modern engineering had arrived, with a major assist in the HVAC field from ASHRAE's forerunner, the American Society of Heating and Ventilating Engineers (ASHVE), and subsequently from ASHRAE. Established in 1894, ASHVE sought to raise standards in the field by incorporating applicable science and by using the experimental methods of science as a basis for drawing conclusions and formulating design rules. Chapter 9 tells ASHVE's story.

ROOTS OF CHANGE: 1550-1600

The scientific roots of HVAC&R reach directly to the first modern experimental scientist, Galileo Galilei, and to the early Greek science and mathematics that influenced him. Galileo began the long journey toward a science of heat with his invention, in 1592, of the first device to use the expansion principle to indicate changes in temperature.

Often called the first thermometer, Galileo's classroom air-and-water thermoscope was crude by today's standards. It was not portable, it was unsealed and therefore subject to changes in atmospheric pressure, and it did not incorporate markings to indicate gradations of temperature (it is thought that a separate scale was used). Nevertheless, the idea of measuring and comparing the intensity of heat at different times or different places represented an important conceptual leap.

The thermoscope aroused great interest and led, ultimately, to the ability to measure temperature or degree of heat with consistent, reproducible results based on a common scale. It would be 170 years, however, before Joseph Black drew a clear distinction between the concept of temperature—intensity or degree of heat—and that of heat quantity or heat capacity.

Galileo had been influenced profoundly, as had many of his contemporaries such as Kepler, by the rediscovery in Europe of early Greek science and mathematics. Among other works, that of the first applied mathematician, the brilliant Archimedes, excited great interest. The agent of rediscovery was the printing press, which, by the 1500s, made accessible to great numbers of people information previously available only to an elite few via painstakingly hand-copied manuscripts.

The classical concept of mathematics as a critical means to truth had a powerful impact in the intellectual environment of sixteenth- and seventeenth-century Europe. Something else from the ancient works also had an impact: ideas so rare that most scholars agree that "unlike technology or religion, science originated only once in history, in Greece . . . no other society independently developed a scientific mode of thought, and all later developments in science can be traced back to the Greeks."[3]

Implicit in the rediscovered works of Aristotle and others from the third to sixth centuries B.C. was the unprecedented attempt to understand and explain natural phenomena on their own terms, to satisfy curiosity, rather than to fit the tenets of particular myths or religions. Also implicit in Greek "natural philosophy" was the assumption that it is possible to discover and understand the physical reality of natural phenomena.[4]

These were stunning conceptual innovations. They were not, however, modern science. The key missing ingredient, which would not appear until the late sixteenth and the seventeenth centuries, was the methodical use of controlled experiments, empirical data gathering, and data analysis to confirm or disprove scientific assumptions—what we know as the experimental method.

Why, one can't avoid wondering, did the impressive early Greek work in exploring biology, physics, medicine and mathematics not lead to greater scientific and technological progress in the classical world? After all, in addition to their theoretical work, the Greeks made an enormous number of concrete observations.[5] Furthermore, although the first-century inventor Hero of Alexandria did not understand the nature of compressed air, artificial vacuums, or steam, wind, and water power, he used them all in various small devices he developed.

The answer provides clues to the dynamics of later progress. These were among the reasons: (1) Thinkers of the time, including the "natural philosophers," were disdainful of manual labor, the domain of slaves and craftsmen, and did not regard applied science as a suitable occupation for the philosopher class. (2) There was little communication between the natural philosophers (scientists) and craftsmen (engineers of the time). The principal area in which technological development was encouraged was weaponry. (3) There was little motivation to increase production, since slaves managed to satisfy the material needs of those in authority.

As for Hero's devices, it seems clear they were intended to amuse or impress but not to serve productive ends. As J. Lindsay points out, "no attempt was made to combine the inventive faculty, so evident in a range of thinkers from Ktesibios to Heron [Hero], with such possibilities as were present in the existing technological level, especially in metallurgy."[6]

Contrast this situation with the dynamic, changing economic and social conditions in Europe from the sixteenth through nineteenth centuries. Early in this period, the new medium of printed books contributed greatly to intellectual ferment and cross-communication between scientists and engineer-inventors. Reaching a wide audience for the first time were such works as Georgius Agricola's *De Re Metallica* (1556), a study of state-of-the-art technology in mining and metallurgy, including ventilation in mines, and Francis Bacon's *The Advancement of Learning* (1605).

Bacon's influence was incalculable. He articulated the scientific method that was to revolutionize human understanding and spark an explosion of useful technology. As the sixteenth century gave way to the seventeenth, the concept of verifying scientific theories by independent measurement was not yet part of the culture in Great Britain, Europe, or anywhere else.

Bacon was an impassioned advocate of rational experimentation to uncover the fundamental laws of nature:

> He felt sure that he knew the right method [of inquiry], and that, if only this could be . . . applied on a large enough scale, there was no limit to the possible growth of human knowledge and human power over nature. . . . [This] was not in

the least obvious at the time; it was, on the contrary, a most remarkable feat of insight and an act of rational faith in the face of present appearances and past experience.

What was wrong with the methods in use up to Bacon's time? . . . In the first place [in Bacon's view], there was an almost complete divorce between theory, observation and experiment, and practical application. [Furthermore, too often,] . . . scientists decided all questions, not by investigating the observable facts, but by appealing to the infallible authority of Aristotle.[7]

Bacon's view that "theory must hence-forward learn from craft practices, and vice versa" had a lasting impact, influencing, for example, the activities and deliberations of the Royal Society of London, established in 1660, as well as the French Académie des Sciences.[8] From the 1640s on, there was a group at Oxford University, which included Robert Boyle and which evolved into the Royal Society, that was dedicated to Bacon's experimental method.

INDISPENSABLE INSTRUMENTS: 1600-1660

Two instruments invented in this period, the barometer and the air or vacuum pump, aroused great interest and stimulated both scientific and technological advances of enormous significance to the future of HVAC&R. S. Lilley provides insight into an even more fundamental significance of these and other seventeenth-century scientific instruments (thermometer, telescope, microscope, etc.). Noting that instruments designed specifically for scientific purposes were used in this period on a "big scale for the first time in all history" and "opened up vast new fields of discovery," he observes:

[Their use] did more than merely lead to new discoveries. It played a major part in establishing the *experimental method*—the method that characterizes modern science. Without special instruments . . . [experiments] don't really get you very far—not far enough to show clearly that experiment is a better method than the old method of just thinking about things. Then, when the new instruments came along, experiment produced such remarkable results that it only took a few decades to demonstrate that the experimental method is better than any other.[9]

By the seventeenth century, water pumps—ordinary suction pumps—were fairly common. At the same time, the mining industry was expanding, mines were growing deeper, and problems with water standing in mines had focused attention on how pumps could be improved and on related scientific issues.

Evangelista Torricelli, a student of Galileo, shared Galileo's curiosity about why ordinary lift pumps could not raise water more than about 32 feet above its external level. Torricelli suspected that pressure from the external air—atmospheric pressure—played a role.

In 1643 he devised a new instrument, the mercury barometer, to test his theory about how high mercury could be raised by a vacuum. His predictions, based on the relative weights of mercury and water and the effects of external air pressure, proved accurate, and he correctly attributed day-to-day variations to changes in atmospheric pressure.

Torricelli's experiments, carried out with assistance from Viviani, another student of Galileo, demonstrated both atmospheric pressure and the existence of a vacuum—a proposition much in doubt at the time. Torricelli died soon after, and it took confirmatory work by Blaise Pascal and further work by Otto von Guericke to convince the many skeptics that a vacuum could indeed exist.

Meanwhile, another major invention was just around the corner. It would lead directly to Robert Boyle's historic work on the physical properties of gases and the importance of air to respiration and combustion. The inventor was Otto von Guericke.

[Von Guericke] was remarkable for an emphasis on experiment, which was something new in Germany; and he was among those who prepared the way for the rise of experimental science in northern Europe.[10]

Controversies about the vacuum prompted von Guericke to develop a new kind of pump, one that would suck air out of a vessel. Von Guericke completed his air vacuum pump in 1645, two years after the invention of the barometer, and performed experiments related primarily to the force of atmospheric pressure.

Von Guericke later dramatized both the tremendous power of atmospheric pressure and the vacuum phenomenon in a much-talked-about demonstration. (He fitted together two hollow bronze hemispheres, evacuated the air between them, and then showed that two teams of eight horses each, straining in opposite directions, could not pull the hemispheres apart.)

Robert Boyle took the basics of von Guericke's air pump and created an instrument capable of much broader scientific investigation. He constructed it so that he "could put various objects into the receiver—as he called the vessel from which the air was pumped out—and see how they were affected by being deprived of air."[11]

PIONEERING THE GAS LAWS

Robert Boyle is one of the giants of science. Experiments of 1658-1659 using his new air vacuum pump, reported in "New Experiments Physico-Mechanicall Touching the Spring of the Air and its Effects" (1660), were stunning in their immediate, obvious implications. Beyond that, they led to his assertion, two years later, of what came to be known as Boyle's Law and was later accepted as a fundamental principle of thermodynamics: At a given temperature, the pressure and volume of a gas are inversely proportional, that is, volume decreases when pressure increases and vice versa.

Boyle's were the first experiments on the physical properties of gases. More than 100 years later (1787), Jacques Charles stated the role of temperature or thermal expansion in the pressure-volume-temperature relationship. In what came to be known as Charles' Law, he discovered that if he heated a gas while keeping the pressure constant, the change in volume was proportional to the change in temperature. Joseph Gay-Lussac independently discovered this relationship in 1802.

These two gas laws, Boyle's Law and Charles' Law, have since been combined as follows:

The volume of a gas varies directly with its temperature and inversely with its pressure.[12]

Boyle's Law is also known, in some parts of the world, as Mariotte's Law. Edme Mariotte conducted exeriments with apparatus just like Boyle's,[13] and in 1676 he stated the same law, emphasizing that temperature must be kept constant for the law to be valid.[14]

Following significant progress from the 1750s through the 1770s in identifying constituents of air, in 1801 John Dalton formulated his theory of partial pressures, known as Dalton's Law: The total pressure of a mixture of gases is the sum of the pressures of its constituent gases. Stated another way, "each component of a mixture of gases in a given region produces the same pressure as if it occupied the region by itself."[15]

OXYGEN AND RESPIRATION

Robert Boyle's experiments in 1658-1659 with his air vacuum pump demonstrated, among other things, which phenomena required air and which did not. For example, deprived of air in his "receiver," animals died and fires were extinguished. Without air around it, a watch continued to run but its ticking could no longer be heard. Boyle showed that heat and light can travel through a vacuum, but the transmission of sound and magnetic attraction require the presence of air. With these experiments, Boyle sowed the seeds of future inquiry in many scientific fields.

Having shown that both respiration and combustion require some (not all) of the air, Boyle came close to discovering oxygen. His research assistant and instrument maker, Robert Hooke, who himself became a respected scientist, advanced this aspect of Boyle's work by identifying the air required by both respiration and combustion as the same part or type of air.[16]

In the 1750s Joseph Black isolated "fixed air" (carbon dioxide), and in the 1770s Joseph Priestley demonstrated that fixed air "would not support combustion and that mice soon died when placed in it, but that both the respirability of the gas and its ability to support combustion were improved by growing a plant in it."[17]

Priestley isolated "dephlogisticated air" (later recognized as oxygen) in 1774 and observed that "a candle burnt in this air with a remarkably vigorous flame. . . ."[18] He found that a mouse placed in the dephlogisticated air could survive "at least twice as long as a mouse placed in an equal amount of ordinary air."[19] He did not realize he was dealing with a distinct constituent of air, but instead thought of it as "pure" air.

Antoine Lavoisier is credited with the discovery of oxygen. Lavoisier is also considered the founder of modern chemistry. Within two decades (1770-1790), his work and influence overthrew the well-entrenched phlogiston doctrine and replaced it with the oxygen theory of combustion, helped effect a total reform in chemistry's nomenclature, and established the modern concept of an element.[20]

Lavoisier had studied combustion and calcination and by 1772 had concluded, contrary to accepted theory, that phosphorus and sulphur "combined with air when burnt and that their weight was increased by this combination with air."[21] His finding contradicted the general belief that combustion released "phlogiston," thought to be a kind of subtle fire material that escaped from burning substances.

Learning of Priestley's work in 1774, Lavoisier concluded that metals also combine with air on calcination. Based on further experiments, he established in 1777 that Priestley's "dephlogisticated air" is one part of the air and that this part—which he named oxygen—is absorbed during combustion, calcination, and respiration.

Lavoisier also showed that respiration converts oxygen into fixed air (carbon dioxide). Subsequently, he and Pierre Laplace, using the ice calorimeter they had developed, demonstrated similarities between respiration and combustion.

Chapter 3 explores the increased focus on ventilation stimulated by Lavoisier's and related findings, and chapter 7 describes the nineteenth-century evolution of ventilation standards. Work done by Max von Pettenkofer in 1862 led to the use of air's carbon dioxide level as one general indicator of ventilation adequacy.

SCIENCE OF HEAT TO CARNOT

In the fifth century B.C., the Sicilian Empedocles formulated a theory involving heat, which, as expanded by Aristotle in the following century, remained influential for some two thousand years. According to Empedocles, all things were made up of four basic elements or "roots"–fire, earth, water, and air; varying the proportions of the elements produced different substances.[22]

As reformulated by Aristotle, the theory appeared to explain a wide range of observed phenomena, which accounts for its longevity. Aristotle emphasized the idea of transformation. Associated with the four basic elements were four primary qualities: dry, wet, cold, and hot.

> Earth was dry and cold, water was cold and moist, air was moist and hot, and fire was hot and dry. One element could, in principle, be converted into any other by the addition and removal of the appropriate qualities. Every substance on earth was composed of combinations of the four elements, and changes which we now call chemical were explained by an alteration in the proportions of the four elements.[23]

Although several seventeenth- and eighteenth-century scientists believed that heat is a kind of motion rather than a substance, the "caloric" or material theory dominated eighteenth-century beliefs about heat and was not overthrown until the 1840s. "Caloric was conceived as a kind of all-pervading, imponderable, highly elastic fluid the particles of which were attracted by matter and repelled by one another."[24] Caloric, it was thought, flowed from hotter bodies to adjacent colder ones.

Progress in understanding heat continued despite the material theory's dominance, thanks to scientific experimentation and the new instruments. In 1701, for example, based on a series of thermometric experiments, Isaac Newton stated what came to be known as Newton's law of cooling. In order to extend the temperature scale and determine high temperatures by extrapolation, Newton found that a solid's rate of cooling is proportional to the temperature difference between the hot body and its surrounding

Science Applied to Heating Technology

Scientific principles and the scientific method were applied to heating technology in a significant way for the first time in Nicolas Gauger's 1713 work, *La Mechanique du Feu*. In this regard his book was a turning point in the long journey from the hearth fire of *Homo erectus* to modern heating.

Based on a series of floor-to-ceiling thermometer readings, Gauger determined that hot air rises and is replaced by colder air. He used this principle and others—such as Newton's hypothesis that "heat radiates and reflects just like light"[25]—to develop numerous fireplace innovations to increase warmth and eliminate smoke.

Gauger's work unquestionably stimulated Benjamin Franklin and others to attempt to advance the scientific design of fireplaces and stoves, as described in chapter 4. However, as I.B. Cohen points out, there was a limit to how successful these efforts could be during the 1700s, since the phenomenon of convection was not yet fully understood. "Only after the later [scientific] work of Rumford [1797] could truly efficient stoves or fireplaces be designed."[26]

Early Kinetic Theory

Daniel Bernoulli quantified an early version of the dynamic, kinetic theory of heat in his famous *Hydrodynamica*, published in 1738. His was not a kinetic theory in the modern sense,[27] but his work was "far in advance of the times." He dispensed with "fire particles" and "subtle fluids"[28] and considered oscillations and collisions of constituent atoms or particles.

Bernoulli pioneered kinetic theory in 1738, but it would be one hundred years before the material theory of heat was abandoned and the mechanical theory accepted. As Cardwell suggests, "Only with the establishment of the doctrine of the *conservation of energy* in the mid-nineteenth century could the dynamical theory come into its own."[29]

Latent Heat and Heat Capacity

Joseph Black is a key figure in the science of heat. Black had been a student of William Cullen, who in 1755 wrote of producing ice by evaporation under high vacuum. In advances that were indispensable to future progress in heat studies, Black distinguished between temperature and quantity of heat and, between 1757 and 1762, defined the concepts of *heat capacity* and *latent heat*.

Building on the work of Hermann Boerhaave and Daniel Fahrenheit, Black discovered that the capacity of substances to absorb heat varies according to the substance. This work eventually led to use of the concept of *specific heat capacity*, i.e., the amount of heat required to raise the temperature of one pound of a substance by one degree Fahrenheit (or one gram by one degree centigrade).

Black discovered that a boiling liquid absorbs a large quantity of heat without having its temperature raised and that the heat can be recovered from the steam. He determined that the unrecovered heat existed in "some sort of inactive or *latent* state," and he called it the "*latent heat of vaporization*."[30] Similarly, heat absorbed when a solid melts was called the *latent heat of fusion*.

Within two decades, Joseph Lavoisier and Pierre de Laplace had developed their ice calorimeter to measure heat flow. Devised for Lavoisier's combustion experiments, the calorimeter measured heat quantity by determining how much ice the heat would melt.

Heat as Motion

As the eighteenth century drew to a close, the material theory of heat—the belief that heat is a substance—reigned virtually unchallenged. What accounted for its staying power, despite the fact that Newton, Boyle, Bernoulli, and others had favored the "heat is motion" idea? Cardwell explains:

> The merits of the theory were considerable, for it provided a very convincing explanation of the process of thermal expansion in solids, liquids and gases; it accounted for the latent heats of fusion and of vaporisation and it harmonised very well with the phenomenon of compressive heating or expansive cooling of a gas—indeed the picture of material heat being squeezed out of a gas was a particularly persuasive one.[31]

In 1798, Benjamin Thompson—Count Rumford—dealt the first blow to the material theory and laid the initial groundwork for later acceptance of the dynamic or kinetic theory of heat as motion. The American-born Rumford was a highly ambitious adventurer, scientist, and inventor who won titles and important posts in both London and Munich, eventually marrying the prominent widow of Antoine Lavoisier in Paris.

While supervising cannon boring at a Munich arsenal, Rumford was struck by the tremendous amount of heat generated by the process. He devised an experiment, famous in the annals of heat studies, in which he duplicated the boring of a cannon inside a box filled with water. The intentionally dull borer was connected to a lathe turned by two horses.

Rumford demonstrated that friction from boring could bring the water to a boil within two and one-half hours and that there appeared to be no limit to the amount of heat that could be generated this way. This result was inconsistent with the idea of heat as substance, he maintained:

> It appears to me to be extremely difficult, if not quite impossible, to form any distinct idea of anything capable of being excited and communicated in the manner the Heat was excited and communicated in these experiments, except it be MOTION.[32]

He buttressed his hypothesis with experiments demonstrating that heat is weightless.[33] He weighed a block of ice before and after it had melted. Rumford found that, although a considerable amount of latent heat had entered the ice as it melted, there had been practically no change in weight.

Rumford's heat-related discoveries and inventions were remarkably wide-ranging. He discovered convective currents in liquids and examined their role in oceans. He made the "fruitful suggestion that radiant heat is propagated by undulations in an aether and is therefore of the same nature as light."[34] He made the significant discovery that the shinier a surface was, the more slowly it cooled.[35]

Rumford was a new kind of scientist-engineer-inventor. His keen interest in heat phenomena was practical as well as theoretical. He knew that an understanding of the natural laws or forces involved would help him achieve his practical design goals. When faced with a design problem or the need to invent, his starting point frequently was fundamental scientific experiments.

For example, his study of the insulating characteristics of various clothing materials, undertaken when he was responsible for army supplies, won him the highest award given by London's scientific pinnacle, the Royal Society. He also used experiments with conduction, convection, and radiation to effect major improvements in fireplace and stove design, as described in chapter 4.

As for the kinetic or "heat is motion" theory, Rumford promoted it at every opportunity. His opponents—most of the scientific establishment—attacked it with equal vigor. A significant amount of supportive quantification had grown up around the prevailing caloric or material theory; at the turn of the century, the kinetic theory, by contrast, was too embryonic and its data too incomplete to compete on equal terms. The kinetic theory would not be accepted fully until the concept of energy emerged half a century later.

Key Role of Radiant Heat

Studies of radiant heat and other forms of heat transfer had important consequences during the first quarter of the nineteenth century. They greatly expanded knowledge of heat's role in geophysical and meteorological phenomena. Thus they heightened awareness of heat's vast, all-pervading significance on earth and, indeed, in the universe.

Furthermore, by the time these studies culminated in 1822 in Joseph Fourier's analytical theory of heat conduction, they had raised the science of heat, in Cardwell's words, to "advanced mathematical theory: the first branch of theoretical physics to be established independently of classical [Newtonian] mechanics."[36]

This story starts with William Herschel, who, in 1800, set out to determine which colors of the solar spectrum produce the most heat. Herschel wanted to filter out those colors so he could re d u c e g lare when studying the sun. He set up his experiment to admit light to a dark room through a slit and a prism. A table placed in the light's path held a series of thermometers.

Herschel found that temperature rose toward the red end of the spectrum (away from the violet end). He was astonished to discover that the temperature *continued* to rise *beyond* the visible red end of the spectrum. He had discovered infrared radiation, which he called an "invisible radiant energy" in his paper "An Investigation of the Powers of Prismatic Colours to Heat and Illuminate Objects."

John Leslie contributed to a growing interest in radiant heat with his 1804 study:

[Leslie] establishes that the absorptivity of a surface equals its emissivity and that the reflectivity of a surface decreases as its emissivity increases. He also shows that as heat is radiated from a point on a surface, the intensity of the radiation from that point in an unobstructed direction varies proportionally to the sine of the angle to the surface.[37]

The work of Herschel, Leslie, Macedonio Melloni, and others in the early decades of the century drew attention to the many similarities between heat and light. S. Brush summarizes the principal results of Melloni's extensive experiments of around 1830 to 1832 as follows:

Radiant heat shares all the qualitative properties of light: reflection, refraction, diffraction, polarization, interference, etc. This meant that heat and light must be fundamentally the same, even though quantitative differences in such properties as wavelength might lead to different effects on the human sense organs.[38]

The focus on similarities, coupled with a revival of the wave theory of light, brought brief popularity in the 1830 to a "wave theory of heat." The wave theory held that heat is a wave vibration in the "universal ether." It is worth mentioning primarily because it helped loosen the hold of the caloric theory (heat as substance) and prepare the way for the kinetic theory (heat as motion).

Implications of Dew Formation

William Charles Wells's 1814 *Essay on Dew and Several Appearances Connected with It* gave an original, experimentally well-documented, important explanation of dew's source and causes. His theory advanced understanding of the extent of moisture vapor in the air, the conditions under which it condenses, and the role of radiant heat in the relation of earth to space.

Wells showed that nocturnal heat radiation to space cools the earth's surface and, in varying degrees, the objects on it. Dew, he explained, is moisture condensed out of surrounding air onto cool objects from which heat has radiated. During the day this radiation to space is "overbalanced by the radiation to the earth from the sun";[39] as W.E.K. Middleton notes, "Wells had an extremely clear view of what is now called the radiation balance of the atmosphere."

Clouds can block much of the outward radiation, Wells found, so on cloudy nights there is less cooling and less dew. There is less dew on windy nights than on still nights, since air has less opportunity to remain in contact with cooled objects and deposit dew. Wells also showed that "a dark substance, charcoal, accumulated more dew than pale material, such as chalk, and that poor conductors of heat such as plants, were covered with more dew than good conductors, such as metal objects."[40]

Fourier, Heat Conduction, and the New Science

Jean Joseph Fourier was a brilliant, pathbreaking mathematician who elevated heat studies to the status of a theoretical science. In his 1822 paper "The Analytic Theory of Heat," he presented a sophisticated, mathematical theory of heat conduction and radiation that included what came to be known as Fourier's law of heat conduction:

He found that the rate of conduction of heat through a body is a function of the difference in temperature between the hot side and the cold, with the conductivity of the body a constant.[41]

Significantly for the future kinetic theory of heat, Fourier's work was independent of the caloric theory. Without explicitly rejecting the material (caloric) theory, Fourier's work helped prepare the way for its demise.

Fourier had taken little interest in the evolution of the heat engine. His historic paper appeared two years before that of Sadi Carnot, often called the father of thermodynamics, whose work remained virtually unnoticed for a quarter of a century. Cardwell concludes, "[Fourier] can hardly be blamed for failing to realise that a close study of the operations of this machine [high-pressure steam-engine] would lead to the establishment of a science of heat even more general than the one whose principles he had announced in 1822."[42]

HEAT ENGINES AND THE BIRTH OF THERMODYNAMICS

In the first century A.D., Hero of Alexandria invented a steam device called an aeolipile, which was, in effect, a toy that he did not adapt to any useful purpose. Giambattista Della Porta was probably the first to scientifically examine the use of steam.

In 1601 Della Porta reported his experimental observations that, by condensing steam in a vessel, one could create a vacuum that would act as a suction pump to draw water into the vessel. Near the end of the century, Della Porta's suction-lift idea—and Torricelli's 1643 work on vacuums—was incorporated into the first useful heat engine, invented by Thomas Savery.

Savery started a pattern in 1698 that would recur with Thomas Newcomen in 1712 and James Watt in 1765: periodically, a gifted engineer-inventor would use the latest scientific understanding, available technology, and his own creative insights to give a significant boost to heat engine design and practicality. These advances required tenacious self-motivation, since there were no schools of engineering at the time; engineers had to seek out, from the mathematicians and physical scientists of the day, information that might be helpful.

> [Despite these impressive efforts,] for 150 years the heat engine developed very slowly because there was no fundamental theory or understanding of the energy and forces with which it operated.[43]

Then, out of the cradle of heat engine technology, from an engineer-turned-scientist seeking the theoretical basis of a perfect heat engine, came one of the great scientific breakthroughs: Sadi Carnot's "Reflections on the Motive Power of Heat" (1824). At first it went unrecognized; a quarter of a century later, it sparked a true scientific revolution comparable to Newtonian mechanics. With Carnot's work as a basic building block and catalyst,

> . . . in the middle of the 19th century, a very small group of mathematical and experimental physicists, in a brilliant burst of creative effort seldom seen in the history of science, formulated the theory of heat, work, and energy, on the foundation of the First and Second Laws of Thermodynamics.[44]

The interaction of science and technology from Savery's engine to the birth of thermodynamics sheds light on the dynamics of progress in this period. It also includes key figures in HVAC's historical pantheon such as William Cullen and Joseph Black.

Savery's "Fire" Engine

Thomas Savery was an English engineer who in 1698 invented an engine that generated great excitement in the mining industry. This was the first useful mine-draining engine, which could "do what teams of horses could not do. Flooded mines could now be reopened."[45] Savery put together ideas from Della Porta (suction lift), Torricelli (vacuum), and others as follows:

> In Savery's engine . . . a large metal cylinder is filled with steam from a boiler and then, the supply having been turned off, is drenched with cold water so that the steam condenses, a vacuum forms in the cylinder and water is sucked up a pipe from a well or reservoir, which is not more than 32 feet below the engine. When the cylinder is full of water the steam is turned on again and its pressure drives the water out of the cylinder and up the rising pipe to a storage tank or drainage channel. When the cylinder is once again full of steam the supply is turned off and the cycle repeated.[46]

Savery's "fire" engine, as it was called, "used fire (heat) to raise water (do useful work), but no one really understood what was happening. For example, Savery could not test his engine to measure its efficiency."[47]

Savery's engine was displaced by Newcomen's much more practical and versatile engine in little more than a decade. Nevertheless, it represented real progress; it demonstrated the potential of pumping engines and stirred intense activity to develop improvements.

Newcomen's Engine

Thomas Newcomen, an engineer who numbered among his friends Robert Hooke, by then a distinguished physicist, concluded that he could devise a better pumping engine. His success was spectacular. His 1712 invention was used widely, largely unchanged, for close to seventy years. Cardwell calls it "the first really successful prime mover . . . apart from the immemorial ones of wind, water and muscle" and concludes: "It belongs to that small . . . select group of inventions that have decisively changed the course of history."[48]

Newcomen's invention, described by Ferguson as "an inspired *tour de force* of engineering design . . . [for which] there was no prototypical machine to adapt," put together existing ideas with ingenious new ones. It used atmospheric pressure to power the downstroke of a piston, an idea he got from previous work by Denis Papin and discussed with Robert Hooke.[49] It condensed steam in the cylinder to create a vacuum, as had Savery's engine, but it did so more effectively—by injecting a stream of cold water *inside* the cylinder rather than by drenching the outside.

The Newcomen engine had a huge overhead beam, pivoted at its center, with heavy chains suspended from each end. On one side hung the piston, within its cylinder, and on the other a pump rod connected to a water pump in the mine. When the piston drew down, it provided power via the beam to the water pump. The new engine incorporated a clever automatic valve mechanism operated by the movement of the great beam:

> At the bottom of the piston stroke the water injection valve was shut off and the steam valve reopened. In this way the vacuum was broken, and the weight of the pump rod raised the piston; the cylinder refilled with steam at atmospheric pressure, thus completing the cycle.[50]

Cullen, Black, and the James Watt Engine

James Watt's great advance in heat engine technology—a separate condenser, developed in 1765—was informed by a much deeper understanding of heat. Watt was a skilled instrument maker employed by the University of Glasgow, where William Cullen had investigated evaporation in a vacuum and where Cullen's student, Joseph Black, professor of chemistry and Watt's friend, had identified the concepts of latent heat and heat capacity.

Watt was asked to try his hand at repairing a Newcomen engine model owned by the university. After concluding that "only one-third of the total steam consumed in the Newcomen engine was being used for the purpose intended—to fill the cylinder and produce a vacuum,"[51] Watt became deeply interested in the general questions of what happened to steam in the engine and how to minimize steam input without reducing engine effectiveness (power output).

He took extensive measurements of steam consumption throughout the engine cycle and compared these with a theoretical minimum requirement ("the volume of the cylinder multiplied by the number of cycles performed"). He concluded that waste was significant and that the excess or wasted steam appeared to equal the quantity required "merely to heat up the cylinder after it had been cooled down by the cold condensing water."[52]

While exploring ways to reduce steam consumption, Watt made use of Cullen's work as well as that of Black, with whom he discussed his experiments. Watt integrated his own insights and experimental results about specific problems with the deeper scientific understanding of Cullen and Black; the resulting synthesis was applied science at its best, given the state of knowledge at the time.

In 1781 the first large-scale Watt engine was produced, introducing the separate condenser—to keep the primary cylinder hot—and other innovative techniques to minimize steam consumption. The Watt engine's "power output per unit of steam was four times that of the [Newcomen engine]." By 1800 there were approximately five hundred successful applications.[53]

Heating for buildings also took a significant new turn as a direct result of Watt's work. Based on his understanding of latent heat and his work with steam boilers, in the 1780s Watt built what appears to be the first central steam-heating system, with piping and radiators. He and his partner Matthew Boulton and others then developed and applied steam-heating systems in mills and elsewhere, as described in chapter 5.

Ingenious as Newcomen and Watt were, both lived at a time when heat was still considered a material substance by many scientists, and there was no real understanding of the relationships among heat, work, and energy. It took the science of thermodynamics to produce engines that were efficient and versatile enough to revolutionize society.

CARNOT'S CONTRIBUTION

Nicolas Leonard Sadi Carnot, known as Sadi Carnot, published only one paper in his lifetime, in 1824 at the age of 28. He died eight years later, after a period in the military and before he could carry out planned experiments on the relationship of heat and work. Nevertheless, that one paper, "Reflections on the Motive Power of Heat and on Machines Appropriate for Developing this Power," secured a place for Carnot among the immortals of science.

Carnot took "a giant step forward in understanding the heat-to-work process."[54] He provided, for the first time, a standard of maximum theoretical heat-engine efficiency by which all heat engines could be judged. In presenting his concepts of the ideal (reversible) heat engine and cycle, Carnot reached conclusions that were at the core of, and the first statement of, what would one day be known as the second law of thermodynamics. (The second law was formulated fully and accepted as a fundamental law a quarter of a century later—after rediscovery of Carnot's paper and further work by Clausius and Kelvin.)

Trained in both engineering and science, Carnot had a keen appreciation of heat engines' enormous potential. "They seem destined to produce a great revolution in the civilized world," he wrote in the introduction to his paper. If the heat engine could be developed to "a powerful and convenient motor that can be procured and carried anywhere," he continued, it could cause "rapid extension in the arts in which it is applied, and . . . even create entirely new arts."

Carnot's interest was scientific, a search for general principles, as he made clear in "Reflections":

> Notwithstanding the work on all kinds of steam engines, their theory is very little understood, and attempts to improve them are still directed almost by chance.
>   If the art of producing motive power from heat were to be elevated to the stature of a science, the whole phenomena must be studied from the most general point of view, without reference to any particular engine, machine, or operating fluid.[55]

To explore the work effect of heat, Carnot realized, the appropriate object of study was a complete engine cycle. During this cycle, he noted, heat must be *both* received and rejected, and the working fluid must return at the end of each cycle to its original state, ready to start a new cycle.

Reversible Cycle and the Carnot Principle

Carnot's inspired concept of an ideal cycle enabled him to demonstrate the absolute minimum amount of heat required for a given work performance. His ideal (reversible) cycle eliminates friction and maintains equilibrium across all boundaries within the cycle, except by infinitesimal amounts. Thus it eliminates nonproductive energy osses in turning heat into work and, while not achievable n the real world, it provides a quantifiable basis for determining the degree of nonproductive heat loss in a system i.e., departure from the ideal).

One of Carnot's key insights was that, operating under hese ideal conditions, a system's work potential is due iolely to the temperature difference between the high-temberature heat source and the low-temperature sink, indebendent of the fluid used. The greater the temperature difference, the greater the work potential.

What is called the Carnot principle is based on Carnot's recognition that there can be no spontaneous ransfer of heat from a lower to a higher temperature second law). Here is Sandfort's summary of the Carnot brinciple:

> Of all heat engines receiving heat from the same constant temperature source and rejecting heat to the same constant temperature receiver, none can be more efficient than a reversible engine [engine operating in an ideal Carnot cycle].[56]

Carnot's ideal cycle consists of two isothermal processes ieparated by two adiabatic processes. Today the term *Carnot cycle* refers to any cycle comprising these four brocesses. Carnot's concept of *reversibility* relates to equilibrium. In each part of the cycle, only an infinitesimal change could, theoretically, reverse the particular process (e.g., from compression to expansion).

The reversible cycle and the Carnot principle can also be explained as follows:

> [In the ideal, reversible cycle,] the mechanical work W it produces can be used to run an identical machine backwards, returning the quantity Q from the cold to the hot reservoir. It follows that any engine more efficient than Carnot's would be a source of perpetual motion. Ruling out such a possibility, Carnot declared that the maximum theoretical efficiency of a heat engine, W/Q, depends only upon the temperatures of the reservoirs between which it runs, and not at all upon the nature of the gas inside it: $W/Q = C(T) (T_1 - T_2)$.[57]

Carnot's description of the reverse-cycle operation presented, for the first time, the basis of mechanical refrigeration.

The 1824 paper "Reflections . . ." contained one flaw that did not affect the validity of Carnot's conclusions but did cause some later confusion. Carnot used the caloric concept in his analysis, bowing to the dominant scientific view about the nature of heat.

Most historians believe that the notes he left and his planned experiments show that he had serious doubts about the caloric theory or, perhaps, had already rejected it before he died. In any case, when "Reflections" was rediscovered at mid-century, some who recognized its brilliance used it to support the caloric argument.

Others, unable to reject his conclusions but favoring the kinetic theory of heat, remained troubled until the intellectual puzzle was solved. These two great advances—Carnot's work and the kinetic theory—were reconciled as the physicists William Thomson (later Lord Kelvin) and Rudolph Clausius, building on Carnot's foundation and work by Julius Robert Mayer and James Prescott Joule,

developed the "definitive memoirs [papers] that established the classical thermodynamics."[58]

CLASSICAL THERMODYNAMICS: 1840s-1880

In the 1840s Robert Mayer and James Joule did important preparatory work for classical thermodynamics and the kinetic theory. They established the following indispensable cornerstone concepts: the conservation (indestructibility) of energy, the interconvertibility and quantitative equivalence of heat and mechanical work, and, more broadly, the interconvertibility and equivalence of all forms of energy.

Mayer was a physician who, while serving briefly on a merchant ship in the East Indies, became interested in animal heat and the external heat that muscle use can generate (e.g., a blacksmith's heat of percussion). He concluded, in an impressive insight, that "the heat generated must be proportional to the work expended . . . [and that] there must, therefore, be a fixed relationship between heat and work."[59]

Mayer explained, in an 1842 paper, that his theory about heat and work was based on the principle that *force* (energy) is indestructible. His paper was one of the first general statements of the principle of energy conservation. It also included his value for the mechanical equivalent of heat.

His work was virtually ignored, however, due, no doubt, to his lack of standing in the scientific community coupled with the entrenched status of the caloric theory. Only near the end of his life was his work recognized and honored. In the long interim, it was the physicist Joule whose extensive experiments had a major impact on scientific thinking.

Mayer's fellow Germans learned of the energy conservation axiom from the Englishman Joule, not Mayer, even though Joule's work did not precede Mayer's. Actually, Joule's work also faced disinterest for a few years, until William Thomson (later Lord Kelvin) heard him speak in 1847, was profoundly impressed, and drew attention to his work.

Joule's Impact

During his lifetime Joule became a highly regarded experimental physicist. It was due in large measure to his extensive, careful experiments on energy conversion and equivalence that the science-of-heat logjam began to break: the caloric theory began to give way to the concepts of energy, energy conservation, and the equivalence and convertibility of all forms of energy.

Growing up in a family with a large brewery and machine shop in a major industrial center, Manchester, Joule became interested in the technical problems of engineers. He was also influenced by an illustrious tutor, John Dalton, father of the atomic theory, and by Michael Faraday's discovery of electromagnetic induction, the basis of the dynamo and transmission of electricity through wire.

Joule's work in the 1840s "was of fundamental importance in tracing out the network of conversion processes, and in providing experimental confirmation of the quantitative equivalence of heat and mechanical work."[60] In an important early paper, the 1843 "On the Caloric Effects of Magneto-Electricity, and on the Mechanical Value of Heat," Joule described experiments that demonstrated the convertibility and equivalence of electrical, chemical, and thermal phenomena.

In these experiments, mechanical work (falling weights) operated an electromagnetic machine that generated an electric current, which, in turn, generated heat. The current passed through a resistor immersed in water, and Joule compared the water's temperature rise with the mechanical work done by the weights to arrive at a value for the mechanical equivalent of heat.

He next measured the heat changes from air compression and expansion against atmospheric pressure.

At this point Joule faced the unresolved difficulty that had made Mayer's determination of the mechanical value of heat uncertain. What proof was there that *all* the work performed on the gas had been converted into heat; alternatively, that *all* the heat produced was due to the work performed? Might it not be that in compressing the gas—in reducing its volume—some of the heat released may have been due to "latent" heat being made "sensible"?[61]

Describing these experiments in an 1845 paper, Joule reported the significant discovery that "when compressed gas was allowed to expand freely without performing any work, there was no change in temperature."[62] Heat was not lost simply by changing the volume of the gas if the expansion performed no work.

Experiments with friction-generated heat came next, including what is probably his best-known work, the paddle-wheel series. Joule used weights to turn a paddle immersed in various liquids. He measured the temperature rise caused by the aqueous churning. Repeating these experiments with great care in 1850, he derived a value of 772.5 footpounds of work per British thermal unit as the mechanical equivalent of heat. As Fenn wrote in 1982, this figure is "within 1 percent of the present best experimental value!"[63]

Joule's work gained little attention until 1847, when two events began to change his standing. Hermann von Helmholtz, in a key, comprehensive paper entitled "On the Conservation of Energy," cited Joule's experiments in support of his own work as he presented the mathematical principles of the conservation of energy.

Helmholtz [citing Joule's work and that of others] expressed the relation among mechanics, heat, light, electricity, and magnetism by treating these phenomena as different manifestations of energy. Helmholtz formulated the law of the conservation of energy as a mathematical and mechanical theorum, emphasizing the unifying role of the energy concept as an expression of the mechanical view of nature.[64]

A fateful meeting also occurred in 1847. Attending a presentation by Joule at an Oxford meeting of the British Association for the Advancement of Science, William Thomson (later Lord Kelvin) was deeply impressed by Joule's experiments and theory, which Joule summarized as follows:

Experiment has shown that when living force [kinetic energy] is apparently destroyed, whether by percussion, friction, or any similar means, an exact equivalent of heat is restored. The converse is also true. Heat, living force, and attraction through space . . . are mutually convertible. In these conversions, nothing is ever lost.[65]

Thomson's keen interest helped bring deserved recognition to Joule's work. In 1850 the Royal Society published Joule's latest paper on the mechanical equivalence of heat and work. Beyond that, the meeting of Joule and Thomson affected the future development of thermodynamics.

Thomson (Kelvin), Clausius, and the Carnot-Joule Dilemma

On that 1847 evening, Thomson arrived with no expectation that Joule's ideas would have a major impact on his thinking and work. Quite the contrary.

Thomson had been educated at both Glasgow University (from the age of ten) and Cambridge, had spent time at Victor Regnault's experimental laboratory in Paris, and had a thorough knowledge of the great French mathematicians such as Laplace and Fourier. His previous work had focused on heat issues and electrical theory. At the time of his meeting with Joule, Thomson held Glasgow University's chair of natural philosophy.

While in France two years previously, he had learned of Carnot's work from Emile Clapeyron's 1834 mathematical reformulation of it and had greatly admired the power of its reasoning. (Clapeyron had adapted James Watt's pressure-volume indicator diagram to depict the Carnot cycle for both a gas and a saturated vapor and had pointed out that the area enclosed by the curve of the cycle represented work.)

Although Thomson was not a particular advocate of the caloric theory (heat as substance), he thought Carnot's theories depended on it, and he was not prepared to renounce Carnot. He had the impression that one could not support both Joule and Carnot.

Hearing Joule for the first time at the Oxford meeting, Thomson found his careful experiments and conclusions convincing . . . and disturbing. If, as Joule maintained, heat was the "living force [kinetic energy] of the particles of the bodies in which it is induced,"[66] if heat and mechanical effect (work) were manifestations of the same thing, if heat and work had a quantifiable equivalence and interconvertibility, if heat could be *generated* by work or *destroyed* in the process of producing work, where did that leave Carnot?

Thomson also found great merit and authority in Carnot's ideal cycle of the reversible engine and in his proposition that mechanical effect depends upon heat (caloric) entering the cycle from a high-temperature reservoir and leaving it via a low-temperature sink. Carnot, believing caloric to be a kind of massless fluid, conceived the passage of caloric through the cycle to be analogous to water falling through a water wheel. All of the caloric had to cycle out, and the agent of change was its fall in temperature.

Both could not be true. Yet there was such power in each that Thomson spent the next three years seeking the points of agreement and the means of reconciliation. In the meantime he published an account of Carnot's work that brought Carnot out of obscurity, and he clarified the issues in the Carnot-Joule dilemma.

One fruit of his search was the *absolute temperature scale (Kelvin scale)*, developed in 1848. Contemplating Carnot's measure of efficiency—temperature difference between heat source and heat sink, *independent of the fluid used*—Thomson saw a need to measure temperature in some fundamental way that was unrelated to a particular thermometric substance and that would be meaningful in thermodynamic analysis.

If heat were indeed the result of particulate motion, then there must be an *absolute zero of temperature* at which there is no motion. Experiments set this at -273.13°C (-459.6°F) and Thomson proposed that temperatures measured up from this point be called *absolute temperatures*. As T. Benzinger has noted, the Kelvin scale was "indispensable" not only for the development of modern physics, but "for the entire technology of temperature, heat, and power."[67]

Subsequently, the pieces of the Carnot-Joule puzzle came together for Thomson. He found his solution: there were *two* fundamental laws at work, not just one conservation law. But before Joule published his work, the German theoretical physicist Rudolph Clausius published "On the Motive Power of Heat and the Laws Which Can Be Deduced from It for the Theory of Heat" in 1850. By a different avenue, Clausius had found his way to the same fundamental reconciliation.

Clausius credited Thomson with clarifying the issues, and Thomson, publishing in the following year, bowed to Clausius's priority but claimed independent discovery of the solution. Both Clausius's paper and Thomson's 1851 paper, "On the Dynamical Theory of Heat, with Numerical Results Deduced from Mr. Joule's Equivalent of a Thermal Unit, and M. Regnault's Observations on Steam," are classics of thermodynamics.

Reconciliation: Two Laws, Not One

Both found that there was indeed a conservation principle, which came to be known as the first law of thermodynamics. But it was not Carnot's conservation of *heat*—it was *energy* that was conserved. Energy was never created or destroyed, *but it could be transformed*.

Both Thomson and Clausius believed that two fundamental principles were required to explain the motive power of heat. The second, which came to be known as the second law of thermodynamics, expressed the directional flow of energy toward dissipation in irreversible physical processes (all spontaneous natural processes): hot toward cold, available or usable toward unavailable, concentrated toward diffused, high quality toward low quality, ordered toward disordered.

This law was consistent with the first, since energy was not destroyed, it was transformed. P.W. Atkins explains it this way:

> The *Second Law* recognizes that there is a fundamental dissymmetry in Nature: . . . hot objects cool, but cool objects do not spontaneously become hot; a bouncing ball comes to rest, but a stationary ball does not spontaneously begin to bounce. Here is the feature of Nature that both Kelvin [Thomson] and Clausius disentangled from the conservation of energy; although the total *quantity* of energy must be *conserved* in any process . . ., the *distribution* of that energy changes in an *irreversible* manner. The Second Law is concerned with the natur-

al direction of change of the distribution of energy, something that is quite independent of its total quantity.[68]

The two fundamental principles—the conservation and dissipation of energy—explained and reconciled Joule and Carnot, provided each gave up something: Carnot's "conservation of heat as heat" (and its supposed transfer *in toto* from heat source to heat sink) had to go, and Joule's claim that heat could be converted 100 percent to mechanical effect had to be modified.

Work could be converted totally to heat, but heat could never be converted totally to work in any cyclical, ongoing process. Even in a perfectly efficient, reversible engine, to produce work a portion of the heat had to flow (at a reduced temperature) to the low-temperature sink in each cycle. This was the second law at work.

Thomson (Kelvin) and Clausius Statements of the Second Law

Thomson and Clausius arrived at the second law from different mental approaches, and their separate formulations of the principle have come to be known as the *Kelvin statement of the second law* and the *Clausius statement of the second law*. While ostensibly different, the two statements are logically equivalent, based on thermodynamic reasoning. Both express the fundamental dissymmetry of nature, and each implies the other.

The Kelvin statement relates to the fact that a cold sink is necessary when converting heat into work in a cyclic process:

> [*Kelvin statement of*] Second Law: No process is possible in which the *sole result* is the absorption of heat from a reservoir and its *complete conversion* into work.[69]

The Clausius statement denies that heat can ever flow spontaneously from a cold to a hotter body:

> [*Clausius statement of*] Second Law: No process is possible in which the *sole result* is the transfer of energy from a cooler to a hotter body.[70]

Thomson (Kelvin) extended his analysis of the second law in an 1852 paper, "On a Universal Tendency in Nature to the Dissipation of Mechanical Energy." And in the fifteen years from 1850 to 1865, Clausius did "monumental work in . . . developing the classical thermodynamics," writing a series of papers that "advanced thermodynamics rapidly as a highly mathematical and theoretical science."[71]

In this period Clausius evolved the "abstract thermodynamic property he later called entropy,"[72] presenting it in its most mature form in the 1865 paper "On Different Forms of the Fundamental Equations of the Mechanical Theory of Heat and Their Convenience for Application." He derived the term *entropy* from the Greek word for transformation.

Entropy denotes the degree of disorder in a system—the extent to which the system's energy is unavailable for work. The second law is often stated in terms of the entropy concept. The following such statement, also known as the *entropy principle*, implies both the Kelvin and the Clausius statements of the second law:

Entropy principle (and alternative statement of the Second Law): Natural processes are accompanied by an increase in the entropy of the universe.[73]

Thermodynamics and Kinetic Theory

Acceptance of the first two laws of thermodynamics brought rejection of the caloric theory and revival of the kinetic or dynamic theory of heat. Clausius "established the first significant tie between thermodynamics and the kinetic theory of gases,"[74] arguing, as had Joule, that

... the equivalence of heat and work supported the hypothesis that heat consisted in a motion of the particles constituting bodies. Clausius maintained that the living force (kinetic energy) of the motion of these particles could be converted into mechanical work. . . . The hypothesis . . . made the equivalence of heat and mechanical work conceptually intelligible, providing a mechanical basis for the relation between heat and work.[75]

Clausius began the mathematical development of the kinetic theory in 1857 and was able to derive all the familiar gas laws from it. James Clerk Maxwell took this development to another level. Sorting out the relations between the laws of thermodynamics and kinetic theory required, for the first time in physics, the use of statistical theory:

The kinetic theory interprets the pressure, temperature, and other macroscopic properties of a gas as functions of the average values of the momentum and energy of its constituent particles. To compute these averages Maxwell . . . introduced a statistical distribution function for the velocities of the particles of an ideal gas (1859, 1866).[76]

Ludwig Boltzmann carried this work further in a fundamental 1877 paper on statistical mechanics. In it Boltzmann presented a "theoretical explanation of the second law based on a combination of mechanics and the laws of probability applied to a large assemblage of molecules in a gas."[77]

New Energy Paradigm: Significance for HVAC

From the late seventeenth to the mid-nineteenth century, physics had been the science of force, based on the laws of dynamics established by Newton. A profound shift took place in the 1850s.

Due largely to the work of Joule, Thomson, and Clausius, energy emerged as the most fundamental, unifying concept. In the "greatest reform that physical science has experienced since the days of Newton," as Thomson himself called it, crediting Joule,[78] physics became the study of energy and its transformations.

The fundamental status of energy derived from its immutability and convertibility, and from its unifying role in linking all physical phenomena within a web of energy transformations. The relationship between the indestructibility and the dissipation of energy broadened the application of the energy concept to all physical processes.[79]

How did this profound new paradigm of energy and the laws of thermodynamics work its way into the technology of heating, cooling, and ventilating? Its potential was made explicit almost immediately by Thomson.

In addition to his gifts as a mathematical physicist, Thomson had a strong engineering bent. He had grown up, studied, and taught at Glasgow University, where Watt had worked and where interaction between scientists and engineers was common. His father had been both a mathematics and engineering professor.

Within months of the 1852 publication of his theoretical paper on the universal tendency toward energy dissipation, Thomson demonstrated what the theory could mean for HVAC&R technology. That same year he published "On the Economy of the Heating or Cooling of Buildings by Means of Currents of Air," which "established [his] priority as the inventor of the heat pump."[80]

Thomson applied thermodynamic principles in describing, for the first time, a refrigeration cycle that could be used to heat or cool buildings. He compared the energy required to heat air directly from fuel combustion, as was the custom, with that required to do the same job with the thermodynamically designed heat pump.

He demonstrated, clearly and directly, that the fuel savings would be significant, and, although it would be eighty-six years before the first practical heat pump application, Thomson had "clearly enunciated its principle"[81] as a direct result of his theoretical work on the second law of thermodynamics.

From the 1860s through the early 1870s, the entropy concept was not fully appreciated and was often misinterpreted, even in textbooks. Then, within one decade, mathematical physicist Josiah Willard Gibbs, working at Yale University, did extraordinary work that communicated its enormous power and relevance to a much wider audience.

With mathematical clarity and elegance, Gibbs developed a broad range of thermodynamic relationships, making first- and second-law theory much more accessible. In his major 1878 paper "On the Equilibrium of Heterogeneous Substances,"

[Gibbs] vastly extended the domain covered by thermodynamics, including chemical, elastic, surface, electromagnetic, and electrochemical phenomena in a single system. . . .

Gibbs's [300-page paper] showed how the general theory of thermodynamic equilibrium could be applied in phenomena as varied as the dissolving of a crystal in a liquid, the temperature dependence of the electromotive force of an electrochemical cell, and the heat absorbed when the surface of discontinuity between two fluids is increased. *But even more important than the particular results he obtained was his introduction of the general method and concepts with which all applications of thermodynamics could be handled* [emphasis added].[82]

It was clear from his earliest work, the 1873 "Graphical Methods in the Thermodynamics of Fluids," that Gibbs "assumed . . . that entropy is one of the essential concepts to be used in treating a thermodynamic system, along with energy, temperature, pressure, and volume."[83] In this paper he originated temperature-entropy and volume-entropy diagrams, showing the many advantages of the former in the study of cyclic processes and the usefulness of the latter for general thermodynamic purposes.[84]

Gibbs also made a major contribution to the gas laws, reformulating Dalton's law of partial pressures to include thermodynamic concepts. The resulting statement on the properties of mixtures is known as the Gibbs-Dalton law:

The internal energy, enthalpy, and entropy of a gaseous mixture are respectively equal to the sums of the internal energies, enthalpies, and entropies of the constituents.

Each constituent has that internal energy, enthalpy, and entropy, which it would have if it occupied alone that volume occupied by the mixture at the temperature of the mixture.[85]

Due in large measure to the work of J. Willard Gibbs, it took only a few years for thermodynamics to become a major factor in analyses and technological development in the following heating and cooling areas: combustion processes that provided heat for boilers and engines, refrigerants and refrigeration machines, and, after 1900, psychrometry, which was the cornerstone of modern air conditioning.

SCIENCE OF REFRIGERATION AND AIR CONDITIONING

The ancients were resourceful in using the evaporative effect, harvested ice, and packed snow for cooling. Chapter 2 cites interesting examples. It was not until the 1500s, with the recorded use of refrigerating mixtures, that the transition from natural to artificial refrigeration began.

First, water was cooled by adding salts such as potassium nitrate. Then it was discovered—as noted by Della Porta in 1589—that very low temperatures could be obtained when snow rather than water was mixed with salts. Francis Bacon and others gave formulas for the mixtures, and they "were used in scientific research as early as the 17th century . . . by the Accademia del Cimento at Florence (1657), by Robert Boyle (1662) and by Philippe Lahire . . . who produced ice in a phial immersed in ammonium nitrate (1685)."[86]

Evaporation under Vacuum

William Cullen first demonstrated the potential of producing refrigeration mechanically, although the practical applications that lay ahead were not recognized. In his 1755 paper "Essay on Cold Produced by Evaporating Fluids," Cullen described experiments in which he produced ice by evaporating a volatile liquid (nitrous ether) under high vacuum, independent of ambient conditions.

At this point we may wonder why Dr. Cullen did not immediately proceed to exploit his discovery and build machines to manufacture ice. Did he not have all the essential elements at hand? There was the refrigerant nitrous ether, which in high vacuum would boil at a low enough temperature to freeze ice. Furthermore, he had a vacuum pump that could produce a continuous vacuum. These items seem to be basically quite similar to the component parts used in our modern vapor compression refrigeration machines.

But this all seems obvious only in the light of our present-day technology and knowledge of thermodynamics. [This was] sixty-nine years before Carnot's work on the true nature of the motive power of heat was published, and nearly one hundred before Kelvin and Clausius finally resolved the great enigma of heat, work, and energy through the concepts of the First and Second Laws of Thermodynamics.[87]

Chapter 5 provides other examples of eighteenth-century inquiries into methods of producing cold.

Compression and Absorption

In the first year of the nineteenth century, John Dalton studied the compressibility of gaseous mixtures and the relation of their temperature and volume; he determined, independently of Jacques Charles and Joseph Gay-Lussac, that as a gas is heated, its volume increases proportionately with its temperature. As noted in chapter 8, his work contributed to the development of the first air-cycle refrigeration systems some forty years later.

In the same year, Dalton formulated his law of partial pressures, described previously, to explain the characteristics of atmospheric gas mixtures. In 1802 he identified water vapor as a gas, "refuting earlier conceptions of fire-filled bubbles of water," and asserted that "water vapor mixes nonchemically with the other atmospheric gases to form air."[88]

A decade into the new century, John Leslie, continuing William Cullen's work, provided the scientific basis for absorption refrigeration. Leslie attained very low temperatures and produced ice by evaporating water under vacuum, using a desiccant (sulphuric acid) to absorb water vapor. Commercial development of the first crude absorption machines, based on this principle, occurred nearly sixty years later, as described in chapter 8.

In the 1770s Joseph Priestley isolated ammonia and carbon dioxide, among other gases. Then, beginning in 1823, Michael Faraday conducted a series of experiments in which he was able to liquefy chlorine, ammonia, and carbon dioxide—the first refrigerants—as well as other gases. Liquefaction was a prerequisite for the development of compression and absorption machines.

Thermodynamics and Efficient Refrigeration

From the time William Cullen first produced ice in his laboratory in 1755 until the last quarter of the nineteenth century, the science and technology of refrigeration evolved in essentially separate streams with minimal interaction. The scientific building blocks needed for modern refrigeration systems were not yet all in place.

As chapter 8 makes clear, ingenious inventors nevertheless made progress from the early 1800s in the development of refrigeration machines of several types. However, as in the case of heat engine development before Newcomen, progress was slow. Sandfort illuminated the reason in his comment about Jacob Perkins, who in 1834 invented the first vapor-compression system: "Perkins had little, if any, real understanding of the fundamental nature of his cycle."[89]

The key missing ingredient was thermodynamic understanding. With the work of Joule, Thomson (Kelvin), and Clausius in developing the first and second laws and the entropy concept and with the work of Gibbs and others in generalizing this work across disciplines and showing how it could be applied, the stage was set for rapid progress.

Carl von Linde was the "right person at the right time" to pull existing science and technology together in a fundamental way to achieve practical progress. Linde had studied science and engineering, including machine construction, at the Zurich Polytechnicum, where Clausius had been among his teachers and where he had "developed a passion for thermodynamics."[90] He subsequently excelled as an engineer, applied scientist, inventor, teacher, and, later, entrepreneur.

Linde used thermodynamics, particularly the second law, in his study and comparison of "mechanical methods of extracting heat at low temperatures." In 1870 and 1871 papers, he "compared the efficiency of air cycle refrigerating machines, absorption machines and compressors of liquefiable vapours"[91] and concluded that the compression system was superior.

Using the science and technology available to him, Linde demonstrated that a major increase in refrigeration efficiency was now possible. The vapor-compression refrigerator he developed in the mid-1870s became, as chapter 8 points out, one of the most widely used in the world. He selected ammonia as the preferred refrigerant because of its thermodynamic properties. As F. Klemm has noted, "Refrigerators existed before Linde's, but his was especially reliable, economical, efficient."[92]

Science made the difference. Linde had arrived on the scene just as all the scientific building blocks for practical refrigeration had become available, and he was trained and motivated to use them effectively. His work and its impact are detailed in chapter 8, as are other machine and refrigerant developments in the last quarter of the nineteenth century.

Humidity and the Birth of Psychrometrics

By the end of the 1800s, the few comfort cooling systems in place (described in chapter 11) were ad hoc, trial-and-error efforts with uneven results. Another scientific element had to fall into place before consistent, predictable, and reproducible environmental performance, particularly humidity control, became possible.

That scientific element was the application of thermodynamic principles, specifically the Gibbs-Dalton law, to meteorological (weather) data. The result was clarification of the relationships among barometric pressure, water vapor's partial pressure, wet- and dry-bulb temperatures, absolute humidity, relative humidity, dew point, enthalpy, and latent heat, i.e., the birth of psychrometrics.

Development of a usable weather data base required two things: accurate instruments and systematic records of standardized meteorological observations. Both were available by the end of the nineteenth century, as was the Gibbs-Dalton law, which made psychrometric analysis for air conditioning possible.

The first crude humidity-measuring instrument appeared in 1450, more than one hundred years before the first thermometer. German mathematician Nicholas de Cusa suspended a mass of wool from one side of a balance and small stones from the other, the two having equal weight in dry air. As humidity increased, so did the weight of the wool; as humidity decreased, the wool became lighter.

It was not until the seventeenth century, however, that "scientists influenced by Descartes began to accept the theory that water vapor was a distinct substance."[93] As interest in humidity studies grew, improved hygrometers were developed by Robert Hooke (1657), Johann Heinrich Lambert (1768), Jean De Luc (1773), Horace Benedict De Saussure (1783), and others.

Both Lambert and De Saussure published accounts of extensive humidity studies, and by 1800 John Leslie had devised and explained the first wet- and dry-bulb hygrometer. Over the next eighty years, the psychrometer (an instrument that measures relative humidities by means of wet- and dry-bulb temperatures) was developed fully as a scientific instrument by E.F. August, J.A. Mason, and others.[94]

Lambert appears to have been the first, in 1774, to present meteorological data graphically rather than in tables. For example, he compared daily temperature and hygrometer readings for three German cities over time and noted an interesting correlation: humidities were highest in June and lowest in December and January, and "the temperature curve tends to lag the humidity curve by one and a half months."[95]

Weather observations had been recorded from ancient times, but it was not until well into the seventeenth century that temperature, pressure, and humidity appeared in systematic meteorological records.[96]

It is clear from two noted activities of the 1660s that contemporary scientists recognized the value of standardization in data taking and of simultaneous observations in different locations. One example was the historic weather-observing network—forerunner of modern international networks—implemented by the Accademia del Cimento under the patronage of Ferdinand II of Tuscany.

Ferdinand had instruments constructed and sent to observers in seven Italian cities and, later, Paris, Innsbruck, Warsaw, and Osnabruck. Instruments included thermometers, barometers, and hygrometers; Ferdinand also provided standard forms for recording observations. Although the Accademia was dissolved in 1667 due to ecclesiastical pressure after only a decade of activity, its example influenced the development of similar networks in the eighteenth and nineteenth centuries.[97]

At about the same time, Robert Hooke drew up a model weather-reporting form. In a 1663 paper he proposed a "Method for Making a History of the Weather" that stressed the importance of standard instruments and observations. "Hooke's proposal is considered by several historians the turning point in meteorological development. . . . For many, Robert Hooke is the Father of Modern Meteorology."[98]

International networks to record and study standardized weather observations advanced in the eighteenth century and matured in the nineteenth. Meanwhile, in 1751, Charles Le Roy formulated the dew-point concept and suggested that "humidity be recorded as `relative humidity,' comparing the actual amount of water vapor in the air with the maximum possible at the given temperature."[99]

Le Roy observed that, as he lowered the temperature of water in a container by introducing ice, at a certain temperature water condensed on the container's exterior.

This enabled Le Roy to determine the amount of invisible moisture in the surrounding air: "There is at all times a certain degree of cold at which the air is ready to release part of the water that it holds in solution. I call this temperature the 'degre de saturation' of the air."[100]

By the last quarter of the nineteenth century, a meteorological data base of scientific quality was in place. Scientists already had applied heat theory and the first law of thermodynamics—conservation of energy—to develop the awesome model of earth, atmosphere, rains, wind, oceans, etc., as a dynamic thermodynamic machine powered by solar radiant heat.

When Gibbs formulated the Gibbs-Dalton law in the 1870s, integrating the concepts of energy, enthalpy, and entropy with Dalton's law of partial pressures, it became possible to understand and quantify the psychrometric characteristics of a key element of the dynamic earth-atmosphere-sun "heat engine": moist atmospheric air. Using the existing weather data base, scientists now developed the psychrometric relationships that would play a crucial role in the development of air conditioning early in the twentieth century.

Psychrometrics: Impact on Air Conditioning

Appreciating the impact that psychrometrics had on air conditioning early in the twentieth century requires some awareness of the context in which it arrived. Here, then, is a quick sketch of existing design theory and practice.

As recently as 1893, John S. Billings summarized the space-cooling situation in the United States as follows, in two paragraphs at the end of the new edition of his book *Ventilation and Heating*. (Dr. Billings, a former U.S. Army surgeon, was a prominent figure in the United States. Educated at Edinburgh and Harvard and a member of the National Academy of Sciences as well as a noted writer in technical areas, he did the conceptual architectural design for the acclaimed New York Public Library and was its first director and librarian.)

Occasionally there is a demand for some means of cooling the fresh-air supply in warm weather, as in legislative assembly halls, in summer theaters, or for the room of a sick person, and in the description of the ventilating appliances of some buildings it is stated that provision is made for doing this by blowing the air over ice placed on racks, etc. The use of ice for this purpose is a very expensive method. [There follows a description of the use of 436 pounds of ice per hour to cool the dying President Garfield's White House room in 1881.]

If a permanent plant for this purpose be desired, some form of compressed air apparatus in which the heat evolved by the compression of the air is removed by cold-water pipes, and the desired coolness is produced by the expansion of the air will probably be found to be the most satisfactory and economical. It should be remembered, however, that when the air of an assembly room is loaded with moisture the introduction of cold air may precipitate this moisture and produce a fog or cloud if there is dust in the air.

This was actually the result of one experiment of blowing cold air into one of the assembly halls at the Capitol in Washington. . . . A plentiful supply of air is usually the best method to secure relief from the feeling of excessive heat.[101]

Chapter 11 of *this* book describes German professor Hermann Rietschel's 1894 *Guide to Calculating and Design of Ventilating and Heating Installations*, which included a chapter on space cooling. Based on fundamental science such as Newton's law of cooling and Fourier's law of heat conduction, Rietschel developed what appears to be the first rational design methodology for such systems.

What Rietschel did, in effect, was to use his scientific understanding to define the problem in engineering terms, i.e., to identify the variables and present a step-by-step design process. Because he put science into an engineering framework, making it more accessible to engineers, Rietschel was a pioneer of the *engineering science* of air conditioning.

Although Rietschel had developed a general design guide, in practice cooling was much more problematic than heating in the 1890s and early 1900s. Rietschel noted the importance of humidity control and was perhaps the first to identify general approaches to handling it. However, there were formidable barriers to precise and predictable implementation.

For one thing, heating systems had been developed first, and existing technology such as coils had been developed for heating purposes. A fairly common approach was to blow air over coils heated by steam or hot water.

When cooling systems began to be considered during this period, most engineers assumed that air cooling was analogous to air heating and could be accomplished just as easily. There was little awareness that what happens to air at a cooling coil, when there is simultaneous moisture condensation and cooling, is much more complex than the heating process. As a consequence, they did not realize how difficult it would be to get a specific, predictable result.

The prominent consulting engineer Alfred Wolff was one of the most sophisticated practitioners of his time. Wolff was skilled at putting together the latest technology to design cutting-edge heating, ventilating, and cooling systems. His work in cooling evolved from the 1893 use of ice racks at Carnegie Hall to the 1901 New York Stock Exchange design, which incorporated cogeneration and absorption chillers and circulated brine through coils.

Wolff had come to recognize the importance of controlling relative humidity. However, Wolff was not a scientist, and, as Willis Carrier would soon discover, precise, predictable control of temperature and humidity in a cooling process using coils was not possible with existing knowledge. Too little was known about the interactions of fluid flow (air outside the coil and brine inside), mass transfer (moisture condensation), and simultaneous heat transfer through specific coil materials. A long series of experiments and developmental work would take place before cooling and dehumidification via coils became practical for broad application.

Carrier occupies a unique position in air-conditioning history. Before Carrier, there was no practical cooling system that achieved consistent temperature and humidity control under varying loads; thus there was no opportunity for air conditioning to spread into general use. With a large assist from science, Carrier changed all that.

In his attempt to design such a system, Carrier studied United States weather data to gain a fundamental understanding of the psychrometrics of moist atmospheric air. He conducted experiments to discover how, using what was available in equipment and knowledge, he could devise a system to produce consistent temperature and humidity levels in practical applications.

He succeeded so thoroughly that his solution remained the dominant air-conditioning system arrangement, much copied by others, for some twenty-five years. He used the science of psychrometrics (based on the Gibbs-Dalton law) and a rational experimental approach to problem-solving to find what may have been the only way to achieve consistent environmental conditions with the existing science and technology.

When Carrier finally found his solution and it became clear in the industry that his system worked, the power of applying psychrometrics to the cooling process also became clear, for it had been his guide. Further, it became clearer where additional scientific or development work was needed to advance the new air-conditioning industry.

Working for Buffalo Forge, Carrier experimented with three system configurations. With the first he attempted to use a moisture-absorbing desiccant to achieve the desired absolute humidity. Desiccants are materials with a high moisture capacity that dehumidify by attracting water molecules from the surrounding air. This occurs because the surface of the desiccant material, when relatively dry and cool, has a lower vapor pressure than that of water vapor in the air.

Carrier encountered several problems and soon realized that too little was known about the complex interactions of desiccants and water vapor. Although the applicable thermodynamic principles had been formulated by Gibbs, Carrier determined that extensive experiments would be needed to clarify the thermodynamics of the desiccant dehumidification process before the appropriate engineering technology could evolve.

The second system configuration Carrier tried, which in theory appeared to solve the temperature/humidity control problem, used a cooling coil in the attempt to cool the air to the desired dew point. However, this system ran into the limitations cited previously (too little knowledge of the interacting fluid flow, heat transfer, and mass transfer characteristics in relation to specific coil materials). In practice, it did not give him the control he sought.

Carrier did not believe he could achieve his goal in the near future with either of the first two approaches. Too much remained to be learned and developed.

His third attempt proved to be his historic success. He found a practical, reproducible way to achieve the psychrometric process and leaving-air condition he sought. Guided by psychrometric understanding, he realized—in what was a stunning idea at the time, though Rietschel had mentioned the concept—that he could actually remove moisture from the air by spraying chilled water into it!

He realized that, by controlling the temperature of a chilled spray in an air washer or spray chamber through which the air passed, he could produce saturated air at a specific temperature and absolute humidity and when he heated that air to the required supply temperature, he could get the relative humidity he wanted. He was aware that, as he sprayed directly into the air, the temperatures of the air and water would reach an equilibrium that was related to the air's psychrometric properties: at saturation, the air's dew-point and dry- and wet-bulb temperatures would be the same.

Carrier called his air-conditioning method *dew-point control* and it became the standard technique for comfort cooling in the first quarter of the twentieth century. Chapter 11 provides interesting details about Carrier, the problem he set out to solve, his experiment-observation cycles, and his subsequent developmental work as well as that of others.

Carrier made two other contributions that outlived his specific system solution. While conducting his research he realized that relationships derived directly from the Gibbs-Dalton theory were somewhat at variance with results he derived using sling-psychrometer readings. He developed rational formulas that slightly modified the theoretical psychrometric relationships to get accurate, usable results with observed data—results that could be relied on for design purposes.

He published the formulas in 1911 along with his other well-known contribution, the psychrometric chart. The chart, which he developed based on the modified Gibbs-Dalton relationships (and first published in embryonic form in 1908), became a standard design tool.

Willis Carrier stands tall in the air-conditioning pantheon. He helped lay the foundation for this new engineering science, and his work, which made reliable air conditioning possible, gave the industry an enormous boost. Once again, the "right person at the right time" had combined new science with appropriate, existing components to create a new technology.

Modern Physics and Thermoelectric Refrigeration

In the 1820s and 1830s, scientific discoveries related to electricity produced two separate, quite different streams of development. One led to widespread use of electricity as a practical power source; the other eventually led to electronic or thermoelectric refrigeration in which electricity converts directly to cooling or heating without mechanically moving parts.

In the first case, Michael Faraday, building on the work of Hans Oersted and others dating back to William Gilbert in 1600, demonstrated *electromagnetic induction*, inducing a flow of current in a wire. Faraday proceeded to develop a dynamo or electric generator "far superior to any previous ones, creating a continuous flow of electricity from heat and mechanical energy."[102]

Subsequent work by many others, as described in chapter 10, led to electric motors and to a network of power-generating facilities. Both spread rapidly in the first decade of the 1900s and thereafter, eventually replacing steam engines and gas-driven internal combustion machines as the principal power source for fans and refrigeration machines.

Thermoelectric refrigeration was the second stream of development started in the 1820s and 1830s. This stream would take a very different and slower path than the one started by Faraday. A major sea change in physics—the development of quantum physics—would have to occur before solid-state theory could make its appearance and produce the semiconductor materials that would make thermoelectric refrigeration practical. Jean Peltier, a pioneer of thermoelectric effects, could not have realized the "significance that [his discovery] would have more than a century later as the basis of a new method of refrigeration."[103]

In 1821 German physicist Thomas J. Seebeck, the first pioneer of thermoelectric effects, discovered what came to be known as the "Seebeck effect": a temperature differential between the junctions of two conductors made of different metals can create a continuously flowing electric current; put another way, "an electromotive force [can] be produced by heating a junction between two metals."[104] Seebeck's discovery is the basis of measurement by thermocouples.

Little more than a decade later, in a related discovery, French physicist Jean Peltier concluded from experiments that "a junction between two dissimilar metals tends to absorb heat when an electric current is passed across it in one direction but to lose heat when the current is passed in the opposite direction."[105] This thermoelectric extraction or production of heat, the basis of thermoelectric refrigeration, is now called the Peltier effect.

Unlike Faraday's discovery, with thermoelectric effects there was a limitation on how much electrical current one could get with existing materials. Development floundered. One of the most awesome of all scientific journeys of discovery had to occur before the thermoelectric applications of today became possible.

Following the discovery in the 1890s of X-rays, radioactivity, and electrons, scientists were baffled by the vast new array of unanswered questions. It became clear that answers required a deeper understanding of the nature of matter, of atomic structure. Intense effort was focused in this area, and historic insights came after the turn of the century: two classic papers, one in 1901 by Max Planck and one in 1905 by Albert Einstein, "established quantum theory, . . . a cornerstone of modern physics."[106]

In 1910 "the only conductors technically known . . . were metals, [and these] were found to be uneconomical" for thermoelectric cooling and heating.[107] However, quantum theory gave birth to solid-state physics and, by the late 1940s, advances in solid-state physics "contributed to the discovery of semi-conductors that can produce the Peltier effect with higher efficiencies than previously thought possible."[108]

As a result, specialized applications began to evolve for this new kind of cooling and heating, which, though still comparatively costly today, has special advantages. Thermoelectric units "are of small size, are silent, have no moving parts, should have a very long life and contain no liquids or gases. Moreover, it is very simple to control the rate of cooling by adjustment of the current, the response to changes in the supply being very rapid. . . ."[109]

For these reasons, thermoelectric units have been used, for example, to cool space vehicles and electronic equipment. As the technology develops and efficiencies increase or costs decrease, it is likely that thermoelectric refrigeration will be applied more broadly to cooling and heating in buildings.

* * *

The story spread out for the reader in the following chapters reflects the interaction of science, technology, and public needs, of scientists, inventors, engineers, and the public at large. It is more than likely that this story contains the roots of future change that we cannot yet foresee.

One thing is certain. As in the past, the heating, ventilating, air-conditioning, and refrigerating technology of the future will be shaped by the interaction of scientific discoveries, inventions, and environmental or societal requirements. What is not known is which will be the prime catalyst in any particular period. Each is, at times, the dominant factor in determining the direction or pace of change.

REFERENCES

1. Lindberg, D.C. 1992. *The beginnings of western science*, p. 5. Chicago: The University of Chicago Press.
2. Cardwell, D.S.L. 1971. *From Watt to Clausius: The rise of thermodynamics in the early industrial age*, p. 292. Ithaca, NY: Cornell University Press.
3. Wolpert, L. 1993. *The unnatural nature of science*, p. 35. Cambridge: Harvard University Press.
4. Wolpert, p. 36.
5. Wolpert, p. 39.
6. Lindsay, J. 1974. *Blast-power and ballistics: Concepts of force and energy in the ancient world*, p. 338. New York: Harper & Row Publishers, Inc.
7. Broad, C.D. 1959. Bacon and the experimental method. In *A Short History of Science: Origins and Results of the Scientific Revolution* (Symposium), p. 30. Garden City, NY: Doubleday & Company, Inc. (First published in 1951 by the Free Press, Glencoe, IL, as *The History of Science: Origins and Results of the Scientific Revolution*.)
8. *Dictionary of the history of science*. 1981. Edited by W.F. Bynum, E.J. Browne, R. Porter, p. 413. Princeton, NJ: Princeton University Press.
9. Lilley, S. 1959. The development of scientific instruments in the seventeenth century. In *A Short History of Science: Origins and Results of the Scientific Revolution* (Symposium), p. 49. Garden City, NY: Doubleday & Company, Inc.
10. Wolf, A. 1935. *A history of science, technology, and philosophy in the 16th and 17th centuries*, p. 99. London: George Allen & Unwin Ltd.
11. Lilley, p. 45.
12. Sandfort, J.F. 1962. *Heat engines: Thermodynamics in theory and practice*, p. 112. Garden City, NY: Doubleday & Company, Inc.
13. Wolf, 1935, p. 243.
14. Parkinson, C.L. 1985. *Breakthroughs: A chronology of great achievements in science and mathematics, 1200-1930*, p. 116. Boston: G.K. Hall & Co.
15. Hellemans, A., and B. Bunch. 1988. *The timetables of science*, p. 250. New York: Simon and Schuster.
16. Wolf, 1935, p. 342.
17. Hudson, J. 1992. *The history of chemistry*, p. 53. London: The Macmillan Press Ltd., and New York: Chapman & Hall.

18. Hudson, p. 56.

19. Parkinson, p. 194.

20. Hudson, p. 61.

21. McKie, D. 1959. The birth of modern chemistry. *A Short History of Science: Origins and Results of the Scientific Revolution* (Symposium), p. 72. Garden City, NY: Doubleday & Company, Inc. (First published in 1951 by the Free Press, Glencoe, IL, as *The History of Science: Origins and Results of the Scientific Revolution.*)

22. Hudson, p. 7.

23. Hudson, p. 10.

24. Wolf, A. 1939. *A history of science, technology, and philosophy in the eighteenth century*, p. 177. New York: The Macmillan Company.

25. Cohen, I.B. 1990. *Benjamin Franklin's science* (supplement by Samuel Y. Edgerton, Jr., p. 201). Cambridge and London: Harvard University Press.

26. Cohen (not the Edgerton supplement), p. 199.

27. *Dictionary*, p. 179.

28. Cardwell, p. 25.

29. Cardwell, p. 27.

30. Mott-Smith, M. 1962. *The concept of heat and its workings simply explained*, pp. 46-47. New York: Dover Publications, Inc. (Originally published in 1933 by D. Appleton and Company as *Heat and Its Workings.*)

31. Cardwell, p. 95.

32. Thompson, Sir B., Count of Rumford. 1798. An experimental inquiry concerning the source of the heat which is excited by friction. *Philosophical Transactions of the Royal Society of London (P.T.R.S.)* 88: 80-102.

33. Thompson, Sir B., Count of Rumford. 1799. An inquiry concerning the weight ascribed to heat. *P.T.R.S.* 89: 179-194.

34. Cardwell, p. 106.

35. Brown, S.C. 1985. Benjamin Thompson, Count Rumford. *Physics History from AAPT Journals*, Melba Newell Phillips, ed., p. 20. College Park, MD: American Association of Physics Teachers.

36. Cardwell, p. 119.

37. Parkinson, p. 245.

38. Brush, S.G. 1976. *The kind of motion we call heat: A history of the kinetic theory of gases in the 19th century*, book 2, p. 309. Amsterdam, NY, and Oxford: North-Holland Publishing Company.

39. Middleton, W.E.K. 1966. *A history of the theories of rain and other forms of precipitation*, p. 189. New York: Franklin Watts, Inc.

40. Dock, W. 1976. William Charles Wells. In *Dictionary of Scientific Biography*, vol. XIV, p. 253. Ed. in Chief: Charles Coulston Gillispie. New York: Charles Scribner's Sons.

41. Lyons, J.W. 1985. *Fire*, p. 58. New York: Scientific American Books, Inc.

42. Cardwell, p. 190.

43. Sandfort, p. xiv.

44. Sandfort, p. xiv.

45. Sandfort, p. 14.

46. Cardwell, p. 13.

47. Sandfort, p. 13.

48. Cardwell, p. 17.

49. Sandfort, p. 17.

50. Sandfort, p. 18.

51. Sandfort, p. 30.

52. Cardwell, p. 44.

53. Forbes, R.J. 1958. *Man the maker: A history of technology and engineering*, pp. 190-192. London and New York: Abelard-Schuman Ltd.

54. Fenn, J.B. 1982. *Engines, energy, and entropy: A thermodynamics primer*, p. 92. San Francisco: W.H. Freeman and Company.

55. Sandfort (quoting Carnot), pp. 61-62, 64.

56. Sandfort, p. 140.

57. *Dictionary*, p. 180.

58. Sandfort, p. 60.

59. Cardwell, p. 229.

60. Harman, P.M. 1982. *Energy, force, and matter: The conceptual development of nineteenth-century physics*, p. 37. Cambridge: Cambridge University Press.

61. Cardwell, pp. 233-234.

62. Fenn, p. 110.

63. Fenn, p. 111.

64. Harman, pp. 3-4.

65. Lindsay, p. 26.

66. Buchwald, J.Z. (quoting Joule). 1976. Thomson, Sir William (Baron Kelvin of Largs). In *Dictionary of Scientific Biography*, vol. XIII, p. 378. Ed. in Chief: Charles Coulston Gillispie. New York: Charles Scribner's Sons.

67. *Temperature, part I: Arts and concepts*, p. 255 (editor's comments). 1977. (Benchmark Papers). Ed.: Theodor H. Benzinger. Stroudsburg, PA: Dowden, Hutchinson & Ross, Inc.

68. Atkins, P.W. 1984. *The second law*, p. 9. New York: Scientific American Books (distributed by W.H. Freeman and Company).

69. Atkins, p. 24.

70. Atkins, p. 25.

71. Sandfort, p. 86.

72. Sandfort, p. 86.

73. Atkins, p. 32.

74. Daub, E.E. 1971. Clausius, Rudolf. In *Dictionary of Scientific Biography*, vol. III, p. 307. Ed. in Chief: Charles Coulston Gillispie. New York: Charles Scribner's Sons.

75. Harman, p. 53.

76. *Dictionary*, p. 181.

77. Klein, M.J. 1972. Gibbs, Josiah Willard. In *Dictionary of Scientific Biography*, vol. V, p. 391. Ed. in Chief: Charles Coulston Gillispie. New York: Charles Scribner's Sons.

78. Smith, C. (quoting Thomson). 1990. Energy. In *Companion to the History of Modern Science*, p. 326. London and New York: Routledge.

79. Harman, p. 58.

80. *The second law of thermodynamics* (editor's comments). 1976. *Benchmark Papers on Energy*, vol. 5, p. 104. Ed.: Joseph Kestin. Stroudsburg, PA: Dowden, Hutchinson & Ross, Inc.

81. *Second law*, p. 104.

82. Klein, pp. 389, 390.

83. Klein, p. 388.

84. Klein, p. 388.

85. Eastop, T.D., and A. McConkey. 1993. *Applied thermodynamics: For engineering technologists*, 5th ed., p. 150. New York: John Wiley & Sons, Inc., and Longman Scientific and Technical.

86. Thevenot, R. 1979. *A history of refrigeration throughout the world*, p. 24. Paris: International Institute of Refrigeration.

87. Sandfort, p. 161.
88. Parkinson, p. 242.
89. Sandfort, p. 169.
90. Thevenot, p. 445.
91. Thevenot, p. 445.
92. Klemm, F. 1973. Linde, Carl von. In *Dictionary of Scientific Biography*, vol. VIII, p. 365. Ed. in Chief: Charles Coulston Gillispie. New York: Charles Scribner's Sons.
93. Frisinger, H.H. 1977. *The history of meteorology: To 1800*, p. 93. New York: Science History Publications.
94. Frisinger, p. 89.
95. Parkinson, p. 195.
96. Frisinger, p. 100.
97. Frisinger, p. 101.
98. Frisinger, p. 102.
99. Parkinson, p. 169.
100. Frisinger, pp. 87-88 (includes quotation from Le Roy, 1751, *Mem. Acad. Roy. des Sci.*, p. 490; Paris).

101. Billings, J.S. 1893. *Ventilation and heating*, pp. 492-493. New York: *The Engineering Record*.
102. Parkinson, p. 294.
103. Goldsmid, H.J. 1964. *Thermoelectric refrigeration*, p. 1. New York: Plenum Press.
104. Goldsmid, p. 1.
105. Parkinson, p. 302.
106. Adkins, C.J. 1987. *An introduction to thermal physics*, p. 100. Cambridge, New York, Melbourne: Cambridge University Press.
107. Ioffe, A.F. 1957. *Semiconductor thermoelements and thermoelectric cooling*, p. 7. London: Infosearch Ltd. (Originally published in 1956 by the Publishing House of the U.S.S.R. Academy of Sciences, Moscow-Leningrad.)
108. Sandfort, p. 162.
109. Goldsmid, p. 210.

THE MYTHOLOGY OF FIRE

In earliest civilization, fire had a mythical and religious significance. Fires were maintained and transported over great distances in crucibles by fire carriers, who were often the priests or shamans of their society. Mircea Eliade describes fire in primitive society

> as the manifestation of a magico-religious power which could modify the world, and which, consequently, did not belong to this world. This is why the most primitive cultures looked upon the specialist in the sacred—the shaman, the medicine man, the magician—as a "Master of Fire."[1]

In much of ancient mythology, the origin of the art of fire making is simultaneous with the origins of civilization. The Greek myth of Prometheus, to whom is attributed the beginnings of civilization, describes how he stole fire from the gods and brought it to earth hidden in a stalk of fennel.[2] For the Greek philosopher Herakleitos, fire is a symbol of the divine depth; it is the prime substance and, at the same time, synonymous with logos. Eliade notes further that

> primitive peoples are universally known to have conceived the magico-religious power as something "burning" and express it in terms signifying "heat," "very hot," "burns," etc. This is why magicians and sorcerers drink salt or peppered water and eat exceedingly piquant plants; in this way, they seek to increase their "inner heat."[3]

Figure 1-1 *Prometheus grasping the fire from the sun (from Valeriano's Hieroglyphica, 1556).*

The biblical references to the fire-carrier denote a gentle character: "A bruised reed shall he not break, and the smoking flax shall he not quench" (Isaiah 42:3).[4]

Tinder, taken from the old English *tyndre*, to kindle, was the basic material for starting fires and transporting embers over great distances. The Indians of Tierra del Fuego in South America are known to use a method of transporting fire by covering a portion of the floor of "their canoes with clay upon which, as on a hearth, they maintain a fire indefinitely."[5]

The first fires were undoubtedly campfires used for warmth, light, and cooking.

> In the first crude remains of the civilization of the most primitive men, hearths in the deposits show how indispensable it was for cooking and for scaring off wild beasts. From the beginning of the Mousterian (Middle Paleolithic period — Neanderthal man — 100,000 B.C.) with its glacial climate, man lived more in caves, and the hearth was situated at the entrance to the cave near a water supply.[6]

Discoveries in South Africa and Kenya indicate that fire was used in campfires from 1 million to 1.5 million years ago. Charred clay found in archeological sites in Kenya in 1981 indicate man-made or natural fires. However, more recent information confirms "the discovery of fire as a practical tool" from the remains of burned bones of *Homo erectus* and *Australopi-*

Figure 1-2 *Chichen Itza, Mexico, sacrificial sweat room, Cenote.*

thecus robustus in layers of limestone that represent 100,000 years of use. The discovery in the Swartkrans cave, about 35 miles west of Pretoria, was from excavations carried out from 1985 through 1987 (*New York Times*, December 1, 1988).

Other legends of primitive peoples describe the role of fire in bringing nomadic people together under the common necessities of warmth, light, and protection from animals. "Under the bond of the common enjoyment, the incoherent sounds by which they expressed their emotions were by degrees roughly cast into the elements of speech; thus the discovery of fire gave rise to the first social meeting of mankind, to the formation of language, to their ultimate union, and to all the wonders of subsequent civilization."[7] Although this view of the early development of language may be biased and historically inaccurate, it is clear that the discovery of fire is viewed as a most significant milestone in the evolution of mankind.

Central heating systems were developed very early, but the technology was lost for over a thousand years until it was rediscovered by the Romans. "In 1954, at Beycesutan, Turkey, a British expedition dug up the palace of the King of Arzawa, a kingdom that flourished in southwestern Anatolia before 1200 B.C. Here, ducts beneath the floors suggest a central heating plant."[8]

In Pasargadae (city of ancient Persia), in the fifth century B.C., fire temples were built by King Cyrus to protect the sacred fires that were maintained by the Magi, who belonged to a Median tribe specially trained in the study and practice of religious ritual. "These temples were square towers built of well-bonded stone, with mock loopholes and windows in dark materials . . . Similar structures can be found near Persepolis (also in Ancient Persia) and at Naksh-i-Rustam, along with four-sided monuments having ornamental bas-relief battlements that have been identified as fire altars."[9]

The Inca and Toltec cultures of Central America used fire for the central heating of sweat-houses, which were a part of their rituals of sacrifice to the gods. In the excavations of Chichen Itza, Mexico, for example, located above the sacred spring, or *cenote*, is a small sweat-house that was used to prepare individuals for their ritual cleansing before being sacrificed (Figure 1-2). Fire was the medium by which an individual was physically and spiritually transformed.

The small limestone building is composed of three chambers: one chamber that is a hearth for the fire, with an opening in the side for wood and an opening in the top to vent smoke, and two other chambers that are the upper and lower levels of the sweat-house for the individual to be sacrificed.

Heat and ventilation were important considerations in the vernacular building of the Pueblo Kiva of the southwestern United States. The Kiva is a ceremonial meeting room ranging in size from 10 to 14 feet to a maximum of 83 feet in diameter for the Anasazi "Great Kiva" in southwestern Colorado. "Shape, depth, and construction particulars vary from site to site, but the use of an external ventilating shaft is nearly universal. This feature is particularly interesting for it demonstrates a simple but ingenious device for promoting air circulation . . . and is remarkably well adapted to the wildly, fluctuating temperatures of the southwest"[10] (Figure 1-4).

In Egypt the hot climate required ventilation and minimum exposure to the sun, but heating was sometimes required for the cooler winter nights. Open hearth fires, from dried vegetable matter or charcoal, created warmth but also smokey rooms that were barely tolerable. The Egyptians introduced the bellows to concentrate and enhance the heat energy of fires.

> On the authority of Strabo, who quotes from an ancient historian, the invention of the bellows with a bag of air, was assigned to Anacharsis, though in use among the Egyptians long before the time of the Scythian philosopher. Its form, and the method of using it, are represented in a painting executed about the time of Thothmes, who was contemporary with Moses. The machine consisted of two leathern bags fitted into a frame attached to a long pipe, which conducted the wind to the fire. A string attached to each bag was held by the operator in his hand, as he stood with a bag under each foot. When, by throwing his weight on one foot, he had compressed one bag, and expelled the air, he transferred his pressure to the other foot, and pulling the string attached to the flattened bag, he raised it, and permitted it to be again distended with air.[11]

The most interesting aspect of this invention was the Egyptians' understanding of the use of the valve. Although a relatively primitive device, manually opened and closed with strings, it functioned adequately for these early bellows.

One of the earliest uses of steam was described by Hero of Alexandra in the treatise "Pneumatics" including "existing devices of his predecessors and contemporaries but also an invention of his own which utilized the expansive force of steam for raising water above its natural level."[12] The device, referred to as "Hero's Engine," was an ingenious idea, but it was not applied for any specific use and there is no record of its further development or progress (Figure 1-5).

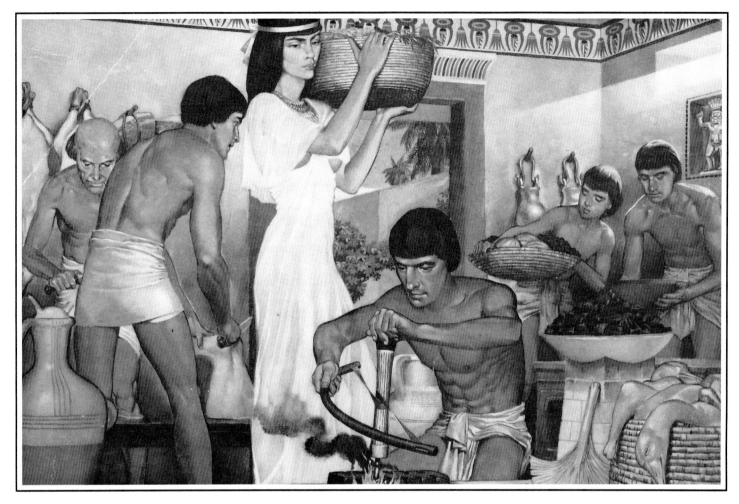

Figure 1-3 *Firemaking in Egypt, 1500 B.C. (from The History of Fire, Universal Match Corp.)*

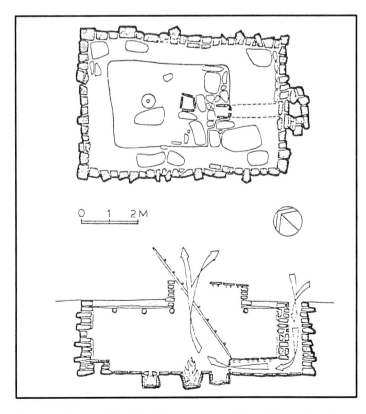

Figure 1-4 *Anasazi Pueblo - Kiva - Antelope Mesa, Arizona (from Labs, K., "The Architectural Underground").*

Figure 1-5 *Hero's Engine, 150 B.C.*

HEATING AND COOLING OF THE ANCIENTS

Heating by Hypocaust—The Roman Baths

Some of the earliest records of central heating date as far back as the third century B.C. when, in the Indus Valley, under-floor heating was used for heating bathrooms.[1] This practice did not become more widespread, however, until central heating was adopted by the Romans. In the Roman Empire, from the first century B.C. to the third century A.D., fire became the basis by which nature was transformed and controlled not only within domestic architecture but also the social centers of the community—the public baths. The baths were the center of the community; they were the source of physical rejuvenation and social interaction.

Domestic buildings such as villas or apartments were usually heated with wood or coal-fired braziers placed in the middle of a room. Smoke was vented through doors and windows or sometimes through vents located at the top of a room. The braziers and tripod supports were made of iron or bronze that were often beautifully detailed and crafted (Figure 2-1).

... the brazier must be regarded as a good method of heating, although the consensus of opinion is that its heating power must have been insufficient. Various facts contradict this view - in the first place, the statements of certain people, such as Winckelmann, who became acquainted with the braziers still customary in Southern countries, and spoke highly of their efficiency. Again, certain discoveries such as those made at the tepidarium of the men's baths in the forum of Pompeii prove that braziers of this kind were capable of heating very large rooms. And lastly, it has been shown by Krell's thorough investigations that rooms of a considerable size can be heated with comparatively small braziers. Krell writes as follows: "The brazier found in the tepidarium of the baths in the forum of Pompeii, standing in the place where it was originally used, had a heating surface of 7 ft. 8 in by 2 ft. 8 in. It is quite sufficient even at the lowest winter temperature to heat a large church with a seating accommodation for over two thousand people, such as the Church of S. Egidius in Nuremberg."[2]

* * *

An interesting variation of the brazier, found at Pompeii, combines the brazier with a boiler. "The plate for firing supports a semi-circular coal pan which is open in the front and

had double walls containing hot water. Its upper edge is adorned with three swans on which is placed the kettle for boiling. Thus the coal fire simultaneously heats the water and the contents of the vessel carried by the swans."[3]

Neuburger describes significant innovations that the Romans brought to the design of the brazier and stove including the use of simple metal fire-grates and cylindrical grate bars with circulating water (Figures 2-2 and 2-3).

One of the earliest recorded developments of the central heating of baths was that of a Roman businessman, Gaius Sergius Orata, who lived near Naples. Around 80 B.C., Orata

built a series of tanks which, instead of building sunken in the earth, were propped up on little brick posts. The smoke and hot air from a fire at one side of a tank circulated through the space below the tank to warm it. . . . Orata bought country houses, equipped them with *balnae pensiles* or "raised bathroom," heated by means of ducts under the floor. . . . Builders learned to apply the Oratan systems, called a *hypocaustum* (from the Greek words for "under" and "burning"), to whole buildings. Under the Principate, Romans who went to live in the northern provinces of the Empire built *hypocaust* houses.[4]

However, the two earliest uses of the true hypocaust—the Stabian Baths (IV period, late second century B.C.) in Pompeii, and the Greek Baths (IV period, c. 100 B.C.) in Olympia—challenge the popular, ancient claim that Sergius Orata, a Roman entrepreneur of the early first century B.C., was the "inventor" of the system.[5]

The Romans used the *hypocaust* method of heating domestic buildings as well as large public structures. Throughout the Roman Empire, from Great Britain to North Africa and Asia Minor, can be found numerous examples of centrally heated structures. "In Rome, a great many of the 170 balnae reported in Agrippa's census of 33 B.C., whose numbers increased to an astounding 856 by the fourth century, must have been arranged along lines generally similar to the Campanian example."[6] The most well known of these are the great imperial baths built in the first and second centuries. Andrea Palladio, in *Les Thermes des Romans*, describes fifteen major public baths which were built over a period of three hundred years.[7]

Figure 2-1 *Roman Braziers, Pompeii.*

Figure 2-2 *Perspective view and vertical section of a compound Brazier, Pompeii (from Neuburger).*

Figure 2-3 *Brazier, stove, and kettle with cylindrical grate (from Neuburger).*

TABLE 1

Major Public Baths Built during the Roman Empire

Agrippa	A.D. 10
Nero	A.D. 64
Vespasian	A.D. 68
Titus	A.D. 75
Domitian	A.D. 90
Trajan	A.D. 110
Hadrian's Villa	A.D. 120
Antonin Caracalla	A.D. 217
Rebuilt original Baths of Nero	A.D. 222-A.D. 227
Alexandre Severe	A.D. 230
Phillipe	A.D. 245
Decius	A.D. 250
Aurelian	A.D. 272
Diocletian	A.D. 295
Constantine	A.D. 324

Prior to the building of the large imperial public baths, there were numerous bathing establishments built in the first century B.C. that used concrete vaulting and dome construction with a great deal of technical sophistication. At Pompeii the Stabian Baths (Figures 2-5 and 2-6) illustrate the organizational layout, which became typical of many later designs, of bathing rooms and plunge baths organized around a central courtyard.

A major restoration of 80 B.C., recorded by an inscription, enlarged the Stabian Baths by adding a (laconicum) and a destrictarium (anointing or scraping room in the traditional Greek palaestra or exercise courtyard). Sometime in the late first century B.C., the circular laconicum was transformed into a (frigidarium) by constructing a circular pool occupying almost the entire floor. (The laconicum of the Forum Baths underwent a similar transformation.) The development of the palaestra's west wing by the addition of an open air swimming pool and a number of adjunct rooms was also

Figure 2-4 *The ancient Roman baths (The Bath, Gerber Plumbing Fixtures Corp.).*

started during this period and continued into the early first century A.D. At the time of the volcanic eruption, only the women's section had been renovated for use; the rest of the building was still under reconstruction.[8]

The Baths of Agrippa were the first public baths built in the city of Rome at the Campus Martius near the Pantheon. Little is known of this establishment today. In 64 A.D. fire destroyed much of central Rome, leaving Nero to rebuild a new city with broad streets, concrete and brick buildings, and large civic structures. The Baths of Nero, built 50 years later, were some of the first imperial baths.

The Baths of Titus were almost four acres in size and consisted of symmetrical, rectangular enclosures of bath buildings and pools. The baths were begun by Vespasian and completed by Titus in 75-80 A.D. and were located on the lower slopes of the Esquiline near the Domus Aurea and the Colosseum. Most of what is known of this complex is from measured sketches from the sixteenth century by Palladio Audrea.

The public baths, or *thermea*, included many different heating rooms, including a *caldarium* or steam room, a *tepidarium* or warming room, a *laconicum* or dry heat room, and a *frigidarium* or public bathing pool. Often included within the facility were toilet rooms, libraries, and meeting halls.

Vitruvius, Roman architect and engineer during the reign of Emperor Augustus (30 B.C. - A.D. 14), gives a description of the methods of construction for the *caldarium* (Figure 2-7)

> The floor of the *hypocaust* beneath the *caldarium* itself is paved with 18" square tiles and is inclined towards the fireplace. On these tiles are placed 8" square brick pillars 2' high and cemented with a clay and hair mixture. On these pillars are placed 2' squares to form the ceiling of the *hypocaust* or floor of the *caldarium*. Air is admitted into the *caldarium* chamber through an oculus in the roof, from which a bronze shield is suspended by chains. By raising or lowering the shield, the aperture is open or closed and the heat is regulated.[9]

Exhaust venting of the smoke was usually done through an opening in the *hypocaust* chamber itself to eliminate the problem of smoke within rooms. Distribution of heat within a building was often done with clay tile risers or chimneys built within the walls, which were open to the *hypocaust* at the bottom and to the outside at the top.

The Roman pursuit of physical comfort was further enhanced by the use of glass. The Romans knew of the use of glass from the Egyptians and employed it in domestic architecture as well as public buildings. Although not common, due to its scarcity and expense, glass was used by the wealthy in their villas and, in some instances, for the large public baths. Sheets of talc and mica were used as "weather screens" as described by the Roman statesman Seneca (4 B.C. - A.D. 65).[10] In Ostia, sheets of mica were used to glaze window openings in baths, and in Pompeii, greenish colored glass was used in both villas and baths.

The Temple of Sulis Minerva—Bath, England

One of the early and most well preserved of the Roman baths is that of *Aquae Sulis*, the Roman name for what is

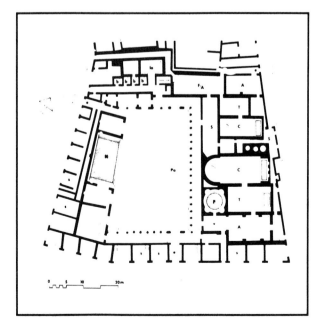

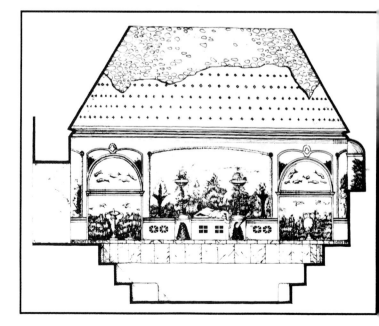

Figure 2-5 *Stabian Baths, 80 B.C., Pompeii. Site plan and section through circular frigidarium (originally laconicum). Wall painted in garden and marine scenes (Eschebach).*

Figure 2-6 *Women's apodyterium in Stabian Baths, Pompeii (Fototeca).*

Figure 2-7 *Hypocaust chamber (from Bernan).*

now the town of Bath, England. The first architectural development around the hot springs (which yield roughly one quarter of a million gallons of water daily) under the Romans may have begun late in the first century but the actual use of the site as a curative center, where the Celtic god Sul was worshipped, definitely goes back to the Iron Age.[11] After the Roman conquest of Britain in 43 A.D., the Romans discovered the hot mineral springs in Bath around which they built the baths and a temple to the goddess *Sulis Minerva*. Current archaeological excavations indicate that the baths were expanded during four major stages of construction. From the original construction in the first century, the baths were expanded in scale and complexity throughout their life to the fourth or fifth century. The baths were fed by the sacred, underground spring of *Aquae Sulis* located in the northeast corner of the baths and piped directly to the Great Bath. "The spring held a considerable power over visitors to the temple because it was here that they could come closest to the divinities of the underworld and in particular to Sulis Minerva who presided over the waters."[12]

The overall bathing facility included (from west to east) a series of individual baths of diminishing size and temperature, referred to as the Great Bath, the Lucas Bath, the 1923 Bath (after its excavation—Natatio from period I), and a series of small, semi-circular cold immersion baths located on opposite ends of the Lucas Bath (period IV) (Figure 2-8). On the western end of the bath were all of the earliest heated baths, which "were different in function and architecture" from those on the eastern end. These included the *fridgidarium* pool and *tepidarium* and *caldarium* chambers. Later, expansion to the east of the Lucas Baths replaced the 1923 Bath with the construction of additional *tepidarium* and *caldarium* chambers.

The Great Bath was 72¼ by 29¼ by 5 feet deep and was surrounded by an open arcade (53 m x 74 m). Within the arcade were alternating rectangular and semi-circular niches that were filled with sculpture. It was used as a meeting place and for a "warm gentle swim rather than for hot treatments."[13] The floor of the bath was lead-lined to retain the water and prevent minor springs from leaking to the surface. The hot spring water was directed to the Great Bath directly from the spring through a lead-lined boxed pipe. This pipe also served a fountain on the north side of the Great Bath.

The West Baths included a *frigidarium* and *tepidarium* and *caldarium* rooms. A *laconium* was introduced by the Romans in the second century.

The *East Baths*, the center of which was the Lucas Bath, were discovered in 1755.

This was a warm plunge bath, although the water would have been cooler than the Great Bath, as it had further to travel. It had steps leading into it and was probably lead-lined, although no trace of lead now remains. The water came from the Great Bath and originally was let out again to feed yet another bath, smaller and cooler in temperature. This smaller bath disappeared as the facilities were improved and, in its place, the Romans built heated rooms or a Turkish Bath. First was the *tepidarium* where warm air entered from the *hypocaust*; then a room called the *caldarium* where the temperature was warmed with hot air circulating directly below the floor; and then a further *tepidarium* in which to cool off slightly.[14]

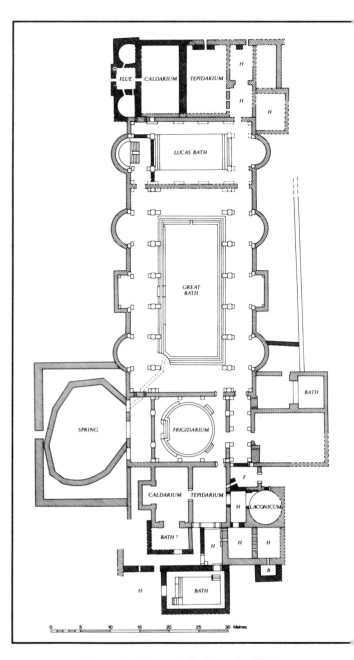

Figure 2-8 *Aquae Sulis (from Cunliffe).*

On the north side of the East Bath was a sunken immersion pool fed from a lead pipe. The circular bath was 30 ft in diameter and 4 ft deep with steps leading into it.

This was a cold plunge bath built in the second century A.D. in the period after the main construction when this whole area was altered and extended with the addition of further heat rooms and an area for vigorous exercises. It was customary to take a cold plunge after using one of the hot treatment rooms before taking a relaxing swim in the warm waters of the Great Bath.[15]

Throughout the four-hundred-year history of Aquae Sulis, alterations and additions to the baths, reconstruction of *hypocaust* chambers, and structural modifications such as roof vaulting over the Great Bath and lateral reinforcement continued to be carried out. The floor of the Great Bath was lowered and repaved with limestone slabs and additional sources of heat were provided for *tepidarium* and *caldarium* chambers.

Figure 2-9 *Hypocaust Chamber of Tepidarium, west bath (from Cunliffe).*

Eventually, flooding from underground springs and the continual seepage of mud into the *hypocaust* chambers and the baths themselves rendered the establishment unusable. Ultimately it had to be abandoned "and the centre of Bath reverted once more to a marsh" until it was rediscovered in the eighteenth century.

The Baths of Trajan

The Baths of Trajan, built between A.D. 104 and 109 in Rome, were designed by the architect Appolodorus of Damascus who adopted the concrete medium of *opus caementicium* to the vaulted structures of the baths. The entire complex, almost 23 acres in size, was a symmetrical enclosure with all of the bathing structures and pools occupying 10 acres of the north side of the complex. The baths of Trajan incorporated a large swimming pool (1), frigidarium (2), caldarium (3), and palaestrae exercise yards (4) in a formal, axial symmetry (Figure 2-10). Yegul refers to the innovation of establishing the frigidarium and caldarium at the center of large axial compositions of cross-vaulted bays, introducing double palaestra symmetrically on either side of the frigidarium, the introduction of a large, open air swimming pool as a major element, and the use of an "outer girdle of secondary elements and supporting functions enveloping the bath block on three or four sides."[16] "It introduced, perhaps for the first time in Rome, intellectual as well as hygienic, recreational, and athletic concerns into the program of the imperial thermae."[17]

Hadrian's Villa

The complex of buildings at Hadrian's Villa in Tivoli were built as a country residence and pleasure spot for the Emperor Hadrian. The complex was built between 118 and 125 A.D. and was occupied by the Emperor Hadrian for only a short period of time before his death. The villa occupied over one hundred acres with many buildings and pavilions, and it included a number of pools and fountains, as well as baths heated by *hypocaust*. The three major baths at Hadrian's Villa include the Large Baths, the Small Baths, and the Heliocaminus Baths. "The Large Baths display a remarkably orderly distribution, balancing a straight frontal row of heated halls with an amply disposed progression of spaces (palaestra, entrance hall (B), natatio (N), and cross-vaulted frigidarium) perpendicular to them which constitute an axis terminating in the round heliocaminus (I)."[18] The Small Baths, located on an axis immediately to the west of the Large Baths, compress a number of facilities into a complex geometric assemblage of rooms and pools. "The urge for experimentation and surprise seems to have reached a peak in the tightly composed, dynamic spatial units of the Small Baths. This building is a rare gem in Roman thermal design and a worthy exponent of the revolutionary architectural thinking that typifies the villa and its celebrated master."[19]

The Forum Baths at Ostia

The Roman Baths at Ostia were built in the second century. Ostia, on the Mediterranean coast directly west of Rome, was (and is today) a popular resort for Romans who wished to get away from the hectic pace of urban life. The town of Ostia included private residences and various public and private baths, many of which were heated by the method of *hypocaust*. There were "some twenty small and medium-sized baths, in addition to several thermae, . . . integrated into the dense fabric of the crowded port city."[20]

One of the local public bathing facilities in Ostia is the *Terme del Foro* or Forum Baths, which included libraries and gymnasia as well as various bathing chambers controlled at different temperatures (Figure 2-14). The octagonal room 1 is referred to as a *heliocaminus*, which is for sunbathing and,

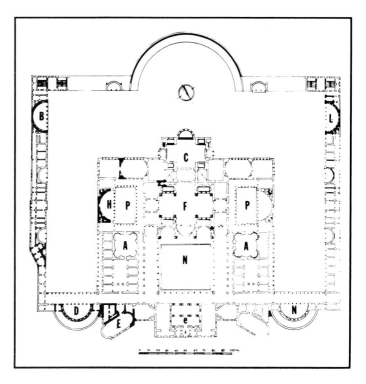

Figure 2-10 *Baths of Trajan, Rome.*

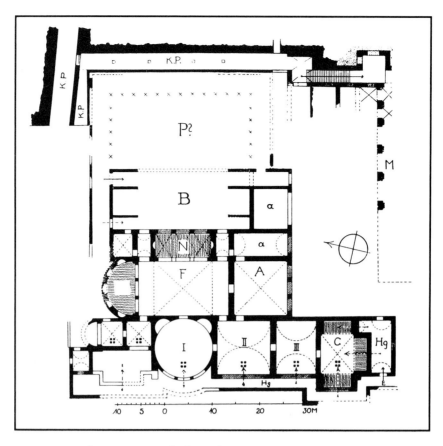

Figure 2-11 *Large baths, Hadrian's Villa, Tivoli (Krencker).*

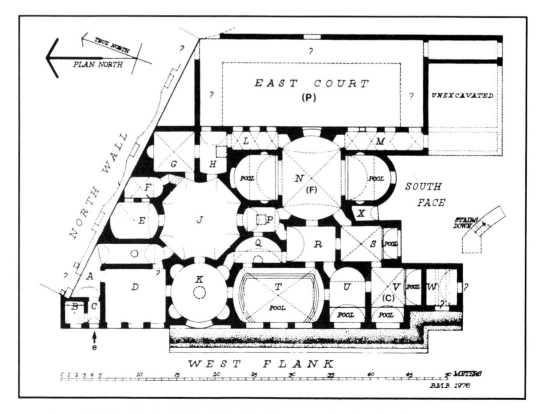

Figure 2-12 *Small baths, Hadrian's Villa, Tivoli (courtesy of B.M. Boyle and W.L. MacDonald).*

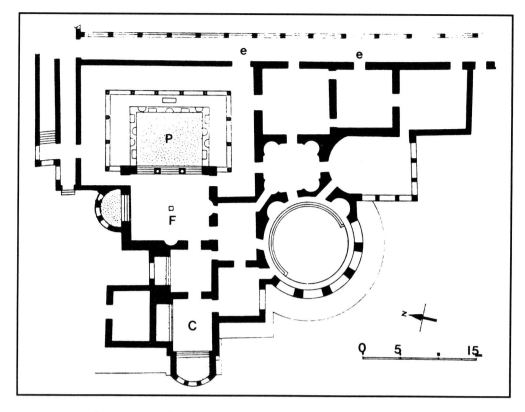

Figure 2-13 *Baths-with-Heliocaminus, Hadrian's Villa, Tivoli (Hermann).*

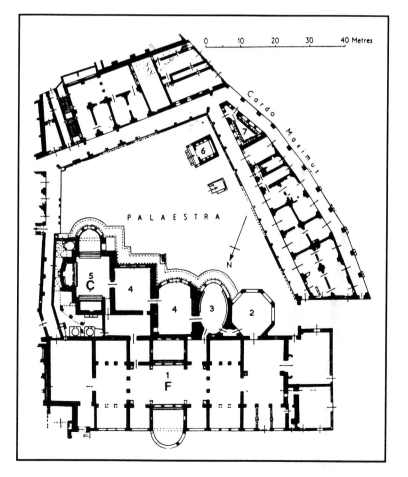

Figure 2-14 *The forum baths, Ostia (from Meiggs).*

therefore, has the greatest solar exposure. Room 2 is a *laconicum*, or dry heat sauna-type space; rooms 3 and 4 are *tepidaria*; room 5 is a *caldarium* steam room with three hot pools, one of which faces an opening onto the courtyard. Room 7 is the service area that contained the brazier heaters for the three *caldarium* pools. Rooms 10 and 12 are *tepidaria* flanking a *frigidarium* cold plunge bath (11) that is connected to the *tepidaria* rooms 2 and 6. Rooms 9 and 13 are libraries. Rooms 8 and 14 are entrance lobbies.

The plan organization of the Forum Baths and the orientation to the sun allow for a flexibility and diversity of use that was one of the most luxurious of its time. The spaces that face onto the courtyard or piazza were originally glazed in thin sheets of translucent mica to allow sunlight in and retain the warm heat of the *tepidaria* and *caldaria* chambers. The orientation of rooms 1 through 5 is such that each room has a southwest exposure to take greatest advantage of the warm afternoon sun. Other establishments such as the Baths of the Seven Sages were built in Ostia.

With further development of Roman baths in the second century, technology remained essentially the same. However, their size and stature grew considerably from the Baths at Hadrian's Villa to such grand designs as that of Caracalla and Diocletian.

The Baths of Caracalla

According to Cameron in his *Baths of the Romans*, the Baths of Caracalla in Rome were begun by Septimius Severus in the beginning of the third century—206 - 216 A.D. They were built over a large *hypocaust* heating system for the numerous chambers and pools. The Baths of Caracalla occupy an area of almost 120,000 square meters or about 30 acres. It could seat as many as 1,600 bathers. It was "restored for the last time by Theodoric in the early 6th century but fell into disuse soon after 537 when the aqueducts of Rome were severed by the Goths."[21]

The Baths of Caracalla included a very large central *frigidarium* (A) adjacent to an equally large *tepidarium* (B) and a circular *caldarium* chamber (D) (Figure 2-15). The main *tepidarium* is flanked on both sides by courtyards (G) and gymnasia (F). To the southwest of the main buildings of the baths are the gardens and libraries (T). The entire complex is enclosed and surrounded by walls of traditional tufa construction.

The great *frigidarium* at Caracalla was the main intersection of the primary axes of the building and a significant focal element of the architecture. The frigidarium "at 170 feet long by 82 wide by more than 100 feet high, this perhaps most sublime of all antique secular spaces richly deserved the careful attention Palladio devoted to its reconstructions."[22] The large domed *caldarium* also had a dramatic focus emphasized by its formal references to the Pantheon, its location within the overall symmetry, and its enormous size. Both of these structures became prototypes for later Roman buildings and for many examples of buildings in western architecture since. Maxentius borrowed the form of Caracalla's *frigidarium* for the Basilica he built near the Forum; and the form of Caracalla's *caldarium* can be seen in the Piazzo d'Oro at Hadrian's Villa in Tivoli.

Unlike *Aquae Sulis*, there were no hot springs at Caracalla, hence, the water had to be heated by fires. The immense amount of water in the baths was heated in 28

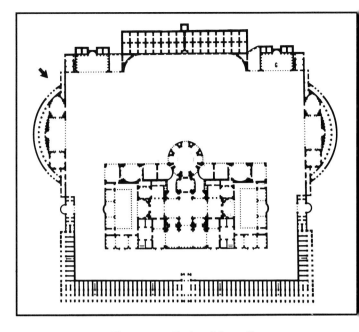

Figure 2-15 *Baths of Caracalla.*

chambers in two rows of 14 on each side (S). Each chamber was 49 feet 6 inches long by 27 feet 6 inches wide by 30 feet-0 inches high and held approximately 41,000 cubic feet of water over 1,361 square feet of floor area that was heated by the *hypocaust* below.

However, the *hypocaust* by itself would not have been sufficient to heat such a volume of water to an acceptably warm temperature.

Hence, the Romans developed an ingenious method of heating that both increased the efficiency of heat transfer and provided a practical means of separating the heat source from its medium of distribution. Essentially a heat exchanger, this heating device, called a *milarium*, was comprised of a brass furnace surrounded by a leaden vessel filled with water circulating from the pools. Thin brass pipes, called *dracones*, led from the perimeter vessel of water to the core of the furnace, and acted as heat exchangers to heat the water. One end of the *dracone* was inserted in the bottom of the *milarium* and another at the top.

> *Thermea* (public baths) of large dimension might have had several milaria (heating devices) connected with them, but those of moderate capacity, and more especially private baths, were probably sufficiently supplied with one. Its great value to the Romans arose from the facility it gave of heating elevated or hanging baths. In these structures it was a principal object not only to have them as large and commodious as those placed on the ground, but to insure an extensive prospect to the bathers. The milarium put this in their power. The *draco* could be carried from a furnace below to any height, and it was a more manageable and compact apparatus than a *hypocaust*, if erected on an upper floor.[23]

Roman Baths throughout the Empire

John B. Ward-Perkins describes numerous baths built by the Romans throughout the provinces outside Italy in terms of three predominant types: (1) "the ancestor of the modern spa. . . . characterized by the number and size of the plunge baths, . . . (2) the huge, symmetrically planned imperial baths; and (3) the more intimate, domestic versions (*balnae*)."[24]

The spa-type bathing establishments were often built on the source of mineral springs, such as *Aquae Sulis* in Bath, England; in Baden, Baden and Badenweiler, Germany; and at Glanum (St. Remy-de-Provence), France. In Badenweiler, "four major rectangular halls with large pools, outlying courtyards and vestibules, and changing rooms (A1-A2) are laid out on both sides of the axis as mirror images. This section comprises the unheated, thermal baths."[25] "The complex at Badenweiler was definitely associated with the cult of Diana Abnoba, the local protectress of the curative waters, whose altar, bearing a votive inscription, was found in the building."[26] Even to the far reaches of the Roman Empire, baths were built in regions as diverse as Augusta Traiana (Stara Zagora), Bulgaria; and Aquae Flavianae (El Hamman), Algeria (Figure 2-16). "The thermo-mineral baths at Augusta Traiana itself (c. 15 km. west of Stara Zagora, on the slopes of Sredna Gova) are more elaborate, consisting of a compact group of four major rectangular

halls with numerous annexed rooms. Two of the large halls contain pools (A and B). The water was supplied from a vaulted square reservoir located in the main hot spring, positioned diagonally against the building. According to the dedicatory inscription, the baths and a shrine to the nymphs (possibly a yet unexcavated nymphaeum) were erected c. 163 by Ulpius Hieronymous, a citizen of Augusta Traiana."[27]

The Hadrianic baths at Leptis Magna (Tripolitania), Libya, were derived from symmetrical "Imperial" baths such as Trajan and Caracalla. The Huntings Baths at Leptis Magna were derived from the smaller scale domestic *balnae*.

As the Romans expanded the Empire into Europe, North Africa, and Asia Minor, they brought with them the knowledge and skills of construction as well as their taste for the

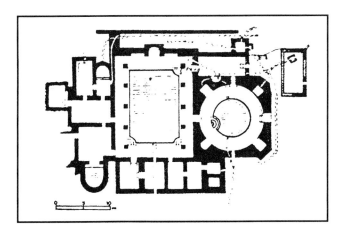

a) Aquae Flavianae, Algeria thermal baths (Krencker).

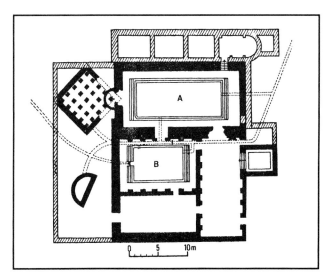

b) Augusta Traiana, Mineral baths (near Stara Zagora, Bulgaria, Hoddinott).

Figure 2-16 *Roman baths.*

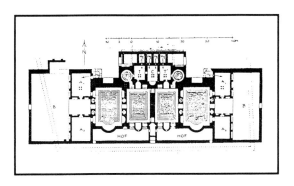

c) Badenweiler, Germany.

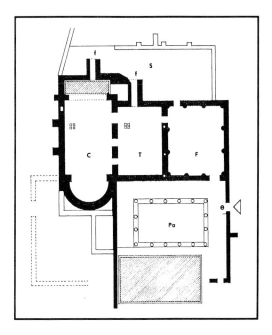

d) Glanum, St. Remy-de-Provence, France (40 B.C.) (Yegul after Grenier).

comforts of their homeland. The construction of *thermea* and other centrally heated buildings continued throughout the Roman Empire with examples such as the Baths of Khirbat al-Mafjar and Qusayr Amra (Figures 2-17 through 2-19). The traditional symmetry of the Caracalla or Diocletian plan gives way to a more loosely symmetrical assemblage of buildings that is typical in many examples of Islamic architecture. Qusayr Amra (the little palace of Amra), located in the desert about 50 miles east of Amman, Jordan, is a relatively small limestone structure including a main entrance hall and a bath consisting of three rooms extending east from the main structure. The structure, built by Al-Walid in the eighth century (711-715), has been referred to as a permanent encampment for the Nomadic family members of the Umayyad Khalif of the Byzantine Empire. The three rooms of the bath include an *apodyterium*, a *tepidarium*, and a *caldarium*. The caldarium is "a dome resembling the vault of heaven . . . for the chief constellations of the northern hemisphere are depicted there, together with the signs of the Zodiac. In the centre are the Great Bear and the Little Bear, separated by the tail of the Dragon."[28]

During the decline of the Roman Empire, sometime around the end of the sixth and the beginning of the seventh century, the use of central heating by *hypocaust* disappeared. In some rare examples, during the twelfth and thirteenth centuries, *hypocaust* heating was used for bathing establishments as well as buildings. It may even be that the concept was reintroduced to western Europe by the Moors.

In Spain, *hypocaust* systems were built by Ibn el-Ahmar (Alhamar the first King of the Nasrids) in the 1240s at the Alhambra in Granada. The *Baños Arabes* (Arab Baths) were used by the Sultan's favorite concubines (Figures 2-20 and 2-21).

Refrigeration and Cooling of the Ancients

It has been suggested that the history of refrigeration (and other advances as well) begins not with art or science but with instinct. The basic drive to avoid extreme heat or cold was followed by observation of these phenomena. As humankind progressed in its thinking ability, mere observation gave way to attempts to imitate, harness, and use the forces of nature. Observation of the cooling effect of snow and ice led to its harvest and storage. Realization of the cooling effect of sweat evaporation led to the storage of drinking water in porous leather bags and jars and ulti-

mately to ice making and primitive air conditioning using the evaporative effect.[29]

Evaporative Cooling

Ice was a yearly natural occurrence in areas with cold winters; however, examples of natural refrigeration were seen in warmer areas as well. "Ice wells" or "ice caves" were found in some locations. For example, in Sicily the presence of porous volcanic rock makes examples of ice wells numerous. Air blowing through moist rock results in such evaporative cooling that ice is formed in some deep holes or wells. Interestingly, this ice is prone to form in the warm months while it usually proceeds to melt when winter arrives. No doubt the initially warm air's relative humidity is lowered as it passes through the cooler rocks,

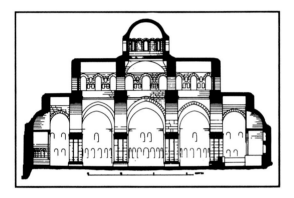

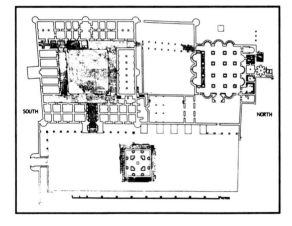

Figure 2-18 *Khirbat al-Mafjar (from Ward-Perkins).*

Figure 2-17 *Qusayr Amra (from K.A.C. Creswell).*

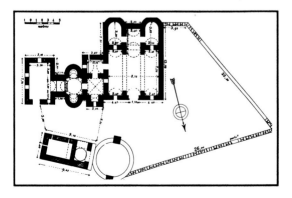

Figure 2-19 *Qusayr Amrah (from Ward-Perkins), eighth century (711-715).*

Figure 2-20 *Alhambra, Granada—Arab baths.*

Figure 2-21 *Alhambra, Granada—Arab baths.*

resulting in enhanced evaporative cooling when it reaches a moist rock area.[30]

The evaporative cooling effect evidenced in these wells and caves was not recognized as such by the ancients, and this phenomenon probably seemed miraculous to many.

Perhaps the earliest attempts to apply the evaporative effect mechanically were those of the Egyptians. Some frescoes dating to 2500 B.C. show slaves fanning porous water jars.[31] The ancient Egyptians later made ice by evaporative cooling. Protagoras, the Greek sophist, describes a fifth century B.C. method of cooling water in his "Comic Histories":

> For during the day they expose it to the sun, and then at night they skim off the thickest part which rises to the surface, and expose the rest to the air, in large earthen ewers, on the highest parts of the house, and two slaves are kept sprinkling the vessels with water the whole night. And at daybreak they bring them down, and again they skim off the sediment, making the water very thin and exceedingly wholesome, and then they immerse the ewers in straw, and after that they use the water which has become so cold as not to require snow to cool it.[32]

Ice and Snow

Although written records of early attempts at refrigeration and cooling are few, compared to the many other accomplishments of early peoples, we do have some examples of the methods used by early civilizations to produce cold.

The need for refrigeration in early civilization was limited. Food supplies were usually sought or grown and then consumed immediately. The distance between food supply and those using it was short. The presence of naturally occurring ice stirred the imagination of some to use this source of cold. There does not seem to be any realization that cold would prolong the shelf life of food, and in many cases, we know that ice was harvested and stored, but we do not know the purpose for which it was collected.

Exactly when the first harvest, storage, or use of ice occurred will probably never be known with certainty. Apparently such an example did exist as long as 4000 years ago. One study concludes that an "ice-house" was built in the Assyrian city of Assur about 2000 B.C.[33]

A collection of ancient Chinese poetry, the *Shi Ching*, dating from about 1175 B.C., describes harvesting ice from deep recesses of hills, after which a thanksgiving sacrifice is offered to the spirit of the cold:

> In the bitter cold days of the second month, The ice flows are as hard as rocks; The axes ring with a merry clang, as we hew out the ice in blocks. The third month comes, Ere the thaw begins, The ice in a cave we store; Then our ploughs made ready to till the land, for spring is at hand once more. When the hot days come, we must open the cave Wherein we have stored our ice; But first to the gods, at the dawn of the day, A lamb we must sacrifice.[34]

Differing translations of this poem exist; however, all are similar in the harvest and storage of ice.[35] Historian Albert

Neuburger says that the type of construction of these cellars is unknown.[36]

Enough information has been preserved from the ancient Romans that we have some examples of methods of their storage and uses. The Romans were famous as heating engineers but they seemed to lack the same sophistication in refrigeration. Johann Beckmann, in his history of inventions, says that he was unable to find any examples of Roman or Greek ice houses.[37] But the Romans did collect snow, for example from Mount Albanus, and stored it in deep pits lined with straw and tree prunings, covering the pit with a thatched roof[38] (see Figure II, color section). This snow was used to directly cool beverages, particularly wine, or was melted and drunk or used for cold baths (frigidaria). It seems that cold beverages became such a hit that Seneca commented: "No running water seemed cold enough for us."[39] Cold water was seen as particularly useful for reviving Romans who had drunk themselves into a stupor! Seneca described these practices and raged against "the shops and storehouses for snow, and so many horses appointed to carry this snow."[40]

Mixing dirty snow into drinks caused enough health problems that the Emperor Nero "fiddled" with the accepted method and developed a more sanitary method: immersing glass containers filled with boiled water into the snow. Pliny noted that Nero's method ensured "all the enjoyment of a cold beverage without any of the inconveniences resulting from the use of snow." Pliny credits Nero with this invention; however, Nero's desire for clean water and wine apparently blinded him to the real significance in his use of secondary heat transfer.[41] R.J. Forbes' technology studies contain an extensive discussion of the use of snow by the Romans.[42] The ancient Greeks seemed to match the Romans in their use of snow cooling of favorite beverages. One ancient Greek, Strattis, said: "No man would prefer to drink wine hot; rather one likes it chilled in the well or mixed with snow." Chares of Mitylene, in recounting Alexander the Great's siege of the Indian capital of Petra, tells how Alexander dug thirty pits, filled them with snow, and covered them with oak branches.[43] Apparently, all this effort was done to ensure that the troops would not suffer tepid wine.

Early Comfort Cooling

Beyond the casual use of cold water, snow or fans to cool the brow, or the drinking of chilled beverages, there is little information on any use of comfort cooling by ancient peoples. Solomon's praise of "the coolness of snow in the heat of the harvest" (Proverbs 25:13) shows that refuge from summer heat was desired and perhaps realized. One of the earliest recorded attempts at lowering the air temperature for comfort cooling is that of the Roman Heliogabulus, who told of Emperor Varius Avitus ordering mountain snow to be formed in mounds in his garden so natural breezes might be cooled.[44] No doubt the ingenuity of ancient peoples resulted in other, unrecorded examples. There are records of an eighth-century Baghdad caliph using snow packed between the walls of his summer villa for cooling.[45]

EARLY VENTILATION

Traditional building design, especially in hot climates, has resulted in a variety of ingenious methods for natural ventilation. Victor Olgyay refers to town planning on the African shore of the Mediterranean where streets are laid out "to bring the coolness of the sea breezes into the heart of the city" and Persian houses that orient large window openings, "the *iwanis*, in the direction of beneficial air movements."[1] The wind scoops of Hyderabad, India, the roof ventilators, or *mulquf*, of Egypt, and the wind towers, *barjeel* or *badjeer*, of Dubai are but a few examples of natural ventilation devices. The wind towers of Dubai, rising 5 to 15 meters above the buildings and open on four sides, can direct prevailing breezes from any direction downward to cool spaces below (Figures 3-1 and 3-2).

Natural cooling of a hospital in Cawnpore, India, has been attempted by supplying air to a space through underground tubes (Figure 3-3). The concept of cooling air by introducing it into the building by underground channels or ducts was used in many applications in hot climates. It was to be used later in some of the designs by William Strutt for the Derbyshire Infirmary (1806 - 1810) and Dr. Reid for the Houses of Parliament.

Vitruvius referred to the use of fire to induce ventilation in areas where breezes were not available. Ventilating fires were used by the Romans and were the most common means of ventilating until the end of the eighteenth century when J.T. Desaguliers introduced fans in the Houses of Parliament.

In Korea, the Buddhist grotto structure of Suk-

kuram (eighth century) is naturally ventilated from humid sea breezes that are treated by "soots (charcoal made of oak) placed in between the stone walls. A hole is placed in the top of the dome in such a way that the air coming in through the main entrance is mixed in the main grotto and ventilated out through the top of the dome to keep fresh air"[2] (Figure 3-4).

The natural ventilation of buildings in the heat of these equatorial climates was primarily for comfort. There was no understanding of ventilation requirements for health and certainly no theoretical basis for design.

Regional architecture of hot climates is typically responsive to prevailing breezes and the advantages of natural ventilation utilizing courtyard plans and open verandas, loggias, or porches for greatest exposure to breezes. Interiors take advantage of large open stairwells to induce vertical air circulation and high ceilings or domed ceilings to ventilate rising hot air. Screen walls and windows, cupolas, roof dormers, and roof vents are all used to enhance ventilation.

Many of these elements can be seen in the early colonial architecture of the United States in Virginia and elsewhere in the South. Thomas Jefferson's Monticello takes advantage of the prevailing breezes with its open verandas and cupola but most notably in the bedroom, where the winds are funneled directly across Jefferson's bed (see Figure III, color section). Openings were provided high over the wall of the bedroom to ventilate his closet area and ensure that his clothes would not become stuffy.

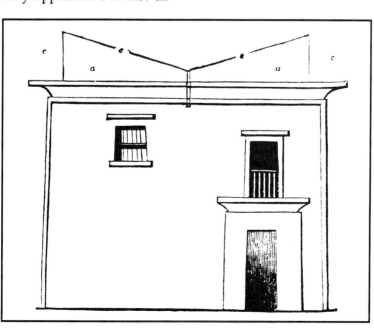

Figure 3-1 *Egyptian wind conductor, or mulquf (from Bernan).*

Figure 3-2 *Wind towers, Dubai (United Arab Emirates)—Sheikh Saeed House (nineteenth century).*

Early Mechanical Ventilation

The development of mechanical ventilation and its application to building comfort is a more recent consequence of rationalism and scientific inquiry that began in the sixteenth century and flourished throughout the Enlightenment. As Reyner Banham describes, "whenever heat or cold could be satisfactorily measured with relatively simple instruments and their causes identified, the `freshness' or `stuffiness' of air could not, largely because their causes could not be identified."[3] But as Bruegmann notes, it is clear that "forced ventilation was from the beginning motivated by considerations of health."[4]

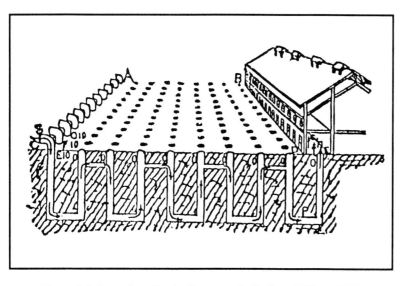

Figure 3-3 *Ground cooling in Cawnpore, India (from Billings 1889).*

From the sixteenth through the eighteenth centuries, methods were developed for improving the effectiveness of ventilation and establishing a scientific basis for its design. The earliest ventilation techniques were applied only to the most extreme conditions such as mining, where the miserable air quality and high concentrations of toxic elements would render working conditions crippling or lethal. Later, as requirements for "fresh air" were better understood, ventilation was applied to the more general needs of industrial, commercial, and domestic buildings. Ventilation by means of fires to induce air movement and by fans to mechanically move air were both used.

Georgius Agricola's *de re Metallica* (1556) illustrates methods of ventilating mine shafts by means of fans and bellows, using manpower and horsepower.[5] Fires were used in vertical shafts to create upward drafts to pull foul or vitiated air from the mines. Bellows were used to pump air into especially foul tunnels, and rotating fan wheels were used in ventilating horizontal shafts (Figure 3-5).

These fan wheels are some of the earliest recorded examples of vertical axis fan systems, but the principles of fan-powered ventilation illustrated by Agricola were not to be used widely in buildings for another two hundred years. One reason for this is that there was no understanding of the properties of air, nor was there any understanding of the physiological requirements of health and comfort.

Later, in the seventeenth and eighteenth centuries, with the discovery of oxygen and other gases, the formation of theories for temperature/pressure relationships and numerous advances in medicine and health gave rise to the beginnings of mechanical engineering.

Seventeenth-Century Experimentation

"Experimentations in the measurement of temperature and atmospheric pressure were being carried out in 1643 by Evangelista Torricelli, a student of Galileo, and his friend, Viviani."[6] Torricelli's invention of the mercury barometer, later to be followed by Blaise Pascal, showed that it was possible to create a vacuum, contradicting two thousand years of philosophical belief from Aristotle to Descartes of the "horror that nature has for empty space—the *horror vacui*." "Except for the telescope, no scientific discovery of the seventeenth century excited wonder and curiosity to a greater degree than did the experiments with the barometer and the air pump."[7]

Investigations of the physical properties of air led to a broader understanding of their application to principles of heating and ventilating. The most important contribution at this time was by Robert Boyle (1627-1691), who developed his kinetic theory of gases—Boyle's Law—in 1662, which describes the relationship between the temperature, pressure, and volume of a gas as a constant.

One of the earliest designs for ventilating systems was that of the Houses of Parliament in the 1660s under the direction of Sir Christopher Wren, who, as a physicist, applied the newly acquired knowledge of his contemporaries to the mundane task of health and comfort. Although the system was not entirely successful, it is one of the first large central ventilating systems for buildings and has been referred to as the beginning of the history of ventilating.

Sir Isaac Newton first described laws of cooling in 1701 in his *Principles of Natural Philosophy*. Newton states the relationship between thermal transfer, surface area, and temperature difference.[8]

The widespread use of open-hearth fires and oil lamps undoubtedly forced the need for better ventilation in buildings. The development of the fireplace flue helped greatly, as did the introduction of the openable sash window. The openable sash window "first appeared in 1300, but not until 1700 was it fairly common."[9]

Eighteenth-Century Developments in Ventilation

Most of the advances in heating and ventilating design during the first half of the eighteenth century were from France and England. It was not until the second half of the century that innovative ideas and products began to emerge from the United States. The experiments of eighteenth-century inventors and engineers were based on a body of scientific and medical theory about the virtues of air, water, and steam heating for comfort, health, and economy. There was a great deal of controversy about which was the best heating method, and, in general, there was a widespread belief that the heating of air to excessively high temperatures would "scorch" it, making it unfit for breathing. This misconception continued through most of the eighteenth and nineteenth centuries.

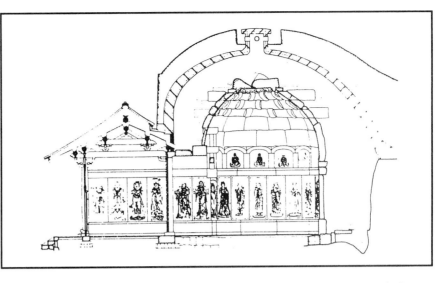

Figure 3-4 *Sukkuram Temple, Korea—eighth century (from ASHRAE Insights).*

The publication of *La Mechanique du Feu* in 1713 by Nicolas Gauger and its English translation in 1716, *The Mechanism of Fire Made in Chimneys* by Dr. John Theophile Desaguliers, may have been the first discussions of the physical properties of air and theories for the heating and ventilating of buildings. Based on many of the methods and experimental principles laid down in *La Mechanique du Feu*, Desaguliers introduced a fanning wheel in 1734 at the Royal Society in London. Similar to those in the sixteenth-century mines of Saxony, the fanning wheel was to "show how damp or foul air may be drawn out of any sort of mines."[10]

In fact, Desaguliers' design was originally made in 1727 for the Earl of Westmoreland to clean foul air out of mines. "The engine worked with a great deal of ease, and there being little atmospheric pressure or weight to be removed, and only the resistance from friction in giving moderate velocity to the air in the pumps, one man was able to discharge 10 cubic feet in a minute."[11] From 1734 to 1736, he applied his fan "engine" to ventilate the House of Commons. Desaguliers' design for the House of Commons was to correct the problems of his initial 1723 system that relied on ventilating fires. He claimed that, to some extent, the failure of his first system was a result of poor cooperation from the housekeeping staff. "Mrs. Smith the Housekeeper, who had possession of the Rooms over the House of Commons, not liking to be disturbed in her use of those Rooms, did what she could to defeat the Operation of these Machines; which she at last compass'd [sic] by not having the Fire lighted."[12] It is claimed he invented the term *ventilator* "to describe the man who turned the crank of the centrifugal fan he was proposing."[13]

In the year 1736, Sir George Beaumont, and several other Members of the House of Commons, observing that the Design of cooling the House by the Fire-Machines above described, was frustrated, ask'd me if I could not find some Contrivance to draw the hot and foul Air out of the House, by means of some Person that should entirely depend upon me; which when I promis'd to do, a Committee was appointed to order me to make such a Machine, which accordingly I effected, calling the Wheel a centrifugal, or blowing Wheel, and the Man that turn'd it a Ventilator.[14]

Figure 3-5 *Ventilation of mine shafts (from Agricola).*

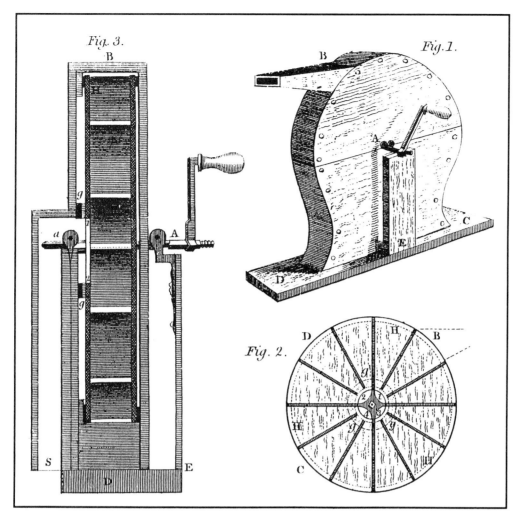

Figure 3-6 *Desaguliers—Fanning wheel, 1735 (from Philosophical Transactions [abridged], VIII, 1735, Plate II).*

This ventilation apparatus consisted of a wooden paddle wheel 7 feet in diameter with radial blades 1 foot wide in a wood casing with rectangular ducts (Figure 3-6). It remained in use until 1791, when the system was redesigned by an architect, Henry Holland.

A little later, also based on Gauger's principles of airflow, Samuel Sutton experimented in 1741 with fires to extract air out of ships, which was demonstrated at a meeting before the British Lords of the Admiralty, and Colonel William Cook introduced steam heating as a means of extracting foul air out of ships.

Ventilation by fans and bellows was proposed by the Reverend Stephan Hales in his *Treatise on Ventilators* of 1758. Hales' main interest was with the ventilation of ships using 20-foot-long inject and exhaust pumps similar to a blacksmith's bellows (Figure 3-7). He estimated that his machine would expel a ton of air at each stroke, or six tons a minute by two men working at the lever . . . " but, according to Bernan, "modern experience would not, perhaps, rate its effect at more than two fifths of the doctor's estimate."[15] Hales also worked on the designs for bellows ventilation of the county hospital and county jail in Winchester, the Savoy Prison, and Newgate Prison.

For mechanical ventilation, the greatest obstacle to overcome was "securing an ample power supply." In 1845, for example, the *Builder* revealed that ventilation of the Queen's opera box by fans required the simultaneous labor of two men during the entire evening.[16]

Based on the principles of heating by Nicolas Gauger, Benjamin Franklin, and Count Rumford, Sir Humphrey Davy developed theories of combustion and heating efficiency as a function of the amount of oxygen supplied to the fire.

Measurements of the content of air and the effects of respiration were being made by Sir Humphrey Davy and later by Prout and Max von Pettenkoffer (1862). They determined the concentrations of carbon dioxide and moisture in air as a result of respiration and perspiration.

However, it was not until the 1770s that scientific research into the properties and components of air resulted in the discovery of oxygen. Dr. Joseph Black first isolated carbon dioxide in the 1750s and his student, Dr. Daniel Rutherford, isolated nitrogen twenty years later. By 1775, Joseph Priestley had successfully isolated nitrous oxide and *phlogiston*. Priestley's experiments were followed by Lavoisier's experiments with phosphorus and sulfur and his discovery of oxygen in 1777.

After Lavoisier and his associates had given the world a clear conception of the constituents and properties of air, interest in the subject of ventilation was immediately aroused, and Lavoisier himself offered some theories that were accepted for many years. He believed that an excess of carbon dioxide in the air caused by respiration and combustion was the principal source of contamination.

A few years previous to the announcement of Lavoisier's work, a tragedy occurred that stirred the civilized world and focused attention on the subject of ventilation. It was the incident of the Black Hole of Calcutta. In June 1758 . . . the Fortress of Calcutta in India was captured during a native insurrection under the leadership of Suras-Ud-Dowa, and the British garrison numbering 146 were incarcerated in the dungeon of the Fortress. This so-called dungeon was, in fact, a room about 18 x 20 feet, with a rather low ceiling.

When morning dawned, 23 of the original 146 were found to be alive.[17]

John Dalton (1766-1844), an English chemist, formulated that the total pressure of a gas is equal to the sum of the pressures of its constituents. In 1802 Dalton published "Experiments and Observations on the Heat and Cold produced by the Mechanical Condensation and Rarefaction of Air" and in 1803 published "Experimental Essays on the Constitution of Mixed Gasses, etc.," where he discusses the thermodynamic properties of air and its components. Dalton's Law became the basis for later measurements of ventilation in terms of oxygen and carbon dioxide levels for respiration.

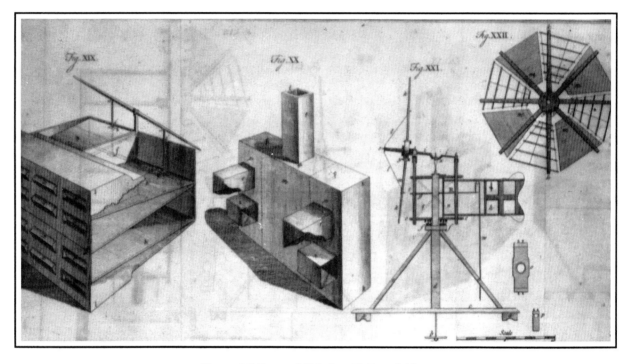

Figure 3-7 *Reverend Hales' ventilation of ships.*

CHAPTER FOUR

EARLY HEATING
AND REFRIGERATION

Prior to the development of the chimney, heating was provided by burning coal or wood in open braziers, often made of iron or bronze and supported on three legs. These offered very little heat, except by direct radiant effects, and they were quite smoky. Neville Billington describes these "forerunners to the enclosed stove," including the Roman tripod braziers of bronze, Spanish braziers illustrated in nineteenth-century texts, and Persian braziers, or *kourey*, which "consisted of a jar containing fuel sunk into the earth in the centre of the room, and the mouth of the jar was covered with a board to serve as a table."[1]

But the fireplace as an enclosed hearth had been in use sometime between the eleventh and thirteenth centuries. The use of smoke vents was introduced in the Alhambra at Granada in the early eleventh century. "It has been claimed that the first chimneys were erected in Italy; the earliest account was given in 1347."[2] During the seventeenth and eighteenth centuries, further developments of the fireplace hearth and chimney began to replace older forms of heating. The most important developments involved the design of the hearth, the chimney, and the damper to increase overall fuel and heating efficiency as well as to reduce smoky backdrafts.

Fireplace Design

The distinction between the fires in Norman castles and at Abingdon Abbey (thirteenth century) and the chimney as we know it is slight, and perhaps we may say that the idea was "born in Britain."[3] The "hooded chimney," or Norman fireplace, first appeared sometime early in the thirteenth century. The central hearth had been moved to the face of an outside wall and a funnel vent with a mantle was first introduced (Figure 4-1 and Figure IV, color section). Bernan described the earliest fireplace of this type at Connisborough Castle and the castles at Rochester, Norwich, and Colchester. He points to the important development of the fireplace being built within the thickness of the wall itself instead of being placed against the wall (as at Connisborough). Similar fireplaces can be seen in Heidelberg Castle in Germany.

In 1600, Louis Savot, a Paris physician, introduced the fireplace grate and in 1624 determined rules for the proportioning of fireplaces.

The earliest attempts to improve the stove are probably those of Kesslar of Frankfurt, in 1618. He designed a round metal stove, with a separate fire-box, a zig-zag flue way within the stove body, and controls for the inlet air and a chimney damper. He also described a sinuous flue pipe to be suspended above a fire on a central hearth. Many stove designers adopted Kesslar's ideas (Bockler 1666; Sturm 1700; Schubler 1728; and others) for both masonry and metal stoves, by providing extra heating surface. Some used extended flueways; others passed the flue gasses into boxes or domes before they entered the chimney (and so obtained a greater area); yet others used simple heat exchangers. One at least used a spiral flue; and Parrot (1795) sought to increase heat transfer by putting a metal spiral in the flue itself.[4]

In 1658, Sir John Winter improved fireplace design by the introduction of outside air beneath the fire. An unusual metal stove design was invented by M. Dalesme in 1680, which burned fuel from the top downward (Figure 4-2).

In the middle and latter end of the seventeenth century, a M. Dalesme, a French engineer, invented a domestic stove or furnace, with the view of giving out nearly all the artificial heat to the apartment, whilst it was calculated to consume the smoke at the same time. The apparatus, which is the invention of Dalesme, improved by Dr. Leutmann, a German, is represented by the following woodcut.[5]

The Dalesme design was exhibited at a fair at St. German in Paris in 1680. "He combined downward combustion with secondary air provision, and was the first to attempt smokeless burning. To light the stove the flue-pipe was warmed by a lamp to induce a current of air, and the top of the fuel in the firepot was then ignited by a burning brand. Much later, American stove-builders (e.g., Nott, 1830) made stoves using downward combustion, combined with an extended flue, to burn anthracite."[6] Leutmann followed on Dalesme's downdraft design in his "vulcanus famulans" or "smoke consuming" stove of the 1680s.

Until the eighteenth century, the typical method of heating was from open hearth fireplaces, most of which were of brick or stone designed by masons and were relatively ineffective in providing good heating.

The increasingly rational attitude toward natural phenomena in the late seventeenth and early eighteenth cen-

25

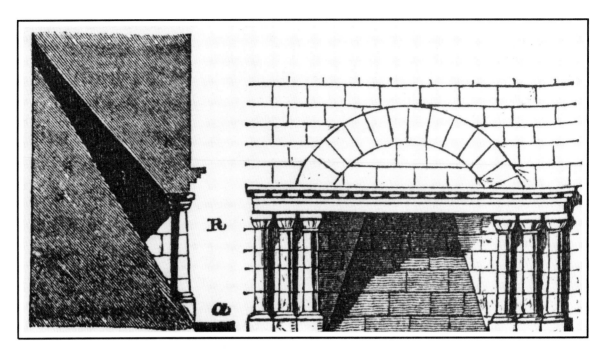

Figure 4-1 *Norman fireplace—Connisborough Castle (from Bernan).*

turies gave rise to scientific experimentation and empirical studies on the design of the fireplace. Bernan describes a Cardinal Polignac who, in 1713, wrote *Le Mecanique a Feu*, regarding "how to make a fire speedily, and make it burn vividly without the aid of a bellows; to heat a capacious room with a small fire, and at the same time, breathe an air fresh and pure, as well as healthily warm."[7] Doctor Desaguliers translated the text into English in 1715 and added an appendix expanding the Cardinal's descriptions of wood-burning fireplaces to include coal-burning fireplaces as well. Although it is not entirely clear, the original French text was written either in collaboration with or under the nom-de-plume of a Monsieur Nicolas Gauger, who history has credited with having written the treatise.

Nicolas Gauger's *La Mechanique du Feu*, published in 1713, was the first analytical study of this type. It influenced both Benjamin Franklin and the Count of Rumford in their studies of fireplace design at the end of the eighteenth century. Gauger's experiments included testing the direction and rate of airflow through a fireplace chamber as a function of temperature. He tried different baffle systems with this method to compare heating efficiency.

Cast-iron stove making existed in Europe and the United States around the end of the seventeenth century, but they were not available in quantities until the second quarter of the eighteenth century.

> These first stoves of German design, are called five-plate or jamb stoves. The five plates formed an open box that was placed against an aperture in the wall that opened into the kitchen fireplace of the next room.

* * *

> By the 1740's, six-plate stoves, also called close stoves, were manufactured as well. These free-standing box stoves have a fuel door at the front end and a smoke pipe that rises from the back connecting to a chimney.

* * *

Ten plate stoves, similar to but longer than those with six plates, have four additional cast-iron plates to form an oven.

Two hinged doors opened on either side of the oven and the smoke from the fire passed around the ends of the oven and out a smoke pipe. Ten plate stoves, popular after 1760 and the likely forerunner of all cookstoves, were used in homes as well as public buildings and halls because the increased surface area radiated more heat.[8]

Benjamin Franklin (1706-1790) worked on the problem of fireplace design and in 1740 invented the "Pennsylvania" fireplace to solve the inconveniences of smoky downdrafts and provide an efficient means of heating. Franklin commented on his new fireplace that "my common room is made twice as warm as it used to be, with a quarter of the wood formerly consumed there." Franklin gave the model to a friend, Robert Grace, who manufactured it at his iron works, and some were sold at Franklin's post office and by his brothers John and Peter.[9] One was purchased by Governor Thomas of Pennsylvania, who was so pleased with the results that he offered Franklin an exclusive patent which Franklin declined. He felt inventions should serve society, not enrich inventors (Figure 4-3).

Figure 4-2 *Dalesme stove, 1680 (from Billington and Roberts).*

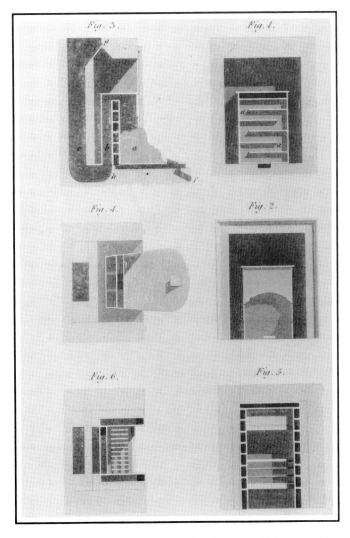

Figure 4-3 *Ben Franklin's Pennsylvania stove, 1745 (from "An Engineer," 1825).*

Figure 4-4 *"Fancy Grates" (from Benjamin Franklin's* Observations on Smokey Chimneys, *1793).*

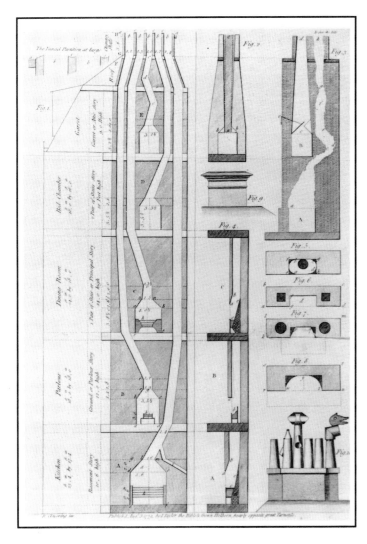

Figure 4-5 *Multiple flues (from Franklin 1793).*

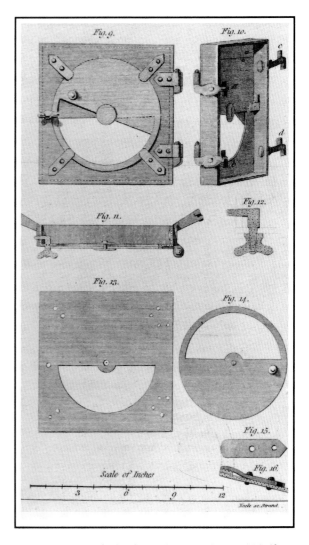

Figure 4-6 *Rumford ash pit door regulator, 1798 (from Rumford's Essays, 1798).*

Benjamin Franklin published his *Observations on Smokey Chimneys* in 1793, proposing rules for the proportioning of fireplaces, as well as the design of various fireplace types. In determining the source of the problem of smoky chimneys, Franklin pointed out nine reasons for the cause of smoke:

- want of air,
- openings being too large,
- too short a funnel (flue),
- chimneys overpowering one another,
- downdrafts due to higher buildings or hills,
- positive pressure built up by the house,
- improper door location,
- descending smoke due to warm outside air and cool inside air,
- strong winds that blow smoke down the chimney.

Franklin described the design of multiple flues in a single chimney, which allowed for the heating of multi-story buildings and apartments (Figures 4-4 and 4-5).

Franklin's recommendations were later expanded in the work of Benjamin Thompson, Count of Rumford (1753-1814), in his rules for fireplace design described in a 1796 pamphlet on *Chimney Fireplaces* and later in his *Essays* published in 1798. Count Rumford, born in Woburn,

Massachusetts, had "collaborated with the British in Boston in 1774 and was obliged to leave the country, and much of the rest of his life was spent in Europe."[10]

Sir Benjamin Thompson, was an extremely busy man. After being an Under-Secretary of State in Lord North's Government, he entered the service of the Elector Palatine and became Chamberlain, Privy Councillor of State, Lieutenant-General, Colonel of the Regiment of Artillery and Commander-in-Chief of the General Staff of the Bavarian Army. He was created Count of Rumford in recognition of his many valued services, both military and civil.

Rumford was a Fellow of the Royal Society and he not only made a most valuable contribution to the theory of heat but he had always before him the importance of employing science in the service of man, and no one has pursued industrial research with greater fervor.

This is not the occasion for a review of his achievements and it must suffice to indicate that he devised methods of measurement and made determinations not only of the specific heats of various substances and the thermal conductivities of insulating materials but also of the calorific values of fuels. On the more practical side he showed, among other things, how steam could be used for heating liquids, and in 1800 this principle was applied in the extensive dye works of Messrs. Gott & Co. at Leeds, where all the coppers were heated by steam from one steam boiler situated in a corner

Figure 4-7 *Benjamin Thompson, Count of Rumford (1753-1814).*

of one of the rooms, almost out of sight. This was a great advance upon the previous arrangement of a separate fire under each copper.

Rumford made notable contributions to fuel economy and showed himself the greatest "chimney doctor" of all time: it is some indication of his capacity for work that, within a period of two months during a holiday in London, more than a hundred and fifty fire-places were successfully altered under his direction.[11]

An important innovation Rumford introduced was the regulator, which provided a means of controlling fresh air intake and, therefore, the rate of burning within the stove (Figure 4-6). Rumford directed his attention to the problem of stove design for heating steam, based on his knowledge of the work of James Watt and Robertson Buchanan in England.

> As to the means of heating, it is certain, from the results of several decisive experiments, that steam stoves are preferable to every other sort, especially for large apartments.
>
> 1st. The heat which these stoves distribute in a room is singularly soft and agreeable, and never causes headache, as iron stoves do which are heated directly by the burning fuel.
>
> 2nd. The temperature of a room warmed by steam can be regulated at pleasure with the greatest ease by means of a simple cock to close more or less the tube which conducts the steam from the boiler into the stove.[12]

His first design of 1798 was made of sheet iron (Figure 4-9). A subsequent design of around 1800 is described by Rumford in his *Essays*.

Rumford's work became the basis for fireplace and stove design throughout the rest of the nineteenth century.[13]

Figure 4-8 *Cartoon by Gillray showing early experiments in pneumatics at the Royal Institution. Rumford is standing on the right.*

Heating with Stoves

Open Hearth Stoves

Open stoves for radiating heat were developed by Franklin and Rumford in a variety of designs. Rumford's contribution of reducing the size of the fire chamber and utilizing the back and side firewalls to radiate more heat into the room was an essential improvement.

Some of the early closed-chamber stove production in Europe was based on sixteenth- and seventeenth-century terra cotta and ceramic designs. These were often large, massive stoves designed especially for cold, northern climates such as Scandinavia and Russia. The northern European, German, and Russian stoves all represented variations on the basic concept of the closed-chamber stove. According to M. Morveau, "M. Moutalambert . . . is due the first introduction into France of stoves on the Russian construction. He called them cheminées poëles, and about 1767 several were erected at Paris."[14] Many of these stoves were formed with ornate detailing and colorful glazes to enhance their appeal.

> The Dutch stove suffered from three main defects—the high temperature of the surface, the high temperature of the flue gases, and the lack of proper control, with large consequent variations in output. Subsequent improvements consisted in the use of fins and ribs attached to the body of the stove, and an air jacket around it, lining the stove with refractory material, and the provision of a magazine for fuel. There was thus a trend towards the design of the Swedish type of stove—greater weight, tortuous flue passages, greater fuel capacity and continuous, slow combustion.
>
> The massive Swedish brick-and-tile stove was also described by Kesslar. The distinguishing feature of this type was the enormous weight of material used in its construction, which served to make the heat output more uniform and to reduce the surface temperature. The stove was, and is, "a common article of furniture in Northern Europe" (Tomlinson) and was often arranged to heat two rooms and to incorporate a boiler and an oven.
>
> In Britain the closed stove has never been in popular favour.[15]

Some fine examples of Dutch porcelain stoves in traditional "Delft blue" and in Chinese pagoda forms can be seen outside the city of St. Petersburg in the summer palace of Czar Peter-Petrodvortz (Figures 4-10 through 4-20 and Figure V, color section).

For the first time, heating was no longer tied to the architectural form of the central hearth, the vertical continuity of the flue, or the distinctive silhouette of the chimney. The introduction of cast iron and terra cotta to stove making provided an efficient means of heating that was separate and independent of the architecture. As such, the stove became the predecessor of today's complex building systems that can be characterized in terms of their performance, manufactured as a series of components, and operated as independent systems.

Caloriferes and "Cockle" Stoves

Improvements of stove design and applications for warm air heating continued into the early nineteenth century. The French chemist Guyton de Morveau attempted improve-

Figure 4-9 *Original model of a Rumford boiler, ca. 1798.*

ments to Swedish and northern European stoves and is one of the first individuals to introduce an air stove with baffles (based on the designs of Franklin and Rumford) to the rest of Europe.

The calorifere, or "fire tube stove," is a French invention described by the Marquis de Chabannes in 1818 as follows: "The principle of the Patent Calorifere is to surround a fireplace with air tubes so disposed, that a much greater surface is brought into immediate contact with the fire. . . ."[1] (Figure 4-21).

> Dingler's Polytechnical Journal, 1824, describes a type of furnace used in a factory in Bavaria in which 60 cast iron pipes, about 6 in. in diameter and 3 ft. long, with a pitch of 25 to 30 degrees, were built in a brick furnace. These furnaces were a French invention and were termed "Calorifere." In England also these "fire-tube stoves" were used and are described by John Hart, Esq., in the New Philosophical Journal, Edinburgh, 1829, as follows: "It is a sort of gas stove in which six iron pipes 7 in. in diameter and 9 ft. long, with a pitch of 10 degrees, are built into a brick furnace supplied with a magazine feed, the fire gases passing around these six pipes and the air passing through them."
>
> An interesting pamphlet by Capt. C. von Bruckmann, 1829, describing the system installed in high school in Hellbronn, says: "The Calorifere is composed of two concentric iron cylinders, thus differing from all other constructions. These cylinders are set in brick."[17]

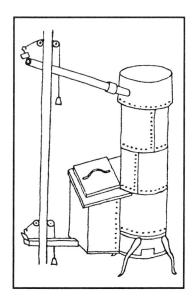

Figure 4-10 *Old German stove, ca. 1600 (from Billington).*

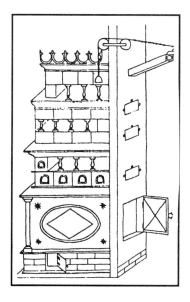

Figure 4-11 *Swedish stove, ca. 1614 (from Billington).*

Figure 4-12 *Russian stove, Dutch style (Petrodvortz, St. Petersburg).*

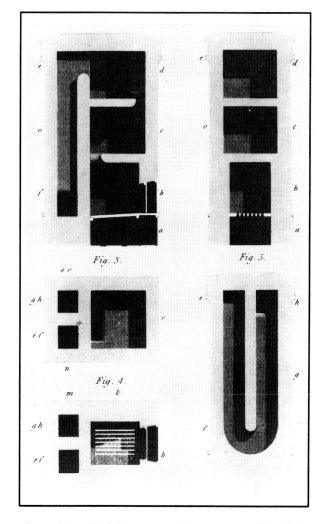

Figure 4-13 *North European or Russian stoves (from "An Engineer," 1825).*

Figure 4-14 *Parlor stove (from* Practische, *Leipzing, 1827).*

Figure 4-15 *Perspectivische Darstellung des Ofens in seinem Aeussern (from Aug. Wilh. Schwartze,* Practische Auleitung zom Bau vou Ofen und Kuchenherden, etc., *Leipzing, 1827).*

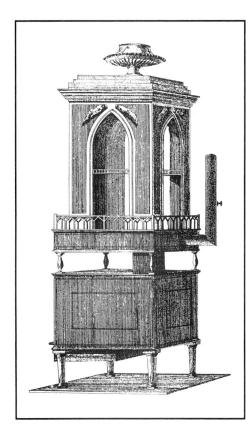

Figure 4-16 *Ein Stuben-Heizofen (from* Practische Auleitung zom Bau vou Ofen und Kuchenherden, etc., *Leipzing, 1827).*

Figure 4-17 *Sein Aeusseres Mit Der Oeffnung des Feuerkastens und des Aschenbehalters (from* Practische Auleitung zom Bau vou Ofen und Kuchenherden, etc., *Leipzing, 1827).*

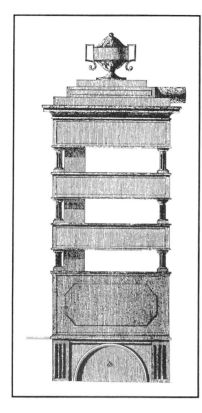

Figure 4-18 *Aufriss des Ofens Vollkgmmen (from* Practische . . ., *Leipzing, 1827).*

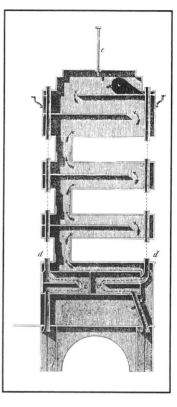

Figure 4-19 *(from* Practische . . ., *Leipzing, 1827).*

Figure 4-20 *Russian stove (Petrodvortz, St. Petersburg).*

The "cockle" stove is described in great detail by Mickleham ("An Engineer") as a confined fire chamber stove based on the "Dutch or German plate iron stoves" and first improved upon by "Mr. Strutt of Derbyshire; for the purpose of warming his extensive cotton-works. . . . This iron fire-room, . . . from its figure has obtained the name of the cockle."[18] Strutt's design used a cylindrical iron fire chamber set on a brick base with a fine-grate and ash pit beneath. The fire chamber is surrounded by brickwork with a space between for air circulation. This air is heated by the iron fire chamber where, by gravity, it then passes to the rooms to be warmed. A variation on this basic design uses a fire chamber with a serpentine chimney to increase the surface area and heat transfer to the air (Figures 4-22 and 4-23).

Another variation is the vase "cockle" stove made from a single cast-iron fire chamber set on thick masonry with multiple openings for air circulation to the space being heated. The vase "cockle" stove represents "a very simple and economical stove on the principle of the lime-kiln. . . . The fuel is applied at the top, which is closed by an iron plate or fire-tile."[19]

The largest and most well-known application of the "cockle" stove was for the Derby Infirmary by William Strutt.

Temperature-Regulated Stoves

Further designs for thermo-regulated stoves were developed by Atkins and Marriott in 1825 and by Dr. Neil Arnott in 1834. Arnott continued the tradition of Franklin and Rumford in his concerns with efficient heating and providing adequate comfort. He was concerned with physiological issues such as the body's own heat capacity, the problems of "noxious" contaminants, and the need for adequate

Figure 4-21 *De Chabannes' calorifere stove (from Billington 1955).*

ventilation. In Arnott's *On Warming and Ventilating*, published in 1838, he states "that a man of sound constitution, and who remains uninjured by poisons or violence, may have uninterrupted health for the full period of human life, there are only four things or conditions which he can ever be required to provide or secure; namely air, warmth, aliment, and exercise of his bodily and mental faculties."[20]

Arnott's thermometer stove automatically regulated the fire by a damper that was controlled by pressurized air heated by the fire itself. Arnott's stove was regulated by a steel/brass compound metal bar, or "pyrostat," that roughly doubled the volume of air for a 480°F temperature rise (Figures 4-24 and 4-25).

Bernan describes an invention by Atkins and Marriott in the appendix to *The Theory and Practice of Warming and Ventilating* of 1825, which was referred to as the "thermoregulator" stove that worked on a similar basis as Arnott's. It was an open grate, coal-burning stove that could regulate the burning as well as feed coal to the fire-grate (Figure 4-25). Like Arnott's thermometer stove, the "thermoregulator" was supplied with an independent, controllable source of combustion air through an air pipe.

> This air pipe is provided with a stop cock, and is carried under, or through, the flooring, to a vessel or reservoir of condensed air. The air-vessel, may be formed of sheet-iron, or wood with iron hoops like a cask; and is to be filled with air (to the amount of several atmospheres if desired) by a condensing pump or a pair of small strong bellows worked by a lever.[21]

These stove designs might be considered some of the early efforts at automatic temperature control, but their popularity remained somewhat limited. Not until the late nineteenth century, with the applications of electricity to thermostatic control, would it become widely accepted.

Nineteenth-Century Cast-Iron Stove Manufacturing

Throughout the nineteenth century, stove manufacturing flourished in the United States, especially in the colder states of New England.

> Records from the first quarter of the nineteenth century indicate that stove plates made in New Jersey and Pennsylvania were shipped to Albany and Troy in great quantities and then assembled and sold by area merchants. Business correspondence from the Cumberland Furnace in Pennsylvania states that stove plates cast there in 1812 were brought to Troy. According to the 1826-1827 account books of the Atison Iron Works located in New Jersey, that foundry carried on a brisk trade with merchants along the Hudson River. "In order to take care of this trade, a schooner, named the Atison, plied regularly between the Mullica River and Albany, New York." Stove types mentioned include cook-stoves, box stoves, six-plate and nine-plate stoves, Franklin-types, and stoves made especially for Sylvester Parker of Troy and William Shaw of Albany. In 1830 the company of Heermance and Rathbone, and of Gill and Cooper, both of Albany, sold respectively 750 and 300 tons of stove plates brought from Philadelphia.
>
> The earliest known stoves cast in Albany were by Warner Daniels in 1808 at the Eagle Furnace, 110 Beaver Street. From 1815 through 1825, Spencer Stafford, of Stafford, Benedict and Company, cast stoves at a foundry at the junction of Washington and Central Avenues, and operated a hardware store at the "Sign of the Gilt Stove," 387 South Market Street.
>
> Troy's iron industry began in 1807 with the building of the Albany Rolling and Slitting Mill by John B. Brinkerhoff. There, Russian and Swedish pig iron was rolled and slitted to form iron hoops and nails. Many years later at this foundry, the iron plates for the Monitor were rolled and forced.
>
> During the nineteenth century between three and thirty-two foundries were operating at any given time in Albany and Troy.[22]

The great variety of ornamental stove castings is illustrated in parlor stoves, cook stoves, and base-burning stoves used in dwellings and public buildings (Figures 4-26 and 4-27).

Early Attempts at Refrigeration

Before the Enlightenment, there does not seem to be any serious attempt to refrigerate by chemical means. However, references to such methods began to appear in the early 1500s in Italy. It seems that the Italian nobility had discovered that their water and wine could be cooled by immersing it in a container of water into which saltpeter (ammonium nitrate) had been stirred. Marcus Antonius Zimara published an account of this as his "Problema 102," apparently about 1525. Another doctor practicing in Rome, Blasius Villa-franca, published a more detailed account in 1550, in which he used the term "refrigerate," and Levinus Lemnius mentioned the salt method as early as 1559 from Antwerp, noting that wine can become so cold as to be uncomfortable to the teeth. Within another 100 years, it had been observed by the Jesuit priest Cabeus before 1646 that ice could be made by such methods. Augmentation of the action of water and ammonium nitrate by the addition of snow, so as to make ice, is mentioned by two Italian authors: Della

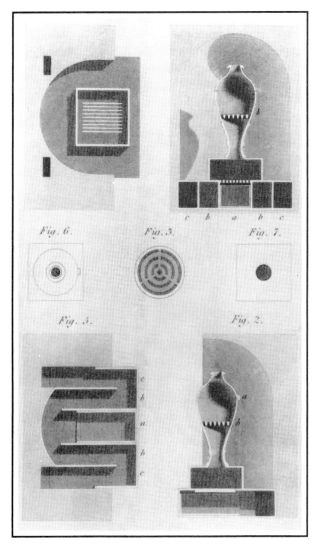

Figure 4-22 *Vase cockle stoves (from "An Engineer," 1825).*

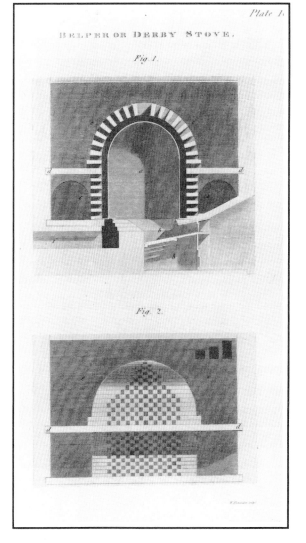

Figure 4-23 *William Strutt-Belper or Derby stove, Derby Hospital, 1806 (from "An Engineer," 1825).*

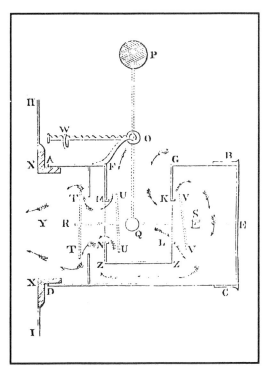

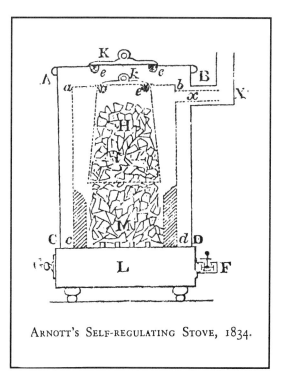

Figure 4-24 *Dr. Arnott's thermometer stove, 1834 (from A.F. Dufton).*

Porta in 1589 and Latinus Tancredus, a professor at Naples, in *De Fame et Siti* in 1607.[23][24]

Genuine scientific study of refrigeration began shortly after, the result of a new way of thinking. The individual was assuming power, and this allowed a search for knowledge that was no longer hindered by states, churches, or tribes. The pseudo-science of alchemy was being replaced by the scientific method. The result was an explosion in science and technology, in entrepreneurship and industry and politics. The new freedom of thought was probably most advanced in Scotland and England. For example, by the mid 1600s the many English "scientists" saw the need for greater association with each other, meeting as "The Invisible College" for discussion and debate. This informal gathering quickly led to a formal organization, the Royal Philosophical Society of London (Figure 4-28). One of the principal movers of the Royal Society was Robert Boyle, who is probably best known today for his gas laws. Boyle applied the scientific method to refrigeration, experimented with freezing mixtures using various salts, and published the results in the *Experimental History of Cold*. Boyle investigated many substances, some of them seemingly unlikely refrigerating agents. One summary notes

> that not only all sorts of acid and alkalized salts, and spirits, even spirits of wine; but also sugar and sugar of lead mixed with snow, are capable of freezing other bodies . . .
>
> That among substances capable of being frozen, there are not only all gross sorts of saline bodies, but such also as are freed from their grosser parts, not excepting spirit of urine . . .

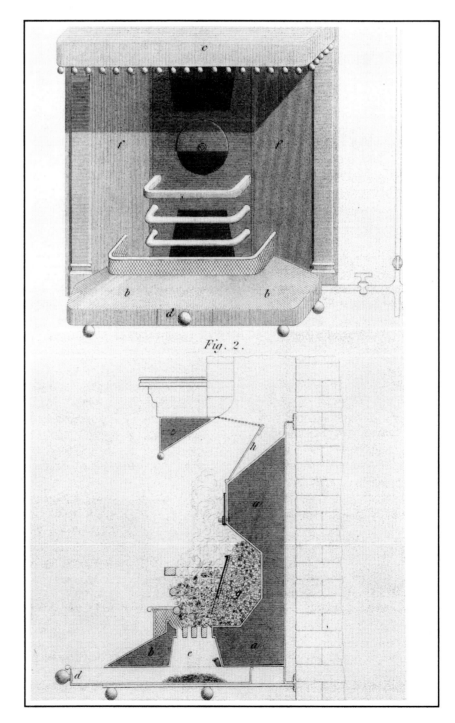

Figure 4-25 *Atkins and Marriott thermoregulator stove (from "An Engineer," 1825).*

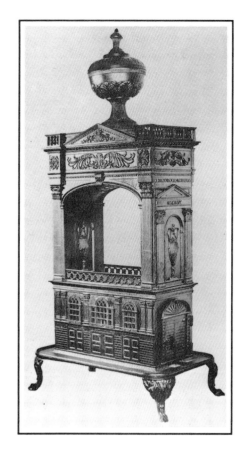

a) Column parlor stove, Pratt & Treadwell, Albany, ca. 1834-36.

b) Base-burning stove, Nott's patent, ca. 1832 (Schaffer Library, Union College, Schenectady, NY).

Figure 4-26 *Nineteenth-century cast-iron stoves (from T.K. Groft).*

a) Two-column parlor stove, J. Rathbone, Albany, ca. 1835-39.

b) Two-column parlor stove, Low & Leake, Albany, patented August 10, 1844.

Figure 4-27 *Nineteenth-century cast-iron stoves (from T.K. Groft).*

That many very spirituous liquors, freed from their aqueous parts, cannot be brought to freeze, neither naturally, not artificially; and here is occasionally mentioned a way of keeping moats unpassable in very cold countries . . .[25]

and goes on to describe all manner of experiments on the relation of cold to animal, vegetable, and mineral materials and for investigating and measuring expansion and contraction caused by cold. Boyle's experiments apparently led him to believe that sal ammoniac (ammonium chloride) was better than ammonium nitrate for freezing mixtures.[26]

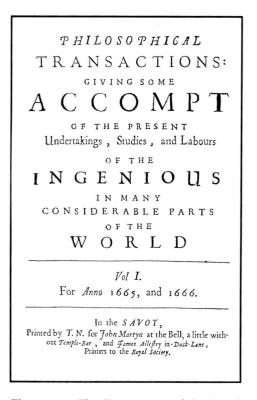

Figure 4-28 The Transactions of the Royal Philosophical Society of London *became an important commentary on scientific pursuit by the late seventeenth century.*

Figure 4-29 *Robert Boyle (1627-1691) was one of the first scientists to pursue orderly investigation into the production of cold (by permission of the President and Council of the Royal Society).*

EIGHTEENTH-CENTURY HEATING AND COOLING

The eighteenth century was the beginning of the practical application of the boiler, first to provide power for industrial expansion and later for the heating of buildings. Thomas Newcomen (1663-1729), an ironmonger from Dartmouth, England, who supplied Cornish tin miners, developed the first steam engine in 1712 for the purpose of draining deep mine shafts of water. "History records his steam engine, but the fact remains that this would have been useless without his invention of the boiler that went with it."[1]

In 1660, Sir Hugh Platt proposed the use of steam for heating in his book *The Garden of Eden*.

"For the keeping," says Sir Hugh, "of any flowers or plants abroad, as also of those seeds sowed within doors, or other pots of flowers or dwarf trees, in a temperate heat, with small charge you may perform the same, by hanging a cover of tin or other metall over the vessel wherein you boil your beefe or drive your buck, which having a pile in the top, and being made in the fashion of a funnel, may be conveyed into what place of your orchard or garden you shall think meete; which room if it were so made as that at your pleasure it may become either close or open, you may keep it in the nature of a stove in the night season, or in any other cold weather, and in the summer weather you may use the benefit of the sun beames to comfort and cherish your plants and seeds; and this way, If i bee not deceived, you may have both oranges, lemons, pomegranates, yea peradventure, coloquintida, and pepper trees and such like. The sides of this room, if you think goode, may bee plastered, and the top thereof may be covered with some strained canvas to take away at your pleasure. Quaere, If it be the best to let the pipe of lead to breathe out at the end only, or else at divers small vents which may be made in that part of the pipe which passeth along the stove. I fear that this is but a meer conceit, because the steam of water will not exceed far; but if the cover to your pot bee of metall, and made so close that no air can breathe out saving at the pipe which is soldered or well closed in some part of the cover, then it seemeth probable that this cover may be put on after the pot is scummed."[2]

One of the earliest references to the use of steam for heating was by Col. William Cook in a paper read before the Royal Society of London and published in the *Philosophical Transactions* in 1745.

In 1745, Colonel William Cook improved on Sir Hugh's suggestion and gave a diagram of an engine for heating all the rooms in a house from the kitchen fire. [In Figure 5-1,] a is a copper with a still-head; b, a copper or lead pipe through which the steam from the head of boiling water heats. In its passing through the eight rooms, the pipe is fixed to the wall or side of the room; in the place of the chimney, c, are stopcocks by which the steam may be suffered to pass as fast or as slow as you please; d, vent for steam to pass out at; and e, cistern of water to replenish copper as it boils away.

The Colonel's scheme was propounded as a saving, and was so far practicable, that there is no doubt, with a tithe of the coals wasted in the fireplace, he could have heated three times the number of rooms enumerated in his proposal. In 1755, it was suggested as a method for forcing fruits.[3]

But it was not until later in the century that others would develop workable heating systems and practical applications for buildings.

The earliest inventions of steam heating systems appear to be those of James Watt in 1784 when he tried to heat his house by using a central steam boiler with a tin plate radiator. The radiator box was 3½ feet long, 2½ feet wide, and 1 inch thick but did not provide adequate heat. "Not long after this, Matthew Boulton, Watt's partner, heated one of the rooms in his house by steam, including a bath, and used the installation for many years."[4] James Watt continued to work on the problems of heating buildings through the firm of Boulton, Watt and Company, which was responsible for many heating installations as well as the first use of cast-iron pipes for heating.

The developments of steam heating and the steam engine allowed first for the relatively efficient distribution of heat in larger buildings and second for the replacement of manually powered fan ventilation with mechanically powered fan ventilation.

Greenhouse heating by steam was also attempted in 1788 by T. Wakefield, Esq., of Norwich.[5] His experiments were continued for several years with considerable success, and in 1792 the plan was adopted at Lord Derby's gardens at Knowsley, apparently on the model of Mr. Wakefield's and was attended with perfect success.[6] John Hoyle of Halifax

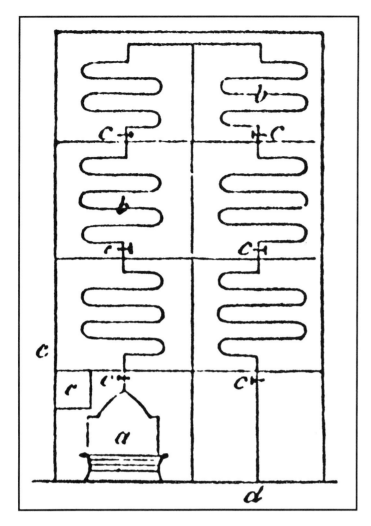

Figure 5-1 *Col. William Cook's design for steam heating (based on Sir Hugh Platt), 1745.*

obtained a patent in July 1791 on improvements to steam heating apparatus. Hoyle describes his steam system as:

An apparatus for generating steam applicable to the warming of buildings. From any part of the boiler above the surface of the water, one or more pipes or tubes to be charged with steam from the boiler, are to ascend or be otherwise conducted into, round, or through the rooms of building to be warmed or heated, and are to be either attached to the ceiling or cornice, or placed lower, as may be best approved of; observing that from the highest elevation they must form a gentle declivity, so as more readily to deposit the condensed steam or water into a cistern or reservoir, into which they are to be for that purpose conveyed, and which reservoir is to be placed as near to the boiler as circumstances will admit. The boiler is to have a communication with the reservoir by means of a pipe intended to supply the water necessary; and that this may be properly and regularly effected in proportion to its evaporation and escape, a cock and floating ball is fixed in the same manner as in cisterns or reservoirs withinside the boiler, which will at all times preserve the water in the boiler nearly on the same level.[7]

* * *

A very extensive system of hot-houses was heated by steam at Dalry, in Scotland, in 1793. The boiler was of cast iron, 3 ft. in diameter, and 14 inches deep, covered with a large flat stone. On one side of the boiler, under the cover, was a projecting nozzle, to which was connected the earthenware pipe which conveyed the steam to the houses. These pipes were so arranged as to allow the water to return to the boiler. This apparatus was in constant use for seven years, until the death of the owner.

About 1793, Messrs. Todd & Stevenson, of Glasgow, heated their mill by steam, using pipes in tin plate. The steam from the boiler in this arrangement ascends in a vertical pipe to the highest story, where, going along the floor horizontally to the further end, it descends to the story below,

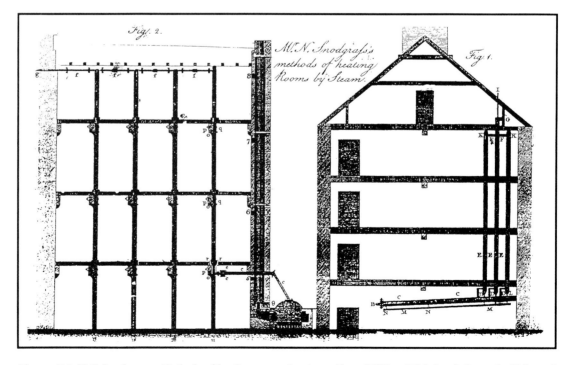

Figure 5-2 *Neil Snodgrass—Methods of heating rooms by steam (from William Nicholson's Journal of Natural Philosophy, Chemistry, and the Arts, vol. XVI, London, 1807).*

where it is again carried along horizontally, and thus continues until it arrives at the bottom; there the water of condensation is carried through a syphon, and the air allowed to escape between the steam pipes and the syphon, or just above the water-line.[8]

In 1799 the first practical use of steam was applied by Neil Snodgrass for the heating of the silk/woolen manufacturing works of Mr. Dale and Mr. McIntosh on the banks of the Spey (Figure 5-2). After this, a number of engineers applied the principles of steam heating to mills to replace the older "cockle" stove heating and provide a more fire-safe method of heating.

Count Rumford, known for his improvements to the fireplace, also worked on methods of heating by steam. In 1801, he developed steam heating for his lecture room using a steam boiler and a three-foot-diameter drum "heat exchanger" located in the basement feeding to eight-inch copper tubes divided in the lecture room into two horizontal branches located under the seats. Rumford was interested in the economics of fuel use as well as better comfort.

Hot Water

The availability of thermal springs offered some of the first inspiration for hot water heating. The Romans took advantage of this natural resource in the construction of baths, and there is evidence of other ancient applications as well. One such record describes a Nicholas Zeno, who, during his travels in 1394, discovered a monastery at East Bygd, Greenland, where hot water from springs was used to heat the buildings. The monks of the monastery of St.

Olaus also used the hot water from the springs for bathing and domestic purposes since "this water as it came into the kitchen was hot enough to boil meats and vegetables."[9] However, the development of hot water heating, using boiler and distribution piping, would not actually be realized until much later.

In 1653 Sir Hugh Platt published *Jewel House*, in which he proposed the use of hot water heating for the drying process in gunpowder manufacturing but not for general applications in heating.

Near the end of the eighteenth century, central heating with hot water was attempted by a few individuals but was not developed further until the late nineteenth century. Sir Martin Triewald is said to have attempted the first successful use of hot water in 1716 for heating a greenhouse. "Sir Martin Triewald, a Swede, who lived for many years in Newcastle-on-Tyne, before he finally settled in his native country, about 1716, described a scheme for warming a greenhouse by hot water. The water was boiled outside of the building, and then conducted by a pipe into a chamber under the plants"[10] (Figure 5-3). A Frenchman named Bonnemain had tried to heat a chicken incubator using hot water in 1777. "As water circulated among the racks of eggs, one loop of the pipe warmed the chicks. At the top of the incubator, a funnel permitted addition of water and a valve was available to release air from the pipes. A diagram shows the mechanism by which the expansion and contraction of a long rod (x) within the boiler controlled the damper(s) that admitted air to the fuel."[11] In the same year, he also designed a system for heating the greenhouses of the Jardin des Plantes at Paris. The hot water circulated by

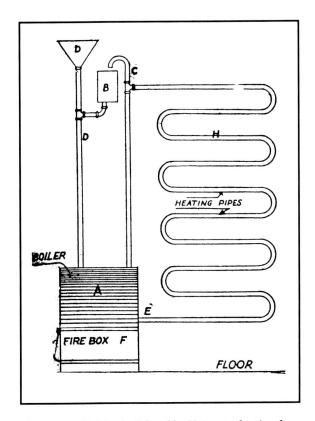

Figure 5-3 *Sir Martin Triewald—Hot water heating for a greenhouse, Sweden, 1716 (from E.W. Riesbeck, "50,000 Years of Heating," Domestic Engineering, January 10, 1925, p. 119).*

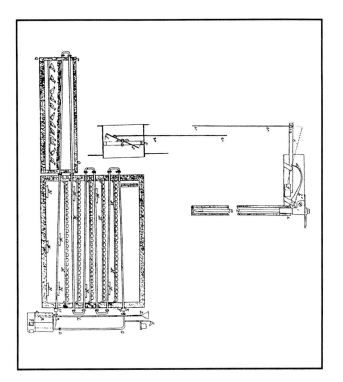

Figure 5-4 *Bonnemain hot water incubator, 1777 (from Gesundheits-Ingenieur, 1907).*

gravity from the "water stove" using piping of relatively small diameter (Figure 5-4).

The Marquis de Chabannes introduced the concept of hot water heating to England in 1816 and claimed it as his own invention.

Refrigeration in the Eighteenth Century

The 1700s saw science and technology developing in parallel but converging paths. As new theories emerged, devices were being invented to allow the theories to be tested. Observations made using the technological devices frequently led to new theories. Thus science utilized technology for its advancement and for inspiration to study a new idea. Likewise, technology developed because of a need for experimental materials and equipment. Since the technology was often inadequate to the needs of science, technology was inspired to refine and improve itself. So science and technology, each borrowing from and inspiring the other, continued their expansion at an ever faster pace.

Inquiries into methods of producing cold proceeded in two directions in the eighteenth century. The investigation of chemical freezing mixtures, begun in the last century, continued. An example of this was the extensive discussion by Richard Walker in England before the Royal Philosophical Society of London and published by him in 1796.[12] However, a new area of investigation emerged, that of cold produced by evaporation, made possible by the development of mechanical pumps.

The application of the vacuum pump, invented by Otto von Guericke, began by the late 1600s. Various experiments were conducted with this new device; however, results were compromised by difficulty in sealing the piston to the cylinder, making high vacuums difficult. Still, slow progress was made in improving these pumps, and the availability of such new tools opened up a new area for scientific experimentation. One who took advantage of the new knowledge of the air pump was Denis Papin, who reported his trials with mechanically evacuated vessels in Paris in 1674.[13] Papin observed that if water in a vacuum were heated, it would boil, but the boiling vessel would not be hot to the touch. Papin further noted that a more volatile liquid, in this case "spirit of wine" (alcohol), would boil even more readily and that this boiling could be accelerated by immersing the vessel in cold water, the cause being that "the vapors of the spirit were condensed, and so made the receiver more empty; which is sufficient to make the spirit of wine boil, even though it were not hot."[14] Papin's

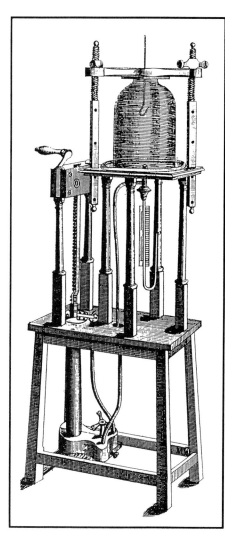

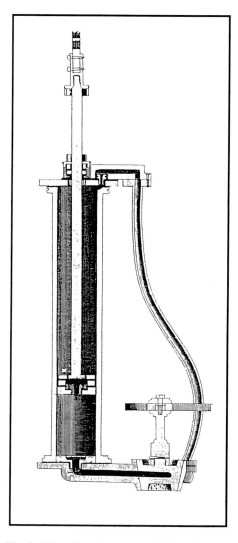

Figure 5-5 *Smeaton's 1751 apparatus for creating a vacuum. Specimens for test were placed under the bell jar, and the air was exhausted using the air pump. A similar device was used by William Cullen to freeze water by causing an ether bath to boil at a low temperature (from Philosophical Transactions, vol. 47, 1752).*

Figure 5-6 *The double-acting piston pump designed by Smeaton for his apparatus. Such a pump was used by Edward Nairne in 1777 to perform experiments that were similar to William Cullen's (from Philosophical Transactions, vol. 47, 1752).*

observations, with their potential application to refrigeration, were apparently not pursued further.

Although the phenomenon of cooling by evaporation was not new, observation of it became more scientific by the mid-1700s. The invention of the thermometer provided an opportunity to see a quantitative cooling effect for the first time. For example, G. Richmann presented a series of papers at the St. Petersburg Academy of Sciences in 1748 that reported on his experiments with cold.[15] In some of these experiments, Richmann noted that a wet thermometer bulb resulted in lower temperatures as measured by the thermometer and that these temperatures rose as the bulb dried. (These particular experiments were translated from Latin into French by Augustine Roux.[16]) Richmann ascribed the result to the cooling effect of the atmosphere on the wet thermometer bulb but had no explanation for the exact cause, speculating that some type of "cooling agent" was present in the atmosphere. Noting further that the cooling effect varied under different conditions, Richmann speculated that the unknown cooling agent was apparently present in differing amounts at different times.[17]

The idea of enhancing the evaporative cooling effect with a vacuum pump seems to have first occurred to William Cullen, professor of medicine at Glasgow, Scotland. Before 1755, one of Cullen's students noticed

phenomena similar to that reported later by Richmann. Cullen was aware that this phenomenon had been observed by de Mairan in France about 1749 and suspected that the evaporation of water or of other fluids was the cause of a lowering of temperature. Cullen repeated de Mairan's experiments more carefully and concluded "that the power of evaporating fluids in producing cold, is nearly according to the degree of volatility in each. If to this we join the consideration that the cold is made greater by whatever hastens the evaporation; and particularly that the sinking of the thermometer is greater, as the air in which the experiment is made is warmer, if dry at the same time; I think we may now conclude, that the cold is produced by the effect of evaporation." Cullen knew that volatile substances would cool to a greater degree if placed under a vacuum than they would in the normal atmosphere. Cullen carried Denis Papin's idea one step further by ascribing the effect of cooling to the evaporation of the liquid, hastened by the vacuum, and by recognizing that more volatile liquids would cool further. Cullen tried various volatile liquids, and in one experiment he froze a dish of water by cooling it with a smaller dish of ether evaporated under a vacuum.[18] Other, similar experiments, using vacuum pumps and volatile liquids, were conducted by Edward Nairne in 1777[19] (Figures 5-5 through 5-8).

Figure 5-7 *William Cullen, medical doctor and professor of medicine at the University of Glasgow, Scotland, is credited with creating low temperatures by boiling a volatile liquid in a vacuum (from Smithsonian Institution, Division of Engineering and Industry).*

[117]

Of the Cold produced by evaporating Fluids, and of some other means of producing Cold ; by Dr WILLIAM CULLEN.

A Young Gentleman, one of my pupils, whom I had employed to examine the heat or cold that might be produced by the solution of certain substances in spirit of wine, observed to me, That when a thermometer had been immersed in spirit of wine, tho' the spirit was exactly of the temperature of the surrounding air, or somewhat colder ; yet, upon taking the thermometer out of the spirit, and suspending it in the air, the mercury in the thermometer, which was of Farenheit's

heit's

Figure 5-8 *The first page of Cullen's treatise on production of low temperatures by evaporation. Cullen's experiments of May, 1755, were reported in the Edinburgh Philosophical and Literary Essays and republished in 1782.*

Figure 6-1 *From The Ice Industry, September 1921.*

THE NATURAL ICE INDUSTRY

Prior to the nineteenth century, ice harvesting and storage were pursued mostly as individual or local enterprises. There were some scattered instances of an "ice industry," as in France beginning at the end of the seventeenth century, where the sale of snow was a profitable trade.[1] At the beginning of that century, the freezing of juices and fruits refreshed the wealthy. One method was described in the *Argenis*, as described by Johann Beckmann: "Arsidas finds in the middle of summer, at the table of Juba, fresh apples, one-half of which was encrusted with transparent ice. A bason, made also of ice and filled with wine, was handed to him; and he was informed that to prepare all these things in summer was a new art. Snow was preserved for the whole year through in pits lined with straw. Two cups made of copper were placed one within the other, so as to leave a small space between them, which was filled with water; the cups were then put into a pail, amidst a mixture of snow and unpurified salt coarsely pounded, and the water, in three hours, was converted into a cup of solid ice, as well formed as if it had come from the hands of a pewterer. In the like manner apples just pulled from the tree were covered with a coat of ice."[2]

Even drinking cups were made of ice and these, as well as iced fruit, were a "grand invention for the art of cookery; which became common among the German cooks, both male and female, about the middle of the [eighteenth] century."[3]

About 1630, French descendants of Italian liqueur merchants invented an iced drink they named "lemonaid." About 1660, a Florentine Italian, Procope Couteaux, began selling solidly frozen lemonaid. By the end of the 1600s, vendors (called lemonadiers) selling iced liquors or frozen drinks were very common in France. This industry used large quantities of ice.[4]

The Rise of the Ice Industry

As the demand for ice increased, local harvesting became inadequate to supply the needs. Soon, even the supply within some entire countries was inadequate, giving rise to the possibility of an international ice trade. Apparently this trade arose in the early nineteenth century. By the 1820s, large quantities of ice were being exported, mainly from Norway and the United States. Most of the ice used in Europe and England was imported from Norway, cut from inland lakes and shipped out of ports Christiania and Krageroe by steamer. The largest user in England was the fishing industry.[5]

The natural ice industry of the United States came into being mainly due to the vision of one individual, Frederic Tudor of Boston (Figure 6-2). Frederic Tudor was a 23-year-old commodities merchant when he decided to seriously pursue his brother William's idea that ice could be harvested and sold in the hot climates of the Caribbean. Tudor's spirit can best be seen in the inscription he wrote on the cover of his first business journal-diary: "He who gives back at the first repulse and without striking the second blow despairs of success, has never been, is not, and never will be a hero in war, love, or business."[6] In 1805, Tudor invested $10,000 to begin his venture. He purchased a brig, the *Favorite*, and shipped a cargo of ice to Martinique after first having sent his two business associates, William Tudor and James Savage, to negotiate exclusive rights to ship ice to the West Indies. Their negotiations failed, and Frederic was left without a place to store the ice or a means to distribute it. Undaunted, he received permission to sell the ice from the ship (Figure 6-3). Although he lost almost $4,000, he sent ice to Havana the next year and obtained licenses from England and France to sell ice in their colonies. Tudor's promising business was almost ruined by the international tensions of 1807-1814, during which time he was technically bankrupt and was arrested numerous times for debts. "Pursued by sheriffs to the very wharf," Tudor fled Boston for Havana in 1815 after scraping together a couple thousand dollars so he could pay for an ice shipment and for construction of an ice house. The Havana government bureaucracy stalled ice house construction until only twelve days before the ice shipment arrived in February 1815. Overcoming these difficulties, Tudor began selling ice at the beginning of March, writing in his diary, "Drink Spaniards and be cool, that I, who have suffered so much in my cause, may be able to go home and keep myself warm."[7] It was another four years before the ice business had grown profitable

Figure 6-2 *Frederic Tudor (1783-1864), "Ice King of the World" (from Library of the Boston Atheneum, Boston, Massachusetts).*

enough so that Frederic Tudor no longer had to sneak back into Massachusetts. Within another year, the economic depression in the United States resulted in another financial crisis for Tudor, leading to his nervous collapse in 1822. However, his business quickly recovered, and shipments to the Caribbean and southern United States cities steadily increased, from 1,200 tons in 1816 to 65,000 tons in 1846. Still, he was not able to completely repay his debts, totaling $280,000, until 1849, when he was 65 years old. During that time, Boston ice came to be shipped to every major seaport in South America and the Far East, including those of China, the Philippines, India, and Australia. Henry Pearson, whose 1933 paper on Tudor is summarized above, said of Frederic Tudor:

> [He] was a striking example of nineteenth-century individualism in its American form. What he created was the work of his own hand, even as the achievement of an artist is, and, like an artist with a new message, he fought his way to fame sustained only by his belief in himself and by his iron resolution: "I have so willed it" was his motto. The revolution which he brought to pass in the habits of dwellers in the West Indies and in this country has a niche in social history, and the use of ice in the preservation of food and in the treatment of illness owes much to him.[8]

By the time Tudor died at age 80 in 1864, he was known as the "Ice King of the World."[9] Frederic Tudor's success with the ice business led to imitators. Addison Gage of Boston attempted to interest England in Boston ice in 1842 with a shipment to London, where the "Boston notion" of iced drinks was not well received. Within several years, ice exports to England did become successful, the result of the efforts of Gage's fellow Bostonians Charles B. Lander and Henry T. Ropes. Ropes established himself in England and abandoned Boston ice about 1850 for less expensive Norwegian ice. Still, the demand in the United States grew steadily, so that by 1880, an estimated 8 million tons of ice were commercially harvested. So much ice was being sold that supplies of sawdust, shavings, and marsh hay used in

ice storage were severely strained. The prices of these commodities, almost worthless before, skyrocketed, and even abandoned sawmills were mined for their sawdust treasure. The shipbuilding industry also benefited, as more and more ships were needed to carry increasing amounts of ice from northern ports to southern cities. More than 150 ice houses supplied the demand on New York's Hudson River alone.[10] In 1855 it was estimated that 9,000 persons were employed in the United States ice industry.[11]

By the late 1850s, the ice industry was clearly becoming a major one. In 1857, "the Report of the Committee of the Boston Board of Trade on the subject of the ice trade" noted that in Boston and the vicinity, 60,000 tons of ice were retailed to 18,000 customers using 93 wagons and 150 horses.[12] A new demand for ice appeared, the result of the tremendous growth of the brewing industry in the United States and Europe beginning in the 1860s. In some areas, the high demand for ice by brewers caused ice shortages and skyrocketing prices. Increasing amounts of ice were being exported from the countries that produced it. Two hundred twenty thousand tons of ice were exported from the United States in 1872, although this figure dropped subsequently as mechanical refrigeration began to be applied at points of use.[13]

Technology of the Ice Industry

As ice use and harvesting grew, specialized technology developed to meet the needs of the new industry. Harvesting tools were modified, and new ones invented. Ice house construction techniques were developed to minimize "spoilage" of ice. Refrigerators were conceived so individual consumers would have a convenient way to store food and, at the same time, create a continuing need for ice. Most of these developments were preceded by "cut and try" methods, honed by observations of their effectiveness or usefulness.

One of the earliest renditions of this technology can be found in an 1803 pamphlet written by Brookeville, Maryland, civil engineer and farmer Thomas Moore.[14] Moore discusses ice and heat and proposes that ice houses be constructed underground. The construction is somewhat crude, and the insulation technology is really not much more advanced than the pits used by ancient cultures. Most interesting is Moore's description of a refrigerator he patented in 1803 and developed so that the butter he was transporting twenty miles to market in Washington would not melt. The patent specification stated:

> The principle of this refrigerator is the application of ice in such a manner that it can receive little or no heat, except from the matter intended to be rendered cold or deprived of its heat. The trials hitherto made have been made by an internal vessel of tin surrounded by an external vessel of wood, so as to leave a small interstice between them filled with ice. The external vessel [has] a coat of woolen cloth lined with rabbit skins, the fur included between the cloth and the pelt. The point to be aimed at in constructing this refrigerator, is to choose for the internal vessel, separating the thing to be made cold from the ice, a substance the best conductor of heat, and for the external vessel, separating the ice from the common atmosphere, the best non-conductors, provided they be sufficiently cheap for common use.[15]

Figure 6-3 *Model of one of Frederic Tudor's ice ships, the Ice King. Early shipments of ice were not always warmly received. About 1820, New Orleans Mayor Augustin McCarthy was reported to have said, "Iced drinks chill the innerds and make consumptives of the people who drink them" when he met the first sailing vessel to deliver ice to the city. He then shocked the crew by ordering every block of ice to be thrown into the sea ("It's On Ice" by M. Presley Dixie, Nov. 25, 1973, p. 29) (from Historical Collections, Baker Library, Harvard University Graduate School of Business Administration).*

Moore's nephew described the actual construction:

The first was made of a size to be carried on horseback. The later ones were large and made in a different manner for family use and dairy purposes. Two square cedar boxes, one of a smaller size to be placed in the larger, and this space filled with pulverized charcoal well packed in, a tin box fastened to the inner side of the lid contained the ice, and the whole covered with coarse woolen cloth. Since this was made to be used by people who had ice houses, and there were not many; Thomas Jefferson had one and some of the cabinet members also, and people of wealth—it was not extensively used. The patent expired in 14 years. It was not renewed, so the public received the benefit of it.[16]

The original letters of patent, signed by Thomas Jefferson and James Madison,[17] were destroyed in a fire in 1945.[18]

Frederic Tudor improved upon Moore's ideas. After reading Moore's pamphlet, Tudor wrote, "The author is correct in principle, but I shall differ in practice." Tudor decided upon above-ground construction for his ice houses. His early refrigerators used sheep fleeces for insulation.[19] Tudor and his contemporaries experimented with ice houses and refrigerator construction, continually improving the designs (see Figure VII, color section).

Harvesting the ice itself presented a challenge. At first, the pond or river ice was simply hand sawed into irregular pieces. These pieces did not store neatly, and ship captains disliked the oddly shaped chunks because they were hard to secure on board. Ice production became more streamlined when a Cambridge hotel manager, Nathaniel Jarvis Wyeth, developed improved harvesting methods for procuring the Fresh Pond Hotel's ice supply. Wyeth's most useful invention was an ice cutter (or ice plow), conceived in 1825 and patented in 1829, which greatly simplified harvesting. Wyeth used horse-drawn, parallel-toothed steel blades to score the ice into uniform rectangles, which could be split off one at a time. The ice blocks were floated to a submerged elevator next to the ice house, pulled to a chute at the top of the house, and slid down into the house. Wyeth's improvements quickly came to the attention of Frederic Tudor, who contracted with him for supply and to supervise Tudor's own operations. Wyeth continued to improve harvesting methods, developing a horse-powered circular ice saw so far ahead of its time that it was of little use until the end of the century. Wyeth's inventions shaved about two-thirds of the cost of harvesting ice, resulting in a lower retail price (Figures 6-4 and 6-5).

Wyeth's devices were widely copied, and their use spread throughout the United States. Frederic Tudor at first had attempted to monopolize the ice business (for example, by securing U.S. Patent 726 of 1838 for the use of sawdust, etc., between blocks of ice); however, he was quickly overwhelmed by increasing competition. Much to his surprise, the resulting lower prices so increased demand that he was making more money than ever before.[20]

Improvements in ice-harvesting and storage technology accelerated as the nineteenth century wore on, this progress spurred by the continuous growth of the industry. Ice tools were improved, with the goal of making ice easier and less expensive to harvest. Later, some of the saws, elevators, etc., used gasoline engines, followed later by electric motors.[21]

Figure 6-4 *Frederic Tudor's ice-harvesting operation at Spy Pond, West Cambridge, Massachusetts (from Library of the Boston Atheneum, Boston, Massachusetts).*

Figure 6-5 *Nathaniel Wyeth's ice cutter, patented in 1829, was a horse-drawn device used to score the ice into blocks. After grooves were cut several inches deep by repeated crossings of the cutter, the blocks were broken off by inserting a tool into the groove. Wyeth, a hotel manager, possessed a creative mind. Frederic Tudor described him thus in 1828: "I found Wyeth wandering about the woods at Fresh Pond in all the lonely perturbation of invention and contrivance. . . . For minds highly excited and in great activity there is no Sunday" (Pearson 1936, p. 196) (from Cliff Petersen Collection of U.S. Patent models).*

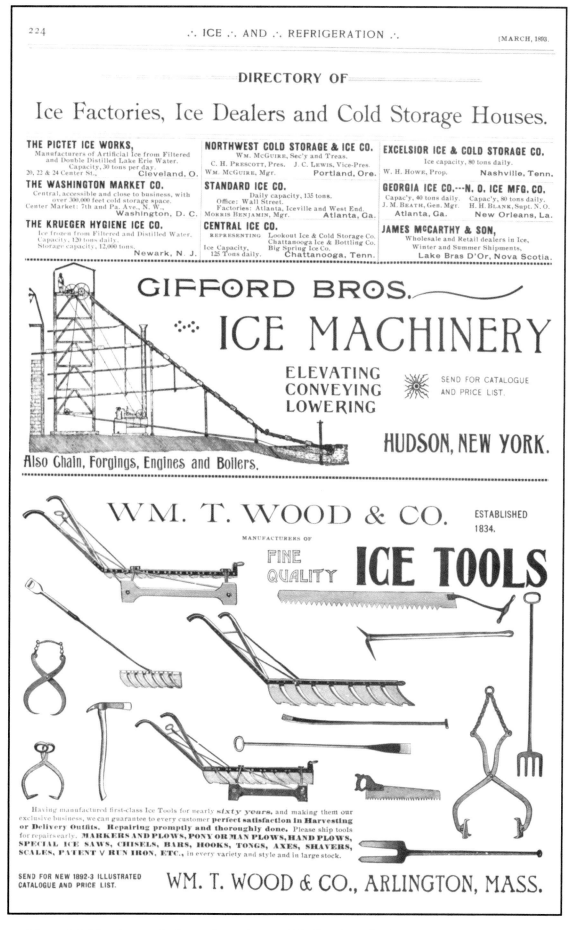

Figure 6-6 *Advertisement, ice-harvesting equipment, 1893 (from Ice and Refrigeration, March 1893, p. 224).*

Figure 6-7 *Advertisement, ice planers, 1905 (from Cold Storage and Ice Trade Journal, 1905).*

Figure 6-8 *Advertisement for ice coupons, which were purchased from ice dealers to be used in lieu of cash (from Ice and Refrigeration, March 1923). Ice picks were imprinted with dealers' names and given to customers, much the same as ballpoint pens are given away today.*

The Refrigerator

As the ice industry proceeded, so did the technology of refrigerators, or "iceboxes" as they later came to be called. Thomas Moore's crude refrigerators were improved upon by the various ice companies, which found a profitable sideline in selling the devices to customers. Flaws in the design of early refrigerators became evident as they were used. The early boxes used no moisture barrier, and condensed water on the inner parts of the boxes rotted the wood, giving rise to foul odors. Water condensed on the cold food too, and this was found to be undesirable if food was to be kept for any length of time. Various attempts were made to correct these problems. Henry Hill was granted U.S. Patent 750 in 1838 for his method of impregnating the inner wood liner of refrigerators with hot rosin and

beeswax. The inner metal lining normally used was dispensed with, eliminating the tendency of moisture to condense on the metal, wetting the wood. Thomas King, in U.S. Patent 4,086 issued in 1845, attempted to dry the air in the refrigerator by drawing a vacuum on the refrigerator box and then admitting air through a coil immersed in ice. In 1848, John Schooley began experiments along the same lines, developing a version of a refrigerator where air flowed over ice in a separate compartment, the dry air then flowing into the bottom of the food storage chamber and rising as it was heated to a vent at the top.[22] Schooley also advocated his method for building cold storage houses and received U.S. Patent 12,530 in 1855. Joseph Locke, a chemist, was solicited by Schooley to write a testimonial to the use of dry, cold air, and he demonstrated his devices from his home in Cincinnati, Ohio.[23] Although Schooley himself

Figure 6-9 *Ice store room, about 1910 (from Ice and Refrigeration [unknown date], Nickerson and Collins Co. photo collection, Smithsonian Institution, Division of Engineering and Industry).*

does not seem to have revolutionized refrigerator construction, the idea that air should pass over ice contained in a separate compartment became widely employed. Refrigerators that deposited moisture on the ice, rather than the insides of the refrigerator, were less objectionable. Larger, commercial refrigerators used these same ideas, although they became more sophisticated in design, for example, through the efforts of Azel Lyman, who obtained various U.S. patents after 1856 (Figure 6-16).

Widespread use of refrigerators seems to have occurred first in the United States, and the production and sale of refrigerators for household and commercial use was a rapidly growing business. For example, even as late as 1904, few household refrigerators were in use in England, where their introduction was strongly advocated by some.[24] Besides, much more ice was used in the United States. It was noted that an Italian province of almost one million people used less ice than a United States town of ten thousand in 1892.[25] Judging by the number of patents issued and by the number of advertisements appearing in the media, the refrigerator business seems to have taken off in the United States, beginning in the 1870s. By the turn of the nineteenth century, the array of differing types of refrigerators was amazing. These ranged from the simplest,

unadorned boxes to intricately carved and mirrored gaudy pieces of furniture made with fine woods. Many of them were poorly constructed, while others were good pieces of engineering. The efficiency of the ice-type refrigerators was only marginally addressed until the 1920s, when increasing competition from the mechanical refrigerator forced the "icebox" manufacturers to design refrigerators for minimal ice use (Figures 6-17 through 6-20).

Decline of the Natural Ice Industry

The natural ice industry began to decline after the 1890s in the most developed countries, the result of several causes. The rapid advance of cities along rivers and major lakes brought with it increasing pollution of those waters by sewage and refuse. Ice harvested from polluted waters was unsightly, frequently smelly, and dangerous to health with its concentrations of harmful bacteria. In many areas, cities banned the sale of ice harvested from polluted sources.

Mechanical refrigeration technology had progressed so much by 1890 that it became increasingly cost-effective as a means of producing ice. Although refrigeration technology was still too unreliable and costly to be applied directly in stores and homes, it had shown its usefulness in the brewing industry, where mechanical systems were seriously dis-

lacing ice. Large refrigerating systems could easily be designed for ice factories, and they were, spurred by the desire of the refrigerating machine companies to develop new outlets for their wares. The restriction of the supply of natural ice caused by polluted supplies and the increased cost of natural ice brought about by the need to go farther away from the cities gave impetus to the rise of the "manufactured ice" industry. Furthermore, the vagaries of winter weather made the steady supply of manufactured ice more desirable, particularly when a warmer than normal winter caused a serious "ice famine" in the United States in 1890. The editors of *Ice and Refrigeration* reported:

Nearly all will agree that the ice season of 1890 has had the most unfortunate results. The previous winter was an open one, and very little ice was harvested in the North. As a consequence, the supply in that section was not equal to the demand and a rise in the price followed. This and the erec-

tion of ice machines in several of the larger cities of the North, furnished ample food for discussion by the newspapers of the country, and as is usually the case . . . a large amount of misinformation was scattered abroad.[26]

The natural ice industry did not take the assault on its status quo lying down. A furious media battle took place for a time, as those ice men who had an interest in natural ice tried to convince the public that their product was better than manufactured ice. It was noted that "a state of belligerency exists between the dealers in natural and in manufactured ice."[27] Others simply resolved themselves to join rather than fight, building ice plants to supplement or replace their natural sources. Although the total use of ice increased into the early twentieth century, less of it was supplied from natural sources, until the natural ice industry all but died out (Figures 6-21 through 6-25; also see Figure VI, color section).

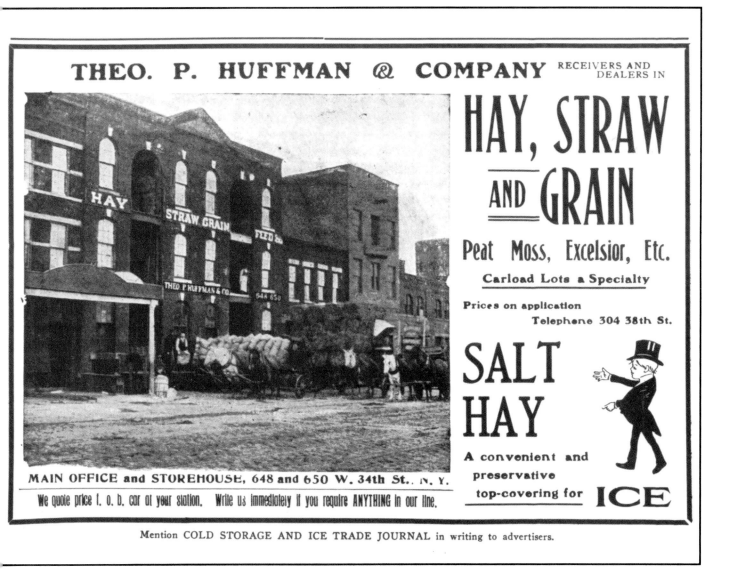

Figure 6-10 *Hay, straw, or sawdust was frequently used as a covering for stored ice. It was also placed between the ice blocks so they would not freeze together (from Cold Storage and Ice Trade Journal, 1905).*

Figure 6-11 *Loading ice wagons at Keystone Cold Storage Co., Reading, Pennsylvania, in 1900 (from Ice and Refrigeration, August 1900, p. 45).*

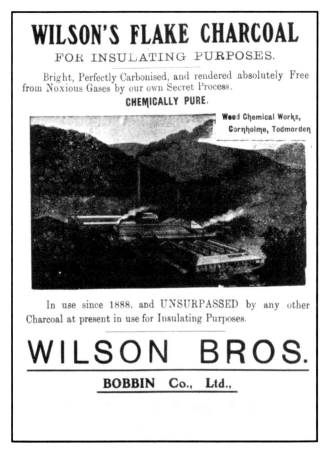

Figure 6-12 *Advertisement, insulation, 1895. Early ice houses used various materials for insulating the walls and roof (from Refrigerating Machinery by A.R. Leaske).*

Figure 6-13 *Loading delivery wagons, 1880s (from Harper's Weekly, August 30, 1884, p. 562).*

Figure 6-14 *"Jitney stations" dispensed ice on the spot to customers who loaded the ice in whatever means of transportation they possessed. Usually the ice was hauled home in small carts or "jitneys." Ice sales locations were a favorite gathering spot for children, who vied for chips of ice on hot summer days (top illustration from Ice and Refrigeration, September 1919; bottom illustration from Ice and Refrigeration, July 1908, p. 14).*

Figure 6-15 *Most portraits of ice men depict them as burly fellows. Actually, many of them were rather slender—but strong—as shown by these photos. The ice cakes weighed 300 to 400 pounds! The "youngest ice man" shown at lower right can't wait! (From left to right, top to bottom, Ice and Refrigeration, April 1905, p. 81; August 1904, p. 55; July 1908, p. 23; October 1910, p. 163.)*

Figure 6-16 *Design for an ice-type commercial refrigerator, about 1870 by Azel Lyman, who recognized the importance of baffles in directing air currents over the ice (from Lyman's Patent Dry Air Refrigerator and Ice House, New York [no date], Stephen Cutter).*

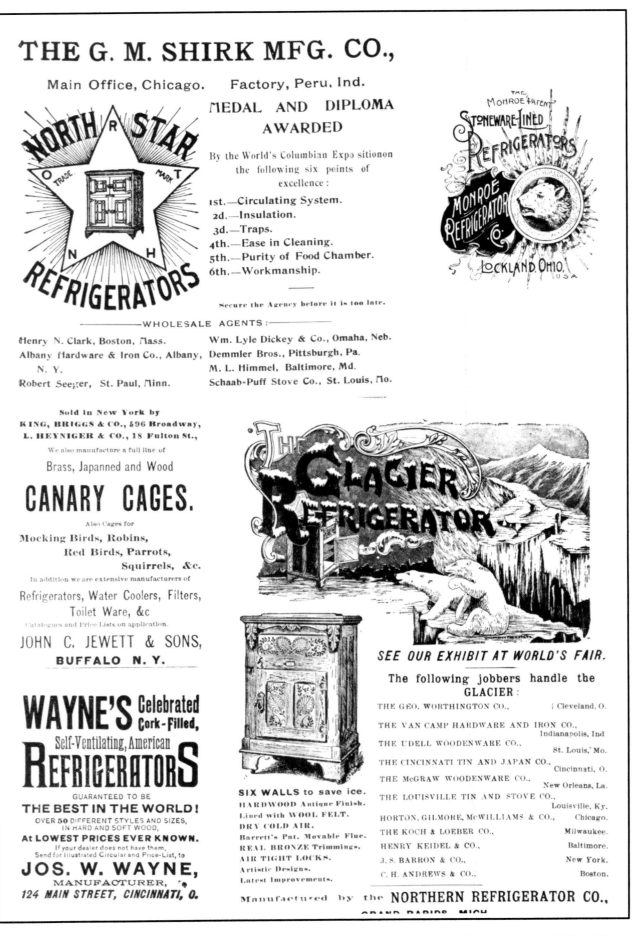

Figure 6-17 *Refrigerator ads, 1890s (from The Metal Worker, March 31, 1894, p. 58; February 1895; and April 8, 1893, p. 37).*

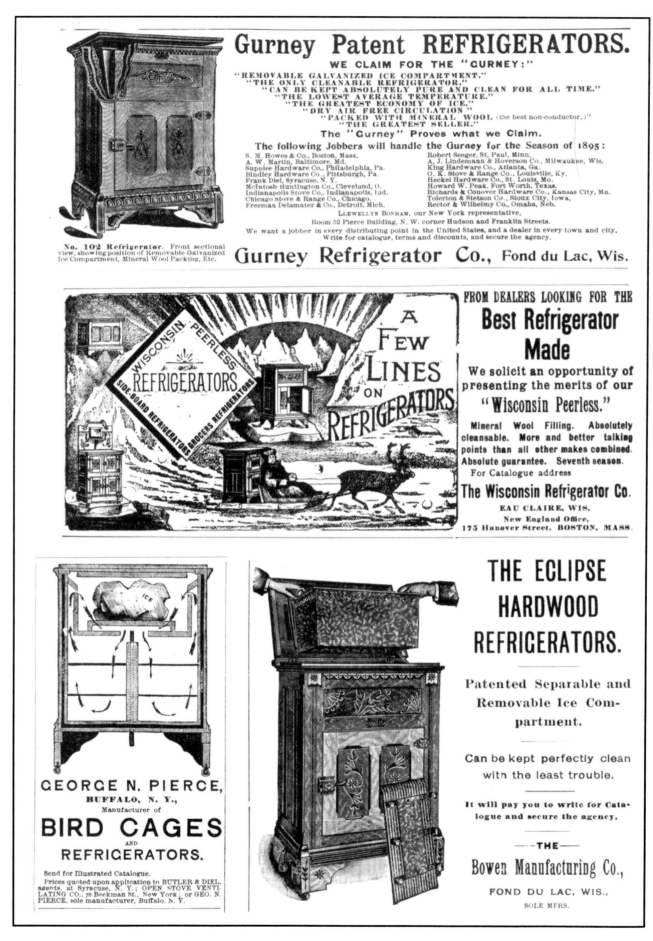

Figure 6-18 *Nineteenth-century refrigerator advertisements (from The Metal Worker, January 12, 1895, p. 28, and July 16, 1881, p. 31).*

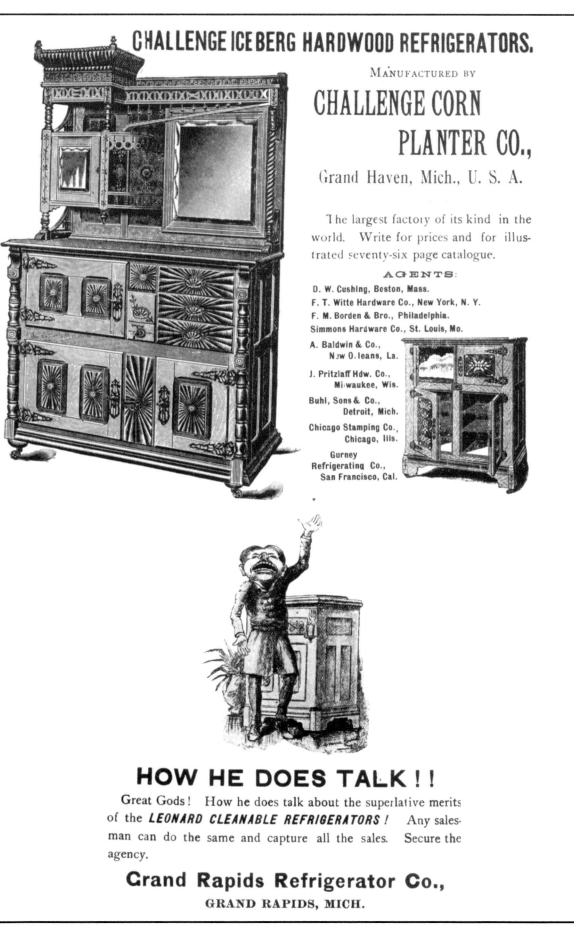

Figure 6-19 *Refrigerator advertisements, 1890s (from The Metal Worker, May 17, 1893, p. 29, and February 2, 1895, p. 27).*

Figure 6-20 *Advertisement, White Enamel Refrigerator Co. (from The Saturday Evening Post, April 29, 1911, p. 48).*

Figure 6-21 *An ice company display at San Antonio, Texas, in the 1920s showing the public the purity and clarity of ice (from Ice and Refrigeration [unknown date], Nickerson and Collins Co. photo collection, Smithsonian Institution, Division of Engineering and Industry).*

Figure 6-22 *Editorial cartoon—proponents of natural ice waged a furious media battle against ice that was manufactured, which they scornfully referred to as "artificial ice" (from Cold, September 1910, p. 185).*

Figure 6-23 *Editorial cartoon (from Cold, January 1914, p. 59).*

Figure 6-24 *Editorial cartoon (from Cold, August 1912, p. 248).*

Figure 6-25 *Editorial cartoon (from Cold, May 1911, p. 143).*

NINETEENTH-CENTURY HEATING, VENTILATING, AND MECHANICAL COOLING

THE BEGINNING OF AN ENGINEERING DISCIPLINE

The nineteenth-century growth of industrialization and the urbanization of centers of trade and commerce created new concerns about health and comfort as well as new opportunities for the fledgling heating and ventilating industry. Eighteenth-century developments in the theoretical sciences were applied in the nineteenth century to the increasingly complex needs of society. Further technological innovation, the growing importance of manufacturers, and the increased scale and complexity of buildings led to the application of large-scale heating and ventilating systems. Near the end of the nineteenth century, mechanical cooling and automatic temperature control were introduced.

Thomas Tredgold (1788-1829)

The empirical, sometimes trial-and-error approach of the eighteenth century matured to become a coherent body of theoretical and practical knowledge that could be applied to the basic needs of health and comfort. One of the most influential treatises in heating and ventilating practice, which continued to be an important authoritative resource for much of the nineteenth century, was Thomas Tredgold's *Principles of Warming and Ventilating Public Buildings, Dwelling Houses, Manufactories, Hospitals, Hot Houses, Conservatories, etc.*, published in 1824. Thomas Tredgold (Figure 7-1) was a self-taught engineer who in his early years as an apprentice studied cabinetmaking and architecture. He devoted his relatively short life to the study of engineering and eventually "worked himself to death" at the age of 40. Tredgold, who codified much of the engineering practice of his time, is credited by the Royal Charter of the Institution of Civil Engineers with defining the profession of civil engineering as "being the art of directing the great sources of power in nature for the use and convenience of man."

Tredgold's work became the basis for the design of many large public projects, such as the Houses of Parliament in London and St. George's Hall in Liverpool by Dr. Boswell Reid, St. Thomas' Hospital in London, and others. He recommended the use of open fireplaces, warm air, and steam heating of individual spaces for dwelling houses as well as the relative safety of steam heating and ventilation of hospitals. His preference for the use of steam, however, is clear.

> One important advantage is obtained by a steam apparatus, which distinguishes it from every other method of distributing heat, which is, that it can be extended to a very great distance from the boiler, in every direction: we can cause it to ascend, descend, or move horizontally, with equal facility; the loss of heat is inconsiderable in conveying it to a distant point: hence, one single fire is sufficient for an immense establishment. . . .[1]

Marquis de Chabannes

In France, Jean Frédéric, Marquis de Chabannes, concerned with the problems of fresh air and respiration, developed a system of heating and ventilating in 1814 for which he received a British patent in 1816. It was described as a

> method of conducting the air, and regulating the temperature in houses and other buildings . . . by producing a current of air in flues or chimnies, or through a tube or tubes, or other aperture or apertures, which is effected by means of the air-pump or pneumatic machine hereafter described, forcing a current of air through every winding, or even through liquids and also by means of the ventilator hereafter described, to be placed on the summit of the flue or chimney, which by its peculiar form, when the wind blows upon it, causes a draught upwards in powerful, according to the action or strength of the wind, but most powerful when the wind acts strongest.[2]

Chabannes' "Patent Calorifere Fumivore Ventilating Furnace," manufactured in his factory and foundry at 121 Drury Lane in London, was used in a variety of industrial, commercial, and domestic heating and ventilating applications. His design for ventilating the Covent Garden Theater in London used his "ventilating furnaces" and gas "ventilating chandeliers" to induce air movement and provide adequate ventilation "for drawing off continually the air breathed by two or three thousand persons."[3] The "calorifere" system of heating became popular in both England and France (Figure 7-2).

Figure 7-1 *Thomas Tredgold (1788-1829), civil engineer (from Andrew Ure,* A Dictionary of Arts, Manufactures and Mines, *1856).*

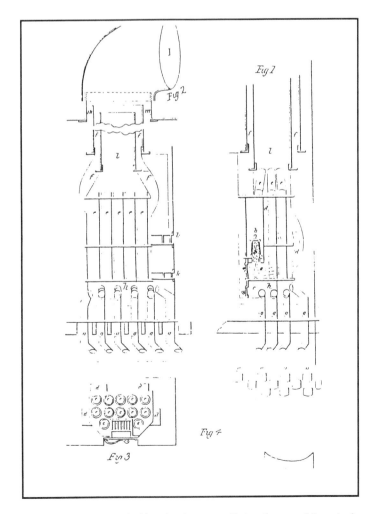

Figure 7-2 *Patent calorifere fumivore ventilating furnace, Marquis de Chabannes, 1818.*

The Houses of Parliament, London

The history of attempts to heat, cool, and ventilate the Houses of Parliament illustrates the changing attitude about engineering design, as well as managing technologies in the first half of the nineteenth century.

One of the original fans for ventilating the Houses of Parliament was designed by John Desaguliers in 1734 (see Figure 3-6). The earliest design, which operated in the House of Commons for many years, was a paddle-wheel type of fan seven feet in diameter, with radial blades one foot wide rotating in a casing.

In 1811, Sir Humphrey Davy took over the responsibility for improving the ventilating system. Davy introduced numerous holes in the floor to distribute heat more evenly throughout the rooms. He installed ceiling screens with heated metal tubes to accelerate velocity of the upward air movement and increase the overall ventilation (Figure 7-3).

The Marquis de Chabannes later provided steam heating for the House of Commons (Figure 7-4) based on design theories of Sir Thomas Tredgold's *Principles of Warming and Ventilating Public Buildings.*

> The progress of ventilation received a great impetus from the appointment of a Committee of the House of Commons, on Acoustics and Ventilation, in the year 1835, on the motion of Benjamin Hawes, Esq., M.P. Numerous parliamentary documents, not only connected with the House of Commons, but also with other public buildings, with private dwelling-houses, and with mines, ships, and manufactories, show the extent to which it has lately formed a leading object of consideration.
>
> It constitutes one of the most important items to which the attention of the Health of Towns' Commission is directed. The various statistical and sanatory reports that have been issued from the Home Office, and from the Medical Departments of the Army and of the Navy, under the direction of Sir James M'Grigor and Sir William Burnett, add much interesting information on the same question. And, if we look to the medical profession generally, the observations of Sir James Clarke on Consumption, and on the Sanative Influence of Climate, the remarks of Dr. Combe, Dr. James Johnston, Dr. Forbes, Dr. Southwood Smith, and numerous others, and the ingenious suggestions and improvements introduced by Dr. Arnott, all show how broadly the necessity of improved ventilation is appreciated, more especially since Tredgold had the merity of placing this subject in a more consistent position than it had ever been previously presented.[4]

Dr. Boswell Reid

The subsequent development of techniques for heating and ventilating reached a much more sophisticated level of complexity in the systems designed for the Houses of Parliament by Dr. David Boswell Reid, a professor of chemistry. With the burning of the Houses of Parliament in 1834 and their later rebuilding, Reid was commissioned to improve upon the previous heating and ventilating systems. Heating was provided in both the House of Lords and House of Commons by batteries of steam heaters, or steam cockles as they were called. The air was brought into equalizing chambers, or plenums, where it was heated. The House of Lords had four rows of three heaters and the

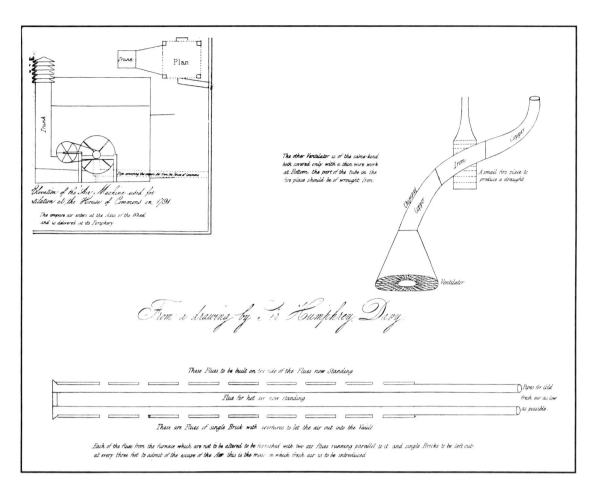

Figure 7-3 *Sir Humphrey Davy, ventilation for the House of Commons, 1811 (from C.J. Richardson, 1837).*

Figure 7-4 *Interior, House of Commons.*

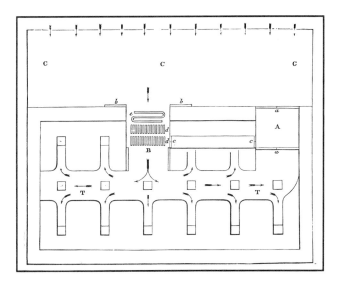

Figure 7-5 *Heating system, House of Commons (from Reid, 1844).*

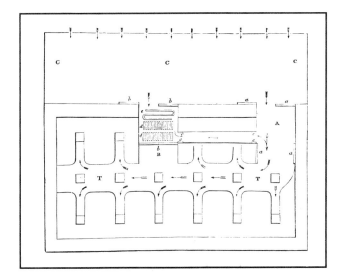

Figure 7-6 *Mixed-air heating and ventilating system, House of Commons (from Reid, 1844).*

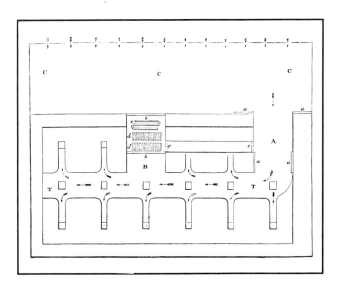

Figure 7-7 *Ventilation system, House of Commons (from Reid, 1844).*

House of Commons had twelve separate heaters. A series of large, manually operated air intake dampers controlled the mixing of outside air with the heated air to maintain desired temperatures (Figure 7-5).

Reid introduced air conditioning, artificial humidification, and chemical air purification. Use of a large chimney to increase ventilation significantly improved the system's performance. The chimney—120 feet high, 8 feet at the top and 11 feet at the bottom—provided a ventilating capacity that was estimated at a 25-horsepower equivalent. The fire grate was 25 square feet in area.

Fresh air was brought in through louvered openings from the courtyards on both sides of the building. The air was filtered and purified by a system that Reid employed, called Guy Fawkes' Vault (Figure 7-9). It filtered, washed, and chemically purified the air with gauze filtering screens soaked with chlorine, carbonic acid, or nitrous acid.

Artificial humidification of ventilating air was first attempted by Reid in 1836.

> Perhaps no buildings have been subjected to such numerous experiments as the Houses of Parliament, to which Sir Christopher Wren, the Marquis of Chabannes, Mr. Davies, Sir Humphrey Davy and many others directed their attention; and it may afford some clue to the diversity of practice if it be remembered that the *area of discharge provided by Sir Humphrey Davy in the present House of Commons, at that time the House of Lords, was one foot, whereas at present it is fifty feet.* Reid goes on to describe the scheme of 1836: "A chamber was provided for moistening, drying, cooling, and producing other alterations in the air, besides those effected by the hot-water apparatus." The air was filtered through a veil, 42 feet long and 18 ft. 6 in. deep; and it was introduced into the chamber through nearly a million holes in the floor. This was similar to the arrangement made by Davy, and about which it was said "For boring twenty thousand holes, The lords gave nothing—damn their souls."[5]

Recent air-conditioning and ventilation research and practice have seen the introduction of chemical additives for deodorizing or as bactericides. It is perhaps not so well known that Reid was first here also. For air purification in large cities, he adopted the following measures:

- exclusion of soot by filtration,
- washing,
- washing with lime water and the addition of ammonia (to neutralize acids),
- addition of chlorine or nitrous oxides to decompose, and
- warming by steam or other means.

St. George's Hall, Liverpool

Between 1851 and 1854, the Irish population of Liverpool increased by nearly 23 percent as a result of the potato famine. "The 1841 census recorded that over a third of the population in Liverpool parish lived in courts or cellars and in 1844, the first of *Two Reports of Commission on the State of Large Towns and Populous Districts* stated that Liverpool was 'the most unhealthy town in England.'"[6]

Liverpool's first Medical Officer of Health, Dr. W.H. Duncan, was of the opinion that lack of through draught in court housing contributed to the spread of infectious diseases, such as cholera, with which Liverpool was plagued in the 1840's. It is not surprising, therefore, that the committee was keen to adopt the City Surveyor's recommendation to employ Dr. Reid even though it involved additional expenditure.[7]

Dr. Reid's designs for heating and ventilating St. George's Hall in Liverpool expand on the concepts he had begun in the Houses of Parliament. St. George's Hall is the largest public building he designed in his career. He worked in an early collaboration with the architect Harvey Lonsdale Elmes, and he prepared a series of experiments to establish a basis for his ventilation design. The experiments

clearly demonstrated the necessity not only for a more ample supply of air than had been previously given in public buildings, but also of the introduction of much more specific means for regulating its ingress, and controlling its temperature, state of moisture, and discharge, according to the ever-varying circumstances under which they are occupied.[8]

St. George's Hall, completed in 1854, includes numerous large public spaces, such as the Great Hall, the Law Courts (the Crown Court and Civil Court), the Concert Room, and various "apartments" comprising almost 150,000 square feet. The Great Hall is 169 feet by 74 feet with an arched ceiling that is 84 feet from the ground. The heating and ventilating system includes hot water heating for spaces; steam heating for spaces and special applications such as humidification, driving ventilation fans, and driving an organ; fireplace heating; ventilation; and cooling (Figure 7-10).

Hot water heating was the primary means of warming the Great Hall, the courts, and the Concert Room and was provided by five hot water coils served by two Cornish-type hot water boilers, each 5 feet in diameter and 15 feet long (Figure 7-11).

Each boiler is provided with a large cylindrical dome, which is placed a few feet from the front of the boiler. From this dome the flow pipe, 12 in. diameter, rises to the expansion tank on the floor above.... The hot water flows to junction boxes placed in the air chamber, and from thence distributed through large valves and pipes to the manifolds of the heating coils.[9]

Hot water piping was insulated with hair felt and canvas that was painted and varnished.

Reid's efforts to introduce more advanced temperature control are especially interesting. Thermometers were installed in front of each of the two boilers and each of the five hot water coils as well as the main hot water return pipe to measure the temperature difference between the supply and return flow.[10] Fifty years later, most of this system was still in operation.

The steam heating apparatus was used primarily to preheat the various spaces in the building prior to "the commencement of business" and was shut off when the hot water was sufficient to maintain comfortable conditions. Steam was supplied by two boilers, each 5 feet in diameter by 15 feet long. There were 27 steam coils (three are shown, L, M, N) constructed of 2-inch or 1-inch-diameter wrought iron tubes and located in various air shafts (Figure 7-11). Steam was distributed at a pressure of 40 psi.

Steam was also used to humidify by its introduction directly into the air shafts. Heated in a small copper steam

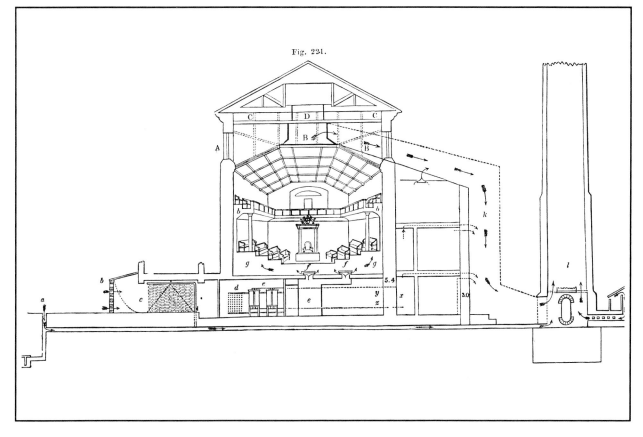

Fig. 221.

Figure 7-8 *Chimney of the House of Commons (from Reid, 1844).*

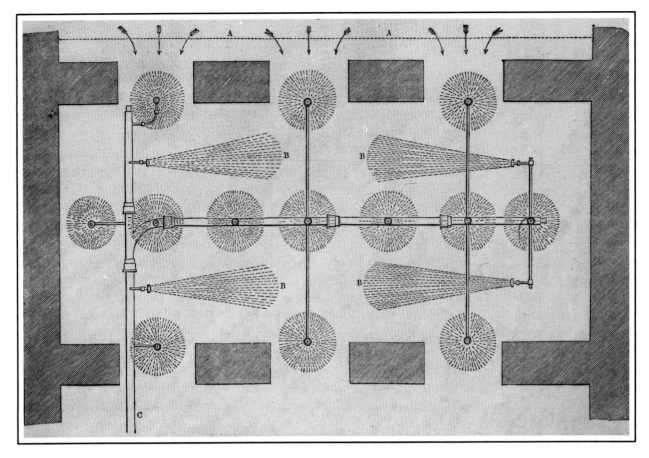

Figure 7-9 *Guy Fawkes' vault (from Reid, 1844).*

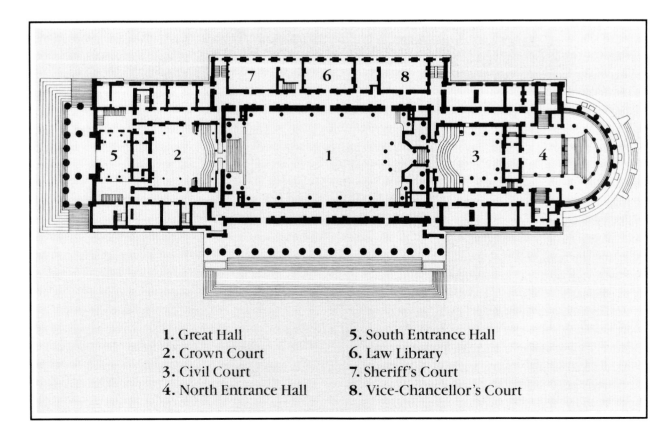

1. Great Hall   5. South Entrance Hall
2. Crown Court   6. Law Library
3. Civil Court   7. Sheriff's Court
4. North Entrance Hall   8. Vice-Chancellor's Court

Figure 7-10 *Plan, St. George's Hall, Liverpool, 1854 (from Knowles).*

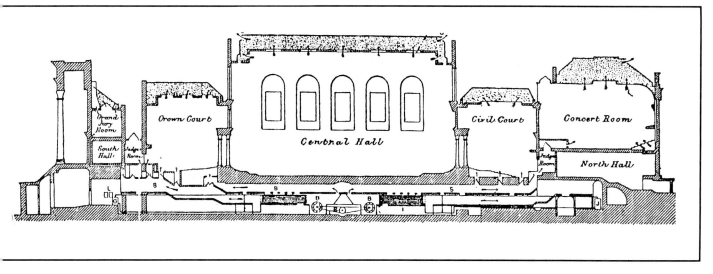

a. Longitudinal section of St. George's Hall.

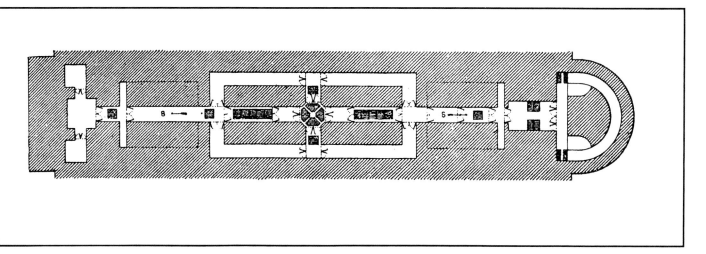

b. Basement plan, St. George's Hall, at level of upper air channels.

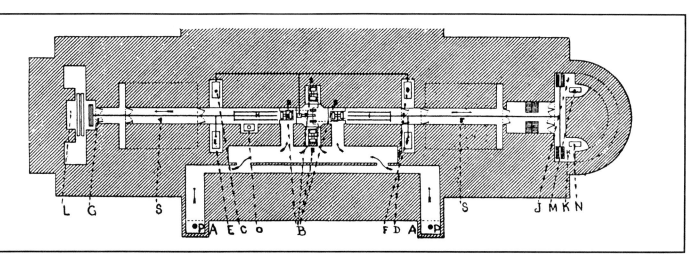

c. Basement plan, St. George's Hall, at level of lower ducts.

Figure 7-11 *Section and plans, St. George's Hall, Liverpool, 1854 (from Honiball).*

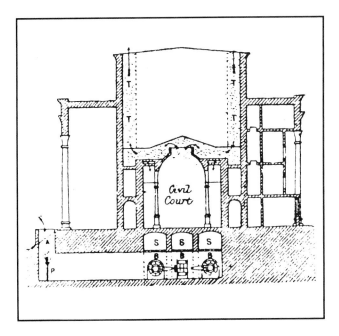

Figure 7-12 *Transverse section through Civil Court (from Honiball).*

boiler, the steam was introduced in front of each heating coil according to the operation of valves by the building superintendent and checked with hygrometers to ensure that there was not "excessive moisture."

All of the smaller spaces of St. George's Hall had fireplaces for heating as well. However, these were not considered to be a primary source of warmth but only "for enabling those who have been chilled out of doors to expe-

rience at once the effect of a powerful warmth, which is s grateful to many, and often so demanded."[11]

The ventilation of St. George's Hall involved the mechan ical supply and distribution of air, as well as its remova and exhaust. "The ventilation arrangements were designe to supply from 7 to 10 cu. ft. of air per minute to each per son occupying the building: the extent of opening of th supply valves is, therefore, regulated by the number of per sons present, the quantity of air driven through the build ing varying from 1,000 to 50,000 cu. ft. per minute."[12]

Air was supplied to the building through two majo shafts (A, A) at each end of the east portico. These were con nected to a main shaft extending the entire north-sout length of the building. This shaft intersected with four lat eral arches under the middle of the Great Hall, from whic four ventilating fans (B), driven by a 16-hp steam engine distributed air through the building. The fans were each 1 feet in diameter with 2½-foot-wide blades and driven at speed of 45 to 60 revolutions per minute (Figure 7-11).

Air was exhausted through openings in the ceiling above each space to ceiling chambers or plenum spaces an then directly to the outside or to four shafts (T) (Figure 7 12). The Great Hall was exhausted directly to the outside The Concert Room, the Crown and Civil Courts, and othe smaller spaces were exhausted to the four shafts. Ceilin panels in each of these spaces were controlled by valve and opened depending upon the quantity of supply a from below. The vaulted ceiling of the Great Hall was bui with hollow brick, set vertically upward, to allow for a di fuse area of more than 400 square feet required by Reid t exhaust the "vitiated" air (Figure 7-13).

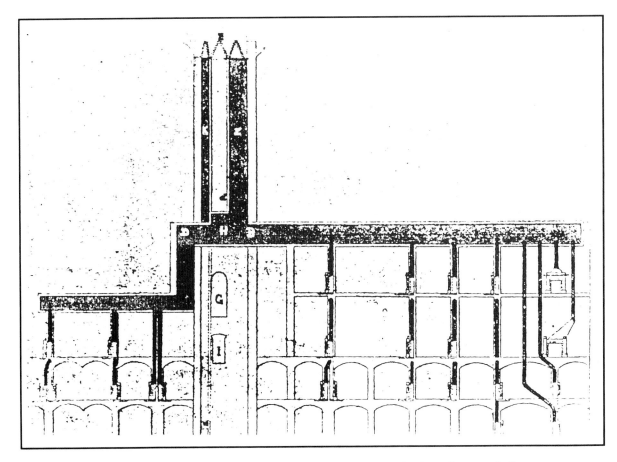

Figure 7-13 *Section of southwest shaft showing course of open fire flues (from Honiball).*

Figure 7-14 *Hollow-brick construction above the Great Hall (from Knowles).*

Figure 7-15 *Flaps covering the ventilation grilles above the small concert room (from Knowles).*

The various fireplace chimneys exhausted to a horizontal passageway, which was also connected to the four shafts (Figure 7-14). The four shafts were each divided into three compartments, two being for the smoke of the fireplaces and one for the "vitiated" air. Each of the four boilers had its own individual flue.

> Control of the incoming and outgoing air was largely manual and was achieved by a veritable army of workers opening and closing a series of canvas flaps and doors which could be individually adjusted by ropes and pulleys.[13]

St. George's Hall, the "immense pneumatic machine of Dr. Reid," continued to operate with many of its original systems intact throughout the rest of nineteenth century.

HOT WATER HEATING SYSTEMS

High-Pressure Hot Water Systems

Angier Marsh Perkins was born in 1799 in Newburyport, Massachusetts, son of Jacob Perkins, and went to England as a young boy and became interested in the problems of heating. He worked on high-pressure hot water heating systems utilizing small-diameter piping, which were developed by the firm of John Russell & Sons of Staffordshire in 1825 for this purpose.

The Perkins system, patented in 1831 (Figures 7-16 and 7-17), consisted of a series of coils passing through a furnace to a steam riser. The apparatus was intended to maintain water temperatures around 350°F, but this was often exceeded, reaching 550°F (1,100 pounds per square inch) or more. The system was popular in England between 1830 and 1840 and was used by Sir John Soane in his house in London and for the heating of the British Museum.

> This principle has been applied at the British Museum on a very extensive scale, there being upwards of five miles of one inch tubing placed in various parts of that building heated by twenty-four furnaces, all of which answer the purpose perfectly.
> Previously to this plan being adopted at the British Museum, four hot water apparatuses upon another plan, and a number of hot air stoves had been put up there, none of which can be compared in point of economy of fuel with the small pipe system, as can be at once ascertained by examining the relative heat of the flues.[14]

"The Perkins system was the forerunner of modern medium and high-pressure hot-water systems. There was, however, no continuous development: the Perkins system was little used after the mid 1800's, while modern pressurized systems did not appear until about 1925."[15]

Edward Weeks received a patent in 1830 to "convey hot water in tubes extending round a hot house, in order to heat the air, for the purpose of promoting vegetation."[16] The system was improved upon by George Knowles that same year.

Charles Richardson, influenced by the work of Angier Perkins, goes on to describe the use of high-pressure hot water heating for both heating and ventilating in *A Popular Treatise on the Warming and Ventilation of Buildings* (1839).

Richardson defends his position by describing the deficiencies of alternative heating methods, such as air stoves or steam, in comparison to hot water heating.

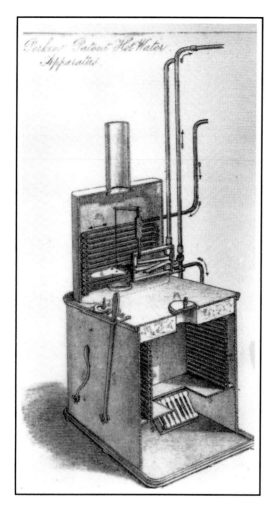

A section on the line C, D of the plan. aa is the fire coil, b the grate, and c the lever attached to the axis that supports the grate, here shown in the position of being thrown down to clear the furnace of scoria.

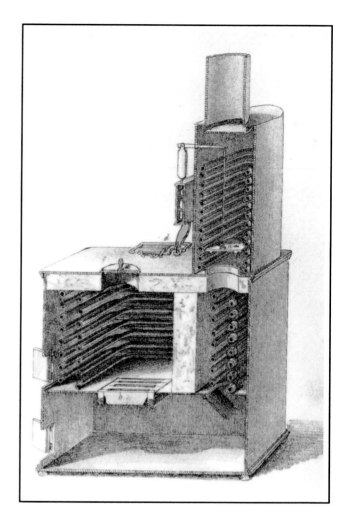

A section on the line A, B.

Figures 7-16 and 7-17 *Perkins patent hot water apparatus (from Perkins, 1840).*

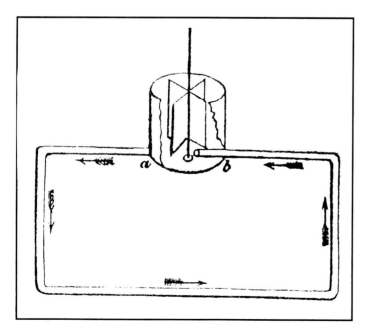

Figure 7-18 *Rotary float (from Hood, p. 123).*

. . . by the latter method, the air receiving its heat from substances at a low temperature, not sufficiently high to separate or change its constituents parts, it cannot be deteriorated; whereas by the pernicious hot air stove, the air, in passing through circuitous flues, and coming into contact with iron plates of a high temperature, its oxygen is more or less absorbed by the iron . . . and thus the remedy becomes more injurious than the evil it was intended to remove.[17]

The pernicious system of warm air from stoves, and the costly, and therefore unattainable air of steam have lately been superseded in a great measure by the more simple and less expensive method of a circulation of hot water through iron tubes.[18]

High-pressure hot water systems received some attention for a short time in England, but they did not continue to be popular or gain widespread use.

Low-Pressure Hot Water Systems

The early development of low-pressure hot water heating was described most clearly by Charles Hood in his publication *A Practical Treatise On Warming Buildings by Hot Water*

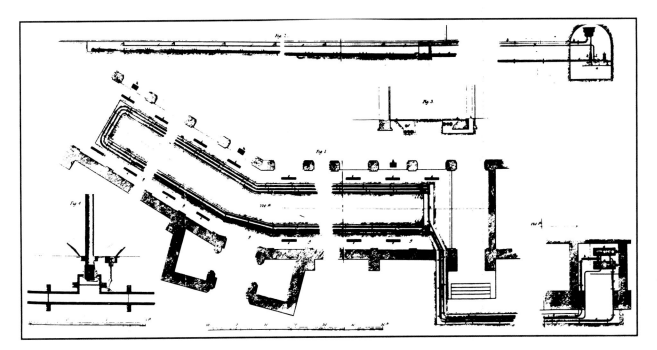

Figure 7-19 *Orangery, Royal Palace at Windsor, J. Bramah & Sons, 1829 (from Tredgold, 1836).*

(2d ed., 1844). An essential element of low-pressure heating systems was the hot water circulator. Hood describes a "rotary float" (Figure 7-18) by which the force of gravity is overcome by centrifugal force in the circulation of hot water.

> The float, or circulator, has motion given to it by means of a fly, similar to a smoke-jack, which is placed in the chimney, and is turned by the smoke of the fire that is used to heat the boiler—the float being fixed on centres, and revolving freely in the boiler. The centrifugal force imparted to the water by the rapid rotation of this float causes it to rise higher at the periphery than in the centre of the boiler; and the velocity with which the float moves determines the extent of this deviation from the level.[19]

The relatively ingenious drive mechanism was still dependent upon the thermal "chimney-effect" from the boiler fire and, therefore, difficult to regulate with any degree of control.

Hood goes on to describe a number of low-pressure hot water heating systems for greenhouses, which achieved considerable popularity.

> From 1801 to 1806 the use of hot water, flowing through leaden pipes placed about nine inches below the surface of the mould, was employed by T.N. Parker, Esq., of Sweeney Hall, Oswestry, for giving bottom heat for melon pits, the water circulating through a single pipe only, which was attached to a small copper boiler. Mr. Weston, of Leicester, in 1800, employed for the same purpose leaden pipes [of] three inches diameter, filled with hot water, which, from the slow conducting power of the metal, retained the heat for a great length of time. In 1826, Mr. MacMurtie, gardener to Lord Anson, described a method of giving bottom heat jointly by flues and steam, which he had successfully employed for a period of twelve years; and in 1831, the author applied the circulation of hot water, on the common plan, through iron pipes of four inches diameter, for producing bottom heat in forcing pits, without the use of dung.[20]

* * *

Hot water heating has always been used, and is chiefly employed at this period, for the same purpose for which is was originated—warming green-houses. This method is preferred because the lower temperature of the pipes containing the water is not so likely to injure plants, also the water is a long time giving out all its heat, in case the fire is neglected, thus keeping the temperature above a dangerously low point for hours. For the same reasons, hot water is being used for warming dwellings, and by many is preferred to any other mode.[21]

Later in the century, there was widespread commercial and domestic use of low-pressure hot water heating. The relative safety, ease of installation and maintenance, and low cost were influential factors in its popularity.

Early Steam Heating Systems

The earliest engineering literature pertaining to steam heating appears to be that of Glasgow civil engineer Robertson Buchanan, who published a pamphlet, *Essay on the Warming of Mills and Other Buildings by Steam*, in 1807. Buchanan then wrote his *Practical Essays on the Economy of Fuel and the Management of Heat* in 1810. This work contained three parts: "On the Effects of Heat, Means of Measuring It, Fuel etc."; "On Heating Mills, Dwelling Houses, and Public Buildings, by Steam"; and "On Drying and Heating by Steam."

The English obsession with their gardens continued to focus the attention and interests of inventors and engineers on methods of heating. In 1829, the Orangery of the Royal Palace at Windsor was one of the first applications of the use of steam heating on a large scale with a system developed by J. Bramah & Sons. The system, described in detail by Tredgold, was intended to maintain temperatures in the Orangery at 55°F and to provide "artificial dew" or humidity to the conservatory by a manually operated valve that admitted steam into the space (Figure 7-19). The system consists of two steam boilers (both of which are only used in cases of extreme cold) and 185 feet of steam piping running in three rows in a trench below the floor. In Figure 7-19, Figure 1 is a plan of the system and Figures 2 and 3 are longitudinal and transversal sections through the pipe trench. The boilers are shown (aa), the service main is shown (bbb) as three four-inch-diameter pipes, and the warm air openings are shown (ee).

Providing better control of health and comfort conditions in hospitals was also an important concern of heating and ventilation design. The earliest applications of steam heat-

ing in the United States were for cotton mills in Massachusetts. A variety of materials and systems were tested with little or moderate success. Tin plate pipes and copper piping were eventually replaced with cast-iron.

Between 1830 and 1835, steam was introduced in pipes made of tin plate, and used for warming and at the same time for escape into the rooms to afford the proper degree of moisture. The pressure was from two to three pounds, and the boiler was supplied from a tank, automatically, by means of stone floats, the same as used first in England. Copper pipes were next used, about three to four inches in

Figure 7-20 *Pioneers of Walworth Manufacturing Company (from the Walworth Co.).*

diameter, and were discarded because every little while when the pressure went down the pipes would collapse. Lines of four-inch cast-iron pipe were then put up; some carried first to the top floor, and then back and forth through the building to the basement; others branching from a main pipe on each floor with the ends projecting through the walls of the building, allowing the water and more or less steam to escape freely into the atmosphere. In each case, the pipes were carried near the ceiling, and no effort was made to retain the water of condensation. In one case, the system of four-inch pipes carried first to the top story without distribution was removed, and six-inch pipes put up, branching from the main, on each floor. With the cast-iron, of course, a greater pressure was possible, and by placing the tank for supplying the boiler in the upper story, fifteen pounds pressure was employed, and the water of condensation removed through traps and other contrivances, some imported from England being in use at the present time.[22]

EARLY U.S. BOILER AND HEATING MANUFACTURERS

Many of the earliest steam heating systems and technologies were exported from England to the United States. The

pioneering work of James Watt influenced the early manufacturers of steam boilers and radiators in the United States. "The first patent for making a welded tube, was issued in England in 1813, and all wrought-iron pipe used in this country previous to 1835 was imported."[23] However, the development of the steam heating industry—its principles of engineering, processes of manufacturing, and experienced tradespeople—are all contributions from the United States.

The origins of steam heating in the United States began with a patent issued on June 12, 1835, to Robert Rogers of South Berwick, Maine, for a device for "warming buildings by radiated and steam heat." However, the papers and drawings connected with the patent for steam heating were destroyed in 1836 during a fire in the patent office building, and it is believed that Rogers died the same year.

Walworth & Nason

In the middle of the nineteenth century, steam heating became the popular method of warming buildings in

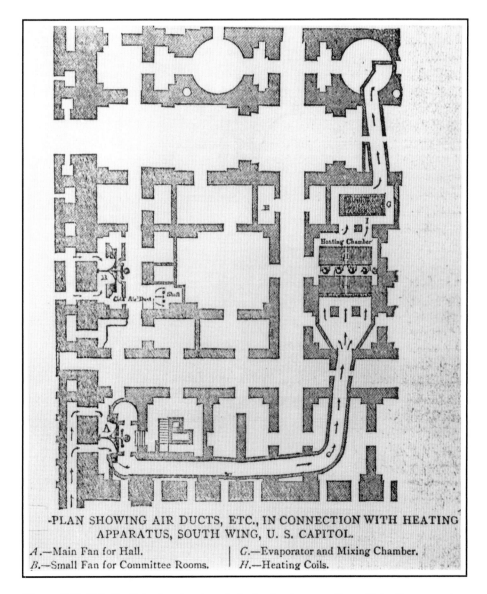

-PLAN SHOWING AIR DUCTS, ETC., IN CONNECTION WITH HEATING APPARATUS, SOUTH WING, U. S. CAPITOL.

A.—Main Fan for Hall.
B.—Small Fan for Committee Rooms.
G.—Evaporator and Mixing Chamber.
H.—Heating Coils.

Figure 7-21 *U.S. Capitol, plan showing air ducts, etc., in connection with heating apparatus, south wing (from J.S. Billings, 1886, p. 124).*

Europe and the United States. The introduction of steam heating to the United States is credited to Joseph Nason (1815-1872), who, through the firm of Walworth & Nason, was the first to demonstrate the use of steam as a practical means of heating. While traveling to London, Nason met Angier Perkins and worked for a period of time in his heating business. Through Perkins, he met with Thomas Russell (of the pipe manufacturing family), who had attempted unsuccessfully to start a business in New York City. Russell sold his stock to Joseph Nason and a partner, James Walworth. With this, the firm of Walworth & Nason began in June 1841. In 1842, Walworth & Nason moved to Boston where their first commission was to heat the "counting-room" of the Middlesex Mill in Lowell, Massachusetts (Figure 7-20).

The firm developed steam heating systems using piping of smaller diameter. The first steam heating installation was in 1845 for the Eastern Exchange Hotel in Boston. The heating of the rooms was accomplished by pipecoils, predecessors to the cast-iron radiators that replaced them later in the century. That same year they installed steam heating for a woolen mill in Burlington, Vermont.

The first application of a fan ventilation apparatus in the United States was by Walworth & Nason on the Boston Custom House in 1846.

> The amount of the contract was $6,750. . . . The fan used was a paddlewheel like that used on steamboats which was mounted in a case fitting the ends of the blades with fair accuracy, but leaving area enough about the periphery to permit free escape of air. The air was heated by coils of 3/4 inch pipe, the water of condensation being discharged through a Nason steam trap which had been invented by Mr. Nason for use with heating apparatus, a sufficient pressure being carried on the boiler to run the small steam engine that drove the fan, the exhaust steam being used to heat one of the coils.[24]

Joseph Nason constructed a small, upright water-tube boiler in 1851 to take the place of the coils of wrought iron pipe that was typical of the earlier work of Walworth & Nason. In 1852, the partnership between Nason and Walworth was dissolved. Joseph Nason went to New York to manage the firm's business there.

In 1855, Nason, at the request of Captain Montgomery C. Meigs, planned the heating and ventilating system for the United States Capitol, which has been described as "the first really scientific and complete job of its kind done in the country."

THE U.S. CAPITOL

General Montgomery C. Meigs, who was responsible for coordinating the overall design and installation of the first heating and ventilating system in the U.S. Capitol, worked closely with Robert Briggs, a consulting engineer from Boston, and Joseph Nason from New York. The heating and ventilating systems were used in the south and north wings of the Capitol for the House of Representatives and the Senate, respectively. The systems included heating and ventilating for the legislative chambers of the House and Senate, as well as the numerous committee rooms, corridors, and the "great stairwells."

General Meigs wrote to his chief, the Honorable J. Floyd, then Secretary of War, that:

> The most difficult piece of engineering and construction which I have yet had to undertake is the heating and ventilating of the Capitol extensions (that is, the House and the Senate Wings). There is none which requires more laborious, complicated and tedious calculation, drawings and studies, none which requires so extensive an acquaintance with the general principles of science and physics of the properties of caloric and its effects on gases and solid bodies. There is none in which so many failures have been made, both in this country and in Europe. The history of the heating of the Houses of Parliament, in England, is a history of failures and blunders, of ignorance and waste.[25]

The heating system consisted of twenty-six indire heaters built into brick chambers in the sub-basement each wing. "These chambers were connected by means subterranean airways of generous proportions, with a fa chamber in each building. The outside air was draw through tunnels of approximately 64 sq. ft. cross-sectio each tunnel terminating at the base of an open toppe tower in the park west of the Capitol and some 400 ft. di tant from the building"[26] (Figure 7-21). Vertical flues bui into the massive brick masonry were used to distribute tl heated air to "hooded outlets" near the floors of variou spaces (Figure 7-22).

> The heaters were of a "box" pipe-coil pattern, each vertical trombone coil begin connected into a steam manifold at top and a corresponding condensate manifold at bottom. The number of trombone coils, or sections, in the heaters, varied from six for the smallest heater to eighteen for the largest. The number of pipes in vertical order in the trombone sections varied from 14 to 24. Each one of all these trombone sections, or elements, was valved at both the steam and condensate connections with respective manifolds, the valves being embodied in the manifolds[27] (Figure 7-23).

The air was carried to a 16-foot-diameter fan from whic "was intended to supply at 60 revolutions per minu 50,000 cubic feet of air against a resistance of about half a inch of water column, and when running from 100 to 1 revolutions to give 100,000 cubic feet of air, which was su posed to be the maximum amount required."

> At the Capitol the system recommended and adopted was that of a forced or plenum ventilation, the entering air being propelled by two large centrifugal fans, one 16 ft. and one 12 ft. in diameter, motive power being applied to the fan by vertical engines, the cranks of which were keyed on to the fan shaft. The volumes of air to be moved were much larger than had been handled in earlier work and a more refined analysis of the form and construction of the fan than previously had been made was deemed advisable, and, therefore, a long and costly series of experiments were made by Mr. Nason, in cooperation with Captain Meigs as to the best possible obtainable form for the fans. These fans as built were really air turbines reversed. They consisted of circular iron discs of diameters mentioned above on the periphery on one side of which were bolted cast-iron quadrilateral vanes.
>
> These vanes were curved and placed on the line of a logarithmic spiral of 45 degrees. The fans were centered in a

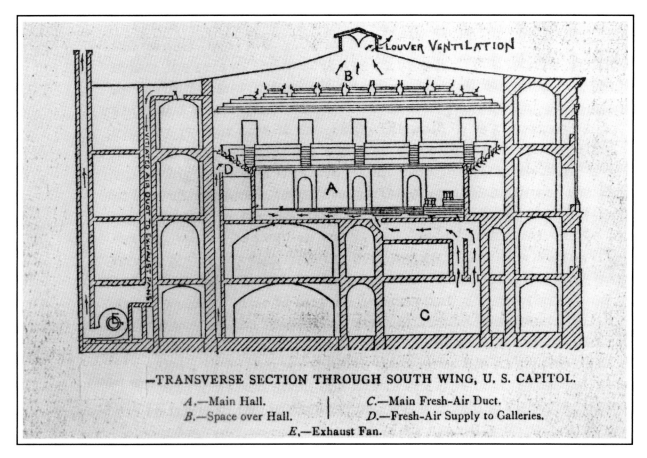

Figure 7-22 *Transverse section through south wing, U.S. Capitol (from J.S. Billings, 1886, p. 125).*

Figure 7-23 *Section through air ducts and heating apparatus of south wing, U.S. Capitol (from J.S. Billings, 1886, p. 126).*

ring of brick work the surfaces of which next to the moving parts was swept in mortar by the fans themselves. They were predecessors of the cone fan of today. The Boston Custom House fans were no doubt built of wood but the fans in question were built of iron by Morris, Tasker & Morris, of Philadelphia, who afterwards made many more for Walworth & Nason for use in insane asylums and hospitals.[28]

Despite the best of available design expertise and the latest heating and ventilating technology at this time, there still remained significant problems with the comfort of its esteemed occupants.

Experience has shown two errors in the design of the system; first, in the method of temperature control involving the human factor to an excessive degree; and, second, in the absence of means for tempering the air before reaching the heaters whose construction and valving exposed all trombone sections unfilled with steam to the liability of freezing cold weather.[29]

Robert Briggs visited the Capitol to examine the heating and ventilating system and was convinced that its proper operation was not clearly understood by those who controlled its operation. He commented that:

The prime object of the entire apparatus is to give the largest quantity of air at the lowest temperature that will answer to

Figure 7-24 *Type of fan installed at the U.S. Capitol, 1857 (from Engineering Review, September 1922, p. 27).*

heat the rooms. The occupants of rooms will only tell you when they are too hot or too cold, but that they have enough air—which in the long run is the most important—rests upon your own care and observation.[30]

This system remained in operation until the beginning of the twentieth century, when, in 1906, it was upgraded.

Nason introduced an innovative radiator design in 1862 "built of pipes screwed into a cast-iron base and so adjusted that each pipe and the base for it contained exactly one square foot of superficial surface. This radiator was the first to be constructed on strictly scientific lines and I think it can be fairly stated that all radiator ratings in use today in this country are primarily based upon the Nason radiator."[31]

In this way, from 1862 to 1879, the vertical-pipe wrought-iron radiator business fell into the hands of concerns of great capital and great business ability. These were the men who had the inventive power and the business capacity to make the steam-heating development in this country in those 17 years one of the business marvels of the nineteenth century. After the close of the Civil War, the heating-business began to attract the attention of the manufacturers of cast-iron.[32]

The firm of Walworth and Nason continued to thrive during the next thirty years, designing and installing steam heating and fan-powered ventilating systems in many large projects throughout the northeastern United States. Walworth and Nason ultimately merged into "the great manufacturing concern" known as the Walworth Manufacturing Company.

Stephen J. Gold and Samuel F. Gold—The H.B. Smith Company

"In the year 1860 the modern steam boiler, either for heating or for power, was still an infant."[33] The development of steam heating for domestic purposes had been limited by problems of explosions and overall safety of operation. The earlier type of shell boiler was a "menace" because of explosions, and the fire tube boilers required constant maintenance and supervision.

Stephen J. Gold, an inventor and iron stove manufacturer from Cornwall, Connecticut, attacked this problem through a series of experiments leading to four patents obtained in 1854 and 1856.

In 1859, Stephen Gold formed the firm of Gold, Foskett & Gold to sell steam boilers and met with the H.B. Smith Company to discuss terms for the lease and manufacture of his steam boiler. This was an upright, wrought-iron shell boiler with a cast-iron internal fire box.[34] Gold developed a radiator to eliminate the extensive wall piping and costly coils that were typical of the work of Joseph Nason. His radiator design, made of riveted sheet iron resembling a mattress, is referred to as the "mattress type" radiator. The radiator was made of two thin plates of sheet iron fastened together by rivets at the bottom of depressions in the outer plate, and the edges were made tight by being rolled up with a piece of cord between them, in such a way as to make them "resistant to the steam pressures." The radiator was equipped with a cock to admit steam and another to let out the air. It was noisy and unsightly and tended to leak.[35] The discussions resulted in an agreement that Gold would eceive a 10 percent royalty on the first $15,000 in sales, which marked the beginning of a successful relationship for many years to come.

The H.B. Smith Co., founded in April 1854 from the original location of Lewis' Stove Works in Westfield, Massachusetts, continued to manufacture all the work of Stephen and Samuel Gold during the rest of the nineteenth century.

The design of hot water and steam boilers attracted the attention of a number of competing firms. In 1857, William C. Baker (who had previously worked with Stephen Gold) and John Jewell Smith formed a partnership as Baker, Smith & Co. in New York and were the first to introduce a water-tube boiler with a box coil for indirect steam heating.[36] Stephen Wilcox of Westerly, Rhode Island, patented a "little pipe boiler" in 1856, which was later manufactured and "perfected" in the first boiler manufactured by the firm when it was organized in Providence in 1867.[37] The water-tube boiler was very successful for the next decade, and its applications for high-pressure steam became especially attractive later in the century for large-scale electrical generation.

Samuel Fay Gold (1840-1907), son of Stephen, who had worked with his father in Cornwall since childhood, received a patent in 1859 for a low-pressure, cast-iron, vertical-section boiler and again turned to the H.B. Smith Company of Westfield, Massachusetts, to manufacture and sell his "Gold boiler" (Figure 7-25). Gold had adapted his original boiler designs from previous work by George B. Brayton of Providence, Rhode Island. Brayton's work involved experiments with a sectional cast-iron boiler in Westerly, Rhode Island, where in 1849, "in the winter of that year," according to his own account, he mounted such a boiler on a locomotive which made a few trips on the ice. Between that date and 1864, he secured several patents, one of which included the means of heating a building.[38] In 1865, four years prior to the second Gold boiler patent, the Brayton "Exeter" boiler (named after the Exeter Machine Works of Boston and Exeter, New Hampshire) received the highest honor of the Massachusetts Mechanics Association and was exhibited at the Centennial in Philadelphia in 1876[39] (Figure 7-26).

However, the Gold sectional, fire-tube-type boiler for heating buildings was "superb and, with constant improvements, held its own for half a century."[40] Samuel Gold also adopted the concept, initially conceived by Thomas T. Tasker of Philadelphia, of returning the water of condensation to the boiler, and in 1862 he, with William Foskett, patented the "Gold Pin" radiator that offered an indirect means of heating.

The Gold boiler introduced low-pressure steam heating with indirect cast-iron radiators that "not only caught the public fancy, but practically changed the entire heating methods of the whole country."[41]

John Henry Mills (1834-1908)

The practical application of steam heating was greatly advanced by the work of John Henry Mills, a "mechanical genius, who was in turn craftsman, inventor, heating contractor, scientific investigator, and engineering consultant." He became one of the most widely renowned engineers in

Figure 7-25 *Original Gold boiler, 1859. "The original Gold boiler—first boiler to be manufactured by H.B. Smith & Co.—in its first form consisted of an assembly of vertical cast iron sections held together with draw bolts and gasketed at the joints. These boilers were invariably installed in brick chambers and fed steam to indirect pin type radiators in the same chambers thereby warming air that was duct conducted to the rooms. Steam also could be fed directly to crude radiators or pipe coils in more distant rooms"* (Stifler, 1960. H.B. Smith Co.).

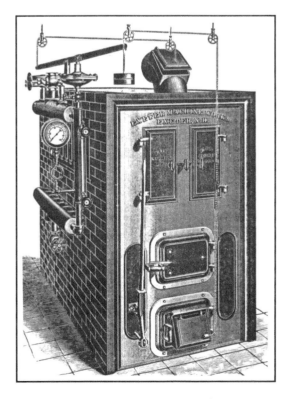

Figure 7-26 *The Exeter steam boiler (from* Heating and Ventilation, *April 15, 1894).*

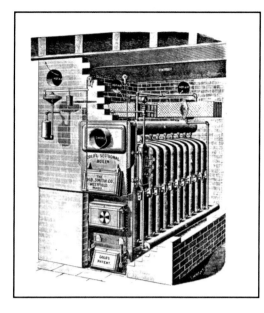

Figure 7-27 *Gold boiler, 1880s. "By the eighties, the Gold boiler had become considerably more sophisticated. Exterior drums with nipple connections to the sections had replaced the old direct connection method although draw bolts were still used. The fire travel remained two pass through horizontal fire tubes formed by the sections themselves, with the smoke outlet discharging at the front of the boiler (Stifler, 1960. H.B. Smith Co.).*

the United States during the last quarter of the nineteenth century.[42]

Following Brayton's lead, John H. Mills in 1867, patented his first cast-metal sectional boiler. This one was designed for use with an engine but others, for heating, appeared in the years between 1869 and 1874. A Walworth catalog of 1892 makes the statement: "It was at our factory in Cambridgeport, Massachusetts, in 1870 that the first Mills Sectional Boilers were made and a little later his direct and indirect radiators." Mills himself regarded his third boiler as his "first practicable boiler," the manufacture of which, he says, was begun by George W. Walker & Co. at Watertown, Massachusetts, in the foundry of Miles Pratt & Co.

The first reference to a Mills Product which appears in the records of the H.B. Smith & Co. is under date of 28 August 1871, when 300 pounds of Mills boiler grates at 7 cents a pound were ordered by the Union Steam and Water Heating Company of New York through the Westfield firm. Eighteen months later (1 March 1873), the Smith Company was in complete control of Mills boiler manufacture.[43]

"In spite of his success with steam, Mills soon turned to water as a superior heating agent. As early as 1877, he had observed its increasing popularity and admitted that it was more silent and steady than steam and more economical of fuel. His extensive work with water began in the mid-eighties."[44] Mills worked on water-heating systems for a number of notable projects, such as the Pierce Building (1887) in Boston and substituting a hot water system for the existing air system in Trinity Church (1888), also in Boston.

In 1877, John Mills wrote a small treatise on *Heating by Steam*, and between 1888 and 1890, he wrote his two-volume book *Heat, Science and Philosophy of its Production and Application to the Warming and Ventilation of Buildings*, which

was published in 1890. "The book is a curious mixture of science, history, and current practice, but is a mine of miscellaneous technical information, with elaborate diagram and charts."[45] This two-volume opus was an important resource for boiler and steam heating engineers for years to come.

In his later years, John Mills achieved enormous success in his industry. "Money came so easily before 1897 that, as he grew older, with no one dependent on him, Mills was inclined to indulge in ultra extravagant experiments."

There is a story, still current at the Westfield foundry, that at some time in 1905 or 1906, John Mills drifted into town shabbily dressed and practically penniless. J.R. Reed, shaking his head sadly but with a characteristic twinkle in his eye, remarked: "John Mills, I always warned you of this. Didn't I say that if you kept on at the rate you were going you would surely scratch a poor man's pants?" Then, putting a check in the old man's hand, he added, "You are not going to give this money away or use it for any more experimenting. It is to take care of John H. Mills." This was the last time that Mills was seen in Westfield. The check was for $5,000.[46]

Frederic Tudor

Frederic Tudor, son of the "ice king" (Figure 7-35), grew up in Boston familiar with the heating and ventilating industry and, like many of his colleagues, an inventor. He was interested in "the comfort and convenience of the average citizen, and especially the average woman (who) had not been considered by steam heating engineers."

All these objections were perfectly plain to me when I entered into the business of heating, but previous to 1880, I had all that I could attend to in improving the art of ventilation in connection with heating, and I had very little to do with heating by direct radiation. After all its advantages have been summed up, in the important respects of health and comfort, it is seen to be a vile system, and it did not interest me, except to imagine how it could be improved. This feeling led to the invention of the jacketed direct radiator with definite air supply and immunity from freezing. The invention is shown in U.S. Patent No. 185,146 [Plate I, Figure 7-36, top]. This patent covers a radiator having a combination of castings and air passages with valves whereby the volume of fresh air admitted and the temperature of the air warmed are easily regulated; in combination with the radiator are a reservoir of water heated by the steam in the radiator. The drawing of this radiator pretty clearly explains it, Figure 3, showing the air damper.

This system affords heat regulation without manipulating valves. It was installed in the Hotel Cluny and a Boston office building in 1876, no valves being used. The Cluny system is in use today.

The evaporator has been used only with large radiators for indirect heating with fans, in connection with the air-mixing valves as shown. Bechem & Post usually omit the manual steam and return valves. It seemed to me about this time that the growth of the high office buildings would make it very desirable to adapt a system of graduated control to direct radiators, whether fresh air was in question or not.

Plate 2 (Figure 7-36, bottom) shows patent 278,636 (May 28, 1883), covering a combination steam and hot-water system, the principal parts of which are the boiler, A, the expan-

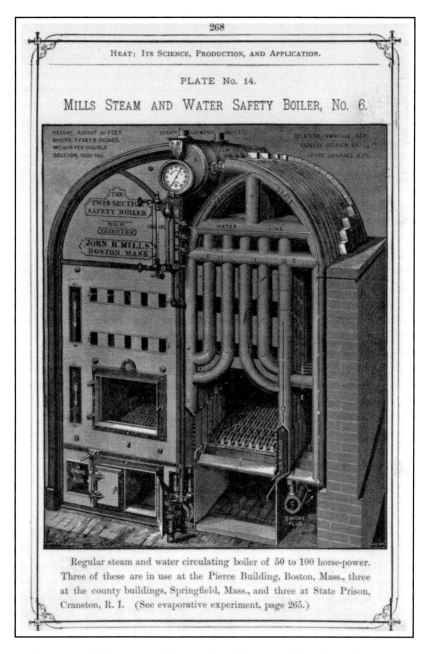

Figure 7-28 *Mills steam and water safety boiler, no. 6 (from J.H. Mills, 1890).*

sion tank, H, the indirect radiator, K, and a direct radiator at the top, put in later, in dotted lines.

The peculiarities of this system are, first: the air trap O, which acts both as a safety valve for the system, and as an air valve for the indirect radiators; and the stand pipe, I, above the expansion tank.

If in this apparatus the fire is forced so as to make steam, the steam will drive the water out of the air trap, O, the indirect radiator, K, and down in the pipe, G, and boiler, A, to the water line, y. In doing this it will raise the water in the expansion tank up into the stand pipe, I, to the upper water line, y, where it will be discharged and relieved of further pressure. In order to accomplish this the size of the expansion tank and the height of the stand pipe must be properly proportioned to the volume of water in the rest of the system.

In this condition the apparatus will run as a steam-heating plant and is equipped with the ordinary damper regulator to check the fire when it gets too hot.

When steam heat is no longer desired, and the fire is allowed to go down, the steam in the top of the trap and in the radiators will gradually condense, and the water will come down from the expansion tank and stand pipe and fill the boiler and radiators just as they were in the first place.[47]

Frederic Tudor continued to work on the design of ventilating systems and designed the heating and ventilating system for the Metropolitan Opera House (1883) and the Union League Club (1887), both in New York City; however, most of his innovations saw more use in Europe than in the United States.

Steam and Hot Water Radiators

As boiler design continued to progress during the last half of the nineteenth century, radiator design was especially important to achieving more widespread acceptance of steam heating by the public. "The first variation from a single pipe around the wall was what was called the `flat-coil.' This was either pipe or gun-barrels from 30 to 48 in. long,

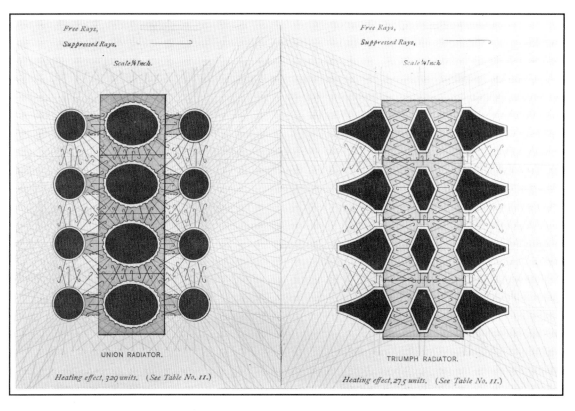

Figure 7-29 *Diagrams of radiant heat (from J.H. Mills, 1890).*

screwed into return-bends. This was followed by what was known as `two-section coils,' which were simply two `flat-coils' fastened up side by side with a `chuck-spacer' to fix the distance between them. Following this came what were known as `manifold-coils,' the pipes being three or four pipes wide. The `box-coil' came into use for indirect work, taking its name because it was boxed close into its place in the cellar."[48] Some pipe coils were enclosed in ornamental baseboards (Figure 7-37), while some had extended surfaces (Figure 7-38).

The original steam distribution systems designed by Joseph Nason in 1845 were pipe coils located in the space that they heated. Nason's design for the U.S. Capitol in 1855 used "box-coils" referred to as "trombone coils" because of their distinctive shape. Stephen Gold introduced his "mattress" radiator in 1854, which was "amazingly like James Watt's invention of 1784"[49] (Figures 7-39 and 7-40). Samuel Gold did not introduce his cast-iron "pin" radiator until 1862 (Figure 7-41).

Wrought-iron radiators were eventually replaced by the more popular cast-iron radiators that could be manufactured in sectional components and with a variety of ornamental finishes. The earliest of these cast-iron radiators were considered to be "of homely design and were known as the Ox-bow and Wash-board" and were typically single castings or halves bolted together (Figure 7-42).

Cast-iron radiators were being manufactured by a number of foundries, and "fitters of those days made many attempts between 1848 and 1862 to produce vertical radiators from pipe, but with slight success, and it was not until 1862 that the problem was solved."[50] Joseph Nason and Robert Briggs received a patent in March 1863 for a steam radiator made up of vertical tubes screwed into a horizontal cast-iron base. Following this, numerous radiator

patents were given out and the vertical-pipe wrought-iron and cast-iron radiator business began to flourish.

However, different radiator sizes and capacities create problems of engineering and proper sizing for rooms "From 1862 to about 1892, the practice of furnishing piping plans to any one who would buy boilers was the universal habit in this country. In this way men who were totally incompetent for the work came in time to the doing of the plan-making work for some of the manufacturers. That the results were not more disastrous than they often proved is a matter of wonder to some of those who look back upon those days from the standpoint of present knowledge."[51]

The Nason and Briggs radiator solved some of this problem by offering wrought-iron pipes and their proportionate amount of the cast-iron base and cap to be exactly one square foot of surface area to the air. The availability of radiators that could be selected according to absolute units of one square foot greatly simplified the design. Steam fitters requiring a specific area of surface, such as 24 square feet, could order standard radiators as 1 x 24, 2 x 12, 3 x 8 or 4 x 6. The most popular width, however, was the two column type.

"The first cast-iron radiator to catch the popular fancy was the `Bundy' radiator. This was brought out in 1869 and was the invention of Nelson H. Bundy, of the firm of Bundy & Healy, of New York. With some minor changes from the original `Bundy' the radiator manufactured by the late A.A. Griffing Company of Jersey City, New Jersey, was the same as this first real competitor of the wrought-iron radiations"[52] (Figure 7-43). Bundy had worked in the New York office of Joseph Nason until 1859, where he worked on a number of large steam heating designs including the insane asylums in Utica, New York, and Macon, Georgia.

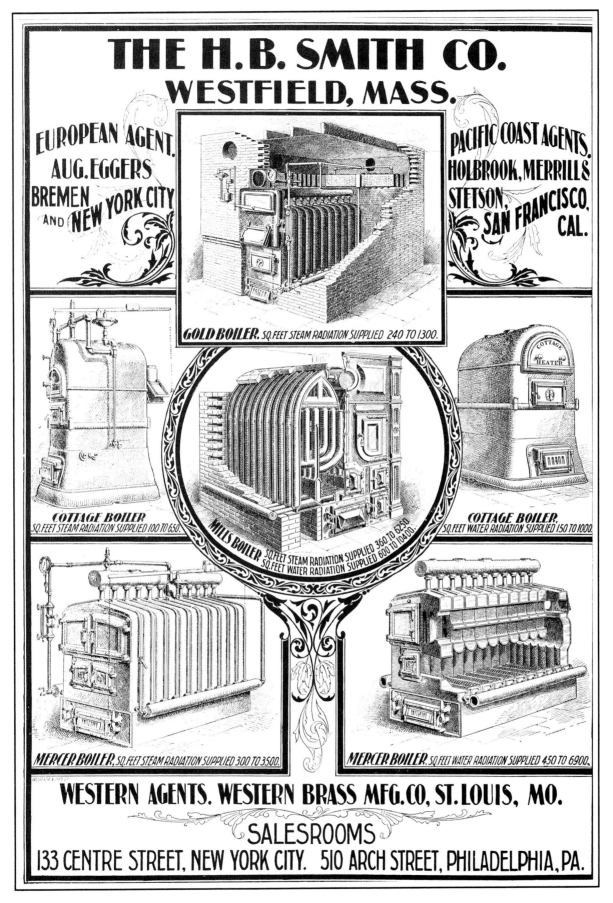

Figure 7-30 *Advertisement, H.B. Smith Co., Westfield, Mass. (from* Domestic Engineering, *April 1900, p. 46).*

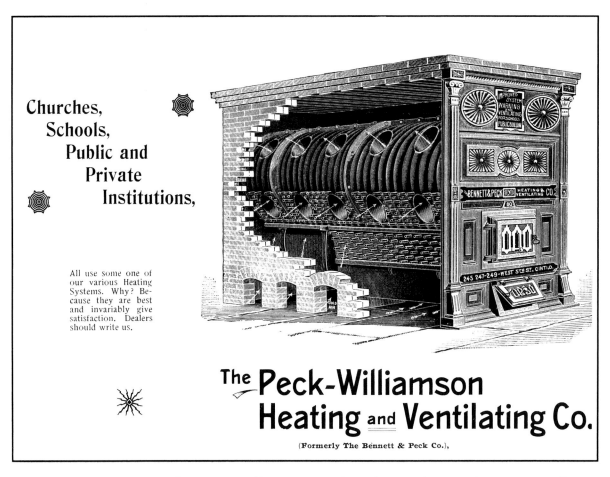

Figure 7-31 *Advertisement for heaters, 1894 (from* Heating and Ventilation, *vol. 4, December 15, 1894, p. vii).*

Most of the early radiator designs were for low-pressure steam, and often the joints, which were made with rubber packing, leaked. John Mills attempted to solve this problem by eliminating joints altogether and making a radiator in a single casting. This radiator was patented in 1873, but the pattern did not go beyond the experimental stage of development.

In the remaining years of the century, radiator manufacturers fine-tuned their designs to offer greater heating capacity, better control, and cheaper construction. Radiator designs were available in numerous styles and finishes. Some were painted and varnished, and scale-model versions were made for a salesman to demonstrate to a potential buyer (see Figure IX, color section). Others were cast with ornate surfaces and cap pieces in the many heating and plumbing shops that flourished during this period (Figures 7-46 and 7-47 and Figure X, color section).

DISTRICT STEAM HEATING

In the 1880s, applications of steam heating were advanced considerably by the introduction of remote, central steam plants, first attempted by Birdsall Holly at Lockport, New York, in 1877, and later carried out by the New York Steam Company in 1880 when it "began laying pipes in the streets of New York, building stations, and manufacturing the various appliances that were found to be necessary as the work progressed."[53] The New York Steam Company was founded by Wallace C. Andrews, an associate of John D. Rockefeller, and members of the first board of directors of the Standard Oil Company. Andrews was fascinated by the experimental work of Birdsall Holly in Lockport and was convinced of its application in a city like New York.[54] However, since this was a pioneering effort, there were many obstacles to overcome, such as the expansion and contraction of pipes where "a new and perfect diaphragm joint was devised . . . called the variator . . . made with cast iron backing plates, with a corrugated copper diaphragm, which provides for the yielding and reflex action for varying lengths in the sections of the pipe . . . steam was first furnished to consumers on April 27, 1882 over five miles of pipe having been laid"[55] (Figures 7-48 through 7-53).

In 1880, the New York Steam Company installed about six miles of steam mains under the streets of New York for power and heating purposes. All the joints in this pipe above eight inches in diameter were made by expanding the pipe into recesses in the flanges, and then beating the ends of the pipe over the edges of the flanges. This was done by machinery, and was well done, and at the time was considered a great improvement over threading or riveting, but in five years, every joint had to be taken out on account of leaks and threaded joints were substituted. These threaded joints lasted until 1895, when all the pipes were renewed with new mains having heavy wrought steel flanges welded on the pipe. These welded flanges when turned true in the lathe make the most workmanlike and perfect steam joints in use at the present time, and their cost alone prevents their general use. Corrugated copper gaskets placed inside the bolts and well pulled up will make a joint which will last as long as the fittings. When the owner's bank

Figure 7-32 *Advertisements for heaters and furnaces—1904 (top) and 1898 (bottom) (from* Engineering Review, *February 1904, p. iv;* Heating and Ventilation, *June 1898, p. xxvi).*

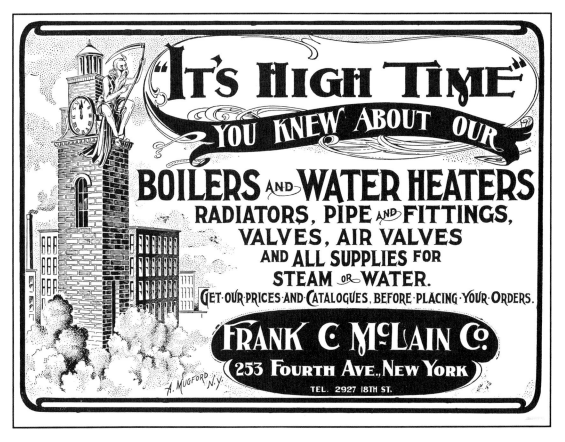

Figure 7-33 *Advertisement for boilers and water heaters—1901 (from* Engineering Review, *September 1901, p. v).*

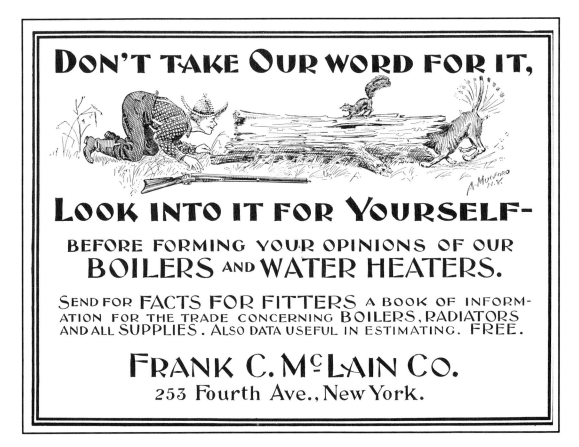

Figure 7-34 *Advertisement for boilers and water heaters—1900 (from* Engineering Review, *December 1900, vol. 10, p. viii).*

Figure 7-35 *Frederic Tudor (from* Heating and Ventilating Magazine, *June 1929, p. 113).*

account is strong enough, ground joints without any gaskets are used. This makes a first-class job, but the price is all but prohibitive.[56]

The original plant on Cortland Street, referred to as Station B, was the largest steam plant in the world with "58 boilers in all, aggregating 16,000 horsepower. The total grate area is 3,495 square feet and the entire heating surface is estimated at 153,600 square feet; 120,000 tons of buckwheat coal are consumed annually. . . . A general pressure of 80 pounds is carried throughout the system. This is reduced by the usual devices according to the needs of the buildings for which the power or heat is furnished, some dwellings receiving their supply at only two pounds pressure."[57]

One of the early followers in the move toward district heating was the Philadelphia Electric Company, which in 1887 ran a steam line to an adjacent building. In generating electricity great quantities of steam were exhausted and wasted. Since at that time electric stations were usually located at the fringe of a city's business district, they were near office buildings large enough to be profitable users of that exhaust steam. Philadelphia's system grew slowly. A line was extended to the company's offices about a block away, but it was 19 years before Jefferson Hospital contracted to buy steam and two department stores joined the system. Competition in providing electric services was keen. At one time there were 20 electric companies and four district steam systems operating in Philadelphia. The sale of waste steam was a profitable activity for electric companies, for replacing boilers in the basements of large buildings usually meant also supplying the electric power that had been generated by the building's own steam engine.

This was the nature of district heating until the start of the century when the Illinois Maintenance Company introduced a different service to owners of Chicago buildings.

The company undertook the operation of existing plants in downtown buildings, connecting them with underground steam lines in order to close down the smaller and less efficient plants. Soon similar companies commenced operations in Boston and New York, the latter adding equipment to manufacture ice during the summers. Seasonal differences in the use of steam were not so great as one would suppose. Records of a large Chicago office building indicate that during a cold day of winter the amount of steam used to generate electricity during office hours was almost equal to that required for heating. District heating systems were established in France, Germany, and other north European locales, but Great Britain apparently did not have an installation until around 1911. Where circumstances offered an

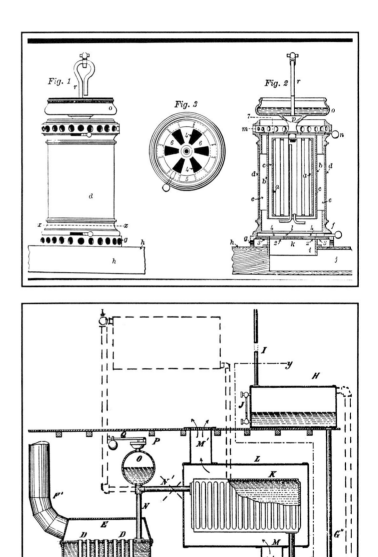

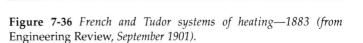

Figure 7-36 *French and Tudor systems of heating—1883 (from* Engineering Review, *September 1901).*

Figure 7-37 *Ornamental baseboard heater, late nineteenth century. Baseboard heat was applied as early as the 1830s using Angier Perkins' high-pressure hot water heating system (from* Domestic Engineering, *November 1889).*

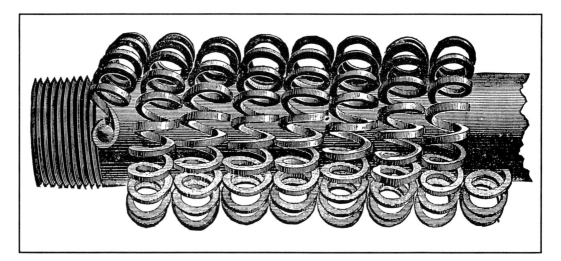

Figure 7-38 *Pipe coil with extended heating surface (from J.H. Mills, 1890).*

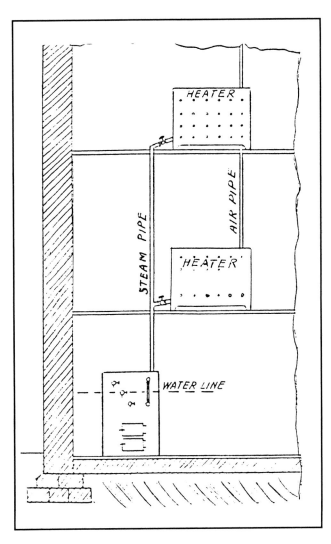

Figure 7-39 *Stephen Gold's single-pipe, low-pressure steam system, showing his "mattress" radiator of 1854.*

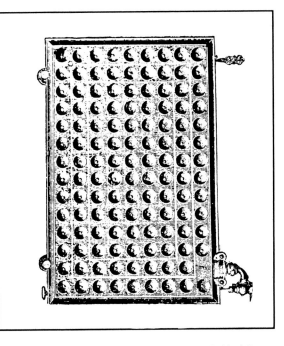

Figure 7-40 *"Mattress-type" radiator, patented in 1854 by Stephen J. Gold of Connecticut, inventor of a popular home heating boiler. This radiator, in which two embossed iron sheets were fastened together by rivets, was similar to James Watt's steam radiator of 1784 (from Susan R. Stifler,* The Beginnings of a Century of Steam and Water Heating, *1960).*

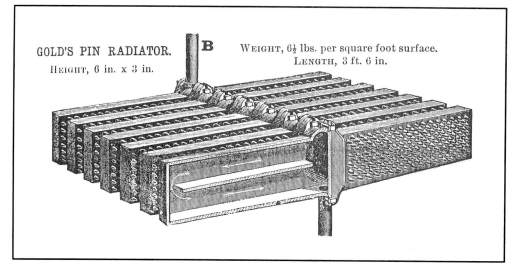

Figure 7-41 *"Pin-type" radiators were patented by Samuel Gold in 1862. These were concealed in ducts or boxes inside walls or below floors, thus their generic name: "indirect radiators." Indirect radiators were usually used with fan-type heating systems, which supplied forced air over the indirect radiator into the heated space through ornamental registers (from J.H. Mills, 1890).*

Figure 7-42 *Cast-iron radiator, Howard Steam Heating Co., Springfield, Mass., 1856 (from Smithsonian Institution, Division of Engineering and Industry).*

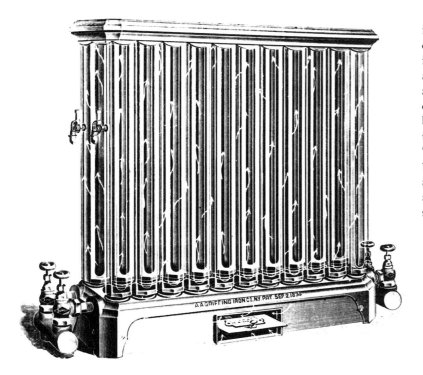
Figure 7-43 *Radiators, 1896 (from* Domestic Engineering, *January 1896, p. 19).*

economical source of heat, district heating was not limited to densely built metropolitan locations. Reykjavik, Iceland, employs natural hot springs. In Virginia, Minnesota, a town of about 10,000 population with a climate similar to that of Moscow, the city system began in the nineteenth century with steam from a local sawmill and was augmented by steam from an electrical power company when that was established. Now the city has over 14 miles of mains operated by the city administration.[58]

EXPERIMENTS WITH SOLAR HEATING FOR STEAM AND HOT WATER

Applications of solar energy for heating and driving machines had interested many inventors since Hero of Alexander introduced his solar devices in the first century. However, the industrial revolution in Europe and North America created an enormous growth in the use of machines that increasingly demanded more and more fuel. France was at a disadvantage compared to other industrial countries because she had to import almost all of her coal. As a consequence, she lagged far behind rapidly industrializing England."[59] The concerns of limited energy resources led a few Frenchmen to investigate alternatives such as the harnessing of solar energy.

Augustin Mouchot, a professor of mathematics at the Lycée de Tours, spent two decades (1860s-1880s) studying solar power. He developed a large "sun machine" for the Universal Exposition in Paris of 1878. The most ambitious efforts were to drive a steam engine with sun power, the first of which was successfully attempted in 1866 by Mouchot. It "vaporized waters into steam at a pressure of 45 pounds per square inch."

Mouchot's assistant, Abel Pifre, took over in research after 1879. Pifre "built several sun motors and conducted public demonstrations to gain support for solar power. At the Gardens of the Tuileries in Paris, he exhibited a solar generator that drove a press which printed 500 copies of the *Journal Soleil.*"[60]

Eight years after Augustin Mouchot began his first experiments, an American engineer named John Ericsson also voiced the hope that someday solar energy would fuel the machines of the Industrial Age. Born in Sweden in 1803, Ericsson emigrated to America in 1839. By that time, he was already well known for such inventions as the screw propeller, which made steam navigation practical. He later achieved widespread recognition for designing the ironclad battleship *The Monitor*, which defeated the Confederate iron ship *The Merrimack* off the Virginia coast on March 9, 1862.[61]

Ericsson worked throughout his life on solar-heating applications, and he developed a number of solar-powered steam engines. He constructed his first solar-powered steam engine in 1870 and after a number of experi-

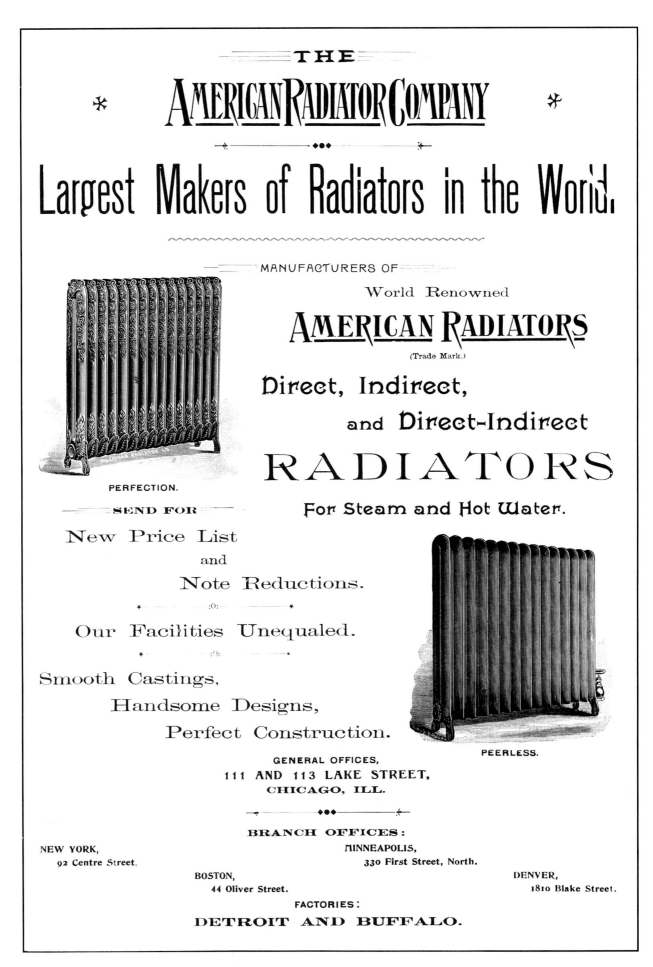

Figure 7-44 *By 1900, the American Radiator Company business trust controlled most of the radiators manufactured in the U.S. This company later merged with the Standard Sanitary Manufacturing Co. to form what is now American-Standard Inc. (from* Heating and Ventilation, *October 1894).*

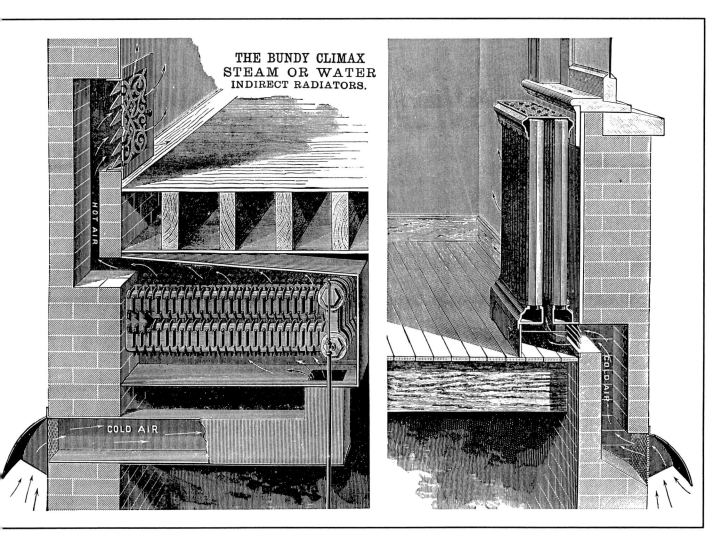

THE BUNDY CLIMAX
STEAM OR WATER
INDIRECT RADIATORS.

Figure 7-45 *Indirect (concealed) radiator at left. At right: direct radiator with indirect feature, admitting fresh air over the heated surface (from J.H. Mills, 1890).*

ients realized that "'although the heat is obtained for nothing, so extensive, costly, and complex as the concentrating apparatus' that engines powered by solar energy were actually more expensive than similar coal-fueled motors."[62]

In 1884, Ericsson introduced a lower cost reflector design but required another four years to perfect its operation. In 1888, his sun motor was ready for production, but within seven months, he died at the age of 86. The detailed plans for his design were never revealed, and the sun motor was never produced.

A number of engineers continued to work on designs for solar heaters and solar-powered motors, but most of the work remained experimental or for very limited applications.

VENTILATION

One of the most influential works in establishing a rational approach for the ventilation of buildings was Thomas Tredgold's *The Principles of Warming and Ventilating Public Buildings, etc.* Tredgold sets minimum standards for the design of ventilating systems: "for each individual we should have 800 cubic inches per minute," which was required for respiration (to purge carbon dioxide).[63] He

reasoned that an additional amount of air was required to remove body moisture and to supply oxygen for candles and/or lamps, providing a minimum ventilation requirement of about 4 cubic feet per minute.[64] Tredgold was one of the first to understand that ventilation was dictated, not only by the amount of oxygen needed for respiration, but also by the "poisons" in the air itself. "Hygienic wants" and the "general disregard of suitable architectural provisions for a supply of sunlight and fresh air, with great inattention to cleanliness and drainage, are continually acting causes of disease and general deterioration of the public health."[65]

Charles Hood was especially concerned with the need to provide adequate ventilation for comfort and health. In his publication *On Warming Buildings by Hot Water, etc.* of 1837, he describes the properties of air, the problems of contaminants and impure air, and the importance of ventilation to health.

Hood used the latter data to estimate the quantity of air needed to carry off the water vapour, arriving at a figure of 3.5 to 5 cu ft/min. Eugéne Peclét made some observations of the odour in a school and in the Prison Mazas in France. As a result, he recommended 300 cu ft/h per person for ordinary rooms and 212 cu ft/h for schools. Morin asked for three times as much fresh air for schools. Thomas Box, in 1875, estimated the fresh air requirements as follows:

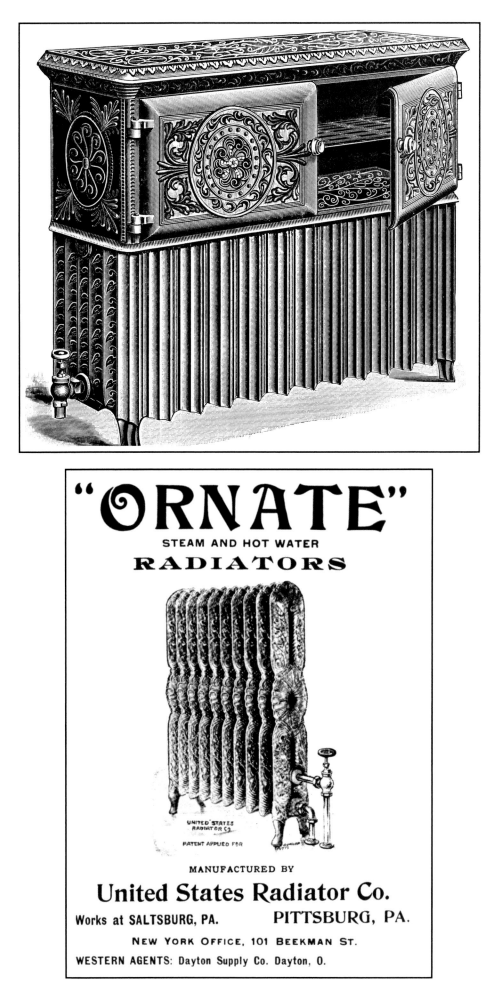

Figure 7-46 *Radiators, 1896 (from* Domestic Engineering, *February 1896, p. 59; January 1896, p. 19).*

Figure 7-47 *Heating and plumbing shop (from* Domestic Engineering, *June 1896, p. 39).*

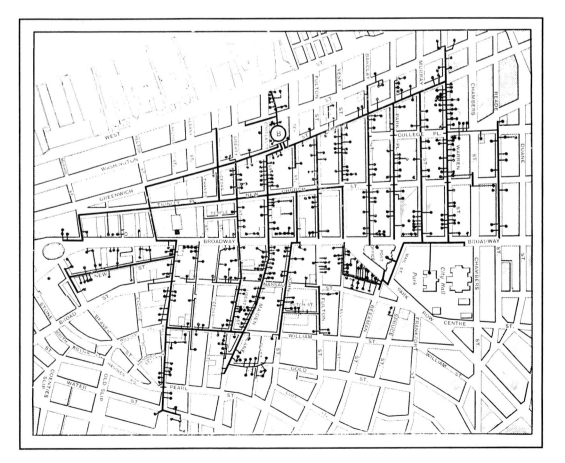

Figure 7-48 *New York Steam Company distribution.*

Figure 7-49 *Many district steam heating systems used piping encased with wood, usually cypress (from* Engineering Review, *November 1908, p. 12).*

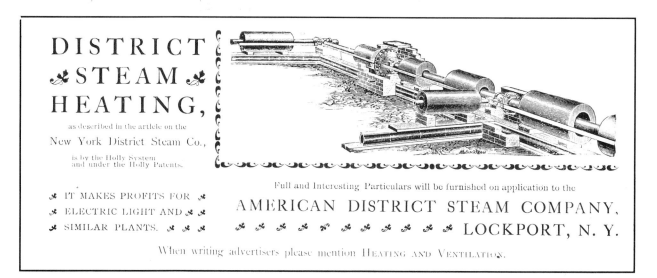

Figure 7-50 *Advertisement, American District Steam Company, Lockport, New York (from* Heating and Ventilation, *July 1897, p. x).*

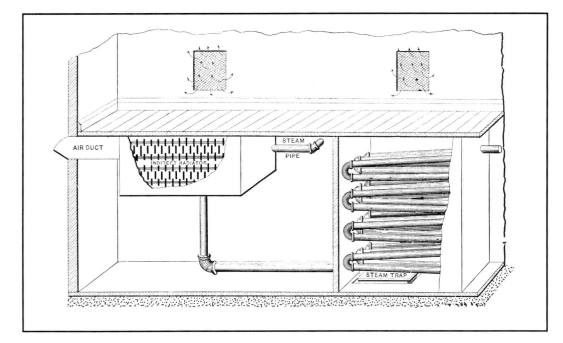

Figure 7-51 *Indirect system of house heating employed by New York Steam Co.*

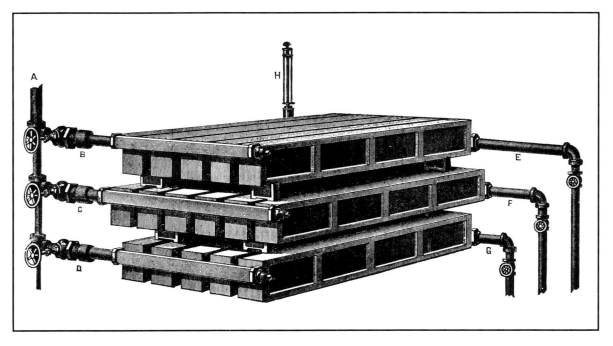

Figure 7-52 *Bank of indirect radiators (from* The Metal Worker, *November 18, 1882, p. 32).*

Figure 7-53 *Indirect radiator for steam or water (Corry Radiator Company, 1896).*

for life	22 cu ft/h
for removal of water vapour	237 cu ft/h
for removal of heat (incl fuel)	220-500 cu ft/h
for removal of odours (after Peclét)	250-300 cu ft/h

He realized that all of these functions could be fulfilled by 250 cu ft/h per person, rising to 500 cu ft/h in crowded rooms.

Rather earlier than this Dr. Reid had formed the opinion that 10 cu ft/min per person was required, on a basis of "an extreme variety of experiments made on hundreds of different constitutions, and also in numerous assemblies and meetings."[66]

General Arthur Morin proposed ventilation for "the renewal of air in buildings . . . only rendered necessary by the vitiation resulting from the respiration and exhalations of the occupants, and by the accumulation of the products of combustion from artificial lighting."[67] Morin's proposals were for ventilation rates much higher than had been previously used.

Between 1857 and 1860 the experiments of von Pettenkofer, Roscoe and other physiologists and chemists had shown that the old ideas as to the amount of air required to so dilute the exhalations of men that there should be no unpleasant odor—were totally inadequate—and the data collected by the Army Sanitary Commission showed that ill health and excessive mortality prevailed among the troops in proportion to the defects in the air supply of their barracks. The Barracks Commissioners fixed 20 cubic feet of fresh air per minute, or 1,200 cubic feet per hour per man, as the minimum requirement. In 1860 General Morin gave the figures required for barracks as 1,059 cubic feet per hour by day and twice that amount at night for each man, and in the first edition of his "Manual of Hygiene," published in 1864, Dr. Parkes states that at least 2,000 cubic feet per hour must be given to entirely free the air from unpleasant odor.[68]

Dr. Boswell Reid directed his attention to the problems of health and sanitation in cities and towns and especially in individual dwellings. "Dr. Reid's experiments and observations to ascertain the amount and proportions of fresh atmospheric air required for personal comfort and the preservation of health, were not confined to Great Britain they were also conducted in numerous investigations in many of the cities of continental Europe; particularly in Paris, Berlin, Munich, Stockholm, and St. Petersburg."[6] Reid himself describes the importance of ventilation for individual dwellings: "Few practical questions are more important to man than the construction and condition of the habitation in which he dwells, and its right adaptation

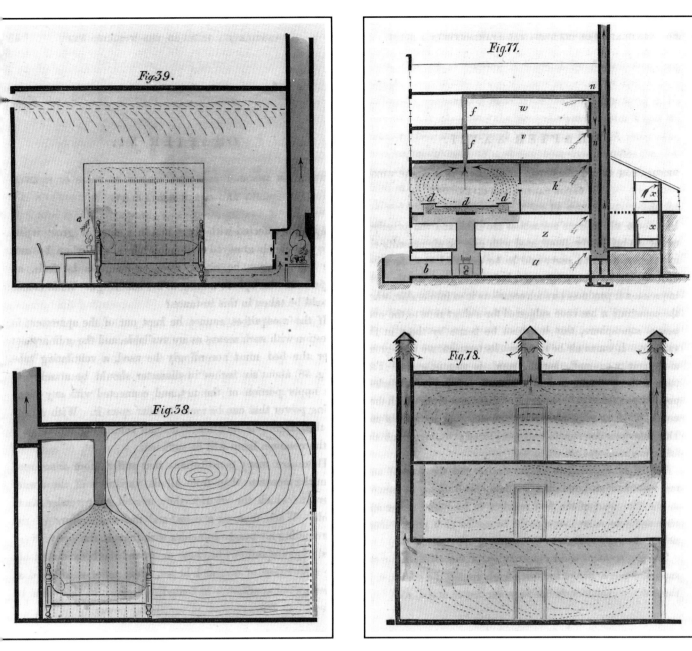

Figure 7-54 *"Ventilation through the mosquito-net in cases of sickness and great irritability" (from Reid, 1858).*

Figure 7-55 *"Ventilation of the principal apartments in a house when large parties are given" (from Reid, 1858).*

CHARACTER OF OCCUPANTS.	For Respiration.	For Vapor.	For Exhalation.	For Heat.	For Lights.
Room with single occupant, cleanly and healthy.......	22	237	250	220	60
Room with single occupant, healthy, but not cleanly. ..	22	237	350	220	60
Room with single occupant, cleanly, but sick..........	22	237	1,000	220	60
Crowded room, healthy and cleanly persons.	22	237	250	500	60
Hospitals (ordinary cases)...........................	22	237	2,000	220	60
Hospitals for fevers, etc.....	22	237	4,000	220	60

Cubic Feet of Air required for the different purposes of Ventilation.

Figure 7-56 *Thomas box—Cubic feet of air required for the different purposes of ventilation (from Billings, 1884, p. 38).*

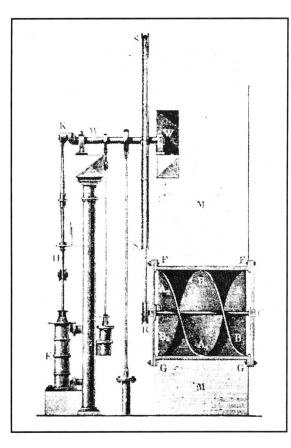

Figure 7-57 *A.M. Motte—Archimedian screw fan, 1834 (from Billington and Roberts).*

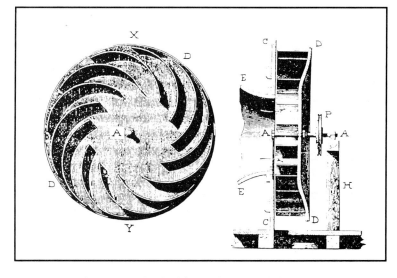

Figure 7-58 *Combes' fan with curved-blade design.*

to his moral, physical, and social wants"[70] (Figures 7-54 and 7-55).

In the United States, Lewis Leeds devoted his attention to the ventilation of government buildings, especially hospitals, during the Civil War. He was heavily influenced by Dr. Reid from his work on the Houses of Parliament, and he lectured extensively on the subject at the Franklin Institute during 1866-1867 in a series of lectures called "Man's Own Breath Is his Greatest Enemy." Demonstrating his concept in a hospital design for the U.S. Surgeon General and Quartermaster General, he was awarded a grand prize at the Paris Exhibition.

Although Thomas Tredgold and Dr. Boswell Reid had defined much of ventilation theory in the first half of the nineteenth century, developments in the areas of physiology and health gave a quantifiable basis for design. The later developments of steam and electric power in the last half of the nineteenth century provided a mechanical means for ventilation and temperature control and created an industry.

> Although it is scarcely eight years since the first edition of this treatise was issued, this comparatively brief period has witnessed an almost phenomenal change in public opinion regarding the absolute necessity of good ventilation. That the evil effects of foul air are now generally appreciated is best evidenced by the legal enactments which control the application of ventilating systems in many of our States and municipalities.[71]

The concerns for public health and ventilation in particular became a major focus of attention in the second half of the nineteenth century with the formation of sanitary com-

missions and boards of health to address the special problems of growing cities and the increased public responsibilities of governments. "The early recognition during the late war, both by the Sanitary Commission and the government officials, of the important fact that many more men are killed by breathing foul air than are killed by the enemies's bullets, led them to use very active exertions to secure good ventilation in hospitals and camps, and to teach the men themselves the value thereof."[72]

Minimum quantities of fresh air were proposed by numerous engineers and physicians. In 1862, Max von Pettenkofer stated that discomfort was primarily due to organic substances, in contrast to the widespread view that excess carbonic acid was the cause of discomfort. In 1872, Alexander Saeltzer reconfirmed this view in his publication of *A Treatise on Acoustics in Connection with Ventilation . . .*, where he describes "this lower strata is the resting place of the organic impurities caused by the exhaled air, evaporations, etc., producing the actual poison which the lungs detest, and sound abhors."[73] By 1883, Hermans in Amsterdam developed a theory that discomfort was a result of poor ventilation interfering with the mechanism of the body's heat loss.

In addition to the overall concerns of health and sanitation and the development of theories on physiology and comfort, many inventors and engineers were developing the technology of fan design itself. Some of the earliest fans, such as those described by Agricola in the sixteenth century, were developed for ventilating mines. Desaguliers introduced his paddle-wheel fan in 1734, and a number of open paddle-wheel-type fans were used prior to 1830, primarily for exhaust. The first "cased" fans "had circular casings, fitting close to the wheel, with an opening at one point to serve as the outlet. . . . A scroll casing, fitted eccentrically, was shown in a drawing in Dr. Ure's *Mechanical Dictionary* published in 1844. A similar arrangement, but using a convolute casing, was illustrated by Reid at about the same time. With this form of casing, the outlet was normally a plain rectangular opening without any further expander."[74]

An unusual fan design, based on the principle of the Archimedian screw, was invented by Mr. A.M. Motte, for

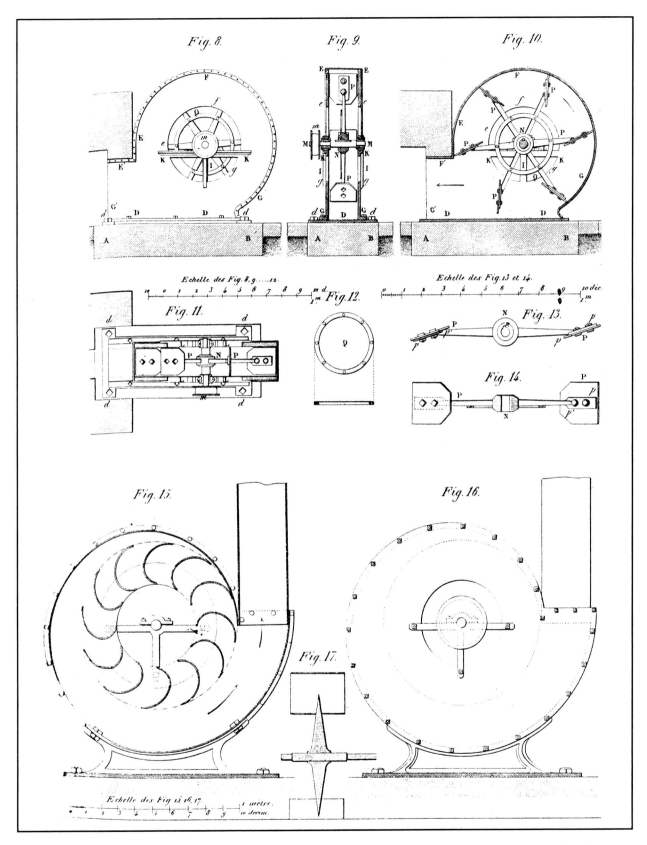

Figure 7-59 *E. Peclét—Forward/backward blade blower (from* Traité De La Chaleur, *3d ed., Paris, 1844, plate 7).*

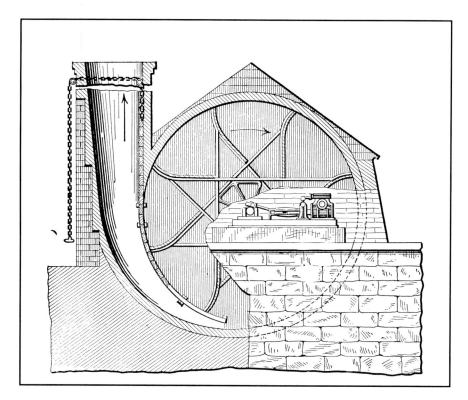

Figure 7-60 *Guibal fan, c. 1878.*

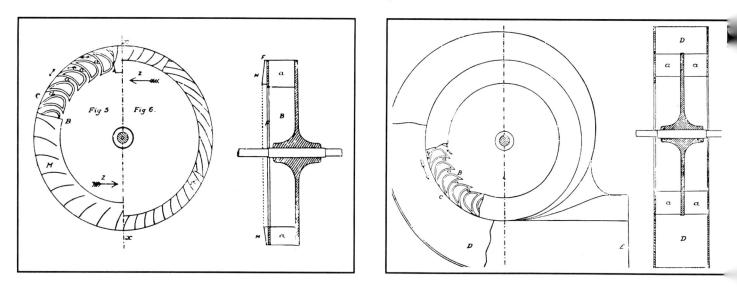

a) Sections showing various blade forms, curves, etc.

b) Longitudinal and transverse sections.

Figure 7-61 *Barlow fan, 1878.*

which he received a prize in 1834. This fan was used to a limited extent in Belgium but "soon fell into disuse" (Figure 7-57).

Some of the earliest curved-blade designs are attributed to Combes. Reid refers to the use of curved-blade fans in 1844, and Eugéne Peclét, in *Traité De La Chaleur*, published in 1844, illustrates a Combes fan but felt that the curved-blade fan was no better than the straight-blade fan (Figure 7-58). Peclét, a French physicist, focused on theories of ventilation as well as fan design. (Figure 7-59). Peclét also developed theories of heat loss and coefficients of heat transfer for different materials, as well as experiments on radiation and convection.

The principles and mechanics of fan design were of particular concern to French inventors during the last quarter of the nineteenth century. "There exists, happily, a very efficient means for improving the resultant of ventilators—it is that connected with the name of M. Guibal. The ventilator is enclosed in a cover, more or less eccentric, which does not permit of the exit of the air except by a narrow passage. . . . The effect, so remarkable in the Guibal chimney, has surprised many persons not familiar with the theory of the flow of fluids."[75] The Guibal fan, invented in 1860, was enclosed in what was referred to as an évasée chimney which was a form of venturi (Figure 7-60).

Another Frenchman, Daniel Murgue, an engineer at the Colliery Company of Besseges, carried out extensive experiments during the 1880s on the efficiency of different fan installations for industrial mines. Murgue established the "manometric yield" as the "coefficient of reduction to be applied to the theoretical depression to obtain the initial depression," or, in other words, the pressure drop across the fan. He also established the "mechanical yield" for a number of types of ventilator systems:

- ventilators by direct impulsion;
  ventilators by centrifugal force, without cover;
  ventilators with centrifugal force, covered, without chimney;
- ventilators with centrifugal force, with cover and rectangular chimney; and
- ventilators with centrifugal force, with cover, slice, and évasée chimney (Guibal type).

Murgue noted that, "In theory every deprimogen ventilator turning under the action of a motor, gives a certain depression depending entirely on the tangential speed, and consequently independent of the volume of air which it yields."[76] Murgue "developed the first satisfactory theory

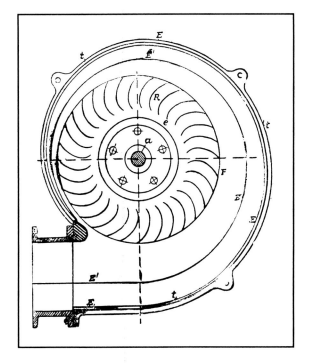

Figure 7-62 *"Ser" fan, longitudinal section, patented 1884 (original design 1878).*

Figure 7-63 *73 B.F. Sturtevant hot air furnace, 1869 (from Smithsonian Institution, Division of Engineering and Industry).*

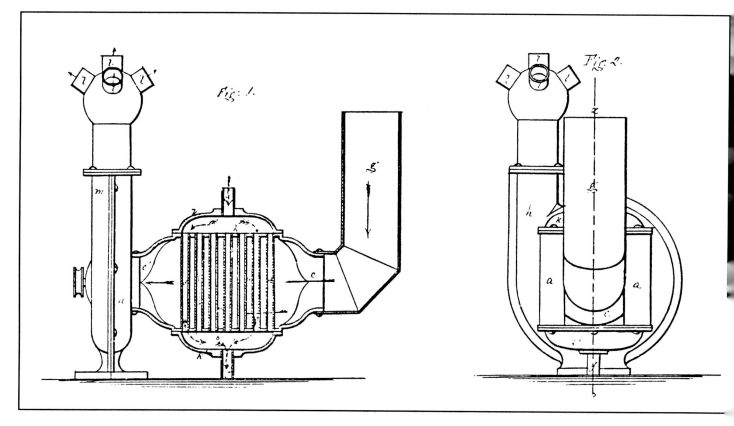

Figure 7-64 *B.F. Sturtevant, compound air heater and steam condenser, patent drawing, February 22, 1870.*

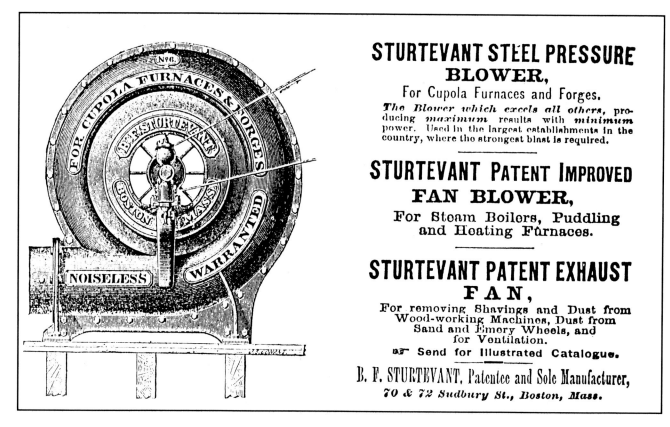

Figure 7-65 *Advertisement, B.F. Sturtevant Blower Company, 1872.*

of fan operation . . . and he showed that simple plane radial blades were not compatible with high efficiency."[77] He admits his clear preference for the Guibal ventilator as being the most efficient design of its day.

The earliest multivane fan (Figure 7-61) is said to have been invented by Mr. Charles Barlow of London, who

> invented and patented a multivane fan, in which, as he explained in his specification (No. 3252, A.D. 1878), the fan blades are stated and claimed to be only one-fourth or even less in radial depth of the radius of the fan wheel; which, it will be noticed, is practically identical with the 1898 Sirocco patent claim (20 years later) of employing blades of a depth not greater than about one-eighth of the diameter of the fan wheel.
>
> Barlow, however, did not even limit the axial length of his said blades; the drawings in his specification show the blades to be nearly three times the length axially, that they are radially deep, but the blades may be (as he claims) shorter or longer axially, as occasion may require.[78]

Marie Antoine Ser patented a forward blade fan design in 1884 that shows the "sectional curve form of blades to be practically identical with the curve form of blades shown in the Sirocco Patent drawings in 1898, and the said Ser blades also have their concave surfaces shown running in the direction of rotation, . . ."[79] (Figure 7-62). "Ser fans were made in sizes up to 2.5 m diameter and 0.5 m wide. A fan of this size, running at 186 rev/min. could deliver 40 cu.m./s."[80]

In the later years of the nineteenth century, fan design was focused primarily on the development of the centrifugal fan. During the 1890s, a number of French engineers continued to patent new designs for centrifugal fans. M. Levet was granted a patent in 1890 for a forward blade centrifugal fan, and Fournier and Cornu received a patent in 1896 for a "narrow blade multivane type" centrifugal fan. "The Rateau fan (1892) was a centrifugal fan with shaped inlet eye, and the blades were three dimensional and of prescribed form."[81]

THE GROWTH OF MANUFACTURING

In the last thirty years of the nineteenth century, a number of companies were formed for manufacturing and engineering of heating and ventilating equipment and systems. These companies transformed the concepts and inventions of this fledgling industry into new products and new markets. Some of the more important companies of this time were founded on technological innovation and business skills that were both essential to their survival during these turbulent and competitive years.

Warren Webster and Andrew Paul

During the late nineteenth century, important enhancements were made to steam heating systems, improving their efficiency and applicability to large building systems. Although many different types of systems were developed

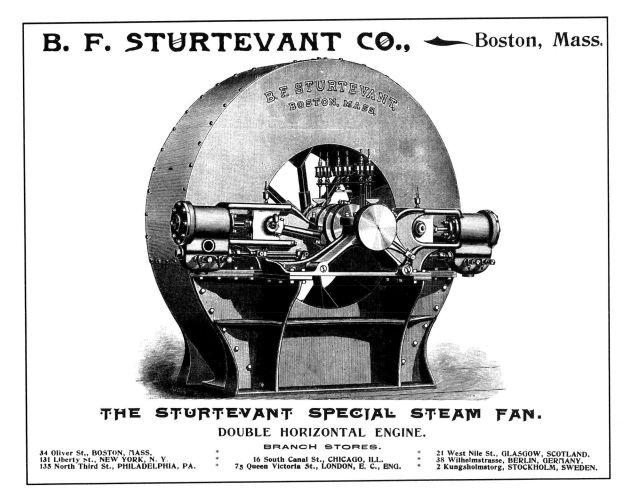

B. F. STURTEVANT CO., Boston, Mass.

THE STURTEVANT SPECIAL STEAM FAN.
DOUBLE HORIZONTAL ENGINE.

BRANCH STORES.

34 Oliver St., BOSTON, MASS.
131 Liberty St., NEW YORK, N. Y.
135 North Third St., PHILADELPHIA, PA.

16 South Canal St., CHICAGO, ILL.
75 Queen Victoria St., LONDON, E. C., ENG.

21 West Nile St., GLASGOW, SCOTLAND.
38 Wilhelmstrasse, BERLIN, GERMANY.
2 Kungsholmstorg, STOCKHOLM, SWEDEN.

Figure 7-66 *B.F. Sturtevant Co., early steam fan (from* Heating and Ventilation, *June 1895, p. xvii).*

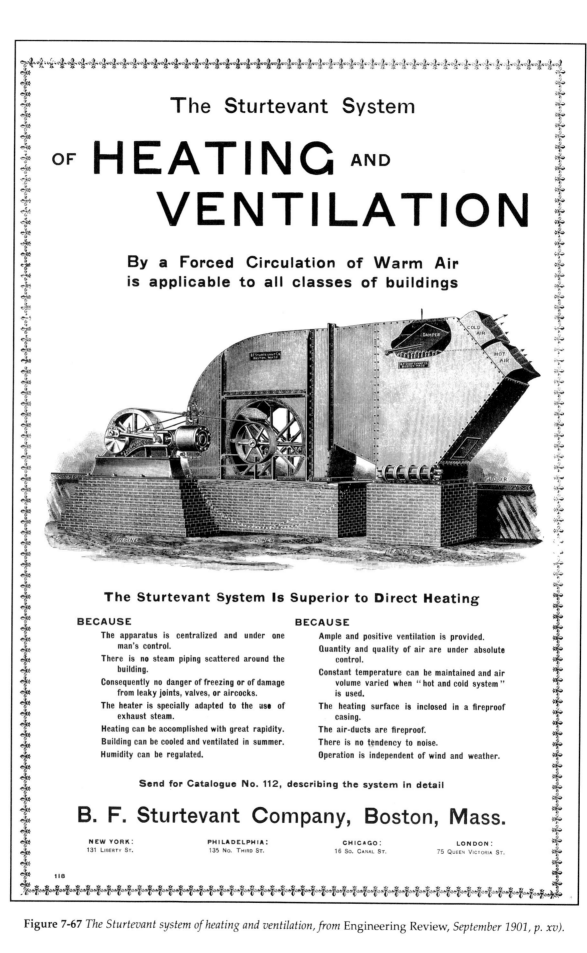

The Sturtevant System

OF HEATING AND VENTILATION

By a Forced Circulation of Warm Air
is applicable to all classes of buildings

The Sturtevant System Is Superior to Direct Heating

BECAUSE

The apparatus is centralized and under one man's control.

There is no steam piping scattered around the building.

Consequently no danger of freezing or of damage from leaky joints, valves, or aircocks.

The heater is specially adapted to the use of exhaust steam.

Heating can be accomplished with great rapidity.

Building can be cooled and ventilated in summer.

Humidity can be regulated.

BECAUSE

Ample and positive ventilation is provided.

Quantity and quality of air are under absolute control.

Constant temperature can be maintained and air volume varied when "hot and cold system" is used.

The heating surface is inclosed in a fireproof casing.

The air-ducts are fireproof.

There is no tendency to noise.

Operation is independent of wind and weather.

Send for Catalogue No. 112, describing the system in detail

B. F. Sturtevant Company, Boston, Mass.

| NEW YORK: | PHILADELPHIA: | CHICAGO: | LONDON: |
| 131 LIBERTY ST. | 135 NO. THIRD ST. | 16 SO. CANAL ST. | 75 QUEEN VICTORIA ST. |

118

Figure 7-67 *The Sturtevant system of heating and ventilation, from* Engineering Review, *September 1901, p. xv).*

Figure 7-68 *Benjamin Franklin Sturtevant, tired of the dust formed in his shoemaking equipment business, built a centrifugal exhaust fan by 1855 and began commercial manufacture of the fans in 1856. Samuel Davidson developed a curved-blade fan, the "Sirocco," in 1900. James Inglis was responsible for the success of the American Blower Company (from Howden Sirocco Inc.).*

From the 1890s through the 1920s, the two principal advances were those of Warren Webster and Andrew Paul. Vacuum return steam heating, in which the return side of a two-pipe steam system is kept below atmospheric pressure to enhance circulation, traces its origins to the U.S. patents of DeBeaumont and of Williames, issued in 1878 and 1882, respectively. In 1888, Warren Webster (1863-1938) purchased a partial interest in a steam heating system patent held by George Barnard that utilized the vacuum principle. Shortly thereafter, Webster's firm, Warren Webster & Company, acquired the patents of DeBeaumont and Williames and became the principal manufacturer of vacuum return systems for many years. The vacuum system was enhanced by the development of the thermostatic return trap, first patented in 1891 by Willis Hall.

At the same time the vacuum return steam heating system was introduced, William Skiffington, suffering as an employee in a cold office at the Fairbanks Company in New York, devised a method of pulling more steam into the heater in his office. Skiffington employed the vacuum principle; however, his approach differed from Webster's in that he exposed the heating surface itself to a vacuum. A separate vacuum line was attached to the radiator and connected to a vacuum pump. Skiffington's idea caught the eye of the office manager, Andrew G. Paul, who saw its potential. He and Skiffington patented the idea; however, Paul was not very successful in promoting his system. He sold his rights in 1898 to Albert Cryer, who established the Paul System Company and proceeded to equip hundreds of buildings with the system, particularly in New York City.[82]

B.F. Sturtevant—The Sturtevant Blower Company

Probably the most important name in ventilation during the last half of the century was Benjamin Franklin Sturtevant, who "started out as a shoemaker and cobbler. Being a very large man he was greatly bothered with the heat . . . so he rigged up, (in) about 1850, a stand with a disc (4 blade) fan run by a belt on to an eccentric pulley to a foot

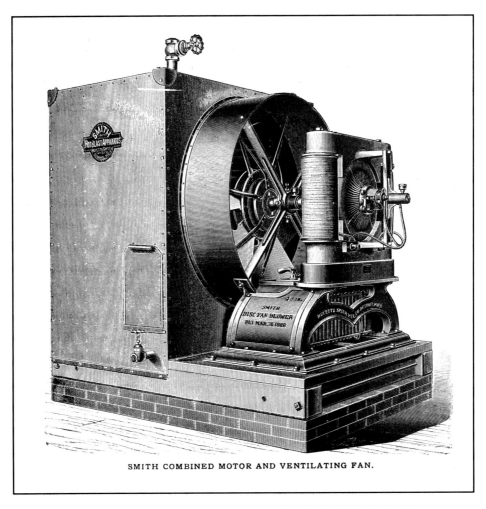

SMITH COMBINED MOTOR AND VENTILATING FAN.

Figure 7-69 *Huyett and Smith disc fan blower—patented March 30, 1888, for hot blast apparatus.*

Figure 7-70 *Advertisement, American Blower Company (from* Engineering Review, *vol. 12, November 1902).*

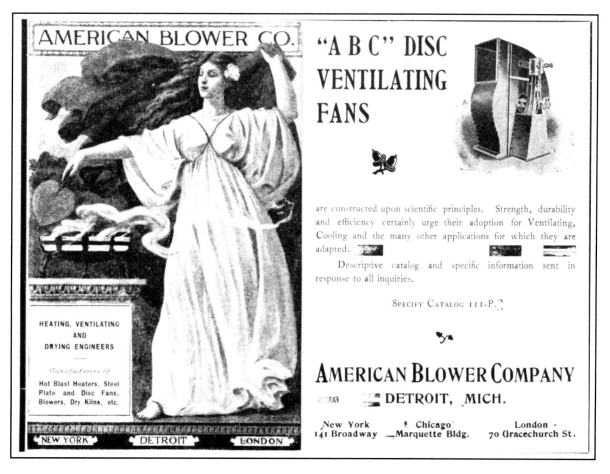

Figure 7-71 *Advertisement, American Blower Company (from* Engineering Review, *vol. 12, February 1902, p. xxi).*

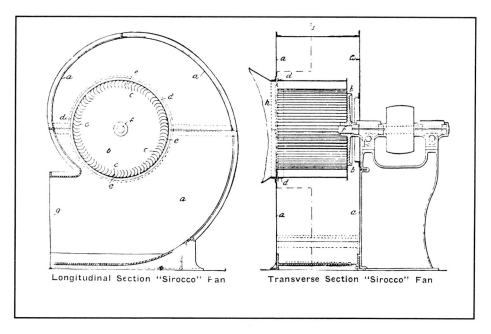

Longitudinal Section "Sirocco" Fan

Transverse Section "Sirocco" Fan

Figure 7-72 *"Sirocco" fan with multiblade vane wheels with shallow blades and wide configuration (from* Engineering Review, *May 1908).*

pedal which he worked with his foot."[83] In 1861, Sturtevant invented a pressure blower, "made with cast-iron split housing, wheel, and spiders made of bronze. The journals were cast-iron, half-boxes with a hardwood plug in each end."[84] In 1869, Sturtevant patented a blower for a hot air furnace (Figure 7-63) and in 1870, he

patented a compound air heater and steam condenser (Figure 7-64).

The Sturtevant Blower Company of Boston was in full operation by 1872, manufacturing fan blowers for heating systems, industrial dryers, ventilation systems, and a variety of other uses (Figure 7-65). The Sturtevant Blower

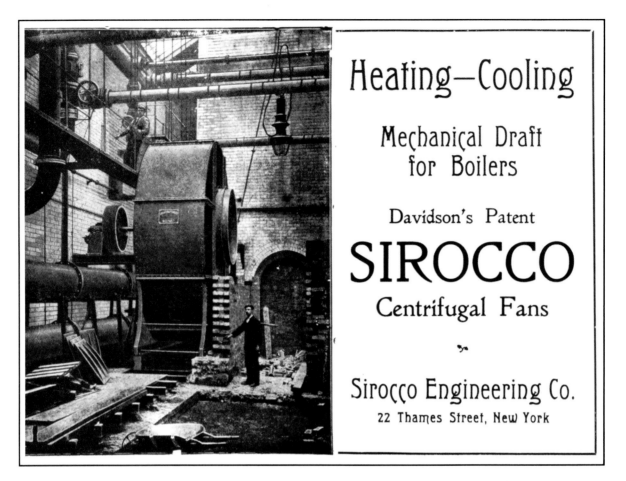

Figure 7-73 *Sirocco Engineering Co., mechanical draft for boilers (from* Engineering Review, *September 1906, p. xxxvii).*

Figure 7-74 *Alfred R. Wolff (from Robert Wolff family).*

Company eventually changed its name to the B.F. Sturtevant Company, with offices in the United States and Europe. The company was then manufacturing steam fan drives and electric fan drives (Figure 7-66), as well as a large variety of fans ranging from small direct-drive electric fans to large-scale closed and open fan systems (Figures 7-67 and 7-68).

The Buffalo Forge Company

"In 1878, Charles F. Brunke and Chas. Hammelman, partner, began the manufacture of the portable forge originated by Mr. Hammelman. After a year of disappointments, the two partners sold Mr. W.F. Wendt, then a bookkeeper in his early twenties, a half interest in this apparently hopeless business. The first little shop was located on the fifth floor of a very humble building located at Washington and Perry Streets, Buffalo."[85] But it was not until 1884 that the company began to manufacture heating and ventilating equipment. Although they continued to make forge equipment, the manufacture of heating and ventilating equipment proved to be very profitable for them. Immediately after the turn of century, in 1903, the company acquired the George L. Squier Manufacturing Company and the Buffalo Steam Pump Company and the business continued to grow throughout the twentieth century. For a number of years, Willis Carrier was an engineer for the company, where he developed the idea of washing air with water sprays (a concept originally introduced by Reid in the 1820s).

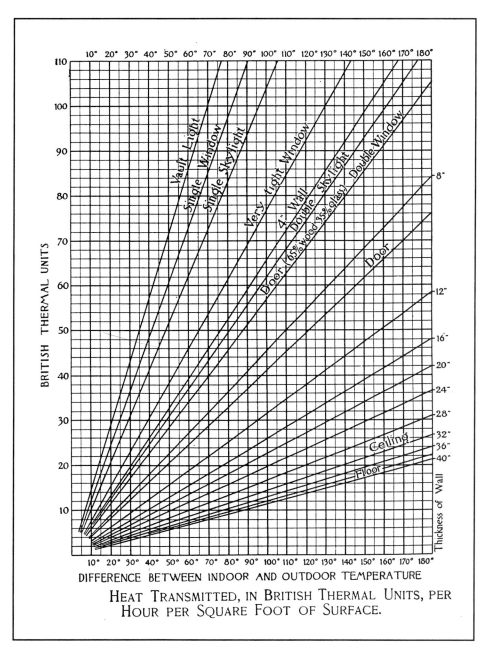

Figure 7-75 *Alfred Wolff—"heat transfer coefficients" (from* The Heating of Large Buildings, *by A. Wolff).*

Huyett and Smith

Mr. Huyett, who was operating a flourishing lumber yard in Detroit, had a young shop foreman named W.D. Smith, who had developed a novel exhaust fan for the removal of wood shavings. "It had a double cut-off and double discharge and believed by Mr. Smith at least, to have a high efficiency and wonderful possibilities. Patents were obtained on this device and in 1881, a co-partnership was formed by Huyett and Smith to manufacture and sell the fan, particularly to lumber mills, etc., Huyett furnishing the necessary funds, Smith the inventive genius."[86] During the next decade, the company manufactured a number of heating and ventilating systems, such as the patented disc fan blower and hot blast apparatus (Figure 7-69). In 1895, the Huyett and Smith Manufacturing Company became the American Blower Company.

American Blower Company

The American Blower Company continued to develop heating and ventilating systems. The "ABC System of Heating and Ventilation" was the trademark of its advertising (Figures 7-70 and 7-71). The company offered a full line of steam heating systems and a variety of low- and high-speed electric and steam fan motor drives.

Sirocco Engineering Company

The Sirocco Engineering Company of New York marketed a low-pressure multivane curved-blade fan patented by Samuel Davidson in 1900. This centrifugal fan had narrow, closely spaced radial blades that were three times longer than typical designs (Figures 7-72 and 7-73).

During the first decade of the twentieth century, the Sirocco fan went through numerous modifications, includ-

Figure 7-76 *View of Fifth Avenue South from East 58th Street, New York City. Includes Cornelius Vanderbilt mansion. Photograph by W.J. Roele, New York, c. 1920 (courtesy of the New York Historical Society, New York City).*

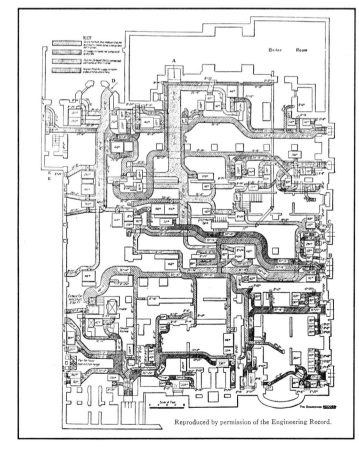

Reproduced by permission of the Engineering Record.

Figure 7-77 *Cornelius Vanderbilt II house, basement plan, heating/ventilating (from* Heating and Ventilation, *June 15, 1897).*

ing changes to the blade design and single- or double-inlet design. In 1908, the Sirocco rights were sold to the American Blower Co.

At the end of the century, there were numerous manufacturers of heating and ventilating equipment competing for a larger and more diverse market. The industry grew very rapidly with the introduction of temperature and humidity control, safety governors, and a variety of new technologies. Concerns for health and sanitation were even more important than at the beginning of the century as cities and towns became more crowded and polluted.

ENGINEERED BUILDING SYSTEMS

Alfred R. Wolff

At the time the New York Steam Company was expanding its steam distribution, numerous commercial and residential buildings were going up throughout New York City. One of the most prolific and influential individuals involved in many of these projects was Alfred R. Wolff, a consulting engineer for the design and installation of heating and ventilating systems and power plants (Figure 7-74). Wolff designed many of the most important projects of the time including the Siegel-Cooper Co. Department Store, the Hotel Astoria, St. Luke's Hospital, Carnegie Music Hall, the New York Life Insurance Building, the Metropolitan Life Building, and others. His works also span the breadth of engineering practice in his use of steam, hot water, and hot air systems, all in a variety of configurations. He was one of the first to apply coefficients of heat transfer for different

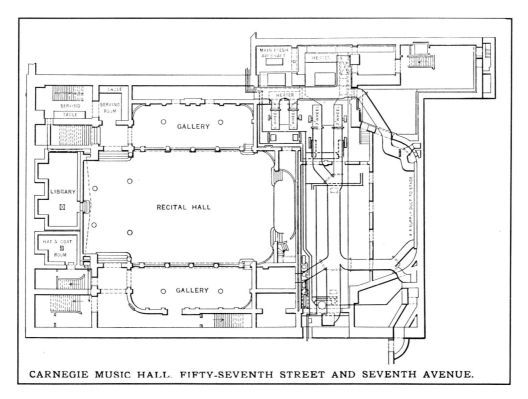

CARNEGIE MUSIC HALL. FIFTY-SEVENTH STREET AND SEVENTH AVENUE.

Figure 7-78 *Carnegie Hall, basement plan, heating/ventilating (from* Heating and Ventilation, *June 15, 1897).*

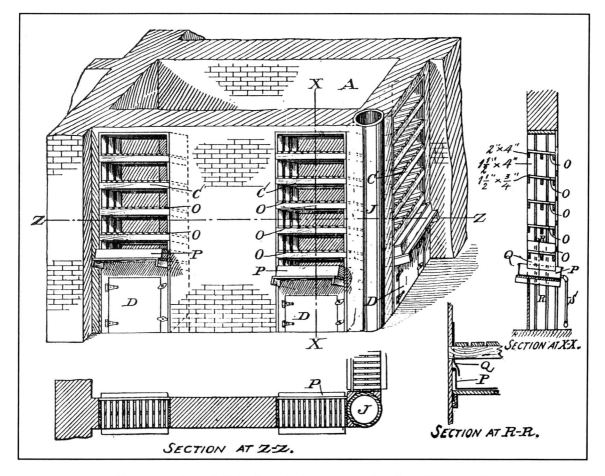

Figure 7-79 *Carnegie Hall—Ice racks for summer cooling (from Billings, 1893).*

materials, initially developed by Eugéne Peclét and Thomas Box (Figure 7-75).

The New York Life Insurance Building (1896-99), designed by McKim Mead & White, architects, and Alfred R. Wolff, consulting engineer, was heated by steam from four water-tube boilers distributed through direct and indirect radiation. The system was controlled by thermostats from the Johnson Electric Service Co. The first seven floors were heated "by indirect radiation to 70_ in zero weather with a pressure of not more than five pounds by means of two central heating stacks and two of B.F. Sturtevant's 7-foot ventilating fans. Air filters clean all entering air from soot and dust. . . . For indirect radiation Bundy loop radiators and coils are used (A.A. Griffing Iron Co., Jersey City, N.J.). Radiators are placed in halls, vestibules, and toilets."[87]

Alfred R. Wolff was also the consulting engineer for a number of large residences, such as the Cornelius Vanderbilt II house and the John Jacob Astor IV house. The Cornelius Vanderbilt house (1879-83 and 1892), designed by Richard Morris Hunt and George B. Post, was a large French chateau-style mansion on Fifth Avenue between Fifty-Seventh and Fifty-Eighth streets (Figure 7-76). The heating and ventilating were provided entirely by ducted air distribution, which was gravity fed or induced by indirect coils so that none of the system was under pressure. Fans were used only for exhaust. "Ninety-seven indirect stacks, having a total heating surface of 19,565 square feet, serve to warm the building, and to supply the hot air for this surface three horizontal tubular boilers are provided. . . . The ducts for supplying fresh air to the indirect stacks are divided into four general classes . . . (and) are provided with switch dampers by which the temperature of the air is regulated."[88] Hot water boilers provided heat from a central distributing tank (Figure 7-77).

The John Jacob Astor IV house (1891-95), designed by Richard Morris Hunt, was also in the French chateau style. The heating and ventilating were provided entirely by hot water, and air was distributed through heating stacks cased in galvanized iron with galvanized iron fresh air ducts leading to them. The building was ventilated by means of exhaust fans discharging into shafts provided for that purpose.[89]

Alfred R. Wolff's design for Carnegie Music Hall used large ventilating and exhaust fans to provide comfort for the main music hall. The heating and ventilation were provided by two 8-foot fans that discharged into a main distribution duct with a face area of more than 50 square feet. Exhaust was provided by fans located on the roof of the building (Figures 7-78 and 7-79).

Figure I *Firemaking by reflection of the sun's rays in the days of the Incas of Peru (from* The History of Fire, *1944, Universal Match Corp.).*

Figure II *Snow harvesting by the Romans. The ancient Romans developed a technology of sorts for harvesting snow and storing it in insulated pits (from the Smithsonian Institution Division of Engineering and Industry).*

Figure III *Monticello, Thomas Jefferson's bedroom (R. Lautman, Thomas Jefferson Memorial Foundation).*

Figure IV *Heidelberg Castle, thirteenth-century hooded chimney (B. Donaldson).*

Figure V *Russian stove, Chinese style (from Petrodvortetz, St. Petersburg).*

Figure VI *By the 1940s, this scene had virtually disappeared from American cities—a result of the success of domestic mechanical refrigerators (from Frigidaire Collection, Collection of Industrial History, General Motors Institute, Flint, Michigan).*

Figure VII *This striking ice house was constructed by Frederic Tudor at Madras, India, where Tudor was conducting a spirited ice business by the late 1830s (from Historical Collections, Baker Library, Harvard University Graduate School of Business Administration).*

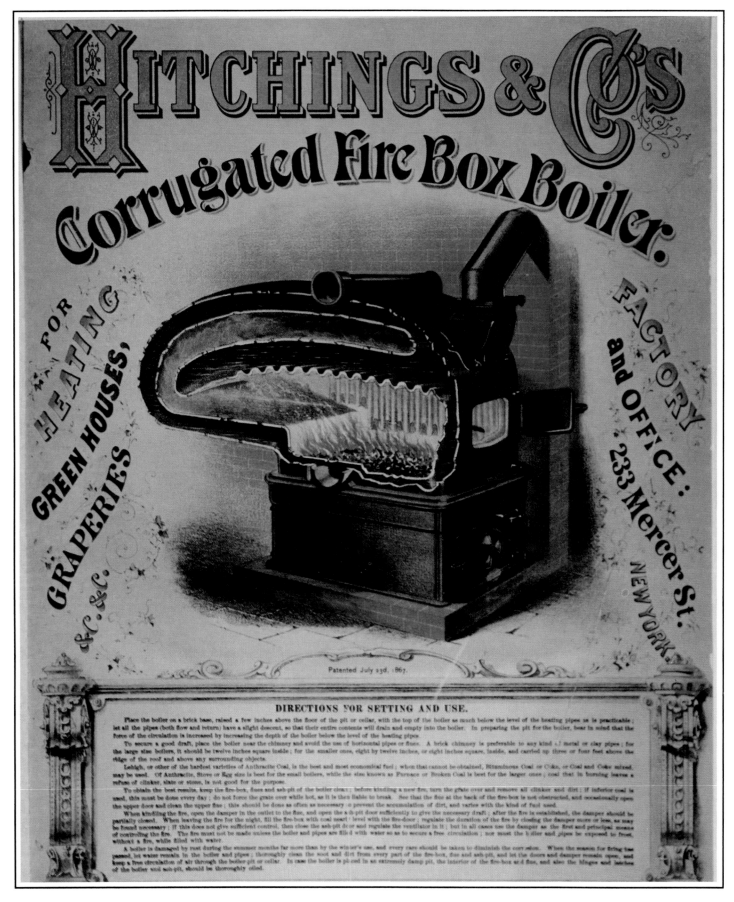

Figure VIII *Nineteenth-century advertising broadside for a "saddleback" steam boiler (from ASHRAE Centennial collection, donated by Ms. Janet Alford)*

Figure IX *Steam radiator (from Smithsonian Institution Division of Engineering and Industry)*

Figure X *The new "Elwood" radiators (from Domestic Engineering, ca., 1890).*

Number 410

Figure XI *Grocer's refrigerators, typical of the ice-type refrigerators coming into widespread use in the United States by the late nineteenth century. The ice bunker (top center door) could be easily converted to mechanical refrigeration with a brine or direct expansion coil installed in the ice compartment (from* Refrigerators for Groceries, *catalog 67, McCray Refrigerator Co., Kendallville, Indiana, 1910).*

Figure XII Ice and Refrigeration *cover, 1891.*

Figure XIII *Advertisement from the Guide International Refrigeration Exposition, 1913.*

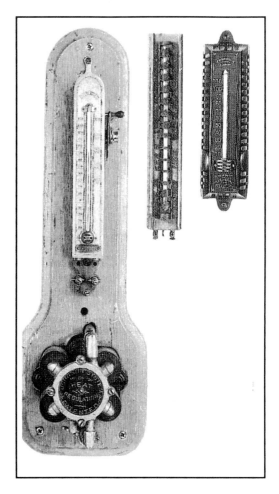

Figure XIV *Johnson's "Electro-Pneumatic" valve thermostat, 1885 (from Johnson Controls, 1984 Annual Report, p. 12).*

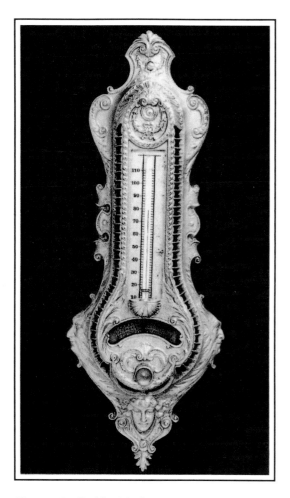

Figure XV *Residential thermostat, Johnson Electric Service Company, ca., 1890 (from Johnson Controls).*

Figure XVI *The cover of one of the first sales brochures for "The General Electric Refrigerator." Placement of the refrigeration unit, with its warm condenser coils, on top of the refrigerator incited some curious service problems. Housewives found that their dish towels dried out more quickly if draped over the warm refrigeration unit. Once a bed for the house cat was found on top of the unit. These user innovations did nothing for the operating efficiency of the refrigerator! One housewife, complaining about her high electric bill, thought that the ice cubes had to either be used or thrown out as fast as the refrigerator made them! A similar complaint was solved when it was discovered that an imaginative homeowner frequently sat in front of the opened refrigerator cooling herself off on hot summer days (from General Electric Hall of History, Schenectady, New York, publicity binders).*

Figure XVII *Frigidaire developed an extensive service organization to install refrigeration systems in homes (from General Motors Institute, Collection of Industrial History, Flint, Michigan).*

Figure XVIII *The last version of the Isko refrigerating machine used a rotary gear compressor and a water-cooled condenser. It seems there was such trouble with the machine that the company was forced into bankruptcy by 1921 and was subsequently purchased by Frigidaire which wanted to obtain the air-cooled condenser patents (from Refrigeration Without Ice-Isko, 1919, Chicago, Illinois, The Isko Company).*

Figure XIX *Porcelain-finish-steel cabinets were introduced by Frigidaire in 1928. By this time, Frigidaire had become immensely successful. Almost ten years before, engineer Glenn Muffley had uttered prophetic words concerning Frigidaire. In 1919, on his way home from work, Muffley observed a store window displaying an ice-frosted sign "FRIGIDAIRE." He heard a prosperous-looking woman say to her husband: "Frigidaire—I wonder if that is something like FREEZONE?" (the widely used corn cure for the feet). Muffley's conclusion: "Give it ten more years and it ought to arrive." By 1928, Frigidaire had sold one million refrigerators (from General Motors Institute, Collection of Industrial History, Flint, Michigan).*

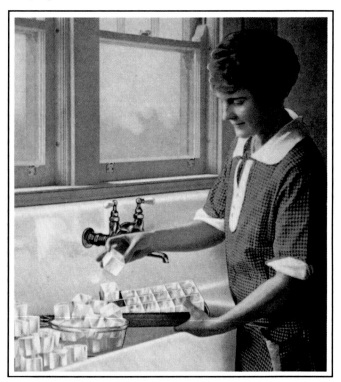

Figure XX *The ice cube trays of the 1920s, made of tin- or nickel-plated copper with plated brass dividers, required immersion under running water to remove the ice cubes. In the late 1920s, one engineer, Lloyd Copeman, introduced a rubber ice cube tray, which could be twisted to remove the ice, much the same as modern plastic trays. Copeman got the idea while duck hunting after noticing that ice frozen on his rubber boots easily broke off when the boots flexed as he walked (from General Motors Institute, Collection of Industrial History, Flint, Michigan).*

Figure XXI *Once electric refrigerators were perfected, they were aggressively promoted. In 1926, six refrigerator manufacturers established a $100,000 fund with the Society for Electrical Development to embark on an advertising program promoting electric refrigerators. The key point to be put forward to the public was "to protect food is to protect life." One of their ads beckoned: "Hundreds of thousands of housewives are enjoying the dependable, economical service of electrical refrigeration. You also should have this modern convenience. For authoritative information see your electric refrigerator dealer" (Electric Refrigeration News, 1927). Figures from late 1920s, unknown periodical.*

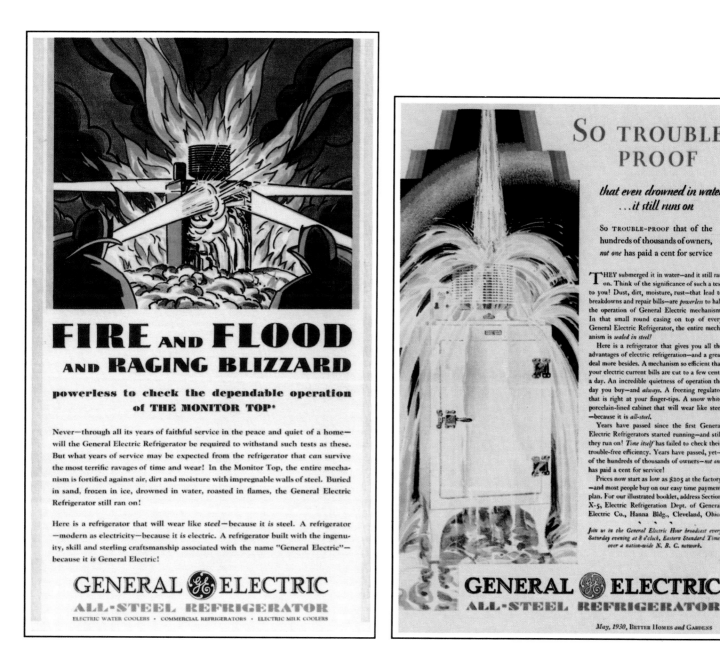

Figure XXII *"As soon as the refrigerators rolled off the production line at Schenectady, "Drowned in Water" demonstrations were held to show the public that these self-contained units were far superior to all...." "An intensive ad campaign showed Monitor Tops being sandblasted, dumped in the Erie Canal, permitted to stand under running water in freezing weather until completely covered in ice, and finally, put through fire tests. Hundreds of dealers were sent special glass tanks to put over Monitor Tops and filled with water for attention getting store-front displays." A General Electric salesman sold a refrigerator to some inhabitants of Java so they could keep their cigars dry enough in the hot, humid climate to smoke (Anonymous 1977). "A roaring 20's success." General Electric Co. Syndicated News, August 15) (from* Better Homes and Gardens, *May 1930).*

Figure XXIII *GE and other manufacturers boasted of the freedom their products gave to the housewife (from General Electric 1933 brochure, courtesy of Harold Briggeman, Fort Wayne, Indiana).*

Figure XXIV *Advertisement, "Cease Firing By Hand," automatic-feed coal stokers (from* Automatic Heat and Air Conditioning, *December 1936, p. 25).*

Figure XXV *Domestic heating, "Modernize Your Heating—This Easy Way!" Although the industry continued to push coal-fired heating as "modern," domestic and commercial heating was being converted to oil or gas (from* Good Housekeeping, *May 1930).*

Figure XXVI *Advertisement, "Univent Ventilation" (from The Herman Nelson Corp., Univent Ventilation, 1924).*

REFRIGERATION OF THE NINETEENTH CENTURY

PRECURSORS TO DEVELOPED MECHANICAL SYSTEMS

The nineteenth century saw an emphasis on practical application of the scientific developments and experiments of the previous century, leading to the beginnings of what would become a mechanical refrigeration industry (Figure 8-1).

The absorption refrigeration system could be said to have antecedents in the work of John Leslie of England in the early 1800s (Figure 8-2).

Leslie experimented with the freezing of water by evaporation by exposing it to a rarified, dry atmosphere. Leslie placed a dish of water and a dish of sulfuric acid under a bell jar, which he evacuated with an air pump (Figures 8-3 and 8-4). The air pump as well as the affinity of sulfuric acid for water vapor caused the water to evaporate rapidly and thus freeze.[1] The use of sulfuric acid to absorb water vapor had been used previously by Edward Nairne in 1777 to permit a drier vacuum than could be had by an air pump alone; however, Nairne did not use the absorption idea to produce cold itself as Leslie did.[2] When Leslie continued his refrigeration experiments for some time, trying to improve the process.[3] Leslie's ideas were further improved by John Vallance, who received two British patents (4884 and 5001) in 1824 in which he outlined a machine that repeated Leslie's process more efficiently by increasing the surface area of the water. Vallance provided a rotating spray device for the water, an increased surface for the sulfuric acid absorbent,

and larger pumps.[4] Any dreams of commercial use that Leslie or Vallance may have had were not realized. True success in the use of the absorption approach to refrigeration was not attained until the work of Carré in France many years later.

John Dalton, a professor at New College, Manchester, England, is today best known for his work on the law of partial gas pressures[5] but less known for his observations in the development of mechanical refrigeration. Dalton conducted a series of experiments in 1802 wherein he noticed the cooling or heating effect upon air depending on whether it was rarified or compressed.[6] These observations would be put to practical use forty years later by Charles Piazzi Smyth and John Gorrie as they experimented with the first air-cycle refrigeration systems.

The idea that cold could be produced by the forced evaporation of a volatile liquid under reduced pressure had been previously pursued by William Cullen in the eighteenth century. That these same volatile liquids could be condensed from a vapor state by application of cooling and compression was also known by the 1800s. Combining these two ideas led to the development of what would ultimately become the dominant means of cooling—the vapor-compression refrigerating system.

The first realization that cold could be produced by evaporating a liquid, then condensing it, and repeating the process in a continuous closed cycle seems to have occurred, not to a scientist, but to a practical inventor-mechanic, Oliver Evans of the United States (Figure 8-5). Evans, who was a steam engine specialist and thus familiar with piston pump technology, proposed in 1805:

Figure 8-1 *"Science presenting steam and electricity to commerce and manufacture," from a painting by Edwin H. Blashfield executed for the U.S. Bureau of Engraving and Printing.*

Figure 8-2 *John Leslie (1766-1872), professor of mathematics at Edinburgh, Scotland, experimented with absorption and vacuum refrigeration beginning about 1815 (from the Smithsonian Institution, Division of Engineering and Industry).*

Figure 8-3 *John Leslie's absorption and vacuum freezing device, 1823. dish of water is suspended above a flat tray of sulfuric acid under a sea glass bell jar. The air pump at left is used to draw a vacuum on the The water boils at a temperature below freezing, not only due to action of the air pump, but also due to the absorbing effect of the a which absorbs water vapor, permitting an even greater vacuum. Le later discovered that parched oatmeal was a better absorber than sulfu acid. The oatmeal had an added advantage of being reusable—it coul regenerated by heating on a stove or in the sun (from* Mechani Magazine, *1823, p. 313).*

For instance, to cool wholesome water . . . for drinking. . . . A steam engine may work a large air pump, leaving a perfect vacuum behind it on the surface of the water at every stroke. If ether be used as a medium for conducting the heat from the water into the vacuum, the pump may force the vapor rising from the ether, into another pump to be employed to compress it into a vessel immersed in water; the heat will escape into the surrounding water, and the vapour return to ether again; which being let into the vessel in a vacuum, it may thus be used over and over repeatedly. Thus it appears possible to extract the latent heat from cold water and apply it to boil other water; and to make ice in large quantities in hot countries by the power of the steam engine. I suggest these ideas merely for the consideration of those who may be disposed to investigate the principles, or wish to put them in operation.[7]

Evans goes on to give a detailed description of how such a system might be constructed.

Oliver Evans never pursued his idea for a closed vapor-compression refrigeration system; however, his friend Jacob Perkins did (Figure 8-6). Perkins was a prolific

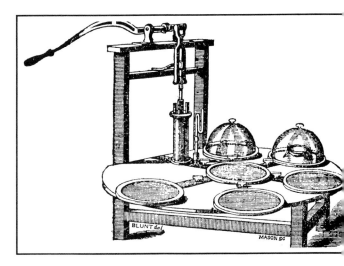

Figure 8-4 *John Leslie's freezing table of 1823. This modification to device shown in Figure 8-3 allowed successive bell jars to be evacua by one pump. As each jar was evacuated, the valve on the evacuation was shut off and the sulfuric acid was allowed to absorb the water va until the water was frozen (from* Mechanic's Magazine, *1823, p. 31*

Figure 8-5 *Oliver Evans (1755-1819) was apparently the first to completely describe the closed vapor-compression refrigeration cycle in 1805 (from Smithsonian Institution, Division of Engineering and Industry).*

Figure 8-6 *Jacob Perkins (1766-1844) patented the closed vapor-compression refrigeration cycle in 1834 (from Andrew Ure,* A Dictionary of Arts, Manufacturers, and Mines, *1856).*

inventor (receiving 21 U.S. and 19 British patents during his lifetime), involving himself in many varied industrial ventures ranging from nail making to his most profitable and enduring pursuit, production of bank notes using engraved steel printing plates.[8] In 1819, Perkins, hearing of a prize being offered by the British government for a foolproof bank note, left for London to pursue the venture. Although his printing firm was unsuccessful in obtaining the Bank of England contract, so much other business was to be had that Perkins remained in England for the rest of his life. Perkins devoted much of his time in England to improvement of the construction of steam engines and boilers.[9] Perhaps it was this work and his familiarity with Oliver Evans' accomplishments that led him in 1834 to apply for and receive British Patent 6662 for a closed-cycle vapor-compression refrigerating system similar to the one proposed by Oliver Evans in 1805 (Figures 8-7 and 8-8).

The Perkins patent was the basis upon which the first refrigerating system was constructed. John Hague, a mechanic in Perkins' employ, together with his apprentices, Crampton and F. Bramwell, constructed a working, modified example of Perkins' machine that was used to produce a small quantity of ice[10] (Figure 8-9).

THE FIRST SUCCESSFUL REFRIGERATION SYSTEMS

John Gorrie Pioneers Air-Cycle Refrigeration

The earliest success in mechanical refrigeration, where an individual pursued development and built actual systems over an extended period of time, can be found in the work of the American John Gorrie, a physician of Apalachicola, Florida[11] (Figure 8-10). Gorrie became interested in the possibilities of using mechanical refrigeration for humanitarian reasons. As early as 1842, he proposed cooling entire cities so as to relieve the inhabitants from the unhealthful effects of excessive heat and humidity. In an anonymous article, Gorrie described the problems of summer heat and humidity in the southern United States, including "malarious" diseases. The author proposed that cities should be cooled by artificial means "to counteract the evils of high temperature, and improve the condition of our cities . . . [by] the rarefaction and distribution of atmospheric air, previously deprived of large portions of latent caloric by mechanical condensation."

Wherever the escape of air . . . takes place, it will expand, and in the process, precisely the quantity of heat which was

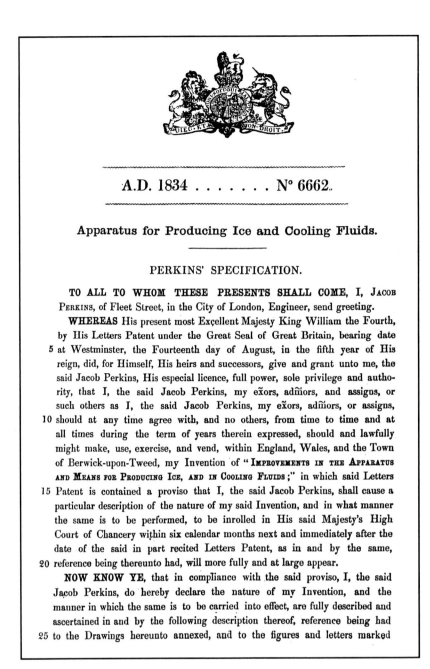

Figure 8-7 *The cover page of Jacob Perkins' patent of 1834.*

previously obtained from it will be absorbed from all surrounding substances, and rendered latent. Acting on this powerful source of heat, by means of water, wind or steam power, into suitable reservoirs in the suburbs of cities, and thence to transmit it through conduits, like water or gas, so that it may be distributed to, and set free in the houses, and even in the streets and squares of the city.[12]

A discussion of the "condensation" (compression) and "rarefaction" (expansion) of air followed. The advantages of cool, dry air were emphasized, with evaluation of costs in the application of a conditioning system for an entire city.

During the next two years, Gorrie constructed a working air-cycle refrigerating system, which he described in a series of articles for the *Commercial Advertiser*, a local Apalachicola newspaper, using the nom-de-plume "Jenner."[13] Gorrie repeated a large part of the thought from the 1842 article, but he left out his plans to cool and ventilate entire cities. Instead, he concentrated on the interaction of climate with humans and diseases, particularly malaria.

Let the houses of warm countries be built with an equal regard to insulation, and a like labor and expense be incurred in moderating the temperature, and lessening the moisture of the internal atmosphere, and the occupants would incur little or no risk from malaria . . . high atmospheric temperature . . . prevents a large portion of the human family from sharing the natural advantages they possess. It is a source of evil that has a double operational; first in causing the mental and physical deterioration of the native inhabitants; second in inducing, or rather, creating malarial diseases. Atmospherical temperature determines, or at least greatly modifies the character of our race.[14]

Gorrie then describes "an engine for ventilation, an cooling air in tropical climates by mechanical power. . . . The machine compressed air with a double-acting pisto pump, forcing it into a storage tank, through a "weighte

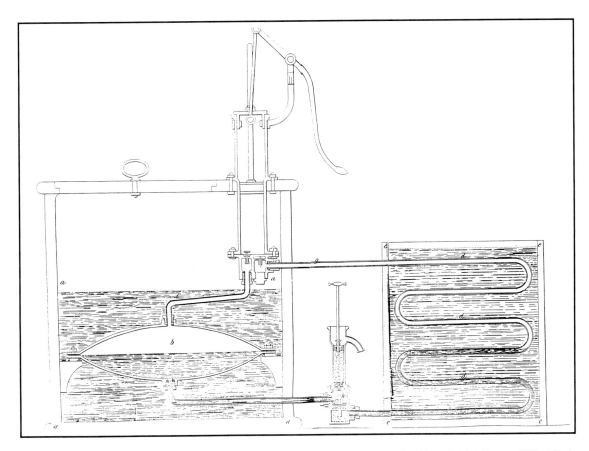

Figure 8-8 *Drawing of Perkins' proposed refrigerating machine of 1834 using ether (from British Patent 6662, 1834).*

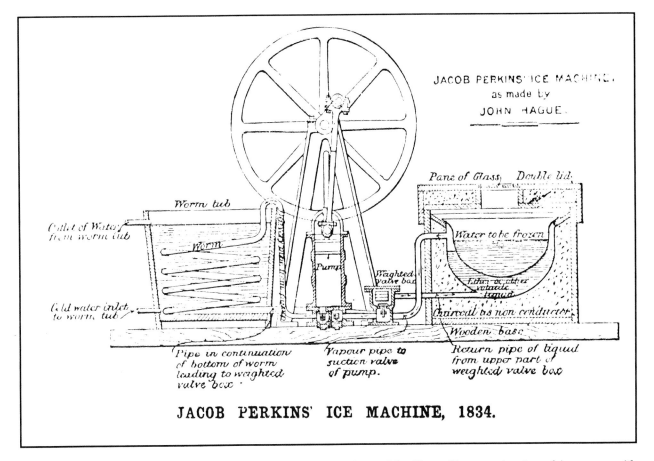

Figure 8-9 *Refrigerating machine made for Jacob Perkins by his assistant, John Hague. Hague used a steam-driven pump with "caoutchoucine" as a refrigerant. Caoutchoucine was a very bad-smelling solvent, obtained from the destructive distillation of India rubber, which Hague apparently had used in Perkins' bank note engraving business. An interesting feature of the design is the use of a weighted expansion valve, a crude precursor of the automatic expansion valve (from Smithsonian Institution, Division of Engineering and Industry).*

Figure 8-10 *John Gorrie (1802-1855) beginning in 1842 devoted the rest of his life to promotion of the air-cycle type of refrigeration system (from Florida State Archives).*

Figure 8-11 *Gorrie's improved ice machine of 1854, which he tried to promote in New York. Multiple ice cans would be cooled in an insulated room, with the incoming water cooled in a shell-and-tube heat exchanger (from Dr. John Gorrie's Apparatus . . ., 1856).*

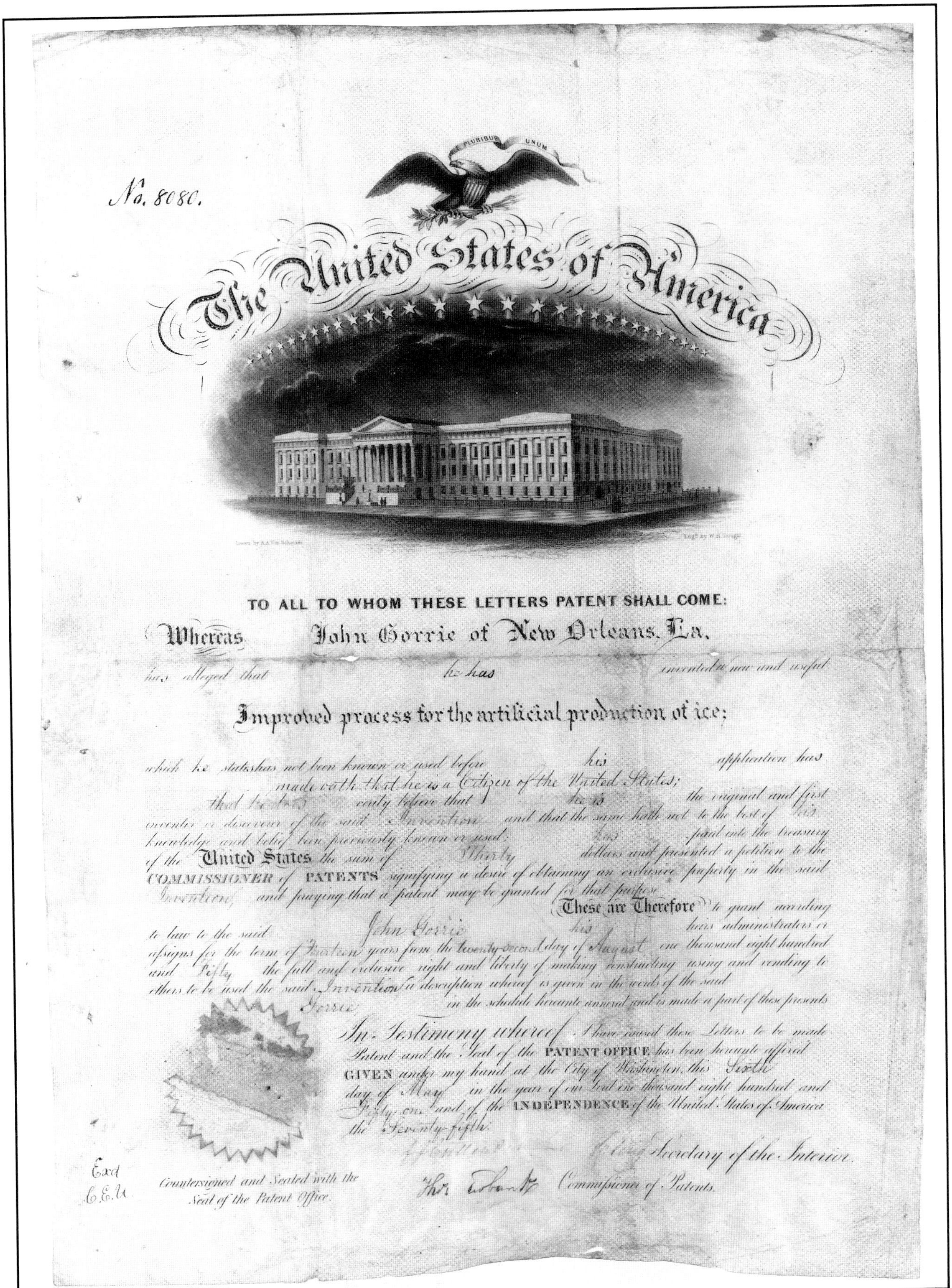
No. 8080.

The United States of America

TO ALL TO WHOM THESE LETTERS PATENT SHALL COME:

Whereas John Gorrie of New Orleans, La.

has alleged that he has invented a new and useful

Improved process for the artificial production of ice;

which he states has not been known or used before his application has made oath that he is a Citizen of the United States; that he does verily believe that he is the original and first inventor or discoverer of the said Invention and that the same hath not to the best of his knowledge and belief been previously known or used; has paid into the treasury of the United States the sum of Thirty dollars and presented a petition to the COMMISSIONER of PATENTS signifying a desire of obtaining an exclusive property in the said Invention, and praying that a patent may be granted for that purpose.

These are Therefore to grant according to law to the said John Gorrie his heirs administrators or assigns for the term of fourteen years from the twenty second day of August one thousand eight hundred and Fifty the full and exclusive right and liberty of making constructing using and vending to others to be used the said Invention a description whereof is given in the words of the said Gorrie in the schedule hereunto annexed and is made a part of these presents.

In Testimony whereof I have caused these Letters to be made Patent and the Seal of the PATENT OFFICE has been hereunto affixed.

GIVEN under my hand at the City of Washington, this Sixth day of May in the year of our Lord one thousand eight hundred and Fifty one and of the INDEPENDENCE of the United States of America the Seventy-fifth.

[illegible] Secretary of the Interior.

Countersigned and Sealed with the Seal of the Patent Office.

Thos. Ewbank Commissioner of Patents.

Exd C.E.U.

Figure 8-12 *The first of three applications by Gorrie for a U.S. patent was filed February 27, 1849. U.S. Patent 8080 was granted May 6, 1851. Gorrie also obtained British Patent 13,234 in 1850. The patented machine is similar to the device described in 1844, with the addition of small pumps to inject cooling water into the compression cylinder and brine into the expansion cylinder. The brine is used to freeze a can of ice. The chilled air exiting from the expansion cylinder is used to cool the incoming water that would be used to make the ice (from Smithsonian Institution, Division of Engineering and Industry).*

valve," then into a double-acting "expansion engine." This engine was connected to the compressor so as to "exert the same mechanical force that was required" to compress the air. The compressor could be operated by horse, water, or steam power. Gorrie also proposed wind-driven sails mounted on the house roof that could "by a slight modification of the present modes of constructing roofs, be so easily screened from view, that they would present no unsightly object." The cool, dry air would be distributed though fireplace chimneys "with the addition of valves to close the top, and valves to shut out or admit the entrance of air into rooms. . . ." Gorrie notes that besides having the benefit of cool air, the humidity of the rooms would also be lowered.[15]

Although John Gorrie had high aspirations for refrigeration, he evidently realized that the only way to realize his humanitarian dreams would be to commercialize his refrigerating machine. In the 1840s, the only possible commercial application of refrigeration was ice making. After 1844, Gorrie's work seems to have shifted more toward the goal of commercial ice manufacture. Gorrie had obtained development capital from a New Orleans businessman and conducted experiments with his machine in New Orleans and Cincinnati, Ohio.[16] Gorrie also attempted to obtain financial backing from a Boston man. The New Orleans financiers failed to pursue Gorrie's project and his northern patron died, erasing any hope of commercial development for the moment.[17] In the meantime, Gorrie obtained British and U.S. patents on his ice-making machine[18] (Figure 8-11).

Gorrie next attempted to license his machine, utilizing the services of a New York agent, and published a pamphlet in 1854 that described and illustrated a much refined ice-making machine[19] (Figure 8-12). Subsequent literature makes no reference to Gorrie's apparatus being licensed or produced; however, there is contemporary mention of two systems based on Gorrie's machine. One was in Cuba, near Havana,[20] and another was constructed by Wollaston Blake on the outskirts of London. The latter system did not work well and was the subject of a critique by William Siemens, who pointed out that with modification the machine could be greatly improved. Many of Siemens' suggestions were used by later air-cycle refrigeration pioneers.[21]

The failure to realize his dream took a toll on John Gorrie's health, and he passed away in 1855 at age 53.[22]

Other Air-Cycle Efforts

About the same time that John Gorrie was beginning his experiments with air-cycle refrigeration in the United States, similar experiments were taking place in Great Britain. Charles Piazzi Smyth, the Astronomer Royal for Scotland, had similar aspirations as John Gorrie—the use of mechanical refrigeration for comfort cooling. In 1850, Smyth iterated the history of his experiments:

The mere fact of compression and expansion having a thermotic effect on air had long been known, but no one seems to have thought of applying it to any decidedly useful purpose, certainly not this one; and for that reason, perhaps, the exact quantity of thermotic effect had never been investigated with precision; and when this idea first occurred to me in 1843, I could procure no data which would enable me to cal-

culate its practicability within any moderate limits. The next year, however, I had a small apparatus constructed for testing the matter experimentally; and though no great exactness was arrived at, still it appeared that sufficient grounds were obtained to warrant the communication of the idea to several friends in 1845, as a possible mode of accomplishing the end in view. In 1847, I had a larger apparatus made; and in the beginning of 1849, communicated an account to the Royal Society of Edinburgh. . . . But in the latter end of 1849, I was enabled, through the kind intervention of Mr. (Robert) Stirling, C.E., to try the experiment on as large a scale as could be possibly be desired.[23]

Smyth goes on to discuss his proposed machines, powered by oxen, to be used to provide cool air for the tropics. Smyth's ideas engendered some interest in the scientific community of Great Britain. For instance, William Petrie proposed alternative power methods using water. Smyth's early proposals used simple expansion of air through weighted valves; however, it seems that William Macquorn Rankine explained to Smyth "the proper thermodynamical method for dealing with a compressible gas,"[26] which resulted in the addition of an expansion cylinder in 1851.[27]

The air-cycle approach to mechanical refrigeration saw intensive development in Great Britain beginning in the 1860s.

Figure 8-13 *Alexander Catlin Twining (1801-1884) was not only a scientist and inventor but also an accomplished civil engineer, specializing in railroad and canal engineering. Twining also pursued interests in astronomy and mathematics and was considered an expert in constitutional law. During his long career, Twining held such positions as professor of mathematics, astronomy, and civil engineering, guest lecturer, and church deacon (from Twining family).*

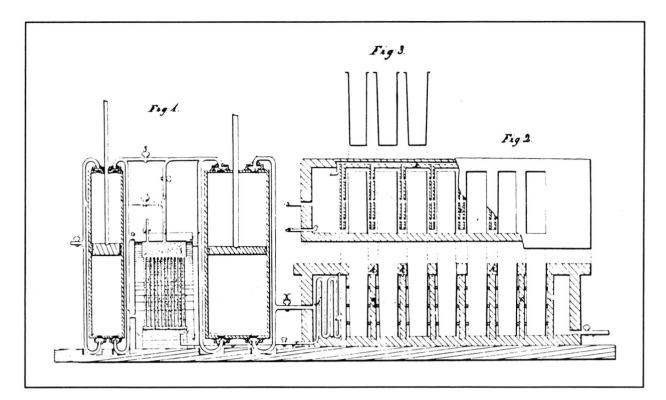

Figure 8-14 *Patent drawing showing Twining's ice-making plant of 1853 upon which the Cleveland, Ohio, plant was based. This plant is a forerunner of the later can ice plants, where water was frozen in metal cans. Twining's system used direct expansion coils wrapped around each ice can, whereas later plants used a secondary refrigerant, such as brine, around the cans. The ether compressor shown on the right side of the shell-and-tube condenser is double acting. The smaller compressor at left was used for nonrefrigeration purposes such as air evacuation. The* Cleveland Leader *reported in 1855 that Twining's machine was freezing ice blocks one-half cubic foot in size.*

THE VAPOR-COMPRESSION SYSTEMS OF TWINING AND HARRISON

Twining Builds the First Ice-Making Plant

The American civil engineer and professor Alexander Catlin Twining (Figure 8-13) is generally credited with being the first to advance the earlier work of Evans, Perkins, and Hague[28] with the vapor-compression method of refrigeration. None of the published information about Twining, his own publications, or personal papers indicates that he had any familiarity with Perkins' work.[29] In fact, there does not seem to be any indication as to why Alexander Twining pursued his interest in refrigeration. For whatever reason, Twining became interested in this area, and he summarized his pursuit as follows:

The first experiments were mere elementary trials, made as far back as the year 1848. By maintaining a vacuum in a small reservoir of ether immersed in water, the weight of ice which the evaporation of a given quantity of ether would produce, was proved. Next, by computing the power necessary to effect that evaporation, there was found a sufficiently promising result to encourage a prosecution of the subject. The experiments were repeated, till 1850, under different forms and with accordant results.

The next question arising was whether the ether vapor could be recondensed with sufficient rapidity. By numerous experiments it was ascertained that only two hundred superficial feet of thin copper pipes would form an adequate surface for the manufacture of 2000 lbs. of ice in a day

Figure 8-15 *James Harrison (1816-1893).*

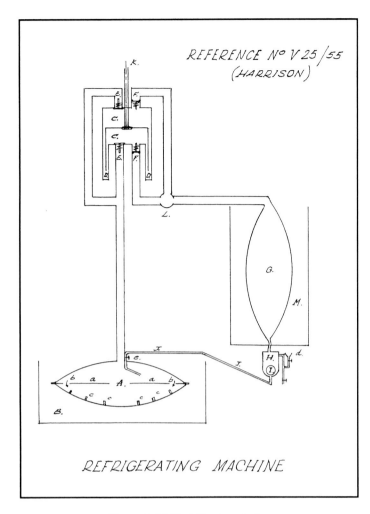

REFERENCE Nº V 25/55
(HARRISON)

REFRIGERATING MACHINE

Figure 8-16 *First Harrison design.*

ued in operation for at least the next two years Cleveland. Twining, like John Gorrie, attempted to intere financial backers for construction of an ice-making plant New Orleans and issued a proposal to interested parties. Unfortunately for Twining, the Civil War scuttled ar progress on the venture. Twining had attempted to set u an improved system at the Morgan Iron Works of New Yor City in 1863, but "without fault of the invention itself, b through accidents, imperfections in the cold-producir constructions, and the failure of funds, the enterprise resul ed in no profit, but in an increase of the inventor's outlay in the aggregate of $40,000, of which only $3000 has ev been realized in return. . . ."[34]

Not only did the Civil War physically prevent Twining efforts to make ice in the South, but Twining also felt that gave others, particularly Ferdinand Carré and Jam Harrison, the opportunity to steal his ideas for their ow use. Twining's feelings are obvious in reading his 1870 pe tion to the U.S. Congress for extension of his 1853 patent. Still, Twining's method of making ice, to be known later a the "can ice" system, would become the most comm method used throughout the world. Twining's 1855 ic making plant at Cleveland was the earliest success at usir the vapor-compression refrigerating system to manufactu ice beyond the experimental, in commercial quantities. N only did the Cleveland system work successfully, but el ments of his patent were incorporated into the first con mercial ice plant operated in the southern U.S. at t Louisiana Ice Manufacturing Company in 1862.[36] Sti Twining's system did not see commercial manufacture. was his contemporary, James Harrison, of Australia, wh would succeed where Twining failed.

Harrison, Seibe, and the First Commercial Vapor-Compression System

Australian printer and newspaperman James Harriso although by trade a printer, apparently had extensive scie tific and mechanical knowledge that enabled him to deve op a can-ice-type ice-making system about the same tin that Alexander Twining did. Harrison served his printir apprenticeship in Glasgow, Scotland, and availed himself the educational opportunities there in the early 183C Harrison attended Anderson's University and the Glasgo Mechanics Institution. He was employed as a printer London and was later hired by Tegg & Co. printers for position in their Sydney, Australia, branch. Harriso allowed that he was only a printer and not a missionary ar was able to convince the ethically minded Tegg to give hi the position. Emigrating to Australia in 1837, Harrison lat began experiments in vapor-compression refrigeratic about 1854 (Figure 8-15). Harrison's biographer, W.R. Lan concludes that about 1854, Harrison and his blacksmi friend John Scott built some form of ice-making machine which "nobody was precise in recording it but many we imprecise in reporting it."[37] Harrison's first experimen resulted in his receipt of a patent from the Colony of Victor in 1855.[38] This patent covers a simple vapor-compressic refrigeration system using ether for a refrigerant and a con pressor. The evaporator and condenser are simply met vessels, the condenser being submerged in water. A hig side float expansion device is employed. Most interesting

of twenty-four hours—even employing water of the temperature of the Earth's Equator.

It was next to be ascertained whether the evaporation itself could be made sufficiently rapid.

The first attempt at a complete freezing machine was made in the summer of 1850. The machine had only capacity to freeze a pail full of water at one operation. It embraced the evaporating, the condensing, and the freezing parts of my present engine and apparatus. But the mode of applying the freezing power was widely different. Six months were consumed in trials with this machine; and the most discouraging practical difficulties were brought to light. It was not till long afterwards that the inventor could discover the proper modes of obviating these difficulties. Nevertheless this first small machine served as a complete verification of the facts, principles and numerous small experiments which had been relied upon; and it thus became an encouragement, in the end, to attempt a vastly larger construction.[30]

Twining had been so sure of success that he filed a caveat with the U.S. Patent Office in November 1849, and soon after filed for a British as well as a U.S. patent[31] (Figure 8-14).

The larger machine mentioned above was constructed at the Cuyahoga Steam Furnace Company in Cleveland, Ohio (where Twining was doing some railroad work), with freezing trials beginning in February 1855. By the summer, the machine was capable of producing almost 1,700 pounds of ice.[32] This machine, based upon Twining's patents, contin-

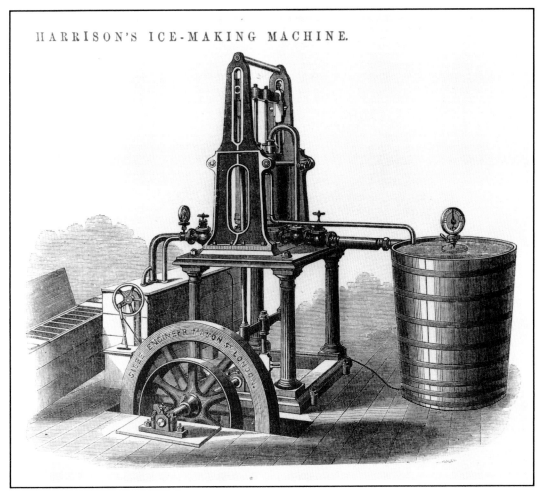

Figure 8-17 *Harrison-Siebe design.*

his patent is Harrison's listing of alternative means of compressing the ether, other than the piston-type compressor: a bellows, centrifugal blower, mercury or water column, diving bell, Archimedes' screw, reversed chain pump, or a reversed overshot water wheel.[39]

Recognizing the limits of available technology in Australia, Harrison and his family sailed for England for what was to be a two-year stay. Harrison's purpose in England was to consult with Daniel Siebe of the British steam engineering firm Siebe & Company. The result was a new design, suitable for production, which was covered by British Patent 2362 of 1857 (Figures 8-16 and 8-17). The first machine of improved design was sold to the Truman, Hanbury and Buxton Brewery in London in 1857.[40] Another machine, with an ice-making capacity of up to 8,000 pounds per day, was constructed by Siebe and exhibited in London before being exported to Australia.[41] In 1858, Harrison returned to Australia, set up an ice-making plant, and continued to promote and sell his ether machine. More machines were built by Siebe in London and by P.N. Russell & Co. in Sydney.[42,43] Thus, James Harrison was the earliest mechanical refrigeration pioneer to see actual commercial production of his invention. This commercial production, made possible by the expertise of a steam engineering firm, was the first of many examples to come and demonstrated the usefulness of the advances in the technology of steam engines to the vapor-compression refrigeration industry.

BEGINNINGS OF COMMERCIAL REFRIGERATION

The middle of the nineteenth century saw the beginnings of a mechanical refrigeration industry, symbolized by the entrepreneurial attempts of Gorrie, Twining, and others and finally realized by Harrison. These beginnings accelerated as the second half of the century wore on. The centers for these developments were in several places.

The Carrés and Tellier of France

As early as 1836, Ferdinand Carré (Figure 8-18) of France had done some experimenting with the vapor-compression idea; however, it was not until 1857 that these experiments were considered a success.[44] Although Carré began his refrigeration work with ether vapor compression, it is his work in absorption refrigeration for which he is most famous. His investigation into the affinity of water for ammonia resulted in his perfection of an intermittent aqua-ammonia absorption refrigerating system in 1859[45] (Figure 8-19). This machine was of a small size, suitable for households, and was to see extended use for many years. It was manufactured at different times, most successfully beginning in 1927 in a modified version known as the Crosley "Icy Ball." About 1859, Carré also developed a continuous absorption machine for commercial use.[46] This continuous machine was manufactured in Paris by Mignon & Rouart

Figure 8-18 *Ferdinand Carré (1824-1900) "was a researcher of great intellectual power and creative capacity. He obtained more than 50 patents on refrigeration techniques, not counting numerous patents in other fields. He was a quiet man, little interested in industrial use of his inventions. He left no written records, apart from his patents" (Thévenot, p. 436). In his patents, "Carré dealt with membrane compressors, various construction of condensers, evaporators, air coolers, and heat exchangers, also crystallizers for freezing out salts from their mother liquor, and ventilating systems. He described the submerged, double-pipe, and vertical and horizontal shell-and-tube types of heat exchangers, and at that early date, an application of the flexible tube, such as now used as bellows for glands and thermostats. Even the modern glandless valve with flexible diaphragm was described by Carré" (from International Institute of Refrigeration).*

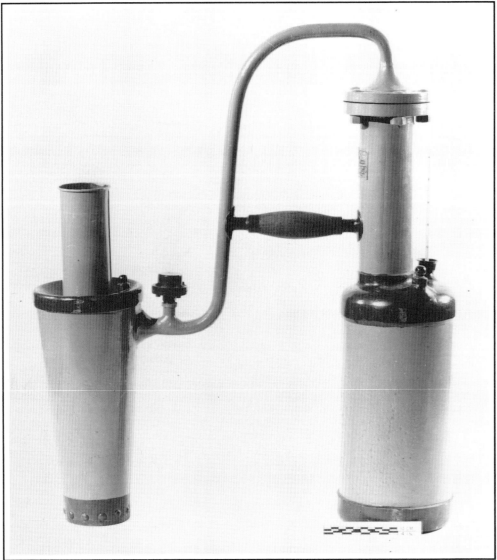

Figure 8-19 *Carré absorption device (from Smithsonian Institution, Division of Engineering and Industry).*

Figure 8-20 Louis Charles Abel Tellier (1828-1913), son of a Normandy textile mill owner, was forced to abandon his father's business after the 1848 French revolution caused a commercial crisis. Tellier next built a unit that used ammonia as a motive power. He next turned to an enterprise that would use "human manure" to manufacture compressed air and distribute it throughout cities in pipes to be used as a motive power. His idea was scornfully criticized, but Tellier was convinced by a country administrator to apply his inventive talent to devising a means of producing ice by mechanical means. Thus his life's work began with his first vapor-compression machine produced in 1868 (from Compte rendu Officiel De La Manifestation Internationale En L'Honneur de Charles Tellier "Pere du Froid," *1913, pp. 71-72) (from International Institute of Refrigeration).*

Figure 8-21 *Refrigeration plant built and operated by Charles Tellier in 1869 at Marseilles using methyl ether refrigerant. Charles Tellier is seated to the right of two unnamed Americans who came to France to purchase the plant in 1870. Tellier later said, ". . . sometime after that, they left. But a short time after they arrived in their country, the 1870 War broke out. One of the two was of German origin. Naturally, I didn't see him anymore. The other person died at this instant. Thus ended the business, so well begun, and this photograph was the only profit I got out of it" (from:* Compte Rendu Officiel De La Manifestation . . ., *1913).*

beginning in 1861. Much of the commercial success of Carré's system has been credited to the onset of the Civil War, which hampered the American refrigeration developments of Gorrie and Twining, while allowing Carré's invention to be smuggled through the Union blockade into the southern U.S. The Carré machines did not operate very satisfactorily at first but were improved by Daniel Holden at New Orleans beginning in 1866. Holden used steam coils to power the system and used distilled water so as to produce clean, nonmineralized ice.[47] Ferdinand Carré continued his refrigeration work, at least through the 1870s.[48]

Edmond Carré, younger brother of Ferdinand, was also active in refrigeration developments. He commercialized the combination evaporation-absorption approach in freezing water, as experimented with by John Leslie and John Vallance. It seems that "this apparatus found some use in Paris cafes, especially after the firm of H.A. Fleuss developed a simple pump."[49]

Charles Tellier, the French "Father of Cold" (Figure 8-20), constructed a vapor-compression machine using methyl ether as early as 1868. In that year, he attempted to ship refrigerated meat to London aboard the *City of Rio de Janeiro*; however, his ether refrigerating equipment failed, and the meat spoiled. Undaunted, Tellier next established a plant to produce ice and "carafes frappées" (frozen bottles) in Marseilles in 1869 (Figure 8-21). This venture was not a commercial success. Tellier next built what is possibly the first mechanically refrigerated cold storage plant in the world in Auteuil. This venture also failed due to the outbreak of the Franco-German war in 1870.[50] Tellier continued to promote his refrigeration ideas, which were unique in that he used forced refrigerated air as a cooling means (Figure 8-22). Tellier successfully demonstrated the system in 1879, when he refitted an English packet-boat, renaming it *Le Frigorifique*, and transported a shipload of meat and poultry chilled to 0_C from France to South America (Figure 8-23). The return trip was not as successful in keeping the meat and Tellier did not pursue commercializing the idea.[51] Although he was active in refrigeration research for most of the rest of his life and despite all his contributions to the advance of refrigeration, he died in relative poverty in 1913.[52]

Figure 8-22 *Tellier was the earliest pioneer to construct refrigerating plants that mimicked the "refrigeration by cold, dry air" ideas being advanced by some of the ice refrigeration advocates. Shown is Tellier's model for U.S. Patent 85,719 of 1869. Tellier employed a shell-and-tube heat exchanger to refrigerate air, blowing the air though the heat exchanger with a steam-driven fan. The refrigerated air was the distributed through the cold storage building (from Smithsonian Institution, Division of Engineering and Industry).*

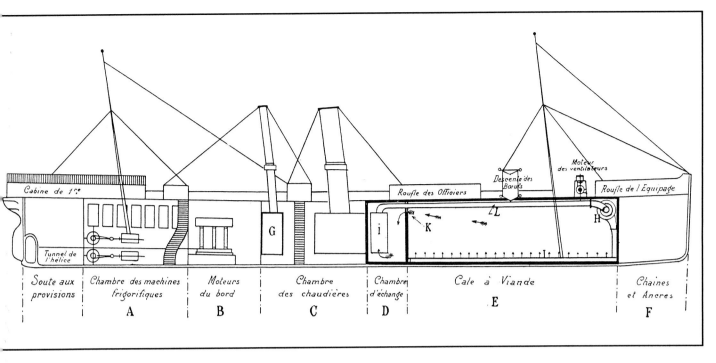

Figure 8-23 *Cutaway of "Le Frigorifique" (from* Compte Rendu Officiel De La Manifestation . . ., *1913).*

Carl Linde and the Thermodynamic Approach

Attempts at mechanical refrigeration before 1870 had yielded results that could hardly be termed efficient in energy use. These early attempts were lucky to achieve even a 10% efficiency.[53] It appears that the first rigorous thermodynamic approach to refrigeration was taken before 1870 by Carl Linde in Germany (Figure 8-24). Linde's 1870 paper, "The Extraction of Heat at Low Temperature by Mechanical Means," was the beginning of what was possibly the earliest attempt to approach the design of refrigerating systems by considering scientific theory first. The next stop was to design the equipment, which Linde addressed the next year in his paper "Improved Ice and Refrigerating Machines."

This paper clearly disclosed the involved theoretical and thermodynamic considerations. It provided a real scientific basis, and as such became immensely valuable in the further technical development of refrigerating machinery . . . which in a short time led to such improvements in general design that practical efficiencies were boosted to fifty percent of the possible thermodynamic maximum. Dr. Linde himself, was the first to make use of his theoretical deductions in the design and construction of refrigerating equipment.[54]

Linde was convinced that the vapor-compression system offered the best possibilities. Persuaded that the brewing industry was the area most in need of mechanical refrigeration, Linde delivered a paper at the Vienna brewers' conference in 1873. This attracted the financial backing of Munich brewer Gabriel Sedlmayr, who allowed him to experiment with refrigerating machinery at the Spaten Brewery. His first machine, using methyl ether as a refrigerant, was completed in 1874, and tests proved that its efficiency was double that of other existing equipment.[55] Still, his first machine was not considered satisfactory in its construction, and Linde proceeded to construct an improved

Figure 8-24 *Carl Linde (1842-1934) was a professor of mechanics at the Munich, Germany, technical college when he saw an advertisement that offered a prize for the best method of paraffin crystallization and separation by mechanical refrigeration. Dr. Linde immediately proceeded with the work of establishing a basis upon which the theory of mechanical refrigeration might be safely developed. Linde was different from the early commercial refrigeration pioneers in that he approached the problem of refrigeration from a theoretical standpoint. Refrigeration historian Roger Thévenot (1979) said that Linde was outstanding ". . . at one and the same time as a scientist, professor, engineer, and industrialist, qualities rarely united in one man" (p. 445) (from* Ice and Refrigeration *vol. 35, 1908, p. 123).*

Figure 8-25 *Model of Carl Linde's first ammonia refrigeration system. The system was installed in 1877 at the Dreherschen Brauerei at Trieste, Austria, where it was in operation until 1908. The original system still exists, and is apparently the oldest ammonia vapor-compression system in the world (from Smithsonian Institution, Division of Engineering and Industry, Washington, D.C., photo no. 50595).*

design using ammonia as a refrigerant in 1877. These fir two machines were vertical, two-cylinder compressors. Th second system employed a brine chiller, the brine bein used in a spray-type device to refrigerate the air. The vert cal cylinder compressor, which used a complicated glyce ine sealing system for the pistons and shaft, was considere unsuitable for commercial production and was abandone in favor of a horizontal, double-acting type (Figures 8-2 and 8-26). This approach produced a lower cost compresso by combining the two single-acting cylinders into a double acting one. The glycerine sealing system was eliminated i favor of an oil-sealed stuffing box at the shaft, as well as th use of mineral oil as a lubricant and piston seal.[56] This nev design was considered suitable for production, and con mercialization began in 1879 with the establishment c Gesellschaft für Linde's Eismaschinen in Weisbaden Germany.[57] The Chicago engineer Fred W. Wolf was one c Linde's early advocates and secured rights to manufactur and sell Linde's refrigerating systems in the U.S. in 188: The Linde machine and refrigerating systems became por ular throughout the world.

The Beginnings of Commercial Refrigeration in the United States

Although Gorrie and Twining had attempted to commer cially develop refrigeration, it was not until the 1860s tha any sort of refrigeration business began. Refrigeration eng neer and historian Justus Goosmann notes that:

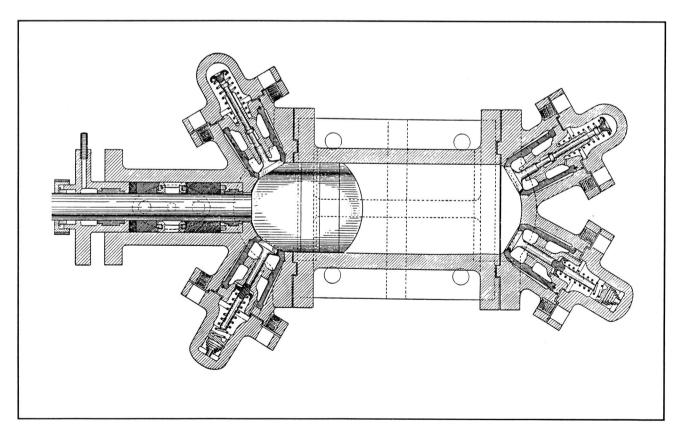

Figure 8-26 *Linde's improved horizontal ammonia compressor. Although Linde was not the first to use ammonia as a refrigerant, his double-acting design was more efficient than others of the 1870s, and was widely used for many years (from J.A. Ewing, 1908,* The Mechanical Production of Cold, *p. 87).*

ure 8-27 *Daniel Livingston Holden (1837-1924) was the first in the*
. to actively pursue commercial refrigeration. As a Boone County,
tucky, schoolboy, Holden froze ice on the underside of a plate con-
ing evaporating ether. Later, as an engineer with Mepes, Holden &
ntgomery & Co., he was sent to San Antonio, Texas, to supervise the
allation of a Carré aqua-ammonia absorption refrigeration system in
5. Dissatisfied with its operation, Holden improved the machine by
rating it with steam heat and substituting distilled water for river
ter so as to make clear, nonmineralized ice. In 1866, Holden secured
rights from Peter Van der Weyde to use a petroleum spirit called "chi-
gene" as a vapor-compression system refrigerant and commenced
nufacture of ice-making plants. One system was erected in New
leans in 1867 to produce ice by the "plate" method (from unknown
iodical source).

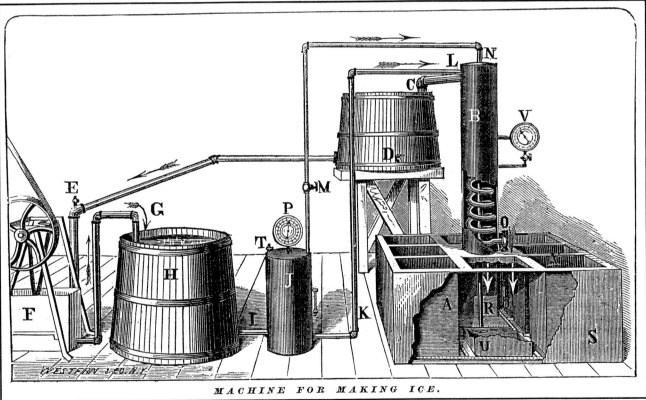

MACHINE FOR MAKING ICE.

Figure 8-28 *Ice-making plant erected at New Orleans in 1869 by D.L. Holden, which used "chimogene" as the refrigerant. The design fea-*
tured some advanced design ideas. The device at the right marked B was a suction-to-liquid heat exchanger, and the vat marked D contained
water to be frozen, which was cooled by the suction gas before it entered the compressor. The tube M-N served to remove flash gas from the
receiver J, admitting it underneath the liquid refrigerant in the evaporator at point U, which served to agitate the boiling liquid and increase
heat transfer. The plant was of the "can" type, the ice cans being inserted into the cavities in the evaporator. The heat transferred from the
ice cans to the evaporator walls (unlike most later plants, which used brine, etc. as a secondary heat transfer agent) (from "Making ice by
machinery," 1869, The Manufacturer and Builder, *vol. 1, December, p. 353).*

. . . nearly all of the pioneer engineers were what is often termed ambitious dreamers. Very few were equipped with even fundamental engineering knowledge. Nearly all of them possessed an undeniable talent for mechanics and in the art of invention. Their acquired momentum of enthusiasm carried them over obstacles, initial failures, financial difficulties, and hardships of various kind to a considerable measure of practical success. Very few of these early pioneers had the advantage of having within their control machine-shop and foundry facilities necessary for this class of work. Hence, the first move was to interest manufacturers to undertake the building of these machines and equipments in accordance with the enthusiastic ideas of these promoters. When the first efforts did not meet with the anticipated success, as was the often the case, the manufacturers, having no particular knowledge of this subject, often lost heart and refused to go on. It was then necessary to begin all over again with increased energy and enthusiasm in order to inspire others.[58]

Perhaps the earliest of the successful commercial pioneers in the U.S. were Daniel Livingston Holden and David Boyle. Daniel Holden entered the ice-making business in 1865 and by the 1870s was engaged in building refrigerating plants using a petroleum ether refrigerant called "chimogene" (also spelled "chymogene" or "cryogene"). Holden had purchased rights to the use of this refrigerant from its patentee, Peter Van der Weyde, about 1870[59] (Figures 8-27 through 8-30). Holden was a prominent manufacturer of refrigerating systems through the end of the century.[60]

David Boyle (Figure 8-31) is probably the best known the early U.S. refrigeration entrepreneurs. He is often cre ited, along with Carl Linde, as "the inventor of the amm nia compressor"; however, neither Boyle nor Linde was t first to propose use of ammonia or construct compresso for its use.[61] David Boyle began his refrigeration work 1865 at Demopolis, Alabama. Boyle recounted his expe ence, saying:

> I was keeping store and making and selling ice cream and lemonaid. A brigade of Federal troops were stationed there, and it were a bonanza to me. I had a shipment of ice from New Orleans delayed in transit three or four days, and when it reached Demopolis its actual cost was about seventy-five cents per pound. The weather was hot, and it did not take long to get rid of it. I used it to cool lemonaid, and sold it at a good profit to the yankee soldiers. The unreliability of transportation, the high cost, and the absolute need of ice at Demopolis set me to thinking and determined me to attempt the making of a machine to supply the wants of Demopolis. Just think of it! The wants of Demopolis! And that was my idea.[62]

Hearing of an ice-making machine backed by parties New Orleans, he went there only to conclude that tl machine (which was probably a Carré apparatus) was tc expensive for commercial use. During the next sever years, he searched for information on availability of refri; erating machines, finally hearing of a Van der Weyc machine being set up in New Orleans (probably t

Figure 8-29 *Holden's improved ice plant. The large device in the center is a condenser featuring a "zig-zag" heat exchanger. To its left is the shell-and-tube brine chiller marked B. By 1878, Holden was in business with his two brothers building machines at the Penn Iron Works in Philadelphia (from* Scientific American, *May 22, 1880, p. 322).*

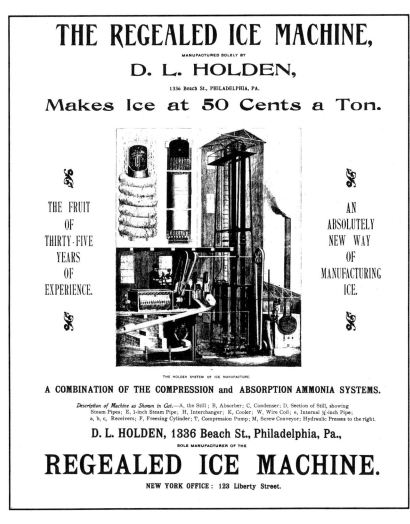

Figure 8-30 *"The regealed ice machine" was Holden's most sophisticated system. Flake ice was made and then compressed into blocks (from* Cold Storage, *vol. 3, May 1900, p. 99).*

(olden). Boyle sold most of his assets and purchased a machine, which was a total failure. In 1869 he took his family to San Francisco and spent a year going through the library of the Mechanics' Institute there. During that time, he learned of Harrison's machine and purchased one from Beibe in London but had to sue to recover his money since the machine was never shipped. Frustrated at his attempts to find a satisfactory machine made by others, he moved back to New Orleans, constructed a one-ton machine, and then went to Jefferson, Texas (probably to the Louisiana Ice Manufacturing Co.), with the half-done machine and only $175 to his name. Upon completing the machine, Boyle found that "it leaked like a sieve" and he had to completely remake it.

My brother and I sat down in the wood pile to cool off. We were worn out with the worry and disappointment, and the machine was a wreck. All was gone, and I was at the end of my tether. I had success within reach, but lacked the means to secure it. My wife joined us, and, after listening to any complaints, made a most astounding statement. She could furnish me with money—money that she (cramped financially as we were) had managed to lay by for darker days. The amount was not large, but it was enough to start me on the final success.[63]

It was not until 1874 that the system was satisfactory in producing ice. Receiving offers of financial backing, Boyle

Figure 8-31 *David Boyle (1837-1891), a Scottish emigrant, was said to have become interested in refrigeration after he made $8,000 selling iced lemonade at Demopolis, Alabama, in 1865 (information and photo from* Ice and Refrigeration, *vol. 1, July 1891, p. 24).*

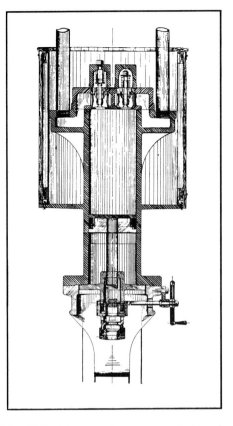

Figure 8-32 *David Boyle's ammonia compressor design, after the 1870s. The vertical, single-acting cylinder design incorporating suction and discharge valves in the compressor head came to be known as the "Boyle pattern" and was used by many manufacturers, even to the present day (from catalog,* Ice Making and Refrigerating Machinery, *1894, Pennsylvania Iron Works Co.).*

moved to Quincy and then Chicago, Illinois. The Boyle Ic Machine Co. was organized about 1877, after Boyle cor tracted with Crane Brothers in Chicago to manufacture h ammonia vapor-compression systems. His earlier attemp had been ice-making plants of the "plate" type, but Boy expanded his horizons to general refrigerating purpose with the sale of a refrigerating plant to the Bemis & McAvo Brewing Co. in Chicago in 1877.[64] Boyle's systems wei manufactured by his and successor companies until 1905' (Figures 8-32 through 8-34).

Before the 1870s, the limited attempts at commerciali; ing mechanical refrigeration centered on ice makinj However, it was the beer-brewing industry that adde enough potential business to that of ice making to provid the financial environment for a refrigeration industr Brewery money financed Carl Linde's first refrigeratio experiments in Germany, as previously seen. German lage beer, which required cool temperatures for fermentatio; became popular in the United States as waves of Germa immigrants entered the U.S. in the latter half of the nine teenth century. An enormous demand for lager beer aros for example, expanding production from two million ba rels in 1863 to more than five million in 1866.[66] For lage beer to be made year-round, refrigeration of the fermenta tion and storage areas became necessary. At first, ice wa used for that purpose, and some mechanical ice-makin plants were installed in breweries to supply ice for brev ing. However, direct application of mechanical refrigera tion was pursued, and the result was that breweries pro vided much of the refrigeration industry's business up t the 1890s.[67] For example, an 1895 advertisement for the L La Vergne Refrigerating Machine Co. listed 583 refrigera tion plants installed, and 369 were breweries.[68] By the la

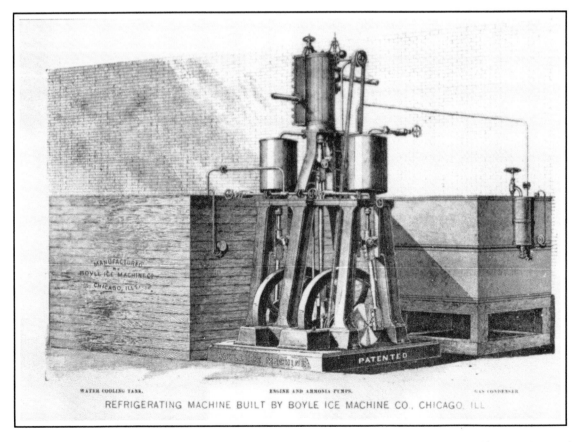

Figure 8-33 *Refrigeration machine for breweries, etc., as manufactured by the Boyle Ice Machine Co. in the 1880s (from catalog,* Boyle Ice Machin Co. Patentees and Manufacturers of Refrigerating Apparatus and Ice Machines, *Chicago, c. 1881).*

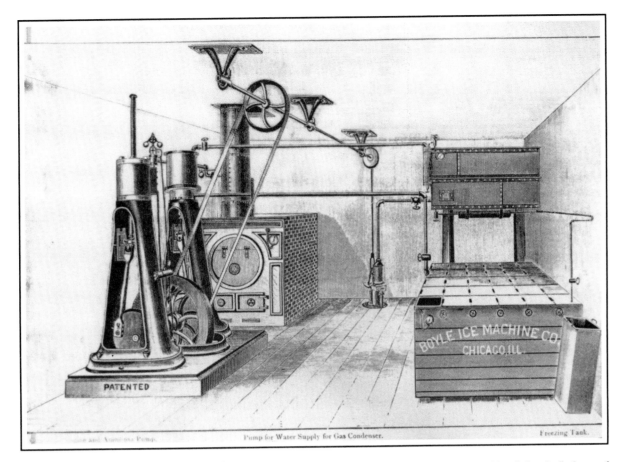

Figure 8-34 *Ice-making plant by Boyle Ice Machine Co., 1879. It appears that Boyle had abandoned his "plate ice" plants of earlier years in favor of the "can ice" type of system. Early ice plants did not always perform up to expectations. "When the machine started, our troubles began. It made ice, all right, but such ice! Not being lasting, it could not be utilized for tomb stones. Being made from hard limestone water, over-ripe hen fruit was its only competitor in smell and taste" (W.J. Rushton, 1916, "Early days of the manufacture of ice,"* Ice and Refrigeration, *November, p. 152) (from catalog,* The Boyle Ice Machine and Refrigerating Apparatus as manufactured by the Boyle Ice Machine Co., *Chicago, 1879).*

er part of that century, most breweries had been equipped with mechanical refrigeration, and this fact so alarmed the U.S. refrigerating machine companies that six leading company representatives attended a secret meeting to address the looming reduction of business. Everyone agreed that the best solution was to consolidate into one firm on the East Coast and another one on the West coast. After months of "discussion," the attempt ended in failure because no agreement could be reached on which of them would be the surviving firms. Their worries proved groundless, however. Two years later, the failure of much of the eastern U.S. natural ice crop gave impetus to the erection of mechanical ice-making plants, and soon there was more than enough business for everyone![69] This was augmented by additional business in equipping packing-houses and cold storage facilities. Thereafter, the mechanical refrigeration industry had plenty of customers.

DEVELOPMENT OF REFRIGERANTS

During the nineteenth century, the vapor-compression refrigeration system became the dominant type used throughout the world. The earliest systems used ether; however, its use declined rapidly as the century progressed. As the refrigeration industry developed, numerous volatile fluids were tried as refrigerants,[70] but most of them proved to be experimental or they saw only limited use. Those that

did see long-term use were ammonia, sulfur dioxide, methyl chloride, and ethyl chloride.

Ammonia

Alexander Twining and James Harrison had received patents in 1850 and 1856 (mentioned previously) for refrigerating machines in which ammonia and other refrigerants were specified. However, both men used ethyl ether in the machines they actually constructed. Charles Tellier of France began his long history of refrigeration accomplishments by experimenting with ammonia in 1862.[71] However, Tellier chose to use methyl ether for his early systems.

Eugene Nicolle, a French engineer from Sydney, Australia, and a pioneer in the export of refrigerated meat, claims that he made an ammonia compressor in 1863-1864 but did not develop it further because absorption-type systems looked more efficient to him.[72] A British patent (3062) was issued to R.A. Brookman in 1864 for an ammonia compression machine for ice making and refrigerating. There seems to be no further mention of Brookman or his system in the sources checked. John Beath of San Francisco built several ice-making plants using ammonia compression systems in the period 1868-1872, but by 1873 Beath abandoned further attempts with vapor-compression systems, concluding that they had too many problems, and turned his efforts to absorption systems.[73] Beath was obviously a ded-

ARCTIC

MACHINES INSTALLED IN 1879
STILL IN CONTINUOUS SERVICE

COMPLETE ICE MAKING and
REFRIGERATING PLANTS
OF ANY SIZE.

Pipe...Fittings   Ammonia
Cans...Tanks   Supplies

STYLE B.

Correspondence Solicited.
Send for Catalogue.

THE ARCTIC MACHINE CO.

CLEVELAND, OHIO, U. S. A.

Figure 8-35 *The Arctic Machine Co. of Cleveland, Ohio—and its successor, Arctic Ice Machine Co. of Canton, Ohio—was one of the earliest manufacturers of refrigerating equipment in the U.S. The company was ultimately absorbed by the York Ice Machinery Corp. (from Selfe, 1900, Machinery for Refrigeration, p. 397).*

icated engineer. Of his early experiences he said, "Peop thought I was trying to make money, but I was really tryi to find out how to make ice."[74]

Probably the first to use ammonia as a refrigerant su cessfully was Francis DeCoppet of the U.S. A Telli machine using ammonia had been installed in 1869 1 George Mertz in New Orleans.[75] It had severe problem with leaks, most probably due to the lightweight constru tion (considering that Tellier's machines were made f methyl ether). Mertz engaged DeCoppet to correct t problem, which he did by constructing a double-acti ammonia compressor in 1870. DeCoppet had to make h own anhydrous ammonia by passing it through quicklin and caustic soda. The compressor operated successfully f two seasons.[76]

John Enright of the U.S. designed an ammonia compre sion system as early as 1876. One was installed at Ziege brewery in Buffalo, New York, about 1877. Enright w engineer for F.M. McMillan & Co. and its successor, Arc Machine Co., which continued to manufacture ammon systems well into the twentieth century[77] (Figure 8-35). Th McMillan Co. was apparently the first to manufactu anhydrous ammonia on a commercial scale, having begu production in the period 1876-1879.[78] The lack of availab ity of dry ammonia caused some early refrigeratir machinery manufacturers to supply stills and lime drye with their equipment so that anhydrous ammonia could b produced from aqua-ammonia, which was commercial available.[79] By the end of the century, refrigerant-grac ammonia was being produced by a number of manufactu ers (Figures 8-36 through 8-38).

Carbon Dioxide

Carbon dioxide (also known in early references as ca bonic acid gas and carbonic anhydride) was first propose as a refrigerant for vapor-compression systems b Alexander Twining, who mentioned it in his 1850 Britis patent. Thaddeus S.C. Lowe experimented with carbo dioxide for military balloons in the 1860s and recognize the possibilities of using it as a refrigerant. He went on t build refrigerating equipment, obtaining British Patent 9! in 1867, and erected an ice machine about 1869 at Jackso

Figure 8-36 *Advertisement, ammonia (from* Ice and Refrigeration, *June 1906, ad section, p. 55).*

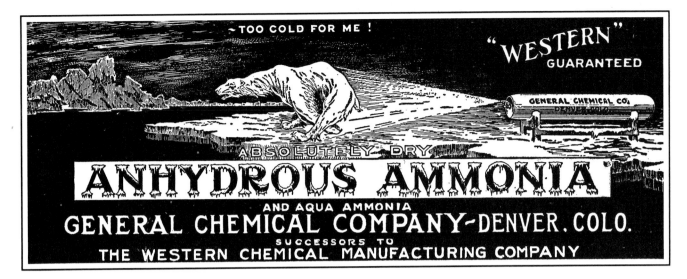

Figure 8-37 *Advertisement, ammonia (from* Ice and Refrigeration, *September 1918, ad section, p. 15).*

Mississippi. He also constructed a machine on board ship for transport of frozen meat in the Gulf of Mexico. Lowe did not develop his ideas further.[80]

Carl Linde also experimented with carbon dioxide when he designed a machine for F. Krupp at Essen, Germany, in 1882.[81] W. Raydt received British Patent 15475 in 1884 for a compression ice-making system using carbon dioxide. British Patent 1890 was granted to J. Harrison in 1884 for a device for manufacturing carbon dioxide for refrigeration use. Still, the use of carbon dioxide did not really advance until Franz Windhausen of Germany designed a carbon dioxide compressor, receiving British Patent 2864 in 1886. Windhausen's patent was purchased by J. & E. Hall of Great Britain, who improved it, commencing manufacture about 1890. Hall's carbon dioxide machines saw widespread application on ships, replacing the compressed-air machines theretofore used. Carbon dioxide systems were used universally on British ships into the 1940s, after which they began to be displaced by chlorofluorocarbon refrigerants.[82] In the U.S., carbon dioxide was used successfully beginning in the 1890s for refrigeration and in the 1900s for comfort air cooling. Its principal advocate in the U.S. was the Kroschell Brothers Ice Machine Co., which manufactured systems under patents purchased from the Hungarian Julius Sedlacek.[83]

Sulfur Dioxide

Sulfur dioxide (also known as sulphurous acid, sulphurous anhydride, or anhydrous sulphurous oxide) was proposed as a vapor-compression refrigerant as early as 1869 by A.H. Tait in his U.S. Patent 94,450. Daniel Holden claims that he experimented with sulfur dioxide refrigerating systems about 1870.[84] However, the earliest successful continuous commercial use was by the Swiss Raoul Pierre Pictet, who perfected his machines about 1876. It appears that Pictet was trying to address the various problems of high-pressure ammonia machines when they were operated in the tropics, as well as air leakage into low-pressure ether machines, which rendered them inoperable, and the mechanical imperfections of compressed-air machines. He proposed sulfur dioxide as an ideal refrigerant, having the advantage of low cost and operating pressures that were low enough for warm climates but high enough to prevent entry of air into the system.[85] Pictet obtained British Patent 2727 in 1875 and manufactured his machine through the Societe Genevoise beginning in 1876 and soon after by a successor firm in Paris[86] (Figure 8-39). Pictet's machines were being sold in a number of industrialized countries by the 1880s. They were more popular in Europe than in the U.S. and were used mainly in small- to medium-sized applications. Sulfur dioxide did not reach its heyday until after 1900 when it was increasingly experimented with by those who desired to perfect the electric household refrigerator.

Methyl Chloride

Methyl chloride (also known in early literature as chlormethyl ether) was discovered in 1835 by the French chemists Dumas and Peligot. Methyl chloride was manufactured in Germany after 1874 for use in making dyes.[87] It was apparently used on French battlefields as a "refrigerant"; however, this probably referred to its use as a topical anesthetic for amputation of arms and legs. Camille Vincent of France used methyl chloride as a vapor-compression refrigerant about 1878, receiving British Patent 470 of 1879, using a two-stage compressor. Cassius C. Palmer in the U.S. also perceived of use of methyl chloride at about the same time, as his British Patent 1752 of 1880 specifies the refrigerant, although Palmer seems to have preferred to use the higher boiling point ethyl chloride instead.

Vincent's ideas were advanced by manufacturers Crespin & Marteau and their successor, Douane of Paris, beginning in 1884.[88] The first successful Vincent machine was installed in Tunis, but his early machines were marked with problems. Glycerine was first used as a compressor lubricant; however, it absorbed moisture and clogged the expansion device. The early machines also experienced breakdown of the methyl chloride, and the resulting chlorine compounds played havoc with the machinery. Most of these problems were overcome when an oil called "valvoline" was substituted for the glycerine.[89] The French machines continued to be manufactured and used mainly in Europe into the 1900s.

Figure 8-38 *Advertisement, ammonia gas mask (from* Ice and Refrigeration, *September 1918, ad section, p. 93).*

Figure 8-39 *Raoul Pictet's sulfur dioxide ice-making machine, 1875. A unique feature of Pictet's compressor was the lack of oil or grease: ". . . a very important part is the fact that it is a lubricant. It follows that if the cylinder is water jacketed to promote slight condensation on its interior walls, no oil whatsoever need be fed to the piston" (W.S. Douglas, 1911, "Sulphur dioxide as refrigerating agent,"* Ice and Refrigeration, *vol. 41, October, p. 114) (from* Les Machines a Glace *by Auguste Perret, Paris, 1904, Figure 94).*

Figure 8-40 *Refrigeration by pipeline, or "district refrigeration," became fashionable at the end of the nineteenth century. Central stations were connected to houses, stores, offices, etc., by underground pipe mains carrying chilled brine or ammonia. Such systems were attempted in many cities, such as New York, London, Paris, Boston, Louisville, and Nashville. It is generally acknowledged that the first successful pipeline refrigerating system was installed in Denver, Colorado, in 1889. Another system was installed in St. Louis in 1891. The illustration is of insulated pipes used in a private district system at the Quincy Cold Storage Company, Boston, about 1895. For detailed information about pipeline refrigeration systems, see the reference cited in this chapter (from Pennsylvania Iron Works catalog of 1895, p. 87).*

Figure 8-41 *Machine room of the Colorado Automatic Refrigerating Co. about 1889. This "central station" for the pipeline system used absorption refrigerating machines, and one of its designers was John Starr, first president of the American Society of Refrigerating Engineers (from* Ice and Refrigeration, *vol. 6, June 1894, p. 402).*

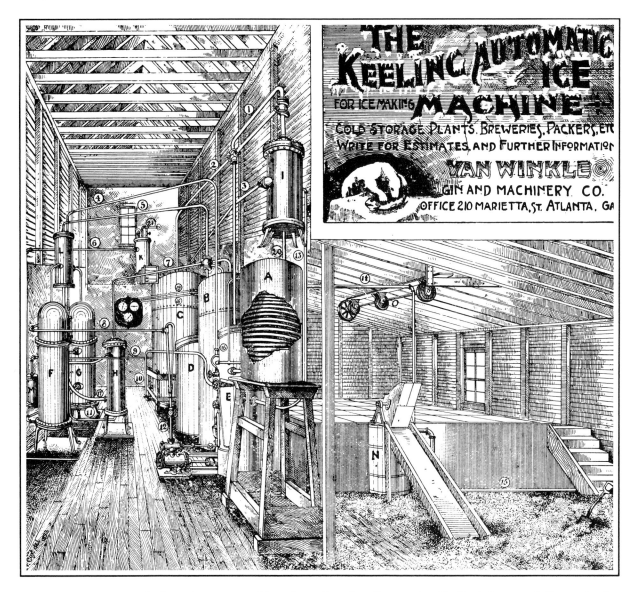

Figure 8-42 *Aqua-ammonia absorption system used in an ice-making plant (from catalog,* Keeling's Improved Absorption Ice Machines, *Atlanta, Georgia, 1892, Van Winkle Gin and Machinery Co.)*

Figure 8-43 *Delivery wagons containing a 15-ton, a 10-ton, and two 100-ton refrigerating machines. Early worries of a lack of business for refrigerating machines due to the saturation of the brewery market proved needless as the ice-making business expanded and new uses for mechanical refrigeration were found (from catalog,* Larsen Ice Machine Co., Inc. Engineers, Manufacturers and Builders of Ice Making and Coldstorage Plants, *Chicago, Illinois, c. 1912).*

Figure 8-44 *The manufacture of ice, sarcastically called "artificial ice" by those engaged in the harvest and sale of natural ice from rivers and lakes, became an important source of business for refrigerating machine companies by the late 1890s. Machine manufacturers strived to produce crystal-clear ice and used imaginative methods to convince potential customers for their machinery (from catalog,* Distilling Water for Ice Making, Bulletin 513, Triumph Ice Machine Co., Cincinnati, Ohio *[no date]).*

Methyl chloride was used sparingly or not at all in the U.S. until after World War I, when it was manufactured and used in some small refrigerating systems.

Ethyl Chloride

Ethyl chloride, like methyl chloride, was used as a topical anesthetic. One reference[90] says that in Switzerland liquid refrigerant was expelled onto an area of skin to be numbed before a medical operation took place. Before that, ethyl chloride was already in use as a refrigerant. Cassius C. Palmer of the U.S. began to study refrigeration in 1867 and was "in business" by 1870. By the 1880s, he began to take out British and U.S. patents, the earliest of which was U.S. Patent 290,600 in 1883 for a refrigerating system for railway cars. All his machines used ethyl chloride.[91] Palmer may have been the first to use a rotary vane compressor for refrigerating purposes. This type of compressor, using glycerine as a lubricant, was a feature of his equipment from the 1890s on. It appears that he was operating his business out of Chicago in 1898.[92] Palmer later advertised as the Railway and Stationery Refrigerating Co. of New York City, and his systems used ethyl chloride under the trade name CLOTHEL. Palmer's system was apparently very successful, as his company and its successor, Clothel Refrigerating

Co., were still advertising in the 1920s. Ethyl chloric (sometimes mixed with ethyl bromide to reduce flammabi ity) was used in some household refrigerators after 1900.

COMMERCIAL AIR AND ABSORPTION CYCLE SYSTEMS

That compressed air could provide cooling when it pe formed work was a phenomenon observed as early as tl eighteenth century.[93] Nothing was pursued beyond obse vation until the next century saw the experimental work Gorrie and Smyth. As previously discussed, neith Gorrie's nor Smyth's machines were commercially deve oped. The Scot, Alexander Carnegie Kirk, developed closed-cycle air refrigeration machine before 1862 as replacement for a Harrison ether vapor-compressic machine that had been installed in a paraffin works England. The management of the works was concerne about the danger of using flammable ether, and Kirk wa asked to find a safe substitute. Influenced by Robe Stirling's air cycle heat engine, Kirk continued constructin experimental closed air cycle machines, some of whic operated satisfactorily for 10 years or more.[94] Frar Windhausen of Germany patented his air cycle machine 1869[95] and Thévenot[96] notes that about 100 of the

Figures 8-45 *Cold storage warehouses, refrigerated with mechanical equipment, became popular in the U.S. by the late 1890s, and soon thereafter in many other countries. Some of these buildings were of elaborate construction, as seen in the Burnham advertisement showing a cold store erected for the World's Columbian Exposition held in Chicago in 1893. (During the exposition, the building was destroyed by fire.) Most of these plants used wrought-iron pipe evaporators. When the ice built up on the pipes to an excessive degree, the refrigeration cycle was reversed, and the compressor discharge of hot gas was used to loosen the ice, which was literally beat off the pipes with wooden clubs (from Burnham ad,* Ice and Refrigeration, *March 1893, p. 220).*

Figures 8-46, 8-47 *Cold storage was popularized at public exhibits, such as this one at the 1904 Louisiana Purchase Exposition, which featured elaborate figures sculpted from butter. Some cold stores operated at low temperatures, allowing meat or fish to be stored in a frozen state (from exhibit scene,* Ice and Refrigeration, *vol. 27, September 1904, p. 84; man with fish,* Ice and Refrigeration, *vol. 91, 1936, p. 281).*

machines were sold. Apparently they were not that successful, being prone to clogging with snow.[97] Paul Giffard of France developed an open-cycle cold air machine about 1870.[98] Giffard experimented for several years, focusing on snow clogging, but was apparently unsuccessful in totally overcoming the problem.[99] Perhaps the first air cycle machine to see extended commercial development was the British machine known as the Bell-Coleman. Wholesale butchers Henry and Joseph Bell of Glasgow wished to pursue the refrigerated transport of fresh meat by ship and con-

sulted with William Thompson (Lord Kelvin) concerning refrigerating machinery. Thompson, in turn, directed them to chemist Joseph Coleman, who studied the Giffard machine and reviewed 100 or so existing patents on cold air machines. Finding no suitable machines, Coleman and the Bells produced a machine of their own design in 1877 under the name Bell-Coleman Mechanical Refrigeration Co. Within two years, perfected machines were installed on board the steamships[100] *Circassia*, for trips to New York, and the *Strathleven*, placed in operation between England and

Figure 8-48 *Editorial cartoons from the trade press illustrate the increasing applications of cold storage and the horror of the new cold storage industry when faced with attempts to restrict them through legislation. Initially there was some opposition to centralized cold storage, the result of some instances of tainted products and the attempts of some to preserve old ways of doing business when faced with new competition (from* Cold, *November 1911, p. 7; January 1911, p. 62; May 1912, p. 155; June 1915, p. 110).*

ustralia.[101] About this time, J. & E. Hall produced an nproved Giffard machine in England.[102] Air cycle refrigerating machines were popular from the 1880s, promoted ainly by British firms, but declined in use by the turn of the ntury as they were displaced on shipboard by smaller, ore efficient carbon dioxide vapor-compression systems.

The absorption-type refrigerating machine initially saw me use after Carré had perfected his aqua-ammonia sysm. During the 1870s and 1880s, Carré's approach was nproved upon by various individuals in different countries; owever, the absorption machine declined in popularity ward the end of the century, displaced by improving apor-compression systems. In fact, the absorption machine as to again see increased use as the century turned. The evelopment of electric power, with its steam-driven plants, rovided a ready source of "exhaust steam" that could be sed to power absorption machines. For a time there was a urry of activity in supplying centrally manufactured refrigation through pipes in city streets (Figures 8-40 and 8-41). oon after, exhaust steam absorption systems were used in ne first cogeneration air-conditioning systems.[103]

HE REFRIGERATION INDUSTRY EGINS TO EXPAND

As the nineteenth century was drawing to a close, refrigation was truly developing into an industry. Numerous rms had been established in various countries to provide echanical refrigerating equipment. Early on, much of eir business came from the beer-brewing industry; hower, the gradual perfection of refrigerating equipment made it more competitive with the natural ice industry, and by the 1890s, ice-making machinery had become a large part of the refrigerating machine companies' business (Figure 8-42). The natural ice industry had promoted a taste for local preservation of food, and the presence of "icebox" household and merchant refrigerators created a demand for refrigerated meat, dairy products, and produce (Figures 8-42 and 8-44). A new cold storage industry arose to provide central storage of refrigerated goods, and this further added to the refrigerating machine companies' sales (Figures 8-45 through 8-51). Unfortunately for the natural ice business, most of the older cold stores converted to mechanical equipment, and the new ones being built to take advantage of the demand that the natural ice merchants had helped create were mechanically equipped. In New York City, two millon tons of natural ice were used in 1890, and by 1905 it was estimated that five million tons of ice were being used; however, three million tons of that total was manufactured ice.[104] Not only was the natural ice business threatened by the introduction of mechanical ice plants, but the entire ice industry, regardless of source, was threatened by the invasion of mechanical refrigerating equipment into the end uses themselves.

> During the last ten years the ice trade of New York City has undergone a very great change. Formerly, hotels required large quantities of ice. All new hotels and many of the old ones now have their own refrigerating and ice making plants and buy no clear ice except for bar and table use. Many office buildings have their own refrigerating plants and pipe ice-cold drinking water to every office. Flats and apartment houses have their own refrigerating plants, refrigerating every family box, pipe ice-cold drinking water to every apartment and use no ice at all in the building.[105]

Ice itself was receiving a bad name as increasing pollution of natural sources caused health and aesthetic problems with natural ice in many places. For example, a story in the *Detroit Tribune* commented:

> For a long time intelligent people have realized that sewage infected ice is rather more than it is cracked up to be. It is probable that many of the summer ailments of the digestive tract are due to the use of villainously impure ice, which is loaded with dormant bacteria. . . . Some of them produce typhoid fever and other filth diseases that frequently end in death. . . . Frozen river water that is contaminated with sewage does not warn the consumer unless the filth is present in large chunks that will not strain through the teeth.[106]

The article went on to say that the consumers' salvation was in the rise of the gas and oil industry that had so polluted the rivers with oily scum, which served as a warning by its presence on the ice that such ice was polluted, even if it looked clean. Such problems gave manufactured ice a bad name as well, especially if the ice was not clear or if it had any odor to it. These devel-

igure 8-49 *Ice-skating rinks, made possible by the application of mechanical refrigation, were constructed in many major cities in the 1890s (from* Ice and efrigeration, *vol. 22, 1902, advertising section, p. 26).*

Figure 8-50 *Refrigerated storage of furs and clothing became another application for mechanical refrigeration. This scene is from the trophy room of the Lincoln Safe Deposit Co. in 1901 (from* Ice and Refrigeration, *vol. 21, October 1901, p. 132).*

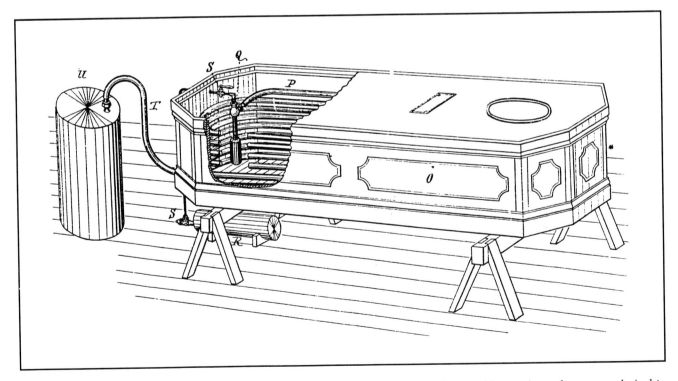

Figure 8-51 *In the 1890s embalming bodies of the deceased was uncommon. To prevent decomposition, various schemes were devised to preserve bodies before burial. At first, ice was used, but with the advent of mechanical refrigeration, inventors turned its application to "corpse cooling." Numerous U.S. patents were issued for corpse coolers after the 1880s, such as this one from U.S. Patent 332,150 of 1885.*

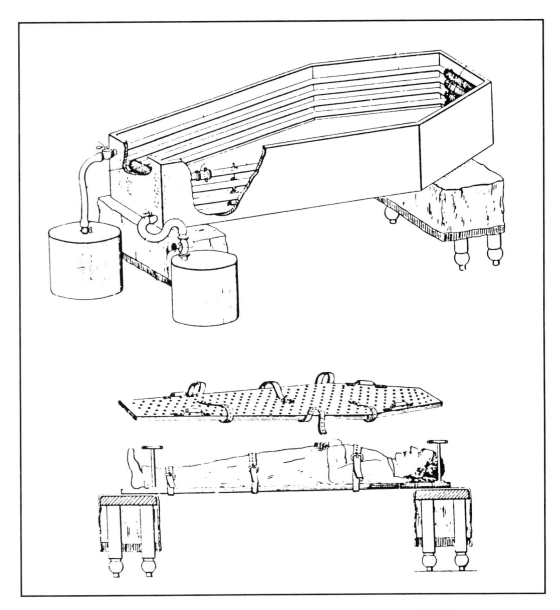

Figure 8-52 *Corpse cooler and preserver, patented October 20, 1885, H.C. Johnson.*

...ments allowed the mechanical refrigeration industry to ...pture more and more of what had been the ice industry's ...omain.

...Numerous other applications were found for mechani-...l refrigeration, some of them quite amusing from ...day's standpoint (Figures 8-52 and 8-53). Many of these ...pplications had previously been supplied by ice. ...nprovements in vapor barriers, insulants, and equip-...ent proceeded rapidly as the end of the century ...pproached. Most of the major scientific theories affecting ...frigeration were firmly established, allowing an indus-...y to develop, so that most of the effort of those engaged ... that industry centered on refining technology and ...pplying those improvements to equipment, thereby ...nproving its efficiency and reducing its cost (Figures 8-54 ...rough 8-70).

The advance of refrigeration from theory to commercial ...pplication was summarized by Auguste Rossi in 1892:

... we see how rapidly after the physical laws and properties of matter began to be better known they received scien-

Figure 8-53 *Advertisement, insulating paper (from* Cold Storage, *unknown date, c. 1900).*

tific as well as practical applications. We see as early as 1835, the first machine producing cold by the evaporation and compression of the vapors of a volatile liquid, soon followed by the air machine based on another principle. For many years these two methods were the only ones resorted to and the only ones to receive improvements. Gradually other principles furnished a new field to inventors; new processes made their appearance, the development of the mechanical arts, of chemistry in all its branches, of metallurgy itself, paving the way to successive improvements in the apparatuses adopted, and the requirements of industry opening new fields of usefulness. From 1835 to our day, each inventor may be said to have contributed a stone to the construction of the ediface which stands now on a firm basis and asserts more and more every day its value and importance by applications in directions least expected.[107]

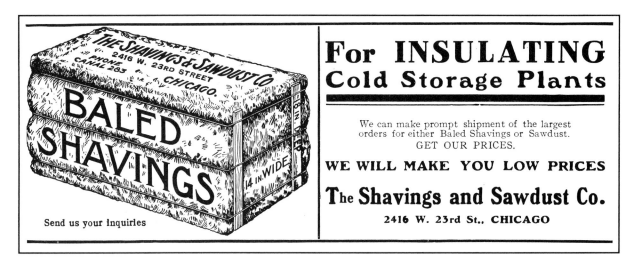

Figure 8-54 *Baled shavings for insulating cold storage plants (from* Ice and Refrigeration, *August 1912, p. 48).*

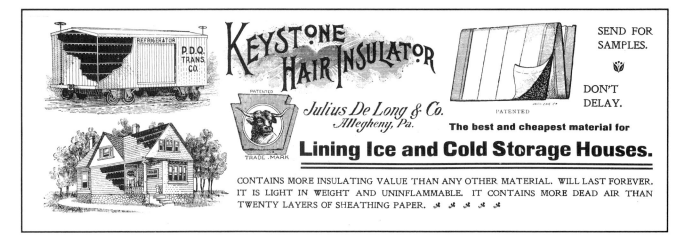

Figure 8-55 *(From* Cold Storage, *1900).*

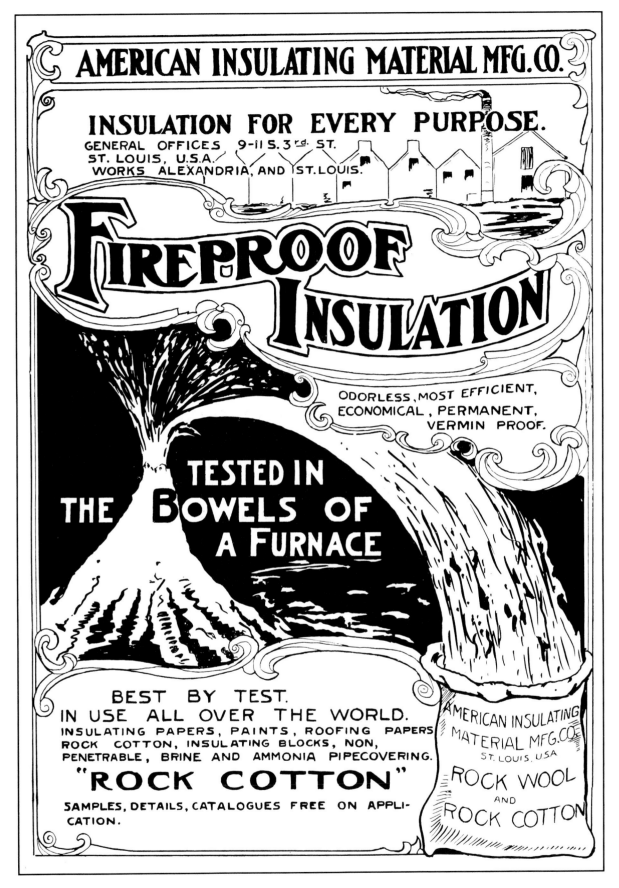

Figure 8-56 *(From* Ice and Refrigeration, *vol. 27, November 1904, advertising section, p. 4).*

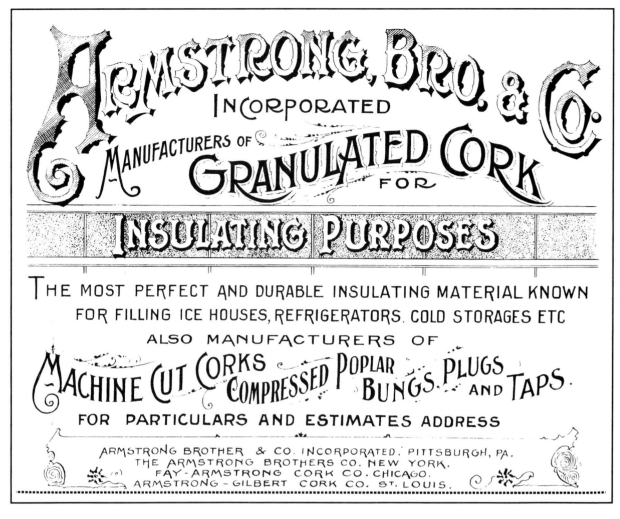

Figure 8-57 *(From* Ice and Refrigeration, *January 1892, p. 58).*

Figure 8-58 *Installing corkboard insulation. The cork was dipped in hot asphalt to provide a vapor barrier and a means of gluing the slabs together (from Cork Insulation Manufacturers Association, photo from* Refrigerating Engineering, *1934).*

Figure 8-59 *Typical open-crankcase, steam-engine-driven ammonia compressor from late 1800s. The machines weighed tens of thousands of pounds, oper-ated at slow speeds, and seemed to last forever if properly cared for. The machine in the photo was made by the De La Vergne Refrigerating Machine Co. (from National Gallery of Canada; photo provided by Smithsonian Institution, Division of Engineering and Industry, Washington, D.C., De La Vergne file).*

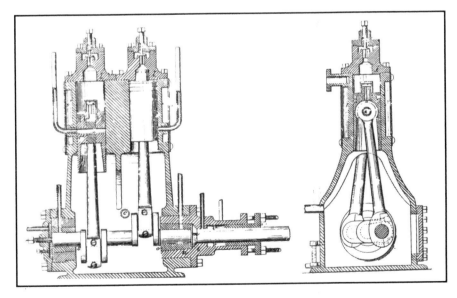

Figure 8-60 *A new way of compressor construction appeared by the turn of the nineteenth century. By enclosing the crankcase and replacing the rod crossheads with piston wrist pins, compressors could be constructed less expensively and operated at higher speeds. The enclosed-crankcase, wrist-pin design seems to have been first proposed by Alexander Ballentine of the U.S. in the 1870s. This drawing is from Ballentine's U.S. Patent 191,638 of 1877. Ballentine's radical design was not easily accepted by the industry, especially after a large Ballentine compressor exploded due to improper casting. Still, the superiority of Ballentine's design caused it to be universally adopted by reciprocating compressor manufacturers later.*

Figure 8-61 *(From* Ice and Refrigeration, *March 1893, p. 263).*

INTERIOR OF ONE OF OUR MAIN ERECTING SHOPS.
Showing Refrigerating Machinery in Progress.

Figures 8-62, 8-63 *Turn-of-the-century "erecting shops" showing assembly of Frick compressors (top view) at Waynesboro, Pennsylvania. The lower view shows assembly of Linde horizontal compressors at the manufacturing plant of the Fred W. Wolf Co. in Chicago (top view from* Cold Storage, *vol. 3, 1900; bottom view from catalog #4,* Linde Ice and Refrigerating Machines, *Chicago, no date (c. 1891).*

Figure 8-64 *(From* Ice and Refrigeration, *March 1923, advertising section, p. 111).*

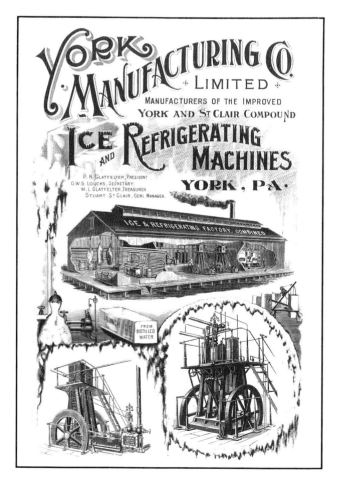

Figure 8-65 *(From* Ice and Refrigeration, *October 1891, inside back cover).*

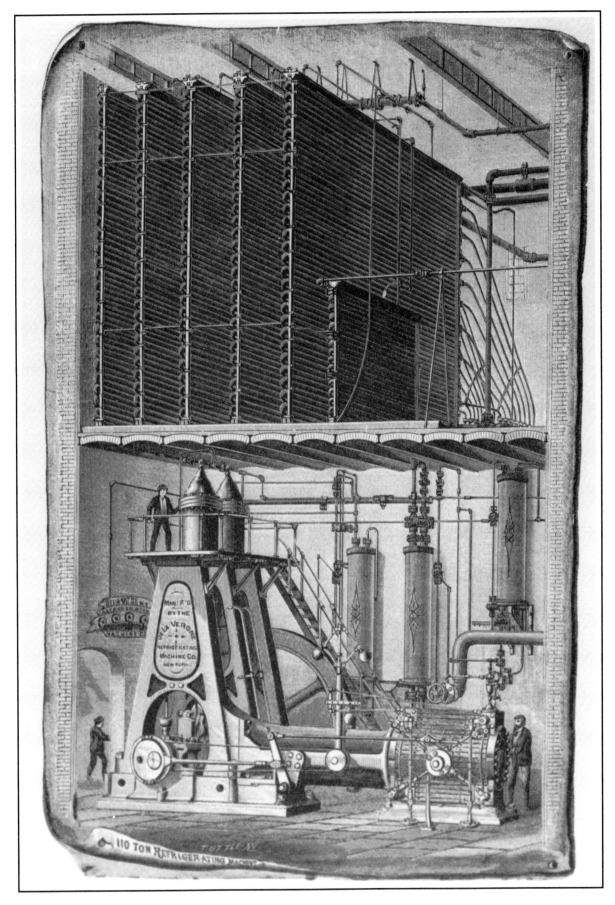

Figure 8-66 *A 110-ton refrigerating machine of 1887. The water-cooled condenser, mounted above the compressor, is of the "atmospheric type" in which the refrigerant was condensed within wrought-iron pipe banks by cooling water that was dispensed from perforated troughs located above each pipe bank. The cooling water dripped from pipe to pipe. Although shell-and-tube, as well as shell-and-coil, heat exchangers were also used in some early refrigerating equipment, the atmospheric type was most popular in the late nineteenth and early twentieth centuries (from catalog,* Mechanical Refrigeration, Processes and Apparatus *of the De La Vergne Refrigerating Machine Co. of New York, 2d ed., 1887).*

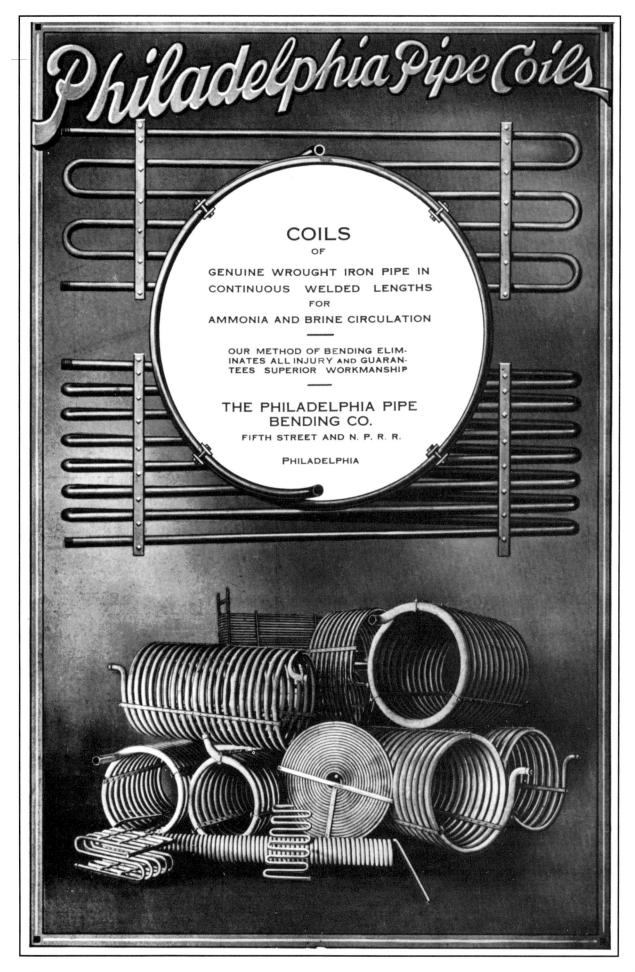

Figure 8-67 *The manufacture of wrought-iron pipe into various configurations was a big business for several decades after the 1880s. The trade magazines of the time featured numerous ads, such as this one (from* Ice and Refrigeration, *September 1919, advertising section, p. 75).*

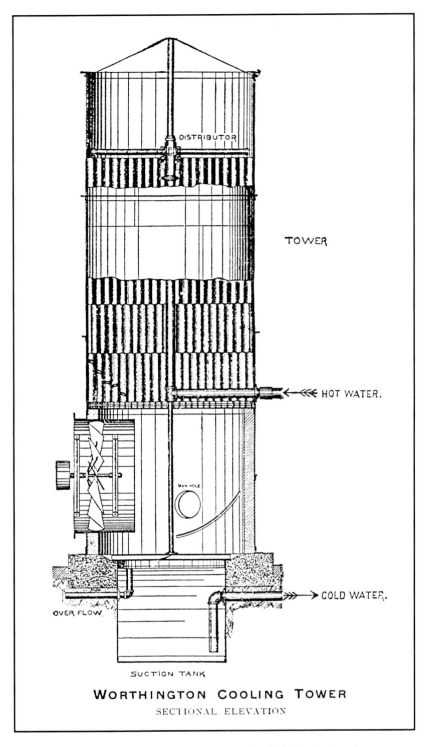

Figure 8-68 *Evaporative cooling towers for condenser water saw use by the 1890s. In fact, there were several manufacturers. The wood "Gradirworks" tower was sold in Europe and the U.S. George Stoecker manufactured one of wood or brick in St. Louis. Henry Worthington seems to have pioneered the use of steel in cooling towers in the 1890s in the U.S. One of his towers "consists of a steel tower enclosing the evaporating surface, which is made up of a vast number of tubular or other sectional elements, arranged in courses, each breaking joints with the next. At the bottom of the tower is a fan, and at the top is a distributing device. The water to be cooled is pumped or allowed to run to the top of the tower, where, in passing through the distributing device, it is evenly spread over the upper course of the evaporating surface, trickling over the successive courses to the cold water tank at the bottom of the tower."*
"A rapid circulation of a large volume of air generated by the fan constantly passes up over the evaporating surface, opposite to the direction of the flow of the water. By breaking joints at each course, the most thorough and efficient contact between water and air is assured, giving the maximum evaporation and consequent cooling effect" ("Annual convention, Southern Ice Exchange," Ice and Refrigeration, March, p. 186) *(from catalog,* The Worthington Cooling Tower, *Henry R. Worthington Hydraulic Works, Brooklyn, New York, 1897).*

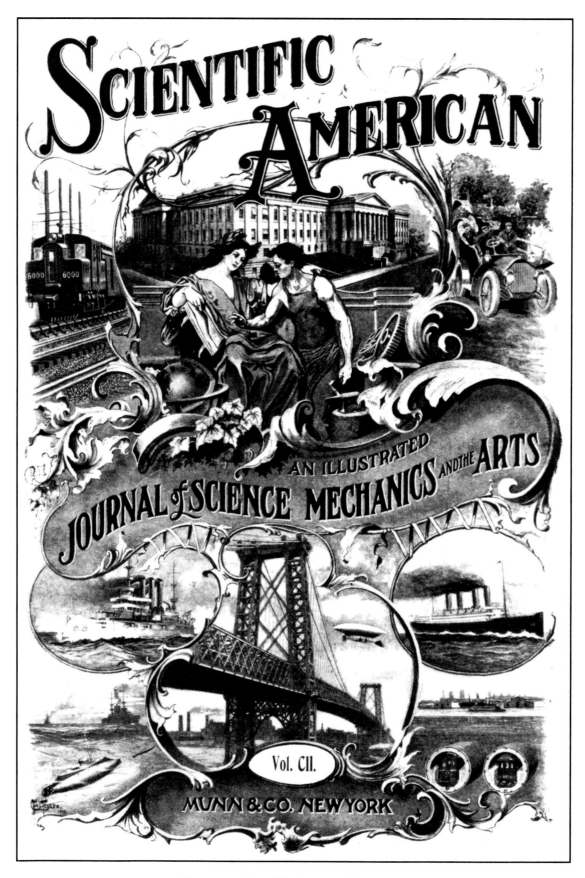

Figure 8-69 Scientific American *illustration.*

THE ENGINEERS ORGANIZE

THE AMERICAN SOCIETY OF HEATING AND VENTILATING ENGINEERS

Factors Leading to ASHVE's Organization

As the art and science of engineering specialties progressed into the twentieth century, engineers began to associate with each other to share their experiences, much as the scientists of the previous two centuries had associated themselves. In the beginning, engineering was divided into broad specialties, which narrowed as the profession advanced. Commenting on this specialization in the United States, Professor John Kinealy noted in 1902:

During the first half of the nineteenth century engineers were classed under two heads: military and civil. The military engineers were those who did work of an engineering character in connection with military operations. They built forts, military roads, bridges and other structures whose primary purpose was for military operations: for facilitating offensive and defensive movements. Military engineers were, as a rule, soldiers first and engineers second. Under the head of civil engineers were classed all those men who had to do with engineering work which did not pertain to military operations. All engineering work of whatever character which was not military was done by the civil engineers.

Towards the middle of the nineteenth century, the civil engineering work became so varied and diversified that engineers were classed under two heads; namely, civil and mechanical engineers. Civil engineers were those who built structures which were at rest, structures such as bridges, buildings, viaducts, sewage systems, water works, etc. Mechanical engineers were those who built machines, objects which were to be for the most part in motion. They built steam engines, machinery for factories, locomotives, etc. The civil engineer had to do largely with that part of mechanics called statics, while the mechanical engineer had to do largely with that part called dynamics. Later, each of these large branches, civil and mechanical engineering, was subdivided into a number of smaller divisions, and the engineer who did work pertaining to one of the smaller divisions was termed an electrical engineer, a sanitary engineer, a steam engineer, a bridge engineer or a structural engineer, depending upon the branch of work in which he was

engaged. Among the latest of the engineers to acquire a distinct title was the heating and ventilating engineer. . . . It is his duty to supply the occupants of buildings with heat to keep their bodies warm during cold weather, and with fresh air for the preservation of their life and health. The heating engineer should be a mechanical engineer. He should know about engines, boilers, steam piping, shafting and other things about which the mechanical engineer must know; and in addition he must have to a certain degree, the kind of knowledge which a physician has, in order to enable him to determine what are the effects of too high or too low a temperature upon the human body, what are the effects of too great or too small an amount of moisture in the air breathed by human beings, and what are the effects of impure air upon the health and well-being of the occupants of rooms. He must know these things not only from the stand-point of the physician, but also from the stand-point of one who, knowing the good or bad effects of certain things, is capable of devising means by which the bad effects may be eliminated and the good effects only preserved"[1] (Figure 9-1).

In the case of heating and ventilating, the specializing that Kinealy spoke of as part of his opening presidential address to the still young American Society of Heating and Ventilating Engineers resulted in the desire to associate in a formal organization in 1894. Interestingly, however, the desire for this new society of engineers was driven as much by anger as it was by idealism!

The Master Steam Fitters

The American Society of Heating and Ventilating Engineers could be said to have had its antecedents in an earlier association, the Master Steam and Hot Water Fitters Association of the United States. The Master Fitters Association held its first annual convention in September 1889 (Figure 9-2). The association, which had received a charter in April, was formed simply because heating and ventilating contractors wanted to protect their interests. John A. Fish, managing director of the Gurney Hot Water Heater Co. of Boston, addressed the first meeting concerning the purpose of the new organization:

Every newspaper contains intelligence of newly-formed associations and as we read, if we think at all, we recognize

One day three men, a lawyer, a doctor, and an engineer, appeared before St. Peter as he stood guarding the Pearly Gates. The first man to step forward was the lawyer. With confidence and assurance he proceeded to deliver an eloquent address, which left St. Peter dazed and bewildered. Before the venerable Saint could recover, the lawyer quickly handed him a writ of mandamus, pushed him aside, and strode through the open portals.

Next came the doctor. With impressive, dignified bearing, he introduced himself: "I am Dr. Brown." St. Peter received him cordially. "I feel I know you, Dr. Brown. Many who preceded you said you sent them here. Welcome to our city."

The engineer, modest and diffident, had been standing in the background. He now stepped forward. "I am looking for a job," he said.

St. Peter wearily shook his head. "I am sorry," he replied, "we have no work here for you. If you want a job you can go to hell."

This response sounded familiar to the engineer and made him feel at home. "Very well," he said. "I have had hell all my life and I guess I can stand it better than others."

St. Peter was puzzled. "Look here, young man, what are you?"

"I am an engineer," was the reply.

"Oh yes," said St. Peter, "do you belong to the Locomotive Brotherhood?"

"No, I am sorry," the engineer responded apologetically. "I am a different kind of engineer."

"I do not understand," said St. Peter. "What on earth do you do?"

The engineer recalled a definition and calmly replied: "I apply mathematical principles to the control of natural forces."

This sounded meaningless to St. Peter, and his temper got the best of him. "Young man," he said, "you can go to hell with your mathematical principles and try your hand on some of the natural forces there."

"That suits me," answered the engineer. "I am always glad to go where there is a tough job to tackle." Whereupon he departed for the Nether Regions.

And it came to pass that strange reports began to reach St. Peter. The celestial citizens who had amused themselves in the past by looking down upon the less fortunate creatures in the Inferno commenced asking for transfers to the other domain. The sounds of agony and suffering were stilled. Many new arrivals, after seeing both places, selected the Nether Regions for their permanent abode. Puzzled, St. Peter sent messengers to visit hell and report back to him. They returned, all excited, and reported to St. Peter.

"That engineer you sent down there," said the messengers, "has completely transformed the place so that you would not know it now. He has harnessed the fiery furnaces for light and power. He has cooled the entire place with artificial refrigeration. He has drained the lakes of brimstone and has filled the air with cool perfumed breezes. He has flung bridges across the bottomless abyss and has bored tunnels through the obsidian cliffs. He has created paved streets, gardens, parks and playgrounds, lakes, rivers, and beautiful waterfalls. That engineer you sent down there has gone to hell and has made of it a realm of happiness, peace, and industry." (From *Ice and Refrigeration*, July 1934, p. 39).

Figure 9-1 *The Engineer—A Parable.*

Figure 9-2 *The first convention of the Master Steam and Hot Water Fitters Association of the United States was held in September 1889 in Chicago. Many of the charter members of the American Society of Heating and Ventilating Engineers were members of the Master Fitters (from* Engineering Review, *July 1905, p. 26).*

Figure 9-3 *The top advertisement is indicative of the competition that the early heating contractors faced from those they felt were incompetent to sell or install heating equipment. One response was to establish trade schools, as shown in the lower illustration. Another response was to band together to fight inept competition, as they did when the Master Steam and Hot Water Fitters Association was formed (from* Heating and Ventilation, *April 1900, p. 17; May 1898, p. 17).*

Figure 9-4 *Hugh J. Barron (1856-1918) is considered the founder of the American Society of Heating and Ventilating Engineers. Angry with the Master Steam and Hot Water Fitters Association's limited discussion of papers presented at its meetings, he and L.H. Hart decided to form a new organization (from* Heating and Ventilation, *July 1898, p. 5).*

that the purpose held primarily in view is the material and not the social or religious advancement of the signers of the roll. So common, indeed, has the formation of business associations become that the social reformers and managers of legislatures now so far recognize them as to appeal to the public in tones of alarm, seeing in each an incipient trust. As I look about me today and see men who have traveled from 100 to 1000 miles to reach this meeting, I have no difficulty in arriving at the conclusion that, although there may be no purpose to form a trust or even a business combination, there are material considerations which call for adjustment. In the few moments which I propose to take I would discuss, suggestively, two points: 1, the establishment and maintenance of confidence among ourselves; 2, the establishment of greater confidence among the public in the professional skill of our craft.[2]

The men who organized the Master Fitters Association were mainly of a practical bent—they were manufacturers,

salesmen, and contractors (Figure 9-3). But the importation from Europe and Great Britain[3] of more sophisticated scientific approaches to the heating and ventilating industry resulted in the evolution of some of the "fitters" into engineering contractors. A review of the meeting reports after 1889 shows that at first much of the energies of the organization were devoted to non-engineering pursuits. In fact the editor of *The Metal Worker* said of the 1891 meeting:

> The objects of the association include protective measures for the trade, and also for the furtherance of technical knowledge concerning steam and hot water heating and pipe fitting. Comparatively little attention has been given to the latter subject so far, but there is every reason to hope that with the increasing strength of the organization the members will realize that the annual gatherings may be made very profitable if the leaders of the trade will undertake to discuss practical heating problems.[4]

About this time, the organization began to expand its interests into standards, and within two years papers dealing with practice began to appear. While some members desired detailed presentations of the developing art and science of heating, it seems that there were many who did not

Hugh Barron's Anger Results in a New Engineering Society

The American Society of Heating and Ventilating Engineers began when Hugh J. Barron, a New York contractor (Figure 9-4), took steps to found it. At the tenth anniversary of the ASHVE, Stewart Jellett related the instances of the Society's founding:

> Until about 1890, the business of heating and ventilating had been largely based on the most ancient rule known to engineers, the rule of thumb. Why a business of such importance and of such magnitude as the heating and ventilation of buildings had not been placed on a more scientific basis many years earlier it is not the purpose of this paper to discuss. I believe it was the stress of competition, the commercial side of the business, that finally forced the recognition of the necessity for more scientific consideration, both in regard to the manufacture of the apparatus used and in its application for regular work.
>
> Many master steam fitters, members of the Master Steam & Hot Water Fitters' National Association which had been organized in 1889, feeling the need of more information regarding the engineering side of their business, introduced the feature of reading papers on questions of interest at the national conventions of their association. As most of those who attend these annual conventions were the men who handled the business matters of their concerns, and not the engineering questions, and as it was their opinion that the conventions were principally for the discussion of business matters, but scant courtesy was given to the reading of these papers, and practically no discussion followed.
>
> I believe the last meeting in which papers of this kind were presented, was that held in New York City, in 1894. At this meeting, papers were presented by Mr. D.M. Nesbit (Figure 9-5) of London, England; Mr. E.P. Bates of Syracuse, N.Y., and Mr. Arthur Walworth, of Boston—all of them able papers, which should have received very careful consideration, but were not given the consideration they merited, and but little discussion followed.

As a result, some of the Master Fitters present at the convention, who were specially interested in the engineering side of their business, became very much disgusted with the manner in which the papers were received. One of them, Mr. Hugh J. Barron, a member of our society, wrote some comments on the papers presented at this meeting, together with a criticism of the action of the Master Steam Fitters' which was published in the *Heating and Ventilation* in the issue of July 15, 1894. The concluding paragraphs of this criticism will, I think, be of interest to our members, and are as follows:

Hugh Barron's comments:

There was one thing conclusively shown by this convention, and that was that engineers are in a decided minority; the majority are more anxious about getting work and money than about the mere art of heating. Imagine any other society in the world inviting men to give them the results of their thoughts, and one gentleman actually coming three thousand miles to do so, and then having a resolution passed that in the future, papers must only take ten minutes to read.

We have lots of time for excursions, but only ten minutes to hear the result of your thoughts.

The facts are that the majority of American Heating and Ventilating Engineers are not members of the Master Steam and Hot Water Fitters' Association, and that a majority of the association are really business men only. These gentlemen cannot appreciate an engineer's feelings in regard to technical matters. It is a pity that there were not at least a thousand present to hear Mr. Nesbit's paper, and to intelligently discuss it, as English Societies of Engineers would discuss a paper presented to them by an American engineer of equal eminence.

The technical side will have to come more to the front at national conventions, the business side being left to the locals, where it belongs, the national convention to be a grand interchange of views, where all designers, constructors, and engineers interested in heating and ventilating can exchange views for the purpose of elevating and ennobling the art which gives them their daily bread.[5]

ugh Barron was known for his outspoken manner. After s death in 1918, his friends recalled that he was ". . . an ishman by birth and had all of the proverbial Irishman's it and spirit. At meetings of the heating engineers' society e members always knew something unusual was coming hen Mr. Barron took the floor. His frankness was equally nphatic, whether in criticism or praise. Mr. Barron considered himself a radical and was prone to take the opposite de in a discussion. One of his remembered hits was made a meeting of heating engineers, when, after he had gone n record as differing pointedly from the view taken by the her speakers, Professor William Kent obtained the floor id said: `Mr. Chairman, I have not always agreed with Mr. arron, but on the matter under consideration, I am happy state that we are for once in a complete accord.' As quick a flash Mr. Barron spoke up: `Mr. Chairman, then I am ndoubtedly wrong!'"[6]

Barron's criticisms had been given to *Heating and entilation* Business Manager Louis Hart (Figure 9-6) for ublication, and Hart discussed with Barron the idea of rming a new organization dedicated to the engineering pects of heating and ventilation. Hart further discussed

Figure 9-5 *English heating engineer David Nesbit was perhaps the first "international member" of the ASHVE. The tepid response of the Master Fitters convention to his paper delivered at its 1894 convention was one of the factors that led to the formation of the ASHVE by several "disgusted" individuals (from* Heating and Ventilation, *January 1899, p. 9).*

the idea with William Mackay (Figure 9-7) and the three men succeeded in generating sufficient interest within three weeks that a meeting of 16 interested individuals held at Hart's office resulted in the following agreement:

We the undersigned, agree to become members of a Society of Heating and Ventilating Engineers, as suggested at the temporary meeting held this date at the office of Heating and Ventilation, 145-146 World Building, New York City. (Signed) Fred P. Smith, Percival H. Seward, Wm. A. Russell, Albert A. Cary, Hugh J. Barron, Wm. Mackay, Albert A. Cryer, Geo. B. Cobb, Thos. Barwick, O.L. Breckenridge, Jas. A. Harding, L.H. Hart, Edward A. Munro, Morris S. King, W.B. Wilkinson, H.M. Swetland.[7]

Smith, Barron, Harding, Mackay, and Carey were appointed to plan the organization, and, after several meetings in Barron's office, they decided on September 10, 1894, as the date for the first general meeting of the new society, to be held at the Broadway Central Hotel in New York City. Charter membership invitations were sent to 157 individuals, and 75 agreed to join.[8]

The Heating Engineers' Charter Meeting

September 10, 1894, was one of the hottest days of that summer, but the heat and humidity (air conditioning still being a novelty at that point) did not prevent those present

Figure 9-6 *Louis H. Hart (1859-1897) was the business manager for the trade magazine* Heating and Ventilation *when Hugh Barron came to him to discuss the limitations of the Master Fitters Association. Hart had been a telegraph operator, state legislator, railroad ticket agent, journalist, and advertising manager for the trade magazine* Electrical World. *Hart, as secretary of the newly formed ASHVE, was apparently responsible for writing the Society's constitution. He died unexpectedly at age 38 in 1897 (from* Heating and Ventilation, *February 1897, p. 31).*

Figure 9-7 *William Mackay of New York helped convince others of the need to form a new engineering society. Mackay became the fourth president of ASHVE in 1897 (from* Domestic Engineering, *January 29, 1898, p. 12).*

from enthusiastically receiving the opening address of Fre[?] P. Smith, who outlined the purposes of the new society:

Gentlemen: The Committee has put me down for what they call an address, but I am not making addresses when the temperature is anything like this, upon the objects, advantages, and policy of the Society of Heating and Ventilating Engineers. We are to have an association, so far as I understand it, for "the promotion of the arts and sciences connected with heating and ventilation, and to encourage good fellowship among its members." Of course there is no use in enlarging much upon these points, for we all understand what is meant by them; still I think if we were to start with that one object, and follow it out conscientiously and to the best of our knowledge and ability, we would do much toward furthering the interests of the heating and ventilating business. I think there is nothing so detrimental to the interests of this business and to the interests of heating and ventilating engineers as the lack of good fellowship among its members. I have often found it to be the case that plans suggested by one engineer would be almost certain to meet with disapprobation by another; that courtesy is not generally extended by one to another, and that it is very frequently the case to find persons praising themselves and their works and belittling their neighbors, letting it be understood that all other devices were failures and extolling the workings of their own systems.

It should be the effort of this society to overcome this feeling among the members of our profession, and by honest, hearty co-operation much could be done toward increasing our income, enhancing the dignity of our business, and elevating the work of the heating and ventilating engineer. As matters stand to-day, good fellowship is a thing unknown among that class of men who call themselves heating and ventilating engineers. No member of a society of architects should say anything derogatory of another member; no member of a society of civil engineers would in any way run down the work of his competitors. They may criticize their engineering work (that is bound to be done in any class of work), and offer plans and suggestions, but they do not go to the extent of saying that their competitors are not competent to do the work, and what applies with other societies should certainly apply with us. . . . Our second object is improvement in the mechanical construction of the various appliances used for heating and ventilating. This is a matter of great importance, in my judgement. Every engineer has worked and planned for new things, and to improve upon what has been done by others in his line, and they are all looking for what we may call "a lead-pipe cinch"—to get something that is different from others and then slap a patent on it, and try to convince the public that nothing else in the world will do the work. If we permit this thing to go on it will surely work to the detriment of the profession. It is only by the united efforts of the members of the society that we may expect to attain that improvement for which we are looking. There is no reason in the world why the society cannot, if properly managed, aid us in raising a high standard of work, and regulate the price we ought to get for our work. What we want is a long, strong pull together, and that is exactly what I meant when I spoke of good fellowship.

We next come to "the maintenance of a high professional standard among heating and ventilating engineers." This does not need explanation. Of course, in the way we are working, made up as we are of a society of engineers, our members will be subdivided into many kinds of engineers. There will be the consulting engineer, who is paid for his professional services; and the contracting engineer, who receives pay for his professional services and a profit on his contract; and the manufacturing engineer, who receives pay for his professional services and a profit on all the goods he sells. We find in the field to-day several classes of incompetents standing ready to be employed in the latter capacity. Would it not be well for all who propose entering this field to prepare themselves especially for it? We can easily have a school for preparation and qualification of such persons, and attendance at such a school for proper Qualification by other means should be the only means by which a man could enter upon his duties as a heating and ventilating engineer. I think this, more than anything else, would tend to a higher professional standard.

"To establish a clearly defined minimum standard of heating and ventilating for all classes of buildings." This is a very important object for our consideration. The idea is this: Massachusetts started out with a compulsory ventilation law. Most of you are aware of this fact, as architects specify "the Massachusetts standard of ventilation" in their plans, and suppose that this is absolute. As a matter of fact there is no standard there and whether or not there are unsatisfactory conditions in the finished work depends largely upon the inspector. They have never formulated any kind of standard. They have had it understood, however, that in schools the standard should be 30 cubic feet per pupil per minute, but further than that they have not gone.

The lack of a definite standard for ventilation in public buildings has very often been the cause of considerable embarrassment. A man may do good work and give entire satisfaction in one district, and go over in to another district and find that he is dealing with a different set of requirements. You will see how easy it is for a man to do first-class work in one place and not come up to the requirements in another under a different inspector, who, while following out the same standard, as he understands it, has a different idea as to how it should be done. To overcome such difficulties as these, every member of our society should do his best to have a universal standard adopted, which shall be definitely known and accepted, in order that every one may be on the same footing.

You can readily see the evil of having instructions so confusing as to lead to work which may be accepted by one man and condemned by another under the same requirements; how annoying that could be, and the necessity that standards should be uniform. . . .

Now, having adopted such a standard, we will want to have all our public buildings ventilated in accordance therewith. Nothing has advanced the work of ventilation in the last three years so rapidly as that rule down in Massachusetts. While architects are all well informed as to their special duties, they are not well informed as to heating and ventilation, and this fact has been brought out more prominently by the requirements of the rule in vogue in Massachusetts than by any other means. The heating and ventilating of a building should be left in the hands of a specialist just as much as should the steam and electric equipment.

"To encourage legislation favorable to the improvement of the arts of heating and ventilation, and to oppose legislation inimical to the business of the engineer." I think I have touched upon that paragraph, and it will not be necessary to add much to it.

The compulsory law in Massachusetts has created a great demand for the services of men skilled in this profession. Down here in New York the demand has not existed to such an extent, but legislation would bring the matter more prominently to the attention of architects and builders.

"The reading, discussion, and publication of professional papers, and the interchange of knowledge and experience among its members." I think it is not necessary to go into that and further at all.

Now, then, there is one other question which comes up in connection with this while judging of the matter of policy, and which I think the society ought to establish. There are architects who think very highly of heating and ventilation, and there are others who have not taken the trouble to go into the matter very thoroughly and have not been talked to about it; and there are many civil engineers who are interested in heating and ventilation. Why not have them join with us in this society? Any man with a technical training and practical experience might be brought into the fold, with good results to all. There are many who already belong to engineering societies. The Society of Mechanical Engineers is large and strong, but ventilation has scarcely been touched upon by that society, and the interests of this profession have not been given the attention and recognition due to them. It is for that reason we are now forming the Society of Heating and Ventilating Engineers[9] (Figures 9-8 through 9-11).

Note that chairman Smith had called the new organization "The Society of Heating and Ventilating Engineers." Although that name had been suggested by the bylaws committee, some were not satisfied with it. Stewart Jellett tells of the discussion of what the Society should be called:

The debate that followed this suggestion was a spirited one. One member objected to the proposed name, and wanted a more definite title, while another thought the name was all right; that other societies might be founded, but they would not count for much, and that the word "THE" in large letters, expressed his idea of what the society was bound to become. Still another member, (our secretary, Mr. Mackay), suggested that the society be called "The International Society of Heating and Ventilating Engineers," inasmuch as foreign engineers had been invited to become members. Mr. Mackay's idea seemed to be to take in the entire world, and prevent infringements, on the general idea expressed by the first member, that we were "The" society, with a capital T.

After a long discussion, the perspiring members reached the conclusion that the heating and ventilating engineering required in America would be a sufficient tax on the society for some years to come, and when Mr. (James) Harding moved, and Mr. Barron seconded the motion, that the society be called "The American Society of Heating and Ventilating Engineers," the motion prevailed.[10]

Hugh Barron, pleased with the birth of the new organization, commented in 1894: "I think the new American Society of Heating and Ventilating Engineers will exercise an excellent influence in our field of effort in various ways. One will be making their plans and specifications so plain and comprehensive that the contractor can figure to a dollar what the work should cost. The second will be to insist that every building that comes under their influence shall be properly ventilated as well as heated; if the engineer is overruled and shouted at he will still insist and again insist, and in a little while he will have his way. The third will be the interchange of knowledge, or rather experience, between engineers of different classes. The consulting engineer will come in contact with the manufacturing engineer,

Figure 9-8 *Charter member Professor John Kinealy, Washingt* *University, St. Louis, Missouri: "In reply to your inquiry, I will say t* *it seems to me that the interests of the members of the American Soci* *of Heating and Ventilation Engineers will be best promoted by encoi* *aging the writing and free discussion, orally or in writing, of papers* *subjects pertaining to heating and ventilation, and the publication a* *preservation of the papers in the transactions of the society. Membi* *engaged in contracting or commercial practice have seldom the desire* *time to write long treatises on any subject, but are usually glad to gi* *to the profession and the world the results of their experiences, in shi* *papers before a society especially interested in the subject discussi* *These short papers often contain the most valuable information and thi* *with the results of scientific investigations, really form the basis of* *books on the subject, and are referred to by those who collect the knoi* *edgement of the subject and put it in convenient book form.*

"It is especially important, therefore, that each member should *encouraged to put his knowledge where it may be used by all the othi* *and the most important work of the society in my opinion is this collei* *ing of individual knowledge and putting it on record for the use of a* (Heating and Ventilation, October 15, 1894, p. 9) *(from* Engineerii Review, *February 1904, p. 16).*

Figure 9-9 *Charter member John Gormly of Philadelphia: "Anotl* *point of advantage to our society would be to have a neat card, with i* *name and address of our society and each member's name and addre.* *sent to the offices of the architects of the United States, and sent yeai* *as their membership changes by death, withdrawal or election. For o* *own office we should have a neat certificate of membership, framed a* *hung conspicuously, to let the world know `we are in it' for business a.* *pleasure and are proud of it"* (Heating and Ventilation, October 1 *1894, p. 8) (from* Engineering Review, *February 1904, p. 3).*

and all will receive pleasure from an interchange of views. Its mission is to secure to society, to the whole world, perfect heating and ventilation. While it cannot reach this high aim, it can approach it; and while it cannot change human nature, its tendency will be to establish a high ethical standard among its members, so that the fact of work being in charge of one of its members will be a guarantee of excellence and of everything that means honest workmanship."[11]

With the election of Syracuse contractor Edward P. Bates as ASHVE's first president (Figures 9-12 and 9-13), the

Society began the difficult task of addressing the needs f engineering standards and accurate equipment data. Th was to be accomplished over the next decades throuj research, first carried out by individuals and corporatioi and later by the Society's own research facility (Figures 9- through 9-16).

In the meantime, the Society continued to grow, ar annual meetings were scheduled at the beginning of ever year. By 1897, a need was felt for meetings at six-mon intervals, so summer meetings were begun that year. The does not seem to be any photographic record surviving

Figure 9-10 *Charter member Harrie Crane of Cincinnati, Ohio: ". . . members will have the opportunity of forming acquaintances, exchanging theories and experiences, and through these associations promulgate a feeling of perfect freedom in consulting one another when in doubt on a subject to the end that the science of heating and ventilation will reach the importance it should in the construction of our homes and public buildings; and to be a member of the American Society of Heating and Ventilating Engineers will be a sufficient guarantee that this branch of the work will receive proper attention"* (Heating and Ventilation, *October 15, 1894, p. 10) (from* Domestic Engineering, *May 28, 1896, p. 18).*

Figure 9-11 *Charter member James Mackay of the American Boiler Co., Chicago: "I would suggest that the object of such a society should be, as far as possible, to embrace all sections of this continent, and it should not be in any sense what might be termed a local organization. I would like to see more charter members enrolled from the West. It is well known that there is more money invested and more men employed in the West than in the East, still a very small proportion of the members of the society are from the West"* (Heating and Ventilation, *November 15, 1894, p. 21) from* Engineering Review, *January 1902, p. 4).*

Society meetings before 1899; however, some of the meetings after that date were visually recorded in the trade journals, and some of the better ones are shown in this chapter (Figures 9-17 through 9-19).

During the several years after its founding, ASHVE went through growing pains as it attempted to form a true identity. Many of the first members became uncomfortable as more and more emphasis was placed on engineering. Commenting on the changing membership at the opening of the fifth annual meeting in 1899, President Wiltsie F. Wolfe noted:

> This society, like others of a technical character, contained at its beginning, members who really were not actively connected within the lines that would properly make them strictly eligible to full membership in such a society, but as

we have progressed and our lines of work have become more clearly defined, many of them, finding the true intent and scope of our work, have withdrawn, and their places have been filled and our membership increased by the addition of others whose work and qualifications bring them into direct touch with the society, and whose connection with it adds to its strength and efficiency. Some old members have withdrawn, feeling, perhaps, that they were not in full accord with the technical and professional spirit that animates our active members. Others, more wisely, I think, have changed their classification and become associate members. Our associate membership could well be extended by the addition of men, who, while not practicing in the engineering lines, are in such sympathy and have such interest in our organization as to impel them to give us the benefit of their efforts and influence. The society as it stands is, therefore, not only improved, as I have previously stated,

Figure 9-12 *Officers, managers, and Council for the American Society of Heating and Ventilating Engineers elected for 1894-1895. Many of those pictured were members of the Master Steam and Hot Water Fitters Association (from* Heating and Ventilation, *January 15, 1895, pp. 12-13).*

W. M. MACKAY, First V.-President.

W. F. WOLFE, Second V.-President.

CHAS. ONDERDONK, Third V.-President.

E. P. BATES, President.

L. H. HART, Secretary.

J. A. GOODRICH, Treasurer.

F. P. SMITH, Chairman B. of M.

Figure 9-13 *Officers, managers, and Council for the American Society of Heating and Ventilating Engineers.*

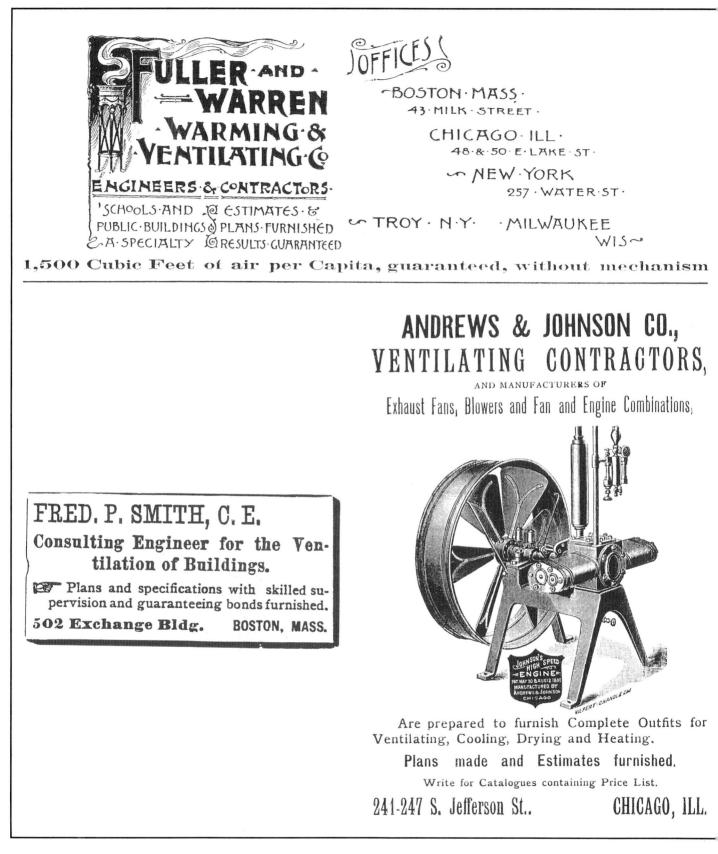

Figure 9-14 *(From* Heating and Ventilation, *January 15, 1894, pp. xvi, xii.)*

Figure 9-15 (*From* Heating and Ventilation, *December 15, 1897, p. xi.*)

Figure 9-16 *The engineering department of the Buffalo Forge Co. in 1902. At the suggestion of the recently hired Willis Carrier (center of top row), Buffalo Forge established a laboratory to conduct equipment tests (from* Engineering Review, *February 1902, p. 23).*

but its standard of scientific attainment is decidedly raised, which is a proper cause for congratulation.[12]

Five years later, charter member Stewart Jellett noted:

It is but natural that a number of men should come into an organization of this kind for commercial reasons, and among those who signed as charter members, and those admitted the first few years were a number of men whose connection with the sale of heating and ventilating apparatus led them to believe that membership in the society would assist them in the sale of their apparatus. It did not take them a very great length of time to disabuse their minds of this idea, and to clearly impress upon them the fact that the commercial side of the business of heating and ventilating was to be left to the Master Steam Fitters' Association, and this fact accounts for the disappearance from the list of members of a large number of names during the first three or four years.[13]

That a more scientific engineering approach was needed was clearly recognized by many. In 1902, then ASHVE President Professor John Kinealy commented:

Without the science, there will be but little progress in the art, and without the art, the science is of little value. Each is dependent upon the other, and the more in harmony they are advanced the more rapid will be the progress in heating and ventilating, and the greater will be the benefit derived by the human race.[14]

Perhaps ASHVE's greatest contribution to scientific engineering was its pursuit of research.

In Pursuit of Research

Some members of ASHVE recognized the need for scientific research from the very beginning of the Society. In fact the Society had hardly begun when one attendant of the organizing meeting, J.J. Wilson, suggested:

I believe it would redound to the benefit of all if a sinking fund were created for the purpose of equipping a laboratory with necessary apparatus, so that standard data could be obtained on the many points of the different systems of heating, and experiments made for the benefit of members. This would also be conductive to giving a high value to such data emanating from this society, and would be beneficial in many ways.[15]

Wilson's suggestion was not cast into reality for some time.

Until 1919, the research activities of the Society were carried on through committees, who without the aid of funds from the Society availed themselves of such facilities as were afforded by educational and governmental laboratories, and the private efforts of engineers and industrial concerns. While these efforts were productive, they were necessarily slow in producing the desired results[16] (Figure 9-20).

The first concrete step leading up to the establishment of the laboratory was taken at the 1917 annual meeting of (ASHVE) . . . when a Committee was appointed to investigate the feasibility of establishing a research fellowship in some university, or a laboratory, in order to more rapidly carry on the needed research.

Heating and Ventilation

NEW YORK.   (Copyright, 1899.)   AUGUST, 1899.   (All rights reserved.)   CHICAGO.

The American Society of Heating and Ventilating Engineers.

Summer Meeting, A. S. H. V. E.

The summer meeting of the American Society of Heating and Ventilating Engineers at Saratoga, July 21 and 22, was duly noticed in our July number, wherein we printed the pa-

this meeting, but at the last moment his calculations were upset.

The secretary announced that at a meeting of the council held June 16, twelve members were elected, whose names were published in HEATING AND VENTILATION for June.

by Mr. McMannis, the reading of the minutes was dispensed with; also the regular order of business customary at the annual meeting.

The first paper read was that by Herman Eisert on "The Calculation of Centrifugal Fans for Ventilating

A GROUP OF MEMBERS AND VISITORS AT THE SUMMER MEETING, A. S. H. V. E.

pers read before the meeting. At the opening the secretary read a letter from President Henry Adams expressing his regret at his inability to be present on account of imperative business engagements; that he had tried for three months to be present at

On motion of Prof. Carpenter, seconded by Mr. James Mackay, it was "resolved that the by-laws be suspended and all business at this meeting be subject to the approval of the society."

On motion of Mr. Wolfe, seconded

Purposes," which was fully reported in HEATING AND VENTILATION last month.

The paper was discussed as follows:

Prof. Carpenter—Mr. Eisert makes a statement which, it seems to me, should be substantiated by considerable data, a!-

Figure 9-17 *The third summer meeting of ASHVE was held at Saratoga Springs, New York, in July 1899. Saratoga was known for its mineral waters and spas, and was typical of the resort areas preferred for these hot weather meetings (from* Heating and Ventilation, *August 1899, p. 1).*

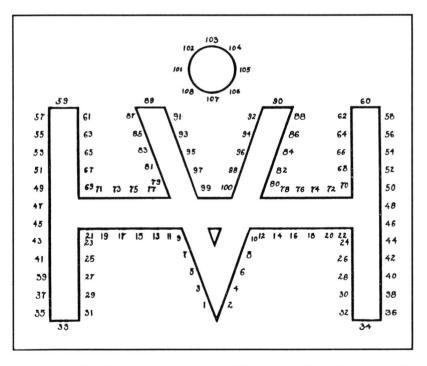

Figure 9-18 *The Chicago summer meeting of 1906 was the first held in air-conditioned quarters. The Auditorium Hotel had just installed a carbon dioxide vapor refrigeration plant to comfort cool two dining rooms and a banquet hall. The seating arrangement was in the form of large crossing letters: H.V.* (from Engineering Review, *August 1906, p. 26).*

Figure 9-19 *The first "talley-ho" coach carrying members and guests to White Fish Bay during the 1907 summer meeting. At the previous summer meeting, President John Kinealy had delivered a toast to the ladies present at the banquet, saying, "Unfortunately for me, the ladies have always gotten me in trouble. Some time ago I responded to a toast similar to this one to-night. It was my intention to say `our wives and sweethearts, may the one always be the other,' but, alas, I made a horrible mistake and said, `may the one never meet the other.'*

"The ladies are a great help to us at our meetings. Those that attend the meetings help by keeping their husbands from staying out at night. Those that stay at home help by allowing their husbands to attend. The Chicago ladies have helped us a great deal at this meeting, and especially in attending this function (the banquet), which is the first occasion of its kind at which the ladies have ever honored us" (Engineering Review, *August 1906, p. 28) (from* Engineering Review, *August 1907, p. 12).*

n 1918, the Committee reported:

> There is no question . . . that the heating and ventilating industry is greatly in need of specific determinations bearing upon the co-ordination and standardization of the practices of this art and the ASHVE is the proper organization, not only to perform some of this work but to assume the direction and encouragement of such of this work as should properly be done by others.

In 1919, the Committee on Research reported a plan of action, which was approved by the Society, and the Research Bureau of the American Society of Heating and Ventilating Engineers opened in August 1919 in the Pittsburgh, Pennsylvania, station of the United States Bureau of Mines, under the direction of John R. Allen.[17] The Research Bureau commenced upon an ever-increasing program with such success that one ASHVE member said in 1931:

> The results which have already been attained indicate the great importance of this line of study and investigation. Progress has already been made in standardizing the condi-

tions of the processes of heating and ventilation. The determination of efficiency of various appliances has already laid the foundation for the future development of the art of heating and ventilation upon defined systems by the use of ascertained methods and reliable apparatus. The work of the Society and of heating engineers in general has thus advanced along lines increasingly directed by accumulated experience, test, and information . . .[18] (Figures 9-21 through 9-24).

Early ASHVE Publications and Displays

From the very beginning, ASHVE published Society business, results of research, and reports of current engineering practice. The official organ for this information was the *Transactions of the American Society of Heating and Ventilating Engineers* beginning in 1895. Much of the material appearing in the *Transactions* also was published in the U.S. trade journals, such as *Heating and Ventilation* and its successor *Engineering Review*, from 1894 to 1912. Material also appeared in *The Metal Worker* and, after its founding by

Figure 9-20 *Before the establishment of the ASHVE research lab, tests were conducted privately. Shown is a test apparatus for establishing steam condensation rates (top view) and for testing cast-iron heating surfaces used in fan-type heating systems. The latter equipment was provided by the American Radiator Co. and the tests were reported before the ASHVE meeting of 1903 by Professor Rolla Carpenter (from* Heating and Ventilation, *January 1900, p. 8; and* Engineering Review, *February 1903, p. 6).*

Figure 9-21 *The unfinished laboratory of the newly established ASHVE research bureau in 1919 at the United States Bureau of Mines, Pittsburgh, Pennsylvania (from* Heating and Ventilating Magazine, *March 1919, p. 56).*

ome ASHVE members in 1904, *Heating and Ventilating.*[19] he *Transactions* were deemed sufficient until 1915 when he *Journal of the American Society of Heating and Ventilating ngineers* appeared to supplement the *Transactions.* In 1929, SHVE decided to discontinue the *ASHVE Journal* and utize the new trade journal *Heating, Piping and Air onditioning* as its official organ for Society business until its 959 merger with the American Society of Refrigerating ngineers. Meanwhile, the *Transactions* continued to be ublished.

A "Publications subcommittee of the Research Bureau ommittee" had suggested in 1917 that the Society publish n engineering handbook, to be written by various expert nembers. Such a handbook could be used by technical chools, and the profit on its sale would provide funds for ne Society's research effort. Nothing resulted from this uggestion, but by 1921 the Research Bureau was in dire eed of funds, and the handbook idea was resurrected and "Guide Publication Committee" was established. The first dition of *The ASHVE Guide,* containing 208 pages, was ublished in 1922.[20]

The purely commercial side of heating and ventilating vas not abandoned, however. An example of this can be een in the pursuit of public advertisement through equip- nent displays, which began as early at 1899. In that year, SHVE member Wiltsie Wolfe reported that he had secured pace for displays in France:

I esteem it an honor to be permitted to appear before this Society and to announce that the science of warming and ventilating has reached such a point of official recognition that an especial department has been devoted to this branch

Figure 9-22 *Margaret Ingels was a staff engineer at the ASHVE Research Bureau from 1921 to 1927. Ingels was apparently the first woman engineer to join the ASHVE, and rose to prominence in the industry with her later work in air conditioning as an associate of Willis Carrier (from* Sheet Metal Worker, *April 4, 1930, p. 193).*

Figure 9-23 *Ladies in attendance at the 1916 summer meeting of the ASHVE in Detroit. When the Society was founded, the very first meetings were attended by the men only, but they soon began to bring their wives and organized activities to be attended by them (from* Heating and Ventilating Magazine, *August 1916, p. 42).*

Figure 9-24 *The heating engineers show their patriotism at the ASHVE annual meeting, Hotel Astor, New York, 1818 (from* Heating and Ventilating Magazine, *February 1918, p. 33).*

in the Paris exposition of 1900. To be sure, the space allotted is very small, being in its entirety 2253 square feet, and sub-divided by several passageways, leaving a clear floor space of only 1385 square feet. Added thereto, there is approximately 1000 square feet of wall surface which can be utilized.

Wolfe then listed the seven classes of the group and the various items in each class.

From this you will realize how difficult it will be to make a representative and typical showing as to the real advancement made in this line. However, small as the allotted space is, it shows progress in the art, and I congratulate you as a Society, and each member individually, fully believing that you and they have helped to do their part in bringing this profession to the world's notice.

This being really the first opportunity ever afforded American manufacturers and engineers to exhibit to the world the progress that has been made in the science, the art and the manufacturer, within the United States, in the several branches of warming and ventilation, the exhibits at Paris in 1900 should be characteristic and typical to the highest degree.[21]

THE AMERICAN SOCIETY OF REFRIGERATING ENGINEERS

Like those who formed an organization for heating and ventilating engineers, the refrigeration engineers felt a need to have their own association. In some ways the birth of the refrigerating engineers' organization was similar to that of the heating and ventilating engineers. Existing organizations ceased to meet the needs of those increasingly specialized in refrigeration. In the U.S., the only engineering organization suitable for refrigerating engineers was the American Society of Mechanical Engineers, where refrigerating engineers "had been in a huddle in some corner discussing their problems." There were also regional trade organizations for the ice business, the largest being the Southern Ice Exchange, where some engineering papers were presented at its meetings. Many of the engineers were also manufacturers and had just formed the Ice Machine Builders Association of the United States in 1903.[22] The

early minutes of this organization show that engineering matters were clearly important to them, as well as the usual business matters.[23]

Unlike ASHVE, where the inspiration for an engineers' organization resulted from one dissatisfied individual, Hugh Barron, inspiring another, Louis Hart, the refrigerating engineers were organized because one person acted directly. But like ASHVE's Louis Hart, the founder of the American Society of Refrigerating Engineers was associated with an industry trade journal. By 1904, William H. Ross (Figure 9-26), in the employ of the *Cold Storage and Ice Trade Journal*,[24] had conceived the idea of forming an association for refrigerating engineers.[25] The American Society of Refrigerating Engineers was officially organized December 5, 1904, and its first official meeting was held December 4-5, 1905, in New York at the "chambers" of the American Society of Mechanical Engineers.[26]

Karl Wegeman, editor of *Cold Storage and Ice Trade Journal*, noted:

The first general meeting of The American Society of Refrigerating Engineers was a most agreeable surprise to everybody, including even the officers and founders. The attendance was much greater than was expected for a first meeting of a new organization, a very large percentage of the members being present. This in itself was sufficiently gratifying, but of even more importance was the fact that the two days' session was brimful of discussions on scientific, theoretical and practical refrigeration, which will certainly be of vast benefit to the industry. Nor was this first meeting indicative of an enthusiasm or earnestness of purpose which may be shortlived. It gave promise of being the first of many annual meetings which will become the guide of the student and the operating engineer in the science of maintaining temperatures below that of the atmosphere. There was an honest ring to the papers and discussions which betokened the purpose of America's foremost experts on refrigeration to get down to facts regardless of anybody's pet theories or interests, but it was also evident that this search for Truth will be fostered without malice or prejudice. In a word, it was an ideal meeting of professional men, gathered together for the promotion of a common purpose in the general interest without selfish purpose or animus[27] (Figures 9-27 and 9-28).

COLD STORAGE AND ICE TRADE JOURNAL

| COLD STORAGE, Vol. XIV., No. 6. | NEW YORK, DECEMBER, 1905. | ICE TRADE JOURNAL, Vol. XXX., No. 6. |

THE REFRIGERATING ENGINEERS MEET

Figure 9-25

Figure 9-26 *The founder of the American Society of Refrigerating Engineers, William H. Ross. Ross was secretary of the organization from 1905 to 1927 (from* Cold Storage and Ice Trade Journal, *December 1905, p. 32).*

Figure 9-27 *John E. Starr (1861-1931), a New York consulting engineer, was elected the first president of the American Society of Refrigerating Engineers in 1904 (from* Ice and Refrigeration, *January 1905, p. 39).*

Charter member Henry Torrance recalled:

that A.S.M.E. members of say 1910 were struck with the way refrigerating engineers got up and said what they had to say without beating around the bush. He also reports that Thomas Shipley, who as president maintained a spirit of fair

play in the general discussion, used to announce as an author concluded his paper, "Fellows, you've heard the paper—are you going to let this fellow get away with it?"

. . . some of the old time members were guilty of lack of information . . . even . . . stupidity. They argued hotly about various matters which could have been settled by referring to existing data, and looked up the data later!

Professor (Denton) Jacobus' role in the Society's first years was to tone down rough talk, polish up papers, and elevate the proceeding in general. . . . And . . . Theodore Vilter, popular because of his humour and good nature, brought life and good fellowship to the ASRE sessions. He was the receiver of many a jest as to where on earth was Milwaukee and what was its leading product[28] (Figures 9-29 through 9-33).

ASRE Publications and Displays

The American Society of Refrigerating Engineers bega publishing the papers read at its meetings right away in th *Transactions of the American Society of Refrigerating Enginee* beginning in 1905.

By 1913 publication of this volume had fallen behind schedule, in fact the 1909 book went into the mail in September, 1912. Reason for this slowness was a lack of funds, since increasing membership had disproportionately increased the cost of running the office. A special committee studied solutions to the problem and a bi-monthly (*Journal of the American Society of Refrigerating Engineers*) was inaugurated in November, 1914, which satisfied many needs besides the financial: it gave the members more frequent touch with the Society and the industry, it provided a means of publishing technical material other than that presented at annual meetings, and it could be used to publicize papers from the local sections, which the Society had hoped to organize within a short time. By 1922, the Society again felt there was need for a change, this time to a monthly publication the size of standard technical and trade magazines. . . .[29]

The result was *Refrigerating Engineering*, which was pub lished from 1922 to 1959.

Refrigerating equipment had been displayed by variou manufacturers at the various "world's fairs" as early as th 1860s. However, the first international exposition devote exclusively to refrigeration was not held until 1913 i Chicago, Illinois, in conjunction with the third internation Congress of Refrigeration[30] (see Figure XIII, color section).

The "Standard Ton" Question

Despite sometimes outwardly raucous meetings, th members of the ASRE did have a serious side. Probably th most important cooperative work done by the ASRE mem bers in the early years of the Society was their effort to sta dardize machine ratings. "The first technical work done b the society was the appointment of a committee of five t work with committees of other engineering bodies to settl upon some standard unit of refrigeration capacity."[31]

The lack of a universal standard for a rating unit fo refrigerating machines caused problems for many year This stemmed from the fact that refrigerating machines ha come to be cataloged and sold by capacity linked to a equivalent of ice. Ice had been sold by the pound or tor

The Refrigerating Engineers in Session, President Parsons Has the Floor and Vice-President Starr Backs Him Up.

Figure 9-28 *Editorial cartoon (from* The New York World, *December 10, 1905, and reprinted in* Ice and Refrigeration, *December 1905, p. 297).*

nd it was logical to sell refrigerating machines by their bility to replace or make ice and to directly rate them in erms of the equivalent amount of ice they would replace. Thus large refrigerating machines were rated in terms of ons of ice rather than by heat units as is now common. Because there was no standard definition of how to rate the machines, games could and were played with the ratings of the machines. One company would try to beat another with ts machine rating in tons, even though a competing machine with a lower capacity might in truth have equal or higher capacity. "The business of rating was taken more eriously than it is now, for purchase specifications were not so closely drawn, and the man with a 100 ton machine might be beaten by his competitor with an 80 ton job."[32] The situation seemed to reach its peak in the 1890s, with several companies trying to outdo the other by advertising that they had "the largest refrigerating machine in the world." The American Society of Mechanical Engineers had a committee to define a "standard ton" as early as 1893, but it seems that the effort was given impetus after the ASRE

was established.[33] A flurry of activity ensued, with suggestions and criticisms scorching the pages of the trade publications. Overcoming corporate suspicion, manufacturers agreed to conduct tests at the plant of the York Ice Machinery Co. in 1903[34] (Figure 9-33). The engineers were reasonably successful during the next years, and the rating controversy subsided.

Both the American Society of Heating and Ventilating Engineers and the American Society of Refrigerating Engineers continued to grow and prosper after their founding. Perhaps this early growth was due to the spirit of progress that seemed to be instilled in the early members. This was perhaps best summarized by *Refrigerating Engineering* editor David Fiske in 1934:

> It seems to be the job of the engineer to use all the theory he can get and if he cannot get any—to go right ahead without it. Repeatedly applications appear before the principles they express. Theory is merely a tool. Science proves nothing in itself. It exists merely to help you do what you want to do.[35]

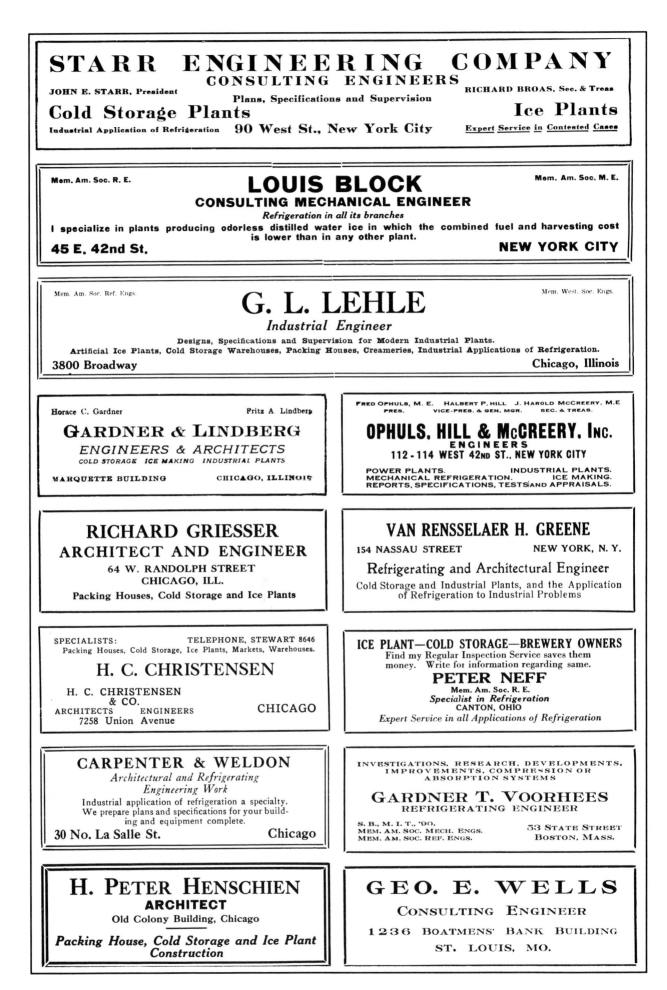

Figure 9-29 (*From* Ice and Refrigeration, *September 1919, p. 69.*)

Figure 9-30 *Refrigerating engineer and manufacturer John De La Vergne was known for his sense of humor, which can be seen in engineer Louis Block's reminiscence of a dinner given in celebration of the sale of the 100th refrigerating plant by the De La Vergne Refrigerating Machine Co. in 1887: "The host of the evening was attired in the superb costume of a Polar Bear, en train, with flashing icicles and boxing gloves. He looked entirely frozen, as is his wont and main characteristic, and whenever he found occasion to use his handkerchief, a sweet yet subdued odor of Rimmel's double extract of anhydrous ammonia filled the lambent air of the banquet hall. He moved among his guests with that air of perfect repose, which is only found among the dwellers on latitudes of a very low thermometer" (L. Block, 1916, "Recollections of a quarter-century experience,"* Ice and Refrigeration, *November, p. 146) (from:* Ice and Refrigeration, *June 1896, p. 387).*

Figure 9-31 *ASRE banquet at the Hotel Victoria, New York, December 4, 1911. "The members of this new society were divided into two sections. One section known as the `pencil pushers' or `blue stockings,' and the other as the `pig irons' or `roughnecks.' For the first 10 years, members would come to the meetings just to hear these two sections fight, and I can say that we used to have battles royal; but out of these battles grew the industry as we know it today. I do not believe that we could have made the progress we did without the kind of men we had at that time. All pioneering is done by hard fighting men. The printed transactions of the Society indicate that the pencil pushers and roughnecks were equally skilled when it came to discussion following the papers" (Helen H. Peffer, 1940, "Early annual meetings,"* Refrigerating Engineering, *January, p. 12) (from* Ice and Refrigeration, *January 1912, p. 16).*

Figure 9-32 *Many of the early banquets were held in interesting places or had imaginative themes. At the December 1913 ASRE meeting in New York, members gathered dressed in butchers' aprons for an "old fashioned beefsteak dinner" at Healy's restaurant (from* Ice and Refrigeration, *January 1914, p. 5).*

Figure 9-33 *Engineering drafting room, 1890s, at the offices of the refrigerating machine manufacturer Fred W. Wolf Co. in Chicago (from* Linde Ice and Refrigerating Machines, *catalog #4, Fred W. Wolf Co., Chicago, Illinois, no date).*

Figure 9-34 *Test apparatus—York Ice Machinery Co.—for standard ton determination (from* Ice and Refrigeration, *August 1904, p. 37).*

ELECTRIC POWER CHANGES THE INDUSTRY

Until the late 1800s, the heating, ventilating, and refrigerating industries had no choice but to use heat-type engines for any motive power required. Toward the end of the century, there was some experimentation with oil and gas engines; however, most ventilating fans and refrigerating compressors were driven by steam engines, usually specially constructed for the purpose by the fan or compressor manufacturer. By the turn of the nineteenth century, steam engines were quite reliable if properly cared for. Unfortunately, care necessitated that the engine be tended by a skilled mechanic, and the expense involved thus restricted use of mechanical ventilation and refrigeration to commercial enterprises large enough to afford the mechanic. However, an event took place in the late nineteenth century that was to result in a democratization of our industries. The introduction of electric power distributed through wires to homes, factories, and stores began in 1879, and this process accelerated in the early 1890s as alternating current polyphase distribution systems were adopted throughout the world.[1] Although many electrical pioneers had developed some of the separate aspects of alternating current, it was Nikola Tesla who envisioned the complete distribution system and all of its components. Tesla recounted that "the idea came like a lightning flash. In an instant I saw it all, and I drew with a stick on the sand the diagrams which were illustrated in my fundamental patents of May, 1888. . . . In the very moment I became conscious of it I saw it fully developed and perfected"[2] (Figure 10-1).

Concurrent with distribution came development of electric motors. Suddenly there was an alternative to steam engines. The electric motor was easily controlled, did not need the continual care of a mechanic, required less floor space, was less expensive, and where the boiler also supplied heating, the boiler could be smaller or eliminated if central steam distribution was available.

THE ELECTRIC MOTOR

The application of the electric motor did not occur overnight, and it was several decades before motors would completely displace steam engines. First, steam engines were continually improved. The introduction of lower-cost high-speed engines, such as those of Porter-Allen and Armington & Sims in the U.S., helped keep electric motors at bay in some applications.[3]

Second, it took some time for electric power to be widely available and especially to be usable at the site of application. Although industrial areas soon had access to electric power distribution of sufficient capacity to meet the high-current demands of electric motors, such was not the case outside industrial areas, where the earliest need for electricity was for incandescent lighting. The electric service provided to homes and stores was neither large enough for motors nor was there any great incentive for power companies to beef up the service, considering that the demand for high-cost mechanical equipment was small.

Third, electric motors themselves were not entirely suitable at first and had to go through a period of development. Their evolution[4] at first seemed to be hampered by the fact that motor patents of Nikola Tesla and others restricted development. "The commercial situation was made very complicated by the uncertainty of the patent situation and a good many concerns in England and America waited many years until the fundamental patents had expired before embarking upon the manufacture of polyphase induction motors."[5] The motors themselves were not entirely reliable at first. Commenting on three-phase motors available in 1894, Charles Steinmetz said:

> If we survey the numerous polyphase induction motors shown at the Chicago Exhibition, we find that all of them (with the exception of a few small three phase motors of the General Electric Co. of 5 to 15 hp) share in having all of the following defects: low starting torque, and, in consequence thereof, abnormal current when starting with full load torque; and, in some cases, complete inability to start against full load torque; high self induction and consequent serious phase-lag; great drop in speed with load, and stalling with overload; all these being properties which, since they can be avoided, must be characterized as faults in design.[6]

Electric motors thus made only slow inroads into the domain of the steam engine. For example, a 1902 survey of 787 large refrigerating plants that appeared in the trade publication *Ice and Refrigeration* showed that 1,447 machines

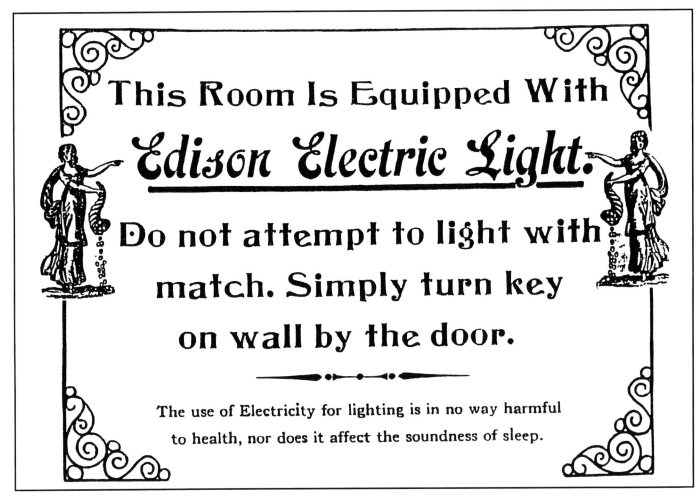

Figure 10-1 *From ASHRAE Centennial Collection.*

were steam engine driven while only 85 were operated by electric motors.[7] One interesting solution to the lack of universal distribution of electric power and of reliable electric motors was to take advantage of the widespread availability in cities of pressurized water systems to drive various types of "water motors" applied to small machines (Figures 10-2 and 10-3). Electric motor design faults were gradually eliminated, so that by 1930, one electrical engineer commented: "But no motor approaches in simplicity and robustness the polyphase squirrel cage induction motor and it has become by far the most widely employed of all types of electric motors."[8]

Although AC induction motors saw increasing use, large ventilating fans and refrigerating systems were operated by steam engines until about 1920. By then electrical engineers had developed synchronous motors with sufficient starting and pull-in torque so that the use of heat engines declined rapidly after that date.[9]

As often seen, the push-pull of development and demand thus affected the heating, ventilating, and refrigerating industry. The progression of the development of the electric motor came at the same time that comfort control and food preservation systems were seeing widespread development and application. Indeed, the growing demand for smaller, reliable systems encouraged electric motor development, while the motor developments made such systems more marketable, creating more demand.

There is no doubt that the small class of refrigeration owes its great progress, if not its very being, to the huge strides made in the production of small motive power, instantaneously applied, . . . which form such a contrast to the clumsy and dirty steam engine and boiler of 20 years ago.[10]

Latter-year improvements have so enhanced the efficiency of small sizes (of refrigerating machines) that the demand has been continually augmented, with the natural result of turning to the electric motor as the most convenient, simple and economical driving power.[11]

At first, the lack of satisfactory single-phase electric motors allowed the polyphase induction motor to move into various industrial uses.[12] While polyphase motors were usable for commercial refrigerating plants, the lack of polyphase residential service restricted any attempted use of refrigeration in the home. The 1880s did see the beginnings of single-phase motor development, and by 1900, the three most commonly used motors in refrigeration, heating, and ventilation had been invented.[13] Systems requiring low starting torque, such as small fans, were able to use the "split-phase" induction motor. The high starting torque capacitor-start induction motor was also invented during this time; however, its commercial use was stalled until the development of inexpensive electrolytic capacitors in the late 1920s.[14] The repulsion-start induction motor had been invented, and it would be this type of motor that would be most often applied to refrig

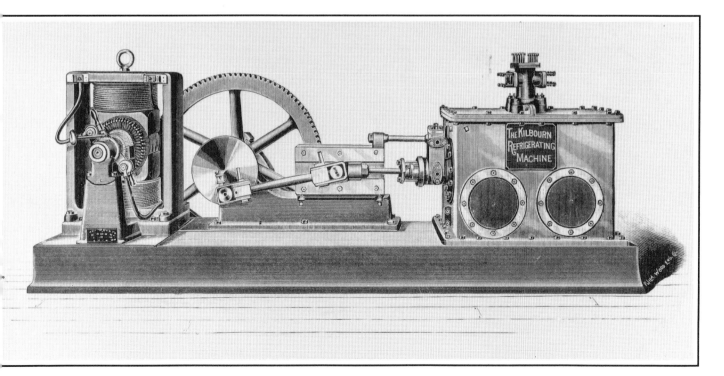

Figure 10-2 *At the turn of the century, widespread use of small refrigerating machines was hindered by lack of an inexpensive driving mechanism that could be left unattended. Typically small steam engines were used as shown, driving duplex compressors manufactured in 1899. Electric motors were supplied when they became available as a manufactured product, but, as this photo of an 1895 electric-driven condensing unit shows, the early motors were of crude construction (from the* Victor Ice and Refrigerating Machines, *1899, Stilwell-Bierce & Smith-Vaile Co., Dayton, Ohio, and from* Ice and Refrigeration, *August 1895, p. 88).*

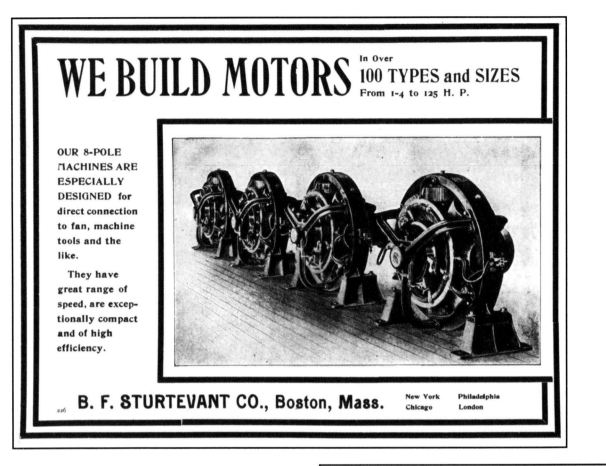

SEYMOUR PATENT PARABOLIC WATER MOTOR.

Figure 10-3 *Use of electric motors progressed at a slow pace due to unreliability and lack of suitable electric service. Some early small systems used motors powered by pressurized city water. Such "water motors" were even used to power small table fans (from* Engineering Review, *February 1902, p. xxi, and May 1907, p. xxxvii; and* Heating and Ventilation, *June 1897, p. xvi).*

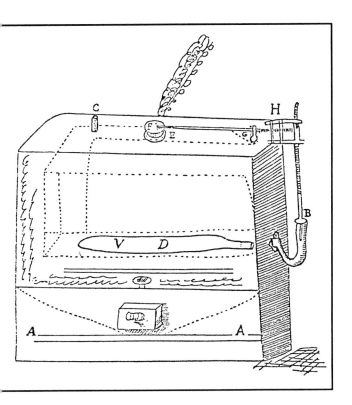

gure 10-4 *Drebbel's thermostat, early 17th century (from llington/Roberts).*

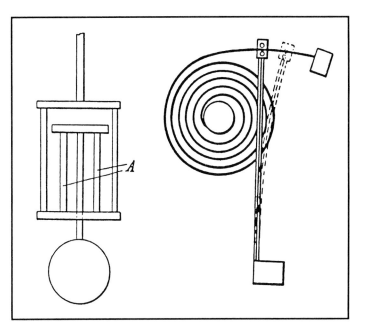

Figure 10-5 *Harrison bimetal devices (from Ramsey, 1946).*

ating systems of less than two horsepower until it was upplanted by the capacitor-start motor in the 1930s.[15] The uccessful development of the repulsion-start motor was eemed significant enough by the Franklin Institute in)02 that it gave its Edward Longstreth Medal of Merit to te Wagner Electric Company. The medal subcommittee ncluded that "the Wagner Electric Co. has developed a ractical single-phase motor which has given satisfactory ervice in commercial use."[16] Small motors soon saw such emand that the General Electric Company's fractional orsepower motor output increased every year from 1902) 1933.[17]

Perhaps the greatest impact of electricity on the heating td ventilation industry during the early twentieth century as in the area of automatic control.

ONTROLS AND AUTOMATION

arly Developments in Automatic Control f Heating

Automatic control of equipment operation as well as eating and ventilating had been attempted on a relatively mple level in the eighteenth century, but there was initial cepticism about its value and efficiency. Initially, the con- ol of temperature was of highest concern to ensure ade- uate comfort and the most efficient use of fuel. In the early venteenth century, Cornelius Drebbel, a Dutch engineer, ad developed a temperature regulator based on pressure td a mechanical damper control (Figure 10-4). "This regu- itor seems to have worked successfully, for Members of te Royal Society of London, including Robert Boyle, hristopher Wren, and in the following generation Robert Iooke, showed interest in it."[18]

Further work on temperature regulation was based on the application of bimetallic strips and the differential expansion of metals. Some of the earliest work in measur- ing the expansion of metals was done in the 1720s and 1730s. John Ellicott invented an instrument for measuring the expansion of metal, which he described in 1736, but the most important influence was the work of John Harrison, who developed compensators to adjust his marine clock for changes in temperature. "His first device, made in 1726, relied on the lengthening of metal rods. . . ."[19]

Harrison's compensated grid-iron pendulum was invent- ed in 1726. In 1761, he produced the first device incorporat- ing a true bimetallic strip. These early bimetals were manu- factured by riveting, but sweating or welding was used before the end of the nineteenth century. The application of bimetals soon spread. M. Bonnemain used a Harrison device in 1777 to control the temperature of both buildings and incubators—probably the first attempt to control space heating automatically. The sensitive element was mechani- cally linked to the ash-pit door of a boiler and served to reg- ulate the rate of combustion (Figure 10-5).[20]

Bonnemain had invented a "heat regulator" for his incu- bation heating systems in 1777.[21] The construction of the regulator was founded upon the unequal dilatation of dif- ferent metals by the same degree of heat. The expansion of the lead was more than the iron for a like degree of temper- ature, and the rod enclosed within the tube being was less easily warmed, so whenever the heat rose to the desired pitch, the elongation of the tube put the collet in contact with the heel of the bent lever; then the slightest increase of heat lengthened the tube anew, and the collet lifting the heel of the lever depressed its other end through a much greater space because of the relative lengths of its legs. This movement operated near the axis of a balance-bar and sank one end of this, thereby increasing the extent of the move- ment, which was transmitted directly to the iron skewer. This pushing down a swing register diminished or cut off the access of air to the fireplace. The combustion was there- by obstructed, and with the temperature falling by degrees,

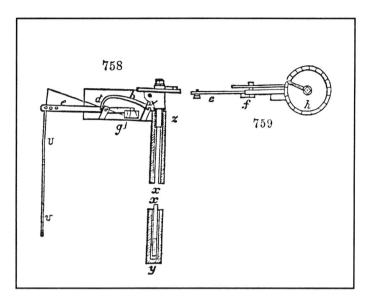

Figure 10-6 *M. Bonnemain, "heat regulator," 1777 (from A. Ure, 1853). A rod of iron, x, is tapped at its lower end into a brass nut, y, enclosed in a leaden box or tube, terminated above by a brass collect, z. This tube is plunged into the water of the boiler alongside the smoke pipe. This figure is a bird's-eye view of the dial.*

the tube shrank and disengaged the heel of the lever. The counterpoise fixed to the balance beam raised the other extremity of this beam by raising the end of the lever as much as necessary to make the heel bear upon the collet of the tube. The swing register, acted upon by this means, presented a greater section to the passage of the air and the combustion was increased (Figure 10-6).

James Kewley's heat governor, patented in 1816, was based on a different principle. It made use of the fact that mercury and alcohol expand and contract at different rates as the temperature changes.[22]

The Atkins and Marriott "thermoregulator stove" described by Mickleham (Bernan) in 1825 and the Arnott "thermometer stove" of 1836 are probably the next examples in the history of automatic temperature control. The Atkins and Marriott design, not entirely automatic, controlled the air supply for burning in the fire-chamber by a stop-cock. "When the fire is sufficiently brisk the further supply of air may be instantly shut off by turning the stop cock."[23]

Neil Arnott was more successful with his "thermometer stove" described in 1836. In one design he used a long bimetallic strip, one end of which was fixed to the casing of the stove and the other was attached to the combustion air damper. Other regulators described by Arnott relied upon the expansion of air in a tube closed by mercury; a float on the mercury surface was linked to the damper. All these devices controlled the temperature inside the stove casing, not that of the room (Figure 10-8). There was also in existence a well-known means of adjusting the temperature of a baker's oven by a self-acting thermometer.[24]

Modern Thermostatic Control—Andrew Ure

Prior to Arnott's work on his "thermometer stove," Andrew Ure (1778-1857) (Figure 10-7) had been working on defining the latent heat of different vapors[25] as well as the design of a thermostat in 1830, which he patented in 1831.

Figure 10-7 *Andrew Ure, M.D., F.R.S., etc. (from* A Dictionary of Arts, Manufactures and Mines, *1856).*

He gained his doctor of medicine degree at Glasgow in 1801 and became a professor of chemistry and natural philosophy at the Andersonian Institution in 1802. He moved to London in 1830 and was appointed analytical chemist to the Board of Customs in 1834. He was the author of a number of scientific and philosophical works; his *Dictionary of Arts, Manufactures and Mines*, published in 1839, was printed in several editions both in England and in the United States. Dr. Ure's claim to fame is based on a patent granted to him in 1830 (No. 6014) entitled "An Apparatus for Regulating Temperature in Vaporization, Distillation and Other Processes." In the specification, several forms of automatic temperature control apparatus are described and shown.[26]

Ure's thermostat, for the control of steam-heating coils, was the first of its kind. It was a bimetallic device of brass and iron whose design could be modified for controlling air or water temperatures.

> THERMOSTAT, is the name of an apparatus for regulating temperature, in vaporization, distillation, heating baths or hothouses, and ventilating apartments &c.; for which I obtained a patent in the year 1831. It operates upon the physical principle, that when two thin metallic bars of different expandabilities are riveted or soldered facewise together, any change of temperature in them will cause a sensible movement of flexure in the compound bar, to one side or other; which movement may be made to operate, by the intervention of levers, &c., in any desired degree, upon valves, stopcocks, stove-registers, air-ventilators, &c.; so as to regulate the temperature of the media in which the said compound bars are placed. Two long rulers, one of steel, and one of hard hammered brass, riveted together, answer very well; the object being not simply to indicate, but to control or modify temperature.[27]

The honor of naming the heat governor the "thermostat" and of indicating wider industrial applications for it than had previously been suggested belongs to Ure.

Altogether Ure was granted five patents in one of which (No. 6016/1830) he described an air-heating stove with a thermostatic control. There is no record of Ure's thermostat ever getting into industrial use, and it is doubtful whether it would have had any success in practice because the riveting together of the two metal strips is unsatisfactory and it was not until a method of firmly uniting them by heat treatment was found that the bimetallic strip became a dependable component for a heat governor (Figures 10-9 and 10-10).[28]

Temperature Regulation for High-Temperature Systems

High-pressure hot water and steam heating posed a special problem of temperature regulation since the high pressures and concern about explosions from boilers required a great deal of attention to their operation. Angier Perkins developed a draft regulator for his high-pressure hot water system in 1840 (Figure 10-11). "The high pressure maintained was regarded, as in England, as a dangerous feature, and the attention of an engineer or skilled mechanic was felt to be a necessity."[29]

Improvements in steam heating required "safe, simple, durable, and reliable boiler" design. In the 1840s, Joseph Nason had developed the "Nason regulator" to control steam pressures. By the 1860s, low-pressure steam systems, popularized by the Gold boiler and others, were typically 2 to 3 pounds per square inch. However, some systems were operated at pressures ranging from 15 pounds per square inch to as high as 40 pounds per square inch. Boiler designs were often tested at ten times the actual operating pressures

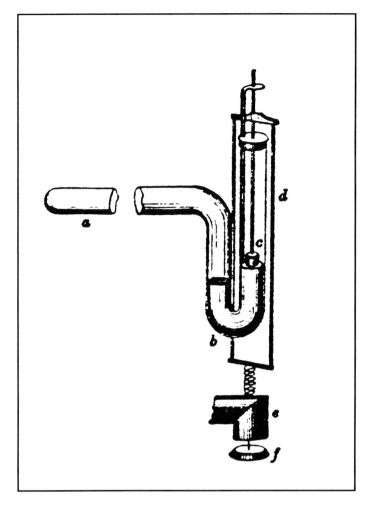

Figure 10-8 *Arnott's thermostat, 1836 (from Edward H. Knight, 1876, Knight's American Mechanical Dictionary, vol. III, Hurd & Houghton, New York).*

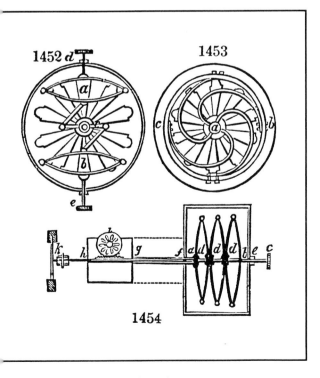

(a) Air register thermostat.

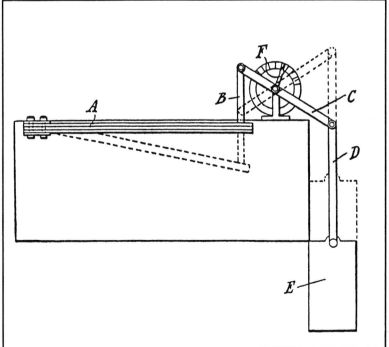

(b) Ure's thermostat, 1830 (from his patent specification).

Figures 10-9 and 10-10 *Andrew Ure, thermostats, 1830 (from his patent specification).*

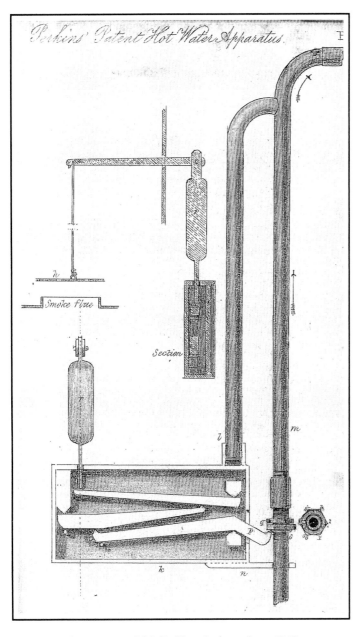

Figure 10-11 *A.M. Perkins, draft regulator, 1840.*

Figure 10-12 *Warren S. Johnson (from Johnson Controls Inc.).*

to ensure their safety. Boilers were furnished with safety valves, glass water gauges, gauge cocks to verify water levels, and draft regulators to maintain desired pressures. By 1878, manufacturers were, by necessity, providing complete systems. "Boilers when furnished complete include all necessary attachments mentioned, viz.: Steam Gauge, Water Gauge, Gauge Cocks, Safety Valve, Blow-off Cock, Feed Valve and Automatic Damper Regulator."[30]

The discovery of practical applications of electricity during the first half of the nineteenth century produced a number of inventions wherein electricity was used as the motive power. Dr. Sternberg's electro-magnetic regulator for controlling the heat of rooms broke new ground in the design of thermostats in that variations of temperature were caused to complete or interrupt an electrical circuit.[31]

* * *

About 1880, evidence first appears of the thermostat beginning to get into practical use, but the form used was unlike any of those so far described. It was invented by Charles Edward Hearson after visiting a poultry farm and being impressed by

the hit-and-miss method adopted in some experiments being carried on for the artificial incubation of eggs. Hearson applied himself to the problem and ultimately found the solution of maintaining the critical temperature level in an incubator by the thermostat. It consists of a capsule formed from sheets of metal sealed together at their edges and enclosing a piece of absorbent material such as blotting paper saturated with gasoline or any liquid which boils at the temperature at which the interior of the apparatus is required to be kept.[32]

The firm of Charles Hearson & Co. Ltd. continued to manufacture incubators controlled by these thermostats until the late 1940s. His shop in Regent Street was referred to in H.G. Wells's *The Magic Shop*, where he describes the shop next door as "the place where the chicks run about just out of patent incubators."

According to a Mr. Wilkinson, the manufacturer of bimetal strips used in thermostats originated in "the sweating together of some silver and copper coins at a fire at Soho Foundry, Birmingham . . ." and that "among the earliest thermostatic uses for (these) bi-metals (known under his registered trademark Thermoflex) was the application to control the temperature in railway coaches in the United States by the Thomson-Houston Co., and to control the pressure in gas lamps."[33]

Although bimetals had been produced previously, "the problem was to find two metals that would give the greatest

ount of movement. A combination of brass and iron was
ed in 1837 and brass and steel 20 years later. Combinations
zinc and copper and of nickel and brass were tried in sub-
quent years. All this was changed about the turn of the cen-
ry when an alloy of nickel and iron was discovered that did
t lengthen when heated. It was called INVAR, a word
ined from its expansion characteristic, INVARiable."[34] In
e 1880s, instruments were used to measure temperature,
essure, and velocity of air (Figure 10-12)

UTOMATIC TEMPERATURE CONTROL
T THE TURN OF THE CENTURY

arren S. Johnson

Although thermostats were manufactured "in consider-
le quantity" prior to 1885, one thermostat design for wide-
read application to heating depended on the combined use

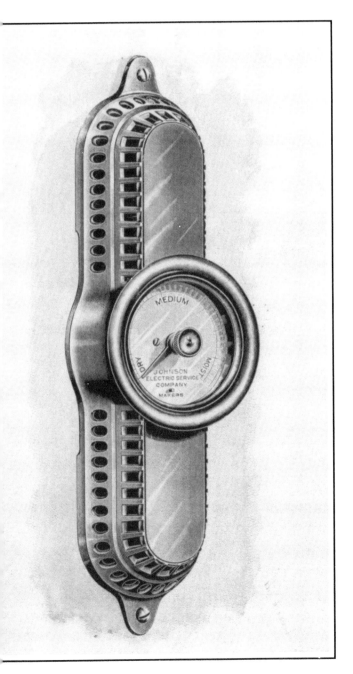

Figure 10-13 *Johnson humidistat, c. 1905 (Johnson Controls).*

of electricity and compressed air, a concept pioneered during
this time by Warren S. Johnson. Johnson was born in Rutland
County, Vermont, and as a young boy showed a strong interest in inventions, from sketches and descriptions "covering a
wide range of subjects in mechanics, chemistry and electricity." He became a country schoolteacher and later a professor
of science and art in Wisconsin. In 1873, he invented an
"annunciator" system at Whitewater College, Wisconsin, to
alert the janitor as to which room required heat, but "his first
bonafide venture was the development of a storage battery
in 1883." In that same year, he began to experiment on electric thermostats and, on July 24, was granted a patent for the
"electric thermoscope."[35]

> The idea of using compressed air to operate his valves and
> dampers suggested itself to Prof. Johnson through his famil-
> iarity with the small hand air compressors used in various
> experiments in his physical laboratory at the Norman
> School. It was both powerful and elastic in its operation. It
> could be used to close a steam valve and hold it closed
> against pressure by means of piston or rubber diaphragm
> attached to the end of the valve stem. Air for his first sys-
> tems was supplied from a hand compressor and by the use
> of a storage air tank, the janitor need pump up air once in a
> while between his other duties.[36]

"Johnson's `electro-pneumatic' valve, patented in 1885,
consisted of a very small compressed air valve which could
be successfully operated by an electric thermostat and
which in turn operated to supply and exhaust compressed
air to and from the diaphragm valve or damper. Electricity
was supplied from salammoniac batteries as dry batteries
were not yet perfected. Compressed air was supplied by a
diaphragm hydraulic air compressor at 15 lbs. per square
inch pressure."[37]

From the invention of the "electro-pneumatic" valve,
Johnson formed the Johnson Electric Service Company to
manufacture temperature control systems to be distributed
through local offices in Wisconsin, Minneapolis, New York,
and Chicago. "The system was first applied to buildings
heated by direct steam radiators with a diaphragm mounted
on top of the valve"[38] (Figure XIV, color section). In 1902, the
company moved to its own seven-story building in
Milwaukee, which it still occupies. From 1914 to 1920, the
company dominated three quarters of the temperature control market and worked on improvements to the design of
thermostats to make them more reliable and serviceable and
to be smaller in size. The Johnson Electric Service Company
produced a number of thermostat cover designs to fit different needs, ranging from an ornate residential thermostat
(Figure XV, color section) to hotel, office, and bath thermostats. During this time, the company also developed an
entire line of temperature control systems (Figure 10-13).

Albert M. Butz and William R. Sweatt

During the early 1880s, Albert M. Butz developed a thermostatically controlled draft damper for heating systems in
Minneapolis, Minnesota. Butz, a partner in the Mendenhall
Hand Grenade Fire Extinguisher Co., received two U.S.
patents (341,092 and 347,866) in 1886 and attempted to sell
his invention through the Butz Thermoelectric Regulator
Company. After Butz left the company in 1888, it was

renamed the Consolidated Temperature Controlling Company.

William R. Sweatt (Figure 10-14) moved to Minneapolis in 1891 at the age of 24, where he began the Sweatt Manufacturing Company to build wooden wheelbarrows, grocery boxes, and wooden washing machines. He "had not been in Minneapolis very long before he was approached by the Electric Thermostat Company to invest some money. It was the old Consolidated Temperature Controlling Company, reorganized and renamed in 1889."[39] The company manufactured a thermostat and a hand-wound, spring-powered motor that controlled indoor temperatures by opening and closing a flapper draft damper on a coal-fired furnace or boiler. However, this first product did not sell and the company continued to have financial problems until 1893, when the company raised funds and was incorporated as the Electric Heat Regulator Company (Figures 10-15 and 10-16). The following years continued to be difficult. In 1905, the company made a thermostat and two kinds of damper motors, one spring powered and the other powered by gravity. W.R. Sweatt introduced a clock thermostat in 1905. In 1912, the company changed its name to the Minneapolis Heat Regulator Company and, by 1913, there were four thermostat models available.

W.R. Sweatt turned more and more to his son H.W. Sweatt to manage day-to-day operations of the company.

Figure 10-14 *W.R. Sweatt in 1891 (from Nessell, 1963).*

H.W. Sweatt called on heating equipment manufacturer to understand their changing needs and maintain the company's leadership. In 1917, the use of oil for domestic heating was dictated by shortages of coal as a result of World War I, and the company shifted its emphasis to oil burner controls.

In the 1920s, the largest competitor was the Honeywell Heating Specialties Company at Wabash, Indiana. "It was started by Mark Honeywell as the Honeywell Heating Specialty Company to manufacture a hot water heating appliance invented by Mark Honeywell and known as `Heat Generator.'"[40] In 1927, W.R. Sweatt and Mark Honeywell met to discuss the possibility of a merger between the two companies. The new company was incorporated in Delaware as the Minneapolis-Honeywell Regulator Company (Figure 10-17).

William P. Powers

William Penn Powers (Figure 10-18) formed the firm of W.P. Powers and Company in LaCrosse, Wisconsin, in 186 to manufacture pumps, shingles, and, later, a chain belt for sawmill operations. In a letter titled "The Result of a Dull Sermon," published in October 1918, Powers described how, in 1887, he became interested in the field of automatic temperature control:

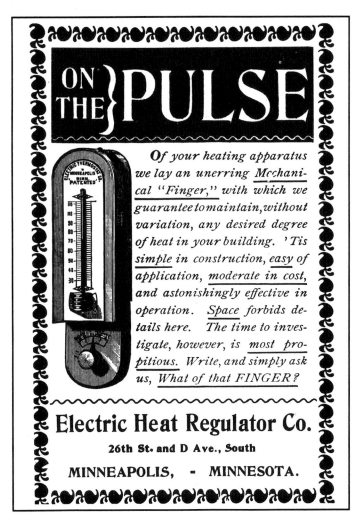

Figure 10-15 *Thermostat, Electric Heat Regulator Co., 1895 (from* Heating and Ventilation, *May 15, 1895).*

One Sunday during the sermon—which may have had some dull passages—the idea occurred to me of utilizing the relative boiling points of water under different pressures to control the draft. I could hardly wait for the benediction in my anxiety to consult the encyclopedia and verify my conception as to the effect of pressure on the boiling points.[41]

Powers went to Chicago in 1890 and formed the Powers Regulator Company. In 1893, the company installed its first thermostat in the First Congregational Church in Nashua, New Hampshire, and exhibited at the Chicago World's Fair that same year. The first thermostat design was round and relatively large, measuring 15 inches in diameter (Figure 10-9). It was connected to a large diaphragm motor that controlled double mixing dampers on a fan heating system.

During the early years of the twentieth century, the Powers Regulator Company manufactured a full line of controls (Figures 10-20 through 10-23) and installed temperature control systems in a number of large projects including many government and institutional buildings and schools. It installed the system in the Minnesota State Capitol and the City Prison ("The Tombs"), the Empire State Building, and the Chrysler Buildings in New York City.

Automatic Control Systems

At the beginning of the twentieth century, temperature control and other forms of commercial and industrial control were dominated by the three companies previously described. However, there were a number of other companies manufacturing controls, such as the Nash Regulating Valve Company, the Compton Electric Service Company, and Foxboro (Figure 10-24).

Automatic Control for Refrigeration

Until the 1890s, mechanical refrigeration was applied as large-capacity systems to breweries, ice making, and cold storage. However, attempts to develop refrigerating systems of small capacity that could be used directly in shops and homes necessitated a new engineering approach. Whereas large systems were continuously attended by skilled operators who constantly adjusted the refrigeration capacity to meet the load demand, small systems could not enjoy the attendance of a human operator if they were to make any economic sense. A small system had to be designed so it would run with little or no attention. To make this possible, the system not only had to be operated by a driving mechanism that needed no supervision but the refrigerating system itself had to automatically adjust to the load placed on it.

Application of thermostats to refrigeration was made possible by the availability of electric power and electric motors. Cycling a refrigerating system to load demand by coupling a thermostat and an electric motor was very simple and inexpensive. Such systems began to make an appearance concurrent with the application of thermostats to heating and with the introduction of electric power systems and electric motors (Figure 10-25).

A precursor to temperature control of refrigeration can be seen in U.S. Patent 105,609 issued in 1870 to Peter Van der Weyde for a refrigerating system that incorporated a crude thermostat:

... an automatic arrangement to keep the temperature at the same height of 32 or 36 degrees Fahrenheit, or any height desired. ... To accomplish this, two platinum wires are melted in the glass of a large mercurial thermometer, one in its lower portion, so as to always be in contact with the mercury, and one at the middle part of the tube as corresponds with 32 or 36 degrees, or any other point of the scale below which we do not desire the temperature to descend. The ends of these wires are connected with the coil of an electro-magnet and a small galvanic battery ... the electro-magnet is, by proper leverage, attached to the power driving the (compressor) in such a way that ... the power is detached from the pump by throwing off the belt, shutting off the steam, or in any other manner.

By the 1890s, when the advent of the electric motor and power systems provided a method of driving systems that was less complicated to control, there were attempts to apply the bimetal type of thermostat to refrigerating systems.

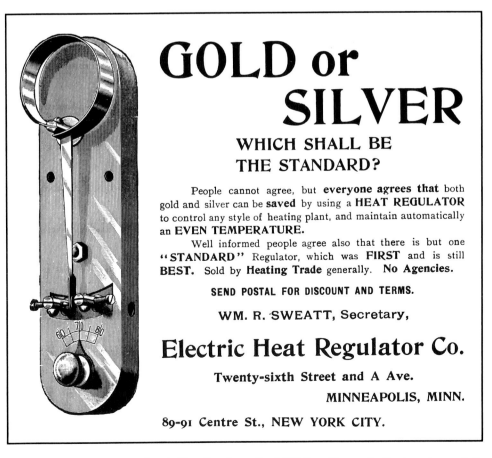

Figure 10-16 *Thermostat, Electric Heat Regulator Co., 1895 (from* Domestic Engineering, *vol. 9, June 1895).*

Figure 10-17 *The Minneapolis heat regulator (from* Engineering Review, *vol. 22, September 1912).*

Quickly, inventors realized that the thermostat itself could not tolerate the heavy current flow an electric motor required, so they devised magnetic relays to indirectly switch the current. Thermostatic control evolved in sophistication into the early twentieth century so that by World War I, the method was developed to the point where it was ready to be perfected for widespread use.[42] Mere cycling of a refrigerating system was not enough to ensure trouble-free operation, however. The evaporator side of a vapor-compression refrigeration system will exchange heat depending on the amount of refrigerant supplied and the suction or "back pressure" applied by the compressor. The amount of heat exchanged also depends on the means provided to transfer heat to the evaporator from the refrigerator load, which varies depending on the heat gained through the walls of the refrigerator and from the product stored in the refrigerator. Thus the load placed on the evaporator changes and requires that the amount of refrigerant supplied to the evaporator be varied for optimum use of the heat exchange surface provided by the evaporator. In large systems, the changing requirements were met by hand-adjusting the refrigerant flow. This method required an attendant who usually observed the amount of frost on the suction line and changed the setting of a throttling valve admitting the liquid refrigerant into the evaporator. If the refrigerating system was shut off for any reason, the expansion valve had to be closed to prevent flooding the system. This use of "hand expansion valves" proved satisfactory where a human attendant was on duty but was an unacceptable method for a small system placed in unattended operation in a butcher shop or home.

Attempts to automatically control the refrigerant flow are actually as old as the vapor-compression system itself. The first vapor-compression system of Jacob Perkins had a

Figure 10-18 *William P. Powers (from* The Aerologist, *June 1927, p. 11).*

Figure 10-19 *Advertisement for Powers thermostat (from* Heating and Ventilation, *May 15, 1895).*

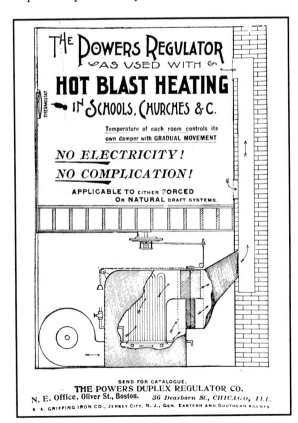

Figure 10-20 *Advertisement, Powers Duplex Regulator Co. (from* Heating and Ventilation, *December 1894).*

Figure 10-21 *Thermostat polishing shop—Powers Regulator Co., early 1900s (from Landis & Gyr Powers).*

weighted expansion valve, in effect a very crude form of a constant-pressure expansion valve. James Harrison employed a "high side float" in his first patents taken out in the 1850s. The high-pressure or "high-side" float device meters refrigerant to the evaporator by using a float that senses the amount of liquid provided by the condenser, metering liquid to the evaporator only as fast as it condens-

es. A changing heat load in the evaporator results in a chang ing refrigerant pressure in the evaporator, and the changin; suction pressure is reflected in the amount of refrigerant cir culated in the system. The float automatically responds to th change in flow by metering more or less liquid refrigerant t the evaporator. After Harrison, the high-side float contro showed up periodically in various systems, but it was no used to any extent in early systems. The han expansion valve was simple and inexpensive, an large steam-engine-driven refrigerating plant required an on-site operator anyway.

As the application of mechanical refrigeratio spread to uses requiring small systems, the nee to control refrigerant flow became evident. / study of United States patents shows that suc attempts to control refrigerant began to appea in the 1880s. The first types of controls were ther mostatically modulated expansion valves tha responded to the temperature of the refrigeratec space. Possibly the first one was incorporated i U.S. Patent 332,150 issued in 1885 to Josep! Holmes for a refrigerated corpse-cooler Numerous other U.S. patents followed for vari ous designs of temperature-controlled valves.[43]

About the same time that temperature-con trolled valves were being developed, expansior valves that responded to the evaporator pressur were also conceived. These constant-pressure valves, now commonly called "automatic expan sion valves," began to appear in United State patents in the 1890s[44] (Figure 10-26).

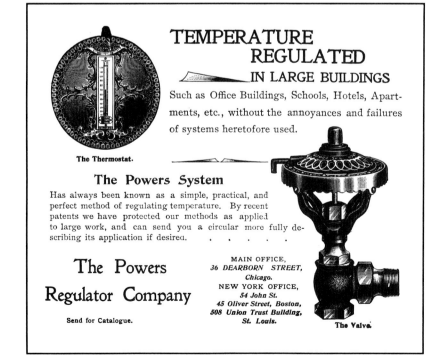

Figure 10-22 *Advertisement, Powers Regulator Co. (from* Heating and Ventilation, *April 1897).*

Figure 10-23 *Powers thermostat, 1903 (from Landis & Gyr Powers).*

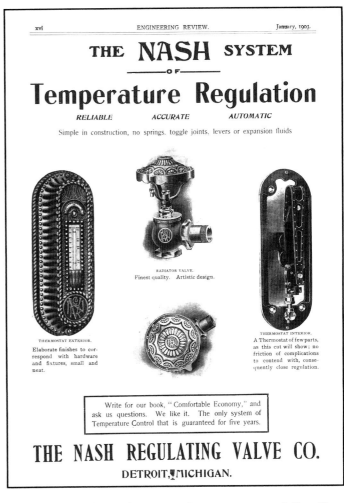

Figure 10-24 *The Nash system of temperature regulation (from Engineering Review, January 1903).*

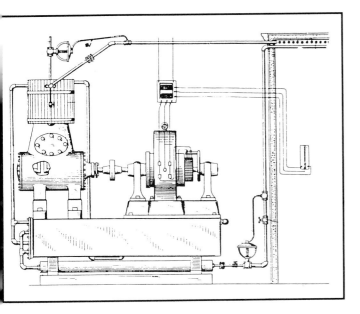

Figure 10-25 *Thermostatic control applied to a turn-of-the-century refrigerating system by William Singer, whose company, Singer Automatic Ice Machine Company, was one of the earliest to manufacture electric-driven, thermostatically controlled refrigerating systems. Singer's company merged in 1902 with others to form the Federal Automatic Refrigerating Co., which became the Automatic Refrigerating Co. in 1905 (from U.S. Patent 697,029 of April 8, 1902).*

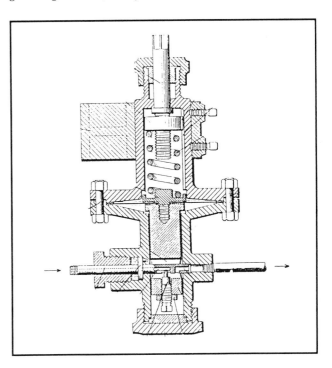

Figure 10-26 *Automatic expansion valve patented in 1905 by Albert T. Marshall. Marshall's patents for automatic control were among those consolidated when the Automatic Refrigerating Co. was formed to develop the market for small refrigerating systems (from U.S. Patent 785,265 of March 21, 1905).*

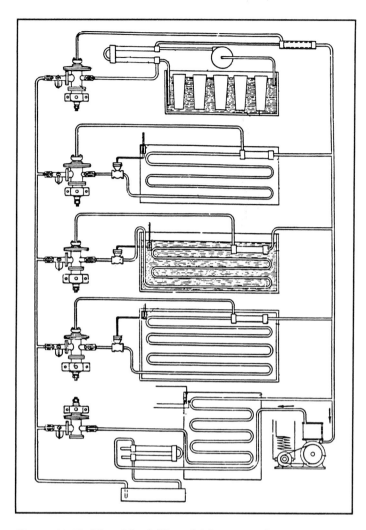

Figure 10-27 *Albert Marshall's multiplex system for operating more than one evaporator at varying temperatures, featuring constant super-heat expansion valves, apparently the first time they were used. For some reason, probably technical, they did not see widespread use until the 1930s.*

It is commonly believed that an even more sophisticated expansion device, the constant superheat expansion valve, now referred to as the "thermostatic expansion valve," was not invented until the 1920s or 1930s[45]; however, such valves did appear before that time. The constant superheat expansion valve, as its name implies, responds to the amount of superheat in the refrigerant after evaporation and acts to maintain efficient use of the evaporator regardless of the heat load.

Albert Tisdale Marshall, who took out numerous automatic control patents featuring thermostats, automatic expansion valves, etc., seems to have invented the constant superheat valve also. His U.S. Patent 1,003,283 of 1911 shows such valves as part of an automatically controlled multiple-temperature refrigeration system (Figure 10-27). Another early constant superheat expansion valve was invented by Fred W. Wolf and Harrison Southworth and patented in 1916 (U.S. Patent 1,166,874 assigned to Iceless Machine Co.).

Numerous other devices were developed around 1900 to control refrigerant flow or other parts of the system. Robert Rollins used a thermostat to operate an electric liquid line valve, a "solenoid valve," to control refrigerant flow in his

U.S. Patent 716,480 of 1902. George Carroll developed an electrically operated expansion valve in 1909 (U.S. Patent 924,964). Robert Massa used a switch operated by evaporator pressure, a "low pressure control," to cycle a refrigerating system in his U.S. Patent 929,151 issued in 1909. The high-pressure safety cutout, known now as a "high-pressure control," was used to stop the refrigeration compressor in the event of condenser coolant failure in U.S. Patent 806,478 issued in 1905 to Albert Marshall. Marshall's patent as well as one issued as U.S. Patent 985,147 of 1911 to Andrew Culver, incorporated an automatically modulated valve to vary the coolant flow to the condenser as needed. As time went on, the various automatic controls were incorporated in progressively more sophisticated systems. It seems that this progress occurred slowly, since many of the aforementioned automatic controls were not at first widely known. For example, a letter was written to the editor of *Ice and Refrigeration* in 1892 asking:

> Do you know of any device by which we can keep our expansion pressure the same at all times—some automatic arrangement? . . . we think an automatic valve of this sort would sell like "hot cakes" and prove a very useful article.

The editor replied: "If any reader can supply the information we would be pleased to receive and publish it for the benefit of the trade in general."[46] A review of subsequent issues of the publication yielded no specific reply, and there was nothing more about automatic expansion valves in the publication until 1897![47]

A NEW ERA FOR REFRIGERATION?—THE SMALL MACHINE

The commercialization of refrigeration proceeded steadily as the twentieth century unfolded. Ice making, cold storage, and brewing provided plenty of business for the manufacturers of refrigerating equipment throughout the developed world. These applications required large-capacity machines, which were steadily improved. However, there was an undercurrent of development for a new application of refrigerating machinery—that of small refrigerating machines that could be located in shops, restaurants, and homes. Such development was to result in the electric domestic refrigerator, a device that could be argued as refrigeration science's greatest contribution of the twentieth century. Although experimentation with small refrigeration systems occurred throughout the world, the United States seemed to be the site of most of the developments. In other countries, use of refrigeration by individuals did not seem to be as advanced.

> Even in London and Liverpool (England) the household refrigerator is comparatively unknown for domestic or household purposes outside the mansions or stately homes of the realm. The Englishman is not a great admirer of ice, and the consumption of the luxury in the United Kingdom is not to be compared in volume to the vast stores required in America.
> . . . the French are sometimes spoken of as the best fed people in the world, (but) they lose much through their strange indifference to the economic uses of ice in the household and market.

In the cities of Germany, as well as in the country, both ice and the refrigerator are in more general use than in any other European country, though not to the extent seen in America. . . .

Italian people do not consider ice necessary at any season. . . . Economy is practiced here to such an extent that fully ninety-seven families out of every one hundred purchase only sufficient foods for daily wants.[48]

In the United States, where use of ice for household purposes had been so effectively promoted by the ice industry, ice-type refrigerators were abundant when compared to Europe. There were also numerous butcher shops, and soda fountains were appearing in cities. Thus there was fertile ground for entrepreneurs willing to try to apply mechanical refrigeration to replace ice. A potential market existed like nowhere else!

The refrigeration of private residences is the next step in the development of mechanical refrigeration. Just what forms this branch of the industry will take, whether it will be had by individual installation or by means of pipe line plants, remains to be seen; though it is likely both systems will be utilized. . . . The subject is one that has not yet been given much attention by manufacturers of machinery, whose efforts have been directed to the greater necessities called for by industrial enterprises, but the day will undoubtedly come when the refrigeration of residences (perhaps by the employment of the electric motor as power) will become an important item, requiring, perhaps, special machines for that purpose and special study of the particular requirements of the field.[49]

A skeptical editor at *Cassier's Magazine* noted:

It, therefore, seems that the facts as they stand at present preclude the possibility of small domestic ice or refrigerating plants, and will so continue until some system may be devised differing widely from those now in use.[50]

In fact a new approach was needed, and those who tried to develop small refrigerating machines were, for the most part, a new breed. These attempts were characterized by novel engineering of systems designed specifically for the purpose, rather than a simple downsizing of existing equipment. These small systems were designed by inventive individuals rather than by the existing refrigerating machine companies. Numerous U.S. patents were granted for mechanical refrigeration systems specifically designed for homes and shops.[51] Some of the inventors were able to go beyond the experimental, obtain financial backing, and bring a product to market. The advertisements shown on these pages are reflective of some of the products actually sold (Figures 10-28 through 10-33).

Possibly the most innovative of these early attempts to successfully market small systems was that of the Automatic Refrigerating Company. The potentially large market for such systems put dollar signs in the eyes of many entrepreneurs, such as Fred Kimball (Figure 10-34), manager of the fractional horsepower electric motor division of General Electric. Kimball saw the potential of enormous sales of small systems. Several companies had been reasonably successful with small systems, among them the Singer Automatic Ice Machine Co. of Bridgeport,

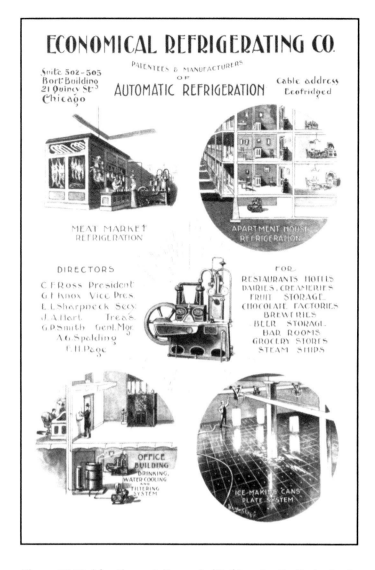

Figure 10-28 *Advertisement, Economical Refrigerator Co. Beginning in the 1890s, there were numerous attempts to bring small refrigerating systems to market. The Economical Refrigerating Co. and its successor, Atlantic Refrigerating Co., tried to promote a small refrigerating system before the turn of the twentieth century, but the system was advertised for only two years (from* Ice and Refrigeration, *March 1896, ad section, p. 216).*

Connecticut, the Marshall Ice and Refrigerating Machine Co. of Boston, and the Automatic Refrigeration Co. of Cleveland. Kimball, in late 1902, convinced a group of investors to form the Federal Automatic Refrigerating Co. in New York City to acquire the above-named companies. This consolidation resulted in the pooling of about 70 patents, including those of William F. Singer, Albert Tisdale Marshall, and Alexander Ballantine, all of whom had made significant progress in applying automatic controls to refrigeration.[52] Edward T. Williams was hired as a consultant to study the patents and design a system incorporating the best features of the various systems[53] (Figure 10-35). Two descriptions from the Automatic Refrigerating Co.'s catalogs (the word "Federal" had been dropped from the company name in 1905) give an idea of its accomplishments.

. . . a special thermostat within the refrigerator, it is claimed, absolutely controls the operation of the motor driven (or

engine driven) compressor, and other automatic devices are in turn dependent upon and regulated by the operation of the compressor itself. As stated in the catalog, the company manufactures and installs complete automatic refrigerating plants from one to ten horsepower capacity or the equivalent of from 800 to 12,000 pounds ice refrigerating per day. The automatic system, it is stated, can be applied to any existing compression plant, and does away with the necessity for constant attention.[54]

* * *

The machines built by this company, as indicated in the show plant in operation at 22 Thames Street, New York, have an automatic valve to control the flow of water to the condenser, and also a safety cut out which serves to shut down the machine and ring a gong in case of abnormal condenser pressure caused by failure of water supply or accidental closing of discharge valve.[55]

THE INITIAL FAILURE OF THE SMALL MACHINE

Although the Automatic Refrigerating Co. and other like it continued to operate for many years, those companies that were successful were few in number. Those that survived seem to have done so by concentrating on light commercial applications of small refrigerating machines such as shops, etc. These applications required smaller machines than the large ones made for industrial refriger

Figure 10-29 *Economical refrigerator, 1895. Patented by Eliel Sharpneck and George Knox in 1896-1897 (U.S. Patents 559,533 and 559,753), the machine is shown hooked to a domestic icebox, as demonstrated at the Chicago Pure Food Show in 1895 (from* Ice and Refrigeration, *November 1895, p. 325).*

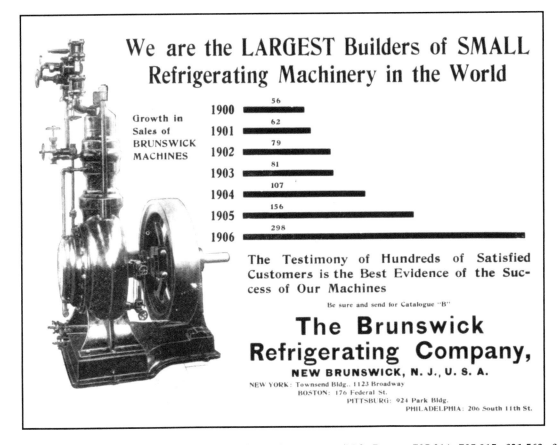

Figure 10-30 *Richard Whitaker patented small-size ammonia refrigerating systems (U.S. Patents 795,014; 795,015; 821,563; 848,277; 911,63 932,599; 936,065; and 1,013,348 issued between 1905 and 1912) that were manufactured by the Brunswick Refrigerating Company, one of the few companies that was successful in this market. Brunswick was one of the first to market a completely self-contained refrigerator, which housed the condening unit in a compartment on the side of the refrigerator, and displayed it at the 1904 World's Fair in St. Louis (see Anonymous, 1904, "Refrigeratin plants at Louisiana Purchase Exposition," *Ice and Refrigeration, *vol. 27, September, p. 89) (from* Ice and Refrigeration, *December 1907, ad sectio p. 73).*

on. However, the seemingly lucrative market for house-old refrigerators required even smaller machines. It seems that the light commercial size of machine was reasonably perfected by about 1910, but perfecting the very small machines needed for home use proved an elusive dream for some time. Most of the earliest small household machines proved to be failures.

John Starr, the first president of the American Society of Refrigerating Engineers, was probably as lucid as anyone when he commented on the subtle difference between the small machines of the turn of the century and an "idiot proof" type of machine needed for the home.

> That "philosopher's stone" of the refrigerating engineer—"the domestic refrigerating machine that could be run by the cook"—was just as active in the minds of the men of 1891 as it is today (1916) and the amount of money and thought spent on this subject was perhaps no less than it is now.
>
> The small machine requiring some intelligent, though not highly skilled attention has, in the period, become an accomplished and accepted and widely used apparatus, and hundreds of them ranging from one fourth to three or four tons in capacity are in successful use.
>
> [However] that supposed line of demarcation between a machine that required a little intelligent attention and no attention at all, was found not to be a line but a gulf which has perhaps not yet been successfully bridged.[56]

By the time Starr made his comments, there were enough ventures in search of Starr's "philosopher's stone" that a leading refrigeration trade journal was able to publish an eight-page article describing most of the 29 different machines it reported were then on the market. Still, it cautioned:

> The advent of the household refrigerating machine that is to "put the ice man out of business" has been prophesied at frequent intervals during the entire twenty five years since *Ice and Refrigeration* started on its career. . . . The little inexpensive machine, that needs little or no attention and that anyone can operate is still wanting. It must be conceded, however, that progress toward the production of such a machine has been made. Hundreds of thousands of dollars have been expended by people who believed the Utopian article had been invented only to learn after sad experience that their confidence had been misplaced and that there is still something lacking in the much desired article.[57]

Given the enthusiasm that seemed to accompany the prospects of household refrigeration, why did it take so long for the dream to be realized? In 1909, for example, of approximately 1,400 refrigerating plants reported to have been installed in the U.S., only five were listed for residences.[58] It seems that Starr had recognized one reason—the machines were still not completely foolproof. Foolproof such a machine needed to be, for as one engineer noted, "it will meet with sufficient human operating intelligence only on rare occasions and is consequently much abused."[59] Or, as another wryly commented, "Just how soon these will come into common use will depend somewhat upon how soon the accomplishments of the cook will include a knowledge of how `to pack the stuff-

ing box,' etc."[60] Even the Curtis Publishing Company concluded that household electric refrigerators had a long way to go when it investigated them about 1917. The company then refused to accept advertising for electric refrigerators in the *Saturday Evening Post*, claiming that the device was not yet a commercial product![61] Most of the engineering thought centered on these problems, all of which were about equal in difficulty:

- The inability to hold the refrigerant charge due to leaky shaft seals, coarse-grained castings, and porous fittings.
- High power requirements needed to overcome shaft seal friction.
- Refrigerants that were toxic or flammable, thereby posing a hazard when they did leak out.
- Impure refrigerants—for example, wet sulfur dioxide, which caused compressor seizure from corrosion.
- The need for more reliable electric motors.
- The need for efficient and inexpensive transmission methods of power from motor to compressor.
- The lack of adequate service when machines broke down.
- The inability to accurately control the small amounts of liquid refrigerant that had to be metered to the evaporator.
- The need for better automatic controls.
- Inadequate insulation and rot and warping from sweating in wooden cabinets.
- The high cost of the equipment and of electricity.[62]

Despite these numerous problems, there was much to be gained if solutions could be found.

> Now here is something that it would seem the public would like to have, and when one stops to consider the field open for such a machine, it is easy to figure a business of such a magnitude as to compare favorably with the telephone, electric lighting, gas and other public utilities.
>
> The attempts to secure this type of machine have been so numerous that space would not permit even a partial list of them. Sufficient to say that they have shown a wonderful degree of ingenuity, and have been based on both the absorption and compression principles, the former appealing to the gas interests while the latter is sought by the electric companies. The expenditure of money has been prodigious and the results not at all in keeping with this expenditure.[63]

Both technical and economic obstacles would ultimately be solved by engineering systems that were both foolproof and less expensive. However, the solution would require even more prodigious expenditures of money.

THE FOOLPROOF HOUSEHOLD REFRIGERATOR

The simplicity, reliability, and low cost that we now take for granted in household refrigerators did not materialize quickly or easily. Much engineering talent was required—even fresh thinking from outside the refrigeration industry. And there was the "prodigious expenditure" that would be required. One estimate concluded that approximately $60

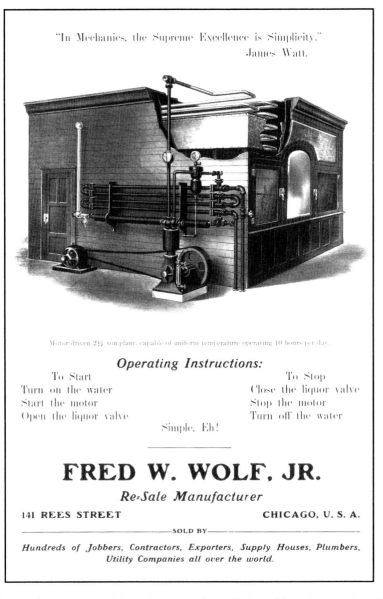

"In Mechanics, the Supreme Excellence is Simplicity."
James Watt.

Motor-driven 2½ ton plant, capable of uniform temperature operating 10 hours per day.

Operating Instructions:

To Start
Turn on the water
Start the motor
Open the liquor valve

To Stop
Close the liquor valve
Stop the motor
Turn off the water

Simple, Eh!

FRED W. WOLF, JR.
Re-Sale Manufacturer

141 REES STREET   CHICAGO, U. S. A.

————————————SOLD BY————————————

Hundreds of Jobbers, Contractors, Exporters, Supply Houses, Plumbers, Utility Companies all over the world.

Figure 10-31 *Fred W. Wolf, Jr., was one of the early pioneers in small-size refrigerating machines. His father, Fred W. Wolf, had introduced the Linde ammonia machine into the U.S., but Fred Wolf, Jr., devoted his efforts to the small machine. His machines became increasingly sophisticated, resulting in a self-contained household machine, the "DOMELRE," in 1913 (from* Ice and Refrigeration, *January 1909, ad section, p. 18).*

million had been spent before 1924 by those trying to develop household refrigerating machines. By 1924, there were about 50 different household refrigerating machines being marketed, and another 50 or so in experimental stages. An unnamed New York interest was said to be advancing $100 million in capital for development of a household refrigerator that would do for refrigerators what the Ford Model T had done for automobiles.[64]

Although numerous individuals and small companies continued to "lose their shirts" in the endeavor, it seems that the talent and the deep pockets were indeed provided from without the refrigeration industry and these outsiders overcame the various technical problems to finally bring the mass market refrigerator into realization.

The Difficulty of Success—The "DOMELRE"

Just how difficult the solution to the mass market household refrigerator would be can be seen in the story of the "DOMELRE" household refrigerator. This device, patent[ed] by Fred W. Wolf, Jr., son of brewery architect and ammon[ia] refrigeration engineer Fred W. Wolf of Chicago, was pos[si]bly the first attempt to manufacture a lightweight, compa[ct] and inexpensive household refrigerating machine.[65] W[olf] brought out the device in 1914,[66] coining the nam[e] "DOMELRE," a contraction of *dom*estic *el*ectric *re*frigerat[or] (Figure 10-36).

It was made by the Mechanical Refrigerator Co. [of] Chicago but did not have extensive sales until Henry B. J[oy] of the Packard Motor Car Company, purchased the righ[ts] from Wolf for $225,000 in 1916 and formed Is[ko] Incorporated, moving the production to Detroit. Howev[er,] various technical problems and low public demand caus[ed] Joy to lose interest and he sold the company. The ne[w] owner redesigned the machine, which caused further pro[b]lems, and the company soon ceased production.[67] It w[as] purchased for a final time in 1922 by Frigidai[re] Corporation. Frigidaire's shrewd patent chief, G. Ral[ph] ehr, wanted to acquire the patents pertaining to the use of n air-cooled condenser. Fehr traveled to the bankruptcy uction and purchased the entire company for $17,400, next pending some time in an unheated warehouse sifting rough the engineering drawings with numbed fingers in ear-zero temperatures.[68]

The Wolf machine featured several novel advances:

The entire unit was self-contained, with the condensing unit mounted on a wooden base and the evaporator hung underneath. The entire assembly could be placed on top of an existing ice box in which a hole had been cut to admit the evaporator (Figure 10-37).

An air-cooled condenser made of bare copper tubing was used. When the design was improved in 1917, fins were added, resulting in a more compact design. Flared joints, borrowed from the automotive industry, were used to minimize the possibility of leaks.

A ¼-hp repulsion-start induction motor was used, and the low current that was required permitted the unit to be "plugged" into an ordinary light socket.[69]

To avoid the slippage encountered when flat drive belts were used on small pulleys, three round rubber cord belts were used to transmit the power to the compressor. (The V-belt drive, which would later be the solution to this problem, was not applied to refrigeration until 1922.)

- An ice cube tray was featured as part of the evaporator (Figure 10-38).
- The retail price was low: $385 in 1916, later dropping to $275 "installed in any ice box"[70] (Figures XVIII, color section, and 10-39).

Considering these features, why did the DOMELRE/Isko machine fail? Frigidaire's G. Ralph Fehr later concluded that the DOMELRE was an idea that had gotten ahead of the mechanical skills needed to carry it out.[71] Frigidaire's first chief engineer, Alfred Mellowes, felt that wet sulfur dioxide refrigerant and a lack of understanding of the conditions in which the refrigerating machine was installed, as well as compressor technical problems, contributed to the failure.[72]

THE DIFFICULTY OVERCOME

The existing industrial refrigeration industry had only half-heartedly attempted to enter the field of household refrigeration in the 1890s. One such industrial company, the De La Vergne Refrigerating Machine Company, had stuck its toes into the household market water in 1893. It "was one of the first companies to experiment with such machines, and sold a number of them, but the business did not prove to be profitable, too much personal attention being demanded."[73] Burned by the household "flash in the pan" experience at the turn of the century, the large refrig-

Figure 10-32 *Cassius C. Palmer began refrigerating work before 1880, and around the turn of the century he developed a small-sized refrigerating system using ethyl chloride refrigerant and a vane-type rotary compressor. The Railway and Stationary Refrigerating Co. and its successor, the Clothel Co., were active until the late 1920s (from* Ice and Refrigeration, December 1907, *ad section, p. 73).*

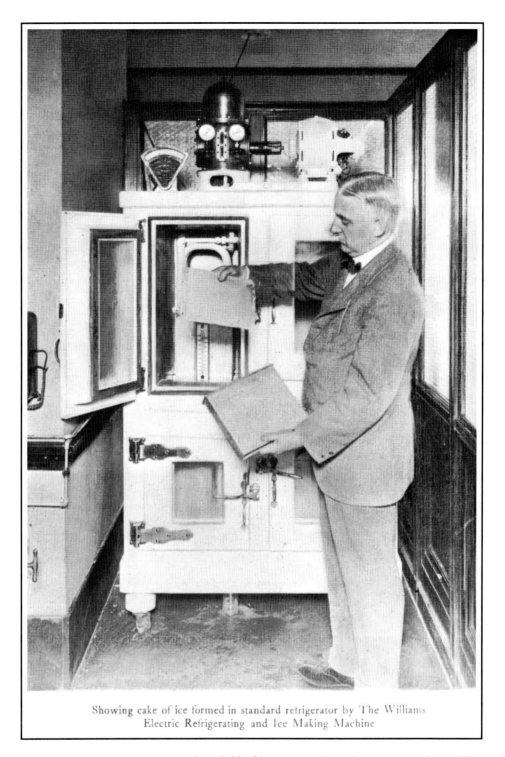

Showing cake of ice formed in standard refrigerator by The Williams
Electric Refrigerating and Ice Making Machine

Figure 10-33 *Edward T. Williams is shown demonstrating his household refrigerating machine about 1919. In 1914, Williams, a New York consulting refrigeration engineer, developed a compact refrigerating system that could be installed on top of an existing icebox (U.S. Patents 1,164,689; 1,165,920; and 1,312,600). A rotary-vane compressor using an ethyl chloride refrigerant featured a rotary mechanical seal to minimize refrigerant leakage and friction. Williams was never able to mass market his invention and, by 1922, he abandoned his system to promote what he thought was a more promising venture, the new electric refrigerator called the SERV-EL (from* The Williams Automatic Electric Refrigerating and Ice Making Machine, *no date, New York, The Electrical Refrigerating Company, Inc.).*

eration companies were conspicuous by their absence in the 1920s. Indeed, even the American Society of Refrigerating Engineers seemed uninterested, publishing few papers concerning household machines. One household refrigerator engineer, John Replogle, who claimed to be the first engineer in that specialty to join the ASRE, said that he "was given pretty much of a `cold' reception at the first meeting which he attended."[74] Like the small entrepreneurial com-

panies at the turn of the century, those companies that perfected the household refrigerator were newcomers.

When *Ice and Refrigeration* felt that it was time to update its 1916 domestic refrigerating machine article in 1923, it required four separate articles to cover the various types then on the market.[75] "In the interim . . . there has been considerable activity in the development and production of a successful household refrigerating machine. Some of the

st engineering talent in the country has been employed to
sign and perfect these small mechanical refrigerating
achines; others are in the experimental stages; and new
vices, processes and machines are being brought out
m time to time."[76]

Although numerous products were listed in these arti-
s, the application of engineering talent and capital was
t uniform. In fact, by 1924, the electric refrigerator market
s 90% controlled by four manufacturers. Despite this, the
ice of the most commonly used refrigerator had
creased from $450 to $250 between 1922 and 1924.[77] The
anufacturers who came to dominate the U.S. market in
e 1920s were all newcomers, established specifically to
pitalize on the household refrigerator. These manufactur-
s were responsible for much of the "considerable activity"
d "engineering talent" devoted to household refrigera-
n. And like the refrigeration industry of the last century,
outside source provided new thinking.

At the beginnings of the refrigeration industry in the
neteenth century, some of the talent entering that new
ld came from or was influenced by the science and indus-
y of steam engines. In the twentieth century, another reci-
ocating engine, the internal combustion engine, and its
ogeny in the automotive industry would provide a simi-
r reservoir of fresh thinking. To this would be added the
fluence of the electrical industry.

Unlike the steam engine influence, which was mainly
chnical, the automotive and electrical industries com-
ned a technical underpinning with a mass market vision
d added the capital necessary to bring a foolproof refrig-
ator to market.

he Automotive Influence—Kelvinator and rigidaire

The potential of what automotive industry capital could
complish was hinted at in the previous story of Isko
corporated, where the automotive money of Henry Joy
ought Fred Wolf's DOMELRE to mass production. Where
ko failed, Kelvinator and Frigidaire would succeed.

At the same time that Fred Wolf, Jr., was conceiving his
OMELRE, Nathaniel Wales, an inventor of automotive
vices and later described as "more full of ideas than a
n-cushion full of pins," teamed up with Detroit engineer
dmund Copeland, who had been the general purchasing
gent for General Motors Corporation. The two wanted to
velop an absorption-type household refrigerator that
ales had conceived. Despite the warnings of General
lotors president William Durant, who told Copeland that
was a fool to put his money into the untested idea, the
vo decided to proceed anyway.[78] Copeland and Wales
ere able to obtain financial backing from Arnold Goss,
irector of the Chevrolet Motor Car Company and an asso-
ate of Durant. A prototype was constructed; however,
oss rejected the machine as impractical. Copeland and
Vales then began working on a vapor-compression-type
stem; however, it was not until 1917 that, after at least a
ozen different models had been constructed, a machine
at operated "reasonably well" was perfected. During that
ear, a new corporation under the name Kelvinator was
tablished.[79] By that time, Wales had departed and Fred
eideman, an assistant of Fred Wolf, Jr., had come over

Figure 10-34 *Electrical engineer Fred Mason Kimball (1861-1930) was
the first manager of General Electric Company's small motor department
established in 1898. Recognizing a potential market for electric motors
convinced a group of investors to merge several companies pioneering in
automatically controlled systems for homes and shops. The Automatic
Refrigerating Company became the first firm to have long-term success
in bringing small-size refrigeration to market (from General Electric Hall
of History).*

from Isko.[80] Heideman seems to have been responsible for
turning Wales's and Copeland's technical problems around
so that by 1918, a prototype machine was installed in a
home for a field test after Copeland had spent $150,000
developing a bellows-type thermostat. The prototype being
successful, a system (which had some features of the
DOMELRE/Isko machine) was placed on the market and
67 machines were sold in 1918.[81] Thereafter, Kelvinator
Corporation was able to make slow progress selling the
public on the new idea of electric refrigeration for the home
(Figures 10-40 and 10-41).

Meanwhile, William Durant apparently had a change of
heart about household refrigeration. About 1916, he
attempted to purchase Kelvinator, whose founding he had
earlier tried to discourage.[82] Unable to make a deal with
Kelvinator, Durant purchased a defunct Detroit firm, the
Guardian Frigerator Company, in 1918. Guardian, founded
in 1915 by Alfred Mellowes and Reuben Bechtold, was one
of the many small companies that had failed experimenting
with household refrigeration.[83] The firm had unsuccessfully tried to market a self-contained electric refrigerator (U.S.
Patent 1,276,612 of 1918) beginning in 1916. Apparently
Durant desired to have an alternative income source should
the automotive industry be ordered to cease motorcar production due to the world war then in progress. Durant felt

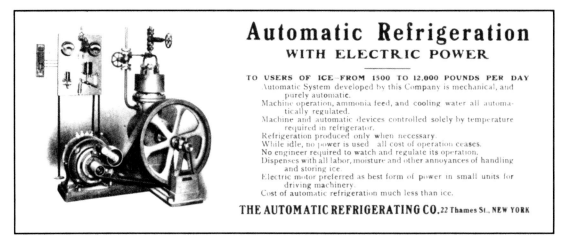

Figure 10-35 *The Automatic Refrigerating Company pioneered the use of thermostats, automatic expansion devices, and safety controls.*

Figure 10-36 *The DOMELRE was probably the first attempt to mass market a foolproof electric refrigerator for the home. Designed to be used with the customer's icebox, a hole was cut in the top of the refrigerator over the ice compartment. The DOMELRE was placed on top of the box, with the evaporator through the hole. The unit was ready to run, featuring thermostatic control and a flexible cord ending in a swivel socket that could be screwed into any Edison-base-type light socket (from* Ice and Refrigeration, *July 1914, ad section, p. 10).*

Figure 10-37 *The ¼-hp DOMELRE was the first household refrigerator produced with an air-cooled condenser. It used a direct expansion evaporator into which the sulfur dioxide refrigerant was fed through an automatic expansion valve. The temperature was controlled with a preset bimetal thermostat. The machine shown, model C.B., saw a production run of at least 75 units beginning in 1914, followed by another 450 using a 12-cylinder wobble-plate compressor ("The first five years in the history of the Isko Company,"* Electric Refrigeration News, *September 12, 1928) (from General Motors Institute, Collection of Industrial History, file 79-10.1-211).*

Figure 10-38 *The DOMELRE was apparently the first household electric refrigerator to feature ice cube trays as part of its design. Supposedly, Fred Wolf, Jr., went to a local 5- & 10-cent store and purchased a muffin baking tin for the purpose. The previous figure shows two of these muffin tins nestled in the evaporator. This figure shows a later production version of the muffin-type ice tray. The "cubes" were released by running water over the tray (from Smithsonian Institution, photo #92-8900).*

that refrigerators would be just the thing to tide his dealers over during the war emergency.[84] Durant renamed the company Frigidaire and, over the objections of his chief engineer, ordered immediate production of refrigerators. However, unexpected trouble developed. The automobile dealers were not as enthusiastic as Durant was for an untried product, forcing General Motors to set up separate dealerships.

By 1920, Frigidaire had produced thousands of refrigerators, but complaints of improper operation flooded in by the hundreds. Durant was embarrassed because many of his wealthy friends who had purchased refrigerators were among the dissatisfied customers.[85] Durant became discouraged and ordered General Motors vice-president John L. Pratt to investigate Frigidaire with the thought that it might be liquidated, an idea favored by a number of General Motors executives. Pratt found that there were many engineering problems in the Frigidaire, but when he went out to talk to the users, he found them very loyal to the product. One woman offered to give up anything in her kitchen but her Frigidaire. He also discovered that there was a lack of adequate service for the refrigerators that were breaking down. If Frigidaire were liquidated, those customers needing service would be left "in the lurch" and General Motors might be left with a "black eye" as a result. Pratt's subsequent report convinced General Motors that Frigidaire was a basically sound product that could be made profitable.

A decision was made to transfer Frigidaire from Detroit, Michigan, to Dayton, Ohio, where it would be operated by General Motors' Delco Light Company division, and where there was ready access to the newly established General Motors Research Laboratory. By that time, Frigidaire was in debt to General Motors for $3.5 million, and there was no prospect for a successful product.[86] Three research engineers—Jesse King, H. Blair Hull, and Sylvester Schweller—were assigned by Delco-Light in July 1921 to the task of improving the Frigidaire refrigerators.[87] They were successful but not until production was completely halted for at least several months. Sales of refrigerators were then resumed in limited numbers; however, sales soon had boomed to such an extent that in 1923, Alfred Sloan (who was Durant's successor as General Motors president) remarked at a sales convention that the profit of Frigidaire in the previous year was sufficient to cover the entire dividend of GM preferred stock[88] (Figures XVII, XX, and XIX color section, and 10-42 through 10-48).

The Influence of the Electrical Industry—General Electric

By the 1920s, electric power was becoming widely used in the U.S. as well as in many developed countries. Various types of appliances, such as clothes irons, washing

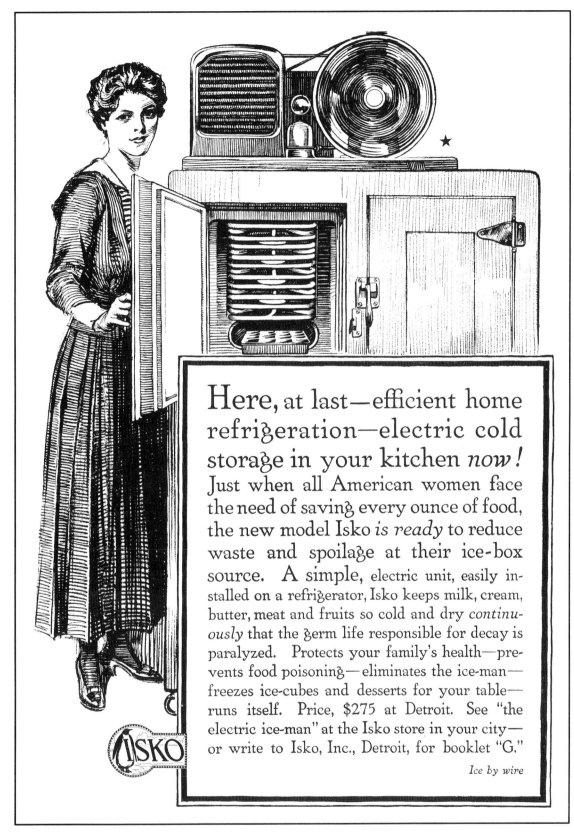

Figure 10-39 *When Henry Joy of Packard Motor Car Company bought out Fred Wolf, Jr., in 1917, the DOMELRE was renamed Isko and was redesigned with a finned-tube air-cooled condenser, apparently the first in the industry. The price was reduced from $385 to $275. About 1,500 of these machines were made (from* Good Housekeeping, *July 1917, p. 145).*

Figure 10-40 *Edmund Copeland inspecting the bellows-type thermostatic control he developed for Kelvinator. A brine-type evaporator, resembling a block of ice, was used. The thermal mass of this type of evaporator reduced cycling of the refrigeration unit. Copeland's thermostat, which cost $150,000 to develop, worked by sensing the temperature of both the evaporator and the refrigerant. The thermostat bellows, containing volatile fluid, was immersed in a copper can of glycerine. The bottom of the can rested on the evaporator casing, while the sides of the can were wrapped with the refrigerant suction line leaving the evaporator. The thermostat operated by turning the refrigerating system on when it sensed that the evaporator had warmed up to its setpoint and turning the system off when it sensed that cold, evaporating liquid refrigerant had reached the suction line coil. The design worked so well that Kelvinator used the Copeland design in its refrigerators for ten years (from Refrigeration Research Corporation Museum, Brighton, Michigan).*

Figure 10-41 *The first successful Kelvinator refrigeration condensing unit featured the "bird cage" type air-cooled condenser of the DOMELRE. This style of condensing unit, manufactured by Kelvinator until 1928, was designed for installation remote from the refrigerator, e.g., in a basement. All of Kelvinator's early systems were designed for conversion of ice-type refrigerators, and Kelvinator did not manufacture a "self-contained" refrigerator until 1925 (from Copeland Corporation, Division of Emerson Electric Corporation, Sidney, Ohio).*

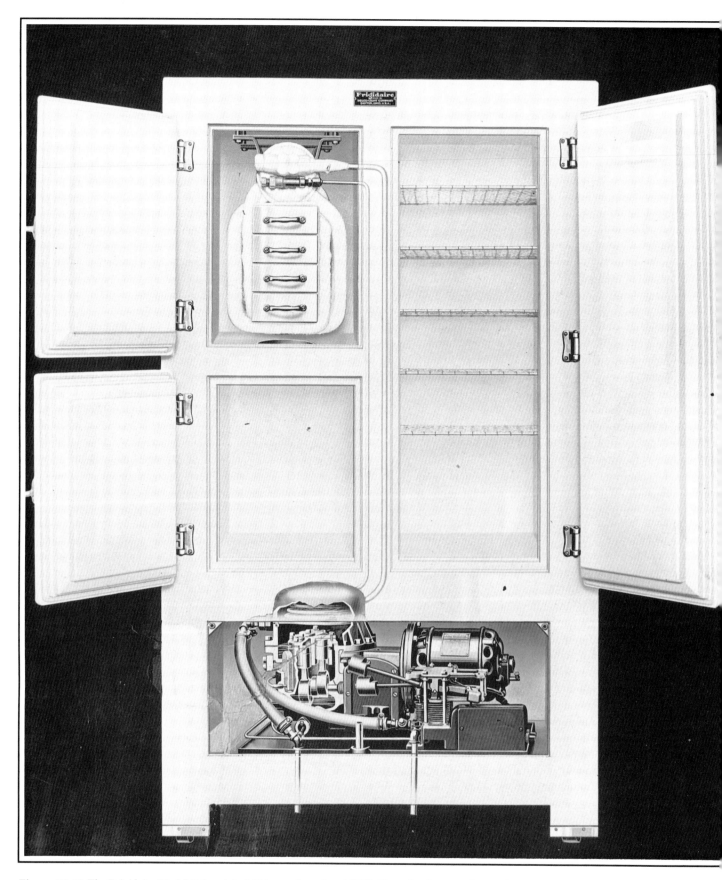

Figure 10-42 *The Frigidaire Model B-9 weighed 834 pounds and cost $775. The price (but not the weight) was gradually reduced until the model was discontinued in 1926 in favor of a metal cabinet. This photo, about 1924, shows a direct expansion evaporator employing a "low-side float" expansion device connected to a water-cooled sulfur dioxide condensing unit (from General Motors Institute, Collection of Industrial History, Flint, Michigan).*

Figure 10-43 *Woodworking department of Frigidaire Corporation, Dayton, Ohio, sometime after 1921. U.S. manufacturers of electric household refrigerators used wooden cabinets until 1926, when metal cabinets were introduced. The result was a lighter, lower-cost refrigerator that was easier to keep clean (from General Motors Institute, Collection of Industrial History, Flint, Michigan).*

Figure 10-44 *Frigidaire's Model B wood cabinet refrigerator was insulated at first with seaweed (eel grass) and later with corkboard. Many of the corkboard-insulated refrigerators caused problems for Frigidaire when food juices seeped through the inside metal liner seal, causing offensive odors. The problem of "the stinkers" (as named by Frigidaire personnel) was solved by dipping the corkboard in "hydrolene," a petroleum-based sealer. The photograph was taken at the Frigidaire factory in the mid-1920s and shows the hydrolene sealing operation (from General Motors Institute, Collection of Industrial History, Flint, Michigan).*

Figure 10-45 *Cabinet assembly at Frigidaire Corporation plant, Dayton, Ohio, 1926. Shown are Frigidaire's first metal cabinet refrigerators, designated as Model M. A wood frame was covered with steel sheets finished in white enamel. The corners were covered with bright metal strips. Whereas the earlier B-9 had weighed 834 pounds and cost $595 in 1922, the introduction of the M-9 in 1926 resulted in a weight reduction to 362 pounds and a price decrease to $405. The Model M was the first Frigidaire to feature an air-cooled condensing unit (McCoy, 1962, part IV) (from General Motors Institute, Collection of Industrial History, Flint, Michigan).*

machines, and electric ranges, were coming into use. The production of electricity was skyrocketing as homes and factories converted to electric power. In the U.S., for example, the amount of electric power produced rose from about 3 billion kilowatt hours in 1900 to about 70 billion in 1925.[89]

Despite the seeming potential for increasing the use of electric power through the promotion of electric refrigerators, the "central station" electric utilities hesitated for some time. "From 1918 to about 1925, the utility companies had seen these refrigerators without taking any action encouraging their use. Two or three years later they began to merchandise electric refrigerators themselves for the purposes of increasing their electrical output."[90] It seems that the daunting technical problems tempered their enthusiasm for a time, but as these problems were overcome and refrigerators became more reliable, the utilities changed their tune.

> Until recently, troubles of various kinds have resulted in household refrigerating apparatus proving unsatisfactory and concerns handling it have been placed in embarrassing positions and suffering heavy losses financially, to say nothing of similar consequences experienced by manufacturers.
>
> All this has resulted in having made it very difficult to convince many central stations that a satisfactory solution of this problem had been really effected.
>
> It is felt, therefore, that these conditions, as much as any, are responsible for domestic electric refrigeration not being much more widely introduced at the present time than it is.
>
> From the above remarks, we draw the conclusion that domestic refrigeration is entitled to the same effort and cooperation from the central stations as had been given the

matter of introducing such devices as the electric range, and with this cooperation there is every reason to expect a very rapid introduction of this equipment into the home, as well as a rapid and continued improvement in perfecting the apparatus itself to the point where there should be no question as to its satisfactory performance.

> For the past three years (1921-1924) or so, there has been a steady increase in the sale and use of domestic electric refrigerating equipment, which has now mounted to such proportions as to make it safe to assume that domestic electric refrigeration has come to stay and it is not going to suffer the setbacks and almost complete demoralization it suffered on several occasions in the past, when it seemed to have received a healthy start.
>
> From the central station standpoint, almost everyone is familiar with the attractive load building possibilities of this device, resulting as it does, in a revenue representing possibly the highest rate per kilowatt of demand of anything connected to the central station system.[91]

In 1925, the managing director of the electric power trade organization in the U.S., the National Electric Light Association, admitted that the group was going to organize a national promotion of electric household refrigerators in the U.S.[92] Thus, by the late 1920s, the electric power interests finally saw the electric household refrigerator as a boon to their sales of electricity.

A principal manufacturer of electrical products was the General Electric Company, which had all but established the electric industry in the U.S.[93] General Electric had been interested mostly in the manufacture of electrical equip-

Figure 10-46 *Model G air-cooled sulfur dioxide condensing unit used with Frigidaire Model M refrigerators. The Model G unit had been introduced in 1924, using a wooden base, for remote installation with the Model B refrigerators in an effort to replace the costly, noisy, water-cooled unit then in production. The unit featured use of the recently introduced V-belt drive. The condenser shown at either side of the compressor was formed of flattened 3/8-inch copper tubing cooled by a fan-type flywheel. Although this construction seems inefficient and expensive by today's standards, widespread use of finned-type air-cooled condensers did not appear until the late 1920s (from General Motors Institute, Collection of Industrial History, Flint, Michigan).*

Figure 10-47 *Frigidaire develped an extensive service organization to install refrigeration systems in homes (from General Motors Institute, Collection of Industrial History, Flint, Michigan).*

ment for central station electric utilities and electrical equipment for industry. Soon, General Electric also developed an interest in household appliances, at first as a means of increasing the electrical load for utilities. The company's first encounter with refrigeration began in this way (Figure XXI, color section).

The Audiffren-Singrun Refrigerating Machine

The Reverend Marcel Antoine Audiffren, a French abbott and physics teacher, developed a hermetically sealed refrigerating system of unique design in the late 1800s.[94] It was said that the system was originally conceived to provide a means to cool wine made by the monks. The system, which incorporated a stationary compressor within a rotating chamber, was commercially produced beginning about 1904 through the efforts of French industrialist Henri Albert Singrun in his Etablissements Singrun at Epinal, France, and later in many other countries.[95] Some years later, an American international trader, Griscom by name, was touring France and, while in Epinal, became convinced that the Audiffren-Singrun machine had commercial possibilities in the U.S. He obtained rights to build the machine in the U.S. Sales of the machine were initially through the H.W. Johns-

Figure 10-48 *Frigidaire refrigerator, 1927. The promotion of electric refrigerators sometimes reached extremes, as shown by this specially painted display model of a 1927 Frigidaire refrigerator. Sometimes refrigerator salesmen went to great ends to sell their product. In 1928, a Frigidaire salesma Alan Richards, took an order for a refrigerator from Alvin "Shipwreck" "Cannonball" Kelley, who claimed to be "the champion flagpole sitter of world." Spending seven days and nights at the top of a flagpole on top of the Andrew Building in Buffalo, New York, Kelley agreed to buy a refrigera if Richards could get the order form to him, so the salesman shinnied up the pole, order in his teeth, and obtained the sitter's signature, to the cheers the many onlookers assembled on the roof (Anonymous, 1928, "Frigidaire salesman climbs flag pole . . .," Electric Refrigeration News, Februa 1) (from General Motors Institute, Collection of Industrial History, Flint, Michigan).*

Manville Company, which had an extensive marketing organization. The machine manufacture was contracted out to the Fort Wayne Electric Works division of General Electric Company, which commenced manufacture in 1912.[96]

Apparently, James Wood, manager of the Fort Wayne operation, was convinced that the A-S machine would prove a boon to the central station utilities, which would benefit from increasing electricity sales as refrigeration was installed in homes. The Audiffren machine was produced until 1928 by General Electric in small quantities, but the bulky, expensive machine was not really suitable for household use. Even so, the Audiffren machine, in its improved versions,[97] proved to be of durable design (Figures 10-49 through 10-52).

General Electric's Refrigerator

The General Electric Company was interested in household refrigerators as early as 1913, apparently as a result of the company's involvement with the Audiffren machine.[98]

About 1917, engineers at General Electric's Fort Way facility began experimentation with domestic refrigerati machines in the hope of finding a replacement for the A machine that could be sold in greater quantities. Cla Orr, who had supervised the manufacture of the A machine from its introduction, tested some open-dri machines but settled on a hermetically sealed compress in 1920. After some experimentation and modificatio fifty samples were built, which incorporated the oscilla ing cylinder design of the A-S machine and a water-cool condenser within the compressor shell.[99] These machin worked reasonably well; however, no action was taken exploit the development. In fact, it was only due to t perseverance of Walter Goll, who had succeeded Jam Wood as manager at the Fort Wayne Electric Works, th experiments with household refrigerators had proceed as far as they had (Figures 10-52 through 10-55).[100] Soo however, a renewed interest was shown by top manag ment, and Francis Pratt, General Electric's vice-preside of engineering, asked Alexander Stevenson, Jr., of the E

M. L'ABBE AUDIFFREN

Figure 10-49 *The Reverend Marcel Audiffren invented a unique hermetical-ly sealed refrigerating system in the late 1800s (from Audiffren Drinking Water System, Bulletin D-201, 1921, H.W. Johns-Manville Co.).*

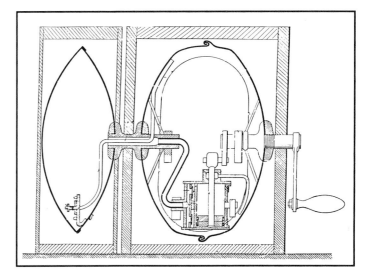

Figure 10-50 *Audiffren's hermetic machine, 1895. A stationary compressor was mounted in a bronze shell at right. Compressed sulfur dioxide refrigerant condensed on the outside of the shell, which was rotated in a water bath. The condensed liquid held against the shell by a centrifugal force was skimmed off, then passed through the shell at left, rotating in the water to be cooled. The liquid refrigerant evaporated as heat transferred from the water being cooled through the bronze shell. The refrigerant vapor thus formed then passed through the shaft, to the right shell, and into the compressor (from U.S. Patent 551,107 of 1895).*

ineering General Department located in Schenectady, New York, to survey the whole field of domestic refrigertion.[101] Stevenson's report, completed in 1923, was probbly the most exhaustive study of the engineering and conomic aspects of the domestic refrigerator done up to hat time. Stevenson not only ttempted to answer the question s to whether General Electric hould formally enter the market, ut he also studied all of the existg household refrigerating machines.[102] As a result, Francis Pratt reported to General Electric President Gerard Swope that the tate of the art of household refrigration had reached a point of sta-ilization and that it was an pportune time to enter into com-ercial exploitation:

It is well understood that heavy financial losses have been incurred in the exploitation of this business, but I suggest that the problem for the General Electric Company to consider is whether the time has not arrived when this business can be made profitable.[103]

Stevenson, aware of the daunt-g task faced by the company, oncluded: "Any scheme for xploitation therefore must include

in its budget a very liberal development account or it is doomed to failure."

It is recommended that the General Electric Company should undertake the further development of an electric household refrigerator as an addition to their string of appliances, and because widespread adoption will increase the revenue of the central stations, thus indirectly benefiting the

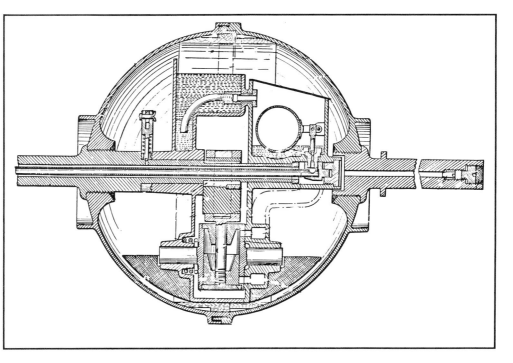

Figure 10-51 *The compressor-condenser end of the improved Audiffren-Singrun machine shows compressor suspended from the shaft, held stationary by a lead weight, with the piston fixed to an eccentric. As the entire shell is turned, the piston oscillates in the cylinder. A high-side float meters condensed liquid refrigerant to the evaporator (from U.S. Patent 1,555,780 of 1915).*

Figure 10-52 *The first Audiffren-Singrun refrigerating machine, produced in the U.S. in 1912 at the Fort Wayne Electric Works Division of General Electric Company. The works manager James Wood (at extreme right) bet a box of cigars that the machine would indeed work. Wood won the bet. Third from right is engineer and master mechanic Clark Orr, who was the principal engineer on the project, and who later designed General Electric's first production household refrigerators. General Electric produced the A-S machine in four sizes, with capacities of 500, 1000, 2000, and 4000 pounds of ice meltage equivalent per day (from* General Electric News, *March 8, 1942, p. 8).*

Figure 10-53 *The first General Electric household refrigerator unit, constructed sometime in 1917-1918 by engineer Clark Orr at the Fort Wayne Electric Works. The open-drive machine failed engineering tests, causing Orr to focus on a sealed compressor design (from General Electric Hall of History, Schenectady, New York, photo 142038).*

Figure 10-54 *The first successful General Electric refrigerating units used a cast bronze casing housing an oscillating cylinder compressor, patterned after the Audiffren-Singrun machine. A water-cooled condenser for the sulfur dioxide refrigerant was housed at the bottom of the casing. A brine-type evaporator was used. The unit featured was internally designed type OC-2, form E, and was constructed before January 1920 (from General Electric Hall of History, Schenectady, New York, photo 142094).*

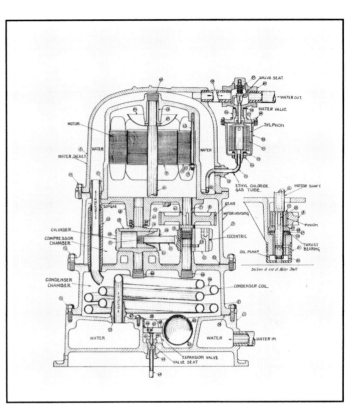

Figure 10-55 *Internal cross section of the type OC water-cooled refrigerating unit (from General Electric Hall of History, Schenectady, New York, photo 142303).*

General Electric Company. But, the General Electric Company should not enter this field in the hope of immediate profits from the sale of these machines. For some years to come, the developmental and complaint expenses will probably eat up all the profits.[104]

The recommendation was accepted by General Electric, and development commenced. Initially, the system developed by Clark Orr at Fort Wayne, internally designated as "type OC-2" (OC—an abbreviation for "oscillating cylinder"), was selected for manufacture after being re-engineered into an air-cooled version as had been recommended by Alexander Stevenson. Twenty test units were built in late 1923 and 1924, followed by another 100 in early 1925.[105] The new design, designated "The General Electric Refrigerator,"[106] was announced in late 1925 (Figures 10-56 and 10-57 and Figure XXI, color section).[107] Within a year, as many as 2,000 OC-2 type refrigerators had been sold by General Electric's Central Station Department through electric utilities. Because the numerous "ice boxes" in public use varied greatly in construction and efficiency, General Electric wisely decided that many potential problems would be avoided if the refrigerators were sold as a complete unit. The wooden cabinet, insulated with corkboard, was manufactured under contract by Seeger Refrigerator Company.

Cabinets were separately shipped from the Seeger factory in St. Paul, Minnesota, directly to the customer, as were the refrigerating units from Fort Wayne, Indiana.

Although the OC-2 refrigerator was a great improvement over the Audiffren-Singrun refrigerating machine, it appears that General Electric felt it still was not the final answer. By late 1925, another round of developmental engineering began, this time centered in Schenectady, New York.[108] Competing teams of engineers were set on the task of developing a mass-production refrigerator.[109] A new design, designated the "DR-2" (the abbreviation DR came from "domestic refrigerator") and engineered by Christian Steenstrup, was selected after extensive testing. The new design, which was advertised as the "Monitor Top," featured an all-steel refrigerator cabinet and a low power consumption of only 50 kWh per month, said to be half the power consumed by competing refrigerators. General Electric committed $18 million for the manufacturing plant and another $1 million for the 1927 advertising campaign.[110] A separate "Electric Refrigeration Department," headquartered in Cleveland, Ohio, was formed.[111] The company opted for mass distribution and sales by dealers, bypassing the electric utilities, which were assuaged by the indirect benefits they would receive from the increase of sales of electric power. The General Electric Monitor Top refrigerator stunned its competition with its advanced features and low price. By 1931, one GE ad claimed that there were one million users! (Figure XXII, color section, and 10-58 through 10-62). The competition from GE resulted in another surge of research and development at other refrigerator manufacturers. For example, Frigidaire Division of

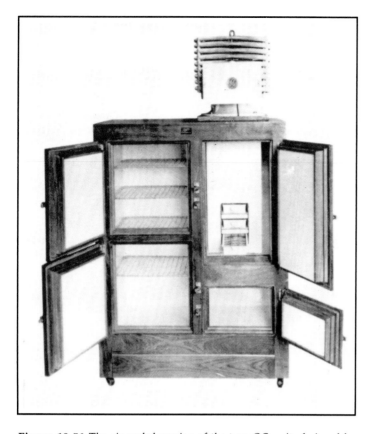

Figure 10-56 *The air-cooled version of the type OC unit, designed by Clark Orr and produced at the Fort Wayne Electric Works. Finned condenser tubes were wrapped around the welded-shell, 1/6-hp hermetic compressor, which used cotton-insulated motor windings. About 2,000 of the "General Electric Refrigerator" were produced. The General Electric Refrigerator was available with an ivory enamel or natural oak finish in a 9- or 15-cubic-foot size (matching exactly the finishes and sizes of Frigidaire's B-9 and B-15 refrigerators) (from General Electric Hall of History, Schenectady, New York, photo 283013).*

General Motors, which had dominated the household refrigerator market in the 1920s, saw its sales lead steadily reduced. The company responded by developing its own sealed refrigerating system, using a hermetic rotary compressor, the "Meter Miser," which used the newly developed chlorofluorocarbon refrigerant, R-114.[112]

A truly foolproof refrigerator had finally been realized, and the public responded by purchasing ever-increasing numbers of household refrigerators (Figure 10-64). By the late 1920s, Frigidaire's president was able to say: "Electric refrigeration for the home has definitely passed out of the `Maybe—some day!' stage. It is entering the `What!—haven't you got it yet?' stage."[113] General Electric's Monitor Top no doubt represented the triumph of technology that ensured a permanent place for refrigeration in the home. General Electric and other manufacturers boasted of their technical advances (Figures 10-65 through 10-67) and the freedom their product gave to the housewife (Figure XXIII, color section). (However, such freedom was short lived, as household work expanded.)[114]

The Ice Industry Response

As household refrigerators were perfected and their sales grew, the ice industry, which once provided all of the refrigeration used in homes, saw a threat to its monopoly. Until the early 1920s, ice men could laugh at the seeming folly of

Figure 10-57 *General Electric installation crews used a specially designed crane to lift the heavy refrigeration unit into place at the top of the cabinet (from General Electric Hall of History, Schenectady, New York, photo 437344).*

mechanical refrigeration for the home; however, by the late 1920s, they no longer laughed. The meetings of regional ice industry associations were full of discussion of the threat of mechanical household refrigeration and how to deal with it. Household refrigeration pioneer Edmund Copeland recalled some of the obstacles thrown in his way:

... in many places the ice men were openly hostile to the new type of refrigeration. In certain cities, . . . where the unions were strong, they put all kind of wiring obstacles in our way. They had ordinances passed to make our jobs difficult of installation. We were required to employ union men instead of our own to do the wiring. We had to employ

gure 10-58 *The first experimental "Monitor Top" refrigerator in the henectady, New York, engineering lab of the General Electric mpany. For the experiment, the type OC compressor was used; how- er, the finned OC condenser was replaced by a bare-tube condenser of ger diameter. The light bulbs in the cabinet produced an artificial load the tests (from General Electric Hall of History, Schenectady, New rk, photo 125779).*

Figure 10-59 *Christian Steenstrup (1873-1955), a "gruff" Danish immigrant, developed General Electric's first mass production refrigerator, the "Monitor Top." Streenstrup's refrigeration system design was one of three considered by GE and was placed in production in 1927 (from General Electric Hall of History, Schenectady, New York).*

Figure 10-60 *Alexander R. Stevenson, Jr., who was at one point president of the ASRE, was placed in charge of the refrigerating engineering efforts at General Electric in Schenectady, resulting in the development of the "Monitor Top" refrigerator. Stevenson is shown admiring an early test model, which had been running for many years. The clock at the top of the photo, shaped like one of the refrigerators, was representative of various items given to dealers and sales personnel as gifts. Monitor-Top- shaped salt and pepper shakers, sugar bowls, etc., sometimes show up in antique stores to this day (from General Electric Hall of History, Schenectady, New York).*

Figure 10-61 *The first advertisement for General Electric's Monitor Top refrigerator in 1927. One million dollars was committed to publicity in the first year (from* Good Housekeeping, *June 1927, p. 135).*

licensed plumbers to install the machines instead of our own skilled and experienced men.[115]

Another commentator noted:

The mere fact that this new invention has stormed the domestic market does not mean that former ice making methods will go into the discard without a murmur. Should anyone, with money at stake, have lulled himself into thinking that the ice man is about to decamp, let him go to a library and read the files of the ice and refrigerating journals for two years past. In the proceedings of national and regional conventions he will find two highly interesting themes. (1) There is much ill-tempered fault finding, but the cursing is not directed altogether, as might be expected, against electric refrigeration for its inroads into their business; rather, the bemoaning is against themselves for short-sightedness in past years for having been slovenly in business methods when the world was at their feet. (2) Amazing reports and surveys appear in the proceedings to indicate the wealth of uncultivated business for "the iceman and his ice." Like the hated coalman of wartime years, the iceman has been so generally scolded by the housewife that she has overlooked his virtues, until now out of clear skies comes an avalanche of double-page spreads from coast to coast extolling the economy and healthfulness of refrigeration.

A chunk of ice in a thoroughly insulated box remains, despite the wonders of electric refrigeration, the most efficient and the cheapest cooling method for the ordinary home. The iceman, individually, may resort to ridicule and vituperation; collectively, however, they are preparing to tell their story as never it has been told.[116]

All of the publicity, both good and bad, only resulted i greater sales of all forms of refrigeration:

. . . a number of advertisements were published in the early stages by both the ice companies and the electric refrigerator advocates that were derogatory to the other's product. Fortunately, both sides of the controversy quickly recognized the uselessness of such a policy and discontinued their vituperative attacks upon each other. As a matter of fact, the publicity now being given to refrigeration, whether it be electric or ice, is increasing business for both, according to experiences from some localities.[117]

Soon the ice companies realized that the large-scal advertising by mechanical refrigerator advocates di indeed help their business:

Eventually they learned that instead of interfering with the sale of ice, it really increased the market for ice because the propaganda on behalf of electric refrigeration taught the people the need of refrigeration, and thousands who had never used ice and who couldn't afford electric refrigeration bought ice boxes and became customers for ice men.[118] (Figures 10-68 and 10-69)

REFRIGERATION TECHNOLOGY EXPANDS

The incredible amount of research and development ger erated in pursuit of the foolproof mechanical househol refrigerator benefited the refrigeration industry at larg. Earlier in this chapter, the discussion of the initial failure the small refrigerating machine began by listing the variou technical problems that had to be addressed. By 1930, all them had been considerably overcome.[119]

- Refrigerant leaks around shafts and within the syster itself had been solved by the development of rotar mechanical shaft seals,[120] close-grained castings, the us of forged brass fittings and flared joints in copper tubin. and the invention of soldered joints for larger diamete tubing.[121] Developments in sealing the compressor an. motor within one enclosure—the hermetic compressor– further reduced leakage problems (Figure 10-70).[122]
- Reduction of leakage lessened the undesirability c toxic and flammable refrigerants, which continued to b used in many small systems until the 1950s.[123] Th problem of refrigerants was addressed successfully b Thomas Midgley, a practical-minded mechanical engi neer who was assigned by Charles Kettering at th General Motors Research Laboratories to search for safe refrigerant in 1928. Midgley, with associates Alber Henne and Robert McNary, developed the chlorofluorc carbon refrigerants, announcing them publicly in 193C Dr. Henne often had to correct Midgley's chemistry, bu saw him as a man of great brilliance, vision, and enthu siasm. Midgley could generate ten ideas a minute, nin of them screwy, but the tenth a "lulu." One of Midgley' "lulus," the CFC refrigerants, in retrospect were one o

Charging the DR-1 unit by a specially developed General Electric process.

Figure 10-62 *Scene from General Electric's production line showing refrigerator units being charged with sulfur dioxide refrigerant. The Monitor Top refrigerators, produced until 1937, used methyl formate or dichlorodifluoromethane (R-12) in later versions (from E.H. Norling, 1932, The Story of Quality, Cleveland, OH, General Electric Co.).*

the great refrigeration advances of the twentieth century[124] (Figure 10-71).

Electric motors were continually improved. During the 1920s, the repulsion-start motor was improved to reduce noise by lifting the brushes from the commutator after starting. Ring-type shaft oilers were eliminated in favor of wick-type oiling. Open-type construction, featuring large holes in the motor casing, was changed to "drip proof" construction. Cotton winding insulation was replaced by varnished windings. Development of electrolytic capacitors spurred use of capacitor-start motors beginning in the 1930s, at first in small sizes. Electric motors in general became lighter and less expensive.

The V-belt drive, which had been conceived as early as 1860, was perfected for the automotive industry in the early 1920s and was applied to refrigeration systems as early as 1922.[125] The V-belt made efficient, inexpensive power transmission possible to such a degree that it was quickly adopted by the heating, ventilating, and refrigerating industries (Figure 10-72).

- Automatic control of refrigerant flow reached a high state of the art by the 1930s with the introduction of two controls, the "thermostatic expansion valve" and the capillary tube.[126] Temperature control became more accurate as thermostats were improved and low-pressure controls were applied to systems[127] (Figures 10-73 and 10-75).

- Refrigerating equipment became more efficient and less expensive after extended-surface heat exchangers were used as air-cooled condensers and evaporators beginning in the 1920s[128] (Figure 10-74).

- Wooden refrigerator cabinets were virtually obsolete by 1930, and metal cabinets, many coated with porcelain enamel, became the norm.[129]

- Service of equipment improved, especially after mechanical refrigerator companies established service departments and schools (Figure 10-75).

- The technology of small refrigeration machines developed for household use expanded, with new approaches—such as improved absorption-type equipment—being marketed[130] (Figures 10-76 through 10-78).

Figure 10-63 *The Frigidaire "Meter Miser" refrigerator was an examp of just how far household refrigerator engineering had progressed by t early 1930s. The hermetic rotary compressor used in the refrigerator w charged with one of the newly developed chlorofluorocarbons, R-11 Power consumption of the 1/20-hp compressor motor was very low, ar the entire refrigerator was priced at $96, an affordable price for mo homeowners. Despite its introduction in 1933 during the Gre Depression, the refrigerator was very successful and was produced various versions for more than 20 years (from* Better Homes an Gardens, *June 1933).*

Household equipment was adapted for light commercial applications as well, resulting in some innovations, such as the electrically refrigerated ice cream cabinet[131] and even refrigerated vending machines (Figures 10-79 and 10-80). A frozen food industry grew, the result of the technology innovations of Clarence Birdseye, M. Zarotschenzeff, and others[132] (Figures 10-81 through 10-84). The technology even caught the interest of physicist Albert Einstein, who developed a magnetically operated refrigerating system for a household refrigerator in the late 1920s[133] (Figure 10-85).

The perfection of small refrigerating systems had indeed reached a point that the engineers of the last century had only dreamed of. Small as well as large system technology continued to develop beyond 1930, and the use of ice and of mechanical refrigeration continually increased (Figures 10-86 and 10-87).

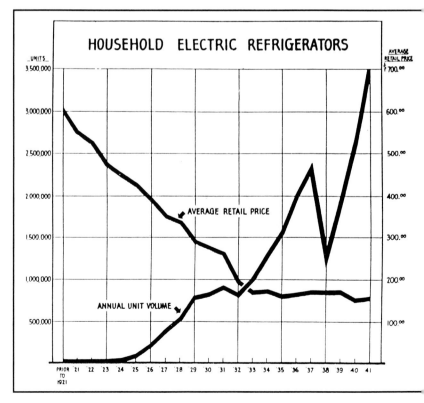

Figure 10-64 *The price of domestic electric refrigerators steadily dropped until the earl 1930s. As refrigerators became more affordable, sales volume rose, interrupted severe only during the U.S. recession of 1938 (from D.C. McCoy, 1949, "The evolution of t household mechanical refrigerator").*

Figure 10-65 *Refrigerator advertising boasted of technological accomplishments and used them to convince customers that electric refrigerators were indeed reliable household products. These scenes are from General Electric Monitor Top refrigerator ads that appeared in the Saturday Evening Post in the 1920s.*

Figure 10-66 *Electric refrigeration was said to have reduced the time needed for food preparation, releasing the housewife from drudgery (from* Good Housekeeping, *December 1925).*

Figure 10-67 *The advertising department of Frigidaire in 1925. Publicity generated by such departments of the household mechanical refrigerator manufacturers not only helped promote sales of mechanical refrigerators but so increased the public's awareness of the importance of refrigerated food storage as to increase sales of ice and iceboxes to those who could not afford the mechanical refrigerators (from* General Motors Institute, Collection of Industrial History, Flint, Michigan).

Figure 10-68 *At first, the ice industry was terrified by the burgeoning mechanical household refrigerator industry; however, the ice men soon realized that their business actually increased from all the publicity generated by refrigerator manufacturers. The ice industry responded to the new competition with better service and more efficient refrigerators (from* Ice and Refrigeration, *July 1926, and Nickerson & Collins photo collection, Smithsonian Institution, Division of Engineering and Industry).*

Figure 10-69 *One response of the U.S. ice industries was to train their employees in the science of food preservation. Here, employees of ice companies are shown studying yeast growth at the first "Household Refrigeration School" organized by the National Association of Ice Industries. The school was directed by Dr. Mary E. Pennington, "noted refrigeration expert and director of the Household Refrigeration Bureau" (from "Household Refrigeration School,"* Ice and Refrigeration, *vol. 74, March 1928, pp. 254-256).*

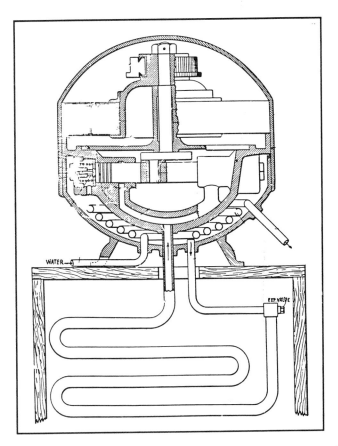

Figure 10-70 *By the 1920s, numerous experiments resulted in the modern hermetically sealed refrigeration compressor. The first to be commercially produced was the "Autofrigor" by Escher Wyss in Switzerland, and featured an external motor stator. Shortly thereafter, Douglas Stokes of Australia patented the compressor shown here, which includes a water-cooled coil to condense the refrigerant within the compressor shell (from U.S. Patent 1,362,757 of 1920).*

Figure 10-71 *Thomas Midgley, a practical-minded mechanical engineer (left) was assigned by Charles Kettering (right) of the General Motors Research Laboratories to search for a safe refrigerant in 1928. Midgley, with associates Albert Henne and Robert McNary, developed the chlorofluorocarbon refrigerants, announcing them publicly in 1930. Dr. Henne often had to correct Midgley's chemistry but saw him as a man of great brilliance, vision, and enthusiasm. Midgley could generate ten ideas a minute, nine of them screwy, but the tenth a "lulu." One of Midgley's "lulu's," the CFC refrigerants, in retrospect, was one of the great refrigeration advances of the twentieth century (from General Motors Institute, Collection of Industrial History, Flint, Michigan).*

Figure 10-72 *Compressors and fans were usually driven with flat leather drive belts. This proved to be unacceptable for operating small refrigeration compressors. There was not enough drive pulley surface, even when an idler pulley was used to increase the arc of belt contact, to prevent slippage when flat gear or chain drive belts were used. However, the solution appeared when General Motors Corporation asked the Dayton Rubber Company to devise a compact belt drive that would transmit a large amount of power without slippage (from Smithsonian Institution, Division of Engineering and Industry).*

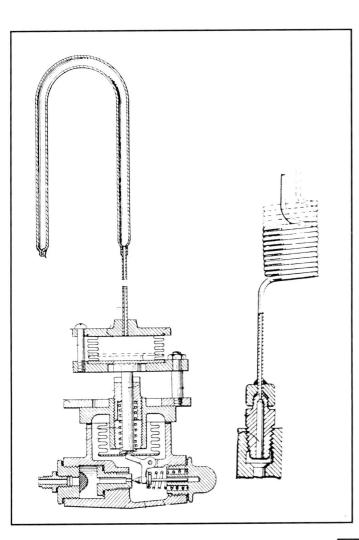

Figure 10-73 *A capillary tube, shown at right in the illustration, was invented by Thomas Carpenter about 1926 (U.S. Patent 1,919,500 of 1933) and used with methyl chloride in the household refrigerator produced by Rice Products, then the idea lay dormant. The constant super-heat "thermostatic" expansion valve invented by Harry Thompson about 1927 (U.S. Patent 1,747,958) resurrected an idea that had been tried around the turn of the century. The late Frank Gleason, an associate of Thompson at Universal Cooler Corporation, recalled that he and Thompson were driving home from a sales meeting when Thompson sud-denly shouted: "I've got it! I've got it!" Thompson insisted that they immediately proceed to the home of Universal Cooler's chief engineer, Oskar Buschmann. Gleason said the two men spent hours discussing and drawing designs for what would be the thermostatic expansion valve. Gleason, a nontechnical type, sat on a couch, bored, reading magazines through all of it! (from patent drawings).*

Figure 10-74 *A successful design for a cross-fin evaporator coil was produced by Lester U. Larkin about 1928 (U.S. Patent 1,776,235 of 1930). The evaporator shown used a low-side float type of refrigerant control contained in the tank at the top of the coil. However, the thermostatic expansion valve was quickly adopted once it became available. Use of extended surfaces on refrigeration evaporators dates at least to the 1890s; however, it was the combination of lightweight fins and tubes that revo-lutionized refrigeration, contributing to the reduction in size and cost (from patent drawings).*

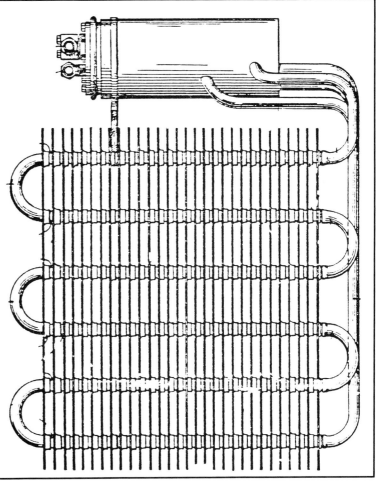

Figure 10-75 *Sulfur dioxide water-cooled condensing unit for commercial installation. The complicated-looking device mounted above the motor is a combination low- and high-pressure control and automatic condenser water valve. The setpoints were adjusted by moving the weights along the levers. The condensing unit shown, Frigidaire's model Y or N (depending on whether a one-third or one-half-hp motor was used), was made from 1925 to 1930 and was mainly used in soda fountains, butcher shops, and apartment houses where several household refrigerators were connected to one large refrigerating unit in the basement. The early commercial refrigeration units were rated in "pounds of ice melting equivalent." That rating, rather than British thermal units, was used because the refrigeration systems were being installed to replace ice in existing refrigerators (Dan McCoy, 1962, "History of Frigidaire") (from General Motors Institute, Collection of Industrial History, Flint, Michigan).*

Figure 10-76 *Two Stockholm, Sweden, engineering students, Baltzar von Platen (left) and Carl Georg Munters (right) demonstrated a gas-fired aqua ammonia absorption refrigerating system for household refrigerators. Their invention was mass manufactured in 1925 by A.-B. Elektrolux in Sweden. In 1927, the system was licensed to Servel Inc. (from Electrolux—Two Epochs That Shaped a Worldwide Group, Stockholm, Sweden, 1988).*

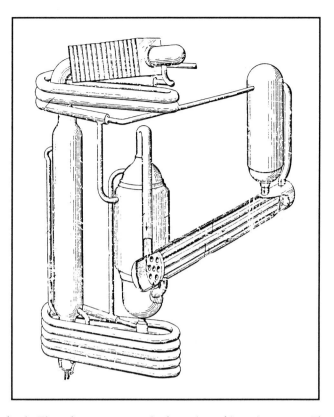

Figure 10-77 *The patent drawing for the Electrolux aqua-ammonia absorption refrigeration system. The noiseless gas refrigerator was promoted as the answer to electric systems: "An over-the-kitchen guest room in a country household where one of those semi-noiseless ice electric ice plants has been installed will be a lot more exciting for a weekend guest than sleeping over the morning coffee grinder. On and off and off and on during the night the said guest will wake from a troubled slumber thinking that maybe there's an earthquake or that maybe something is going to blow up" (W.E. Hill, 1928, "Artificial ice,"* Electric Refrigeration News, *January 4, p. 24) (from U.S. Patent 1,609,334 of 1926).*

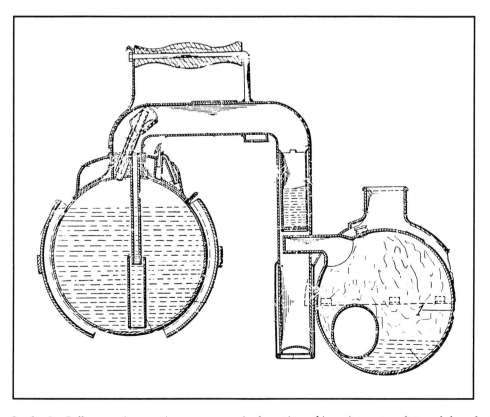

Figure 10-78 *The Crosley Icy Ball was an inexpensive aqua-ammonia absorption refrigerating system that needed no electricity. Produced beginning in 1927, some of these devices are still in use today throughout the world (from U.S. Patent 1,740,737 of 1929).*

Figure 10-79 *The small machine technology of household refrigerators was adapted to ice cream dipping cabinets, which previously used a mixture of salt and ice. The freezing mixture was usually attended to by the ice cream delivery man, often with messy and inconsistent results. This prompted the Arctic Ice Cream Company of Detroit, Michigan, to develop a mechanically refrigerated cabinet at its Nizer Laboratories Company division. John Replogle, formerly Frigidaire's chief engineer, designed a system that was manufactured beginning in 1923. Early electric cabinets used flooded-type refrigeration systems to maintain alcohol, which surrounded wells holding the ice cream cans, at low temperatures. Other companies quickly followed with their own designs. Shown is a 1925 Frigidaire installation (from General Motors Institute, Collection of Industrial History, Flint, Michigan).*

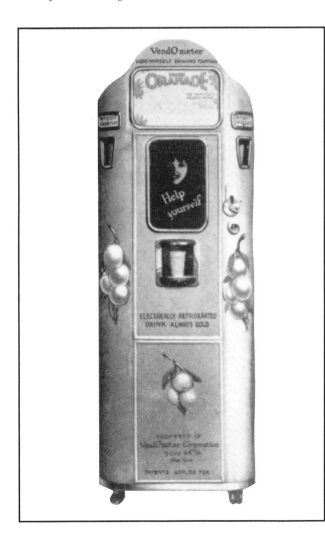

Figure 10-80 *Small refrigerating machines were applied to vending machines beginning in the 1920s, as shown for example in this orangeade dispensing machine produced by the Vendometer Corporation in New York in 1928 (from* Vendometer News, *January-February 1928).*

THE ICE-MAKING ROOM.

THE COLD OR FREEZING ROOM

MILK-PRESERVING ROOM.

Figure 10-81 *Thomas Mort's freezing works at Darling Harbour, Australia, began operating in 1875 and is said to have been the first cold storage-freezing complex using mechanical refrigeration. Designed by Eugene Nicolle, the complex had a central operations desk with gauges, control valves, and remote reading thermometers. Nicolle also employed an air-to-air heat exchanger with the ventilation supply and exhaust to improve energy efficiency (from* Illustrated Sydney News, May 27, 1876).

Figure 10-82 *Clarence Birdseye (1886-1956) began his busines[s] career as a fur trader in Labrador, where he "... saw natives catchin[g] fish in fifty below zero weather, which froze stiff almost as soon as the[y] were taken out of the water. Months later, when they were thawed ou[t] some of these fish were still alive." Amazed at the fish's freshness afte[r] thawing, Birdseye began to conduct experiments in quick freezin[g] from 1916, while he was in Labrador, until the early 1920s, after h[e] had returned to the U.S., and by 1924 had founded the Gener[al] Seafoods Company (with some financial backing of the America[n] Radiator Co.) and established an experimental laboratory i[n] Gloucester, Massachusetts, where he, Donald Tressler, and [A.] Brackett devised a belt-type quick-freezing apparatus as well as car[d]board packaging.*

Figure 10-83 *"Clarence Birdseye, now famous as the man who introduced frozen foods into the diet of millions, came to Frigidaire in 1929 with a request for special purpose refrigeration. Frigidaire built a combination display and storage cabinet for Birdseye's frozen foods at that time. Also in 1929, Frigidaire first placed on the market a low temperature storage cabinet . . ." (McCoy, 1962, part IV, p. 30) (from* Ice and Refrigeration, *vol. 92, 1937, p. 366).*

Figure 10-84 *M.T. Zarotschenzeff, an immigrant from Estonia to the U.S., developed a quick-freezing process using a chilled-brine spray, "the Z process," which was promoted in a number of countries at the same time Clarence Birdseye was perfecting his belt-type quick-freezing method (from* Ice and Refrigeration, *vol. 92, 1937, p. 366).*

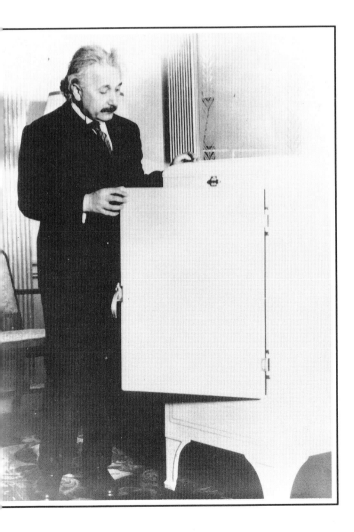

Figure 10-85 *Albert Einstein, admiring Frigidaire's "Meter Miser" refrigerator about 1934. "In the late 1920s, Leo Szillard, Einstein's assistant, proposed a new type of mechanical refrigerator, which, if placed under the great name of Einstein, would surely sell. Einstein [was] totally uninterested in business and money, but Szillard was poor and the idea seemed interesting [to him]." Allgemeine Elektricitaets Gesellschaft conducted tests, which left ". . . Berlin's practical engineers chuckling softly at the great theoretician's mistake" (Anonymous, 1929, "Einstein stumped by ice box,"* Ice and Refrigeration, *vol. 77, December, p. 440) (from General Motors Institute, Collection of Industrial History, Flint, Michigan).*

Figure 10-86 "My dear, you must come over and see our new artifici ice and electric stove combination with radio attachment that broadcas as the ice freezes! Social life in the suburbs has become awfully hect since everybody who is anybody has gone in for plain and fancy ie plants. Time was when you could get a line on a family's social status l the make of their car. . . . Nowadays you can tell whether the so and so are worth knowing by the number of ice cubes per minute their ice box capable of throwing off" (Hill, 1928, "Artificial ice," p. 24). Combinatie refrigerator-stove appliances were introduced by several companies bu were never popular (from General Motors Institute, Collection Industrial History, Flint, Michigan).

Figure 10-87 Combination stove/refrigerator (from General Electric Hall of History, Schenectady, New York).

Figure 10-88 (From Ladies Home Journal, *March 1931).*

THE EARLY TWENTIETH CENTURY: 1900-1930

After the turn of the century, the knowledge and technology of heating and ventilating advanced much more rapidly, and building systems became more independent of the buildings for which they were designed and used. The industry experienced a period of rapid growth in developing large and complex systems as well as small, unitary systems, both in response to a rapidly changing world.

Skyscrapers began to define the skylines of Chicago, New York, and eventually every major city in the world. In 1907, for example, the 52-story Woolworth Building in New York was the tallest building in the world. The increased size and complexity of large commercial buildings required greater attention to their heating and ventilating. Systems had to be larger and more sophisticated, and their engineering had to be executed with much more specialized expertise.

Along with the rapid growth of large cities, the expansion of smaller cities and suburban areas created more apartment buildings, residential communities, and single-family houses. There was a great need and an especially large market for small, simple, and reliable heating and ventilating systems.

Whether the industry had created the market through thirty years of aggressive advertising or was responding to a clear need, heating and ventilating manufacturers responded quickly. Manufacturers began to offer safer and more reliable systems as well as smaller, more lightweight "units" that combined heating, ventilating, and possibly air conditioning with integral but simple control. The end of the nineteenth century gave birth to the heating and ventilating industry, but the beginning of the twentieth century saw it mature. By 1926, the industry finally presented itself to the public in its first National Heating and Ventilating Exposition at the new Madison Square Garden in New York (Figure 11-1).

During the first two or three decades of the twentieth century, advances in the technology of heating and ventilating offered a certain degree of freedom from the extremes of climate. Architectural form, dominated by the aesthetics of the "machine age," could now be relatively independent of climate. Central heating and refrigerating systems were available for commercial buildings and unitary systems were sold in large numbers for domestic use. The availability of manufactured building components initiated the dis-

integration of architecture into individual systems, each with its respective specialty of expertise.

THE RETURN TO THE HEARTH

Although the central hearth was no longer a necessity of comfort, the romantic view of the hearth as the center of the home continued to be a strong influence for domestic architecture of the twentieth century. It is almost as if the hearth, in losing its functional reason for being, was enhanced in its mythological, spiritual, social, and aesthetic significance. The intrinsic power of fire and the hearth continued to be established as the center of domestic and community life.

At the turn of the century, the importance of the hearth was expressed in an enormous variety of designs. From the ornate fireplaces of Charles Rennie Mackintosh to the "austere" fireplaces of Frank Lloyd Wright, a great deal of the attention was devoted to their form and craft.

Frank Lloyd Wright was very much a technical innovator but he favored practical solutions in support of the needs of living in a house. "Wright's houses are remarkably livable, thanks to his central heating system using hot water pipes that encircled the rooms and that were usually concealed in the wainscoting. If there were window seats, these would be warmed by a radiator positioned directly underneath them."[1] Wright's Larkin Building, completed in 1906, was technically advanced in its day, with central heating and ventilating as well as cooling.[2]

For Frank Lloyd Wright, the hearth was the organizational and physical, as well as mythical, center of his domestic architecture. In Wright's "organic architecture," "stoves and radiators have disappeared, lighting fixtures are becoming incorporated. . . . The chimney has grown and is still growing in dimensions and importance. . . ."[3] He applied the principles of climatic design and environmental control to his residential projects to coordinate all the elements of heat, light, and air (Figures 11-2 and 11-3).

> The other aspects of the construction and management of the Prairie houses he did perceive to need explanation, and the essential clues to his method of environment management are found in the text that he wrote to accompany the first European publication of the Prairie houses by Wasmuth in 1910. Thus:

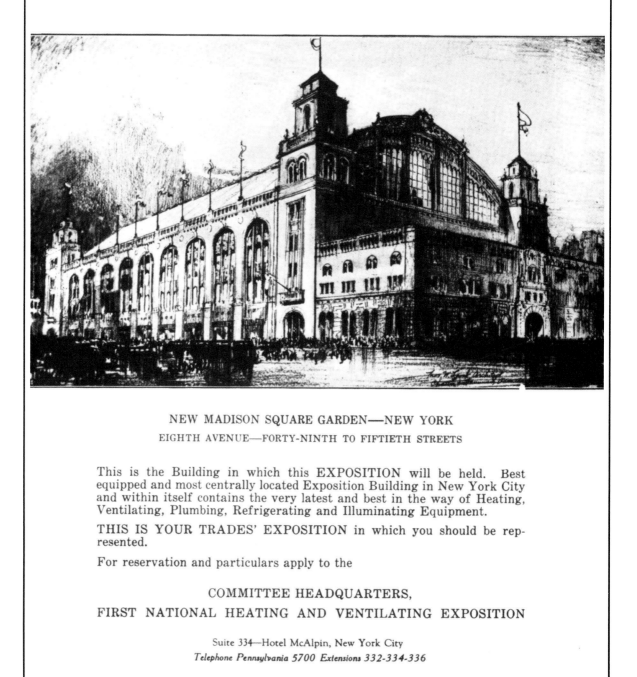

Figure 11-1 *First national heating and ventilating exposition (from* The Heating and Ventilating Magazine, *March 1926).*

Figure 11-2 *Fireplace, W. Willets house, Highland Park, Illinois, 1902 (from Ford).*

Another modern opportunity is afforded by our effective system of hot-water heating. By this means the forms of buildings may be more completely articulated, with light and air on several sides. By keeping the ceilings low the walls may be opened with a series of windows to the outer air, the flowers and trees, the prospects, and one may live as comfortably as formerly, less shut in . . . it is also possible to spread the buildings, which once in our climate of extremes were a compact box cut into compartments, into a more organic expression, making a house in a garden or the country the delightful thing in relation to either or both, that imagination would have it.[4]

Few writings of any architect relate mechanical equipment and plan and section so directly to aesthetic pleasure as does this compact and holistic vision of Wright's. Few statements of method can be so directly and revealingly tested against actual buildings. Although the statement begins with hot-water heating, it proceeds directly to the improvement of aspects and ventilation made possible by articulating the house into more separate parts, and in the process it inevitably involves lightweight construction on two counts.[5]

EATING SEES WIDESPREAD APPLICATION O THE HOME

il Heating

Although oil had been discovered in 1859 by Edwin L. rake in Titusville, Pennsylvania, it did not find its way to plications for heating until later in the nineteenth centu-

ry, when 54 oil-fired boilers were used to heat the buildings of the 1893 Chicago World's Fair.

A "furnace apparatus" was invented in 1885 which burned a mixture of petroleum, air and steam. The 54 steam boilers used to heat the Columbian Exposition in Chicago in 1893 were oil fired. By the early 1900's, more than a dozen heavy duty oil burners were made for industrial users, for heating large buildings, for shipboard use and the like. Few of these ever penetrated the home heating market.[6]

Some of the earliest types of oil heating used vaporizing-type oil burners that used "a woven wick to bring the fuel oil from the fuel container beneath it to heat of the flame and expose it to vaporization and burning." The wick-type stove was later replaced by a wickless type that used perforated metal shells or sleeves to vaporize the oil. These were based on designs made by Jim Breese and Duo-therm. "Thousands were used for kitchen ranges before World War II and since then, an equally fantastic number have been used for stoves and room heaters."[7]

The first approval listing of an oil burner was in 1912, but this listing was withdrawn three years later because the manufacturer stopped making it. The first mechanical draft burner that represented the domestic oil burner as it was subsequently developed was listed and approved by the (Underwriter's) laboratories in 1919. In 1936, when the number of oil burner manufacturers probably reached its peak, there were more than 200 listed burners.[8]

The greatest impetus to the oil heating industry was the shortage of coal during World War I. The War Priorities

Figure 11-3 *Fireplace, A. Heurtly house, Oak Park, Illinois, 1902, Frank Lloyd Wright (from Ford).*

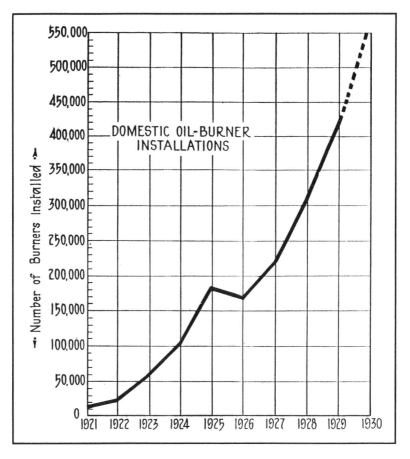

Figure 11-4 *Domestic oil-burner installations, 1921-1930 (from: Past year's progress in the oil-burner industry presages bright future,* The Heating and Ventilating Magazine, *April 1929, p. 82).*

Board in Washington, D.C., had set restrictions on the use of coal, which was being redirected to the war effort. However, there were no restrictions on the use of oil. In 1917, Honeywell received its first large order for oil-burner controls, which at that time only consisted of a damper flapper that was connected to the start/stop mechanism of an oil burner in response to the demands of a thermostat. Honeywell's first oil-burner relay was not available until 1923. The industry grew considerably during the 1920s and domestic oil burner sales soared to more than 400,000 installations (Figure 11-4).

One of the earliest types of automatically controlled domestic oil burners was the pot-type "Nokol" oil burner, referred to as the Doble-Detroit System, which is considered to be the first. The "Nokol" burner was developed from "the essential heat-producing parts of the Doble-Detroit Steam Automobile, which caused quite a furor at the 1917 Automobile Show."[9] Other examples of this type include the Model H Electrol oil burner (1918) (Figure 11-5a) and the McIlvaine early pot-type (Figure 11-5c). Numerous other models were placed on the market in the 1920s (Figures 11-6).

By the 1930s, oil burners were being packaged in compact residential heating units combining burner, boiler, automatic control, and a domestic hot-water heater. The General Electric Company of Schenectady, New York, introduced its G-E oil furnace in 1932. The claim of "completely automatic, trouble-proof oil heating" would continue to change domestic heating for the rest of the century (Figure 11-8).

Heating with Natural Gas

The use of natural gas for heating developed slowly in the nineteenth century with a few examples of gas space heaters in England and the United States. "In Boston, about 1859, a manufacturer introduced a line of small space heaters, referred to as `portable heaters' that were not vented and were connected by a hose to a nearby gas cock."[10] Gas applications for space heating were also limited for many years by a strong coal industry and by gas producers

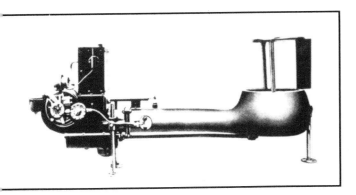

a. Model H Electrol oil burner, 1918. Said to be the first electric ignition burner to use an ignition coil similar to that in the Model T Ford.

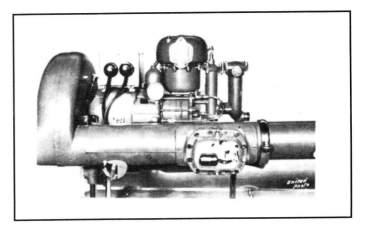

b. Super-automatic oil heater. An atomizing vertical rotary burner with a low-pressure atomizing pump to send an oil froth to a motor-driven spinning nozzle.

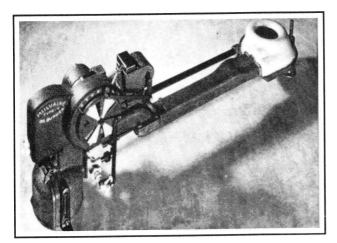

c. McIlvaine early pot-type oil burner. It operated on six fire sizes, matched to the heating load.

d. One of the first high-pressure burners to incorporate a fuel unit. Before this, manufacturers coupled strainers, pumps, pressure regulators, and shut-off valves, often using parts of different makes.

Figure 11-5 *Early oil burners (from: Burners—Then and now, Fuel Oil & Oil Heat, July 1972, pp. 46-47).*

Figure 11-6 *Advertisement, "Electrol, quiet, all-electric oil burner" (from* The Heating and Ventilating Magazine, *December 1926, p. 40).*

Figure 11-7 *Advertisement, "Koolstack Boiler" (from* The Heating and Ventilating Magazine, *August 1928, p. 23).*

themselves, who were poorly organized and relatively content with the domestic lighting and cooking markets. The coal industry was revitalized with the introduction of automatic-feed domestic coal stokers; the oil industry was offering a new source of competition, and electricity was replacing gas illumination.

"However, by 1914, there were five general classifications of gas space heaters on the market . . . one was the *Incandescent Radiator*, which was essentially an open-faced heater with mica-glazed doors with the gas flame heating a refractory that became incandescent. Another was the *Reflector Radiator*, in which the radiation from the flame was reflected into the room from a polished metal surface behind it. Then there was the *Gas Radiator*, which was enclosed with sheet iron and heated the room air from the hot surfaces of the enclosing sheet."[11]

An advertising campaign was begun to emphasize the inefficiency and waste of coal, in contrast to the virtues of "clean" natural gas (Figures XXIV, color section, and 11-9 and 11-10). At the 1922 convention of the American Gas Association in Atlantic City, representatives proclaimed a new era:

Before many years have passed, fuel consumers in great cities, getting all their heat units through pipes, will look back in horror to the day when raw coal was burned and the people submitted to the evils of smoke, ashes, unnecessary waste and needless labor. In this coming time, citizens will regard our present fuel practices very much as we regard the clumsy methods of folks a generation ago, when water was supplied to each household from a well in the backyard instead of from a central reservoir with pipes leading to all the homes in the community. It will be just as easy in the future to turn on the gas in the cellar furnace as it is now to turn on water in the bathtub.[12]

Despite these efforts, the industry continued to grow relatively slowly through the 1920s and 1930s because of its higher cost as compared to coal, inadequate distribution systems, and increased competition from alternative heating fuel sources (Figure XXV, color section).

Figure 11-8 *General Electric oil "furnace," 1932 (General Electric Hall of History, Schenectady, NY).*

Figure 11-9 *"As coal is used at present," describing the disadvantages of coal (from* The Heating and Ventilating Magazine, *November 1922, p. 54).*

Figure 11-10 *Advertisement for gas heating as the "modern road to comfort, convenience, health, cleanliness" (from* The Heating and Ventilating Magazine, *January 1927).*

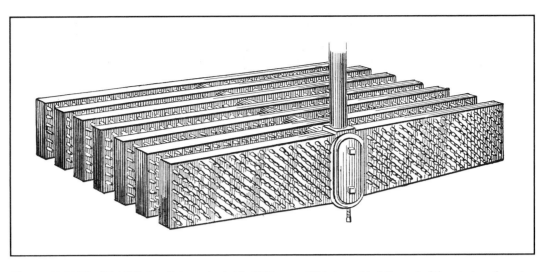

Figure 11-11 *The "Gold Pin" radiator, patented in 1854, was still being sold at the end of the nineteenth century (from* Heating and Ventilation, *March 15, 1898).*

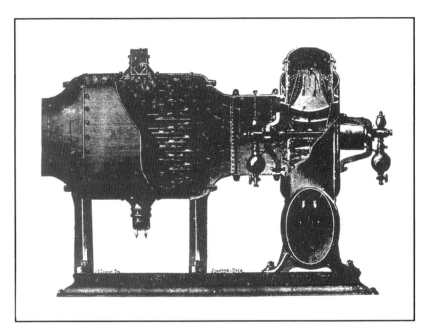

Figure 11-12 *First unit heating apparatus (B.F. Sturtevant, ca. 1870).*

FROM THE RADIATOR TO LIGHTWEIGHT HEATING SURFACES

Once the radiator was introduced in the mid-nineteenth century, there were many efforts to conceal or eliminate this "unsightly" object altogether. Indirect radiators were the first attempt to move the room radiator to the basement and, in effect, provide some of the first examples of the use of a heat exchanger. Samuel Gold's introduction of the "Pin" radiator (Figure 11-11) and the promotion of indirect heating by the New York Steam Company and others did a great deal to advance the widespread acceptance of this concept.

The principles of heat transfer were better understood from the pioneering work of Eugéne Peclét and Thomas Box, and especially from the later work of John Mills. The concealed or invisible radiator, which marked the beginning of the development of unitary heating, was based on the automobile radiator and the unit ventilator. Lightweight heating surfaces were becoming available from a number of inventors and sheet metal fabricators as well. The development the nonferrous radiator reduced the weight of heating unit from 1,500 pounds to 300 pounds.

The unit heater, the predecessor to unit ventilators and fan-coil systems, was developed to compete with hot-blast systems popularized by Sturtevant in the 1880s. Sturtevant himself was probably the first to introduce a unit heating apparatus, known as the "independent unit heater," shown in a Sturtevant catalog of 1870[13] (Figure 11-12). 1898, Henry Baetz of St. Louis invented the Baetz air heater that was sold by the St. Louis Blower and Heater Company (later changed to the Skinner Bros. Manufacturing Company) (Figures 11-13 and 11-14).

The Baetz heater is constructed of steel plates and angles. It will be noticed that the upper part is occupied by steam coils arranged so that they may be removed for repairs. The blower is shown beneath in the same enclosure. Air is drawn in by the fan from two sides and is forced upward

The Baetz Patent Steam Air-Heating Apparatus.... ✋ ✋ ✋

IS designed to make use of the waste or exhaust steam by extracting the heat therefrom and utilizing it for warming the buildings. All manufacturing plants, where steam is used for power, can be warmed comfortably by using the exhaust steam in connection with the Baetz Patent Apparatus. The heating of the feed-water for the boilers with the exhaust steam will not be interfered with by this system.

The cost of operating the apparatus is practically nothing.

The cost of the apparatus, when compared with other heating systems, is very small. The apparatus is very compact in construction, and requires small floor space.

The construction of coil is such that a good circulation of steam is insured. The steam enters at the top and the condensation has a continuous drain to outlet at bottom of coil, keeping all parts of coil well heated. The air, in its course, passes upwards, coming in contact with every inch of heating surface; and the manner of constructing the coil causes the air in its passage to be divided and subdivided many times, and become thoroughly heated before leaving the apparatus.

For the purpose of repairs, it can be taken apart very easily, as can be seen from the description. Live steam at high pressure can be used in apparatus as well as exhaust steam.

Steam (either live or exhaust) is admitted to the coil at inlet pipe A. Water of condensation leaves coil at outlet pipe B. Cold air is drawn into apparatus at blower inlet C; also at opposite side. Hot air is forced out of apparatus at outlet D.

— 3 —

Figure 11-13 *Baetz air-heating apparatus sold by the St. Louis Blower and Heater Company for factories, 1902 (from* Heating and Ventilating, *June 1929, p. 137).*

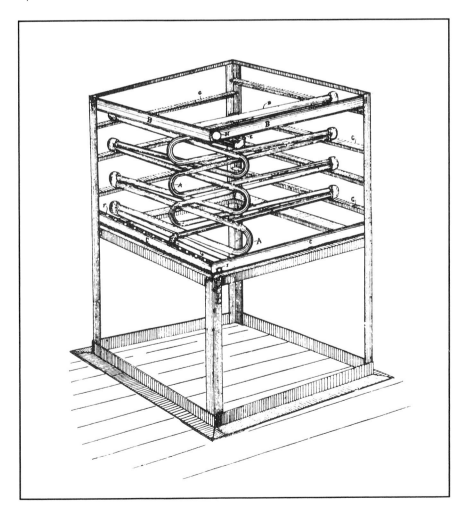

Figure 11-14 *Coil used in unit heater above (from* Heating and Ventilating, *June 1929, p. 137).*

against the steam-heated coils, passing out at the top as heated air. A convenient line shaft, a small engine or a motor may be used to propel the fan. The illustration shows where the steam and return connections are made. When a small engine is used for driving the fan the exhaust steam from the engine can be piped direct into the heater coils.[14]

The American Blower Company of Detroit also manufactured a unit heater based on the same principles, and a few years later the Ilg Electric Ventilating Company of Chicago manufactured the Ilgair unit heater.

"In 1907, Mr. M.C. Hubbard of New York State invented and placed on the market a Unit Ventilator called `The Monarch.' The Monarch ventilator consisted of a small motor, fan and radiator, enclosed in a steel cabinet."[15] The patent rights were purchased by Moline Heat in Moline, Illinois, and the design was modified to use a double radi-

Figure 11-15 *Advertisement, "Univent," Moline Heat (from* The Heating and Ventilating Magazine, *May 1920).*

tor to increase heat transfer area. It was marketed in 1919 under the name "Univent" and was available in capacities ranging from 600 to 1,500 cfm (Figures 11-15 and 11-16).

The Univent unit ventilator patents were then sold to the Herman Nelson Corporation in 1922. Herman Nelson's "Invisible" radiator, introduced in 1926, was made of copper and an alloy of aluminum. The unit was 3½ in. wide and 9 in. high and weighed only 40 pounds. Soon other manufacturers placed unit ventilators on the market (Figure 11-17).

The American Radiator Company was one of the first to apply the concept of the "Pin" radiator to its "Vento" cast-iron heater (Figure 11-18). The original patents for the "Vento" radiator were issued in 1903 to John J. Spear to solve the difficulties of installing pipe coil heaters, "which were used exclusively" at the time. "These heaters with their heavy cast

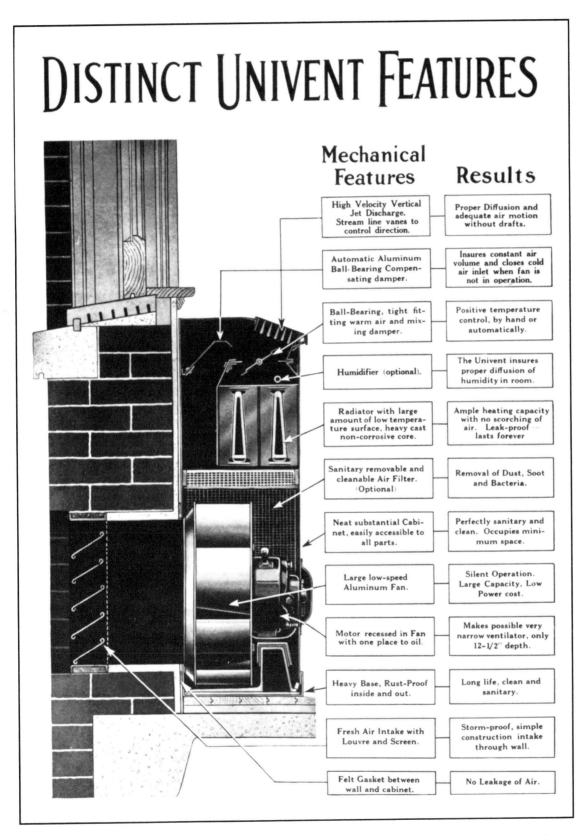

DISTINCT UNIVENT FEATURES

Mechanical Features

Results

Mechanical Features	Results
High Velocity Vertical Jet Discharge. Stream line vanes to control direction.	Proper Diffusion and adequate air motion without drafts.
Automatic Aluminum Ball-Bearing Compensating damper.	Insures constant air volume and closes cold air inlet when fan is not in operation.
Ball-Bearing, tight fitting warm air and mixing damper.	Positive temperature control, by hand or automatically.
Humidifier (optional).	The Univent insures proper diffusion of humidity in room.
Radiator with large amount of low temperature surface, heavy cast non-corrosive core.	Ample heating capacity with no scorching of air. Leak-proof — lasts forever
Sanitary removable and cleanable Air Filter. (Optional)	Removal of Dust, Soot and Bacteria.
Neat substantial Cabinet, easily accessible to all parts.	Perfectly sanitary and clean. Occupies minimum space.
Large low-speed Aluminum Fan.	Silent Operation. Large Capacity, Low Power cost.
Motor recessed in Fan with one place to oil.	Makes possible very narrow ventilator, only 12-1/2″ depth.
Heavy Base, Rust-Proof inside and out.	Long life, clean and sanitary.
Fresh Air Intake with Louvre and Screen.	Storm-proof, simple construction intake through wall.
Felt Gasket between wall and cabinet.	No Leakage of Air.

Figure 11-16 *"Distinct Univent features," p. 35 (from* Univent Ventilation, 1924, *Herman Nelson Corp.).*

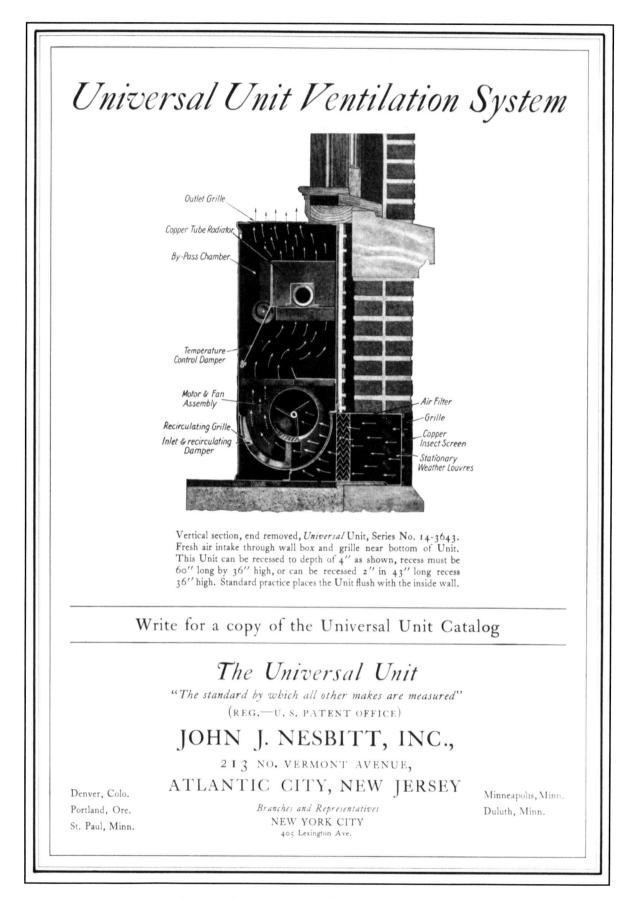

Figure 11-17 *Advertisement, "Universal unit ventilating system" (from* The Heating and Ventilating Magazine, *January 1926, p. 109).*

25 YEARS
without one instance of failure

THIS is the remarkable record of Vento Cast Iron Heaters and one of the reasons why this heating surface is almost always the choice of leading engineers and architects.

Another reason for the widespread endorsement of Vento is its low cost. The superior qualities of Vento cost no more. A review of a number of representative bids show the net installed cost to be invariably in favor of Vento.

Vento Heaters are made of high quality close-grained cast iron that will not deteriorate under the action of air, gases, water or summer dampness. The durability of Vento is actually unlimited. Its life is longer than that of the building.

VENTO
CAST IRON HEATERS

SEND FOR CATALOG
We will send you without obligation a Vento catalog containing complete engineering data—just send us your name and address.

AMERICAN RADIATOR COMPANY
40 West 40th Street, New York   816 So. Michigan Ave., Chicago, Ill.

Figure 11-18 *"Vento" cast-iron heaters, American Radiator Co. (from* The Heating and Ventilating Magazine, *April 1929).*

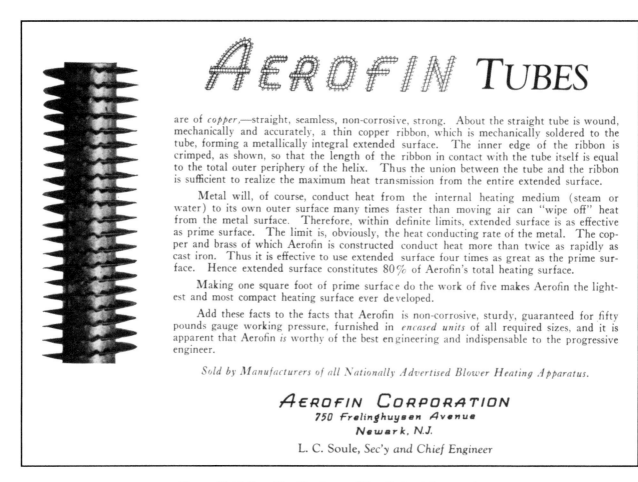

AEROFIN TUBES

are of *copper,*—straight, seamless, non-corrosive, strong. About the straight tube is wound, mechanically and accurately, a thin copper ribbon, which is mechanically soldered to the tube, forming a metallically integral extended surface. The inner edge of the ribbon is crimped, as shown, so that the length of the ribbon in contact with the tube itself is equal to the total outer periphery of the helix. Thus the union between the tube and the ribbon is sufficient to realize the maximum heat transmission from the entire extended surface.

Metal will, of course, conduct heat from the internal heating medium (steam or water) to its own outer surface many times faster than moving air can "wipe off" heat from the metal surface. Therefore, within definite limits, extended surface is as effective as prime surface. The limit is, obviously, the heat conducting rate of the metal. The copper and brass of which Aerofin is constructed conduct heat more than twice as rapidly as cast iron. Thus it is effective to use extended surface four times as great as the prime surface. Hence extended surface constitutes 80% of Aerofin's total heating surface.

Making one square foot of prime surface do the work of five makes Aerofin the lightest and most compact heating surface ever developed.

Add these facts to the facts that Aerofin is non-corrosive, sturdy, guaranteed for fifty pounds gauge working pressure, furnished in *encased units* of all required sizes, and it is apparent that Aerofin *is* worthy of the best engineering and indispensable to the progressive engineer.

Sold by Manufacturers of all Nationally Advertised Blower Heating Apparatus.

AEROFIN CORPORATION
750 Frelinghuysen Avenue
Newark, N.J.

L. C. Soule, *Sec'y and Chief Engineer*

Figure 11-19 *(from* The Heating and Ventilating Magazine*).*

iron bases were very difficult to handle, difficult to vent, and generally unsatisfactory."[16] Spear was interested in a cast-iron heating surface that could be installed in sections.

After developing some sketches on this idea, Spear took them to Mr. Wooley, a vice-president of the American Radiator Company, who felt that it could not be manufactured in the company's foundry. After further discussion with the foundry manager, Mr. Scotty Nelson, it was clear that it could be made, and it was manufactured and marketed by the American Radiator Company in 1903. The first sales were for schools in Denver, Colorado, and for three years the company's sales were poor. James H. Davis was enlisted from the Warren Webster Company to increase the sales effort.

A "Vento" steam radiator was combined with a unit ventilator in 1923 by the Peerless Unit Ventilation Co. This was enclosed in a steel cabinet with two aluminum multi-blade fans, a fresh air inlet, an air-mixing damper, and a thermostat. The Peerless unit and many unit ventilator systems like it were especially popular in school classrooms and retail stores and became known as "classroom units" or "drugstore units" (Figure XXVI, color section).

One of the first lightweight nonferrous heating surfaces was developed by L.C. Soule in the early 1920s. Soule had been an engineer for the American Radiator Company Laboratory of Thermal Research in Buffalo, New York, where in 1912 and 1913, he had done tests on the early "Vento" heater designs.[17] He later became secretary and chief engineer for Aerofin Corporation after he presented

Figure 11-20 *James A. Trane (from* Domestic Engineering, *p. 33).*

Figure 11-21 *Showroom of James A. Trane, LaCrosse, WI (from* Domestic Engineering, *p. 37).*

is concept to Willis Carrier and J.I. Lyle, who offered their support.

Aerofin introduced fin-tube systems for heating and cooling in 1922 that were constructed of seamless copper or brass tubing "about which is wound a thin, narrow, helical extended surface, also of copper or brass." The fin-tube was enclosed in a galvanized sheet-steel casing and supplied in one, two, or three rows of standard widths (Figure 11-19).

The combination of sheet-metal radiation surfaces with copper tubing in "fin-tube" designs was first introduced by a number of companies. Reuben Trane, son of the steam heating system manufacturer James A. Trane, introduced the concept of unitary heating in the form of a "cabinet heater" (Figures 11-20 through 11-22). The Trane Heat Cabinet was first announced to the public in May 1926 (Figure 11-23). This consisted of a U-shaped copper tube and fin design in a sheet-metal enclosure. The cabinet was available in four lengths—13 in., 27 in., 41 in., and 56 in., and three heights—19 in., 26 in., and 38 in., with a standard 4-in. depth.

Willis Carrier had worked on unitary systems for air cleaning and humidification during the time that he had worked for the Buffalo Forge Co. in Buffalo, New York. There he had developed encased fan ventilation and humidification units (Figure 11-24). Later, after forming his own company, he translated this background to unitary systems.

In 1934, Carrier Research Corporation patented an air-conditioning apparatus that combined heating, air conditioning, and ventilation in a single packaged unit (Figure 11-25). Known as the Carrier "Weathermaker," this was the first combination unit for the domestic market. In the following years, the "Weathermaker" continued to be marketed under the same name despite many transformations and advances.

AIR CONDITIONING

Many have thought that comfort cooling, which the general public loosely calls "air conditioning," sprang up soon after the turn of the century.[18] However, it seems that crude forms of air cooling had been evolving along with heating, ventilating, and refrigeration science, which had its mechanical beginnings in the early 1800s. Uses of air conditioning included industrial processes as well as cooling for comfort. This section focuses on the evolution of air cooling for human comfort, which evolved first and which has had such an immense impact on us all.

Early Origins of Mechanical Comfort Cooling

The need to stay comfortable in an oppressive climate no doubt has existed since the dawn of humankind, and there are scattered references to some of the schemes devised by

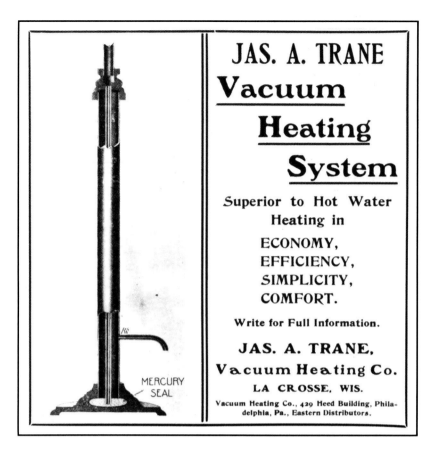

Figure 11-22 *Advertisement, James A. Trane vacuum heating system—from its original days of manufacturing steam heating equipment (from* Engineering Review, *October 1903).*

our early ancestors to stay cool. Some of these were discussed in earlier chapters. The "ancient manner" of comfort cooling, evaporative cooling, had not evolved further even by the seventeenth century, as described by a New Zealand physician visiting England at the time:

> The better to qualifie and mitigate this heate it shal be very good to sprinckle on the pavements and coole the floores of our houses or chambers with spunging water, and then to strew them over with sedge, and to trim up our parlours with greene boughes, fresh herbs, or vine leaves . . .[19]

Mechanical air conditioning was not a practical possibility until the dawn of the Scientific Age and the Industrial Revolution. From the very beginning of this era of technology, ideas were proposed and some experiments carried out regarding artificial air cooling. Sir John Leslie, who experimented with absorption refrigeration in the last century, proposed that artificial cooling be introduced into hospitals and aboard ships in 1813.[20]

What we view as modern mechanical air conditioning could be said to have crude origins in the mechanical ventilation proposals of the Marquis de Chabannes, who advocated use of a centrifugal fan to force heated or cooled air through ducts to rooms. In December 1815, a British patent was granted to Jean Frédéric, Marquis de Chabannes, for "a method or methods of conducting air, and regulating the temperature in houses or other buildings, and warming and cooling either air or liquids in a much more expeditious and consequently less expensive manner than hath hitherto been done. . . ." The patent specification states: "My method of cooling air is by means of the air pump . . . causing the

air to pass through a cool medium." The illustration of th apparatus shows a cooling tower, and thus Chabann intended to cool the air by evaporation of water. Chabann subsequently published his heating and ventilating propo als in 1815 and 1818.[21]

At about the same time, also in England, a "Mr. Deacor introduced his "EOLIAN" heating-cooling apparatus. F cooling purposes, air was drawn by a fan over parallel irc plates that were cooled by a cold-water bath at their bas Although this system was installed in some public building "it failed to bring the merited reward to the inventor."[22]

Robert Salmon and William Warrell were issued Britis Patent 4331 for an evaporative cooler in 1819. Although was not designed specifically for comfort cooling, b rather as a general means of cooling liquids, it exhibite many of the elements to be incorporated into "air washer designed later as coolers for air conditioning. In France b the 1840s, Eugéne Peclét had devised some of the earlie evaporative coolers featuring a modern design.[23] Still, would be another fifty years before air washers wou begin to be used as air coolers. Although the idea of fa forced cooling systems was established by the 1840s, use cold water or evaporative cooling placed a limit on th amount of comfort that could be obtained. A means of dra tically cooling air mechanically did not exist until artifici refrigeration was invented.

Vapor-compression refrigeration had been proposed 1805, a working model had been constructed about 183 and more extensive experiments had been conducted in th early 1850s; however, all of these attempts were devoted refrigeration, although some of the early patents mentio

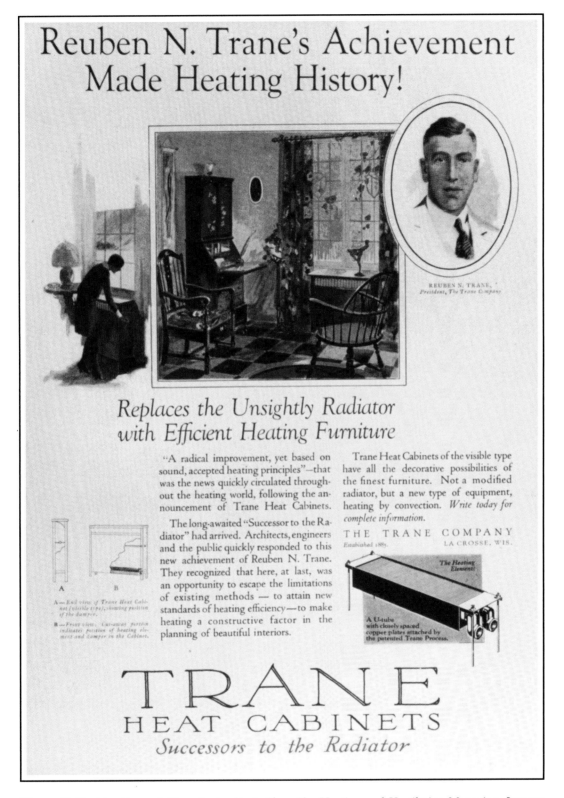

Figure 11-23 *Advertisement, Trane heat cabinets (from* The Heating and Ventilating Magazine, *January 1927, p. 18).*

Figure 11-24 *Advertisement, Buffalo Forge Co. and Carrier Air Conditioning Company, illustrating Carrier's first product, an air washer and humidifier (from* Engineering Review, *May 1912).*

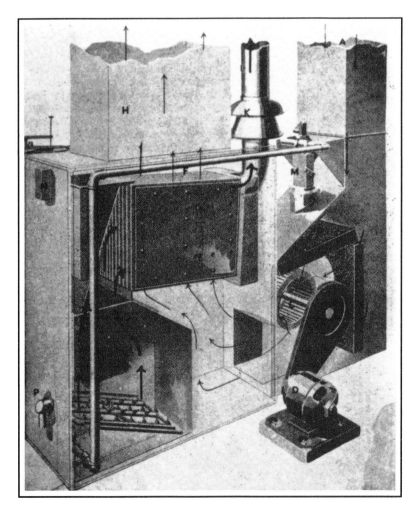

Figure 11-25 *Diagrammatic view of the "Weathermaker"; the heavy arrows showing the path of the products of combustion, and the light arrows, the airflow (from* The Heating and Ventilating Magazine, *October 1928, pp. 101-102).*

Figure 11-26

"I can stand for tainted money, I can stand for tainted grub;
I can drink polluted water and employ it when I scrub,
But since noting this invention I shall never, I declare,
Be content again with breathing anything but laundered air.

Give me clothing filled with shoddy, filled with microbes, if you will;
Let a million microbes bite me when I touch a dollar bill;
Let the germs come swarming o'er me when I take an easy chair,
But I pray you do not give me anything but laundered air.

If ozone may be laundered, can't we neatly crease it too—
Hang it round in snowy bundles like the laundry people do?
Oh, I hope the time is coming when to laundries we'll repair
Bright and early Monday mornings for our week's supply of air."

(An anonymous writer in a Montreal, Canada, newspaper and reprinted in Engineering Review, *April 1906, p. 23) (from* The Aerologist, *February 1927, front cover).*

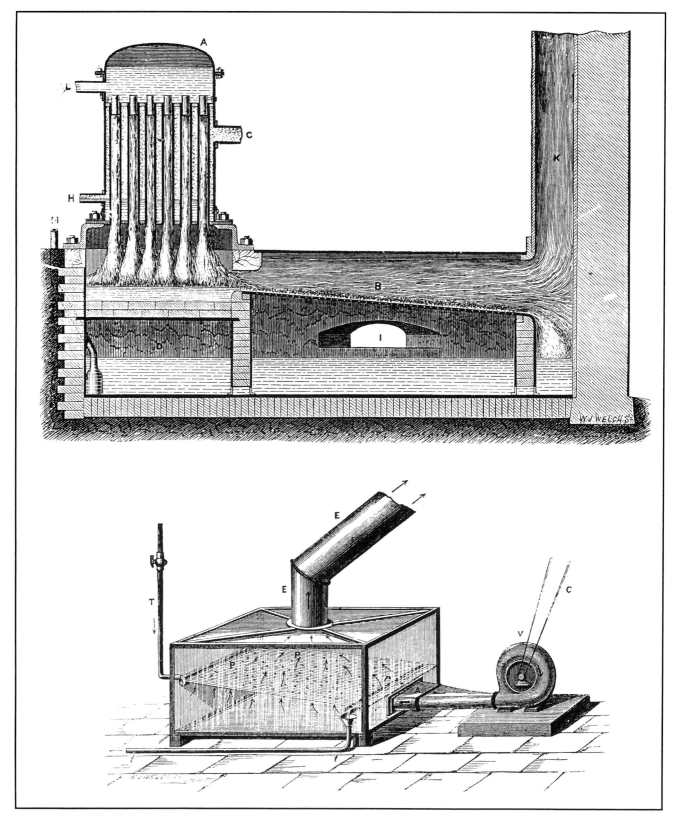

Figure 11-27 *Evaporative air cooler and air washer of the 1870s (from* The Practical Magazine, *1873, p. 459).*

comfort cooling.[24] At the same time, air-cycle refrigeration was experimented with in the U.S. by John Gorrie and in the United Kingdom by Charles Piazzi Smyth.[25] Such a system was also discussed by William Thomson (Lord Kelvin).[26] Curiously, all three air-cycle systems were proposed specifically for comfort cooling for hospitals, etc.; however, the first two were experiments and the last one only a proposal.

In 1856, ventilation pioneer David Boswell Reid had lectured on the desirability of cooling air in temperate and cold climates.[27] Indeed, Reid had already experienced crude air-conditioning design in his work at the British Houses of Parliament twenty years earlier. He had generally proposed the idea of mechanical air conditioning: "By constructing a few chambers in every hospital, where the quality of the air . . . might be entirely under control, and

MR. SOMES'S INVENTIONS

FOR

THE PRESERVATION OF FOOD,

ANIMAL OR VEGETABLE,

FOR THE

COOLING OF HOTELS, THEATRES, HALLS, CHURCHES,

AND ALL OTHER BUILDINGS,

VENTILATION, &c., &c.

NEW YORK:
PRESS OF E. S. DODGE & CO., PRINTERS AND STATIONERS, 84 JOHN STREET.
1865

Figure 11-28 *Daniel Somes may have been the first air-conditioning entrepreneur. Somes proposed that "hospitals may be so arranged that heat, flies, nor dust, need ever be present to harass and torment the patients. This is accomplished also at a cost so comparatively small as scarcely to deserve a mention. Had Mr. Somes made no discovery but this, he would be entitled to (and receive) the gratitude of the (human) race." Somes had been a member of the U.S. Congress—only a politician could promise so much at almost no cost (from Somes, D. 1865.* Mr. Somes's inventions for the preservation of food, animal or vegetable, for the cooling of hotels, theaters, halls, churches, and all other buildings, ventilation, &c., &c. *New York: E.S. Dodge & Co.).*

medicated, heated, dried, moistened, cooled, and applied in any quantity, as circumstances might dictate, . . . in numerous cases of disease."[28] Reid constructed such an air-conditioning system, but not for a hospital. By 1836, he had completed modifications to the heating and ventilating system for the British Houses of Parliament (discussed earlier in this book), wherein his proposals were put into practice. "Much is frequently effected in cooling the House (of Commons) in summer . . . by the evaporation of water, by the contact of air with cold water apparatus (the same that is used as hot water apparatus in cold weather), and, in rare cases, by the use of ice. . . ."[29] Reid had constructed an air washer under the House of Lords in which the air was cleansed, cooled, and disinfected through gauze filters and water sprays located in "Guy Fawkes' Vault." (This room was so named because it had once been stuffed with gunpowder by a revolutionary, Guy Fawkes, who attempted to blow up the Houses of Parliament. The plot was foiled, the gunpowder removed, and the room later served admirably as part of Reid's ventilation system.) During winter, the air could be filtered and humidified. Reid's system was mechanical in the sense that it used a fan to move the air; however, it did not directly use a mechanical refrigeration system. (Refrigerated systems were not applied to strictly defined air-conditioning systems until about the turn of the century.) Given the infancy of refrigeration at that time, Reid had to later admit that the only inexpensive way cooling could be done was to run water from a cold stream through heating apparatus in the airstream of a ventilating system.[30] Even the renowned English civil engineer Isambard Kingdom Brunel, when asked to design portable hospitals for use in the Crimean War, had to resort to simple forced ventilation for cooling purposes.[31]

The 1860s brought a bit more sophisticated approach to the comfort cooling of rooms. In 1864, a hospital cooling system was proposed in *Scientific American* that featured an air washer to clean the air, a fan-coil supplied by melting salted ice to cool the air, and an overhead distribution system with individual dampered outlets.[32] In France, A. Jouglet wrote an early treatise on comfort cooling in 1873, in which he discussed various methods of cooling air. Mentioned were compression-reexpansion of air, cooling by evaporation, cooling by ice or refrigeration machines, and cooling by circulation of air through underground ducts[33] (Figure 11-27).

In the U.S., Daniel Somes obtained numerous U.S. patents for comfort cooling ideas during the period 1867-1869. Some proposed cooling buildings by spraying air mists on building roofs and walls or distributing air to them that was cooled by underground ducts or pipes in which cold water circulated[34] (Figure 11-28). Numerous other patents were issued after the 1870s for comfort cooling schemes.[35]

Later, when mechanical refrigeration systems were becoming available as a manufactured product, they could be incorporated with the many comfort cooling ideas that popped into people's brains (Figures 11-29 through 11-31). Thermostats, which had already been invented, began to be applied to heating systems, and some patented cooling systems incorporated them too. All of the mechanical devices that were becoming more readily available were, however, not much more than "tinkertoys" for grown men to play

with as they constructed systems for this great idea of comfort cooling. That the realization of mechanical comfort cooling was more difficult than most realized can be seen the crude attempts to provide air cooling for the dying U President Garfield at the White House in 1881. Naval engineers, after studying several mechanical possibilities, simply blew air over ice![36] One article of 1887 noted:

> The problem of refrigerating a summer house should seem to offer no insuperable difficulties to the inventive genius of an age that has managed to create an artificial summer amidst the snows of Quebec and St. Paul. . . . Considering the number of refrigerating agencies known to modern chemistry, there would, indeed, be nothing surprising in the invention of a parlor cooler as portable as a small cooking stove. . . .[37]

Another commentator, arriving at the crux of things, aske us to consider ". . . the legitimate question . . . in all enterprises,— 'Will it pay?' Will the advantages to be derive authorize the trouble and expense?"[38] The great idea lacke a scientific basis, a public demand, and organized marke ing (Figure 11-32).

Air-Conditioning Science

The scientific basis for modern air conditioning seems have emerged at the end of the nineteenth century. Befor the 1890s, the numerous cooling systems proposed or con structed were really hit-or-miss approaches. Some mean was used to cool the air and the cooler, sometimes drier a was then used for comfort cooling. Although some rea ized that the air needed to be not only cooled, but als dehumidified, there was no understanding of the scienc involved in these processes. No one seems to hav attempted to approach the problem on a scientific basis order to determine how to size equipment, how to cool a to a given temperature, and, more important, how t remove moisture from air for a desired result in relativ humidity.

But it appears that a genuine scientific approach to coo ing originated in Germany. German heating engineers wer applying the scientific approach first discussed by Eugén Peclét in France for the sizing of heating systems. Heatin science was being taught at German engineering schools. I 1894, Hermann Rietschel, a professor at the Berlin Roya Institute of Technology, published the first of many edition of his *Guide to Calculating and Design of Ventilating an Heating Installations*. Rietschel indicates in his preface tha he desired to present the science of heating and ventilatin in a clear and simplified manner so it would be useful fo the designer and contractor. It could be said that th appearance of Rietschel's handbook marks the transferrin of heating and ventilating practice from scientists or tinker ers to engineers, architects, and contractors. Significantly Rietschel included a chapter entitled "Kuhlun geschlossener Raume" in his book.[39] This chapter on room cooling is perhaps the earliest comprehensive example of real scientific approach to cooling.

Hermann Rietschel advocated a scientific approach before the turn of the century, and he published a step-by-step approach for calculation of cooling plants. The importance of humidity control was established. Now it was pos-

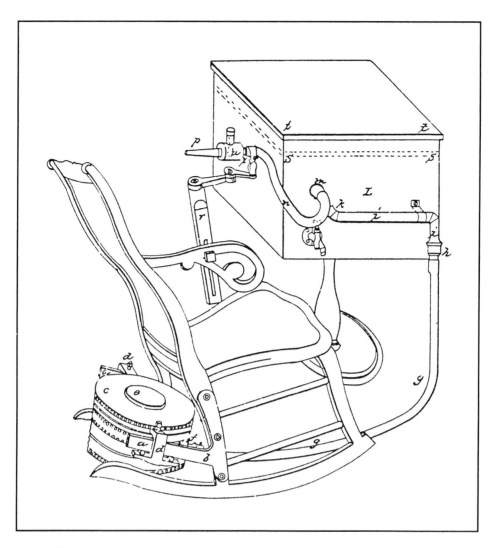

Figure 11-29 *David Kahnweiler's "ventilating rocking chair" was advertised in the* Philadelphia Evening Journal *of June 1, 1859, as ". . . a novelty that commends itself to all who value health and comfort. The invalid will recognize it as an invention especially conductive to his well being, inasmuch as with the addition of, say two cents of ice per day, the luxury of pure air may be fully enjoyed within doors, and the heat of the summer, or the vitiated atmosphere of a closed apartment defied" (from U.S. Patent 18,696 of 1857).*

sible for a designer to engineer a system to condition a room to a predetermined temperature and humidity level. Professor E. Brueckner of Munich discussed the German scientific approach in an article in *Ice and Refrigeration* in 1900.[40]

Early Scientific Air Conditioning in the United States

"The time is not far distant when mechanical refrigerating machinery will be applied to the cooling of hotels and dwellings in summer in a manner similar to that by which the heating is now done in winter, and a portion of the heating apparatus will be used for this purpose . . .," said the editors of the steam journal *The Stationary Engineer* in 1891.[41] Indeed, Professor Rolla Carpenter noted in his heating and ventilating book: "Cooling of rooms . . . bids fair to be at some time an industry of considerable importance. Rooms may be artificially cooled by a system constructed similar to that described for hot blast heating."[42] The heating system that lent itself to easy use for room cooling was the so-called hot blast system. The idea of using ventilating fans to blow air over heated

surfaces was certainly not new, but packaged systems containing a centrifugal fan and a heating coil had only recently become available. In the United States, Benjamin F. Sturtevant patented a combination fan and heat exchanger for cooling or heating purposes in 1869 (U.S. Patent 92460, July 13, 1869). He soon had established a company to manufacture and sell fans and heating systems. Other companies followed so that by the 1890s, the method of using a fan to blow air over a steam- or water-heated surface and then distributing the air to rooms in large buildings was well established. Such "hot blast" systems easily combined the need for ventilation with heating. This type of system lent itself to cooling as well because the heating surface could be cooled in summer by refrigerated brine. These hot blast systems were also being equipped with air washers for filtering and humidifying by the 1890s, and the air washer could be adapted for cooling purposes[43] (Figure 11-33).

One of the earliest extensive discussions of comfort air cooling that addressed the need for dehumidification as well as cooling appeared in 1893.[44] The author, Leicester Allen, illustrated the construction of an air cooler that dried the incoming air with a desiccant before cooling it.

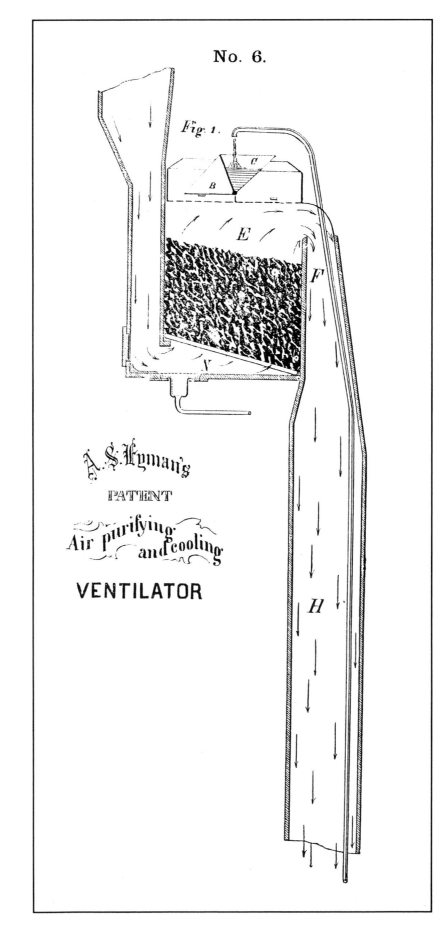

Figure 11-30 *Azel Lyman's evaporative cooler is an example of the many schemes of the 1800s that attempted comfort cooling. Most amounted to no more than curiosities (from* Lyman's patent dry air refrigerator and ice house, *n.d., New York: Stephen Cutter).*

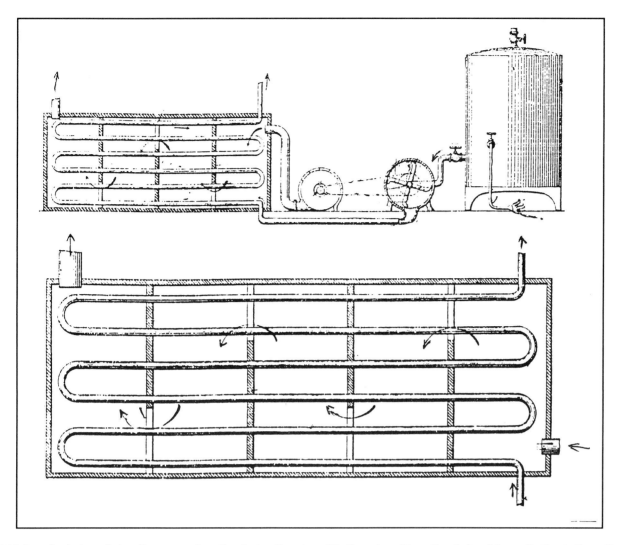

gure 11-31 *A mechanical comfort cooling system from the nineteenth century. The figure is an "invention designed for application to the cooling of build-*
.gs of all kinds, including dwellings, theaters, and halls, packing houses, breweries, hospitals, &c., but is peculiarly adapted for use in hospitals by reason
its two-fold office therein." A liquid refrigerant stored in the tank at the right flows into a motor that is operated by the expanding refrigerant. The motor
erates a fan that blows the room air over a pipe bank cooled by the expanding refrigerant. The "two-fold office" of the device refers to its application as a
om cooler, and the use of the liquid refrigerant to numb limbs needing surgical amputation. This is an advantage, say the patentees, because their sys-
n eliminates the attendants normally needed to spray ether on the body part to be numbed, and who "are not unfrequently so affected by sight of the
eration of the surgeon as to render them unable properly to perform their work. . . ." The surgeon himself could spray the refrigerant using a hose hooked
a rubber surgical glove with a pin hole placed in one of the fingers (from U.S. Patent 262,185 of 1882).

The scientific approach to heating and ventilating as
racticed in Germany seems to have been first introduced
to U.S. practice by heating and ventilating engineer
lfred Wolff after 1889.[45] A discussion of Rietschel's hand-
ook by one of Wolff's associates (Arthur K. Ohmes) leads
the belief that Wolff was aware of Rietschel's work,
cluding that on room cooling.[46] Wolff also may have read
heard Hermann Eisert's recital of Rietschel's methods in
396, in which Eisert said:

> Under all conditions, however, it is advisable to fix the limit
> of the humidity of the air in the rooms to be cooled and to
> proportion the cooling apparatus correspondingly.[47]

Wolff, being a consulting engineer, responded to
emand— and there was little demand for comfort cooling
stems in the 1890s. Still, Wolff did design some cooling
stems combining hot blast heating and cooling appara-

tus. Such systems were designed for the Cornell Medical
College in 1899 and the Hanover National Bank in 1903.[48]
The medical college system cooled the "post graduate dis-
secting room," thereby keeping both the live and the dead
bodies cool! The system was used for graduation exercises
during the summer. The crowning event in Wolff's cooling
career, however, was the cogeneration system he designed
for the New York Stock Exchange in 1901 (Figures 11-34 and
11-35). The system, originally designed to provide 450 tons
of refrigeration from electric generator exhaust steam provided to ammonia absorption brine chillers, was to cool the
Exchange board room and remove the machinery heat load
from several basement levels. The system size was reduced
just before installation to 300 tons and provided comfort
cooling only to the board room.[49] The significance of
Wolff's Stock Exchange job was that it was perhaps the earliest to recognize humidity control as a primary objective.
To the building architect George Post, Wolff wrote:

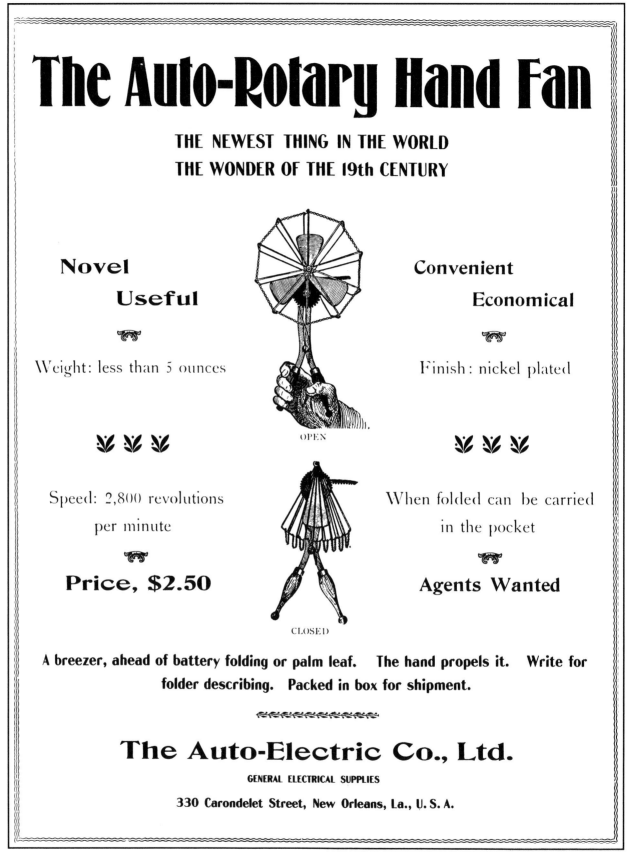

Figure 11-32 *Before the twentieth century, fans were the only means of cooling available to the public (from* Electrical World and Engineer, *May 5, 1900, p. 59).*

THOMAS'

Acme Air Purifying and Cooling System

| Any Degree of
HEATING
COOLING | **AUTOMATIC HUMIDITY CONTROL** | Any Degree of
DRYNESS
MOISTURE |

THE SYSTEM HAS YEARS OF SUCCESSFUL EXPERIENCE BEHIND IT

THE FOLLOWING USE THE ACME:

BANKS
Kuhn, Loeb & Co., New York.
First National, Chicago.
Corn Exchange National, Chicago.
Chicago Exchange National, Chicago.
Northwestern National, Minneapolis.
Western German National, Cincinnati.
Bank of Nova Scotia, Toronto.
Laclede National, St. Louis.
Colonial Trust, Pittsburg.
Land & Title, Philadelphia.
Suffolk Co., Boston.
First National, Kansas City.

SCHOOLS
Horace Man. School, E. St. Louis, Ill.
Morgan School, Cincinnati.
12 Schools, St. Louis, Mo.

MERCANTILE AND OFFICE BUILDINGS
Wanamaker, New York.
H. B. Claflin, New York.
American Optical, Suffield, Mass.
Chamber of Commerce, Minneapolis.

MERCANTILE AND OFFICE BUILDINGS—CONTINUED.
Telephone Co., Minneapolis.
Carlton Building, St. Louis.
Taylor Dry Goods Co., Kansas City.
Edison Electric Co., Chicago.
Sears Roebuck, Chicago.
Hibbard, Spencer & Bartlett, Chicago.
Tribune Building, Chicago.
Swift Co. (Stock Yards), Chicago.
Boston Store, Chicago.
Rookery, Chicago.

HOSPITALS
Providence Hospital, Oakland, California.
Epworth Hospital, South Bend, Ind.
Augustana Hospital, Chicago.
Michael Reese Hospital, Chicago.
Samaritan Hospital, Chicago.
Ravenswood Hospital, Ravenswood, Ill.

COURT HOUSES, POST OFFICES, ETC.
Post Office, Chicago.
Post Office, Milwaukee.
Court House, Des Moines.

COURT HOUSES, POST OFFICES, ETC.—CONTINUED.
Court House, Chicago.
Court House, Syracuse.
Court House, Riverside, California.
City Hall, St. Louis.
Court House, Etc., Pittsburg.
Public Library, Chicago.
Carnegie Library Extension, Pittsburg.
Pittsburg & Lake Erie Station, Pittsburg.
Union Station, Indianapolis.

HOTELS AND RESTAURANTS
King Edward, Toronto.
Great Northern, Chicago.
Seelbach, Louisville, Kentucky.
Jefferson, St. Louis.
Kirkwood, Des Moines.
College Inn, Chicago.
Rectors, Chicago.
Lakota, Chicago.
Board of Trade, Chicago.
Hanna & Hoggs, Chicago.
States, Chicago.
Penobscot, Detroit, Michigan.

If interested write for further list of references from Churches, Schools, Manufacturing and all classes of buildings

MAIN OFFICES

288 HUDSON STREET, NEW YORK   17-19 SO. CARPENTER STREET, CHICAGO

CHEMICAL BUILDING . . . . ST. LOUIS	HICKOX BUILDING . . . . CLEVELAND
ENDICOTT BUILDING . . . . ST. PAUL	POSTAL BUILDING . . . . KANSAS CITY
MERCANTILE LIBRARY BUILDING . . . . CINCINNATI	MAJESTIC BUILDING . . . . DETROIT

Figure 11-33 *Thomas' air washer was apparently the first spray-type washer to be placed in general manufacture. At the turn of the century, these devices were coupled to fan-type heating systems, providing humidification, filtering, and limited cooling. One report of an air washer installation at the Chicago Telephone Company read:*

"That Chicago air is an excellent subject for a washing machine no one will deny, but few are aware that it is being done in the heart of the city every hour in the day. Most people when they first hear of it laugh and decline to believe that such a thing is possible. Only an actual inspection of the operation will convince them. Those who have witnessed it with open-mouthed wonder have uttered enough ejaculations to clog-up the big pipe. A representative of the Chronicle visited this new basement laundry the other day and was shown the engineer. Kneeling down and opening the door into the chamber where the air is drenched with water, the engineer reached a hand in toward the lower tier of pipes into which the damp air passes. The hand disappeared in the spray, and when it came out a moment later it was full of soft, watery mud of a bluish gray color.

"'There! That is what we get out of Chicago air,' said the engineer. 'How would you like to have your lungs lined on the inside with that? We get so much of it out of the air that we carry it away in buckets. On an average about one bucket of dirt is washed out of the air every day. The system works to perfection, and we haven't the least difficulty in mining the mud out of air. Of course, the operation as a whole seems very wonderful, and perhaps it should be so considered, but if you will notice, none of the several operations comprising the washing process is either intricate or complicated. Nothing could be more simple than each one of the steps, but when all are taken together the whole seem stupendous.'

"An attempt has never before been made in Chicago, it is said, to wash air or purify it, so as yet the atmosphere-washing at Franklin and Washington streets is as great a curiosity as a museum freak." (Anonymous. ca. 1896-1904. Domestic Engineering, pp. 43-44).

BIG COOLING PLANT IN STOCK EXCHANGE.

Three 150 Ton Machines Will Try to Keep the Brokers' Tempers Even—This Practically Marks the Opening of a New Era in Refrigeration.

INTERIOR OF THE BOARD ROOM OF THE NEW YORK STOCK EXCHANGE.

Figure 11-34 *The New York Stock Exchange, 1903. The New York Stock Exchange was the sight of the earliest true air-conditioning system successfully designed and operated for comfort cooling. The mechanical system was designed by heating and ventilating engineer Alfred Wolff, who consulted Henry Torrance, Jr., of Carbondale Machine Co. on the refrigeration system. Three 100-ton ammonia absorption chillers provided cooling for the cogeneration-type system that was designed to control humidity and temperature. The machines were powered by the exhaust from the steam engines that operated the electrical generators. The waste water from the refrigeration condensers was stored in roof cisterns and was then used to flush the toilets! Forty-two distribution boxes provided conditioned air through numerous inconspicuous small openings in the ornate ceiling of the "board room," resulting in a uniform downward movement of conditioned air at low velocity during summer months. This system was the forerunner of more sophisticated systems designed two decades later for movie houses, and remained in operation for twenty years (from headline in* Cold Storage, May 1903, p. 206; illustration in The Metal Worker, August 5, 1905).

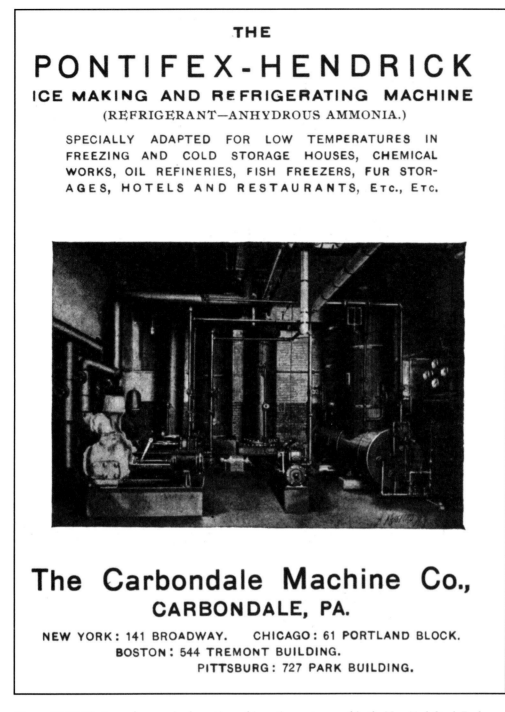

THE

PONTIFEX-HENDRICK

ICE MAKING AND REFRIGERATING MACHINE

(REFRIGERANT—ANHYDROUS AMMONIA.)

SPECIALLY ADAPTED FOR LOW TEMPERATURES IN FREEZING AND COLD STORAGE HOUSES, CHEMICAL WORKS, OIL REFINERIES, FISH FREEZERS, FUR STORAGES, HOTELS AND RESTAURANTS, ETC., ETC.

The Carbondale Machine Co.,
CARBONDALE, PA.

NEW YORK: 141 BROADWAY.   CHICAGO: 61 PORTLAND BLOCK.
BOSTON: 544 TREMONT BUILDING.
PITTSBURG: 727 PARK BUILDING.

Figure 11-35 *The type of ammonia absorption refrigeration system used in the New York Stock Exchange is shown in this advertisement (from* Cold Storage, *June 1903, p. 285).*

The chief advantage of the cooling of the air, however, is that the degree of moisture in the air will be so considerably reduced. . . . The refrigerating plant as designed, will not only lower the air entering the room 8% to 10%, when the external temperature is say 85, but if the humidity of the entering air is say 85%, it will be lowered at the same time to about 55%. What this means in comfort, in ability to transact business, the health and well-being of the members, can scarcely be realized by a mere recital of the above figures, but must be experienced to be thoroughly appreciated. . . . If the refrigerating plant is instituted for the board room and the entering air is cooled . . . and the percentage of moisture lowered, the result will be that this room will be superior in atmospheric conditions to anything that exists elsewhere. It will mark a new era in the comforts of habitation.[50]

Wolff told the Stock Exchange building committee:

> I would like to say that the importance of this plan to the upper portion of the board room is in the abstraction of the moisture and the reduction of humidity. I attach less importance to the reduction of the temperature than to the abstraction of the moisture.[51]

Wolff's calculations of July and August 1901 show that the plant was designed to lower the board room temperature from 85°F to 75°F and the relative humidity from 85% to 55% for 3,570,000 cubic feet of air per hour, and that the entire cooling plant capacity needed was 420 tons.[52] Wolff's New York Stock Exchange system incorpo-

How Dr. Alexander Graham Bell keeps cool in hot weather.

Figure 11-36 *Telephone inventor Alexander Graham Bell was "like a fish out of water" when he tried his hand at air-conditioning engineering about 1911. Bell converted his swimming pool into a study and living room and employed an ice-type cooling system. Unfortunately, his system discharged the cold air at the bottom of the room (from* Scientific American, *July 29, 1911, p. 105).*

rated all the elements of modern air conditioning—humidity control (in winter also), temperature control, and filtering. The system was designed to provide specific results at a design condition. And the system, after design and installation, operated successfully for 20 years.

A few other engineers took a calculated approach to comfort cooling as well. For example, refrigeration engineer Alfred Siebert proposed comfort cooling and, like Hermann Rietschel, discussed the need for lowering the relative humidity of the air by cooling it to saturation then reheating it to the desired temperature and relative humidity conditions. Siebert showed calculation examples in his article.[53] Siebert also received three U.S. patents for comfort cooling devices,[54] and his first patent (issued in 1902) mentions humidity control.

At this time, the early 1900s, a scientific approach to air conditioning had begun to evolve, and more heating and ventilating engineers were becoming interested in the subject. As one ASHVE member said, after a comfort cooling paper was delivered at the Atlantic City, New Jersey, meeting in 1902: "This paper is like the little neck clams we get here at Atlantic City— a kind of sample—but not enough of it."[55] But there also had to be a public demand, and the science of air conditioning had to be more exact to provide a reliable, marketable product (Figure 11-36).

The Public is Exposed to Cooling

Most of us now consider summer cooling a necessity—we have experienced it, we like it, it can be had at a reasonable cost—so we demand it. Such was not the case at the beginning of the twentieth century. Few people anywhere in the world had been exposed to a pleasantly cool, mechanically produced environment during the hot summer. Yes, there were many advocates of comfort cooling in the 1800s, but few real examples. Beginning in the 1890s, summer cooling plants were installed in some public places, and these installations, though few and far between, did begin to expose the public to comfort cooling, creating increased demand for future entrepreneurs.[56]

Sometime prior to 1903, refrigeration engineer Gardner T. Voorhees had cooled his Boston offices for many years. Voorhees was initially in charge of the refrigeration plans for the Louisiana Purchase Exposition (the St. Louis World's Fair) of 1904-1905. Voorhees proposed an ambitious program to comfort cool the Fair's refrigeration bureau office to demonstrate the usefulness of comfort cooling and to entice commercial participants to hook up to the Fair's central refrigeration plant for air-cooling purposes.[57] It seems that the Fair administration broke their contract, and Voorhees later said:

In my opinion, many practical uses of refrigeration were put back twenty-five years or more by the action of the St. Louis World's Fair Officials in breaking their contracts. . . .

It may be stated that with the enormous capacity of the proposed plant at St. Louis and the strong desire of many concessionaires to have their exhibits, theaters, restaurants, etc. thus cooled, a most wonderful opportunity was lost to have shown what I believe is one of the greatest coming uses of refrigeration, that is, cooling of what might be called peopled rooms for the comfort of (those) therein.[58]

At this large public gathering place, the State of Missouri Building contained a rotunda and 1,000-seat auditorium that were cooled during the summer. Approximately 35,000 cfm of partially recirculated air, cooled by direct expansion, was delivered through mid-height wall registers[59] (Figure 11-37). No doubt this installation impressed Fair visitors, many of whom experienced comfort cooling for the first time. But it really caused a stir among refrigeration engineers, causing *Ice and Refrigeration* to run an extended article on the installation. The editors concluded:

The practical application of mechanical refrigeration to air cooling for the purposes of personal comfort, no doubt has a field, . . . and the day is at hand, or soon will be, when the modern office building, factory, church, theater and even residence will be incomplete without a mechanical air cooling plant.[60]

Willis Carrier—The Air-Conditioning Specialist

At the first International Congress of Refrigeration, German refrigeration pioneer Carl Linde discussed comfort cooling but he concluded that, although the refrigeration industry had made as much progress in room cooling as could be expected, it was capable of rendering even more progress for humanity.[61] The science of air conditioning had begun to evolve, comfort cooling had seen limited public display, and the heating, ventilating, and refrigeration industries were well developed commercially by the early 1900s. All these things had to be pulled together into one and sold to the public. An individual came upon the scene who had the brains and the vision to do this. That individual was Willis Haviland Carrier (Figure 11-38).

Willis Carrier was a brilliant but also creative engineer who had gone to work in 1901 for Buffalo Forge Co., one of the principal manufacturers of hot blast heating apparatus, and soon had been assigned to research and development. Buffalo Forge was very weak in the R&D area, even to the extent of having few performance data on its own equipment. The company was asked to solve a humidity control problem at a printing company in 1902, and the job was referred to Carrier. It had been suggested that dehumidification could be accomplished by use of a desiccant (calcium chloride) or by use of refrigerated pipe coils. Instead of taking a hit-or-miss approach, Carrier took a scientific approach—he investigated these ideas theoretically and experimentally in his newly established research laboratory. He decided to control the humidity by use of cooling coils, and the system was designed and installed at the Sackett and Wilhelms Co. in Brooklyn.[62] Unfortunately, the dehumidifying system was retrofitted to an existing hot blast heating system instead of being designed from scratch

MISSOURI BUILDING.
An appropriation of $1,000,000 was made by Missouri for the Fair.

gure 11-37 *The Missouri State Building at the Louisiana Purchase Exposition (the St. Louis World's Fair) of 1904. The building was equipped with ntral air cooling and it was the first time that comfort cooling was experienced by numbers of people from all over the world (from* Sights, Scenes and onders at the World's Fair, *St. Louis, Missouri, Louisiana Purchase Exposition Company, 1904).*

Figure 11-38 *Willis Haviland Carrier (1876-1950). Willis H. Carrier was no doubt the leading air-conditioning expert of the twentieth century. Lik* *many creative individuals, he had some amusing traits. One engineer who knew Carrier during his creative years recalled some amusing situations:*

"Like many able engineers, the Chief (the nickname given to Carrier by his associates) was not an outstandingly good speaker, and on occasion woul *lose some of his audience by going beyond their understanding, failing to make the subject perfectly clear. He was at his best in a one-to-one or a sma* *group conversation in trying to explain ideas for the operation of equipment.*

"What mental characteristics made Willis Carrier such a creative person? Certainly, one of these was his ability to concentrate on a problem to the exclu *sion of mundane interruptions like telephone calls, meals, going home. When he was thinking deeply about a problem, he would frequently go into a* *almost trance-like state from which he could be roused only with great difficulty and reluctance and into which he would readily return again until hi* *thought processes were complete. This was very frustrating to his secretaries, wife and his associates. But they learned to live with it in the knowledg* *that it contributed to his creative results.*

"Willis Carrier's ability to concentrate his thoughts to the exclusion of whatever else was going on around him resulted in many situations which len *themselves to anecdotes, one of which may be apocryphal but at least is in character. This had to do with starting out from Newark on a train. The con* *ductor came around to collect tickets but the Chief couldn't find his. He searched all his pockets and his baggage but no tickets. The conductor said h* *could pay for the tickets and get a refund when he found them. But Willis Carrier said, `That's not the problem—I don't know where I'm going.'*

"Once when the Chief was visiting our house, he seemed to be having trouble with his feet. He complained that one foot felt cold and the other foot hur *We suggested that he take off his shoes and check to find out what the trouble was. He did and found that instead of putting two socks on each foot from* *getting cold feet, as he intended, he had put one sock on one foot and three on the other foot.*

"The Chief was not the best of automobile drivers and many people found being a passenger of his a hair-raising experience. The Chief never seemed t *have a serious accident, but his fenders did suffer. When the move from New Jersey to Syracuse was made, the Chief flunked his driver's test and had t* *wait a period before he was able to make it again. In fact, my same correspondent said that the Chief didn't know that you had to have a driver's license.* *(From ASHRAE Historical Archive and Library, Atlanta, Georgia, and Ashley, C.M. 1980. Recollections of Willis Carrier. Paper presented at the his* *torical seminar conducted at the annual meeting of the American Society of Heating, Refrigerating and Air-Conditioning Engineers, Denver, CO, Jun* *[unpublished]).*

s a total system. The system failed to maintain the design onditions and was removed shortly after installation. Carrier "realized that the design was not the final answer or controlling the moisture content of the air, so began working toward a design that would be the answer."[63]

Carrier was good at visualization upon observation. When conducting the experiments for the printing plant job with refrigerated pipe coils, he

> . . . observed that as dehumidification was taking place, the air was in contact with water on the pipe surfaces; in other words, we had the apparent paradox of reducing the moisture in air by bringing it into contact with moisture. Of course, the explanation was simple. The temperature of this water was below the dewpoint or condensation temperature of the entering air. Why should we not, then, spray the cold water into the air stream, thus increasing the surface of contact and reducing the resistance to air flow.[64]

Carrier had concluded what Hermann Rietschel had written about eight years before—that an air washer could be used to dehumidify air. But Rietschel had also said that control of this process to achieve a desired result needed to be investigated further. Carrier's observations led him to scientifically approach the question of humidity control experimentally. "These early experiments, prompted by a problem based upon a comparatively small printing establishment, started the trend of investigation through which many of the fundamental laws of evaporation, of humidity control and of heat transfer were established. . . ."[65]

Carrier's process of thought during the 1902-1903 experiments was revealed sometime later. Commenting on the experiments with calcium chloride to dehumidify air, Carrier said:

> . . . when calcium chloride, or any other substance, absorbed moisture out of the air an exactly corresponding amount of latent heat was released in the form of sensible heat . . . the observation of this one phenomenon led to a train of thought, which eventually was to become important. This experiment disclosed the inter-relation of latent and sensible heat in the air when its moisture content was altered without the addition or subtraction of external heat. It also led to complementary experiments upon the process of evaporation of water into air and, finally, into the development of the principles upon which air conditioning was founded. . . .[66]

Willis Carrier the scientist was theorizing, experimenting, and observing results from which he learned, leading to more theorizing, experimenting, and observation. But Carrier was also an engineer and a businessman. His scientific process

> . . . also led to a further study of the need for devising suitable equipment for carrying out air conditioning processes,

Interior of Shop, showing Air Washers and Humidifiers under construction

Figure 11-39 *Carrier air washers under construction at Buffalo Forge Co. about 1908. (From: Anonymous. 1908.* Carrier air washers and humidifiers with notes on humidity. *Syracuse, NY: Carrier Air Conditioning Company of America.)*

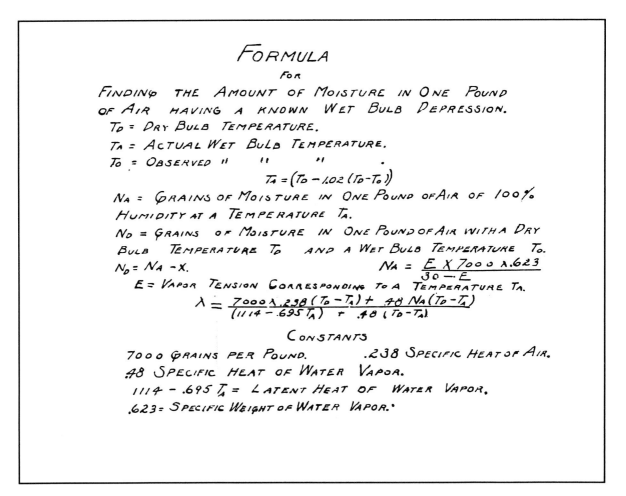

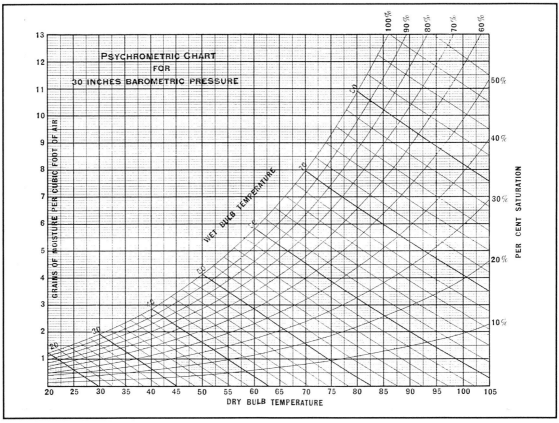

Figure 11-40 *Willis Carrier's psychrometric chart was first published in 1908. This formula is from Carrier's personal engineering data file. Formal publication of Carrier's psychrometric formulas did not occur until 1911, when he delivered a paper on the subject before the American Society of Mechanical Engineers. (From: Anonymous. 1908.* Carrier air washers and humidifiers with notes on humidity. *Syracuse, NY: Carrier Air Conditioning Company of America. Photocopy of Carrier's formula provided by John McClive, manager of marketing [retired], Buffalo Forge Co., Buffalo, NY.)*

as well as to thought upon the need of various industries for maintaining atmospheric conditions, independently of external weather variations.[67]

Carrier the engineer then designed a spray-type air conditioner, a very sophisticated air washer with which he could control the absolute humidity of the air leaving the conditioner, and, ultimately, the relative humidity of the conditioned space. On September 16, 1904, Carrier applied for a patent on the device, "Apparatus for Treating Air," receiving U.S. Patent 808,897 on January 2, 1906. The Buffalo Forge Company began manufacture of the air washers in 1905 (Figure 11-39).

One of the Buffalo Forge engineers, I.H. Hardeman, had studied textile engineering, and Hardeman supposedly told Carrier that his spray conditioner would revolutionize the textile industry, where control of humidity was very important in spinning factories. Carrier the businessman recognized the opportunity, began to study this area, and brashly wrote an article on humidity control for *Textile World* in 1906 "without having ever been in a textile mill." Hardeman sold one of Carrier's spray conditioners to the Chronicle Cotton Mill[68] in Belmont, South Carolina, to control humidity but the very large heat load of the equipment had not been properly taken into account, and the device did not work quite as well as Carrier had hoped. Carrier astutely observed the results, took measurements at the plant, and studied the data.[69] He later said:

> In this study an interesting fortuitous relationship was discovered between the cooling capacity of saturated air and the relative humidity which could be maintained with varying temperature, that is the differential between the dew point of air introduced and the temperature of the room was practically constant for any relative humidity irrespective of the variation in basic temperature. For a fixed room temperature, of course, this would be obvious and was the foundation upon which the basic patent for the dew point method of controlling relative humidity was obtained.[70]

Once again, Carrier had experimented (this time in his customer's plant), observed results, and, upon studying the results, advanced the science of air conditioning to a higher level.

Carrier utilized what he had learned from the cotton mill experience and all he had observed before formulating what many believe was his greatest accomplishment—the development of rational psychrometric formulas and the psychrometric chart. Carrier tells how this came about:

> All of these early experiences in the laboratory and in practical application brought to our attention fundamental relationships and natural laws which we investigated and finally succeeded in rationalizing on a mathematical basis. For instance, it was noticed that the saturation temperature of the air, when passed through a chamber in which the spray water was simply recirculated, was exactly the same as the wet-bulb temperature of the entering air. This same fact subsequently was observed in tunnels in which wet material was being dried. Under these conditions it was noted that the wet-bulb temperature remained essentially constant throughout the length of the tunnel while the dry-bulb temperature of the air was being reduced, due to absorption of sensible heat by evaporation, and coincidentally the dew-point was increasing.

An analysis of this showed that the total heat of the air remained constant throughout such a saturation process and that the wet-bulb temperature could be taken under any condition as a measure of the total heat of the air. These facts were rationalized and formulated, establishing the basis for the Psychrometric Chart, now in general use.

Stuart W. Cramer of Charlotte, North Carolina, independently discovered this same law relating to the wet-bulb when he found that the air leaving his heated humidifiers was the same temperature as the wet-bulb of the room. He utilized this principle in 1906 in the wet- and dry-bulb hygrostat upon which he obtained a basic patent.[71]

Carrier patented his device for dew-point control, filing on July 16, 1906, and receiving U.S. Patent 854,270 on May 21, 1907. During this time, he began development of his psychrometric chart and formulas.[72] The first psychrometric chart was published in 1908[73] (Figure 11-40). His formulas, psychrometric chart, and apparatus for controlling air were discussed in two papers presented before the American Society of Mechanical Engineers in 1911.[74]

In the meantime, Carrier was busy continuing his experimentation both in the lab at Buffalo Forge and at customer sites as each humidity control system was designed and sold. The feedback Carrier obtained from his experiments and installations allowed him to learn and make improvements in his design approach and in the equipment. Carrier had convinced the Buffalo Forge management that humidity control for industry could make money for the company and that Buffalo Forge should be the first manufacturer to pursue this new field and manufacture equipment for it (Figure 11-41).

As a result, the Carrier Air Conditioning Company of America was established as a subsidiary of Buffalo Forge Company in 1907. Now Carrier had a sales staff to sell the new product and an engineering staff to design systems. The Buffalo Forge subsidiary was apparently the first manufacturing-engineering combine in the history of air conditioning, and it came about because one man had a vision of an entirely new industry. Certainly, Carrier did not invent air conditioning nor was he the first to take a scientific approach to it.[75] However, Carrier's work in air conditioning was unlike what anyone had done up to that time. Hermann Rietschel had postulated the early science of air conditioning, but recognized its limits and suggested experimentations. Alfred Wolff had applied a calculated approach to the design of the year-round air-conditioning system at the New York Stock Exchange, but paused until he was asked as a consulting engineer to design another comfort cooling system. Wolff did not design the equipment itself, but utilized what was available in the marketplace. Willis Carrier, when given the printing plant job, had been able to not only define the problem, but came up with what he thought was a workable solution. When that solution did not give the desired result at a cotton mill, Carrier learned from that failure and further observations and experiments to further refine both the theory and the apparatus, ultimately resulting in dew-point control and the psychrometric chart. Carrier's keen powers of observation; his ability to see relationships among various theories, data, and results; his ability to learn from each experiment and job design (a feedback mechanism of sorts); an abstract

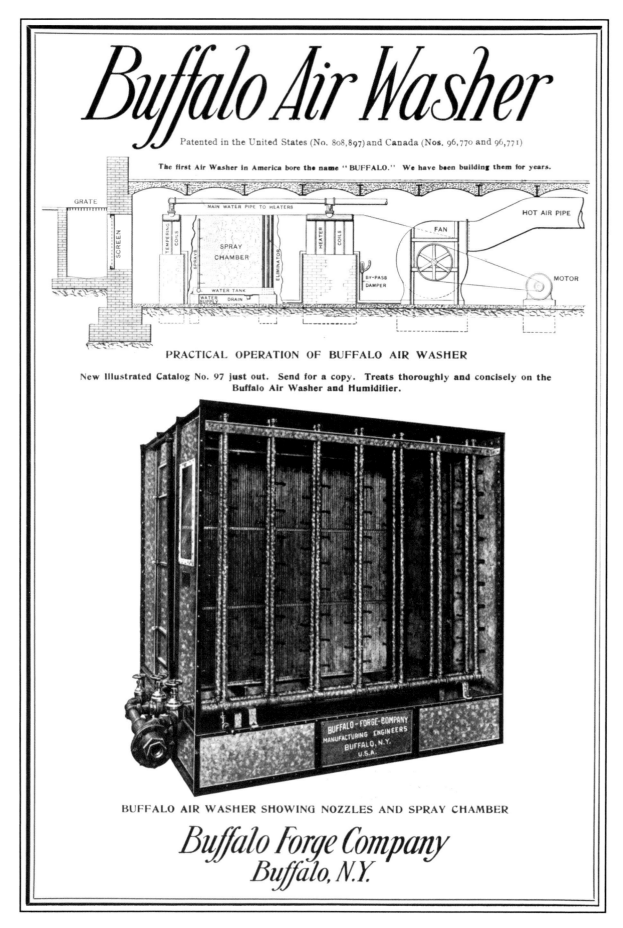

Figure 11-41 *Carrier's spray-type air washer was the basic element for his method of dew-point control of humidity. Carrier's air-conditioning systems were first applied to industrial uses and later to comfort cooling (from* Engineering Review, *June 1906, p. xii).*

thinking ability coupled with a very creative mind; and a very good business sense were combinations rarely seen in one person. Willis Carrier's great contribution was his ability to see that air conditioning could be an industry, and he took the steps to establish such an industry by combining scientific method, engineering, and business.

Air Conditioning Defined

The phrase "air conditioning" first appeared in 1905. Stuart Cramer, a textile engineer from Charlotte, North Carolina, who independently discovered some of the relationships that Willis Carrier had used to arrive at his rational psychrometric formulas, used the term "air conditioning" in a patent filed in April 1906 (U.S. Patent 852,823). Cramer also used the term publicly in a paper entitled "Recent Developments in Air Conditioning" read before the convention of the American Cotton Manufacturers

Association in May 1906.[76] Cramer tells how he arrived at that name:

> When entering this field, several years ago, I was puzzled to find a word that would embrace this whole subject; in casting about, I finally hit upon the compound word, "Air Conditioning," which seems to have been a happy enough choice to have been generally adopted.

Historian Gail Cooper says that the term was "suggested by the use of the term `conditioning' in the treatment of yarn, cloth, or raw materials before manufacture."[77]

Willis Carrier seized upon the new term when he convinced Buffalo Forge Company to establish the subsidiary Carrier Air Conditioning Company of America in 1907. In 1908, G.B. Wilson wrote the first textbook that used the term, in which he defined modern year-round air conditioning:[78]

Figure 11-42 *By the 1920s, the research laboratory of the American Society of Heating and Ventilating Engineers was engaged in air-conditioning-related research. Here, cloth body suits, which could be saturated with water, are modeled. The suits were used to test the reaction of the human body to "wet-bulb" conditions (from: Ku Kluxing in science,* The Aerologist, *January 1927, p. 15).*

Figure 11-43 *Refrigeration systems for Balaban & Katz theaters in Chicago, 1919-1920. Refrigeration systems were installed in 1919 and 1920 to cool Balaban & Katz's Central Park and Riviera theaters in Chicago. The movie theaters were ornate in design, as seen in the view of the Riviera's auditorium. Both cooling systems used direct expansion carbon dioxide systems, with the Central Park theater's compressor shown in the lower view. Designed by Frederick Wittenmeier, a U.S. pioneer of carbon dioxide systems, both systems proved unsatisfactory because cool air was supplied at the floor. Patrons complained of drafts, even resorting to wrapping newspapers around their feet (from a catalog of the Wittenmeier Machinery Co., no date).*

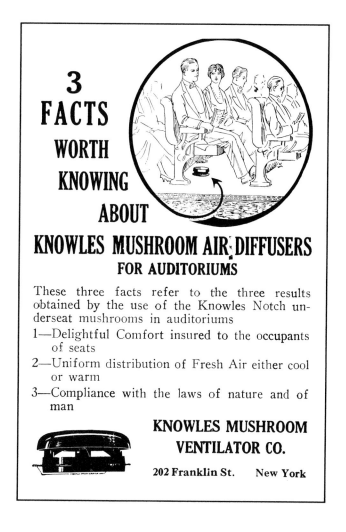

Figure 11-44 *Small floor registers, commonly known as mushrooms, were used in halls and theaters after 1910 for upward air distribution. Such outlets proved unsatisfactory for cooling purposes (from* The Heating and Ventilating Magazine, *June 1929 and January 1925).*

1. To maintain a suitable degree of humidity in all seasons and in all parts of a building.
2. To free the air from excessive humidity during certain seasons.
3. To supply a constant and adequate supply of ventilation.
4. To efficiently wash and free the air from all micro-organisms, effluvias, dust, soot and other foreign bodies.
5. To efficiently cool the air of the rooms during certain seasons.
6. To either heat the rooms in winter or to help heat them.
7. To combine all the above desiderata in an apparatus that will not be commercially prohibitive in first cost or cost of maintenance.

All of this early work to achieve humidity control by Carrier, Cramer, and the aforementioned text by Wilson was applied to industrial process air conditioning, the first area of application being cotton mills. Although Stuart Cramer devoted the rest of his career to textile engineering, Willis Carrier soon saw the possibility of increasing his business by joining the others who had already ventured into comfort cooling.

The public had been exposed to comfort cooling, a science of air conditioning had evolved, and companies, both existing and new, began to try to exploit the possibilities of the new marketplace of air conditioning. As all of this was happening about 1910, there were still two great stumbling blocks before air conditioning could come to the masses-cost and reliability (Figure 11-42).

The Realization of Public Air Conditioning

The heating and ventilation of public halls had been topic of discussion and experimentation for more than or hundred years, and the results saw marked improvemen after the application of mechanical ventilating fans an blowers during the later nineteenth century. A furthe improvement resulted from the manufacture and applica tion of air washers to ventilation by 1900. According to or engineer, many of these devices had been installed in th U.S. before 1910, numerous ones being used for cooling. As cooling devices, air washers were less than effectiv because they did not adequately control humidity in mo cases, unless the water temperature was regulated. Ther were a few early attempts using air washers in general-pu pose theaters at Weisbaden and Frankfurt, German around the turn of the century. These were not considere successful due to the humidity problem. However, a mor sophisticated approach was taken at a theater at Cologn Germany, about 1903, where a brine-to-air heat exchange was used in the ventilating airstream to cool and dehumid ify the air in summer. This system not only used an ammo nia refrigeration system to chill the brine, but also use

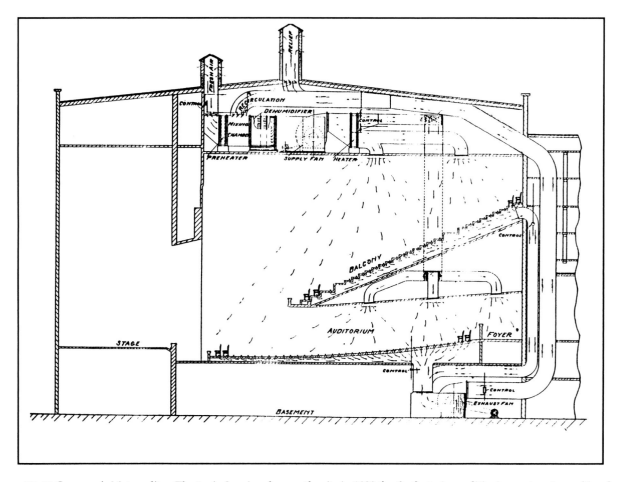

Figure 11-45 *Grauman's Metropolitan Theater in Los Angeles was the site in 1922 for the first air-conditioning system to combine downward distribution of supply air, recirculation of some of the return air, and a bypass of some supply air around the cooling coil, later remixing it to afford better humidity control. Although these individual design elements had been proposed and used before, it was the design by Leo Logan Lewis of Carrier Engineering Corporation that combined all three with automatic control to set a new standard for theater air conditioning (from* The Heating and Ventilating Magazine, *March 1924, p. 58).*

overhead distribution of air, returning it through multiple openings in the floor.[80] Another comfort cooling plant, featuring off-peak storage using 50,000 gallons of refrigerated brine, began operation in July 1909 at the City Theater in Rio de Janeiro, Brazil.[81] In the United States, a theater in Evansville, Indiana, cooled its ventilating air during summers before 1907 by melting crushed ice in baskets placed in the fresh air inlet.[82] The Folies-Bergere Theater in New York installed an air-cooling system in 1911. The system, designed by Walter Fleisher, used a Thomas air washer, apparently with no mechanical refrigeration. Fleisher admitted that the system was not very good, saying, "We were able to cool about 7 degrees below outdoors, but only the inefficiency of the apparatus saved the installation from being unbearable."[83]

The aforementioned installations that did use mechanical refrigeration had one flaw—they used noxious refrigerants, such as ammonia in the Cologne installation, or sulfur dioxide, as was used in Brazil. Such systems presented a real danger in crowded places, where a refrigerant leak could result in panic if not actual death should sufficient amounts of refrigerant escape. When theater cooling began to take off in the second decade of the twentieth century, the danger of poisonous refrigerants in public places was addressed in several ways.

The earliest motion picture theaters employed direct expansion systems using carbon dioxide refrigerating systems.[84] Such was the type said to have been installed in 1911 at the Orpheum Theater in Los Angeles using refrigerating equipment made by Kroeschell Brothers Ice Machine Company.[85]

This system was probably designed by Frederick Wittenmeier. Wittenmeier was a German immigrant to the U.S. who had practiced steam fitting. In 1896, he joined the heating contractor and boiler manufacturer Kroeschell Brothers Company in Chicago. Thereafter, he convinced Kroeschell to enter the ice machine business.[86] Wittenmeier, who claimed to have introduced carbon dioxide refrigeration into the U.S. (using the patents of Julius Sedlacek), designed a number of air-cooling systems, two of which were installed in the Central Park and Riviera theaters in Chicago in 1919 and 1920, after he had left Kroeschell to establish his own company[87] (Figure 11-43).

The carbon dioxide systems did solve the problem of toxic refrigerants; however, the systems in which they were used were not marvels of air-conditioning engineering. These early designs did not effectively address the proper distribution of air, nor did they result in good humidity control. There were really just heating systems to which some refrigerating equipment had been added for summer cooling. For many years, heating and ventilating engineers had argued about the best means to distribute air in the fan-type systems, commonly referred to as "hot blast" heating systems, which had become popular by the turn of the nineteenth century for large buildings. Much of the discussion of distribution had settled on the merits of introducing supply air either at the floor or at the ceiling. Each method had its proponents. Air from above would enter the breathing zone first and flush stale air to the floor. But heated air rose, so many felt it was better to supply it at the floor and let it rise to the ceiling. In the case of a theater, it made sense to introduce heated air at the floor so the patrons would be

cozy in winter, and many theaters employed upward distribution of air. However, upward distribution was unsatisfactory if cool air was employed. European practice was cognizant of the superiority of downward distribution for cooling as early as the 1860s, and at least one article discussing such practice was published in the U.S. before World War I.[88]

To be effective, air distributed for comfort cooling had to be below the room temperature, but cold air introduced in proximity to people could result in very uncomfortable conditions. The first successful air-conditioning systems recognized the necessity of distributing the supply air from many openings in the ceiling, allowing it to diffuse and mix with the room air before striking the occupants, thus arriving at the comfort zone at a reasonable temperature, humidity, and velocity.[89]

Most of the early U.S. theater systems were designed to optimize heating and so used upward distribution from floor outlets (Figure 11-44). Some of them were retrofitted with cooling systems, the previously mentioned Central Park and Riviera theaters being examples, with poor results. The first example of a well-engineered theater system seems to have been provided by Carrier Engineering Corporation. This firm designed and installed an air-washer-type cooling system in 1922 at the Metropolitan Theater in Los Angles using carbon dioxide refrigeration equipment manufactured by the Carbondale Machine Company.[90] L. Logan Lewis designed the system, which incorporated several advances. Lewis had apparently inspected the two Chicago theater cooling installations, which used upward distribution from under the seats. The result was hot, stuffy conditions at upper levels, while the orchestra level became so cold that patrons had to sit on their feet or wrap them in newspapers. Upward distribution also stirred up dirt and dust off the floor.[91] Lewis, possibly unaware of previous discussions and application of downward distribution, observed the bad results of the upward system and independently developed a downward system specifically engineered for theaters. Lewis also applied a design featured in many fan-type heating systems, that is, bypassing some of the airstream around the heat exchanger. When applied to cooling systems, bypassing some of the supply air around the air washer and remixing it before distribution to the theater resulted in better humidity control (Figure 11-45).

The bypass idea had been proposed as early as 1895 by S.H. Woodbridge for an air-cooling system for the U.S. Capitol. Woodbridge proposed:

> . . . a part only of the air may be so sharply chilled as to remove the weight of moisture necessary to insure dryness, and this chilled and dried air may then be passed on and mixed with the untreated part, resulting in the drying and cooling of the entire volume of air.[92]

Bypass was actually used for cooling at a theater in Vienna about 1909.[93] In the 1890s, Professor Hermann Rietschel had proposed that recirculating much of the air supply was necessary for successful cooling systems.[94] Combining the idea of bypass and recirculation was advocated in the early 1900s by Louis Schmidt: "Auditorium cooling would be to a considerable extent on the closed system. To avoid excess of humidity for comfort some of the

Don'ts For Theatre Ventilation

1. Don't use the mushroom system of supply for cold air.

2. Don't pass all air through the cooler.

3. Don't omit complete mechanical exhaust with refrigerating systems.

4. Don't omit automatic temperature control with refrigerating systems.

5. Don't supply cold air at low points and expect to pull it up with the exhaust.

6. Don't supply warm air at high points and expect to pull it down with exhaust.

7. Don't expect to pull air any place. You can push, but you cannot pull.

8. Don't conceive of a theatre as a tight box. It never is.

9. Don't introduce air into a theatre auditorium from the rear unless you know exactly where it is going and can accurately control its temperature and velocity.

10. Don't expect a thermostat on the main floor to maintain conditions of comfort in the balcony, or vice-versa.

11. Don't supply air to the main floor and balcony, or to the main floor and dressing rooms with the same fan.

12. Don't expect air currents to follow trained arrows on the plans, unless you are sure the arrows are thoroughly and properly trained.

13. Don't expect a Rolls-Royce ventilating system at the cost of a Ford.

Figure 11-46 *E. Vernon Hill's rules for effective theater design in 1925 sought to avoid the problems that prevailed in many theaters: "Until recently . . . it was the practice to install one or two noisy exhaust fans and spot a few unvented gas radiators about. When the combination of garlic, Fleur de l'Orient, halitosis, etc., became unbearable, the organ and the big propeller fans would be started. Some of these old propeller fans are quite the equal of the organ in noise-generating characteristics, but they move the air out, and down the aisles comes a flood of cool air, striking the patron on the back of his perspiring neck and legs. Naturally, we are behind in our hospital building program." (Buck, E.S. 1928. Theater air conditioning in the Southwest.* The Heating and Ventilating Magazine, *February, p. 74) (from* The Heating and Ventilating Magazine, *March 1925, p. 45.)*

returning warm air is bypassed and mixed with the cooled air."[95] Lewis combined all three ideas of downward diffusion, bypass, and recirculation into one system with automatic control, making theater air conditioning a workable idea. These new approaches to air-conditioning engineering were further refined in subsequent theater applications by both Lewis and by his competitor, Walter Fleisher.[96] By the late 1920s, a number of engineers were specializing in air conditioning, and numerous engineering articles appeared concerning the air conditioning of theaters and public buildings[97] (Figures 11-46 through 11-50).

The new engineering methods reduced system and operating costs, making air conditioning much more attractive to those responsible for the explosion of theater construction and renovation that began in the 1920s in the U.S. Whereas four theaters were cooled in Chicago in 1922, fourteen were in operation three years later. It was projected that fifty theaters in New York City would be cooled by 1927.[98] As competition among these theaters increased there was further need to reduce installation and operating costs, creating more impetus for better-engineered systems. An outstanding example of engineering for reduced cost may be seen in the story of the application of the centrifugal compressor to the refrigeration equipment of air-conditioning systems.

Better Refrigeration Machines Needed for Air Conditioning

Refrigerating equipment as applied to air conditioning in the early 1900s had severe drawbacks. Not only was there toxic refrigerant hazard, but the equipment was large and costly. The application of automatic controls, necessary to eliminate the employ of an operating "engineer," was still

Ventilation
Complete Air Conditioning Installations
Cooling—Refrigerating—Washing

Wittenmeier Horizontal Compressor CO_2

A Few Representative Installations

CAPITOL THEATRE, New York, N. Y.
WARNER BROS. THEATRE, New York, N. Y.
KEITH'S FORDHAM, New York, N. Y.
LOEW'S NEW ROCHELLE, New Rochelle, N. Y.
FOX ACADEMY OF MUSIC, New York, N. Y.
UNITED ARTISTS THEATRE, Los Angeles, Calif.
METROPOLITAN THEATRE, Boston, Mass.
PYTHIAN TEMPLE, New York, N. Y.
ELKS CLUB, Union Hill, N. J.
MASONIC TEMPLE, Kansas City, Mo.
ILLINOIS ATHLETIC CLUB, Chicago, Ill.
UNION LEAGUE CLUB, Chicago, Ill.
N. Y. COUNTY COURT HOUSE, New York, N. Y.
FEDERAL RESERVE BANK, Chicago, Ill.
U. S. NAVAL HOSPITALS, San Diego, Calif.
CONCOURSE PLAZA APTS., New York, N. Y.
RALEIGH APTS., New York, N. Y.
WEYLIN HOTEL, New York, N. Y.
MONTAUK POINT HOTEL, Montauk Point, N. Y.
RITZ-CARLTON HOTEL, Boston, Mass.
NEW BEDFORD HOTEL, New Bedford, Mass.
AMBASSADOR HOTEL, Chicago, Ill.
WINDERMERE HOTEL, Chicago, Ill.
AUGUSTINIAN FATHERS, Staten Island, N. Y.
BOARD OF EDUCATION, Chicago, Ill.
N. Y. TELEPHONE COMPANY, New York, N. Y.
NATIONAL CITY BANK, New York, N. Y.
WRIGLEY BUILDING, Chicago, Ill.
TRIBUNE BUILDING, Chicago, Ill.
KINGS COUNTY HOSPITAL, Brooklyn, N. Y.
CITY OF NEW YORK NURSES' HOME, Welfare Island, N. Y.
NORTH COMMUNITY HOSPITAL, Glen Cove, N. Y.
MICHIGAN CHILDREN'S HOSPITAL, Detroit, Mich.
ILLINOIS CENTRAL R. R. HOSPITAL, Paducah, Ky.
NORTHERN PACIFIC HOSPITAL, St. Paul, Minn.
LUCKEY PLATT DEPT. STORE, Poughkeepsie, N. Y.
HORNE DEPT. STORE, Pittsburgh, Pa.
CURTISS CANDY CO., Chicago, Ill.
ALBERT PICK & CO., Chicago, Ill.
TRIANON BALLROOM, Chicago, Ill.

WHEREVER comfort and efficiency require cooled or refrigerated air, Wittenmeier-Vitolyzed-Air equipment delivers it.

In hundreds of theatres, hotels, clubs, restaurants, apartment houses, schools, hospitals, and industrial plants our installations give perfect service.

Simple in design, construction and in operation, once installed they become almost automatic, requiring a minimum of time on the part of mechanic or engineer.

No matter what problem of cooling or refrigeration presents itself to you, we have sometime, somewhere faced and solved a problem similar in its main essentials—and installed the necessary apparatus.

Our experience is at your service. Full information supplied gladly upon request.

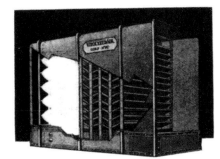

Air washer and eliminator as installed by Wittenmeier-Vitolyzed-Air

One Contract---One Responsibility

WITTENMEIER—VITOLYZED-AIR
1926 BROADWAY—NEW YORK CITY

Figure 11-47 *Advertisement, air conditioning (from* The Heating and Ventilating Magazine, *July 1927, p. 181).*

Figure 11-48 *Advertisements, air conditioning (from* The Heating and Ventilating Magazine, *April 1920 and* Ice and Refrigeration, *July 1927).*

in its infancy. Even where automatic control was used, the "engineer" was still necessary because in 1920 much of the refrigerating equipment being installed was steam engine driven. As a result, mechanically refrigerated air-conditioning systems were expensive. When air conditioning was first applied to motion picture theaters, the first cost was annoying, but it did not keep some movie houses from paying the cost—after all, having the only air-conditioned theater in town did sell a lot more tickets, and the increased

sales volume could justify the higher first cost. But soon, there were many air-conditioned movie houses in a large city, and the novelty and monopoly enjoyed by the first theater in a city were no longer present. Willis Carrier and his group of air-conditioning engineers were successfully capturing much of the new business of air conditioning in offices and industrial air conditioning. Problems with large ammonia refrigeration machines used in one of Carrier's industrial jobs in 1915 convinced Willis Carrier that:

> If air conditioning is going to grow, there will have to be something done about mechanical refrigeration. We must have a refrigerating system that is simple and foolproof—so simple that we can run warm water through a pipe and have it come out cold. . . .[99]

The refrigerating machine companies, satisfied with the slow progress of their low-temperature equipment, were not particularly interested in customizing machines for the high-temperature requirements of a new but tiny area of the industry. As Carrier studied the possibilities of improving refrigerating equipment, he apparently became convinced that his firm would have to design something that would meet all the requirements for air conditioning, reduce equipment cost, improve reliability, and therefore improve his competitive edge in a new business where he was being joined by many participants. Indeed there was the danger that those same refrigerating machine companies that were oblivious to the future of the air-conditioning industry would soon become competitors themselves. (In fact, this nightmare did become reality for Carrier—one of his main suppliers of refrigeration machines, York Ice Machinery Corporation, became his major air-conditioning competitor by the late 1930s.) So a radical departure from existing practice was needed. Willis Carrier was no doubt aware of the European work in centrifugal refrigeration and he seems to have settled on that type of device for his new development.

Development of the Package Centrifugal Chiller

Centrifugal or turbocompressors were employed as early as the 1890s for compressing air; however, it was not until the early 1900s that they saw use for refrigeration. Maurice Leblanc of France seems to have been the first, in the early 1900s, using water vapor and carbon tetrachloride as refrigerants.[100] At about the same time, two Germans, Elger Elgenfeld and Hans Lorenz, independently experimented with centrifugal compressors as refrigerating devices. Lorenz presented a paper in 1910 proposing use of centrifugal compressors with various common refrigerants.[101] W. Hessling received British Patent 13109 in 1908 for a multi-stage ammonia centrifugal refrigeration compressor. In Switzerland, Heinrich Zoelly designed a compressor before 1913 that recognized that a high-density refrigerant was necessary to keep the number of compressor stages to a minimum.[102] Thus turbo-type compressors were being developed in Europe at the beginning of the century for refrigeration, where they saw little use. Air conditioning was to be their first extensive application.

In June 1920, a paper entitled "Development Possibilities for Improvement in Refrigeration," written by Willis Carrier, was circulated to key people within the Carrier

In Industrial Plants

WHERE

Humidifying, Dehumidifying or Cooling

is Desirable for Automatically Maintaining
Certain Temperatures and Relative Humidity

Our Equipment is Unsurpassed

and during the 19 months in which the United States was at war was furnished for the following:

Food Products — Chemical — Steel — Zinc—Hardware—Electric Lamp—Smelting and Refining—Glue-Packing—Electric Storage Battery — Hat Manufacturers — Lithographing—Explosive and Municipal Plants.

Banks—Schools—Department Stores—Theatres—together with a Court House—Stock Exchange—Government Building—Cafe —Restaurant—College—Laboratory—Hotel—State Capitol and a Government Hospital.

The above, in addition to hundreds of installations during the preceding ten years

Our Engineering Ability

demonstrated by the great number of plants satisfactorily equipped, enable us to design and furnish the type of

AIR CONDITIONING APPARATUS

that will meet your requirements

BRAEMER AIR CONDITIONING CORPORATION
Lafayette Bldg., PHILADELPHIA
New York Cincinnati St. Louis Indianapolis Kansas City

Figure 11-49 *William Braemer was an early associate of Willis Carrier at Buffalo Forge Company who later was hired by the steam heating specialists Warren Webster & Co. to form an air-conditioning engineering department there. Braemer developed the Webster air washer before leaving to establish his own firm (from* The Heating and Ventilating Magazine, *December 1918, p. 5).*

Figure 11-50 *(From* Automatic Heat and Air Conditioning, *September 1934, p. 24).*

organization with the caution that it be ". . . not left around where everyone can see it."[103] The paper revealed that Carrier was ready to actively pursue the design and manufacture of a refrigeration system using a centrifugal compressor. One month later, unsuccessful in finding a suitable American manufacturer, Carrier instructed his German representative, Albert Klein, to evaluate possible German firms "who could be trusted with the manufacture." This preliminary evaluation being completed, Willis Carrier went to Germany to select a firm, C.H. Jaeger & Cie. of Leipzig, to manufacture a prototype carbon tetrachloride machine, which was shipped to the U.S. in early 1922.[104] Carbon tetrachloride, corrosive to some metals, was deemed unsuitable for a refrigerant, and Carrier settled upon dichloroethylene, a fluid he discovered quite by accident while studying the characteristics of carbon tetrachloride in a chemistry book. It turned out that dichloroethylene or "dielene" was manufactured in quantity as a cleaning fluid

in Germany. The compressor was only one part of a total package that Carrier was considering, and he and Alfred Stacy experimented with heat transfer devices, methods of shaft sealing, etc. The result was a package chiller incorporating a centrifugal compressor and covered by several U.S. patents.[105] The first machine, incorporating welded steel shell and brass tube heat exchangers, was completed in 1922.[106] This chiller was unveiled before a May 1922 meeting of the New York Chapter of the American Society of Heating and Ventilating Engineers, to which members of the American Society of Mechanical Engineers and the American Society of Refrigerating Engineers had been invited. "The evening was started with an elaborate dinner served in the sheet metal shop, by the feminine members of the Carrier organization. A jazz band of five pieces, recruited from the office force, supplied entertainment during the course of the meal." A 100-ton-capacity machine was then demonstrated, the compressor being less noisy than the

Figure 11-51 *The package centrifugal chiller was shown by Willis Carrier for the first time in 1922 at a joint meeting of ASRE and ASHVE. After the demonstration, the guests were entertained by a boxing match. Willis Carrier describes the demonstration: "It was terrible when I heard that long, loud, rumbling, slowly diminishing b-r-r-r. I visualized the rotor of the compressor tearing itself to pieces. Beads of perspiration came out of my forehead and my hands were soaking wet. But I kept right on talking, trying to act as if nothing had happened. Irvine (Lyle), sitting near the back, casually left the room with an air of calmness I knew he did not feel. Directly, he came back and signaled to me that all was okay. Later he told me the cause of the noise. In arranging the space for the boxing matches, one of our men pulled a large metal dining table across a rough concrete floor. No sound effects could have done any better in imitating the disintegration of a rotative machine" (Ingels, 1952, pp. 60-61) (from* Ice and Refrigeration, *July 1922, p. 44).*

4,000-rpm steam turbine driving it[107] (Figure 11-51). Since the 1922 chiller was not satisfactory for production or sale, experimentation and refinement continued, both before and after the chiller went into production in 1924. The new chiller, combined with the spray-type cooling and dehumidifying system, proved to be a much more reliable and lower cost key to large air-conditioning systems. This new use and improvement of existing technology allowed one company to greatly expand the application of air conditioning, and the competitive threat goaded others to improve their own equipment and designs, with the consumer the ultimate winner.

The First Room Coolers

The proliferation of motion picture houses in the late 1920s exposed much of the public to air conditioning for the first time. The business world was shown that it made economic sense to install air conditioning not only in public places, but also in offices and even homes. Much progress had been made in reducing the cost and improving the design of large air-conditioning systems. However, these large systems were, for the most part, unsuitable for small installations. Still, it seems that a yearning for the comforts of air conditioning had been planted, at least in the U.S. But air conditioning was still too expensive for mass application. "Fifteen dead in Chicago as mercury soars," read a headline in the 1920s. The story following noted:

While beaches and parks were thronged with fugitives from stuffy rooms and apartments, hundreds of persons moved their beds to porches, roofs and in some cases into yards. The boulevards and highways were congested with motorists trying to get out of the sweltering city.[108]

Figure 11-52 *Until mechanical air cooling became cost effective, electric fans were the only inexpensive means to alleviate the effects of heat (from* The Heating and Ventilating Magazine, *August 1918, p. 70).*

Such situations sparked the desire for domestic air cooling, at least during the moment of maximum discomfort. Indeed many attempts to cool dwelling rooms had preceded the 1920s. Inventor Alexander Graham Bell, speaking about "Prizes for the Inventor," told a graduating class of students about 1918: "The problem of cooling houses is one that I would recommend to your notice, not only on account of your own comfort, but on account of public health as well."[109] Household cooling was thus seen as a panacea, relieving the stress of oppressive heat and humidity and even mitigating the side effects of improper ventilation, "elephant air," according to *Scientific American*:

> Elephant air derives its name from the anecdote about the small boy who was invited to a birthday party a few weeks after having seen his first circus. Upon entering the home to which he had been invited, he shouted with glee, "Oh! They're having a circus. I can smell the elephants."[110]

Despite the inviting possibilities of mechanical cooling, electric fans were about the only inexpensive means available for "cooling" (Figure 11-52).

Although many desired to market a small cooling system for homes and offices, the technology of refrigeration systems precluded such devices until the 1920s. The innovative developments in household refrigeration resulted in a refrigeration technology that could be applied to room cooling. It was now possible to produce a system that would be reliable and of a cost that was affordable.[111] In fact, the first such device to be marketed was produced by a household refrigerator manufacturer, Frigidaire. Introduced in 1929, the Frigidaire split-system room cooler ". . . was rather expensive and it required a complicated installation. All had hopes that it would work well, but there was no certainty. The first air conditioning (at Frigidaire) was based on the ductless theory; it was thought wise to have no complicated installations."[112] "During the next few years quite a few commercial installations were made in restaurants and other places using a multiple number of units. An outstanding one was in the Hollywood Night Club in New York where so many units were in use that the bundle of (refrigerant) line tubing leading to the compressor room was approximately one foot in diameter. . . . Sales were quite good . . ."[113] (Figures 11-53 through 11-58).

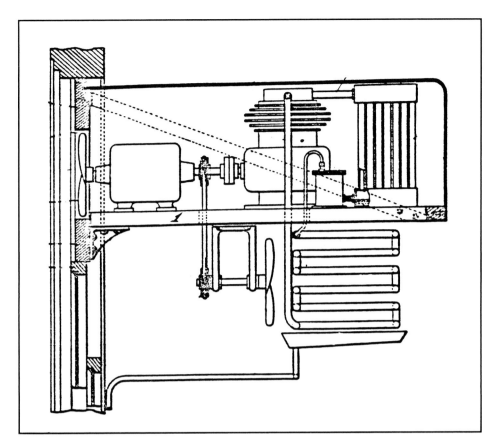

Figure 11-53 *Gustave Kramer developed a through-the-wall room cooler in 1918. His patent also shows a self-contained water-cooled room cooler. His ideas were premature, considering the state of the technology at that time. It was not until the late 1920s that refrigeration equipment was reliable and inexpensive enough for room cooling in homes, stores, and offices to be practical. The technological developments stemmed from those made in the household mechanical refrigerator industry. In fact, Kramer's patent lay dormant until it was acquired by Frigidaire, the principal refrigerator manufacturer in 1928 (from U.S. Patent 1,706,852 of 1929).*

Another refrigerator manufacturer, General Electric, also became interested in room coolers about the same time. In 1928, Frank Faust, development engineer in the Electric Refrigerator Department of GE, was asked ". . . to develop a demonstration of the feasibility of applying the General Electric Refrigerator development to room cooling." Faust designed a water chiller using "Monitor Top" household refrigerator units, the chilled water being pumped to a finned coil in an air handler that had been obtained on consignment from Willis Carrier. The system was installed in the office of a New York psychiatrist, a friend of Gerard Swope, president of General Electric Company (Figure 11-59). Faust recalled:

> I personally tested this system and prepared a technical report. The system worked perfectly. The demonstration apparently was very successful in convincing the top officials of the company to finance further development of room cooling. It may also have influenced Carrier to develop their so-called "Atmospheric Cabinet," first installed in 1931.

Faust was then assigned to develop a room cooler, which, unlike Frigidaire's split system, was to be self-contained. The coolers used the Monitor Top hermetic sulfur dioxide compressor, a water-cooled condenser, and a thermostatic expansion valve with a finned-coil evaporator and fan. The assembly was housed in a specially designed wood hous-

ing resembling a radio cabinet. Thirty-two of these prototypes were produced in 1930 and 1931. In parallel, a self-contained oil-fired boiler-burner unit was developed. On the basis of these two projects, General Electric established the Air Conditioning Department in 1932[114] (Figures 11-60 and 11-61).

Willis Carrier and his engineering staff, apparently busy with industrial and movie house air conditioning, were slow to move into the residential and light commercial room cooler market. Their first venture in this area was the "Unit Air Conditioner," a spray-type conditioner designed by Carlyle Ashley and introduced in 1928 for use in offices, factories, etc.[115] (Figure 11-62). The unit, called the "centrijector" inside the company, incorporated a finned coil for heating. The water spray provided humidity control in winter and, by using chilled water, both humidity and temperature could be lowered in summer. Shortly thereafter, Carrier introduced the "Weathermaker" furnace, which was possibly the first modern design, self-contained cabinet-type forced-air gas furnace. Also developed by Ashley, the Weathermaker furnace was a high-efficiency design similar to today's recuperative condensing-type furnaces.[116] The furnace could be equipped with a cooling coil; however, such combinations were not actually installed until the early 1930s. By 1932, Carrier had also introduced the "Atmospheric Cabinet" or "Room Weathermaker," which

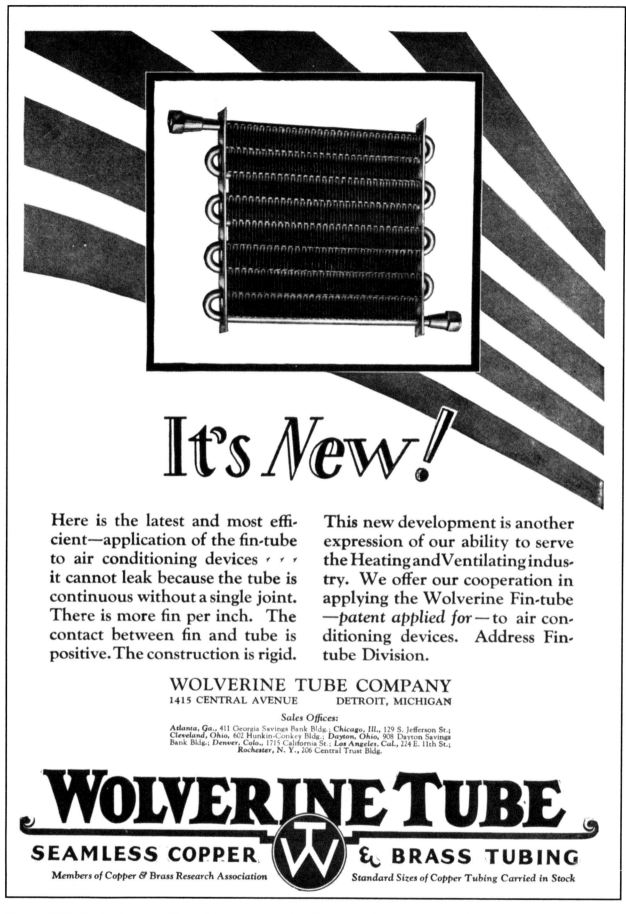

Figure 11-54 *The development of lightweight extended surfaces for refrigeration evaporators and condensers was one factor that allowed the development of packaged air-conditioning equipment (from* The Heating and Ventilating Magazine, *February 1928, p. 155).*

Figure 11-55 *The first Frigidaire room cooler was finished in gray enamel with monel trim. In the 1920s, monel, an alloy of nickel and copper, was used as stainless steel is used today. The cabinet, designed to be connected with a remotely located condensing unit, weighed 200 pounds (from Frigidaire Collection, General Motors Institute, Collection of Industrial History, Flint, MI).*

Figure 11-56 *The inside of the Frigidaire room cooler. A 1/20-hp fan, specifically designed by the Hartzell Propeller Co. (of airplane fame) for quiet operation, drew 450 cfm of air across an eight-row "ribbon fin" coil. The coil was connected to a remotely mounted, 1½-hp air- or water-cooled sulfur dioxide condensing unit (which weighed more than 400 pounds). The typical refrigerant charge was six pounds. Note that there are two suction lines. Copper tubing sizes larger than a ½-inch were unavailable at the time, necessitating multiple suction lines on large equipment. This expensive situation was resolved when larger sizes of rigid tubing with solder-type fittings were made available in the early 1930s. Tradenamed "Streamline" (from Frigidaire Collection, General Motors Institute, Collection of Industrial History, Flint, MI).*

Figure 11-57 *The Frigidaire room cooler was aggressively marketed. The 1930 model (shown) was a bit more stylish; however, the cabinets were still ugly. One newspaperman commented: "Having survived thus far . . . the bad design prevalent in most radio cabinets, the punished public will soon have to accommodate itself to another modern gadget, the air conditioning cabinet. That part of it that is at all sensitive to design is wondering whether the monstrosities of the radio cabinets are to be repeated or whether the makers of coolness will have a little better aesthetic sense than the makers of sound did" (Anonymous. 1937. Will air conditioning cabinets follow radio's bad example?,* Heating and Ventilating, *September, p. 45) (from Frigidaire Collection, General Motors Institute Collection of Industrial History, Flint, MI).*

Figure 11-58 *Advertisement (from* Fortune, *May 1932, p. 7).*

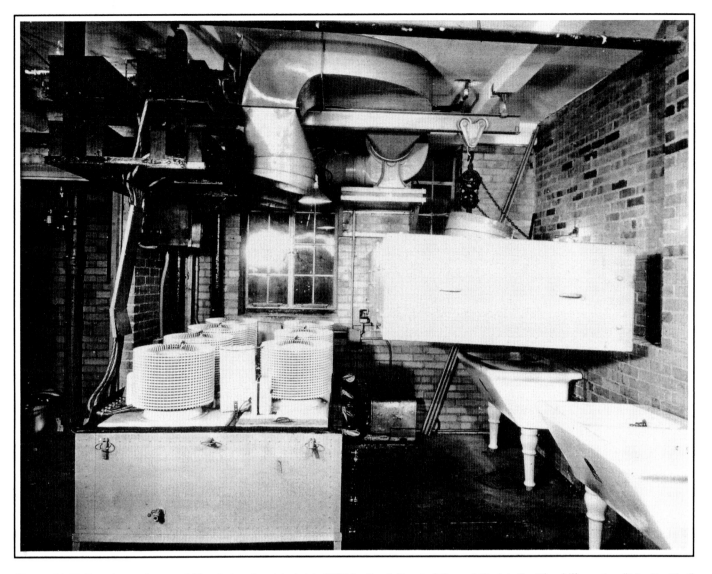

Figure 11-59 *Experimental water chiller designed and tested in 1928 by Frank Faust of General Electric Co. The chiller, using "Monitor Top" household refrigerator units whose evaporator coils were suspended in the water tank, supplied cold water to an air handler for a New York doctor's office. The metal cover lying at right was placed over the refrigerator unit's condensers and a blower forced air over the coils, the rejected heat being ducted outdoors. This installation proved the feasibility of room cooling to the General Electric management, with the result that Faust was asked to develop a self-contained room cooler (from General Electric Hall of History, Schenectady, NY).*

was a cabinet device similar to those being sold by Frigidaire and General Electric.[117] The Atmospheric Cabinet used a remote refrigeration unit; however, by 1933, Carrier had produced a self-contained unit[118] (Figure 11-63). Recognizing the increasing potential of small air-conditioning units, Carrier hired "America's first woman air conditioning engineer," Margaret Ingels, to be in charge of a campaign to educate the public as to the benefits of air conditioning.[119]

Thus by 1930, air-conditioning science and equipment had evolved from curiosity to practicality. It would soon pass from a luxury to a necessity as equipment was improved in both cost-effectiveness and efficiency, thereby making air conditioning available to more and more people throughout the world.

The Heat Pump

The realization that a refrigeration system transferred heat from a lower energy state to a higher one engendered the idea that such a system might be used for heating purposes. Indeed, Oliver Evans, who proposed the closed vapor-compression refrigeration cycle in 1805, had noted: "Thus it appears possible to extract the latent heat from cold water and to apply it to boil other water. . . .[120] By 1852, William Thomson (Lord Kelvin) had proposed that an air-cycle refrigeration system be used to heat or cool the air in buildings, and outlined the design of such a machine.[121] However, the construction of a working heat pump apparently did not occur until Peter Ritter von Rittenger (1811-1872) built such devices in Austria. Von Rittenger published

Figure 11-60 *The first General Electric room coolers were housed in specially designed decorative walnut wood cabinets resembling radios (from General Electric Hall of History, Schenectady, NY).*

an article in 1855, the title of which translates as "Theoretical and Practical Treatise on a New Method of Evaporating All Kinds of Liquids, Based on a Hydro-Mechanical Power System Applied to a Continuous Vapor Circulation with Special Application to the Salt-Brine Evaporating Process." The introduction to the article states:

> Steam can generate mechanical work. Most of today's industrial advances are based on this fact. Physicists have no objections to also accepting that mechanical work can generate steam. As far as I know, however, nobody has tried to take advantage of this fact for the benefit of industry on a large scale. This treatise explores the possibility.[122]

In 1856, von Rittenger constructed an experimental heat pump with an input of 11 kilowatts and said to be 80% efficient. The device was to be used to evaporate salt brine at Ebensee in upper Austria. However, the device, although successful when used with fresh water in experiments, failed to be useful with salt brine due to technical problems associated with the crust formed from the evaporation. Another salt evaporation plant was constructed between 1870 and 1880 at Lausanne, Switzerland, patterned after von Rittenger's ideas.[123] A theoretical discussion of a heat pump appeared in 1886, with the conclusion that an ammonia vapor-compression system would be most suitable.[124]

However, the most extensive work was carried out by T.G.N. Haldane of Scotland beginning in the mid-1920s. Haldane published his work in 1930, after he had tested a system installed at his home. He proposed that the vapor-compression refrigeration cycle could provide a more economical method, in certain circumstances, to heat buildings and swimming pools. He also noted that the system could be used for central cooling as well as ice making.[125]

Perhaps Haldane's work was the trigger that unleashed a flurry of heat pump development, for the 1930s saw considerable effort to apply refrigeration systems for combined heating and cooling. In 1932, three General Electric Company engineers published an article discussing the theory, technical aspects, and economics of heat pumps and listed the reasons they had not been commercially developed.

- No suitable refrigerating machine with the necessary characteristics of safety, quietness, lack of vibration, freedom from service, and high efficiency has been available commercially in sizes of 5 to 25 hp.
- The cost of electricity in most localities has been too high until recently to make this method of heating compare favorably with existing methods.
- Very little has been known of the actual operating costs of a refrigerating system because of the special nature of

Figure 11-61 *Advertisement (from* Fortune, *April 1934, p. 186).*

Figure 11-62 *Advertisement (from* The Heating and Ventilating Magazine, *March 1928, p. 157).*

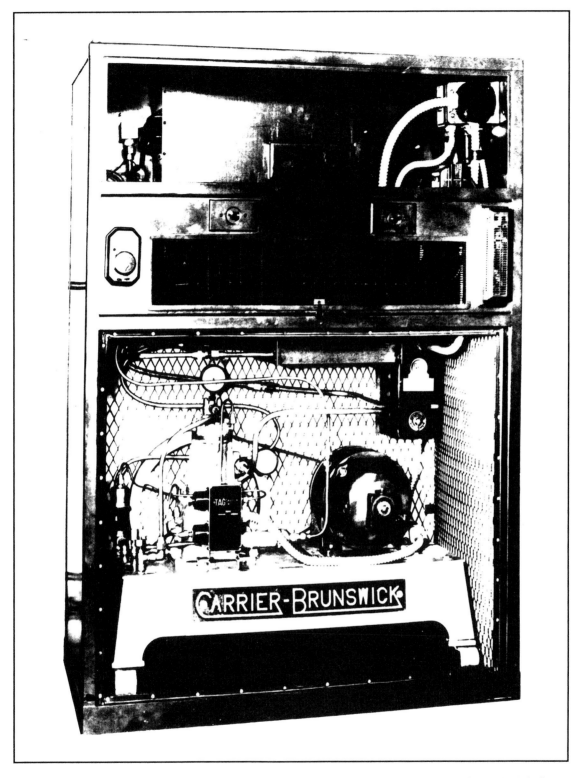

Figure 11-63 *Carrier's self-contained "Atmospheric Cabinet" or "Weather-Kooler" from 1933 featured a belt-driven methyl chloride condensing unit that took up as much space as the blower, controls, and evaporator coil. Such self-contained, water-cooled units were soon being made by various manufacturers and installed in stores, restaurants, and offices. Despite their bulk, they were durable, with many still in operation in the 1970s.*

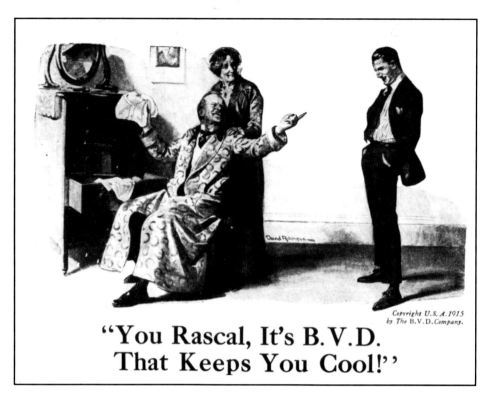

Figure 11-64 *"You rascal, it's B.V.D. That keeps you cool!" If B.V.D. brand underwear didn't keep you cool enough, there was always the "air conditioned bed."*

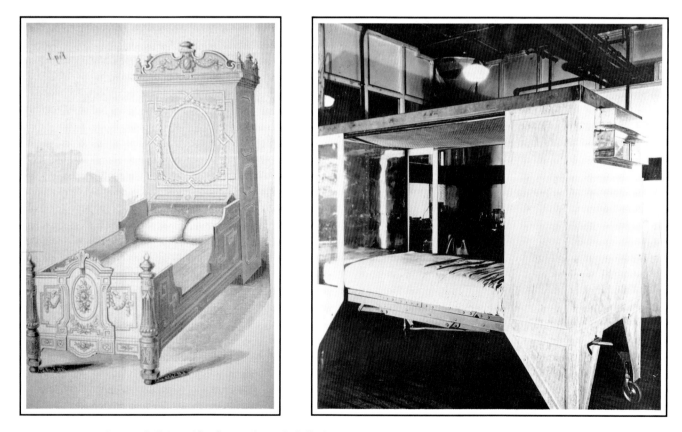

Figure 11-65 *Azel Lyman's "air purifier for ventilating beds," which used ice in the mid-1850s, and the Frigidaire "Air Conditioned Bed" from 1933, which used a supply and return air duct. About that time, Crosley Radio Corporation designed a mechanically cooled bed, and two U.S. patents were granted for cooling methods for beds. As one would expect, these various devices were never popular; (from* Scientific American, *June 5, 1915, p. 564; A.S. Lyman's Patent air purifier for ventilating beds, decks and rooms with pure air, no date; and Frigidaire Collection, General Motors Institute, Collection of Industrial History, Flint, MI).*

refrigerators and auxiliary equipment needed, and the careful study of climatic conditions which is required to predict their performance.

- Very little has been known of the first cost of equipment for heating and cooling electrically because of the special nature of the equipment. . . .
- People have not yet been educated to the needs of air conditioning, including refrigeration. Until they demand cooling equipment, there is little or no advantage of supplying refrigerating equipment for heating only.[126]

During the 1930s, these concerns were being met, resulting in numerous heat pump developments during the following two decades.[127] Some of the effort was directed toward large applications. For example, the Southern California Edison Company applied an 800-horsepower, 480-ton vapor-compression refrigeration system at its office building in Los Angeles in 1931. The installation provided summer cooling as well as heating in winter when the outdoor temperature was above 42°F.[128] One installation by the Atlantic City Electric Company in the eastern U.S. was tested at low outdoor temperatures during 1934-1935.[129] This system used four refrigeration units for capacity control. By 1940, at least twenty commercial installations of heat pumps had been made.[130]

Progress in the design of small refrigeration and air-cooling systems lent itself to application to small heat pumps as well. The first successful package heat pump was apparently the design of Henry Galson, Henry Heller, Charles Neeson, and Hans Steinfeld produced by the De La Vergne Division of Baldwin-Southwark Corporation. The system, placed on the market in 1933, was of "air-to-air" design, rated at 14,000 Btuh. An opposed-piston design, 1½-hp hermetic compressor was used with the newly available chlorofluorocarbon refrigerant R-12. Due to the 750-pound weight of the unit, a duct connection to the outside was to be provided for installation. About 100 units were produced in 1933.[131]

Despite the technical advances in heat pump technology, such systems were never very popular. They had to compete with fossil-fueled heating systems, which themselves were becoming increasingly more reliable and lower in cost.

No Need to Suffer from the Heat
. . . Summer or Winter

You paid for heat this winter...in more ways than one. And you'll pay for it this summer, too...when those long stretches of hot, humid weather set in...when the atmosphere in your home approaches the breathless mugginess of the tropics...when dust and dirt sift through open windows...when mental and muscular energy drops and sleepless nights reduce vitality to an even lower degree.

But there's no need to endure these discomforts. York Air Conditioning for the home substitutes clean, filtered, healthful and invigorating indoor air...cooled and dehumidified to the correct degree. Nerves relax in quiet comfort. Sleep is restful and refreshing. Daily tasks seem lighter. Street noises and dirt are shut out. Summer entertaining becomes a pleasure as guests are welcomed across your threshold to the utmost in hospitality...the air conditioned home.

And when you select air conditioning think of winter, too...think in terms of *year 'round* comfort and health. Central or unit system...York Air Conditioning is designed for both summer and winter service. It lives up to a name that has spelled quality and dependability for the past half-century.

YORK ICE MACHINERY CORPORATION, YORK, PA.

Figure 11-66 *"No need to suffer from the heat"* (from Heating, Piping and Air Conditioning, *May 1933, p. 71*).

POSTSCRIPT

lthough this history of heating, ventilating, air conditioning, and refrigeration ends at the dawn of the 1930s, the pace of new discovery in the field was considerably slower after 1930 and much of what has happened since that time has been a refinement of past achievements. This is not to say that discovery stopped—it did not, as evidenced by, for example, the application of electronics to automation beginning in the 1960s.

The growth of this industry has been explosive in the last six decades. So much innovation and improvement in existing system ideas and equipment has occurred that it would be a monumental task to chronicle it and the space required to cover all of it would be immense. It is true that certain developments could be selected and their story told, much as has been done in this book with earlier advances. However, this presents the problem of weeding out those innovations that truly were great in their effect on the industry and on the human race. Which innovations will be judged by history as great accomplishments and which, although enthusiastically received for a period, will turn out to be mere "flashes in the pan"? The authors do not profess to have the wisdom to guess the answer. The "trees" of the 1930s and beyond stand too close to us now for inclusion in this book. However, time will ultimately provide a horizon to stand upon, to allow us to rise and view the entire forest, giving a clear view of which innovations stand tall and healthy, having survived the trials of scientific inquiry and the marketplace.

Also, individuals from the post-1930s who made or applied their discoveries seem to have a different mind-set than that of their predecessors, particularly those of the last century. Perhaps we have lost some of the characteristics of the last century, where individuals "saw art and science, industry and nature as a continuum of creation and the quest for knowledge as a common activity, shared by chemists and poets, painters and engineers, inventors and philosophers alike . . .," as historian Paul Johnson stated in *The Birth of the Modern: World Society 1815-1830*. This is not to say that the progress made since the 1930s is historically irrelevant. In fact, it should be chronicled.

The achievements of the previous one hundred years are clear in the body of engineering work represented today by the professional societies. The American Society of Heating, Refrigerating and Air-Conditioning Engineers has contributed to the overall growth of the industry during the last 100 years by its promotion of innovation. Its predecessor organizations, the American Society of Heating and Ventilating Engineers (later renamed the American Society of Heating and Air Conditioning Engineers) and the American Society of Refrigerating Engineers, espoused continuous achievement from their founding until their merger in 1959. The promotion of technical excellence, firmly established in its foundation, has continued ever since. This excellence broadened as ASHRAE became an international body, focusing the expertise of members throughout the world for the betterment of humanity. The Society has truly lived up to the slogan of the American Society of Refrigerating Engineers, as stated by its first president, John Starr: "We have undertaken the responsibility of speaking with authority, of finding the truth and proclaiming it."

Starr's words also proclaim the mission of the authors in researching the history presented in the preceding pages. We leave this work with a realization of the truth as described by former U.S. President Harry Truman: "The only thing new in the world is the history you don't know."

REFERENCES AND NOTES

—— Chapter 1 ——

1. Eliade, M. 1971. *The forge and the crucible—The origins and structures of alchemy*, p. 79. New York: Harper & Row.
2. The myth of Prometheus was popularized by the poems of Heisod (700 B.C.) and the fifth-century play "Prometheus Bound by Aeschylus." At Argos, it was believed that the carrier of fire was the hero Phoroneus, son of a tree nymph. Prometheus appears at Athens as one of the gods specifically worshipped by potters and smiths.
3. Eliade, p. 80.
4. Derry, T.K., and T.I. Williams. 1982. *A short history of technology*, p. 230. New York: Oxford University Press.
5. Ibid., p. 230.
6. Huyghe, R., ed. 1962. *Larousse encyclopedia of prehistoric and ancient art*, p. 43. New York: Prometheus Press.
7. Bernan, W. (R. Mickleham). 1845. *On the history and art of warming and ventilating buildings*, vol. I, p. 24. London: George Bell.
8. Sprague de Camp, L. 1963. *The ancient engineers*, p. 171. London: Souvenir Press.
9. Huyghe, p. 299.
10. Labs, K. 1968. The architectural underground. *Underground Space*, vol. 1, p. 4. London: Pergamon Press.
11. Bernan, vol. I, p. 29.
12. Anonymous. 1922. *Steam—Its generation and use*, 35th ed., 6th issue, p. 13. New York: The Babcock & Wilcox Co.

—— Chapter 2 ——

1. Anonymous. 1969. *A history of technology and innovation, progress through the ages*, vol. 1.
2. Neuburger, A. 1930. *The technical arts and sciences of the ancients*, Henry L. Brose, trans., p. 252. London: Methuen & Co. Ltd.
3. Ibid., p. 254.
4. Sprague de Camp, L. 1963. *The ancient engineers*, p. 172. London: Souvenir Press.
5. Yegul, F. 1992. *Baths and bathing in classical antiquity*, p. 48. Cambridge: MIT Press.
6. Ibid., p. 19.
7. Palladio, A. 1730. *Les Thermes des Romans*. Paris: Imprimerie de Firmin Didot Frères.
8. Yegul, p. 61.
9. Bernan, W. (R. Mickleham). 1845. *On the history and art of warming and ventilating buildings*, vol. I, p. 40. London: George Bell.
10. Ibid., pp. 43-44.
11. Yegul, p. 117.
12. Cunliffe, B. 1984. *Roman bath discovered*, p. 74. London: Routledge & Kegan Paul.
13. Ibid., p. 74.
14. Ibid., p. 24.
15. Billings, J.S. 1893. *Ventilation and heating*. New York: The Engineering Record.
16. Yegul, p. 142.
17. Ibid., p. 142.
18. Ibid., p. 86.
19. Ibid., p. 89.
20. Ibid., p. 66.
21. Ibid., p. 152.
22. Lewis, D. 1981. *The drawings of Andrea Palladio*, p. 136. Washington, DC: International Exhibitions Foundation.
23. Bernan, vol. I, pp. 55-56.
24. Ward-Perkins, J.B. 1977. Roman architecture. *History of World Architecture*, p. 234. New York: Harry N. Abrams.
25. Yegul, p. 119.
26. Ibid., p. 120.
27. Ibid., p. 111.
28. Creswell, K.A.C. 1958. *A short account of early Muslim architecture*, p. 91. New York: Penguin Books. Creswell notes that the caldarium at Qusayr Amrah "is of the greatest importance, for it is the earliest existing attempt to portray the vault of heaven on a hemispherical, instead of a flat, surface but the artist must have copied a drawing on a table in front of him, and in doing so has transposed everything from right to left."
29. Oldham, B.C. 1965. The history of refrigeration, 1, Introduction. *The Journal of Refrigeration* 8(May): 147-149.
30. Anonymous. 1901. The tenth anniversary of *Ice and Refrigeration*. *Ice and Refrigeration* 20(July): 2.
31. Oldham, pp. 147-149.
32. Anthenaeus (C.D. Yonge, translator). 1854. *The Deipnosophists, or banquet of the learned*, book III, c. 98. London: Henry G. Bohn.
33. Forbes, R.J. 1958. *Studies in ancient technology* VI: 105. Leiden: E.J. Brill.
34. Allen, C.F.R., translator. 1891. Book XV, Ballads from the country of Pin, #1, vs. 5 from life in the old times. *The Book of Chinese Poetry, Being a Collection of Ballads, Sagas, Hymns, and Other Pieces Known as the Shih Ching or Classic of Poetry*. London: Kegan Paul, Trench, Trubner Co. Ltd.
35. Curtiss, C. 1933. History of refrigeration, some authentic notes. *Refrigerating Engineering* 25(Feb.): 100.
36. Neuberger, pp. 122-124.
37. Beckmann, J. (W. Johnston, translator). 1814. *A history of inventions and discoveries*, III, p. 324. London: J. Walker & Co., et al.
38. Putnam, A.P. 1892. Wenham Lake and the ice trade. *Ice and Refrigeration* 3(July): 14.
39. Curtiss, p. 100.
40. Ibid., p. 100.
41. Plinius Secundus, Caius (J. Bostock and H.T. Riley, translators). 1861. *The natural history of Pliny*, book XXXI, c. 23. London: Henry G. Bohn.
42. Forbes, VI, pp. 108-113.

43. Anthenaeus (C.B. Gulick, translator). 1928. *The Deipnosophists*, book III, c. 124. London: William Heinemann Ltd.
44. Oldham, pp. 147-149.
45. Jaquet, J. 1985. Air conditioning: An historical perspective. *Consulting Engineer*, July, p. 41.

—— **Chapter 3** ——

1. Olgyay, V. 1973. *Design with climate, bioclimatic approach to architectural regionalism*, p. 94. Princeton, NJ: Princeton University Press.
2. Choi, S.H., and C.B. Kim. 1990. Eighth century shrine uses carbon filtration. *ASHRAE Insights* 5(1): 12.
3. Banham, R. 1969. *The architecture of the well tempered environment*, pp. 40-41. Chicago: University of Chicago Press.
4. Bruegmann, R. 1978. Central heating and forced ventilation: Origins and effects on architectural design. *The Journal of the Society of Architectural Historians*, October.
5. The original Latin text by Agricola was translated to English by former President Herbert Hoover and his wife in 1912. Agricola, G. 1556. *de re Metallica* (reprint trans. 1950. Herbert Hoover and Lou Henry Hoover). New York: Dover.
6. Billington, N.S. 1955. A historical review of the art of heating and ventilating. *Journal of the Institution of Heating and Ventilating Engineers* 23(Oct.): 251-252.
7. Halliday, D., and R. Resnick. 1966. *Physics I & II*, p. 433. New York: John Wiley and Sons.
8. Newton, I. 1701. *Principles of natural philosophy*, vol. II, prop. XLI.
9. Billington, p. 263.
10. Desaguliers, J.T. 1727. An attempt made before the Royal Society, to shew how damp, or foul air, may be drawn out of any sort of mines, &c. by an engine contriv'd. *Philosophical Transactions* 35(July-Sept.): 353.
11. Bernan, W. (Robert Mickleham). 1845. *On the history and art of warming and ventilating rooms and buildings*, vol. II, p. 40. London: George Bell.
12. Desaguliers, J.T. 1734. *Course in experimental philosophy*, p. 560.
13. Banham, p. 52.
14. Desaguliers, 1734, p. 563.
15. Bernan, vol. II, p. 53.
16. Bruegmann, p. 150.
17. Sprague, J.F. 1930. Looking backward through the history of ventilation 1880-1930. *The Aerologist* VI(Aug.): 39.

—— **Chapter 4** ——

1. Billington, N. 1959. A historical review of the art of heating and ventilating. *Architectural Science Review*, Nov., p. 121.
2. "An Engineer" (Robert Mickleham). 1825. *The theory and practice of warming and ventilating public buildings*. London: Underwood, Thomas and George.
3. Ibid.
4. Billington, N., and B. Roberts. 1982. *Building services engineering, a review of its development*, p. 93. Oxford: Pergamon Press.
5. Mickleham, R. 1829. *Practical observations on ventilating and warming*, p. 224. London: Thomas and George Underwood.
6. Billington and Roberts, p. 94.
7. Bernan, W. (Robert Mickleham). 1845. *On the history of warming and ventilating rooms and buildings*, vol. II, pp 1-2.
8. Groft, T.K. 1981. *Cast with style, nineteenth century cast-iron stoves from the Albany area*, pp. 12-13. Albany, NY Albany Institute of History and Art.
9. The title page of Ben Franklin's brochure advertised Pennsylvania fireplaces "made in the best manner" by R. Grace in Philadelphia, J. Parker in New York, and J Franklin in Boston. The brochure was printed in 1744 at the expense of Robert Grace.
10. Stifler, S.R. 1960. *The beginning of a century of steam and hot water heating by the H.B. Smith Co.*, p. 17. Westfield, MA: H.B. Smith Co.
11. Dufton, A.F. 1936. Heating research. *Journal of the Institution of Heating and Ventilating Engineers* 4: 199-200.
12. Ibid., p. 201.
13. Thompson, B., Count of Rumford. 1802. On the management of fire and the economy of fuel. *Essays*. In 1946 and early 1947 some members of the Institution of Heating and Ventilating Engineers and of the Society of Instrument Technology met informally on various occasions and, in May 1947, it was decided to form a club to meet at monthly intervals during the winter. "Rumford" was particularly appropriate as a name for the club since he was well known for his work in developing efficient heating and pioneering the application of philosophy to practice. An early meeting of the club was at a luncheon in June 1947 convened at short notice in honor of Willis H. Carrier, who was visiting this country for the centenary celebrations of the Institution of Mechanical Engineers. Carrier was elected an honorary member of the club.
14. Bernan, vol. II, p. 178.
15. Billington, N. 1955. A historical view of the art of heating and ventilating. *Journal of the Institution of Heating and Ventilating Engineers* 23(Oct.): 264-265.
16. de Chabannes, Jean Frédéric, Marquis. 1818. *On conducting air by forced ventilation and regulating the temperature in dwellings*, p. 52. London: The Patent Calorifere Fumivore Manufactory.
17. Vetter, H. 1907. Calorifere. *The Metal Worker, Plumber and Steam Fitter*, Oct. 5, p. 49.
18. "An Engineer," p. 238.
19. Ibid., p. 244.
20. Arnott, N. 1838. *On warming and ventilating*. London: Longman, Brown, Green, and Longmans.
21. "An Engineer," p. 335.
22. Groft, p. 14.
23. Beckmann, J. (W. Johnston, translator). 1814. *A history of inventions and discoveries*, III, pp. 341-344. London: J. Walker & Co., et al.
24. Porta, G.D. 1589. *La magie naturelle, qui est secrets es miralles de nature mis en quatre livres*. Rouen, France: Francois Vaultier.
25. Anonymous. 1665-1666. A further account of Mr. Boyle's experimental history of cold. *Philosophical Transactions of the Royal Society of London* 1-2: 46-52.

26. Anonymous. 1666. A new frigorific experiment showing, how a considerable degree of cold may be suddenly produced without the help of snow, ice, haile, wind, or niter, and that any time of the year. *Philosophical Transactions of the Royal Society of London* 1-2(July 18): 255-261.

—— **Chapter 5** ——

1. Yunnie, P. 1988. Hubble-bubble, boil and trouble. *Building Services, the CIBSE Journal*, August.
2. Bernan, W. (Robert Mickleham). 1845. *On the history and art of warming and ventilating rooms and buildings*, vol. II, pp. 239-240 (taken from Sir Hugh Platt's Garden of Eden, p. 19).
3. Ibid., pp. 240-241.
4. Stifler, S.R. 1960. *The beginning of a century of steam and hot water heating by the H.B. Smith Co.*, p. 13. Westfield, MA: H.B. Smith Co.
5. Hood, C. 1844. *A practical treatise on warming buildings by hot water . . .*, 2d ed., p. 129. London: Whittaker and Co.
6. Ibid., p. 129.
7. Anonymous. 1878. *Steam and hot water for warming and ventilating all kinds of buildings*, p. 5. Boston: Swamscot Machine Co.
8. Ibid., p. 6.
9. Anonymous. 1898. *Domestic Engineering* 11(May 14): 12.
10. Anonymous, 1878, p. 11.
11. Anonymous. 1907. *Gesundheits-Ingenieur*, August 31.
12. Walker, R. 1796. *An account of some remarkable discoveries in the production of artificial cold; with experiments on the congelation of quicksilver in England; likewise best methods of producing artificial cold; and their application to useful purposes in hot climates.* Oxford, UK: Fletcher and Hanwell.
13. Anonymous. 1675. Some experiments made in the air-pump by Monsieur Papin, directed by Monsieur Hugens (as appears in the discourse printed at Paris, 1674). *Philosophical Transactions of the Royal Society of London* 9-10: 443-447.
14. Anonymous. 1675. Promiscuous experiments in the air-pump likewise, by the same persons. *Philosophical Transactions of the Royal Society of London* 9-10: 544-548.
15. Richmann, G.W. 1748. De qvantitate caloris, qvae post miscelam flvidorvm certo gradv calidorvm oriri de bet cogitationes. *Novi Commentarii Academiae Scientiarvm Imperialis Petropolitanae* 1: 152-167; Richmann, G.W. 1748. Formvlae pro gradv excessvs caloris, svpra gradvm caloris mixit ex nive et sale ammoniaco, postmiscelam dvarvm massarvm aqvearvm, diverso gradv calidarvm, confirmatio per experimenta. *Novi Commentarii Academiae Scientiarvm Imperialis Petropolitanae* 1: 168-173; Richmann, G.W. 1748. Inqvistio in legem secvndvm qvam calor flvidi vase coctenti certo temporis intervallo, in temperie aeris constanter eadem decrescit vel crescit, et detectio eivs, simvlqve thermometrorvm perfecte concordantivm constrvendi ratio hinc dedvcta. *Novi Commentarii Academiae Scientiarvm Imperialis Petropolitanae* 1: 174-197; Richmann, G.W. 1748. Tentamen legem evapora-

tions aqvae calidae in aere frigidiori constantis temperiei definiendi. *Novi Commentarii Academiae Scientiarvm Imperialis Petropolitanae* 1: 198-205.
16. Roux, A. 1758. *Recherches historiques et critiques*, pp. 80-91. Paris.
17. Ibid., p. 90.
18. Black, J. 1782. *Experiments upon magnesia alba, quicklime, and other alcaline substances; to which is annexed, an essay on the cold produced by evaporating fluids, and of some other means of producing cold; by William Cullen, M.D.* Edinburgh, Scotland: William Creech.
19. Nairne, E. 1777. An account of some experiments made with an air-pump on Mr. Smeaton's principle; together with some experiments with a common air-pump. *Philosophical Transactions of the Royal Society of London* 67: 614-649.

—— **Chapter 6** ——

1. Putnam, A.P. 1892. Wenham Lake and the ice trade. *Ice and Refrigeration* 3(July): 14-17.
2. Beckmann, J. (W. Johnston, translator). 1814. *A history of inventions and discoveries*, III, pp. 349-350. London: J. Walker & Co., et al.
3. Ibid., p. 349.
4. Ibid., pp. 352-353.
5. Anonymous. 1901. The tenth anniversary of *Ice and Refrigeration. Ice and Refrigeration* 20(July): 1-16.
6. Anonymous. 1935. Supplementary material on Frederic Tudor ice project. *Bulletin of the Business Historical Society* 9(Feb.): 2.
7. Pearson, H. 1933. Frederic Tudor, ice king. *Proceedings, Massachusetts Historical Society* 65: 183.
8. Ibid., pp. 169-215.
9. Putnam, A.P. 1892. Wenham Lake and the ice trade. *Ice and Refrigeration* 3(July): 14-17. Additional information can be found in the following: Anonymous. 1932. Frederic Tudor—Ice king. *Bulletin of the Business Historical Society* 6(Sept.): 1-8. Anonymous. 1935. Supplementary material on Frederic Tudor ice project. *Bulletin of the Business Historical Society* 9(Feb.): 1-6. Cummings, R.O. 1949. *The American ice harvests.* London: Cambridge University Press. Tudor's correspondence, diaries, and other papers are archived at the Baker Library, Harvard University, Cambridge, MA.
10. Putnam, A.P. 1892. Wenham Lake and the ice trade. *Ice and Refrigeration* 3(Aug.): 95-97; 3(Sept.): 179-182.
11. Anonymous. 1855. Ice—How much of it is used and where it comes from. *Debow's Review* 19(Dec.): 709-712.
12. Wood, W.E. 1916. Twenty five years development in harvesting and housing ice. *Ice and Refrigeration* 51(Nov.): 190-193.
13. Goosmann, J.C. 1924. History of refrigeration. *Ice and Refrigeration* 67(July): 33-34.
14. Moore, T. 1803. *An essay on the most eligible construction of ice-houses, also a description of the newly invented machine called the refrigerator.* Baltimore: Bonsal & Niles.
15. Anonymous. 1928. Thomas Moore's refrigerator. *The United Newsletter*, April 16.

16. Ibid.
17. Anonymous. 1931. Early Maryland settler invented refrigerator. *Air Conditioning and Refrigeration News*, March 25, p. 2.
18. Nash, S. 1985. Letter from Sandy Spring Museum regarding Thomas Moore to Bernard Nagengast, ASHRAE Historical Committee, April 13; and Hiratsuka, S. 1985. Letter regarding Thomas Moore to Bernard Nagengast, March 9.
19. Cummings, p. 8.
20. Cummings, pp. 16-22, 29.
21. Wood, pp. 190-193.
22. Schooley, J.C. c. 1856. *John C. Schooley's process of obtaining a dry cold current of air from ice*. Cincinnati, OH: J.C. Schooley.
23. Locke, J.M. 1856. *A monograph upon the preservation of organic substances by means of a current of dry air*. Cincinnati, OH: Moore, Wilstach, Keys & Co.
24. Anonymous. 1904. Refrigeration abroad. *Ice and Refrigeration* 27(Aug.): 72.
25. Anonymous. 1892. Ice in Europe. *Ice and Refrigeration* 3(Nov.): 359-362.
26. Anonymous. 1891. The situation in the South. *Ice and Refrigeration* 1(Sept.): 158.
27. Anonymous. 1892. *Ice and Refrigeration* 2(Jan.): 32.

—— Chapter 7 ——

1. Tredgold, T. 1824. *Principles of warming and ventilating public buildings*, 2d ed., pp. 18-19. London: Josiah Taylor.
2. de Chabannes, Jean Frédéric, Marquis. 1816. Patent specification for ventilating apparatus. *Repertory of Arts, Manufacturers and Agriculture*, No. CLXVIII, Second Series, May, pp. 321-322.
3. de Chabannes, Jean Frédéric, Marquis. 1818. *On conducting air by forced ventilation and regulating the temperature in dwellings*, p. 26. London: Schulze and Dean.
4. Reid, D.B. 1844. *Illustrations of the theory and practice of ventilation*, pp. ix, x. London: Longman, Brown, Green & Longmans.
5. Ibid., p. ii.
6. Knowles, L. 1988. *St. George's Hall, Liverpool*, p. 33. Liverpool, UK: National Museums & Galleries on Merseyside, Liverpool Museum.
7. Ibid., pp. 26-27.
8. Honiball, C.R. 1907. The mechanical ventilation and warming of St. George's Hall, Liverpool. *The Heating and Ventilating Magazine* 4(Oct.): 15.
9. Ibid., p. 18.
10. Ibid., p. 19. Honiball describes Reid's application of thermometers for a unique high-temperature alarm relay: "Originally, each boiler was also fitted with an electric thermometer, which operated an electric bell in the office of the superintendent when the temperature of the water in the boilers exceeded a pre-arranged limit. These thermometers consisted of an iron bottle about 12 in. long, fitted with two glass tubes containing the terminal rods of the circuit. The mercury, which, when expanded by heat, rose in the glass tubes and so completed the circuit by coming in contact with the terminal rods. The temperature at which the bell will operate can be adjusted by raising or lowering the rods accordingly."
11. Ibid., p. 20.
12. Ibid., p. 21.
13. Knowles, p. 27.
14. Perkins, A.M. 1840. *Patent apparatus for warming and ventilating buildings*, p. 5. London: J.B. Nichols & Son.
15. Billington, N., and B. Roberts. 1982. *Building services engineering, a review of its development*, p. 121. Oxford: Pergamon Press.
16. Anonymous. 1830. *London Journal of Arts and Sciences*, vol. 5, 2d series, pp. 83-84.
17. Richardson, C. 1839. *A popular treatise on the warming and ventilation of buildings*, 2d ed., p. 18. London: John Weale Architectural Library.
18. Ibid., p. 21.
19. Hood, C. 1844. *A practical treatise on warming buildings by hot water, on ventilation, etc.*, 2d ed., p. 123. London: Whittaker & Co.
20. Ibid., pp. 128-129.
21. Anonymous. 1878. *Steam and hot water for warming and ventilating all kinds of buildings*, p. 14. Boston: Swamscot Machine Co.
22. Ibid., p. 10.
23. Ibid., p. 11.
24. Walworth, A.C. 1912. First fan installations in the United States. *Engineering Review* 22(Sept.): 27.
25. Anonymous. 1925. Heating and ventilating the United States Capitol. *The Heating and Ventilating Magazine* 22(Mar.): 61.
26. Ibid., p. 61.
27. Ibid., p. 62.
28a. Billings, J.S. 1886. *The principles of ventilating and heating*, 2d ed., p. 127. New York: The Sanitary Engineer.
28. Walworth, p. 28.
29. Anonymous, 1925, p. 62.
30. Ibid., p. 62.
31. Pierce, E.A. 1911. *A practical manual of steam and hot water heating*, 1st ed., p. 149. Chicago: Domestic Engineering Co.
32. Ibid., p. 333.
33. Stifler, S.R. 1960. *The beginning of a century of steam and hot water heating by the H.B. Smith Co.*, p. 80. Westfield, MA: H.B. Smith Co.
34. Ibid., p. 27.
35. Ibid., p. 28.
36. Ibid., p. 34.
37. Ibid., p. 80.
38. Ibid., p. 81.
39. Pierce, p. 200.
40. Stifler, p. 80.
41. Pierce, p. 202. The term "indirect radiator" refers to the placement of the device. A "direct" radiator was placed in the room to be heated, whereas an "indirect" radiator was concealed inside a wall or floor, covered by a suitable grating. Normally, air from a central fan system was forced over the indirect radiator into the room. "Direct-indirect" radiators were placed in the room and were equipped with a base through which air flowed up and through the radiator.
42. Mills. J.H. 1890. *Heat, science and philosophy of its productions and applications to the warming and ventilation of*

buildings. Boston: American Printing and Engraving Co.

43. Stifler, pp. 81-82.
44. Ibid., p. 87.
45. Ibid., p. 78.
46. Ibid., pp. 89-90.
47. Tudor, F. 1901. The "French" system of heating and the Tudor system. *Engineering Review* 11(Sept.): 11.
48. Pierce, p. 332.
49. Stifler, p. 28.
50. Pierce, p. 332.
51. Ibid., pp. 150-151.
52. Ibid., p. 335.
53. Anonymous. 1897. New York Steam Company's plant. *Heating and Ventilation* VII(6), June 15, p. 1.
54. Anonymous. 1932. *Fifty years of New York steam service—The story of the founding and development of a public utility.* New York: New York Steam Corporation.
55. Anonymous, 1897, p. 1.
56. Anonymous. 1903. *Engineering Review* 13(May): 22.
57. Anonymous, 1897, p. 2.
58. Elliott, C. 1992. *Technics and architecture,* pp. 284-285. Cambridge, MA: MIT Press.
59. Butti, K., and J. Perlin. c. 1980. *A golden thread, 2500 years of solar architecture and technology,* p. 63. New York: Cheshire Books, Van Nostrand, Reinhold.
60. Ibid., p. 74.
61. Ibid., p. 77.
62. Ibid., p. 78.
63. Tredgold, T. 1836. *The principles of warming and ventilating public buildings, dwelling houses, manufactories, hospitals, hot houses, conservatories, etc.,* p. 73. London: M. Taylor.
64. Refer to the analysis of Tredgold's ventilation recommendations by A.K. Klauss, R.H. Tull, L.M. Roots, and J.R. Pfafflin in: "History of the changing concepts in ventilation requirements," *ASHRAE Journal,* June 1970.
65. Harris, E. 1858. An introductory outline of the progress of sanitary improvement in: Reid, D.B., *Ventilation in American Dwellings,* 1st ed., p. xii. New York: Wiley and Halsted.
66. Billington, N. 1955. A historical review of the art of heating and ventilating. *Journal of the Institution of Heating and Ventilating Engineers* 23(Oct.): 274.
67. Morin, A. 1867. On the ventilation of public buildings. *Proceedings of the Institution of Mechanical Engineers,* p. 61.
68. Billings, J.S. 1893. *Ventilation and heating,* p. 38. New York: Engineering Record.
69. Reid, D.B. 1858. *Ventilation in American dwellings,* 1st ed., p. xxiii. New York: Wiley and Halsted.
70. Ibid., p. 1.
71. Anonymous. 1896. *Ventilation and heating principles and application.* Boston: B.F. Sturtevant Co.
72. Leeds, L.W. 1868. Lectures on Ventilation, *Man's own breath is his greatest enemy,* being a course delivered in the Franklin Institute during the winter of 1866-67, p. 51. New York: John Wiley & Sons. Leeds' reference to "the late war" refers to the Civil War in the United States.
73. Saeltzer, A. 1872. *A treatise on acoustics in connection with ventilation and an account of the modern and ancient methods of heating and ventilation,* p. 70. New York: D. Van Nostrand.
74. Billington and Roberts, p. 221.
75. Murgue, D. 1883. *The theories and practice of centrifugal ventilating machines,* pp. 15-16. London and New York: E. & F.N. Spon.
76. Murgue, p. 70.
77. Billington and Roberts, p. 229.
78. "An Expert." 1908. Fan notes, design, construction, efficiency, etc. *Engineering Review* 18(May): 18.
79. Ibid., p. 18.
80. Billington and Roberts, p. 225.
81. Ibid., p. 226.
82. Webster, W. 1929. High spots in the progress of vacuum and vapor heating. *Heating and Ventilating* 26(June): 99-100.
83. Sprague, J.F. 1930. Looking backward thru the history of ventilation 1880-1930. *The Aerologist* VI(Aug.): 5.
84. Ibid., p. 6.
85. Anonymous. 1928. The history of the Buffalo Forge Company. *The Aerologist* 4(Dec.): 33.
86. Anonymous. 1930. Interesting people. *The Aerologist* 6(July): 35.
87. Anonymous. 1897. Heating and ventilating plants in a few conspicuous New York buildings. *Heating and Ventilation* VII(6): 6.
88. Ibid., p. 6.
89. Ibid., p. 6.

—— **Chapter 8** ——

1. Leslie, J. 1813. *A short account of experiments and instruments, depending on the relations of air to heat and moisture,* pp. 138-150. Edinburgh, Scotland: William Blackwood. Leslie's thoughts on heat can also be found in: Leslie, J. 1813. On the relations of air to heat, cold, and moisture, and the means of ascertaining their reciprocal action. *Philosophical Magazine* 41(June): 446-457.
2. Nairne, E. 1777. An account of some experiments made with an air-pump on Mr. Smeaton's principle; together with some experiments with a common air-pump. *Philosophical Transactions of the Royal Society of London* 67: 58. Nairne's complete experiments are reported in: Nairne, E. 1777. An account of some experiments made with an air-pump on Mr. Smeaton's principle; also some experiments with a common air-pump. *Philosophical Transactions of the Royal Society of London* (abridged) 19: 220-224.
3. Anonymous. 1823. Professor Leslie's process for making ice. *Mechanic's Magazine* 1: 311-323.
4. Specifications for Vallance's patents can be found in: Anonymous. 1824. To John Vallance for his invention of an improved method of freezing water. *The London Journal of Arts and Sciences* 8: 250-253; and Anonymous. 1826. To John Vallance for his invention of an improved method or methods of abstracting or carrying off the caloric of fluidity from any congealing water; also, an improved method or methods of producing intense cold; also, an improved method or methods of applying this invention, so as to make it available to purposes, with reference to which tem-

perature above or below the freezing point may be rendered productive of advantageous effects, whether medical, chemical, or mechanical. *The London Journal of Arts and Sciences* 11: 298-302.

5. Dalton, J. 1803. Experimental essays on the constitution of mixed gasses; on the force of steam or vapour from water and other liquids in different temperatures, both in a Torricellian vacuum and in air; on evaporation; and on the expansion of gasses by heat. *A Journal of Natural Philosophy, Chemistry, and the Arts* 5: 257-273; and Dalton, J. 1804. Experimental essays on the constitution of mixed gasses; on the force of steam or vapour from water and other liquids in different temperatures, both in a Torricellian vacuum and in air; on evaporation; and on the expansion of gasses by heat. *A Journal of Natural Philosophy, Chemistry, and the Arts* 7: 5-17.

6. Dalton, J. 1802. Experiments and observations on the heat and cold produced by the mechanical condensation and rarefaction of air. *A Journal of Natural Philosophy, Chemistry, and the Arts* 3: 160-166.

7. Evans, O. 1805. *The young steam engineer's guide*, p. 137. Philadelphia: H.C. Carey and I. Lea.

8. Ammons, J. 1972. Jacob Perkins. *Refrigeration Service and Contracting*, February, pp. 7-10; March, pp. 7, 14. For a comprehensive biography of Perkins, see: Bathe, G. and D. 1943. Jacob Perkins, his inventions, his times and his contemporaries. Philadelphia: The Historical Society of Pennsylvania. Bathe's information on Perkins is summarized in Ammons (1972).

9. Ammons, J. 1972. Jacob Perkins. *Refrigeration Service and Contracting*, April, pp. 7-9.

10. Anonymous. 1882. Ice-making. *Journal of the Society of Arts* 31: 76-77. Hague's machine is also illustrated in: Anonymous. 1883. One of the first ice machines. *Scientific American*, January 20, p. 34.

11. For detailed accounts of Gorrie's life and work, the most useful accounts are: Mier, R.E. 1938. John Gorrie—Florida medical pioneer and harbinger of air conditioning. Ph.D. thesis. Deland, FL: Stetson University; Mier, R.E. 1947. More about Dr. John Gorrie and refrigeration. *The Florida Historical Quarterly* 26(Oct.): 167-173; and Becker, R.B. 1972. *John Gorrie, M.D., Father of air conditioning and mechanical refrigeration.* New York: Carlton Press, Inc.; Sherlock, V.M. 1982. *The fever man—A biography of Dr. John Gorrie.* Tallahassee, FL: Medallion Press. Gorrie's work in refrigeration and air conditioning was most recently summarized in: Nagengast, B. 1991. John Gorrie— Pioneer of cooling and ice making. *ASHRAE Journal* 33(Jan.): S52-S61.

12. Anonymous (John Gorrie). 1842. Refrigeration and ventilation of cities. *The Southern Quarterly Review* 1(Apr.): 425-426. Raymond Becker concludes that this article, although unsigned, was written by John Gorrie (Becker, 1972, p. 79). The conclusion seems warranted, since the 1842 article contains wording that is in many cases identical to that used in Gorrie's 1844 articles.

13. "Jenner" (John Gorrie). 1844. On the prevention of malarial diseases. *Apalachicola Commercial Advertiser* I(April 6); II(April 13); III(April 20); IV(April 27); V(May 4); VI(May 11); VII(May 18); VIII(May 25); IX(June 1); X(June 9).

14. Ibid., part V.

15. Ibid., part IX.

16. The experiments in New Orleans and Cincinnati are reported in: Garric (Gorrie), J. 1850. On the quantity of heat evolved from atmospheric air by mechanical compression. *American Journal of Science and Arts* 60(Nov.): 39-49, 214-227. Regarding New Orleans money, see ibid., p. 44.

17. Mier, 1938, p. 72.

18. British Patent 13,234 (1850) and U.S. Patent 8080 (1851).

19. Gorrie, J. 1854. *Dr. John Gorrie's apparatus for the artificial production of ice in tropical climates.* New York: Maigne & Wood Book and Job Printers.

20. Anonymous. 1851. Manufacture of ice—Dr. Gorrie's process. *Mechanic's Magazine, Museum, Register, Journal and Gazette* 54: 87-89.

21. Coleman, J.J. 1882. Air refrigerating machinery and its applications. *Minutes of Proceedings of the Institution of Civil Engineers* 68: 177-186.

22. Becker, 1972, p. 137.

23. Smyth, P. 1850. On a method of cooling the air of rooms in tropical climates. *The Practical Mechanics Journal*, October, pp. 156, 157. Smyth's communication to the Royal Society can be found in: Smyth, C.P. 1849. On a method of cooling the atmosphere of rooms in a tropical climate. *Proceedings, Royal Society of Edinburgh* 2: 235-236. One early example of an attempt to use the air cycle for refrigeration can be seen in Lemuel Wright's British Patent 6655 of 1834, in which he proposes alternative compression and expansion of air in a single cylinder to freeze water.

24. Smyth, 1850, pp. 157, 194-198.

25. Petrie, W. 1851. Simplification of the machinery of Prof. P. Smyth's tropical air-cooling apparatus. *The Practical Mechanics Journal*, January, pp. 270-273.

26. Coleman, p. 211.

27. Rankine, W.J.M. 1852. Remarks on the mechanical progress for cooling air in tropical climates. *Report of British Association for the Advancement of Science*, p. 128. For examples of Rankine's proposals, see this citation and: Anonymous. 1853. Cooling air by expansion. *The Civil Engineer and Architect's Journal*, p. 364.

28. Some sources repeat a reference to a "Hagen," as first reported by Selfe and repeated by Plank (Selfe, N. 1900. *Machinery for refrigeration*, p. 44. Chicago: H.S. Rich & Co.; Plank, R. 1954. *Handbuch der Kältetechnik*. Berlin: Springer-Verlag). In reading Selfe, *Hagen* is obviously a misspelling of *Hague*. Plank also reports that an Englishman, Shaw, worked on a vapor-compression machine about the same time as Perkins, but no source for the information is cited. One source says that Shaw was an English physicist who experimented with, but did not construct, an ether device in 1836. The citation also says that a French inventor, Bourgeois, constructed a vapor-compression device as early as 1840 (Anonymous. 1913. *Compte Rendu Officiel De La Manifestation Internationale En L'Honneur De Charles Tellier, "Pere du Froid."* Paris: Association Francaise Du Froid).

29. Alexander Twining's personal papers and letters are located at the New Haven Colony Historical Society, New Haven, CT.

30. Twining, A.C. 1857. *The manufacture of ice on a commercial economy, by steam or water power*, pp. 4-5. New Haven, CT: Thomas J. Stafford.

31. British Patent 13,167 of July 3, 1850, and U.S. Patent 10,221, issued November 8, 1853. These two patents differ in that the U.S. patent covers only the use of mechanical refrigeration for ice making, while the British patent claims invention of the vapor-compression process itself, a claim that proved to be insupportable.

32. Twining, 1857, pp. 5-6.

33. Ibid., pp. 17-18.

34. Twining, A.C. 1870. *The fundamental ice-making invention; patented November 8, 1853; in a plea for extension . . . .*, p. 2.

35. Ibid.

36. That the U.S. patent was indeed applied to an actual system seems to be verified by royalty payments to Twining, as noted in Twining, 1870, p. 3. Regarding the Louisiana Ice Manufacturing Co., see the following: Anonymous. 1869. Artificial ice. *American Journal of Science and Arts* 98: 440-441; Becker, V.M. 1909. Elemental processes. *Ice and Refrigeration*, February, p. 54; Nickerson, J.F. 1915. The development of refrigeration in the United States. *Ice and Refrigeration* 49(Oct.): 171.

37. Lang, W.R.R. 1992. *James Harrison—Pioneering genius*, pp. 12-14. Newtown, Victoria, Australia: Neptune Press Pty. Ltd.

38. Patent number VP 25/1855 (old series).

39. Patent specification is summarized by Lang, pp. 112, 113.

40. Lang, pp. 58-62; also: Oldham, B.C. 1966. The history of refrigeration, 11, The European influence. *The Journal of Refrigeration* 9(July): 181-182.

41. Anonymous. 1858. Harrison's ice making machine. *Illustrated London News*, May 29. A good description of Harrison's early machines is in: Tomlinson, C., ed. 1868. Ice. *Cyclopaedia of Useful Arts & Manufactures* 3: 410-418. London: Virtue & Co.

42. The Siebe machines were apparently engineered not only by Daniel Siebe, but also by Henry Joseph West, according to: Oldham, B.C. 1966. The history of refrigeration, 8. The formative period. *The Journal of Refrigeration* 9(Jan.): 22-23. The Russell machines, first of horizontal design, and later similar to the Siebe "table engine" design, were engineered by Norman Selfe. Selfe's contributions and comments can be found in the following: Selfe, N. 1895. Refrigeration in the antipodes. *Ice and Refrigeration* 8(Feb.): 83-84; 9(Aug.): 93-94; Selfe, N. 1895. Mechanical refrigeration. *Ice and Refrigeration* 9(Sept.): 168-171; Selfe, N. 1899. A pioneer refrigerating engineer. *Ice and Refrigeration* 16(Apr.): 297-298; Selfe, N. 1901. Pioneers in refrigeration. *Ice and Refrigeration* 21(Dec.): 235-236.

43. For reasonably good histories of the work of various refrigeration pioneers, see the following four article series: Becker, V.H. 1908. Elemental processes. *Ice and Refrigeration* 35(July): 28-29, 35(Aug.): 72-73, 35(Sept.): 112-114, 35(Oct.): 163-165; Becker, V.H. 1908. Elemental progress related to mechanical refrigeration. *Ice and Refrigeration* 35(Nov.): 204-206, 35(Jan.): 18-19, 36(Feb.): 53-56, 36(Mar.): 10-111, 36(May): 252-254; Goosmann, J.C. 1924-1926. History of refrigeration. *Ice and Refrigeration* 66(Apr.): 297-299, 66(May): 446-448, 66(June): 541-542, 67(July): 33-34, 67(Aug.): 110-112, 67(Sept.): 181-183, 67(Oct.): 226-228, 67(Dec.): 428-430, 68(Jan.): 70-71, 68(Feb.): 135-137, 68(Apr.): 335-336, 68(May): 413-414, 68(June): 478-480, 69(Aug.): 99-101, 69(Sept.): 149-151, 69(Oct.): 203-205, 69(Nov.): 267-269, 69(Dec.): 372-373, 70(Jan.): 123-124, 70(Feb.): 197-198, 70(Mar.): 312-314, 70(May): 503-504, 70(June): 611-614), 71(Aug.): 81-84; Rossi, A.J. 1891. Artificial refrigeration. *Ice and Refrigeration* 1(July): 12-13, 1(Aug.): 91-93, 1(Sept.): 141-143, 1(Oct.): 191-192, 1(Nov.): 260-263; and Oldham, B.C. May 1965-March 1968. The history of refrigeration. *Journal of Refrigeration*, vols. 8-11; and the following books: Anderson, O.E., Jr. 1953. *Refrigeration in America*. Princeton, NJ: Princeton University Press; Thévenot, R. 1979. *A history of refrigeration throughout the world*. Paris: International Institute of Refrigeration; and Woolrich, W. 1967. *The men who created cold*. New York: Exposition Press.

44. D'Auriac, F. 1863. *De La Production Du Froid Applications Industrielles Appareils Carré*, pp. 34-35, 45-46. Paris: Victor Masson Et Fils.

45. Ibid., p. 60. Carre began work with a patent in 1837. The first application of his vapor-compression system was at a brewery in Marseilles in 1859. His absorption system was applied at the same brewery in 1853. See: Velten, E. 1908. The promotor of refrigeration in France. *First International Congress of the Refrigerating Industries, Summaries in English*. Paris.

46. These machines were patented: see British Patent 2503 of 1860 or U.S. Patent 30,201 of 1860 to F.P.E. Carré. The first publication of Carré's work, in 1862, was in *Comptes Rendus Academie Sciences*, vol. 54.

47. Anonymous. 1901. Historical review of the rise of mechanical refrigeration. *Ice and Refrigeration* 21(Aug.): 50.

48. Thévenot, R. 1979. *A history of refrigeration throughout the world*, p. 436. Paris: International Institute of Refrigeration.

49. Billington, N.S., and B.M. Roberts. 1982. *Building services engineering, a review of its development*, p. 259. Oxford: Pergamon Press.

50. Anonymous. 1913. *Compte Rendu Officiel De La Manifestation Internationale En L'Honneur De Charles Tellier, "Pere du Froid,"* pp. 72, 75-79. Paris: Association Francaise Du Froid.

51. Ibid., p. 83. It seems that there was an earlier attempt to establish a business in the U.S.—by the Baltimore and Texas Steam Transportation Co. in 1870-1871—to use the Tellier process to ship beef between Baltimore and New Orleans. See: de la Reintrie, H.R. 1871. Statement, Baltimore and Texas Steam Transportation Company (Tellier process). Baltimore, MD.

52. Anonymous. 1913. Charles Tellier, deceased. *Ice and Refrigeration* 45(Nov.): 303; Anonymous. 1914. Tellier starved to death? *Ice and Refrigeration* 46(Feb.): 86.

Charles Tellier's autobiography was published as: Tellier, C. 1910. *Histoire d'une Invention Moderne, le Frigorifique*. Paris: Librairie Ch. Delagrave. Tellier's U.S. Patent 85,719 of 1869 features his forced-air cooler design.

53. Goosmann, 1925, February, p. 136.
54. Ibid., p. 137. The German titles of Linde's papers are Über die Wärmeentziehung bei niedrigen Temperaturen durch mechanische Mittel (1870) and Verbesserte Eis- und Kühlmaschine (1871).
55. Goosmann, 1925, April, p. 336.
56. Mineral oils were now available that were suitable for low-temperature work. A complete discussion of Linde's first compressor designs and of oils for refrigeration can be found in: Goosmann, 1925, May, pp. 413-414.
57. Goosmann, 1925, June, p. 478.
58. Goosmann, 1925, September, p. 149.
59. Chimogene, meaning "cold generator," was said to have a boiling point of about 30_F and was "obtained at the first stage of distillation of petroleum and by the redistillation of benzine and other similar light products . . .," according to U.S. Patent 72,431, issued to P.H. Van der Weyde, December 17, 1867. Daniel Holden used the spelling "chymogene," and others sometimes spelled it "cryogene." Van der Weyde also patented a refrigeration system (U.S. Patent 87,074 of 1869) that was improved upon by Daniel Holden.
60. Some of Holden's U.S. patents are: 95,357 of 1869, "Improvement in ice machines"; 101,876 of 1870, "Improvement in apparatus for the manufacture of ice"; and 123,697 of 1872, "Improvement in body-preservers."
61. For details on the early use of ammonia as a refrigerant, see the discussion of commercial refrigerants later in this chapter.
62. Anonymous. 1891. The late David Boyle. *Ice and Refrigeration* 1(July): 24.
63. Ibid.
64. Skinkle, E. ("The Boy"). 1895. Twenty five years of refrigeration. *Ice and Refrigeration* 9(Dec.): 397-398.
65. According to Goosmann, 1925, August, p. 101, Boyle Ice Machine Company was merged with Empire Ice Machine Company in 1884 to form the Consolidated Ice Machine Company, which, in 1890, became John Featherstone Sons, succeeded in 1905 by Featherstone Foundry and Machine Company. Catalogs of the Pennsylvania Iron Works issued in the 1890s indicate that the firm also was a manufacturer of Boyle's machine.
66. Goosmann, 1924, July, p. 33.
67. A history of the brewing industry in the U.S. can be found in: Seibel, J.E. 1898. Historical outlines of brewing in the United States. *The Western Brewer* 22(Feb. 15): 279-282. A history of the application of refrigeration to brewing can be found in: Anonymous. 1876. Artificial production of ice and cold in fermenting rooms and beer vaults. *The Western Brewer* 1(Oct.): 61-62; Anonymous. 1897. Twenty years' progress in mechanical refrigeration. *The Western Brewer* 22(June 15): 1050e-1050h; Seibel, J.E. 1908. Refrigeration in its relation to the fermenting (brewing) industry of the United States. *The Western Brewer* 33(Dec.): 666-667; and Becker, V.H. 1912. The relation of refrigeration to the art of brewing. *The Western Brewer* 38(May): 221-224.
68. Advertisement. 1896. *Ice and Refrigeration* 10(Jan.): 72.
69. Anonymous, 1891, p. 24.
70. A recent comprehensive history of refrigerants is: Nagengast, B.A. 1989. A history of refrigerants. In: *CFC's: Time of Transition*. Atlanta: American Society of Heating, Refrigerating and Air-Conditioning Engineers, Inc.
71. Anonymous. 1913. Charles Tellier, deceased. *Ice and Refrigeration* 45(Nov.): 303.
72. Selfe, 1899, pp. 297-298.
73. Beath, J.M. 1912. Ice making experiences. *Ice and Refrigeration* 43(Sept.): 81-82.
74. Ibid., p. 82. Some early U.S. patents issued to Beath are: 127,180 of 1872 to Samuel Martin and John Beath for a plate-type ice-making system featuring an evaporative condenser; and 161,976 of 1875 to John Beath for a plate ice system that uses an evaporator plate with embossed sheet-metal serpentine refrigerant passageways riveted to the ice plate. Beath quickly abandoned compression systems in favor of absorption systems. Since both Beath and David Boyle were located in San Francisco in the early 1870s and since both of them constructed plate ice systems, one could speculate that they were aware of each other's work.
75. Anonymous. 1872. Refrigeration by means of ammonia. *Scientific American* 26(June 8): 380.
76. DeCoppet, F.V. 1892. Pioneer ice making. *Ice and Refrigeration* 2(Jan.): 38.
77. Anonymous. 1901. Historical review of the rise of mechanical refrigeration. *Ice and Refrigeration* 21(Dec.): 229.
78. Ibid., August, p. 56.
79. Rankin, T.L., and G. Johnson. 1892. Corrosion of bolts. *Ice and Refrigeration* 3: 428.
80. Anonymous, August 1901, p. 52.
81. Linde, C. 1893. The refrigerating machine of to-day. *Ice and Refrigeration* 5(Sept.): 173.
82. Ewing, J.A. 1908. *The mechanical production of cold*. London: Cambridge University Press; Woolrich, W.R. 1967. *The men who created cold*, pp. 105-107. New York: Exposition Press.
83. Goelz, A.H. 1920. Carbonic anhydride refrigeration. *Ice and Refrigeration* 59(July): 17.
84. Anonymous. c. 1878. *D.L. Holden & Bros., manufacturers of ice machines, also refrigerating machines, for breweries, distilleries, packers, fruit houses, steamships, etc.*, p. 21. Philadelphia: Penn Iron Works.
85. Anonymous. 1876. Raoul Pictet's sulphurous acid ice machine. *Nature* 30(Mar.): 432-434.
86. Thévenot, 1979, p. 56.
87. Churchill, J.B. 1932. Methyl chloride. *Industrial and Engineering Chemistry* 24(June): 623-626.
88. Thévenot, 1979, p. 56.
89. Goosmann, 1924, December, pp. 428-430.
90. Anonymous. 1892. Ice water. *Ice and Refrigeration* 3(Aug.): 124.

91. Anonymous. 1929. Patent suit of Frigidaire vs. General Necessities. *Electric Refrigeration News*, March 27, pp. 47-48.

92. Anonymous. 1898. *Ice and Refrigeration*, March, p. 169.

93. A water-pumping "engine" installed about 1755 by M. Hoell to remove water from a mine at Chemnitz, Hungary, has been described in several references. The pumping machine used a column of water as a piston to compress air, which, in turn, forced water up from the bottom of the mine. After doing its work on the water, which could also be likened to a piston pushed by the expanding air, the air was released at the top of the mine through a stop cock. Frequently, not only air but entrained water frozen into ice pellets would emit from the stop cock at such velocity as to "pierce a hat, if held against them, like pistol bullets." See: Anonymous. 1829. *Library of useful knowledge* 1(1): 17-19.

94. A complete history and detailed description of the machines can be found in: Kirk, A.C. 1874. *On the mechanical production of cold*, pp. 4-29. London: William Clowes and Sons. The original paper by the same name was published in the *Minutes of the Proceedings of the Institution of Civil Engineers* 37. See also British Patents 1218 of 1862 and 2211 of 1869 to A.C. Kirk.

95. British Patent 669 of 1869.

96. Thévenot, 1976, p. 44.

97. Coleman, pp. 153-154.

98. British Patent 627 was issued in 1873 to P. Giffard, A. Sublet, and J. Jeune.

99. Coleman, p. 153.

100. Coleman, pp. 154-158.

101. A complete description of these systems is in Coleman, pp. 158-162.

102. Concerning Hall's contributions, see: Miller, H. 1985. *Halls of Dartford*. London: Hutchinson Benham.

103. Further discussions on pipeline refrigeration can be found in the following: Branson, D. 1894. Artificial refrigeration through street pipe lines from central stations. *Journal of the Franklin Institute* 137(Feb.): 80-93; Branson, D. 1894. Pipe line refrigeration. *Ice and Refrigeration* 6(June): 402-404; Anonymous. 1891. Refrigerating by street mains from a central station. *Ice and Refrigeration* 1(July): 14-17; Anonymous. 1892. A soda water fountain. *Ice and Refrigeration* 2(May): 344-345; Horne, G.A. 1931. The future of central station refrigeration. *Ice and Refrigeration* 80(Mar.): 229-233; Oakley, A.W. 1925. Central station pipe line refrigeration. *Ice and Refrigeration* 68(Jan.): 33-37; Tait, R.H. 1916. Development of pipe line refrigeration. *Ice and Refrigeration* 51(Nov.): 174-176; and Anonymous. 1892. *The new era in refrigeration, cooling by street pipeline*, 2d ed. New York: International Cooling Co. The early pipeline systems in the U.S. were installed by the International Cooling Co. of New York. The systems installed in Denver and St. Louis were under subsidiary companies. See the last reference (*The New Era in Refrigeration . . .*) for information on this. Also see U.S. Patents 489,729 and 489,897 of 1893.

104. The first two were designed by Alfred Wolff for the New York Stock Exchange in 1901 and the Hanover Bank in 1903. Both used aqua-ammonia absorption systems provided by Carbondale Machine Co.

105. Briggs, J.N. 1905. Natural and manufactured ice in New York. *Cold Storage and Ice Trade Journal* 13(Apr.): 28.

106. Anonymous. 1903. Lots to say about natural ice. *Cold Storage* 10(Aug.): 64.

107. Rossi, A. 1892. Artificial refrigeration. *Ice and Refrigeration* 2(Feb.): 100.

—— **Chapter 9** ——

1. Anonymous. 1902. The American Society of Heating and Ventilating Engineers. *Engineering Review* 12(Jan.): 1.

2. Anonymous. 1889. The Master Steam and Hot Water Fitters Association. *The Metal Worker* 32(Sept. 14): 37.

3. Attempts at real heating and ventilating engineering seem to have their origins in the work of Eugene Peclét of France and can be seen in his engineering work *Traité de Chaleur*, published in various editions in the nineteenth century. Peclét's work was introduced into England by Thomas Box, and it also found its way to Germany, where it was refined. At the end of the century, "German theory" was introduced into U.S. practice by New York consulting engineer Alfred Wolff.

4. Anonymous. 1891. The Master Fitters convention. *The Metal Worker* 35(May 30): 25.

5. Jellett, S. 1904. A short history of our society. *Domestic Engineering* 26(Feb.): 171-173.

6. Anonymous. 1918. Deaths—Hugh J. Barron. *The Heating and Ventilating Magazine* 15(May): 64.

7. Jellett, p. 173.

8. Ibid., pp. 173-174.

9. Anonymous. 1894. The American Society of Heating and Ventilating Engineers. *Heating and Ventilation* 4(Sept.): 10-13.

10. Jellett, pp. 174-175.

11. Anonymous. 1894. The American Society of Heating and Ventilating Engineers—Suggestions for its advancement. *Heating and Ventilation* 4(Oct.): 8.

12. Anonymous. 1899. The American Society of Heating and Ventilating Engineers. *Heating and Ventilation* 9(Jan.): 1.

13. Jellett, p. 176.

14. Anonymous. 1902. The American Society of Heating and Ventilating Engineers. *Engineering Review*, January, p. 3.

15. Wilson, J.J. 1894. American Society of Heating and Ventilating Engineers. *Heating and Ventilation*, October 15, p. 16.

16. Houghten, F.C. 1929. The research laboratory of the American Society of Heating and Ventilating Engineers. *The Aerologist* 5(Oct.): 8.

17. Ibid., pp. 8, 9. An early description of the Research Bureau's work can be found in: Allen, J.R. 1920. The work of the research bureau. *Journal of American Society of Heating and Ventilating Engineers* 26(Nov.): 759-765.

18. Bolton, R.P. 1931. Progress in heating and ventilating during the past quarter of a century. *Heating, Piping and Air Conditioning*, January, p. 3.

19. *The Heating and Ventilating Magazine*, later renamed *Heating and Ventilating*, was founded in 1904 by 15

engineers and manufacturers (W. Wolfe, C.B.J. Snyder, H. Hall, W. Mackay, R. Carpenter, H. Crane, F. Williams, W. Webster, J. Heg, J. Kinealy, C. Kellogg, B. Carpenter, E. Smith, A. Kenrick, and A. Cryer). The first issue, edited by H.A. Smith, appeared at the June meeting of the Master Steam and Hot Water Fitters Association in Atlantic City. The magazine was the idea of William Mackay, a New York manufacturer, who had heard the lament of a "prominent English heating and ventilating engineer" about the lack of a U.S. publication devoted exclusively to heating. The English engineer had noted that an earlier U.S. publication had lost its name and identity by covering too many areas (probably *Heating and Ventilation*, which had expanded to plumbing and changed its name to *Engineering Review* in 1900) (Anonymous. 1914. 1904-1914. *The Heating and Ventilating Magazine*, June, pp. 23-31).

20. Stacy, A.E. c. 1953. Progress chart of ASHVE. Typewritten paper in Historical Archive (catalog 91-401) of the American Society of Heating, Refrigerating and Air-Conditioning Engineers, Atlanta, GA.

21. Anonymous. 1899. American Society of Heating and Ventilating Engineers. *Domestic Engineering* 14(July 29): 10-14.

22. Anonymous. 1903. Ice machine builders convene. *Ice and Refrigeration* 24(May): 194.

23. Anonymous. 1903. *Minutes of meeting of Manufacturers of Refrigerating Machinery, later known as the Ice Machine Builders' Association of the United States*, February 18-19, Cincinnati, OH; Anonymous. 1903. *Minutes of second meeting of the Ice Machine Builders' Association of the United States*, April 3-4, Cincinnati, OH; Anonymous. 1903. *Minutes of third meeting of the Ice Machine Builders' Association of the United States*, June 5-6, Cincinnati, OH; Anonymous. 1903. *Minutes of fourth meeting of the Ice Machine Builders' Association of the United States*, September 18-20, Cincinnati, OH.

24. This publication was the consolidation of *Cold Storage* and the *Ice Trade Journal* in 1903.

25. Ross is given credit for the founding by all of the charter members still living in 1940 (see: Peffer, H.H. 1940. Early annual meetings. *Refrigerating Engineering*, January, p. 11). Ross was also identified as the founder by David Fiske in the following: Anonymous. 1934. Charter members of the American Society of Refrigerating Engineers. *Refrigerating Engineering* 28(Dec.): 323.

26. Coverage of the organizational meeting can be found in: Anonymous. 1904. Refrigerating engineers meet. *Cold Storage and Ice Trade Journal*, December, pp. 58-76; Anonymous. 1905. Refrigerating engineers organized. *Ice and Refrigeration* 28(Jan.): 38-49. This article has a list of charter members on p. 49. The first general meeting is extensively covered in: Anonymous. 1905. The refrigerating engineers meet. *Cold Storage and Ice Trade Journal*, December, pp. 21-72.

27. Anonymous. 1905. First meeting of A.S.R.E. *Cold Storage and Ice Trade Journal*, December, p. 100.

28. Peffer, p. 12.

29. Anonymous. 1944. Random items of A.S.R.E. history. *Refrigerating Engineering*, December, pp. 475-476.

30. For contemporary coverage of the International Refrigeration Exposition, see the following: Anonymous. 1913. The international refrigeration exposition. *Ice and Refrigeration* 45(Aug.): 73-75; Anonymous. 1913. International exposition of refrigeration. *Ice and Refrigeration* 45(Oct.): 199-246; and Anonymous. 1913. *Guide to the international refrigeration exposition*. Milwaukee, WI: Vilter Manufacturing Co. The original incorporation papers and minutes of meetings of the exposition committee are in the Historical Archive of the American Society of Heating, Refrigerating and Air-Conditioning Engineers, Atlanta, GA. Most recently, the exposition was summarized in: Woodford, M.W. 1990. The history of international air-conditioning, heating and refrigerating expositions. *ASHRAE Transactions* 96(1): 1182-1186.

31. Anonymous. 1905. American Society of Refrigerating Engineers. *Engineering Review* 15(Feb.): 32.

32. Anonymous. 1934. Ice was the thing. *Refrigerating Engineering* 28(Dec.): 290.

33. Ibid.

34. Anonymous. 1903. First test for unit of refrigeration. *Cold Storage* 10(Oct.): 159. For examples of discussions of standard ratings, see the following: Denton, J.E., and D.S. Jacobus. 1892. Summary of results of principal experimental measurements of performance of refrigerating machines. *ASME Transactions*, p. 507; Anonymous. 1903. Convention of Southern Ice Exchange (standard ton of refrigeration). *Cold Storage* 9(Mar.): 110-111; Anonymous. 1903. Standard unit of refrigeration. *Ice and Refrigeration* 25(July): 16-18; Voorhees, G. 1903. Standard unit of refrigeration. *Ice and Refrigeration* 25(Aug.): 47-50; Skinkle, E. 1903. Standard unit of refrigeration. *Ice and Refrigeration* 25(Sept.): 101-103; Bertsch, J.C. 1903. Another opinion on standard ton. *Ice and Refrigeration* 25(Oct.): 125-128; Voorhees, G. 1903. Standard unit of refrigeration. *Ice and Refrigeration* 25(Oct.): 129-131; Voorhees, G. 1903. Standard unit of refrigeration. *Ice and Refrigeration* 25(Nov.): 195-196; Goosman, J.C. 1903. Standard unit of refrigeration. *Ice and Refrigeration* 25(Dec.): 223; Bertsch, J.C. 1904. Standard unit of refrigeration. *ASME Transactions*, p. 292; Matthews, F.E. 1904. Standard unit of refrigeration. *Ice and Refrigeration* 26(Feb.): 73-75; Anonymous. 1904. Standard unit of refrigeration. *Ice and Refrigeration* 27(Aug.): 37-42; Anonymous. 1905. Preliminary report of committee on standard tonnage basis for refrigeration. *ASME Transactions* 64; Matthews, F.E. 1905. Standard unit of refrigeration. *ASME Transactions*, p. 502; Anonymous. 1905. Standard unit of refrigeration. *Cold Storage*, June, pp. 28-37; Anonymous. 1905. Mechanical engineers meet. *Ice and Refrigeration* 28(Jan.): 57; Anonymous. 1905. Preliminary report on standard unit ton. *Ice and Refrigeration* 28(Apr.): 206; Anonymous. 1905. Standard unit ton. *Ice and Refrigeration* 29(Aug.): 65-66; Anonymous. 1921. Report of committee on standard tonnage basis for refrigeration. *ASME Transactions*, p. 1259.

35. Anonymous. 1934. Landmarks of a generation. *Refrigerating Engineering* 28: 294.

—— **Chapter 10** ——

1. For some recent commentary on electric power introduction, see the following: Hughes, T.P. 1983. *Networks of power*. Baltimore, MD: The Johns Hopkins University Press; and Hunter, L.C., and L. Bryant. 1991. *A history of industrial power in the United States, 1780-1930*, vol. 3, *The transmission of power*. Cambridge, MA: MIT Press.

2. Tesla, N. 1915. Some personal recollections. *Scientific American*, June 5, pp. 537, 576.

3. Ironically, high-speed steam engines were applied by the electrical industry to drive alternators to produce electricity, but their availability hindered application of the electric motors that used the electricity. For a history of high-speed steam engines, see Bowditch, J. 1989. The American high-speed single-valve automatic cutoff steam engine: Its origins and a brief comparison with the Willans central-valve engine. *Transactions of the Newcomen Society* 61: 1-14.

4. Controversy continues over who "invented" the induction motor. See: Dood, K.L., et al. 1989. Communications: Tesla and the induction motor. *Technology and Culture* 30(Oct.): 1013-1023.

5. Hobart, H.M. 1930. Some events in the early days of the polyphase induction motor. GE Historical File, L4249-L4260, p. 5. Schenectady, NY: General Electric Hall of History.

6. Ibid., p. 10.

7. Hunt, A.L. 1902. Manufactured ice. *Ice and Refrigeration* 22(June): insert sheet at p. 220.

8. Hobart, p. 10.

9. Alger, P.L., and F.D. Newbury. 1932. The development of electrical machinery in the United States. *General Electric Review* 35(Sept.): 462. Some articles that discuss the use of electric motors for refrigerating equipment are: Lloyd, R.L. 1908. Electricity in refrigeration. *Journal of the Franklin Institute* 166(Dec.): 453-469; Behan, T.W. 1919. Electricity in household service. *General Electric Review* 22(Mar.): 180-185; Anonymous. 1912. Electric refrigeration in the ice cream business. *Electrical Review and Western Electrician* 60(May 25): 983-987; Lloyd, R.L. 1912. Electrical refrigeration for florists. *Electrical Review and Western Electrician* 60(May 4): 839-842; Tweedy, E.F. 1913. Mechanical refrigeration and ice making from a central station point of view. *General Electric Review* 16(Aug.): 584-593; Anonymous. 1925. Synchronous motor drives. *Refrigerating Engineering* 11(May): 393-398; and Deans, W. 1924. Electricity in automatic refrigeration. *Refrigerating Engineering* 10(Mar.): 335-349. For a comparison of steam engines and electric motors from an economic point of view in the 1920s, see: Anonymous. 1925. Steam vs. electrically driven plants. *Ice and Refrigeration* 69(July): 59 and 69(Aug.): 115.

10. West, E.H. 1904. Small refrigerating plant for shop and private residences. *Proceedings, The British Cold Storage and Ice Association* 4: 5.

11. Lloyd, R.L. 1908. Electricity in refrigeration. *Journal of the Franklin Institute* 166(Dec.): 453.

12. Kimball, F.M. 1907. The utility of the single phase motor. *General Electric Review* 9(Nov.): 243.

13. A good general reference on the history of electric motors is MacLaren, M. 1943. *The rise of the electrical industry during the 19th century*. Princeton, NJ: Princeton University Press.

14. Veinott, C.G. 1948. *Fractional horsepower electrical motors*, 2d ed., p. 122. New York: McGraw-Hill.

15. Veinott, p. 224. The repulsion-start induction motor was invented by Dr. Engelbert Arnold (U.S. Patent 543,836 of August 6, 1895). Veinott notes that ". . . in 1896, the repulsion start motor wiped the capacitor start motor out of existence. Now, 50 years later, the capacitor-start motor is making the repulsion-start motor obsolete for most applications" (p. 122).

16. Anonymous. 1902. Committee on science and the arts. *Journal of the Franklin Institute*, May, p. 397. This type of motor was first patented in 1888 (U.S. Patent 389,352 to Anthony, Jackson, and Ryan), but the patent was for an externally controlled armature circuit. The internally controlled circuit was apparently first used by Engelbert Arnold in his U.S. Patent 543,836 of 1895. By the 1920s, the repulsion-start motor was almost universally used on small, open-drive refrigeration units. Most of the motors were supplied by Century Electric Company, Wagner Electric Corporation, or Dayton Engineering Laboratories Co. (and successor divisions of General Motors Corporation: Delco Light Co., Delco-Remy, and Delco Products Co.).

17. Anonymous. 1934. Fractional hp motor output doubled every 7 years. *General Electric News*, June 8, p. 3.

18. Billington, N., and B. Roberts. 1982. *Building services engineering, a review of its development*, p. 441. London: Pergamon Press.

19. Elliott, C. 1992. *Technics and architecture*, p. 296. Cambridge, MA: MIT Press.

20. Billington and Roberts, p. 442.

21. Ure, A. 1853. *A dictionary of arts, manufactures and mines*. New York: D. Appleton & Co.

22. Billington and Roberts, p. 442.

23. "An Engineer." 1825. *The theory and practice of warming and ventilating public buildings*, p. 336. London: Underwood, Thomas and George.

24. Billington and Roberts, p. 442.

25. See abstracts of the papers printed in the *Philosophical Transactions of the Royal Society of London, 1815-1830*, vol. 2, pp. 97-98. The second section of Dr. Ure's paper relates to thermometric admeasurements and to the doctrine of capacity. He does not consider the thermometer liable to the uncertainty attributed to it by Mr. Dalton, which is an equable measure of heat, in consequence of its possessing an increasing rate of expansion, compensated for by a quantity of the quicksilver getting out of the bulb into the tube and consequently out of the action of the heat, the bulb being the only part heated in all ordinary cases. In the third section, relating to the latent heat of different vapors, Dr. Ure details experiments made to ascertain the caloric existing in different vapors and the temperatures at which they respectively acquire the same elastic force (see p. 97).

26. Ramsey, A.J.R. 1946. The thermostat or heat governor, an outline of its history. *Transactions of the Newcomen Society* 25: 55.

27. Ure, A. 1856. *A dictionary of arts, manufactures and mines*, pp. 843-844. New York: D. Appleton & Co.
28. Ramsey, p. 56.
29. Stifler, S.R. 1960. *The beginning of a century of steam and hot water heating by the H.B. Smith Co.*, p. 23. Westfield, MA: H.B. Smith Co.
30. Anonymous. 1878. *Steam and hot water for warming and ventilating all kinds of buildings*, p. 19. Boston: Swamscot Machine Co.
31. Ramsey, p. 57.
32. Ibid., p. 58.
33. Ibid., p. 59.
34. Nessell, C.W. 1960. The evolution of the thermostat. *Trade Winds*, February, p. 9. Minneapolis: Minneapolis-Honeywell Regulator Co.
35. Hill, E.V. 1927. The story of the thermostat. *The Aerologist* 3(Apr.): 15.
36. Ibid., p. 28.
37. Ibid., p. 13.
38. Ibid.
39. Nessell, p. 9.
40. Ibid., p. 12.
41. Powers, W.P. 1918. Result of a dull sermon. *Tuesday Talks* 1(5).
42. The appearance of systems engineered for automatic control by thermostat can be seen in the various patents issued beginning in the 1890s. For example, see the following U.S. patents: 478,373 of July 5, 1892, to Alexander Shiels, which features thermostatic control of steam to the driving engine; 630,618 of August 8, 1899, to Albert Marshall, which features a thermostat controlling an electric motor drive; 683,186 of September 24, 1901, to William Singer: thermostat; 697,029 of April 8, 1902, to William Singer: thermostat and electric motor; 716,480 of December 23, 1902, to Robert Rollins, which features a thermostat operating a liquid-line solenoid valve; 834,870 of October 30, 1906, to Jacob Chamberlain and Albert Marshall, assigned to the Automatic Refrigerating Co.: thermostat and safety controls for refrigerating systems; and 981,840 of January 17, 1911, and 982,794 of January 31, 1911, to Eugene Carpenter and Fred Kimball, assigned to the Automatic Refrigerating Co.
43. Some examples of temperature-controlled expansion valves are in the following U.S. patents: 406,775 of July 9, 1889, to Charles Sautter; 450,575 of April 14, 1891, to C. Cox and C. Brockington; 458,247 of August 25, 1891, to Lewis Charles; and 853,503 and 853,505 of May 14, 1907, to Arthur Eddy.
44. Some early U.S. patents for automatic expansion valves or for systems incorporating them are 452,536 of May 19, 1891, to Ehregott Winkler; 504,092 of August 29, 1893, to P. Schmaltz; 537,622 of April 16, 1895, to Ehregott Winkler; 549,426 of November 5, 1895, to Alexander Ballentine; 630,617 of August 8, 1899, to Albert Marshall; 740,170 of September 29, 1903, to Eugene Osborne; 785,265 of March 21, 1905, to Albert Marshall; 815,912 of March 20, 1906, to Arthur Eddy; 908,508 of December 12, 1908, to George Carroll; and British Patent 19,335 of November 1891 to L. Stern and T. Murray.
45. Usually Harry Thompson is given credit for the "thermostatic expansion valve," as revealed in his U.S. Patent 1,747,958, filed August 24, 1927, and issued in 1930, and assigned to Universal Cooler Corporation.
46. Anonymous. 1892. Information wanted. *Ice and Refrigeration* 2(Mar.): 182.
47. The automatic expansion valve patented by Alexander Ballantine in 1895 is described in: Anonymous. 1897. Automatic expansion cock. *Ice and Refrigeration* 12(Feb.): 117.
48. Anonymous. 1892. Ice in Europe. *Ice and Refrigeration* 3: 359-361. The situation had changed little almost 25 years later, according to: Anonymous. 1926. Domestic refrigeration abroad. *Ice and Refrigeration* 71(Aug.): 104.
49. Anonymous. 1892. Refrigerating private residences. *Ice and Refrigeration* 3(Aug.): 110.
50. Anonymous. 1901. Domestic ice machines. *Ice and Refrigeration* 21(Dec.): 230.
51. Some U.S. patents for small systems for homes include 46,595 of February 28, 1865, to Daniel Somes, which features multiwalled refrigerators lined with pipes through which cold spring or well water is circulated (also shows the use of underground pipe coils to allow transfer of heat to the ground with recirculating water); 343,035 of June 6, 1886, to Elias Kauffeld for a household refrigerator using the air cycle; 424,747 of April 1, 1890, to Frederick Wolf, which features a steam-engine-driven refrigeration unit mounted on top of a refrigerator; 442,026 of December 2, 1890, to W.E. Facer, which features automatic control by disconnecting the drive mechanism; 476,358 of June 7, 1892, to Alexander Ballentine for a self-contained refrigerator using a water motor drive (see also: Anonymous. 1892. Some new ideas. *Ice and Refrigeration* 2[June]: 428); 511,857 of February 2, 1894, to William Mild: a remote, electric-motor-driven unit; 549,426 of November 5, 1895, to Alexander Ballentine for a self-contained refrigerator using an automatic expansion valve; 559,533 and 559,753 of May 5, 1896, and 578,297 of March 2, 1897, to Eliel Sharpneck and George Knox—this is the "Economical Refrigerating Machine" that was advertised by the Economical Refrigerating Co. or Atlantic Refrigerating Co. in *Ice and Refrigeration* in 1896 and 1897 (the refrigerator is described in: Anonymous. 1895. A new small machine. *Ice and Refrigeration* 9: 325); 577,328 of February 16, 1897, to William Singer for a self-contained, thermostatically controlled electric refrigerator; 630,616 of August 8, 1899, to Albert Marshall for a self-contained, thermostatically controlled electric refrigerator using an automatic expansion valve and an automatic condenser water valve as well as a high-pressure control; 769,969 of August 8, 1905, to William Heister for a self-contained refrigerator with a water-motor-operated unit on top of the cabinet; 962,704 of June 28, 1910, to Ralph Emerson and Frank Bishop for an electric refrigerator with the unit on top; and 1,050,910 of January 21, 1913, to Frank Bishop, assigned to Auto-Electric Refrigerating Co., for a self-contained refrigerator with the unit on top (a thermostat opens the condenser water valve, which

operates a pressure switch to cycle the refrigerating unit).

52. Anonymous. 1929. Inventions of E.T. Williams big factor in growth of domestic refrigeration. *Electric Refrigeration News*, September 12, p. 3; and Anonymous. 1936. E.T. Williams' 1914 design marked his first step in long line of household refrigerator patents. *Air Conditioning and Refrigeration News*, October 7, pp. 24-25.

53. Anonymous, 1936, pp. 24-25.

54. Anonymous. 1905. Trade literature. *Ice and Refrigeration* 28(Feb.): 120.

55. Anonymous. 1906. Trade notes. *Ice and Refrigeration* 30(Apr.): 245.

56. Starr, J.E. 1916. Refrigeration twenty-five years ago. *Ice and Refrigeration* 51(Nov.): 144.

57. Anonymous. 1916. The domestic refrigerating machine. *Ice and Refrigeration* 51(Nov.): 144.

58. Anonymous. 1910. The refrigerating industry in 1909. *Ice and Refrigeration* 38(Jan.): 59.

59. Goosmann, J.C. 1923. Automatic refrigerating machinery. *Ice and Refrigeration* 64(Jan.): 62.

60. Carpenter, M.R. 1905. Requirements of small refrigerating plants of less than one ton capacity. *Transactions of the American Society of Refrigerating Engineers* 1: 162.

61. Muffley, G. 1941. Twenty-five years of household electric refrigerator development. *Ice and Refrigeration* 101(July): 38-39.

62. Some of the discussion of these problems can be found in the following: Muffley, 1941; Neff, P. 1915. The domestic refrigerating machine. *Ice and Refrigeration* 49(Oct.): 143-144; Starr, J.E. 1918. The household refrigerating machine. *A.S.R.E. Journal* 5(Nov.): 157 (discussion in 6[1]: 34-45 and 6[5]: 372); Kramer, G.A. 1920. Some problems of household refrigerating machine design. *Refrigerating Engineering* 7(July): 29-40; Goosmann, 1923, p. 63; Taubeneck, G.F. 1937. The development of the American household electric refrigeration industry. *Actes Du VIIe Congres International Du Froid*, pp. 540-561, Utrecht, the Netherlands; and Williams, E.T. 1929. Shaft seals for small refrigerating machines. *Refrigerating Engineering* 17(Mar.): 73, 77-78.

63. Neff, p. 143.

64. Hardgrave, A. 1924. Development in household refrigeration. *Ice and Refrigeration* 66(Apr.): 329. The "unnamed New York interest" was probably General Electric, which had made a study of household refrigeration in 1923 and concluded that it should enter the market.

65. U.S. Patent 1,337,175, issued April 13, 1920, was the first patent filed by Wolf on December 23, 1913. Others include: 1,222,170 and 1,291,334. Although Wolf had been interested in small machines prior to 1913, he may not be the inventor of the DOMELRE, since one information source says that a patent (specific one unknown) was assigned to Wolf on June 5, 1913, by Earnest F. Nauer. At the very least, however, Wolf was no doubt active in improving the machine. See: Shellworth, P. 1948. Antecedents of Frigidaire. Frigidaire Collection, file 79-10.1-44. Flint, MI: General Motors Institute, Collection of Industrial History.

66. Anonymous. 1914. Electric refrigerating outfit applicable to any ice-box. *Electrical World* 64(Aug. 22): 393.

67. Anonymous. 1957. An early history of the electric refrigerator. *Electrical Merchandising*, July, pp. 116, 117. Authors' note: This article contains numerous misspellings of names of individuals and companies.

68. McCoy, D.E. n.d. Interview with Mr. Fehr. Frigidaire Collection. Flint, MI: General Motors Institute, Collection of Industrial History.

69. Actually the unit was not "plugged in" as we know the meaning of the word today. In 1914, appliances were a new phenomenon and homes were not wired with electrical outlets. Early appliances had a swivel-type male "Edison base," as used on light bulbs, which could be screwed into any handy light socket. Early American kitchens became nightmares of "octopus wiring," with several electrical cords accommodated by multiple-socket adapters screwed into a drop-cord light socket hanging from the middle of the room. The repulsion-start induction motor was well suited for such low-voltage nightmares, having the ability to develop very high starting torque at low line voltage.

70. Anonymous. n.d. Refrigerator cost comparison. Frigidaire Collection, file 79-10.1-44. Flint, MI: General Motors Institute, Collection of Industrial History.

71. Shellworth, P. 1949. Report of interview with Mr. G. Ralph Fehr. Frigidaire Collection, file 79-10.1-43. Flint, MI: General Motors Institute, Collection of Industrial History.

72. Mellowes, A.W. 1926. Memo of the history of household electric refrigeration. Typed copy in Frigidaire Collection. Flint, MI: General Motors Institute, Collection of Industrial History.

73. Doelling, L.K. 1916. Twenty five years' evolution of refrigeration. *Ice and Refrigeration* 51(Nov.): 160.

74. Anonymous. 1936. Replogle tells of Frigidaire's beginnings in refrigeration and of early problems. *Air Conditioning and Refrigeration News*, October 7, p. 27.

75. Anonymous. 1923. The domestic refrigerating machine. *Ice and Refrigeration* 65(July): 1-7; 65(Aug.): 60-65; 65(Sept.): 123-126; 65(Oct.): 190-192.

76. Ibid., July, p. 1. The 1923 article series was further updated in 1925 (see: Anonymous. 1925. Household refrigerating machines. *Ice and Refrigeration* 69(Nov.): 262-265; 69(Dec.): 369-371.

77. The four manufacturers were most likely Frigidaire, Kelvinator, Copeland, and Servel (see: Copeland, E.J. 1924. Relative hazards of gases used in domestic ice machines. *Ice and Refrigeration* 67 (Nov.): 336.

78. Beckman, J.W. 1931. Edmund J. Copeland tells how he developed electric automatic refrigeration and made refrigerated homes possible. Manuscript in Burton Historical Collection, Detroit Public Library, and reprinted as: Beckman, J.W. 1932. Pioneer explains barriers facing early manufacturers. *Electric Refrigeration News*, July 7, pp. 8-11.

79. Long, W.H. 1936. Goss relates story of Kelvinator's early history. *Air Conditioning and Refrigeration News*, October 7, p. 9.

80. Regarding Heideman's influence, see the following: Mellowes, 1926; Anonymous. 1936. Heideman produced unit with Wolf in 1912; some of his early designs still in use. *Air Conditioning and Refrigeration News*, October 7, p. 9; and Hibbard, H.W. 1926. Memo on the history of electric refrigeration. Frigidaire Collection. Flint, MI: General Motors Institute, Collection of Industrial History. Edmund Copeland also gives Heideman credit for assistance but does not mention specifics. See Beckman, 1931.

81. Long, 1936.

82. McCoy, D. 1963. Notes on interview with Mr. L.A. Clark. Frigidaire Collection, file 79-10.16-75. Flint, MI: General Motors Institute, Collection of Industrial History.

83. For a history of Guardian and Frigidaire, see: McCoy, D. 1962. History of Frigidaire (draft copy). Frigidaire Collection. Flint, MI: General Motors Institute, Collection of Industrial History.

84. Shellworth, P. 1949. Report of interview with Mr. A.W. Mellowes. Frigidaire Collection, file 79-10.1-43. Flint, MI: General Motors Institute, Collection of Industrial History.

85. Anonymous. 1936. Replogle tells of Frigidaire's beginnings in refrigeration and of early problems. *Air Conditioning and Refrigeration News*, October, p. 27.

86. McCoy, 1962, part III.

87. Ibid., part IV.

88. Fehr, G.R. 1982. Letter to "Mr. Frpst." Original copy in the personal library of Bernard A. Nagengast, Sidney, OH.

89. Persons, W.M. n.d. *An economist's appraisal of domestic electric refrigeration*, p. 3. New York: Kelvinator Corporation.

90. Beckman, 1931, p. 22.

91. Anonymous. 1924. Electric domestic refrigeration. *Ice and Refrigeration* 66(June): 518.

92. Hardgrave, p. 330.

93. General Electric Company was formed in 1892, the result of the merger of the Edison General Electric Co. and the Thompson-Houston Co. One of the predecessor companies, the Edison Electric Light Co., had begun the electrical industry in the U.S. in 1879.

94. Audiffren was a teacher at Petit Séminaire in Grasse, France, in 1904. See French Patent 238,845 of May 31, 1894; British Patent 22,279 of 1894; or U.S. Patent 551,107 of 1895, issued to Marcel Audiffren.

95. The improved machine is shown in U.S. Patent 764,515 of 1904, issued to Audiffren. See also: Anonymous. 1904. A novel refrigerating apparatus. *Ice and Refrigeration* 26(Apr.): 250; and U.S. Patent 898,400 of 1908, issued to M. Audiffren and H.A. Singrun.

96. The complete story of the Audiffren machine in the U.S. had to be pieced together from several sources: Anonymous. 1912. Motor-driven refrigerator. *Electrical World* 59(June): 1277; Anonymous. 1912. *Audiffren refrigerating machine catalog 50*. New York: H.W. Johns-Manville Co.; Anonymous. 1938. America's first successful electric refrigerating machine. *General Electric Fort Wayne Works News* 21(May 6): 1-2; and Anonymous. 1939. Refrigeration pioneer ends long service. *General Electric Fort Wayne Works News* 22(Oct. 6): 1, 3. The name of the American company holding the rights is variously referred to as the American Audiffren Co. or the Audiffren Refrigerating Machine Co.

97. Improved machines are covered by the following U.S. patents: 1,555,780, issued in 1915 to M. Audiffren and H.A. Singrun; 1,164,243, issued in 1915 to James Wood; 1,273,653, issued in 1918 to Clark Orr, assigned to General Electric Co.; 1,281,820, issued in 1918 to Clark Orr, assigned to General Electric Co.; 1,281,821, issued in 1918 to Clark Orr, assigned to General Electric Co.; 1,326,686, issued in 1919 to Clark Orr, assigned to General Electric Co.; and 1,559,883, issued in 1925 to A. Karr and K. Perkins (an air-cooled version). A complete listing of capacities and dimensions of the Audiffren machines manufactured in the U.S. can be found in: Macintire, H.J. 1928. *Handbook of mechanical refrigeration*, pp. 67-68. New York: John Wiley & Sons. The Audiffren machine continued to be manufactured at least into the 1940s by license from Singrun, and later by Glacia in Denmark. Reports of machines made in the 1920s that were still operating surfaced in the 1950s and 1960s, and some say that there is a good possibility that Audiffren machines are still in operation in underdeveloped countries, where many were sold.

98. In a meeting in 1913, members of the General Electric Consulting Engineering Department, presided over by Charles Steinmetz, discussed a report (given by Chester Rice and Stuart Thompson) on domestic refrigeration that analyzed the Audiffren machine, according to Crosby Field, who attended the meeting, as related in a letter to the editor, *ASHRAE Journal*, December 1969, p. 4.

99. Anonymous. n.d. Home refrigerator got its start here. *Ft. Wayne Journal Gazette*; see also Stevenson, 1923 (note 101). The water-cooled hermetic system developed by Clark Orr is covered by U.S. Patent 1,902,518, filed July 3, 1920, and issued in 1933.

100. Goll was able to convince the Schenectady headquarters of the company to keep appropriating money for the research as it was needed, according to Clovis Linkous, unofficial historian of General Electric's Fort Wayne division.

101. The report was apparently commissioned because General Motors Corporation had offered to buy rights to General Electric's refrigeration technology, according to: Wise, G. 1977. Postlude—50 years ago R&D refrigerators. *Post*, August 13 (General Electric Company, Schenectady, NY). This is plausible, considering that the Frigidaire division of GM was having engineering problems until 1923, and one possible solution would be to obtain GE's household refrigerating technology developed at its Fort Wayne Electric Works division. However, another explanation is that GE was to turn over the household refrigerator technology to GM so that it could develop a refrigerator that would be manufactured by GM for GE (see: Pratt, F. 1923. Domestic refrigerating machines. Letter to Gerard Swope, dated August 17. Photocopy provided by G. Wise, corporate research

and development, General Electric Company, Schenectady, NY).

102. Stevenson, A.R. 1923. Domestic refrigeration. Research report for General Electric Co., originally located in the company's Technical Data Library, Schenectady, NY. (The report was destroyed, along with most of the library, by corporate decision.) A copy of the report was obtained by Ruth Schwartz Cowan, History Department, University of New York, Stony Brook, and this copy, which was probably the only extant example, was recopied for the ASHRAE Historical Archive and Library, Atlanta, GA.

103. Pratt, 1923.

104. Stevenson, 1923, "Summary and conclusions."

105. Anonymous. c. 1970. Outline history of the General Electric household refrigerator. Paper at General Electric Hall of History Collection, Schenectady, NY.

106. According to William Holladay, who worked in Schenectady and Fort Wayne as a newly hired engineer for the refrigeration department, the name "Freosan" was initially selected as the marketing name for the refrigerator but, just before the formal announcement, it was thought that such an obscure name would not catch on with the public. No one could come up with a better name, so the machine was simply called "the General Electric Refrigerator."

107. Anonymous. 1925. G-E announces new refrigerator. *The General Electric Monogram* 3(Oct.): 22. A very complete description of the OC-2 refrigerator can be found in: Anonymous. 1926. An electric refrigerator for the household. *The G-E Digest* 6(June): 22-24. The air-cooled OC-2 system is covered by two U.S. patents issued to Clark Orr— 1,669,141, filed February 2, 1926, and issued in 1928, and 1,725,472, filed December 16, 1924, and issued in 1929.

108. Anonymous. n.d. Unattributed historical notes in files of G. Wise, Corporate Research and Development. Schenectady, NY: General Electric Company.

109. Roider, R. 1952. General Electric refrigerator's silver anniversary. Paper at General Electric Hall of History Collection, Schenectady, NY. According to Harold Briggeman, who was one of the refrigeration engineers at Fort Wayne and the nephew of Clark Orr, one of the competing engineering teams was his uncle's. In an interview with Bernard Nagengast in 1990, Briggeman said he was not surprised that a Schenectady design won out. He related that Alexander Stevenson, who was in charge of the Schenectady efforts, frequently visited Fort Wayne, "nosing around" in the engineering efforts there. Stevenson wanted to know about every breakthrough, but was tightlipped about the efforts in Schenectady. U.S. Patent 1,669,141, filed in 1926, is possibly Orr's modified version developed in response to Schenectady's request for designs from competing engineering teams, which resulted in three different systems being considered for mass production. Orr's design was not chosen, and it was Christian Steenstrup's DR-2 model that saw mass production beginning in 1927.

110. Anonymous, c. 1970.

111. Anonymous. 1927. Formation of electric refrigeration department announced. *The General Electric Monogram* 4(Jan.): 16.

112. The Frigidaire Meter Miser compressor was developed by Andrew Kucher, who had been hired specifically for that purpose. Kucher had developed hermetic rotary compressors for Westinghouse in the early 1920s. The late G. Ralph Fehr, Frigidaire's long-time Patent Department chief, told Bernard Nagengast (in a personal interview given shortly before his death) that General Electric's competition caused Frigidaire management to launch a program to develop a low-cost, sealed refrigeration system that would regain Frigidaire's lost sales. A rotary compressor design was advocated by Frigidaire's engineering department, and Andrew Kucher was regarded as the leading rotary compressor engineer, so Frigidaire decided to obtain Kucher's services "at any price." After some negotiations, Kucher was hired at such a high salary that Fehr said management did all it could to keep it a secret. Word got out, and rumors spread among Frigidaire's other salaried engineers—in Fehr's words, "a scandal." Even at age 99, long after everyone else associated with the incident was deceased, Fehr refused to discuss the amount of Kucher's salary! Fehr said that Kucher was worth the money, turning out a flawless design (to the delight of Frigidaire's managers). Further corroboration of Fehr's story can be found in McCoy, 1962, part IV, p. 12; and McCoy, D. 1964. Notes on interview with Richard S. Gaugler. Frigidaire Collection, file 79-10.16-75. Flint, MI: General Motors Institute, Collection of Industrial History.

113. Biechler, E.G. n.d. New ice age brings food luxuries to the masses. *Chain Store Review*.

114. For a discussion of the increase in housework caused by modern appliances, including the refrigerator, see Cowan, R.S. 1983. *More work for mother*. New York: Basic Books.

115. Beckman, 1931, p. 19.

116. Haring, H.A. 1926. Growing pains of a giant industry. *Advertising & Selling*, May 19, pp. 19, 20, 52.

117. Anonymous. 1926. Status of electric refrigeration. *Electrical World*, October 30, reprint, p. 10.

118. Beckman, 1931, p. 22. Regarding the benefit of mechanical refrigeration to the ice industry, see also: Anonymous. 1927. Mechanical refrigeration and the ice business. *Ice and Refrigeration* 73(Nov.): 350. Although many ice men saw that they could coexist with mechanical refrigeration, some continued to resist. For example, see: Anonymous. 1929. Proposed boycott of mechanical refrigerator manufacturers. *Ice and Refrigeration* 76(Feb.): 75-76. Sometimes opposition reached absurd proportions, as it did when one brochure warned that mechanical refrigerators caused cancer and asked that the U.S. Congress be petitioned to ban them (see: Teigen, F.A. 1933. *Cancer—The potential penalty of electric refrigeration*. Minneapolis: F.A. Teigen.

119. A general idea of the many technological advances over time can be discerned from the various editions of the following: Althouse, A.D., and C.H. Turnquist. 1936. *Modern electric and gas refrigeration*, 2d ed. Chicago: The Goodheart-Willcox Co., Inc.; Althouse and Turnquist, 1944, 4th ed.; Fittz, R.U., and J.A.

Moyer. 1928. *Refrigeration.* New York: McGraw-Hill Book Company, Inc.; Fittz and Moyer, 1932, 2d ed.; Hull, H.B. 1924. *Household refrigeration.* Chicago: Nickerson & Collins Co.; Hull, 1927, 2d ed.; Hull, 1928, 3d ed.; Hull, 1933, 4th ed.; Praetz, J.G., and J.F. Wostrel. 1948. *Household electric refrigeration.* New York: McGraw-Hill Book Company, Inc.

120. See: Williams, E.T. 1929. Shaft seals for small refrigerating machines. *Refrigerating Engineering* 17(Mar.).

121. Taubeneck, p. 547. The "Streamline" solder fittings were developed to solve the problem of running multiple suction lines for commercial refrigeration units greater than ½-hp. Before 1930, refrigeration tubing (most of which was tin-plated on the outside) was unavailable in sizes greater than 1/2-in. O.D.

122. Hermetically sealed refrigeration systems were advocated as early as the 1890s. The Audiffren-Singrun was apparently the first, and has been described previously in this chapter. The A-S was unique in design, but the now-universal idea of enclosing the motor-compressor in a shell can be seen in these early U.S. patents: 597,532 of 1898 to William Singer, featuring an external stator; 1,212,127 of 1917 to Howard Carpenter; 1,263,633 of 1918 to Heinrich Zoelly (this is the "Autofrigor," which featured an external stator; the unit was manufactured by the Swiss firm Aktiengesellschaft Der Maschinenfabriken Escher Wyss & Cie for a number of years); 1,781,082 of 1930 to Edward Rueger is another Autofrigor patent; 1,362,757 of 1920 to Douglas H. Stokes of Australia (this steel-shelled compressor was commercially manufactured); 1,482,028 of 1924 to Earl Oswald and Clarence Holley, assigned to Utility Compressor Co. (a patent for a bolted-shell compressor, originally filed in 1919); 1,568,102 of 1926 to Elihu Thompson, featuring an adjustable clearance volume and using a spring instead of a piston wrist pin; 1,731,009 and 1,736,973 of 1929 to Jesse King, assigned to Frigidaire, featuring pistons driven by a wobbling fulcrum or a rocking fulcrum and sealed by a bellows; 1,744,969 of 1930 to Arthur Kercher, featuring a radial four-cylinder compressor; 1,760,621 of 1930 to Swan Anderson; 1,807,871 and 1,807,872 of 1931 to Osborne Price, featuring a rotary pendulum-type compressor. The hermetic compressor designs of Clark Orr and Christian Steenstrup, manufactured by General Electric, have been previously discussed. The Streenstrup compressor featured such modern advances as hydrogen brazing and glass-sealed electrical connections. Numerous U.S. patents for rotary hermetic compressors were filed as early as 1921, issued to Andrew Kucher, and assigned to Westinghouse Electric and Manufacturing, such as 1,656,917 of 1928; 1,719,808, 1,719,810, and 1,719,820 of 1929; 1,751,209 and 1,763,162 of 1930; and 1,797,287 and 1,798,684 of 1931. Jay Grant DeRemer filed patents as early as 1918 for a unique hermetic compressor based on the Archimedes screw principle, which compressed the refrigerant between slugs of mercury. The design was placed in production about 1927 by Savage Arms Co. using isobutane and then methyl chloride refrigerants. The design, used mainly in Savage's ice cream cabinet line, was produced into the 1930s. Examples are displayed at the Refrigeration Industry Museum in Los Angeles and at the Refrigeration Research Corp. museum, Brighton, Michigan. See U.S. Patents 1,373,174 and 1,373,175 of 1921; 1,537,937 of 1925; 1,589,373 of 1926; and 1,807,774 of 1931. See also DeRemer, J.G., and R.W. Ayres. 1927. A hermetically sealed refrigerating machine using the mercury compressor. *Refrigerating Engineering* 14(Dec.): 169; and DeRemer, J.G., and G.W. Dunham. 1933. Improvements in the mercury-gas compressor. *Refrigerating Engineering* 26(Dec.): 307. A general discussion of early hermetic compressor designs can be found in: Van Deventer, H.R. 1930. Pioneering work on enclosed machines dates back to 1897. *Electric Refrigeration News*, January 15, p. 22, and October 8, pp. 14-15; and Van Deventer, H.R. 1931. Patent situation in enclosed motor refrigeration. *Refrigerating Engineering* 21(Jan.): 1.

123. The purity problem of refrigerants was overcome when large chemical companies, such as Virginia Smelting Co., Carbon and Carbide Co., and Dupont, began manufacturing sulfur dioxide, methyl chloride, etc., on a commercial scale. Various refrigerants used in small systems in the 1930s, in approximate order of popularity, included sulfur dioxide, methyl chloride, isobutane, ethyl chloride, and methylene chloride. Methyl formate was used for a short time by General Electric until it was found to disassociate in use. Ammonia was seldom used in small systems. By the late 1940s, some new systems were still being installed using methyl chloride, which continued in use into the 1950s. The introduction of the chlorofluorocarbons was interrupted by World War II, when their production was co-opted for the war effort.

124. The chlorofluorocarbon refrigerants were developed by General Motors' research laboratory at the request of Frigidaire in an effort to find an ideal refrigerant. The refrigerants were produced by Kinetic Chemicals Corporation, a joint venture of General Motors and DuPont, and were commercially sold beginning in the early 1930s. The original articles by the inventors discussing the development are: Henne, A.L., and T. Midgley, Jr. 1930. Organic fluorides as refrigerants. *Industrial and Engineering Chemistry* 22(May): 542-544; Midgley, T., Jr. 1937. From the periodic table to production. *Industrial and Engineering Chemistry* 29(Feb.): 241-244. The basic U.S. patent covering the chlorofluorocarbon refrigerants is 1,833,847, filed February 8, 1930, and issued in 1931 to Thomas Midgley, Jr., Albert Henne, and Robert McNary, and assigned to Frigidaire Corporation. Recent histories of the development are: Downing, R. 1984. Development of chlorofluorocarbon refrigerants. *ASHRAE Transactions* 90(2B), and reprinted in ASHRAE. 1989. *CFC's: Time of transition*, pp. 16-21. Atlanta: American Society of Heating, Refrigerating and Air-Conditioning Engineers, Inc.; Nagengast, B.A. 1989. A history of refrigerants. *CFC's: Time of Transition*, pp. 11-14. Atlanta: American Society of Heating, Refrigerating and Air-Conditioning Engineers, Inc.; and Nagengast, B.A. 1988. A historical look at CFC refrigerants. *ASHRAE Journal*, November, pp. 37-39.

125. See U.S. Patent 27,846, issued to Henry Underwood in 1860. Underwood's belt was far ahead of its time and the manufacturing methods existing then, and may not have seen commercial use. It seems that the V-belt did not see widespread use until General Motors Corporation pursued the development in the 1920s. The company needed to move large volumes of air over a new automotive power source—the Copper Cooled Engine"—and all existing methods of transmitting power from the engine to a cooling fan were deemed unsuitable. Dayton (Ohio) Rubber Company was asked to devise a new drive belt that could transmit great power with no slippage. Dayton Rubber introduced a V-belt, covered by U.S. Patent 1,537,075 of 1925, issued to Abraham L. Freedlander and William G. Goodwin and assigned to the Rubber Development Co. (This was apparently not the first modern V-belt, as several earlier U.S. patents exist: 1,425,021 of 1922, to Irwin Kepler, assigned to B.F. Goodrich Co.; 1,432,973 of 1922, to Harold Delzell, assigned to B.F Goodrich Co.; and 1,510,449 of 1924, to F.F. Brucker, assigned to Miller Rubber Co.) V-belts were adopted by the refrigeration industry at first for small machines. Apparently the first to use the belt was Lipman Refrigeration in 1922. See: Anonymous. 1936. Lipman developed. . . . *Air Conditioning and Refrigeration News*, October 7, p. 21.

126. The first capillary tube, used with methyl chloride refrigerant, was used in the Rice household refrigerator beginning about 1926. See U.S. Patent 1,919,500, filed July 9, 1926, issued in 1933 to Thomas Carpenter, and assigned to Rice and Barnes. See Rice sales literature, such as: Anonymous. n.d. *These and many of the advantages Rice offers you.* New York: Rice Products, Inc. A similar device, which metered the refrigerant through screw threads, was patented as 1,183,979 in 1931 (filed July 8, 1926) by Frank West, assigned to Rice Products, Inc. A screw-thread-type expansion device (the "Restrictor") was actually produced by Frigidaire in the 1930s as part of the household refrigerator line incorporating the "Meter Miser" rotary compressor and refrigerant R-114. The modern thermostatic expansion valve was perfected by Harry Thompson, as described in U.S. Patent 1,747,958, filed August 24, 1927, issued in 1930, and assigned to Universal Cooler Corporation. The patent was subsequently placed in the public domain by Universal Cooler so as to benefit the entire refrigeration industry. It was further improved and mass-marketed by Detroit Lubricator Co. See U.S. Patent 2,008,663, filed October 14, 1931, by Earnest Dillman, issued in 1935, and assigned to Detroit Lubricator Co.

127. A low-pressure control was marketed as an integral part of Frigidaire's Model G condensing unit introduced in 1924. This may have been the first large-scale use of this type of cycling control. In 1926, Frigidaire introduced an improved spring-type control in response to a need for a means of effectively controlling multiple-evaporator systems being used for soda fountains. The new control, which soon was christened the "rat trap" by servicemen, was produced until the early 1930s and was used in Frigidaire's household refrigerators promoted in advertisements as the "Cold Control."

128. Extended surface had been applied to refrigeration evaporators as early as the 1890s in the form of cast-iron disks bolted to the evaporator pipes; however, the idea was not extensively used in the U.S., being more common in Europe. The idea of using lightweight fins on thin-walled tubes is also an old idea, being seen in various patents issued around the turn of the century, such as: British Patents 17,438 of 1898 to R.C. Ayton; 12,340 of 1899 to H. Rau; 14,155 of 1899 to M.H. Smith; 22,975 of 1901 to F. Sauerbier; 25,214 of 1901 to J. Tarpin; 13,214 of 1902 to W. Walker; 28,954 of 1902 to A. Dumas; and 23,227 of 1903 to W. Proctor; and U.S. Patent 649,204 of 1900 to J. Grouvelle and H. Arquembourg. These ideas do not seem to have been put into commercial use until the 1920s and later. Frigidaire began to use fins on its evaporator coils beginning in 1923. A cross-fin evaporator coil was patented in the U.S. by Lester U. Larkin in 1930 (filed in 1928) as 1,776,235. The design was used in forced-air unit coolers placed on the market about 1930 by Copeland Products Co. Extended surfaces were not used on condensers until air-cooled condensers came into use. The Isko refrigerator model RB of 1917 used spiral-wrapped finned tubes as a condenser, and this may have been the first production use of a finned, air-cooled condenser. The idea was apparently borrowed from the finned radiator used on the Pierce-Arrow automobile, another example of the influence of automotive technology on small refrigerating machine design. The Isko condenser was apparently unique until the major refrigerator manufacturers began to use finned condensers all at about the same time in 1927-1928. At that time, numerous U.S. patents were filed by firms that would serve as vendors to the refrigerator manufacturers. These patents included 1,685,290 of 1928 and 1,760,038, 1,761,981, and 1,777,782 of 1930 to Harry Bundy; 1,709,176 of 1929 to Rollin Hyde, assigned to McCord Radiator & Mfg. Co.; 1,745,544 of 1930 to John Karmazin; and 1,773,249 of 1930 to Henry Yeager, assigned to Fedders Manufacturing Co.

129. Metal cabinets had been tried as early as 1908 in a commercial installation. See: Anonymous. 1909. Refrigeration in the Hotel Anthony. *Ice and Refrigeration* 36(June): 294-298. By 1927, metal cabinets began to be used by household refrigerator manufacturers for both ice and mechanical systems.

130. A general history of household absorption refrigeration can be found in: Anonymous. 1931. Progress of gas refrigeration. *Electric Refrigeration News*, February 25, p. 18. Numerous absorption systems, such as the Keith and the Faraday systems by Frigidaire, were tried in household refrigerators beginning in the 1920s. No doubt the most successful absorption system was developed by two engineering students in Sweden, Baltzar von Platen and Carl Munters, in the early 1920s. Their system, an aqua-ammonia type, was acquired by AB Elektrolux of Stockholm and was sold by licensees in many countries. In the U.S. and Canada, the system, known as the "Electrolux," was sold by Servel Corporation, which had been producing electric refrig-

erators since 1922. The system was later covered by three U.S. patents—1,609,334 of 1926 and 1,613,627 and 1,613,628 of 1927. Soon after the Electrolux system was introduced, a very simple aqua-ammonia refrigerating machine, the "Icy Ball," was placed on the market by Crosley Radio Corporation in 1927. This device, essentially an improvement of one of Ferdinand Carré's inventions, was sold all over the world, and proved particularly useful in rural areas since it required no electricity. A U.S. patent was filed in 1927 by David Forbes Keith of Toronto, Canada, and was issued in 1929 as 1,740,737, assigned to Crosley Radio Corp. Another assigned U.S. patent, 1,811,523, was issued in 1931 to Russell Smith.

131. It seems that the first electrically refrigerated ice cream cabinet was developed by Frigidaire's former chief engineer, John Replogle, beginning in 1921 at Nizer Laboratories Company for the Arctic Ice Cream Company in Detroit. The new appliance was placed on the market in 1923 by Nizer Corporation (which merged with Kelvinator in 1926) and 1,470 machines were sold that year. A complete history of the Nizer development is in: Von Meyer, W.G. 1936. Nizer's rapid growth prelude to steady growth for ice cream cabinet manufacturers. *Air Conditioning and Refrigeration News*, October, p. 20. The Nizer machine was patented by John Replogle as U.S. Patents 1,146,546 of 1923, 1,658,209 of 1928, and 1,716,150 of 1929. Shortly thereafter, Frigidaire began marketing its own ice cream cabinet in early 1924. See: Anonymous. 1924. Ice cream cabinet. *Ice and Refrigeration* 66(Jan.): 95. Lipman also responded to the Nizer challenge with a cabinet of its own, also available in early 1924. See: Anonymous. 1924. Automatic ice cream cabinet. *Ice and Refrigeration* 66(Jan.): 95. A general discussion of the advantages of mechanical refrigeration as applied to ice cream cabinets, and a description of a machine developed at Vilter Manufacturing Co. (but apparently never placed in production), can be found in: Haven, C.D. 1925. The mechanically refrigerated ice cream cabinet. *Refrigerating Engineering* 12(Oct.): 103-110.

132. A general history of early meat freezing can be found in: Critchell, J.T., and J. Raymond. 1912. *A history of the frozen meat trade*. London: J. Raymond. These early methods were slow freezing processes, usually designed for preservation during transport. A good history of modern quick freezing, cowritten by Clarence Birdseye's associate Donald Tressler, is: Tressler, D.K., and C.F. Evers. 1936. *The freezing preservation of fruits, fruit juices, and vegetables*. New York: Avi Publishing Co. Other articles dealing with freezing and its introduction on a commercial scale are: Anonymous. 1930. Development of the frozen food industry. *Ice and Refrigeration* 78(June): 543-547; Anonymous. 1930. Introductory sales campaign for quick frozen products. *Ice and Refrigeration* 78(June): 553-555; Hopkins, G.J. 1930. Low temperature display cases. *Ice and Refrigeration* 79(July): 51-52; Birdseye, C. 1932. Production and distribution of quick-frozen perishable foods in the U.S. *Ice and Refrigeration* 83(Nov.): 223-227; Birdseye, C., and G.A. Fitzgerald. 1932.

History and present importance of quick-freezing. *Industrial and Engineering Chemistry* 24(June): 676-678; Holley, K.T. 1932. Some technical problems of the frozen food industry. *Refrigerating Engineering* 23(Jan.): 58; Burke, F.X. 1933. Frozen foods have an alluring future. *Refrigerating Engineering* 25(June): 314; and Poole, G. 1936. Four years' progress in quick freezing. *Ice and Refrigeration* 91(Nov.): 388-390. The two main pioneers in quick freezing were Clarence Birdseye and M.T. Zarotschenzeff. Clarence Birdseye developed a quick-freezing process in the mid-1920s using a moving belt upon which food packages were placed. Birdseye's method is described in: Anonymous. 1929. Birdseye method of freezing fish. *Ice and Refrigeration* 76(Apr.): 321-324; Birdseye, C. 1933. Preservation of perishable foods by new quick-freezing methods. *Journal of the Franklin Institute* 215: 411-424; Killeffer, D.H. 1931. Quick-freezing solves food problems. *Scientific American* 147(July): 16-18. There is an unpublished biography of Birdseye in: Belfiglio, A.J., Jr. 1984. Clarence Birdseye (photocopy of unissued paper in library of Bernard Nagengast, Sidney, OH). Birdseye related his trials in: Anonymous. 1930. Pioneer. *Electric Refrigeration News*, March 26, pp. 2, 9. Birdseye's early U.S. patents covering his process are 1,608,832 of 1926; reissue 16,740 of 1927; and 1,759,682, 1,773,079, and 1,773,081 of 1930. Regarding the unexpected success of Birdseye frozen foods in 1930, see: Anonymous. 1930. Memo from R.W. Sinks to Engineering Department, Frigidaire Corporation, Dayton, OH (original memo in Frigidaire Collection, General Motors Institute, Collection of Industrial History, Flint, MI). M.T. Zarotschenzeff, an Estonian who was editor of the Russian trade publication *Refrigeration Industry*, began experimenting with freezing about 1913. He emigrated to the U.S. in 1918 and perfected the "Z Process" of quick freezing, patenting it in 1926. The Z Process, which used sprays of chilled brine, was particularly successful for quick-freezing fish. Zarotschenzeff was able to promote the system to such an extent that it saw use in many countries. Regarding Zarotschenzeff's work, see: Thévenot, R. 1979. *A history of refrigeration throughout the world*. Paris: International Institute of Refrigeration; Zarotschenzeff, M.T. 1930. *Between two oceans . . . .* London: *The Cold Storage and Produce Review*; Zarotschenzeff, M.T. c. 1927. *Rapid freezing of meat & fish products*. Tallin, Estonia: Kulmetus Ltd.; Anonymous. c. 1927. *Export bacon factory*. Tallin, Estonia: Kulmetus Ltd.; Zarotschenzeff, M.T. 1932. The "Z" process in America. *Ice and Refrigeration* 83(Aug.): 67-70; Zarotschenzeff, M.T. 1933. The "Z" process in America—New type quick-freezing machine. *Ice and Refrigeration* 84(Jan.): 41-45.

133. See: Anonymous. 1929. Einstein turns ice maker. *Ice and Refrigeration* 77(Nov.): 292; and Anonymous. 1929. Einstein stumped by ice box. *Ice and Refrigeration* 77(Dec.): 440. These articles discuss a system using mercury "pistons" activated by an oscillating magnetic field. The idea was patented and sold to AEG in Germany; however, subsequent tests proved the idea

commercially unfeasible. U.S. Patent 1,781,541 of November 11, 1930, was issued to Albert Einstein and Leo Szilard for an absorption system using butane. The patent was assigned to Electrolux-Servel Corp., but apparently was never placed in production.

—— Chapter 11 ——

1. Secrest, M. 1992. *Frank Lloyd Wright, a biography*. New York: Alfred A. Knopf.
2. Reyner Banham devotes considerable attention to the system. "The internal atmosphere was serviced as follows: air from well above the external pollutants was drawn down capacious ducts in the blank walls of the corner towers, at the sides of the staircases, as Wright indicates. In the basement it was cleaned and heated, or after the installation of the Kroeschell refrigerating plant in 1909, cooled—but never humidity-controlled, and hence Wright's judicious quotation-marks around the words 'air-conditioned' (in the town where Carrier was perfecting humidity control he had better be careful!). The tempered air was then blown up riser ducts in the massive blank brick panels on the exterior walls immediately adjacent to the stair-towers, and distributed floor by floor through input registers on the backs of the downstand beams under the balustrades of the balconies. The same blank brick panels also contain the exhaust ducts through which vitiated air is extracted, and a third duct-space in the panel houses pipes and wiring and other ancillaries. Throughout the interior, extracts are marked by a characteristic and much-used Wrightian device—a pattern of hollow bricks forming a coarse grille, around which even the earliest photographs show the typical staining that commonly marks an exhaust" (from: Banham, R. 1969. *The architecture of the well-tempered environment*, pp. 90-91. Chicago: Architectural Press).
3. Wright, F.L. 1960. *Writings and buildings*, pp. 102-103. New York: Horizon Press.
4. From the English version of the explanatory text to the first Wasmuth volume (*Ausgefuhrte Bauten und Entwurfe*, Berlin, 1910) reprinted in Gutheim. Wright, F.L. 1914. *Frank Lloyd Wright on architecture*, pp. 72ff. New York.
5. Banham, p. 105.
6. Nessell, C.W. 1963. *The restless spirit*, p. 44. Minneapolis: Minneapolis-Honeywell Regulator Co.
7. Anonymous. 1960. Comfort from a tank of oil. *Trade Winds*, February, p. 42.
8. Ibid., p. 40.
9. Anonymous. 1926. Ancient oil burner literature. *The Heating and Ventilating Magazine* 23(Dec.): 104.
10. Anonymous. 1960. The story of how man harnessed the ghost. *Trade Winds*, February, p. 30.
11. Ibid.
12. Anonymous. 1922. Impressions of the recent gas convention. *The Heating and Ventilating Magazine* 19(Nov.): 54.
13. Anonymous. 1919. The development of the individual forced-blast heating unit. *The Heating and Ventilating Magazine*, July, p. 60.
14. Anonymous. 1919. The development of the individual forced-blast heating unit. *The Heating and Ventilating Magazine*, June, p. 20.
15. Richardson, C.S. 1920. How the double radiator revolutionized the best engineering ideas on combined heating and ventilating systems for schools and similar buildings. *The Heating and Ventilating Magazine*, May, pp. 14-17.
16. Hill, E.V. 1927. The story of Vento. *The Aerologist* 3(Feb.): 11-13.
17. Soule, L.C. 1929. The evolution of the lightweight heating surface. *Heating and Ventilating*, June, p. 121.
18. Much of this belief is traceable to the widespread publicity (beginning in the 1940s) given to the air-conditioning work of Willis Carrier, which credited him with its development beginning in 1902.
19. Bernan, W. (Robert Mickleham). 1845. *On the history and art of warming and ventilating rooms and buildings*, vol. I, p. 140. London: George Bell.
20. Leslie, J. 1813. *A short account of experiments and instruments, depending on the relations of air to heat and moisture*, p. 168. Edinburgh: William Blackwood.
21. de Chabannes, Jean Frédéric, Marquis. 1815. *Explanation of a new method for warming and purifying the air in private homes and public buildings . . .*; London: Schulze and Dean; de Chabannes, Jean Frédéric, Marquis. 1818. *On conducting air by forced ventilation and regulating the temperature in dwellings*. London: The Patent Calorifere Fumivore Manufactory.
22. Bernan, vol. II, pp. 88-89.
23. Peclét, E. 1844. *Traité De La Chaleur*, 3d ed., plate 109. Paris: D. Avanzo Et Cie.
24. Use of refrigeration for comfort air cooling is mentioned in the following early British patents: 2503 of 1860 to F.P.E. Carré; 952 of 1867 to T.S.C. Lowe (a carbon dioxide system); 3278 of 1868 to T.S. Mort and E.D. Nicolle; 2171 of 1882 to McMillan and Johnson for a portable room cooler; 2387 of 1885 to E. Fixary; and the following U.S. patents: 47,991 of 1865 to N. Shaler; 85,719 of 1869 to C. Tellier; 87,084 of 1869 to P. Van Der Weyde; 104,614 of 1870 to W. Mason; 110,573 of 1870 to J. Kraffert; and 144,577 of 1873 to A. Tait.
25. See earlier mentions of Smyth's and Gorrie's refrigeration work in this book. A recent discussion of Smyth and Gorrie and their work in comfort cooling can be found in: Nagengast, B.A. 1991. John Gorrie: Pioneer of cooling and ice making. *ASHRAE Journal* 33(Jan.): S52-S61. Cooling of air by compression then expansion was patented in England by John Vallance. See: Anonymous. 1822. To John Vallance for improvements on a patent granted to him, June 1820, for "a method and apparatus for freeing room and buildings from the distressing heat sometimes experienced in them, and of keeping them constantly cool, or of a pleasant temperature, whether they are crowded to excess, or empty, and also whether the weather be hot or cold." *The London Journal of Arts and Sciences* 3: 292-298.
26. Thompson, W. 1852. On the economy of the heating or cooling of buildings by means of currents of air. *Proceedings of the Philosophical Society of Glasgow* 3 (1853-1854): 269-272.

27. Reid, D.B. 1856. Progress of architecture in relating to ventilation, warming, lighting, fire-proofing, acoustics, and the general preservation of health. *Annual Report of the Board of Regents of the Smithsonian Institution*, p. 158.

28. Reid, D.B. 1844. *Illustrations of the theory and practice of ventilation, with remarks on warming, exclusive lighting, and the communication of sound*, p. 217. London: Longman, Brown, Green & Longman.

29. Reid, 1844, pp. 273, 275, 295.

30. Reid, 1856, p. 159.

31. Rolt, L.T.C. 1957. *Isambard Kingdom Brunel—A biography*, pp. 225-230. London: Longmans, Green & Co.

32. Anonymous. 1921. Cooling of hospitals. *Journal of the A.S.H.V.E.* 27(Oct.): 763-764.

33. Jouglet, A. 1873. On the various systems of cooling the air; and their application in factories, public buildings, and private houses. *The Practical Magazine* 1(6): 450-463.

34. For example, U.S. Patents 68,908; 70,909; 73,936; 77,669; and 96,047.

35. For example, see British Patents 15556 of 1890 to W. MacDonald for a room cooler; 26795 of 1896 to J. Stott for a central ventilating system for cooling and heating buildings, and featuring air filters; 4783 of 1898 to A.W. Stewart (the "Thermotank" system); and the following U.S. patents: 14,510 of 1856 to Azel Lyman for an air cooler for refrigeration or comfort cooling using ice (the scheme is also outlined in a catalog issued by Lyman: *Lyman's Patent Dry Air Refrigerator and Ice House* [n.d.], New York: Stephen Cutter); 262,185 of 1882 to Henry Johnson and Francis McMillan for a fan-coil system; 636,886 of 1899 to Louis Bell, assigned to the Bell House Cooling Co., for an evaporative-type cooler in which the air to be cooled is kept separate from the evaporating water by very thin membranes (a brief description is in: Anonymous. 1900. Schemes of house refrigeration. *Ice and Refrigeration* 18[Sept.]: 87); 655,148 of 1900 to Walter Dickerson, assigned to the Tripler Liquid Air Co., for a fan-coil-type cooler using liquid air as the refrigerant (refrigeration using liquid air made a brief appearance around the turn of the century); and 724,145 of 1903 to John and William Titus for a room cooler using ice with a hot water radiator. Some of the air coolers patented in the 1800s were for refrigeration purposes exclusively but are sometimes cited as examples of comfort cooling apparatus. Although they could have been used as such, such patents do not actually state a comfort cooling purpose. A prime example is U.S. Patent 146,267 of 1874 issued to Andrew Muhl and entitled "Apparatus for cooling the air of buildings." A number of schemes appeared around the turn of the century using compressed air, which would be distributed to the points to be cooled, in some cases from central stations throughout a city. One such scheme is outlined in: Harpole, A.J., and A. Flower. 1896. *Heating, cooling and ventilating buildings with purified compressed air.* Union City, TN: Cartan Printing Co. These systems of using high-pressure air distribution through small pipes to nozzles were the very crude antecedents of the high-pressure conduit distribution system developed by Carlyle Ashley and Willis Carrier around 1930 and tradenamed "The Conduit Weathermaster System," which revolutionized air conditioning in tall buildings.

36. A pamphlet, "Reports of officers of the Navy on ventilating and cooling the Executive Mansion during the illness of President Garfield," published by the Government Printing Office in 1882. A brief description is in: Billings, J.S. 1893. Air cooling. *Ventilation and Heating*, pp. 492-493. New York: *Engineering Record*.

37. Oswald, F.L. 1887. Summer refrigeration. *North American Review* 145: 262-263.

38. Anonymous. 1853. Salubrity of cities restored by the introduction of pure air. *DeBow's Review* 14(Mar.): 208-212.

39. Rietschel, H. 1894. *Leitfaden zum Berechnen und Entwerfen Lüftungs-und Heizungs-Anlagen*, pp. 243-254. Berlin: Julius Springer.

40. Brueckner, E. 1900. The refrigeration of dwellings. *Ice and Refrigeration* 17(Mar.): 212-254.

41. Anonymous. 1891. Engineers needed. *Ice and Refrigeration* 1(Sept.): 155.

42. Carpenter, R.C. 1895. *Heating and ventilating buildings*, p. 300. New York: John Wiley & Sons.

43. In 1902, it was reported that B.F. Sturtevant Co. had installed a fan-type heating and cooling system for the Armour Building in Kansas City, Missouri. The system featured an air washer that cooled the air in summer by using chilled water. See: Anonymous. 1902. Heating and cooling the Armour Building. *Engineering Review* 12(Apr.): 29. Recent investigation by the Kansas City ASHRAE Chapter indicated that the building no longer exists. The first installation of a modern spray-type air washer was apparently a Thomas air washer at the Chicago Public Library in 1900. See: Anonymous. 1910. Early air washing installation. *The Heating and Ventilating Magazine* 7(Oct.): 23-25.

44. Anonymous. 1893. Summer ventilation and cooling. *Heating and Ventilation* 3(Mar.): 5-8.

45. A recent study of Wolff's work is: Nagengast, B.A. 1990. Alfred Wolff: HVAC pioneer. *ASHRAE Journal* 32(Jan.): S66-S80.

46. Ohmes, G.R., and A.K. Ohmes. 1936. Early comfort cooling plants. *Heating, Piping and Air Conditioning* 8(June): 310-312.

47. Eisert, H. 1896. The cooling of closed rooms. *ASHVE Transactions* 2: 172-195.

48. The Cornell plant is described in: Anonymous. 1901. The mechanical plant of the Cornell Medical College, New York. *The Engineering Record*, October 5, pp. 319-324. The Hanover Bank installation is described in: Anonymous. 1903. Cooling a modern bank building. *Cold Storage* 10(Aug.): 51.

49. A comprehensive description of the New York Stock Exchange system, including illustrations and calculations, can be found in the following: Anonymous. 1905. Heating, ventilating and air cooling at the New York Stock Exchange—IV. *Engineering Record* 51(Apr. 29): 490-491; Anonymous. 1905. Cooling the New York Stock Exchange. *The Metal Worker, Plumber and Steam Fitter* 64(Aug. 5): 55-58. The system was drafted by

Wolff's associate Werner Nygren, who also supervised the installation. Nygren recalled the experience in: Anonymous. 1930. The old and the new in air conditioning. *Heating and Ventilating* 27(Jan.): 66-71. The absorption refrigeration system was designed by Henry Torrance, Jr., of Carbondale Machine Co., who described the system in: Torrance, H., Jr. 1910. Refrigeration and ventilation of inhabited places. *IInd International Congress of Refrigeration*, pp. 839-848. Vienna: J. Weiner. A nonillustrative description of the refrigerating system is also in: Anonymous. 1903. Big cooling plant in Stock Exchange. *Cold Storage* 10(May): 206-208. A description by the New York Stock Exchange's chief engineer decades later is: Kepler, D.A. 1947. Air conditioning the New York Stock Exchange. *Heating, Piping and Air Conditioning*, April, pp. 69-73.

50. Letter from Alfred Wolff to George B. Post, October 1, 1901. New York: New York Stock Exchange Archives.

51. Anonymous. 1902. *Minutes of the building committee,* January 31, p. 8. New York: New York Stock Exchange Archives.

52. Ibid., March 21, attachment.

53. Siebert, A. 1897. Refrigeration. *Ice and Refrigeration* 13(July): 16-18.

54. U.S. Patents 697,679, April 15, 1902, "Air cooling apparatus"; 734,975, July 28, 1903, "Apparatus for supplying cool air to buildings"; 780,385, January 17, 1905, "Air cooling apparatus."

55. Anonymous. 1902. Cooling an auditorium by the use of ice. *Engineering Review* 12(June): 13.

56. Despite the limitations, there were a number of comfort cooling systems installed around the turn of the century. Ice-type cooling systems installed at the Keith and Broadway theaters are mentioned in the previous note. An ice-type cooling system as designed by Alfred Wolff was installed at the New York Music Hall (Carnegie Hall). See the *Engineering Record* of July 4, 1891, and February 6, 1892, for detailed plans of the mechanical systems. For descriptions of this and some other early installations, see: Billings, J.S. 1893. New York Music Hall. *Ventilation and Heating*, pp. 372-375. New York: *Engineering Record*. In 1891, the St. Louis Automatic Refrigerating Co. installed a district refrigeration system by which ammonia was circulated from a central plant through street pipelines. One of the customers was a restaurant and beer hall called the "Ice Palace," which was cooled in summer by frosted pipe coils on the restaurant walls. The walls were made a bit less unsightly by the addition of painted murals of the Kane polar expedition, sleighing scenes, and "other frescoes of a frigid character." See: Anonymous. 1891. Living room refrigeration. *Ice and Refrigeration* 1(Sept.): 148. The Kansas City Cable Railway Co. experimented with cooling using compressed air to cool passenger cars at the Pullman shops in 1891. See: Anonymous. 1891. Regulating the temperature of rooms. *Ice and Refrigeration* 1: 29. There is also a description of a comfort cooling installation in 1892 by M. Dillenberg in San Francisco. See: Anonymous. 1892. Refrigerating private residences. *Ice and Refrigeration* 3(Aug.): 110. Dillenberg also placed advertising about the same time in *Ice and Refrigeration* showing the apparatus that was designed to cool food as well as the residence. A two-ton ammonia system was installed in 1895 to cool the library of a home in St. Louis (see: Anonymous. 1895. Refrigerating private residences. *Ice and Refrigeration* 9[Aug.]: 104-105). See also: Siebert, A. 1900. Residence cooling in St. Louis. *Ice and Refrigeration* 17(Mar.): 215-216. At about the same time, a one-ton Linde ammonia system was installed to cool a residence in Frankfurt-am-Main, Germany. See: Brueckner, E. 1900. The refrigeration of dwellings. *Ice and Refrigeration* 17(Feb.): 114. An ammonia brine chiller was proposed to cool the air of the U.S. Senate chamber in 1896. See: Woodbridge, S.H. 1895. Report on the heating and ventilation of the Senate wing of the United States Capitol, Washington, D.C. To Joseph C.S. Blackburn, chair, committee on rules, Washington, DC; and Anonymous. 1896. The Senate chamber refrigerated. *Ice and Refrigeration* 11(Dec.): 393. *Ice and Refrigeration* later reported that air-cooling plants had been installed on some hospital ships used in the Spanish-American and Boer wars. Cooling plants were also installed in 1900 on five Mississippi River steam tenders and on one steam dredge. See: Anonymous. 1901. Historical review of the rise of mechanical refrigeration. *Ice and Refrigeration* 21(Dec.): 224. The St. Nicholas Garden in New York City was cooled in summer by circulating air under a temporary floor over the ice-skating rink kept frozen by nine miles of direct expansion ammonia piping (see: Anonymous. 1901. Cooling public halls. *Ice and Refrigeration* 21(Oct.): 135. Pipeline district refrigeration systems similar to the one in St. Louis referenced above were proposed in 1901 for York and Reading, Pennsylvania, for the purposes of refrigeration and cooling homes, stores, etc., as mentioned in: Anonymous. 1902. To cool buildings. *Ice and Refrigeration* 22(Jan.): 18. A combination well water/ammonia brine chiller was used to cool air for a theater in Cologne, Germany, about 1903-1904. A description is in: Musmacher, J. 1904. Cooling plant in Cologne theater. *Ice and Refrigeration* 26(May): 253-256. In 1906, a cooling plant was installed to cool wards of the Boston Floating Hospital; however, the size of the cooling plant was inadequate. New York consulting engineers Westerberg and Williams were hired to redesign the system in 1907. The new system maintained a design condition of 68°F to 70°F indoor temperature at a relative humidity of 50% at an outdoor design condition of 88°F and 85% relative humidity. Air was cooled and dehumidified using ammonia-refrigerated brine coils. The supply air was then reheated with a steam coil. The amount of air to be reheated was controlled by a duct-thermostat-actuated bypass damper. Each of five wards also had its own thermostat-controlled reheat coil. See: Anonymous. 1909. Boston floating hospital. *Ice and Refrigeration* 36(Mar.): 89-91. In 1907, a carbon dioxide direct expansion air-cooling system, designed by Andrews & Johnson Co. and Kroeschell Bros. Ice Machine Co., was installed to cool the banquet room and the Pompeiian meeting room of the new annex of

the Auditorium Hotel in Chicago. The system so pleased the hotel management that they planned to double the size of the system so the corridors and restaurant could be cooled. See: Anonymous. 1907. Cooling public rooms in a Chicago hotel. *Ice and Refrigeration* 33(Oct.): 126-130.

57. Anonymous. 1903. *Ice and Refrigeration* 25(July): 18.

58. Voorhees, G.T. 1916. Observations of a refrigerating engineer. *Ice and Refrigeration* 57(Nov.): 150.

59. Anonymous. 1904. Refrigerating plans at Louisiana Purchase Exposition. *Ice and Refrigeration* 27(Sept.): 83-99.

60. Anonymous. 1904. At the World's Fair. *Ice and Refrigeration* 27(Nov.): 179-180.

61. Linde, C. 1908. Conference de M. Le Professeur C. von Linde La Refrigeration des Locaux Habites. *Comptes Rendus Du Congres, Premier Congres International Du Froid*, Paris, France, part 1, pp. 142-150.

62. Ingels, M. 1950. Willis Carrier, father of air conditioning. Typed manuscript at Department of Manuscripts and Archives, Accession 2511, pp. 50-65. Ithaca, NY: Cornell University. This 400-page manuscript was reduced by "a major rewrite, a massive condensation, and a non-technical edit" to about 16% of the original, resulting in the following published work: Ingels, M. 1952. *Willis Haviland Carrier, father of air conditioning*. Garden City, NJ: Country Life Press. A discussion of the original versus the published book is in: Lewis, L.L. 1959. The father of air conditioning—The book versus the original 400-page manuscript. Internal memo, Carrier Corp., Syracuse, NY. Washington, DC: Carrier File, Smithsonian Institution, Division of Engineering and Industry.

63. Ingels, M. 1949. Letter to Samuel Fletcher, vice president, Sackett & Wilhelms Lithographing Corp., November 14. Accession 2511, Department of Manuscripts and Archives. Ithaca, NY: Cornell University. Researching the Sackett-Wilhelms air-conditioning installation is difficult since there appears to be no contemporary descriptions of the installation or its performance. In fact, the best description is by Walter S. Timmis given to the New York chapter of ASHVE in 1914, detailed in: Anonymous. 1914. The New York chapter discusses control of atmospheric conditions in printing establishments. *The Heating and Ventilating Magazine* 11(Jan.): 48. When Margaret Ingels was working on the manuscript for her biography of Willis Carrier, she did no research on the printing plant installation herself, instead relying on research done by the Carrier advertising department around 1943, according to: Ingels, M. 1964. Letter to L.L. Lewis, July 23, Accession 2511, Department of Manuscripts and Archives. Ithaca, NY: Cornell University. By 1964, when questions arose as to the success of the installation, Carrier's associate L. Logan Lewis investigated and wrote a report that was "not for publication" (Lewis, L.L. 1964. Sackett-Wilhelms Printing and Publishing Co., 1902, a technical review of some heretofore unpublished information. Accession 2511, Department of Manuscripts and Archives. Ithaca, NY: Cornell University). It seems that Carrier's advertising department chose to ignore the following statement:

"My own recollection, however, which is rather clear, was that the installation referred to was never considered a success, and its operation was discontinued within a comparatively short time after completion of that plant," which is contained in: Pratt, H.H. 1943. Letter to Walter A. Bowe, Carrier Corporation, June 15, from the president of Sackett & Wilhelms Lithographing Corp. Referring to the ventilating system itself, Pratt went on to say: ". . . the chances are that the whole plant itself was so constructed that the installation did not have much of a chance." That the installation had been removed before 1910 is documented in: Caffrey, R.J. 1951. Letter to J.R. Vernon, Milwaukee office, Johnson Service Co., September 19. Accession 2511, Department of Manuscripts and Archives. Ithaca, NY: Cornell University. Margaret Ingels told Logan Lewis in 1964: "From memory—I do not believe the Sackett-Wilhelms job operated successfully" (Ingels, M. 1964. Letter to L.L. Lewis, July 9. Accession 2511, Department of Manuscripts and Archives. Ithaca, NY: Cornell University). Carrier's first catalog (see note 73), published in 1908, does not mention the Sackett-Wilhelms plant in the section, "Lithographing and Color Printing Plants" on pp. 17C and 18C, but uses a testimonial from a San Francisco company, which further implies that the Sackett installation was not considered significant enough to be included in the catalog.

64. Carrier, W.H. 1929. Air conditioning—Its phenomenal development. *Heating and Ventilating* 26(June): 116.

65. Ibid.

66. Carrier, W.H. 1936. Progress in air conditioning in the last quarter century. *ASHVE Transactions* 42: 323.

67. Ibid.

68. For a complete description of the cotton mill system, see: Carrier, W.H. 1907. A new departure in cooling and humidifying textile mills. *Engineering Review* 17(July): 25-26.

69. Ingels, 1952, pp. 26-29.

70. Carrier, 1936, p. 324.

71. Carrier, 1929, pp. 116-117.

72. Formulas and psychrometric charts in Carrier's own hand, dated July 20, 1908, were at one time in the Engineering Department files at Buffalo Forge Co. Many years ago, they were photocopied by John McClive, manager of marketing. In 1985, copies of the copies were given to Bernard Nagengast by McClive. Recent attempts to locate the originals have been unsuccessful.

73. Carrier's psychrometric chart was printed on page 33 in: Anonymous. 1908. Carrier air washers and humidifiers with notes on humidity. New York: Carrier Air Conditioning Company of America. A preceding article, "Humidity," by J.I. Lyle, makes no mention of the chart, nor is there any mention of it in the table of contents or any caption under the chart itself.

74. Carrier, W.H. 1911. Rational psychrometric formulae—Their relation to the problems of meteorology and of air conditioning. *ASME Transactions* 33: 1005-1053; Carrier, W.H., and F. Busey. 1911. Air conditioning apparatus—Principles governing its application and operation. *ASME Transactions* 33: 1005-1136.

75. Carrier has often been called the "Father of Air Conditioning"; the term apparently was first used in: Wampler, C. 1949. *Dr. Willis H. Carrier, father of air conditioning*. New York: The Newcomen Society of England, American Branch. However, Carrier himself was not so presumptuous, admitting in 1929: "No individual or no firm can take credit for all or any part of these developments" (see: Carrier, 1929, pp. 115-118). Although Willis Carrier did not "invent" air conditioning, there is no argument about him being its greatest advocate and practitioner in the last 90 years!

76. The term *air conditioning* also appears in: Cramer, S. 1909. *Useful information for cotton manufacturers*, 2d ed. Charlotte, NC: Queen City Printing Co.

77. Cramer is quoted in: Cooper, G.A. 1987. "Manufactured weather": A history of air conditioning in the United States, 1902-1955. Ph.D. dissertation, pp. 41-42. Santa Barbara: University of California.

78. Wilson, G.B. 1908. *Air conditioning being a short treatise on the humidification, ventilation, cooling, and the hygiene of textile factories—Especially with relation to those in the U.S.A.*, p. 112. New York: John Wiley & Sons.

79. Anonymous. 1936. Progress of air conditioning. *Ice and Refrigeration* 91(July): 12. A discussion of the use of air washers for cooling purposes is in: Anonymous. 1907. Air purification and cooling. *The Metal Worker, Plumber and Steam Fitter*, September 21, pp. 48-50; and Anonymous. 1909. Topical discussions, topic no. 3, air-cooling by air-washers. *ASHVE Transactions* 15: 170-173. A specific instance of the successful application of an air washer in a comfort cooling system, installed in 1906, is discussed in: Feldman, A.M. 1909. A combination ventilating, heating and cooling plant in a bank building. *ASHVE Transactions* 15: 252-275. Feldman was an early specialist in cooling installations. He designed comfort cooling systems for residences as well as commercial buildings. See: Feldman, A.M. 1914. A ward-cooling plant in a hospital. *The Heating and Ventilating Magazine* 11(Mar.): 21-23; and Feldman, A.M. 1914. Cooling two rooms in a country residence. *The Heating and Ventilating Magazine* 11(Mar.): 33-35.

80. Musmacher, J. 1904. Cooling plant in Cologne theater. *Ice and Refrigeration* 26(May): 253-256.

81. Anonymous. 1910. Refrigeration abroad. *Ice and Refrigeration* 39(Nov.): 223.

82. Anonymous. 1907. Air purification and cooling. *The Metal Worker, Plumber and Steam Fitter* 68(Sept.): 48-50.

83. Fleisher, W.L. 1929. Notes of a pioneer in air conditioning. *Heating and Ventilating* 26(June): 114.

84. Anonymous. 1927. Ammonia versus carbon dioxide as a refrigerant in air conditioning work. *The Heating and Ventilating Magazine* 24: 61.

85. Cooper, 1987, p. 147.

86. Anonymous. 1928. Fred Wittenmeier, deceased. *Ice and Refrigeration* 74(Apr.): 409.

87. Anonymous. n.d. *Wittenmeier Machinery Company catalog*. Chicago: Wittenmeier Machinery Co.; and Wittenmeier, F. 1922. Cooling of theaters and public buildings. *Refrigerating Engineering* 9(Oct.): 115-118.

88. Arthur Morin mentioned comfort cooling experiments using a downward distribution system at the Conservatoire Impérial des Arte et Métiers in Paris during the period 1864-1867, and contrasted downward flow with the uncomfortable conditions caused by upward distribution, which resulted in ". . . the presence of very disagreeable draughts about the legs of the people, showing the mistake of letting the fresh air enter at the floor" (Morin, A. 1867. On the ventilation of public buildings. *Proceedings of Institution of Mechanical Engineers*, p. 76). An extended discussion of the advantages of downward distribution, as applied in Europe, appeared as a translated article in: Anonymous. 1914. Ventilation and cooling of halls. *The Heating and Ventilating Magazine* 11(May): 33-37.

89. In the U.S., Alfred Wolff's work provides the best example of the recognition of the downward distribution principle, as all of his comfort cooling systems incorporated it.

90. Ingels, 1952, p. 145. A complete description is in: Anonymous. 1924. Downward-diffusion air conditioning system for a large theater. *The Heating and Ventilating Magazine* 21(Mar.): 57-58, 64-65.

91. Anonymous. 1923. The new era, manufactured weather in the motion picture theater. *The Weather Vein* 3: 7-24.

92. Woodbridge, 1895, p. 15.

93. Anonymous. 1909. Air cooling . . ." *The Metal Worker, Plumber and Steam Fitter*, March 27, p. 49.

94. See the discussion of Rietschel's methods earlier in this chapter.

95. Schmidt, L.M. 1908. *Principles and practice of artificial ice-making and refrigeration*. Philadelphia: Philadelphia Book Co.

96. Fleisher, W. 1950. How air conditioning has developed in fifty years. *Heating, Piping and Air Conditioning*, January, pp. 120-123. Also see the following U.S. patents: 1,583,060, dated May 4, 1926, to L.L. Lewis; 1,670,656, dated May 22, 1928, to W.L. Fleisher; and 1,751,805 and 1,751,806, dated March 25, 1930, to W.L. Fleisher.

97. For example: Anonymous. 1912. Heating and ventilating T. Eaton & Company department store, Toronto, Ontario. *Engineering Review* 22(July): 26-28; Goodwin, S.L. 1927. Original design data for theater air cooling. *The Heating and Ventilating Magazine* 24(Mar.): 61-64, 71; 24(Apr.): 66-70; Lewis, A. 1927. Refrigeration as applied to air conditioning. *The Heating and Ventilating Magazine* 24(Jan.): 80-86; and Buck, E.S. 1928. Theater air conditioning in the Southwest. *The Heating and Ventilating Magazine* 25(Feb.): 73-74, 80.

98. Anonymous. 1925. Economy in theater refrigeration. *The Aerologist* 1(Sept.): 5-7.

99. Ingels, 1952, p. 52.

100. British Patents 17,224 and 21,271 of 1904 to Maurice Leblanc. See also: Grant, W.A. 1942. A history of the centrifugal refrigeration machine. *Refrigerating Engineering*, February.

101. Elgenfeld, E. 1911. The working pressures and effects of cold air turbo-engines. *IInd International Congress of Refrigeration, Vienna 1910, English Edition of the Reports and Proceedings*, pp. 123-127, 312. Vienna: J. Weiner; Lorenz, H. 1911. The possibility of employing turbo-blowers as cooling-machine condensers. *IInd*

International Congress of Refrigeration, Vienna 1910, English Edition of the Reports and Proceedings, pp. 128-134, 295-297. Vienna: J. Weiner.

102. Anonymous. 1913. Refrigeration abroad. *Ice and Refrigeration* 45(Aug.): 87.

103. Lyle, J.I. 1920. Confidential memo to A.E. Stacy, Carrier Engineering Company, New York, June 16. Carrier materials. Washington, DC: Smithsonian Institution, Division of Engineering and Industry.

104. Klein, A. 1950. Letter to Margaret Ingels, Carrier Corporation, March 23. Carrier materials. Washington, DC: Smithsonian Institution, Division of Engineering and Industry.

105. U.S. Patents 1,569,214, dated January 12, 1926; and 1,575,817 and 1,575,818, dated March 9, 1926.

106. Ingels, 1950, unpublished manuscript. Excerpts in Carrier materials, pp. 237-267. Washington, DC: Smithsonian Institution, Division of Engineering and Industry.

107. Anonymous. 1922. A new refrigerating machine. *Ice and Refrigeration* 63(July): 43-45.

108. Photocopy of newspaper article, no citation, in Frigidaire Collection, file 79-10.10-7. Flint, MI: General Motors Institute, Collection of Industrial History.

109. Anonymous. 1917. Air cooling schemes for houses. *The Heating and Ventilating Magazine*, September, p. 36.

110. Anonymous. 1930. *Scientific American*, January, pp. 14-17.

111. For a discussion of the advances in technology that affected room cooler development, see: Morgan, R.W. 1950. Room air conditioners—Past and present. *Refrigerating Engineering*, January, pp. 34-41.

112. Shellworth, P. 1949. Summary of interview with Mr. Robillard, March 1. Frigidaire Collection, file 79-10.1-43. Flint, MI: General Motors Institute, Collection of Industrial History.

113. McCoy, D. 1964. Frigidaire air conditioning. *History of Frigidaire*, p. 2. Unpublished manuscript. Dayton, OH: Montgomery County Historical Society.

114. Morgan, 1950, p. 357; and Faust, F. 1986. The early development of self-contained and packaged air conditioners. *ASHRAE Transactions* 92(2B): 357.

115. U.S. Patent 1,883,456, issued in 1932.

116. U.S. Patent 1,948,156, issued in 1934 to Carlyle M. Ashley and Vincent S. Day, assigned to Carrier Research Corporation.

117. Lewis, L. 1959. The evolution of Carrier's first self-contained room cooler, part II (unpublished). Syracuse, NY: Carrier Air Conditioning Co.

118. Lewis, 1959, part IV.

119. Anonymous. 1930. To make the public conditioned-air conscious. *Sheet Metal Worker*, April 4, p. 193.

120. Evans, O. 1805. *The young steam engineer's guide*, p. 137. Philadelphia: H.C. Carey and I. Lea.

121. Thomson, W. 1852. On the economy of the heating or cooling of buildings by means of currents of air. *Proceedings of the Philosophical Society of Glasgow* 3: 269-272.

122. Krenn, K., W. Ritter, and M. Schneeberger. 1986. The world's first industrial heat pump. *Newsletter of the IEA Heat Pump Center* 4(June).

123. Ibid.

124. Richmond, G. 1886. The refrigeration machine as a heater. *Journal of the Franklin Institute* 122(Aug.): 113-119.

125. Haldane, T.G.N. 1930. The heat pump—An economical method of producing low-grade heat from electricity. *Journal of Institution of Electrical Engineers* 68: 666-675. Before Haldane, there was experimentation with heat pumps in Germany. See U.S. Patent 1,214,255 of 1917 to Altenkirch and Tenckhoff.

126. Stevenson, A.R., F.H. Faust, and E.W. Roessler. 1932. Application of refrigeration to heating and cooling of homes. *General Electric Review* 35(Mar.): 145-153.

127. More than 100 citations listing articles, etc., regarding heat pumps are listed in: Anonymous. 1947. *Heat pump bibliography*. Birmingham, AL: Southern Research Institute.

128. Doolittle, H. 1931. Edison building heated and cooled by electricity. *Power* 74(Sept. 8): 348-351.

129. Sporn, P. 1935. An all electric heating, cooling and air conditioning system. *Transactions, American Society of Heating and Ventilating Engineers* 41: 306-326.

130. Penrod, E.B. 1947. A review of some heat-pump installations. *Mechanical Engineering*, August, pp. 639-647; Penrod, E.B. 1947. Air conditioning with the heat pump. *American Scientist* 35(Oct.): 502-524.

131. Neeson, C.R. 1933. Room cooler design. *Refrigerating Engineering* 26(Nov.): 233-238; Steinfeld, H.K. 1986. Pioneer developments in self-contained air conditioning. *ASHRAE Transactions* 92(2B): 366-374; Galson, H.L. 1935. Using the reversed cycle refrigerating principle for a self-contained heating and cooling unit. *Heating, Piping and Air Conditioning*, October, pp. 197-202; Anonymous. 1934. De La Vergne self contained air conditioner. Bulletin 105. Philadelphia: De La Vergne Engine Co.